BUSINESS TAX
AND LAW
HANDBOOK

3rd edition

David Bertram

Richard Lawson

PEARSON EDUCATION LIMITED

Head Office:
Edinburgh Gate
Harlow CM20 2JE
Tel: +44 (0)1279 623623
Fax: +44 (0)1279 431059

London Office:
128 Long Acre, London WC2E 9AN
Tel: +44 (0)20 7447 2000
Fax: +44 (0)20 7240 5771
Websites: www.business-minds.com
www.pearsoned-ema.com

This edition first published in Great Britain in 2001

© Allied Dunbar Assurance plc 2001
www.allieddunbar.co.uk
© Keith Hatchick, Chapters 17 & 19
© Nicholas Marshall, Chapter 11

The right of David Bertram and Richard Lawson to be identified
as Authors of this Work has been asserted by them in accordance
with the Copyright, Designs and Patents Act 1988.

ISBN 0 273 65046 7

British Library Cataloguing in Publication Data
A CIP catalogue record for this book can be obtained
from the British Library

10 9 8 7 6 5 4 3 2 1

Typeset by M Rules
Printed and bound in Great Britain by Biddles Ltd, Guildford and King's Lynn

*The Publishers' policy is to use paper manufactured
from sustainable forests.*

CONTENTS

PREFACE

We have written this book because we perceived a need for a practical guide for businessmen and their professional advisers. Business tax and law are key subjects for any proprietor, director of a private company and for specialists responsible for particular functions such as personnel managers, company secretaries and finance directors. Such business people are typical clients of accountants and solicitors and we know from long experience that they need to be guided through the complex maze of legislation regulation and common law. Very often we are asked specific questions and we find it essential to put our advice into a broader context—half the battle in practice is to identify all pertinent questions and matters to be addressed. We have therefore endeavoured to produce a handbook which describes and explains the main principles that lie behind topics such as employment law, contracts, health and safety at work and taxation. We have sought to identify problem areas and matters on which specific advice should be taken from a professional adviser who specialises in that particular field.

Practising as an accountant or solicitor has changed beyond recognition over the past 25 years. Indeed, much tax law has changed substantially in the last three years, following the 1997 General Election and New Labour's victory. There will always be a need for a professional adviser who gives general advice, helps clients to identify key questions and then interprets the input from specialists and explains to the client what it means in practice.

The law is stated as at 31 July 2000.

David Bertram
Richard Lawson

ABBREVIATIONS

ACAS	Advisory Conciliation and Arbitration Service
ACT	advance corporation tax
ADRs	American Depositary Receipts
AIM	Alternative Investment Market
APPP	Appropriate Personal Pension Plan
CA 1985	Companies Act 1985
CAA 1990	Capital Allowances Act 1990
CFC	controlled foreign company
CGT	capital gains tax
CY basis	current year basis
DDA	Disability Discrimination Act 1995
ECJ	European Court of Justice
EDT	effective date of termination
EIS	Enterprise Investment Scheme
ERA	Employee Rights Act 1996
ESC	extra statutory concession
ETO reason	economic, technical or organisational reason
EU	European Union
EWC	expected week of childbirth
FA	Finance Act
FSAVC	Free Standing Additional Voluntary Contributions
HSE	Health & Safety Executive
HSWA 1974	Health and Safety at Work Act 1974
IBA	industrial buildings allowance
IHT	inheritance tax
IHTA 1984	Inheritance Tax Act 1984
LAPR	Life Assurance Premium Relief
NI	National Insurance
NRE	net relevant earnings
PET	potentially exempt transfer
PHI	permanent health insurance
PPE	personal protective equipment
PPP	Personal Pension Plan
PSO	Pension Schemes Office
PY basis	preceding year basis
QCB	qualifying corporate bond

RRA	Race Relations Act 1976
SDA	Sex Discrimination Act 1975
SERPS	State Earnings Related Pensions Scheme
SDRT	stamp duty reserve tax
SMP	statutory maternity pay
SP	Inland Revenue Statement of Practice
SSAP	Statement of Standard Accounting Practice (issued by the Institute of Chartered Accountants)
SSP	statutory sick pay
TA 1988	Income and Corporation Taxes Act 1988
TCGA 1992	Taxation of Chargeable Gains Act 1992
TMA 1970	Taxes Management Act 1970
TULR(C)A	Trade Union and Labour Relations (Consolidation) Act 1992
TURERA	Trade Union Reform and Employment Rights Act 1978
VAT	value added tax
VATA 1994	Value Added Tax Act 1994

ALLIED
DUNBAR

Other titles in the Allied Dunbar Handbook series

TAX HANDBOOK 2000/2001

Whether you are a financial adviser, accountant, solicitor, company secretary, finance director or private individual who wants to find out about your own tax situation, this thorough guide has to be your first choice for shrewd advice and tax saving hints. Fully revised and updated, this edition incorporates all the latest changes following the Finance Act 2000. It offers sound advice on how to cope with self assessment, as well as offering detailed information on the complete range of taxes including CGT, VAT, stamp duty, inheritance tax, life assurance and national insurance.

INVESTMENT & SAVINGS 2000/2001

The *Allied Dunbar Investment & Savings Handbook* guides you through the complexities surrounding the abundance of financial products available, so that you can make informed choices for your investment strategy. Completely up to date with the latest legislation (it features changes resulting from the Spring 2000 budget and the Finance Act 2000), it highlights the significant changes in the law and how they will impact on your investments and savings.

RETIREMENT PLANNING (7th edition)

The *Allied Dunbar Retirement Planning Handbook* is an essential addition to your bookshelf. It ensures that you are fully aware of long and short term investment opportunities and examines the options available for improving retirement prospects.

EXPATRIATE TAX & INVESTMENT (7th edition)

'Expat's bible' – *What Investment*   'An absolute must' – *Money Magazine*

Written by experts, the *Allied Dunbar Expatriate Tax & Investment Handbook* gives you comprehensive coverage of every aspect of expatriate tax and investment, from the effect of the single currency to advice on working abroad. It is the essential guide for expatriates wishing to manage their financial affairs to their greatest possible advantage.

PENSIONS (7th edition)

This is the complete guide for business owners, company directors, the self employed and professional pension planners. It gives you a detailed investigation of all the choices available for successful pension planning.

ESTATE PLANNING & TAXATION OF CAPITAL (2nd edition)

The *Allied Dunbar Estate Planning & Taxation of Capital Handbook* provides an easy and straightforward way of understanding the principles of capital taxation on personal business and family wealth and how, by careful planning, its impact can be, legally, mitigated.

For further information contact your local bookseller,
telephone Pearson Education Ltd on 01279 623333
or e-mail at customer.orders@pearsoned-ema.com

1

INTRODUCTION

Being in business is not easy and there is a multitude of legal obligations and reporting requirements. A businessman cannot hope to become an expert overnight but he should not just muddle along; if he does so he is bound to come unstuck.

A detailed study of the subject is beyond the scope of this book. Instead, the authors' intention is to describe the basic principles of business tax and law, and to give examples of how these principles work in practice and highlight those areas where the businessman should take professional advice.

The following are key aspects to bear in mind.

1.1 HOW ARE TAXABLE PROFITS COMPUTED?

It is important to appreciate that accounts which have been drawn up according to commercial principles may need to be adjusted for tax purposes. For example, there is no tax relief for depreciation charged in accounts, but relief may be due via the capital allowances system.

Accounts should be drawn up on the earnings basis, ie a trader's stock or work in progress at his year end should be brought into account in arriving at his profit. Certain expenses are not allowable for tax purposes, for example entertaining or gifts to customers. A provision for a bad debt can be allowable for tax purposes but only if it is a specific provision. Bonus payments to employees can be a tax deductible expense even though they are paid after the end of the year. However, they have to be paid within nine months if tax relief is to be obtained for the year to which the bonuses relate. Pension contributions are tax deductible only if they are actually paid during the accounting period.

1.2 CAPITAL GAINS TAX (CGT)

Chapters 5 and 6 cover CGT as it relates to a businessman. Chapter 5 covers general principles such as what assets are chargeable assets and how a gain is computed for CGT purposes. Particular types of assets such as land and buildings, unquoted shares and foreign property are then discussed. Chapter 6 focuses on various business transactions such as tax relief for a person who has lent money to a businessman where that loan has to be written off, and looks at the circumstances in which income tax relief may be available for a person who has subscribed for shares in an unquoted trading company.

Roll-over relief enables a person who reinvests a capital gain to defer tax. It applies to disposals of land and buildings, goodwill and other similar assets. The relief introduced more recently for reinvestment in unquoted shares is also covered.

Retirement relief is being withdrawn progressively. In its place is a new form of relief, 'taper relief' (see 5.6). Indexation is, in effect, frozen at 5 April 1998. Indexation still applies for companies.

1.3 VALUE ADDED TAX (VAT)

VAT affects almost every businessman. Chapter 7 covers the basic rules as well as those which apply to import and export transactions and special schemes available to traders in certain industries. A trader normally needs to account for VAT on a quarterly basis and it is therefore important to understand the procedures properly. The legislation provides certain 'incentives' for traders to comply since interest and penalties may be levied for failure to render returns and pay VAT promptly.

1.4 STAMP DUTY

This tax, established in 1694, is the oldest form of tax in force in the UK. The general principles are covered in Chapter 8. Professional advice should be sought as liability for stamp duty tends to arise only on certain exceptional (but usually larger) transactions such as the purchase, or taking a lease, of premises.

1.5 CONTRACT LAW

In this increasingly litigious age, it is important to understand the basics of the law of contract. Chapter 9 describes the main principles and deals with the situation where things go wrong, eg one party makes a mistake or suffers loss through misrepresentation. The chapter also covers the Unfair Contract Terms Regulations.

1.6 SALE OF GOODS

Sale of goods law is really part of contract law, but it merits a chapter in its own right. The Sale of Goods Act provides that certain terms are taken as being implied when parties enter into a contract. Chapter 10 also covers matters such as product liability and liability under the Consumer Protection Act.

1.7 BUSINESS TENANCIES

For most businessmen, taking a lease of business premises is their largest single commitment. A lease can be a short- or long-term contract and rent may continue to be payable if the business comes to an end and the premises are no longer needed. Most modern leases contain an obligation on the tenant to return the premises in a fit condition at the end of the lease. It is very important for the tenant to be aware of what he may be letting himself in for. Chapter 11 also takes into account the Landlord and Tenant (Covenants) Act 1995.

1.8 EMPLOYMENT LAW

This is an area of the law where the influence of EU legislation is particularly apparent. Even temporary and part-time employees may acquire significant statutory employment protection rights. It is very important to follow the proper procedures where an employee's work is less than satisfactory or where an employer may need to make the employee redundant.

1.9 EMPLOYEE COMPENSATION

In Chapter 13 the rules which require an employer to deduct tax and withhold NI contributions are set out. The chapter covers matters such as Pay As You Earn – how it works and payments from which PAYE must be withheld. It then goes on to look at benefits in kind, the way in which they are taxed and the returns which must be completed at the end of the year by the employer.

An important element of employee remuneration may consist of special share schemes and these are covered in some detail. Also discussed are the treatment of redundancy payments and compensation for loss of office, and the way in which the Revenue ensures that the proper procedures are observed. A businessman may encounter the Collector's Audit Division and he may also undergo an investigation by one of the Schedule E Compliance Units – it is important to be prepared.

1.10 LIFE ASSURANCE, PENSIONS AND PERMANENT HEALTH INSURANCE

Chapter 14 covers the basics of life assurance, pensions and permanent health insurance. It details the different types of policy and sets out the legislation governing them. The second part of the chapter considers the uses of life assurance, pensions and permanent health insurance, with particular emphasis on the business needs of sole traders, partners and small companies.

1.11 HEALTH AND SAFETY AT WORK

There is a mass of legislation and European and Government regulation covering health and safety. In some situations, an employer who has transgressed could be exposed to criminal liability. Even in cases where only civil penalties are involved, it is not a matter to be taken lightly as the Health and Safety Executive or the local authority may have the power to compel a person to cease trading until certain work is carried out to ensure that adequate standards are in operation. Chapter 15 offers a basic introduction to this complex area.

1.12 GENERAL INSURANCE

The subject of general insurance is comprehensively examined in Chapter 16. The need for insurance cover is explained and the main compulsory insurance requirements are set out. The different types of cover available, from physical property to liability and indemnity insurances, are described in detail.

1.13 PARTNERSHIP LAW

The Partnership Act was passed in 1890 and has been supplemented by a number of cases which have come before the courts over the last 100 years. Entering into a partnership requires careful consideration as a partner may be jointly and severally liable for all the firm's debts. The position on tax liabilities is changing with the introduction of self-assessment, but this is merely an exception to the general rule. It is therefore crucially important to carefully regulate certain aspects of the firm's financial affairs to ensure that partners who leave it do not avoid their proper share of any problems and liabilities.

1.14 TAXATION OF UNINCORPORATED BUSINESSES

Not only are there special rules which govern the way in which taxable profits are arrived at, there are also special rules covering the way in which self-employed individuals are taxed.

There are also additional complications for partners, over and above the rules which apply to individuals who carry on business on their own account as sole traders.

1.15 COMPANY LAW

It is all too easy for individuals to acquire a company 'off the shelf' from formation agents and to commence trading with little or no understanding of the proper legal procedures. Companies House and the Revenue are increasingly taking a tough line and the well advised businessman needs to understand the basic reporting requirements.

It is also important to make provision in case things start to go wrong or to develop in an unexpected way. Situations are often encountered where a 50% shareholder wishes to disengage from a company and the other shareholder has quite different views on how this should be dealt with. There may be deadlock from a legal viewpoint which is hardly conducive to achieving an orderly and efficient parting of the ways. Similarly, problems may arise if a director is exceeding his authority and committing the company in ways which are not acceptable to his fellow directors. The position is often made worse because proper procedures were not followed in the past (eg there are no formal minutes of directors' meetings at which policy matters were discussed). As in so many areas, legal disputes may arise simply because a situation has arisen which was not envisaged at the outset; we have therefore endeavoured to provide an overview of relevant aspects of company law which need to be borne in mind by individuals who are directors and/or shareholders in private companies.

1.16 HOW COMPANIES ARE TAXED

If a company is formed to carry on a business, it is important to understand how the company will be treated for tax purposes. A return may be required on a quarterly basis for interest and other annual payments paid by the company. Mainstream corporation tax has to be paid nine months after the year end, although large companies now make their payments by instalments.

Companies are now on the self-assessment system for companies. Automatic penalties and interest charges may apply where accounts are filed late with the Revenue.

There are a number of important claims and elections which may need to be made, usually within a set period of either two or six years. The Revenue normally resists late claims unless there are good reasons why the claim was not made in time.

1.17 TAX PLANNING FOR SOLE TRADERS AND PARTNERS

Chapter 21 covers some of the key issues for self-employed businessmen such as the tax implications of bringing in or buying out a partner. The chapter looks at questions such as whether there are tax benefits in transferring a business to a company and the most tax efficient way in which to achieve such a transfer, and some of the tax aspects which need to be considered where an unincorporated business is sold or closed down.

1.18 TAX AND THE COMPANY PROPRIETOR

Tax is an important consideration for shareholder directors. Chapter 22 looks at points to bear in mind when buying a company, the treatment of shareholder directors, the way in which they are assessed on benefits received by them (or by members of their family) and the tax implications of various transactions with the company. Many shareholder directors tend to use their company as a 'money box' and draw cash during the year in anticipation of bonuses which will be declared at the company's AGM – all very well in theory but doing this may infringe company law and give rise to a tax charge for the company and a separate tax charge for the director.

Matters are considered such as the purchase of assets from the company (or sales of assets to the company), the rules affecting self-administered pension schemes, possible ways in which a shareholder may be bought out (purchase of own shares and demergers) and more technical issues such as CGT planning and anti-avoidance legislation.

1.19 INHERITANCE TAX AND BUSINESS PROPERTY

Inheritance tax may take 40% of an individual's assets on his death after various exemptions and a nil rate band. But there are special reliefs available for businesses and in particular 100% business property relief for unincorporated businesses and substantial shareholders in private trading companies. However, business relief may not always be available as once again there a number of stringent conditions which need to be satisfied.

1.20 CONNECTED PERSONS

Because it would otherwise be possible to manipulate transactions between connected persons to gain tax advantage, the taxing statutes contain a number of provisions aimed at preventing this. As a general rule, transactions between connected persons are deemed to take place at their market value, and not, if different, some other price attributed thereto by the connected parties. The key pieces of legislation are for income and corporation taxes (TA 1988, s 839), for capital gains tax (TCGA 1992, s 286), and for inheritance tax. The definitions found in TA 1988, s 839 and TCGA 1992, s 286 are, for all practical purposes, identical.

1.20.1 Income and corporation taxes and capital gains tax
(TA 1988, s 839; TCGA 1992, s 286)

Individuals

A person is connected with an individual if that person is the individual's wife or husband, or is a relative, or the wife or husband of a relative, of the individual or of the individual's wife or husband. A 'relative' means brother, sister, ancestor or lineal descendant.

Trustees

A person, in his capacity as trustee of a settlement, is connected with:

(1) any individual who in relation to the settlement is a settlor;
(2) any person who is connected with such an individual; and
(3) any body corporate which is connected with that settlement.

A body corporate is connected with a settlement if it is:

(1) a close company (or only not a close company because it is not resident in the UK) and the participators include the settlement trustees; or
(2) controlled (under TA 1988, s 840) by a company falling within (1) above.

Partnerships

Except in relation to acquisitions or disposals of partnership assets pursuant to bona fide commercial arrangements, a person is connected with any person with whom he is in partnership, and with the spouse or relative of any individual with whom he is in partnership.

Companies

A company is connected with another company:

(1) if the same person has control of both, or a person has control of one and persons connected with him, or he and persons connected with him, have control of the other; or

(2) if a group of two or more persons has control of each company, and the groups either consist of or could be regarded as consisting of the same persons by treating (in one or more cases) a member of either group as replaced by a person with whom he is connected.

A company is connected with another person if that person has control of it or if that person and persons connected with him together have control of it.

Any two or more persons acting together to secure or exercise control of a company are treated in relation to that company as connected with one another and with any person acting on the directions of any of them to secure or exercise control of the company.

A 'company' includes any body corporate or unincorporated association, but does not include a partnership, and applies to a unit trust scheme as if the scheme were a company and as if the rights of the unit holders were shares in the company.

Control

Two definitions of 'control' are offered. The first, which is of general application, is that found in TA 1988, s 840, namely that in relation to a body corporate 'control' means the power of a person to secure:

(1) by means of holding shares or possessing voting power in or in relation to that or any other body corporate, or

(2) by virtue of any powers conferred by the articles of association or other document regulating that or any other body corporate,

that the affairs of the first-mentioned body corporate are conducted in accordance with the wishes of that person, and, in relation to a partnership, means the right to a share of more than one-half of the assets, or of more than one-half of the income, of the partnership.

The second definition of control is that found in TA 1988, s 416. Strictly, it is a definition for close company purposes. However, it is frequently brought into other legislation. Under s 416, a person is said to have 'control' of a company if he exercises, or is able to exercise or is entitled to acquire, direct or indirect control over the company's affairs, and in particular, but without prejudice to the generality of the preceding words, if he possesses or is entitled to acquire:

(1) the greater part of the share capital or issued share capital of the company or of the voting power in the company; or

(2) such part of the issued share capital of the company as would, if the whole of the company's income were in fact distributed among the participators (without regard to any rights which he or any other person has as a loan creditor), entitle him to receive the greater part of the amount so distributed; or

(3) such rights as would, in the event of the winding-up of the company or in any other circumstances, entitle him to receive the greater part of the assets of the company which would then be available for distribution among the participators.

Where two or more persons together satisfy any of the above conditions, they are taken to have control of the company.

A person is treated as entitled to acquire anything which he is entitled to acquire at a future date, or will at a future date be entitled to acquire.

There is attributed to any person any rights or powers of a nominee for him, that is to say, any rights or powers which another person possesses on his behalf or may be required to exercise on his direction or behalf.

Associates

There may also be attributed to any person all the rights and powers of any company of which he has, or he and associates of his have, control or any two or more such companies, or of any associate (or any two or more associates) of his, including those attributed to a company or associate as above, but not those attributed to an associate hereunder; and such attributions are made hereunder as will result in the company being treated as under the control of five or fewer participators if it can be so treated.

By ESC C9, companies are not associated merely because they are treated as controlled by the same loan creditor if apart from the common creditor there is no other connection between the companies. Also, companies are not associated by reason of taking into account fixed-rate preference shares if certain conditions exist. Further, it depends on the facts whether companies are associated because a person can exercise the rights and powers of his associates. Trustee companies which hold rights and powers and thereby exercise control are not to be treated as associates where the rights are held in trust and there is no other connection between the companies.

For the purposes of 'small companies marginal relief' (TA 1988, s 13), the Revenue will, by concession, not treat companies in certain circumstances as associated, and 'relative' includes only a husband or wife or minor child where there is no substantial commercial interdependence.

The Revenue have announced that two associated companies are under the control of the same person(s) only if an irreducible group of persons having control of one company is identical with an irreducible group of persons having control of the second company. An irreducible group of persons is one which has control but which would not have control if any one of them were excluded.

1.20.2 Inheritance tax

Control of company
(IHTA 1984, ss 269 and 270)

A person has control of a company at any time if he then has the control of powers of voting on all questions affecting the company as a whole which, if exercised, would yield a majority of the votes capable of being exercised on them.

Shares or securities are deemed to give a person control of a company if, together with any shares or securities which are related property (under IHTA 1984, s 161), they would be sufficient to give him control of the company (as defined in 1.20.1).

Where shares or securities are comprised in a settlement, any powers of voting which they give to the trustees of the settlement are for the above purpose deemed to be given to the person beneficially entitled in possession to the shares or securities (except in a case where no individual is so entitled). Where a company has shares or securities of any class giving powers of voting limited to either or both of:

(1) the question of winding up the company, and
(2) any question primarily affecting shares or securities of that class,

the reference above to all questions affecting the company as a whole have effect as a reference to all such questions except any in relation to which those powers are capable of being exercised.

Any question of whether a person is connected with another is determined as it falls to be determined under TCGA 1992, s 286, but as if 'relative' included uncle, aunt, nephew and niece.

Inheritance tax also introduces two further concepts: associated operations and related property.

Associated operations
(IHTA 1984, s 268)

'Associated operations' means any two or more operations of any kind, being:

(1) operations which affect the same property, or one of which affects some property and the other(s) of which affect property which represents, whether directly or indirectly, that property, or income arising from that property, or any property representing accumulations of any such income, or
(2) any two operations of which one is effected with reference to the other, or with a view to enabling the other to be effected or facilitating its being effected, and any further operation having a like relation to any of those two, and so on, whether those operations are effected by the same

person or different persons, and whether or not they are simultaneous; 'operation' includes an omission.

The granting of a lease for full consideration in money or money's worth is not taken to be associated with any operation effected more than three years after the grant.

Where a transfer of value is made by associated operations carried out at different times it is treated as made at the time of the last of them. However, where any one or more of the earlier operations also constitute a transfer of value made by the same transferor, the value transferred by the earlier operations is treated as reducing the value transferred by all the operations taken together, except to the extent that the transfer constituted by the earlier operations but not that made by all the operations taken together is exempt under IHTA 1984, s 18.

Related property
(IHTA 1984, s 161)

Where the value of any property comprised in a person's estate would be less than the appropriate portion of the value of the aggregate of that and any related property, it shall be the appropriate portion of the value of that aggregate. Property is related to the property comprised in a person's estate if:

(1) it is comprised in the estate of his spouse; or
(2) it is or has within the preceding five years been the property of:
    (a) a charity, or held on trust for charitable purposes only, or
    (b) a political party (IHTA 1984, s 24), a housing association (s 24A) or national purposes body (s 25),

and became so on a transfer of value which was made by him or his spouse and was exempt to the extent that the value transferred was attributable to the property.

The appropriate portion of the value of the aggregate of that and any related property is such portion thereof as would be attributable to the value of the first-mentioned property if the value of that aggregate were equal to the sums of the values of that and any related property, the value of each property being determined as if it did not form part of that aggregate.

The proportion which the value of a smaller number of shares of any class bears to the value of a greater number is taken to be that which the smaller number bears to the greater; and similarly with stock, debentures and units of any other description of property.

Shares are not treated as being of the same class unless they are so treated by the practice of a recognised stock exchange or would be so treated if dealt with on such a stock exchange.

2

SCOPE OF INCOME TAX

DAVID BERTRAM, CLAYFIELD PROFESSIONAL GUIDANCE LTD

2.1 SCOPE OF TAXES ON PROPERTY, PROFITS OR GAINS

TA 1988, s 1 provides that income tax, which applies primarily to individuals, but also to partnerships, trusts, personal representatives, etc, is a tax on all 'property, profits or gains' as described in Schedules A, D, E and F (see TA 1988, ss 15–20).

Capital gains tax (CGT) is levied on chargeable gains realised by individuals, trusts, personal representatives, etc on assets disposed of in tax years for which they are classed as UK resident or ordinarily resident. Non-UK resident and non-UK ordinarily resident individuals may, on the disposal of assets UK situated used in or for the purposes of a trade, profession or vocation carried on through a branch or agency in the UK, be chargeable to CGT on chargeable gains arising in a tax year in which such trade is carried on. This does not apply if double taxation relief is available. (See further Chapter 5 regarding taxation of chargeable gains.)

Corporation tax is charged on the 'profits of companies' (TA 1988, s 6), which means both income and chargeable gains (TA 1988, s 8; TCGA 1992, ss 1 and 8). A non-resident UK company is not subject to corporation tax unless it carries on a trade in the UK through a branch or agency (TA 1988, s 11; TCGA 1992, s 10); again, this does not apply if double taxation relief is available.

Note that a non-resident company which does not carry on a trade through a UK branch or agency is chargeable to income tax (at basic rate only) on any income arising in the UK, unless double taxation relief is available.

If a company receives any payment on which it bears income tax by deduction, and the payment is taken into account in computing the company's income chargeable to corporation tax, the income tax is set off against any corporation tax assessable on that income.

(See further Chapter 20 with regard to taxation of company profits.)

2.2 INCOME TAX CHARGE ON 'PROPERTY, PROFITS OR GAINS'

The rules prescribed for the measurement of income, profits or gains vary according to the type of income, etc (ie the source from which the income, etc arises). The various categories of income, etc are divided, for assessment purposes, into Schedules A, D, E and F (Schedules B and C were repealed). Schedule E is concerned with income from offices or employments (see Chapter 13), while Schedule F (see Chapter 22) deals with the assessment of income from dividends and other distributions. Schedule A is charged on the annual profits from rents or other receipts arising from any estate, interest, or rights in or over land in the UK (TA 1988, s 15).

If income is within the scope of Schedule A, E or F, it cannot be charged under Schedule D (among a number of cases, see in particular *Fry v Salisbury House Estate Ltd* (1920) 15 TC 266). These cases concerned the allocation of profits to Schedule A or D. There are other cases concerned with allocation of profits to Schedule D or E (eg *Mitchell and Edon v Ross* (1961) 40 TC 11; *Fall v Hitchin* (1972) 49 TC 433; *Edwards v Clinch* (1981) 56 TC 367; and *Hall v Lorime* (1993) 66 TC 349). The problem of allocation between Schedules D and E and related matters is ongoing.

For example, if a receipt is to be charged under Schedule D Case I, it must be an annual profit or gain from the trade which is the 'source' of the receipt. The source doctrine prevents any receipt from being chargeable under Case I unless that is clearly the source that gives rise to it. If it is to be chargeable to income tax, another Schedule or Case must be found. Casual or occasional payments may, in some circumstances, be liable under Schedule D Case VI. However, a payment which is genuinely unsolicited (eg a gift) is unlikely to be from any source and is almost certainly outside income taxation altogether.

2.3 SCHEDULE D: ANNUAL PROFITS OR GAINS

In broad terms (see TA 1988, s 18(1)), tax under Schedule D is charged on 'the annual profits or gains arising or accruing' to any person:

(1) residing in the UK from property of any kind, whether situated in the UK or elsewhere, and
(2) residing in the UK from any trade, profession or vocation, whether carried on in the UK or elsewhere, and
(3) although not resident in the UK, from any property in, or from any trade, profession or vocation exercised within, the UK.

Tax is also charged under Schedule D on all interest of money, annuities and other annual profits or gains not charged under Schedule A or E, and not specially exempted from tax.

Although, as noted above, Schedule D taxes *annual* profits or gains arising or accruing, 'annual' here is not restricted to mean profits or gains recurring year by year, nor lasting for a year, nor to be calculated with reference to a year. However, the emphasis here is that it is annual *profits* that are chargeable, not *capital*. In many cases the test in distinguishing between capital receipts and income receipts has been between a sum which is received for the use of an asset (ie income) and a sum received on disposing of an interest in an asset (ie capital). The simile often used is that of the tree, which is capital, and its fruit, which is income.

There are, inevitably, cases where the treatment of revenue capital items is dictated by specific statutory provisions which override the general principles which would otherwise apply (eg certain gains of a capital nature obtained from the disposal of land – see TA 1988, s 776, an anti-avoidance provision).

'Property' in this context is not limited to real property (land and buildings), and means anything which is capable of being owned (eg intangible intellectual property rights such as copyrights and patents).

For income tax, Schedule D is divided into six Cases, each of which has its own specific rules:

Case I: Any trade carried on in the UK or elsewhere but not contained in Schedule A.

Case II: Any profession or vocation not contained in any other Schedule.

Case III: (a) Any interest of money (whether yearly or otherwise) or any annuity or other annual payment, whether payable within or outside of the UK, either as a charge on any property of the person paying it under any deed or will or otherwise, or as a reservation out of it, or as a personal debt or obligation under any contract, or whether it is received and payable half-yearly or at any shorter or more distant periods (but *not* including payment chargeable under Schedule A).

            (b) All discounts.

            (c) Income from securities which is payable out of the UK or Northern Ireland public revenue.

Case IV: Income arising from securities out of the UK.

Case V: Income arising from possessions out of the UK not being income consisting of emoluments of any office or employment.

Case VI: Any annual profits or gains not falling under any other Schedule D case and not charged under Schedule A or E.

For corporation tax the Cases are:

Case I: Any trade carried on in the UK or elsewhere but not contained in Schedule A.

Case II: Any profession or vocation not contained in any other Schedule.

Case III: (a) Profits and gains arising from loan relationships, treated as chargeable under Case III (non-trading loan relationships) by FA 1996, ss 80–105.

(b) Any annuity or other annual payment which:

(i) is payable (whether inside or outside the UK and whether annually or at shorter or longer intervals) in respect of anything other than a loan relationship; and

(ii) is not a payment chargeable under Schedule A.

(c) Any discount arising otherwise than in respect of a loan relationship.

Case V: Income arising from possessions out of the UK not being income consisting of emoluments of any office or employment, but not including any income falling within Case III(a) above.

Case VI: Any annual profits or gains not falling under any other Schedule D case and not charged under Schedule A or E.

Although the Revenue has no right to choose under which Schedule it will charge tax, there is greater opportunity for choice between the Schedule D cases.

Schedule D, as outlined above, is not exhaustive, and there are other tax rules which direct that tax be charged under Schedule D, even if it would not normally fit within the charge, eg:

(1) TA 1988, s 1A (income from savings and distributions chargeable under Cases III–V taxed at lower rate).

(2) TA 1988, s 314 (income from employment as a diver concerned with exploration or exploitation of the seabed chargeable under Case I).

(3) TA 1988, s 347A (exclusion from tax of annual payments which would otherwise fall within Case III, subject to specified exceptions).

(4) TA 1988, s 503 (profits from commercially let furnished holiday accommodation in the UK chargeable under Case I).

(5) TA 1988, s 580A (exclusion from tax of annual payments under a long-term disability insurance policy providing insurance against risk of illness, unemployment, etc, provided that no relief was claimed for payment of the premium (sometimes referred to as 'permanent health insurance')).

(6) F(No 2)A 1992, Sched 10 (calculation of Case I profits under the Rent-a-Room scheme).

Any annual profits or gains not falling under any other Schedule D case and not charged under Schedule A or E can be charged under Schedule D Case VI, which is the residual case. Case VI is also used to charge tax on some surpluses, which on general principles would not otherwise be liable under Case VI (eg gains of a capital nature obtained from the disposal of land – see TA 1988, s 776, an anti-avoidance provision).

Unlike the Schedules, the first five (four for corporation tax) Schedule D cases, which define specific classes of income, are not exclusive. Thus, if income can fall within more than one case the Revenue has the right to choose the case under which the charge is made. For example, interest income can be charged under:

(1) Case I as trading income including, for companies, as a credit under the FA 1996 loan relationships regime;
(2) Case III as interest; or
(3) if the source is foreign, Case IV as income from foreign securities or Case V as income from foreign possessions.

For companies, non-trading credits under the FA 1996 loan relationships regime are charged under Case III.

Under self-assessment, the Revenue's right to choose applies (see TMA 1970, s 28A(7A)) where, in a return:

(1) alternative methods are allowed by the income tax rules for bringing amounts into account in that return,
(2) the return is made, or amended, using one of those methods,
(3) the return could have been made using an alternative method, and
(4) the Revenue determines which of the alternative methods is to be used in relation to the taxpayer for that period (there is no right of appeal against such a determination).

In this event, any enquiry into that return or into an amendment of it is conducted as if the only method allowed were the one determined by the Revenue. There are two cases where the tax rules allow alternative methods for bringing amounts into account in a return – in making a computation for the purposes either of Schedule D Case I or II, or of Cases III–V. Similar rules apply for corporation tax (FA 1998, Sched 18, para 84).

The Revenue option does not apply to Case VI, which is exclusive and does not come into play until all other cases have been considered. However, in some circumstances assessments can be made as alternatives to Cases I or II.

2.4 SCHEDULE D CASES I AND II

As explained in 2.2, all taxable income must be derived from a source specified in one or other of the Schedules. The following concerns income assessable under Schedule D Cases I and II.

Following the 'source' doctrine, income can only be charged to tax under Cases I and II if it is shown that the taxpayer carries on, and the income is derived from, a trade (Case I) or a profession or vocation (Case II).

When considering, for example, whether Case I applies, the general requirements for assessment under Schedule D must be considered along with the specific requirements of the particular case. Thus, Case I applies to the annual profits or gains arising to a UK resident from any trade, whether carried on in the UK or abroad, and to the annual profits or gains arising to a non-UK resident person from a trade carried on in the UK. A similar analysis applies to annual profits or gains arising from a profession or vocation under Case II.

A UK resident who carries on a trade wholly abroad might thus appear to be chargeable under Case I. However, such profits are instead liable under Case V as income from a foreign possession, a principle established by *Colquhoun v Brooks* (1889) 2 TC 490. In this case, a UK resident was a sleeping partner in an Australian firm carrying on a business in Australia. Under the law which applied at the time, he was assessed under Case I on the full amount of his share of the business profits. The House of Lords held that his partnership interest was a possession within Case V.

It could be argued that some activities which produce income from the use of land, or which arise out of land, fall within Schedule A as 'annual profits arising from a business carried on for the exploitation, as a source of rents or other receipts, of any estate, interest or rights in or over land in the UK', and that such activities amount to carrying on a trade. However, Schedule A states that it does not apply to profits arising from the occupation of land. More specifically, it excludes farming and market gardening (TA 1988, s 53) and mines, quarries and other concerns (s 55), the profits of which are chargeable under Case I. Here, the cultivation of short rotation coppice and stud farming are regarded as farming under FA 1995, s 154; however, woodlands and land being prepared for forestry purposes are not regarded as 'farming'.

2.4.1 Profession or vocation

There are no definitions within the legislation for 'profession' and 'vocation'; indeed there are no reported tax cases in which the point at issue was the distinction between the two. There was, however, an exemption for 'any profession the profits of which are dependent mainly on the personal qualifications' of the person carrying on the profession and 'in which no capital expenditure is required, or only capital expenditure of a comparatively small amount' which applied under the Excess Profits Duty, with similar relief available under National Defence Contribution and Excess Profits Tax, which can be regarded as precedents.

CIR v Maxse (1919) 12 TC 41 concerned the owner of a monthly political magazine who wrote much of it himself. It was held that, for Excess Profits Duty purposes, he carried on a separate profession of journalist and editor. It followed that, in arriving at the profits of his publishing business, an allowance should be made for his services. This decision was followed in *Salt v Fernandez* [1997] SSCD 271, in which a lecturer wrote and published a book in 1983. Later, in 1994, he also published in booklet form a lecture which had been given more than 80 years previously. The Revenue issued Schedule D assessments on the basis that he was acting as a professional author. On appeal, the Special Commissioner accepted his contention that, in addition to being a professional author, he had begun a separate trade of publishing when he published the lecture. However, subsequently, as reported in *Salt v Fernandez (No 2)* [1998] SSCD 176, the Revenue had issued Case I assessments. As a result, the publishing trade's profits in 1993–94 were assessed for both that year and for 1994–95 the following year (under the opening years rule which applied for the preceding year basis of assessment then in force). The author's contention was that the profits should not be assessed again, as they were included in the 1994–95 Case II assessment on him as an author. The Special Commissioner, in rejecting this contention, held that TMA 1970, s 32 (relief for double assessment) required that the amount should be taken out of the Case II assessment and assessed under Case I, even though this might result in the amount 'being assessed more than once under the rules applicable to new trades'.

In *Webster v CIR* [1942] 2 All ER 517, it was held that an ophthalmic optician was not carrying on a profession, but was carrying on the business of selling spectacles, to which eye-testing was ancillary and the receipts from which could not be severed (distinguishing *CIR v Maxse*). However, in *Carr v CIR* [1944] 2 All ER 163, the Commissioners held that an optician was carrying on a profession, which was upheld by the Court of Appeal, holding that whether a trade is a 'profession' turns on the facts of the individual case, and not solely on the trader's 'special skill or ability, or some special qualifications derived from training or experience'.

In the context of corporation tax, in *CIR v Peter McIntyre Ltd* (1926) 12 TC 1006 the Court of Session held that a company which carried on business as auctioneers was not carrying on a profession, on the grounds that a company cannot have the 'personal qualifications' necessary to bring it within the exemption.

Billam v Griffith (1941) 23 TC 757 concerned the meaning of 'vocation'. A former barrister had written and sold a successful play. He had also previously written several plays in his spare time without selling them. It was held that he had been carrying on the vocation of dramatist, and that his receipts from the successful play were receipts of that vocation.

Historically, a 'profession' meant the three learned professions of the Church, Medicine and the Law, but today the term is much wider and normally involves some substantial exercise of either purely intellectual skill, or of any manual skill controlled, as in painting and sculpture or surgery, by the operator's intellectual skill, as distinguished from an occupation which is substantially the production or sale of commodities. Three further tests of a profession have been put forward:

(1) its practice is based on preliminary study, training and, possibly, examination in the general principles of the pursuit;
(2) the profits which may be made from its pursuit do not depend primarily on the provision of great quantities of capital; and
(3) it is a pursuit which is followed not solely as a livelihood but always subject to overriding duties, prescribed by a code of professional honour involving, in an especial degree, the strict observance of confidences, in which services must be rendered to the client without stint in proportion to the client's need rather than in proportion to the reward which is received.

'Vocation' has a wide meaning related to the way a person passes his life and indicates a calling. This is not necessarily one related to religion, caring or high-minded service to others. Authors, bookmakers, dramatists, jockeys and professional singers have all been dealt with by the courts on the basis that they carried on vocations.

There is generally little difference between the basis of assessment under Cases I and II, so that the distinction between a 'trade' on the one hand and a 'profession' or 'vocation' on the other is now of very limited importance. This all the more so, now that FA 1998, s 42 effectively has brought to an end the cash basis and bills issued basis of accounting for professional practices by providing that the accounting basis for computing the profits of a trade, profession or vocation must give a true and fair view of the profit or loss. This rule applies to periods of account beginning on or after 6 April 1999.

2.4.2 Trade

'Trade', defined in TA 1988, s 832(1), 'includes every trade, manufacture, adventure or concern in the nature of trade'. Regrettably, this is not a model of clarity, and this lack of an exhaustive definition has given rise to much litigation. On the face of it, 'trade' must take its ordinary meaning – thus, to follow a dictionary definition, 'The practice of some . . . business . . . habitually carried on, especially when practised as a means of livelihood or gain, . . . now usually applied to a mercantile occupation and to a skilled handicraft, as distinct from a profession'. In *National Association of Local Government Officers v Bolton Corp* [1942] 2 All ER 425, it was held that '"trade" refers to the various activities of commerce – the winning and using the products of the earth and selling them, or manufacturing and selling them, the purchase and sale of commodities, or the offering of services for a reward, such as conveyance and the like.'

In many, perhaps most, cases it is self-evident that a trade is being carried on. There are inevitably a large number of marginal cases which require further consideration. As the statutory definition in s 832(1) provides little guidance on what amounts to trading, it is necessary to consider the large volume of tax cases dealing with this issue. In summary, the message from case-law is that trade cannot be defined precisely, but there are certain characteristics which are normally those of trade, and others which would normally prevent a profit from being derived from a trade.

The definition of 'trade' also includes 'manufacture', which should cause few difficulties. The words 'adventure or concern in the nature of trade' are more problematic. Using ordinary, rather than statutory, meanings, it would appear that such activities, while not amounting to full-blown trades, can nevertheless be taxable under Case I, and bring in transactions that, although less than full trading operations, are within its broader meaning for tax purposes. It is sometimes suggested that it is only the word 'concern' that is qualified by the words 'in the nature of trade'. If this were to be the case, the word 'adventure' stands alone. In fact, the courts frequently use the words 'adventure in the nature of trade' to describe the the test for activities within Case I (eg 'To say that a transaction is or is not an adventure in the nature of trade is to say that it has or has not the characteristics which distinguish such an adventure': *Edwards v Bairstow and Harrison* (1955) 36 TC 207). The definition has been held to be wide enough to bring into Case I isolated transactions or speculative adventures that yield unexpected profits (*Martin v Lowry* (1926) 11 TC 297 (purchase and resale of war surplus linen); *CIR v Livingstone & Others* (1926) 11 TC 538 (purchase, conversion and resale of a ship); *Cape Brandy Syndicate v CIR* (1921) 12 TC 358 (speculative purchase and resale of brandy); *Pickford v Quirke* (1927) 13 TC 251 (purchase and resale of cotton mills); *Edwards v Bairstow and Harrison* (1955) 36 TC 207 (purchase and resale of cotton-spinning plant); *Rutledge v CIR* (1929) 14 TC 490 (single purchase and multiple sales of large quantity of toilet paper); *CIR v Fraser* (1942) 24 TC 498 (isolated purchase and resale of whisky in bond); *Wisdom v Chamberlain* (1968) 45 TC 692 (purchase and sale of silver bullion held as a hedge against devaluation))).

However, it does not follow from these cases that every isolated transaction or speculative adventure giving rise to a profit should be within Case I. In *Leeming v Jones* (1930) 15 TC 333 (acquisitions of options to rubber estates assignment of rights to a public company) it was found that the transaction was not a concern in the nature of trade. It was stated that: 'in the case of an isolated transaction ... there is really no middle course open. It is either an adventure in the nature of trade, or else it is simply a case of sale and resale of property.' To be assessable under Case I, a profit must be of an income nature and not a capital accretion.

There is no fixed rule to apply to the question of whether a trade exists, and every case must be decided on its own facts and circumstances. However, the courts tend to review transactions to establish whether they bear any of the six 'badges of trade' identified and summarised in 1955 in the Final Report of the Royal Commission on the Taxation of Profits and Income. Over the years, as circumstances have required it, the courts have added further 'badges'.

Each of these badges is described below, together with a summary of what are regarded as the major relevant criteria that have a bearing on whether a trade exists.

A profit-seeking motive

If it is shown that the sole object of acquiring an asset was to sell it on at a profit, and with no intention of holding it as an investment, the natural conclusion would be that a trade is being carried on. However, while an intention to make a profit is a relevant factor in deciding whether there is a trade, it is not of itself decisive. Indeed, for tax purposes a trade may be carried on even though there is no intention to make a profit. The reverse is also true and the realisation and accumulation of a surplus of receipts over outgoings from carrying on an activity does not necessarily amount to a trade. Important decisions in determining whether a trade is being carried on include *Salt v Chamberlain* (1979) 53 TC 143 (speculative stock exchange transactions by an individual did not constitute a trade – he was seeking to establish a trade loss to set against other income). In *Halefield Securities Ltd v Thorpe* (1967) 44 TC 154, an investment company sought, unsuccessfully, to establish that a substantial loss on disposal of a shareholding should qualify for loss relief from a trade of dealing in securities. However, the taxpayer companies in *Lewis Emanuel & Sons Ltd v White* (1965) 42 TC 369 and *Cooper v C & J Clark Ltd* (1982) 54 TC 570 claimed successfully that losses on investments gave rise to trading losses available for relief.

In general, as shown by *Paddington Burial Board v CIR* (1884) 2 TC 46 (surplus income assessable although applicable in aid of poor rates), the destination of a surplus is irrelevant. Similar decisions were arrived at in *Dublin Corp v M'Adam* (1887) 2 TC 387 (surplus of water undertaking assessable although applicable to reduce indebtedness); *Webber v Glasgow Corp* (1893) 3 TC 202 (local authority profits assessable although applicable for public purposes); and *Brighton College v Marriott* (1925) 10 TC 213 (profits of a school assessable although applicable for charitable purposes).

It is also important to note that a trade may be carried on for tax purposes even though there is no intention to make a profit. If a trade is found to be carried on there is liability to tax on any resulting profits whether or not the trading activities are directed to the making of a profit. In *Carnoustie Golf Course Committee v CIR* (1929) 14 TC 498 and *CIR v Stonehaven Recreation Ground Trustees* (1929) 15 TC 419, where a committee in the first case and trustees in the latter managed public recreation facilities, this was held to be trading. In the latter case it was held that although the trustees' object was never intentionally commercial, it was what they did, and not what they intended to do, that decided whether they were carrying on a trade.

The realisation's subject-matter

While almost any form of property can be acquired to be dealt in, those forms of property, such as commodities or manufactured articles, which are normally the subject of trading are only very exceptionally the subject of investment. Problems may be encountered with assets that are generally bought:

(a) as an investment that usually, but not necessarily, yields income (eg shares); or
(b) for personal use or enjoyment (eg works of art); or
(c) as a fixed asset of an admitted trade (eg machinery and plant).

It is the nature of such assets that leads to an initial presumption that they are not acquired as a subject of trade.

Property which does not provide its owner with an income or personal enjoyment merely by virtue of its ownership is more likely to have been acquired with the object of a deal than property that does not (see eg *CIR v Fraser, Rutledge v CIR, Edwards v Bairstow and Harrison* and *Wisdom v Chamberlain* above). However, the fact that an asset does not produce income before realisation is no more than a pointer to the possibility that it is held as a trading asset. In most cases the benefit to the holder comes as an enhancement in the asset's capital value (see *Marson v Morton (and related appeals)* (1986) 59 TC 381).

Transactions involving financial assets such as shares, options and futures do not normally amount to trading for tax purposes. In particular, shares are usually held for investment with a view to providing income or capital growth. Yet there are many short-term transactions which cannot be classed as investments, but which fall short of trading. There is now a range of provisions which ensures that surpluses from transactions involving various financial instruments are brought into the scope of taxation in income form.

There are also assets which do not produce income, but which are acquired for the pleasure which ownership brings to the owner (eg antiques or works of art). The owner may well hope for an increase in value in due course. However, this does not bring the transaction within the ambit of trading unless there are other significant indications of a trading intention.

If the subject of the transaction is normally used for investment – land, houses, stocks and shares – the inference that the venture was a trading one is not so readily to be drawn from an admitted intention to sell on the arrival of a suitable, preselected time or circumstance (see *CIR v Reinhold* (1953) 34 TC 389).

The quantity purchased can also be a factor. In *CIR v Fraser* and *Rutledge v CIR*, the commodities in question, whisky and one million toilet rolls respectively, had been bought in quantities which were far in excess of anything which could be used by the taxpayer personally.

Transactions involving land are among the most difficult to categorise as land is capable of functioning both as an investment or trading stock.

Number or frequency of similar transactions by same person

If realisations of the same sort of property occur in succession over a period of years, or there are several such realisations at about the same date, there is a presumption that there has been dealing in relation to each (eg *St Aubyn Estates Ltd v Strike* (1932) 17 TC 412 (breaking up an estate via a company formed for the purpose); *Martin v Lowry* (above) (disposal in small lots of a large quantity of government surplus aeroplane linen)). A large number of similar transactions is also indicative of a trade (eg *Pickford v Quirke* (above); *Leach v Pogson* (1962) 40 TC 585 (setting up and selling driving schools); and transactions in shares in *Lewis Emanuel & Sons Ltd v White* (above), although this was not thought to be conclusive in *Salt v Chamberlain* (above).

Addition of value to asset(s)

What (if anything) is done to an asset pending resale is a relevant factor. If modifications are carried out to the asset by way of processing or manufacture, or some kind of adaptation to make it more readily marketable, or if any special exertions are made to find or attract purchasers, such as the opening of an office or large-scale advertising, these are actions typical of trading activities. Similarly, breaking down assets into smaller lots to facilitate a sale may be a pointer to a trading motive as in *Edwards v Bairstow & Harrison* (above). Likewise, in *Cape Brandy Syndicate v CIR*, the work related to a large quantity of Cape brandy which was shipped to the UK, blended expertly with French brandy, re-casked and sold in numerous lots was all part of the evidence leading to a conclusion that a trade was carried on. In *CIR v Livingstone* (above), work was undertaken to convert and refit a ship for subsequent sale, and in *St Aubyn Estates Ltd v Strike* (above) roads were laid on an estate in preparation for its break up and sale.

When there is an organised effort to obtain profit, there is a source of taxable income. However, expenditure on an asset after purchase and before resale is not always strong evidence of a trading motive. It will depend on the nature and scale of the expenditure (eg insurance against loss, normal maintenance to prevent deterioration, or to maintain the asset in working condition, would add little weight in favour of trading). However, if an asset did not need any modification or other work then absence of any modification etc is neutral.

Manner of acquisition

It is less likely that the sale of an asset acquired in some way other than by purchase will be classified as a sale by way of trade than one which was acquired by a purchase (eg land acquired by reclamation under an agreement rather than by purchase was held not to be a trade when the land was subsequently sold in *Hudson's Bay Co Ltd v Stevens* (1909) 5 TC 424, but the formation of a company between the inheritor of an estate and its development and sale led to the opposite conclusion in *St Aubyn Estates Ltd v Strike*).

If an asset is acquired by gift or inheritance, it is probable, although not inevitable, that a subsequent sale is not by way of trade. However, the sale may give rise to a trading profit if at some point before the sale the asset became trading stock of a trade or an adventure in the nature of trade.

Circumstances of the disposal

The way in which a disposal is carried out is of considerable significance. Thus, the conclusion that a trade is being carried on is likely if the transactions were undertaken in the same manner that an undisputed trader would carry them through. The test which must be used to determine whether a venture is 'in the nature of trade' is whether the operations involved in it are of the same kind, and carried on in the same way, as those which are characteristic of ordinary trading in the line of business in which the venture was made (see *CIR v Livingstone*). In *CIR v Fraser* and *Rutledge v CIR*, it was important that the commodities concerned were sold in much the same way as would apply in the course of an ordinary trade in that commodity. Any organised activity intended to promote sale is evidence of trading (eg a sales campaign by advertisement or canvass or the organisation or employment of a selling agency or sales staff: see *Martin v Lowry*). The formation of a syndicate or company solely or mainly for the purpose of the particular transaction is evidence of trading (see *St Aubyn Estates Ltd v Strike*, above, and *California Copper Syndicate Ltd v Harris* (1904) 5 TC 159).

The 1955 Final Report suggested that the circumstances responsible for the realisation should be considered. There may be some explanation, such as a sudden emergency or opportunity calling for ready money, that negatives the idea that any plan of dealing prompted the original purchase. Such a conclusion might be drawn where a sale of a property, intended to be held as an investment, is a forced sale brought about by pressure from bankers to repay a loan at short notice.

Substantial advertising and the creation of an organisation to deal with sales enquiries etc indicated trading in *Martin v Lowry* and in *Cape Brandy Syndicate v CIR*. The absence of an organisation, because none was necessary, was held to be irrelevant in *Edwards v Bairstow and Harrison*. There may be some explanation, such as a sudden emergency or opportunity calling for ready money, that negates the idea that any plan of dealing prompted the original purchase.

Period between purchase and sale

Generally speaking, purchase and sale transactions carried out over a short period indicate trading (eg *Martin v Lowry*, *Wisdom v Chamberlain*, *Pickford v Quirke*, *Leach v Pogson* and *Lewis Emanuel & Sons Ltd v White*, but not *Salt v Chamberlain* (above), nor *Johnston v Heath* (1970) 46 TC 463 where an agreement to sell a plot of land was made *before* the land was purchased. At the other extreme is *Orchard Parks Ltd v Pogson* (1964) 42 TC 442, where the period between the purchase of land for development (although the project had to be abandoned) and when the land itself was ultimately sold, was 25 years!

Association of disposal with seller's other interests

It is likely that a transaction that is related to a trade already carried on by the seller will be looked upon as itself being a trading transaction (*Cape Brandy Syndicate v CIR*; *Pickford v Quirke*; and *Gloucester Railway Carriage & Wagon Co Ltd v CIR* (1925) 12 TC 720).

If there is an admitted trade, then a similarity to the transaction under consideration may be a pointer to that transaction having a trading character. However, in *Harvey v Caulcott* (1952) 33 TC 159, where a builder claimed successfully that certain properties that he had built and then sold many years later were investments and not part of his trading stock, it was held that the fact the man was a builder put the onus on him to show that the profit was from an investment and not from trading stock.

Other relevant cases include *CIR v Fraser*, where it was held that where there is 'a single transaction entered into by an individual in the line of his own trade (although not part and parcel of his ordinary business)', is easier to hold that it is an adventure in the nature of trade than 'a transaction entered into by an individual outside the line of his own trade or occupation'. In *Lynch v Edmondson* 1998 SSCD 185, the purchase by a bricklayer of a plot of land and the building thereon of two flats was held to be 'a typical trading transaction'. This case was distinguished from *Marson v Morton* (above), where the question was posed: 'Is the transaction in question in some way related to the trade which the taxpayer otherwise carries on?'.

Method of finance

If a transaction is financed by means of borrowing, and it is clear that the borrowing is in due course to be repaid in the short term from the proceeds of sale from the asset concerned, it is likely that trading will be inferred. This conclusion was also drawn in a case where there was an agreement to sell land before it had been purchased in *Johnston v Heath*. In *Tebrau (Johore) Rubber Syndicate Ltd v Farmer* (1910) 5 TC 658, a company had acquired rubber estates in Malaya, planted them, but then before any rubber was produced sold the estates. In this case the profit was held to be a capital profit. A purchase of eg silver bullion futures was undertaken in the expectation that it would be paid for out of the proceeds of the sale in *Wisdom v Chamberlain*. Furthermore, in this case such activity was entirely outside the taxpayer's normal show business occupation.

The sale by a builder of shops he had built and subsequently let, and a house in which his foreman had lived, was held in *Harvey v Caulcott* to be the realisation of investments. This was despite the fact that the purchase was made out of the resources of an admitted trade that the taxpayer was already carrying on. The court did not consider that the payment of the sale proceeds into the existing business was significant. It could not offset a finding that the asset had been an investment from the beginning.

If an asset provides an income such as rent, interest or dividends, it is more likely to be an investment than if it produced none. But the income has to be considered alongside any expenses associated with the transaction. Suppose that the purchase of an asset is financed by borrowings on which interest is payable, that interest may match or exceed the income. In that event, the asset's income-bearing nature is of less importance. The conclusion is that any benefit can only come from the actual disposal of the asset, allowing the loan to be repaid, the income being merely set against the outgoings until that surplus is available (see *Cooke v Haddock* (1960) 39 TC 64).

Miscellaneous matters

The Revenue takes the view that transactions undertaken solely for fiscal purposes are not trading, even if the outward characteristics of trading are present, because they lack an underlying commercial purpose. In some cases, the real purpose behind transactions is to obtain a tax advantage by eg establishing a loss to obtain repayment of tax paid at source, or to set against other profits. This view is supported in such cases as *Lupton v FA & AB Ltd* (1971) 47 TC 580; *Coates v Arndale Properties Ltd* (1984) 36 TC 275; *Reed v Nova Securities Ltd* (1988) 59 TC 516; *Overseas Containers (Finance) Ltd v Stoker* (1989) 61 TC 473; and *Ensign Tankers (Leasing) Ltd v Stokes* (1992) 64 TC 617.

Revenue extra-statutory concessions, statements of practice, interpretations etc deal with a number of marginal situations and should always be consulted.

Two matters arise:

(1) If it is shown that profitable transactions do not amount to a trade there can be no Case I charge.
(2) If it is shown that loss-making transactions do amount to a trade, such losses can be offset against other income and, in certain circumstances, against chargeable gains.

2.5 SCHEDULE D CASE III
(TA 1988, s 64)

Income under Case III broadly comprises interest, but does not include any payment chargeable under Schedule A, discounts, and income from securities which is payable out of the UK or Northern Ireland public revenue (see 2.3).

Case III charges income tax on the full amount of the income arising within the tax year, and is paid on the actual amount of that income without any deduction. Different rules apply for corporation tax, and most interest, discounts etc are dealt with under the FA 1996 loan relationships regime.

2.6 SCHEDULE D CASES IV AND V
(TA 1988, ss 65–68)

Income under Cases IV and V comprises income arising from securities out of the UK, and income arising from possessions out of the UK not being income consisting of emoluments of any office or employment respectively.

Cases IV and V charge income tax on the full amount of the income arising in a tax year, whether or not the income has been or will be received in the UK. This is subject in the case of income not received in the UK to:

(1) the same deductions and allowances as if it had been so received, and
(2) a deduction on account of any annuity or other annual payment (not being interest) payable out of the income to a person not resident in the UK.

Income chargeable to tax under Case IV or V from carrying on any trade, profession or vocation either solely or in partnership is computed following the normal Cases I and II rules.

The rules described above do not apply to any person who is not UK-domiciled or, being a Commonwealth or a Republic of Ireland citizen, is not UK-ordinarily resident. In such event tax is computed under:

(1) Case IV on the full amount, so far as it can be computed, of the sums received in the UK in the year of assessment, without any deduction or abatement; and
(2) Case V on the full amount of the actual sums received in the UK in the tax year without any deduction or abatement other than is allowed under Case I.

The meaning of 'received in the UK' in this context is widely drawn, and includes sums received from remittances payable in the UK, or from property imported, or from money or value arising from property not imported, or from money or value so received on credit or on account of any such remittances, property, money or value brought or to be brought into the UK.

There are extensive rules for looking through 'back-to-back' loan transactions designed to receive benefit in the UK without bringing the income back to the UK.

Relief is available (under TA 1988, s 585) if a person can show that he was unable to transfer income to the UK owing to the laws of the territory where the income arose, or to executive action of its government, or to the impossibility of obtaining foreign currency in that territory; and that the inability was not because of any want of reasonable endeavours on his part.

A special rule applies where a person is chargeable to income tax under Case V on income which arises from rents or other receipts from a business carried on for the exploitation of any estate, interest or rights in or over land outside the UK, and is not income derived from carrying on a trade, profession or vocation. All such businesses and transactions carried on or entered into by a particular person or partnership, so far as they are chargeable to tax under Case V, are treated as, or as entered into in the course of carrying on, a single 'overseas property business'. The income from an overseas property business is computed under Schedule A rules. It is important to note that an overseas property business is dealt with entirely separately from any actual Schedule A business.

The special treatment under TA 1988, ss 503 and 504, CAA 1990, s 29 and TCGA 1992, s 241 (furnished holiday accommodation) does not apply to the profits or losses of an overseas property business.

Income chargeable to tax under Case IV or V is, in the case of property situated and profits arising in the Republic of Ireland, computed on the full amount of the income arising in the tax year, whether or not the income has been or will be received in the UK. This is subject, in the case of income not received in the UK, to:

(1) the same deductions and allowances as if it had been so received, and
(2) a deduction on account of any annuity or other annual payment (not being interest) payable out of the income to a person not resident in the UK.

This does not apply to any income derived by a person from the carrying on by him of any trade, profession or vocation, either solely or in partnership. Tax on any such income arising in the Republic of Ireland is computed either on the full amount thereof arising in the tax year on broadly the same basis as if it had arisen in the UK.

2.7 SCHEDULE D CASE VI

Income tax under Case VI is computed on the full amount of the profits or gains arising in the tax year.

2.8 SCHEDULE E

For a discussion of the income assessable under Schedule E, see Chapter 13.

3

COMPUTING TRADING PROFITS FOR TAX PURPOSES

DAVID BERTRAM, CLAYFIELD PROFESSIONAL GUIDANCE LTD

This chapter covers the way in which a business's taxable profits are ascertained, and deals with some of the more common of the adjustments to the accounts of a business which are required for business purposes.

3.1 HOW TAXABLE PROFITS ARE ARRIVED AT

3.1.1 Introduction

The tax legislation provides no firm rule for what expenditure is deductible in computing, for tax purposes, the profits of a trade, etc. The charge to tax under Schedule D Case I is on 'the full amount of the profits of the year of assessment' (TA 1988, s 60(1)). For income tax this is generally the profits of a 12-month period ending within a tax year (TA 1988, s 60(3)), although there are special rules which apply on commencement and discontinuance (TA 1988, ss 61–63A). For corporation tax purposes, income under Case I for an accounting period is computed on 'the full amount of the profits or gains arising in the period' (TA 1988, s 70(1)).

As there is no specific definition, 'profits' must be taken to have its natural and ordinary meaning in a commercial context. It can thus be arrived at by taking the receipts of the trade and deducting from them the expenditure necessary to earn those receipts (*Gresham Life Assurance Society v Styles* (1890) 3 TC 185).

An item of expenditure should be deductible in computing the profits of a trade if the expenditure can be justified on commercial accounting principles (*Usher's Wiltshire Brewery Ltd v Bruce* (1915) 6 TC 399; *Lothian Chemical Co Ltd v Rogers* (1926) 11 TC 508). Where there is a specific statutory prohibition, that expenditure cannot be deducted even if, as a matter of accounting principle, it would be proper to deduct it.

3.1.2 Accounting practice

The measure of profits for tax purposes is, first and foremost, a question of law. However, the courts consider evidence as to how accounts are drawn up in practice.

The Accounting Standards Board (ASB), set up under the CA 1985, is responsible for setting Accounting Standards. The ASB adopted the existing Statements of Standard Accounting Practice (SSAPs) and has also issued its own Financial Reporting Standards (FRSs). These are, initially, issued for discussion and comment as Financial Reporting Exposure Drafts (FREDs). Additionally, for particular industries, Statements of Recommended Practice (SORPs) are issued. Particular issues are dealt with by the Urgent Issues Task Force (UITF).

A company's balance sheet must give a true and fair view of its affairs at the end of its financial year and its profit and loss account must give a true and fair view of its result for the year. For those companies for which an auditor's report is required, such report must state whether, in the auditor's opinion, the balance sheet and profit and loss account give a true and fair view of the companies' affairs and of its profit or loss. The auditor must qualify his report if the accounts do not represent a true and fair view.

SSAP 2 (Disclosure of accounting policies) distinguishes between:

(1) *Fundamental accounting concepts* – SSAP 2 sets out the fundamental accounting concepts which underlie the periodic financial accounts of business enterprises.
(2) *Accounting bases* – These are the methods for expressing or applying the fundamental accounting concepts to financial transactions and items.
(3) *Accounting policies* – These are the specific accounting bases judged by a business to be the most appropriate to its circumstances and adopted for the preparation of its financial accounts.

SSAP 2 identifies four fundamental accounting concepts:

- going concern
- accruals
- consistency, and
- prudence.

The going concern concept makes the assumption, where it is appropriate to do so, that the business will continue to operate for the foreseeable future. The profit and loss account and the balance sheet are prepared on the basis that it is neither intended nor necessary to liquidate the business or to reduce its operations significantly.

Under the accruals concept, income and costs are accrued. This means that they are recognised as they are earned or incurred rather than according to when money is received or paid. In general, income (or 'revenue') and costs should be matched so that revenues are set against associated costs and expenses, so far as a relationship can be established or reasonably assumed. They should be dealt with in the profit and loss account for the period to which they relate. However, if the accruals concept is inconsistent with the prudence concept, the prudence concept prevails.

The consistency concept requires that the same accounting treatment is applied to like items within each account and from one period to the next. The need for consistency has been recognised by the courts. For instance, its importance in relation to the valuation of stocks was stressed in *Ostime v Duple Motor Bodies Ltd* (1961) 39 TC 537. However, it is important to take account of changing facts. For example, a fixed percentage addition for overheads in a stock valuation may lead to inconsistency if there are marked variations in the ratio of overheads to direct charges. The principle of consistency, however, also means that there must be a good reason for a change from one existing valid basis to another (eg a company is taken over and adapts its basis to that of its new owners, or there is some alteration in the nature of a business's trade). If an invalid basis has hitherto been followed in the accounts, together with an adjustment in the tax computation (so that the profits are computed on a valid basis), a business may want to change its accounts to a valid basis other than the one adopted in the tax computations. The Revenue generally accepts this change unless the existing taxation basis has been applied for so long as to raise the question of consistency.

The prudence concept requires that revenue and profits should not be anticipated but rather should be recognised only when realised. Moreover, provision should be made for all known liabilities. If necessary, a provision should be made for costs or expenses for which liability has arisen, with the provision being made on an estimated basis in the light of the information available.

SSAP 9 deals with the valuation of stocks and long-term contracts. As noted above, SSAP 2 recognises the 'consistency concept' and requires the matching of costs with related revenues. The cost of unsold goods or unconsumed materials will have been incurred in the expectation of future receipts. Accordingly, such costs are carried forward and matched with the revenue when it arises. If, for example, stocks have deteriorated or become obsolescent and there is no reasonable expectation that sufficient revenue will arise to cover the costs which have been incurred, the irrecoverable costs are charged to revenue in the accounts under review. Thus means that, as a general rule, stocks are stated at the lower of cost or net realisable value. For long-term contracts it may be appropriate to release profit to the profit and loss account as various stages in the contract are reached.

FRS 12 sets out the principles of accounting for provisions, contingent liabilities and contingent assets. Its purpose is to ensure that appropriate recognition criteria and measurement bases are applied thereto.

A provision is a liability that is of uncertain timing or amount, to be settled by a transfer of economic benefit.

A contingent liability is either

(1) a possible obligation arising from past events the existence of which will be confirmed only by the occurrence of one or more uncertain future events not wholly within the business's control; or

(2) a present obligation that arises from past events but is not recognised because it is not probable that a transfer of economic benefits will be required to settle the obligation or because the amount of the obligation cannot be measured with sufficient reliability.

A contingent asset is a possible asset arising from past events the existence of which will be confirmed only by the occurrence of one or more uncertain future events not wholly within the business's control.

Most small companies can now dispense with an audit. Their directors must ensure that the accounts show a true and fair view, and that other Companies Act accounting, reporting and record-keeping requirements are satisfied. This applies to companies with a turnover of:

(1) £90,000 or less, which are entitled to dispense with the audit without any replacement independent check; and

(2) above £90,000, but not more than £100,000 (for financial years ending after 26 July 2000) (£250,000 for charitable companies), which may replace the audit with a 'compilation report' signed by the 'Reporting Accountant'. This is broadly similar to the certificate normally given to the accounts of an unincorporated business prepared by an independent qualified accountant.

There are a number of circumstances where, even though they fall within the above turnover limit, the companies concerned may not dispense with an audit. These apply where the company is a plc, or has a balance sheet gross asset value exceeding £1,400,000, or is regulated under the Financial Services Act or, when brought into force, by the Financial Services and Markets Act 2000, or is a member of a group, or if sufficient shareholders object.

It is a recommendation of the accountancy bodies that the accounts of unincorporated businesses should generally comply with SSAPs and FRSs even though there is no mandatory requirement to do so.

Financial Reporting Standards for Smaller Entities (FRSSE) is a simplified version of the requirements for larger entities. It should be used by those businesses that fall within its scope and have chosen to adopt it. Two points are worthy of note:

(1) 'the treatment prescribed by the standard or requirement is compatible with that already used, or expected to be used, by the Inland Revenue in computing taxable profits'; and

(2) the FRSSE represents 'a pragmatic relaxation of disclosure rules rather than any new form of financial reporting tailored to the needs of small businesses'.

The current size limits are (under CA 1985, s 247(3)) a turnover of not more than £2,800,000, a balance sheet gross asset value not exceeding £1,400,000, and not more than 50 employees. However, the FRSSE does not apply to large or medium-sized companies, groups etc; plcs; banks, building societies or insurance companies; authorised persons under the Financial Services Act; or members of groups containing companies within the last three categories.

Under FRSSE, a provision is defined as 'a liability of uncertain timing or amount'. A liability is 'an entity's obligation to transfer economic benefits as a result of past transactions or events'. An obligation is 'either a legal obligation (derived eg from a contract or legislation) or a constructive obligation, where the entity has indicated to other parties that it will accept certain responsibilities and has created valid expectations in those other parties that it will discharge those responsibilities'. In summary it states that

> 'A provision should be recognised when, and only when, it is probable (i.e. more likely than not) that a present obligation exists, as a result of a past event, and that it will require a transfer of economic benefits in settlement that can be estimated reliably. The amount recognised as a provision should be the best estimate of the expenditure required to settle the obligation at the balance sheet date.'

So far as concerns individuals and partnerships, there is, under self-assessment, no statutory requirement to prepare a profit and loss account. Unless the business is large or complex (eg partnerships with turnover in excess of £15m) the Revenue does not require businesses to send in accounts rather than completing the standardised accounts information. However, a business must keep certain records of its dealings, as follows:

(a) details of the amount and description of all receipts and expenses in the course of the trade;

(b) where the trade involves dealing in goods, details of all purchases and sales of goods in the course of the trade; and

(c) supporting documents to the above including accounts, books, deeds, contracts, vouchers and receipts.

A sole trader or partnership whose gross annual turnover is below £15,000 need not submit accounts. The return must, however, show turnover, total business purchases and expenses and net profit. However, the trader should keep records to substantiate the figures in the return if necessary.

The amount shown as profit by the profit and loss account is not usually the amount of profit to be assessed, for in nearly every case it is necessary to make the adjustments required by the Taxes Acts. For example, accounts prepared for commercial reasons may include a provision for the wear and tear to a building. However, such a provision must be 'added back' (ie it is disallowed as a deduction in computing the profit of a business). Although no relief is available for wear and tear or for depreciation in value as such, a form of relief may be given, for appropriate expenditure, through the capital allowances system.

Although, for sole traders and partnerships, there is no statutory authority for the form that accounts are to take, the profit figure must be computed on an accounting basis that provides a true and fair view, subject to any adjustments required by tax law. A profit and loss account is usually accompanied by a balance sheet drawn up as at the date on which the accounting period ends. The purpose of the balance sheet is to show a 'snapshot' of the assets and liabilities of the business at that date, along with details of any provisions and reserves and the interests of the proprietors.

There are statutory requirements relating to the allowability of provisions as follows. First, under FA 1989, s 43 a deduction is allowed for emoluments provided that they are actually paid (or made available eg by transfer to a directors' current account having been subjected to PAYE and NICs) within nine months of the period of account to which they relate. This could cause problems in relation to long-term contracts. If a provision for losses on a long-term contract include amounts related to employees' remuneration it would have to be disallowed for tax, notwithstanding that the requirements of FRS 12 are satisfied. This should be borne in mind when periodically releasing profit on a long-term contract into the profit and loss account.

Secondly, any sum which is paid by an employer as contribution under an approved occupational pension scheme is allowed (under TA 1988, s 592(4)) to be deducted as an expense incurred in the chargeable period in which the sum is paid, but no other sum is allowed to be deducted as an expense relating to making, or any provision for making, any such contributions. The amount of an employer's deductible contributions must not exceed the amount contributed by him under the scheme for employees in a trade or undertaking the profits of which are assessable to UK income or corporation tax. However, a sum not paid by way of ordinary annual contribution may be treated, as the Revenue may direct, either as an expense incurred in the chargeable period in which the sum is paid, or as an expense to be spread over such period of years as the Revenue thinks proper. The Pension Schemes Office determines the period of spread. For chargeable periods ending after 31 May 1996, the period of spread is as follows:

Amount of special contribution	No of years
£500,000–£999,999	2
£1,000,000–£2,000,000	3
£2,000,000 or more	4

The Revenue's discretion cannot be reviewed by Commissioners (see *Kelsall v Investment Chartwork Ltd* (1993) 65 TC 750).

Pension contributions for an unincorporated business proprietor are not an allowable deduction in computing profits, although relief is available as a deduction from taxable profits (see Chapter 14 for details of proprietors' personal pension contributions).

Relief is available, under FA 1989, s 76, for contributions to UK pension schemes solely for overseas employees, and to overseas pension schemes which correspond to UK approved pension schemes if the payments are for employees who receive foreign emoluments or are non-resident and working wholly abroad.

However, expenses relating to an unapproved retirement benefit scheme are precluded from relief in computing business profits, if no-one is chargeable to income tax on the sum paid or on the benefits provided or to be provided (see *Tax Bulletin* 17 (June 1995), p 225).

Thirdly, FA 1996, Sched 9, para 2 deals with late payment of interest under the loan relationships rules. Specifically, it applies for the purpose of bringing debits into account in respect of a debtor relationship of a company where an authorised accruals basis of accounting is used for that relationship. If interest payable under that relationship is not paid within 12 months following the end of the accounting period in which it would otherwise be treated as accruing, and credits representing the full amount of the interest are not brought into account for any accounting period in respect of the corresponding creditor relationship, then debits relating to that interest are brought into account on the assumption that the interest does not accrue until it is paid.

Fourthly, FA 1996, Sched 9, para 5 allows a departure from the assumption in the case of creditor relationships that every amount payable under those relationships will be paid in full as it becomes due. This is allowed to the extent only that:

(a) a debt is a bad debt;
(b) a doubtful debt is estimated to be bad; or
(c) a liability to pay any amount is released.

Such a departure is allowed only where there is an appropriate adjustment if any part of an amount taken or estimated to represent an amount of bad debt is paid or otherwise ceases to be an amount in respect of which such a departure is allowed. Where a liability to pay any amount under a debtor relationship of a company is released, and the release occurs in an accounting period for which an authorised accruals basis of accounting is used in that relationship, no credit in respect of the release is required to be brought into account if the release is part of a relevant arrangement or compromise (voluntary arrangements under Insolvency Act 1986, or a compromise or arrangement under CA 1985, s 425), or the relationship is one as respects which FA 1996, s 87 requires the use of an authorised accruals basis of accounting.

If a company makes a provision for a bad debt due from a connected party, the assumption that every amount payable under the relationship will be paid in full is applied. There is one exception to this rule where:

(a) in consideration of, or of any entitlement to, any shares forming part of the ordinary share capital of the company on whom the liability would otherwise have fallen, the creditor company treats the liability as discharged; and

(b) there would be no connection between the two companies for the accounting period in which that consideration is given if the question whether there is such a connection for that period was determined by reference only to times before the creditor company acquired possession of, or any entitlement to, the shares in question.

Bad debt relief is also denied even if the parties cease to be connected. ESC C28 alleviates potential obstacles to the provision of venture capital and to company rescues.

3.2 PERIOD IN WHICH RECEIPT ASSESSABLE OR DEDUCTION ALLOWABLE

3.2.1 Introduction

The profit or loss of a trade from the sale of goods for a given period depends on four factors:

(1) the sales made in the period;
(2) the cost of acquiring or manufacturing goods for resale;
(3) overhead or establishment expenditure or other expenditure of a revenue nature incurred in carrying on the business; and
(4) the valuation of stock of unsold goods, materials or work in progress.

In the trader's accounts, these matters should be dealt with following accepted accountancy principles applicable to the trade. For tax, this treatment is followed subject to specific statutory provisions and case-law. Although it might be thought that such considerations merely allocate income between one period of account and the next, there are cases where the effect can be of great significance. The inclusion of general reserves or the undervaluation of trading stock may postpone tax liabilities for many years.

BSC Footwear Ltd v Ridgeway (1972) 47 TC 495 upheld the Revenue's right to challenge a method of stock valuation which had been adopted for more than 50 years, saying that while the basis used by the company may have given a true picture of the trading results 'over the years', it did not produce 'the profits for 1959 taken in isolation, as was required for tax purposes'. The questions to be asked are thus:

(1) Have all the sources of profit relating to a particular accounting period been reflected in the profit and loss account on which an assessment is based?
(2) Has all allowable expenditure been charged in the appropriate period?
(3) Have trading stock and work in progress been valued on an acceptable basis?

In *Gardner, Mountain and D'Ambrumenil Ltd v CIR* (1947) 29 TC 69 it was held that for completely rendered services or supplied goods, where payment is not made until a subsequent tax year, the absence of payment in the tax year of supply cannot be treated as a loss; nor can the later payment be treated as pure profit in the subsequent tax year. Instead, in calculating the taxable profit under Schedule D, the net profit must be accounted for in the year of supply, even though payment has not yet been received.

3.2.2 Timing

The timing of receipts and expenses is governed by the general requirement that persons carrying on a trade or profession are assessable on 'the full amount of the profits or gains' (TA 1988, s 60(1) for income tax, and s 70(1) for corporation tax) of the relevant period. The starting point is the business profits as shown by the accounts drawn up in accordance with the ordinary principles of commercial accounting. In *Gallagher v Jones* (1993) 66 TC 77, the Master of Rolls held that subject to express or implied statutory rules, accepted commercial accountancy principles, as modified over time, should be applied in ascertaining business profits and losses. Over many years, the courts have held that the principles of commercial accounting are of assistance in determining the period in which costs and receipts are recognised for tax purposes.

In *Southern Railway of Peru Ltd v Owen* (1956) 36 TC 602, the company operated a railway in Peru, and at the time, under Peruvian law, an employee was entitled to statutory compensation on the termination of his services. The amount which an employee would receive was calculated by reference to the length of service and the rate of salary for each month of service. The company argued that on proper commercial accountancy principles it became liable year by year to pay a specific amount of 'deferred remuneration' when the employee's services terminated, and that the amount thereof accrued due to each employee from year to year and should be allowed as a deduction in computing the company's profits for each year.

The case is interesting because, although it went against the company, it was held that the company was not prevented by any rule of law from making a deduction for the deferred remuneration, and that a provision in its accounts for its prospective liability is permissible if capable of sufficiently accurate calculation. Unfortunately, the company's calculations were not sufficiently accurate.

Certain types of expenditure are disallowed for tax purposes even though it may be sound accounting practice to deduct such costs in a trader's accounts. However, in *Johnston v Britannia Airways Ltd* (1994) 67 TC 99, the High Court upheld the company's appeal to allow provisions made in its accounts for the future overhaul of jet aircraft. This was done by taking the average cost of the ten most recent overhauls. This was then converted to an average cost per flying hour, taking account of the history of the engine concerned. The provision in the accounts was arrived at by taking the average cost multiplied by the actual hours flown by each engine in the accounting period. The Special Commissioners had held that the provision gave a 'true and fair view' of the company's trading position. This case establishes an important precedent.

In a Privy Council case, *Bombay IT Commr v Ahmedabad New Cotton Mills Co* (1929) 9 ATC 574, stock was found to be grossly undervalued, and it was held that an assessment to rectify the closing undervaluation had to be reduced by the opening undervaluation to bring out the true profits. But where a company altered its method of dealing with accrued profits on long-term contracts, and the closing work in progress in the first year accounts on the old basis was substantially below the opening figure in the second year accounts on the new basis. Held, distinguishing *Ahmedabad*, the difference must be included in the second year profits (*Pearce v Woodall-Duckham Ltd* (1978) 51 TC 271).

In *Pearce*, there was a change in the valuation of work in progress from an on-cost method to an accrued profit method. The change in the method of valuation had increased significantly the opening value which was brought into the company's accounts as a separate item 'surplus arising on change in valuation of contract work in progress at 31 December 1968'. It was held that this surplus, representing anticipated profits for work carried out prior to 1969, ought to be taxed in 1969 when it was first revealed and brought into account. If, however, those profits were not all received in 1969, that sum could be apportioned between 1969 and subsequent years. The decision was confirmed in the Court of Appeal: 'The company was entitled to produce accounts based on its on-cost method prior to 1969. The company was entitled, but not bound, to produce accounts for 1969 and subsequent years by the accrued profit method. The change was made for sound commercial reasons.' Equally, the Revenue's view is that where a basis which is valid for tax purposes has been adopted in a taxpayer's accounts, the taxpayer does not have the right to adopt a different basis in computing the profits figure to be entered on his tax return.

Pearce applies for accounting periods ending up to 5 April 1999. For changes of accounting basis taking effect after 5 April 1999 the case-law rule is made statutory (FA 1998, s 44 and Sched 6). Positive prior year adjustments are charged under Schedule D Case VI rather than as Case I or II receipts. Negative adjustments continue to be treated as deductible expenditure for Case I or II.

3.2.3 Period in which receipts are to be included

The general principle is that an item becomes a trade receipt on the day on which it becomes a debt receivable, even though the date of receipt is postponed. This is the 'accruals' concept. Thus, when a sale is made in an accounting period, the sale price should normally be brought into account for tax purposes in that period even if the proceeds are not received until after the end of the period, although this may be subject to a possible provision for bad debts. Inevitably there are exceptions to this general rule.

In *JP Hall & Co Ltd v CIR* (1921) 12 TC 382, it was held that the date at which a transaction becomes a sale depends on the terms of the contract: it may be the date of delivery of the goods.

In *Symons v Weeks* (1983) 56 TC 360, a proportion of progress payments received by an architect that related to future work were excluded from the profit for a period, as they represented work to be done in future periods. Held, the amount to be included is the value of the work in progress estimated in accordance with the correct accountancy principles. Progress payments are only taken into account in the period in which they fall due to the extent that they represent the value of work done in that period.

In *Rownson, Drew and Clydesdale Ltd v CIR* (1931) 16 TC 595, a company varied the terms of an existing agreement under which it would receive additional sums, calculated with reference to sales results. The additional sums cannot be apportioned over the whole period of the agreement. The payment was to be made at the conclusion of the contract, dependent on results, and arose as a profit at the date when it became ascertainable.

In *Eckel v Board of Inland Revenue (Trinidad and Tobago)* (1989) 62 TC 331, consideration for a sale cannot be treated as a trade receipt until the trader has fulfilled all the conditions necessary for him to be entitled to the payment.

In *Morley v Tattersall* (1938) 22 TC 51, unclaimed balances of purchase money in the hands of a firm of auctioneers did not, on being subsequently distributed among the partners, become trading receipts. But in *Jay's The Jewellers Ltd v CIR* (1947) 29 TC 274, a pawnbroker came into possession of unclaimed surplus money on the sale of unredeemed pledges. It was held that the surpluses were not receipts of the company's trade when they were received, but became receipts of the trade when the company's right to retain the sale proceeds became absolute on the borrowers' failure to claim the surpluses within the statutory time limit.

In *Elson v Prices Tailors Ltd* (1962) 40 TC 671, unclaimed deposits left by customers who had failed to collect their made-to-measure suits or claim their deposits were true deposits and not sums in part payment. Thus they were to be included in the computation of profits and gains on the dates when they were received.

3.2.4 Period in which expenses are to be included

The normal accountancy practice is to deduct as an expense in the profit and loss account a sum actually accrued during the accounting period; such deductions are usually allowed in computing that period's taxable profit. In some circumstances, a deduction may also be made in the accounts for a liability which has not yet accrued but for which there is an expectation that it will arise in the future. The tax treatment of such a deduction depends on the facts of a particular case, the nature of the business concerned and, particularly, the degree of contingency. Deductions of this kind are often referred to as 'provisions' or 'reserves'.

Where a provision relates to specific expenditure which has already accrued or which the trader knows will arise and the amount of which can be calculated with a reasonable degree of accuracy, it is known as a 'specific provision' and is allowed for tax purposes. By contrast, a trader may create a general reserve (eg for repairs to property) against which expenditure is charged as and when it arises. This 'general provision' is not usually allowed for tax purposes.

A provision to meet contingent liabilities is only allowed as a deduction if it can be shown that it is an essential charge against the receipts of the accounting period concerned for the true profit to be stated.

In *Peter Merchant Ltd v Stedeford* (1948) 30 TC 496, it was held that a distinction must be drawn between an actual liability already accrued, which is deductible, and a liability which is future or contingent and for which no deduction can at present be made.

Insurance agents often receive a commission on selling a policy, subject to the liability to repay part of it if the policy lapses at an early date. If the commission is recognised as income at the outset, the Revenue accepts that the agent is entitled to make a provision for the contingent liability to repay it. However, in calculating the amount of the provision, the agent must make a proper valuation, taking into account factors such as the lapse rate among customers and the proportion of commission which is usually repayable on the relevant policy (see RI 30).

In *Naval Colliery Co Ltd v CIR* (1928) 12 TC 1017, a company was forced to close its mines owing to a strike. The complete work stoppage resulted in severe damage to the mine, and heavy expenditure had to be incurred for pumping and restoring pit props. The amount of this expenditure was charged in the account in the period before reconditioning work began. It was held that the cost of reconditioning was not a proper deduction in that accounting period. It is only when liability for expenditure is incurred that it becomes a proper charge for tax purposes; the fact that circumstances exist in a given period necessitating the expenditure is not the test to be applied. See also *Johnston v Britannia Airways Ltd* at 3.2.2, in which the company successfully made provision for the cost of major overhauls of each of its aircraft.

The Revenue has indicated that it considers provisions for future redundancy payments to be deductible provided that:

(1) the provision is made in accordance with generally accepted accounting principles, including FRS 3.18;
(2) a decision is made during the period to proceed with a redundancy programme;

(3) an accurate calculation (usually including the identification of individual employees) is made in line with SSAP 17; and

(4) payment is made within nine months of the end of the period of account as required by FA 1989, s 43.

3.2.5 Anticipated losses

In *H Ford & Co Ltd v CIR* (1926) 12 TC 997, a company entered into contracts for the sale of grain from Argentina and undertook liability for detention of the ships. Labour troubles ensued and the ships were delayed. The company never admitted liability for a claim, and ultimately never paid it, but deducted the amount of the claim in its accounts. This amount was an anticipated liability only and therefore was inadmissible for tax purposes.

More recently, following the decision in *Herbert Smith (a firm) v Honour* (1999) STC 173, which concerned a provision for future rent payable on surplus business premises, the Revenue now accepts that there is no tax rule that denies a deduction for provisions made for 'anticipated losses'. Accurate provisions for foreseen losses on long-term contracts made in line with correct accounting practice are deductible.

3.2.6 Delivery and passing of ownership of goods

The strict position is that before goods are treated as sold or purchased for tax purposes, the property in the goods should have passed from the seller to the purchaser. For this purpose it is not essential that the goods should have been physically delivered. The time when the property in the goods has passed depends on the parties' intention, as evidenced by the contract terms and, in the absence of such evidence, is governed by the provisions of the Sale of Goods Act 1979, ss 17–19. In practice, and where considerable sums are not involved, the Revenue may be prepared to accept other methods of valuation of stock in trade at a particular date, so long as the particular method is followed consistently.

Certain traders sell goods on special terms whereby they retain (or reserve) the title to the goods until payment is made. This should be distinguished from the supply of goods as consignment stocks (eg on a sale or return basis), which are normally to be treated as stock in the hands of the supplier until disposed of by the consignee. For accountancy purposes, if the circumstances indicate that the reservation of title is regarded by the parties as having no practical relevance except in the event of the buyer's insolvency, the goods are, notwithstanding the strict legal position, treated as purchases in the buyer's accounts and sales in the supplier's accounts. The Revenue has agreed (in ESC B6) that for sales subject to reservation of title, the above recommended accountancy treatment is accepted for tax purposes provided that both parties to the contract follow it.

3.2.7 **Pre-trading expenditure**
(TA 1988, s 401)

Relief is available for costs incurred before start of trade. If the normal tests for deductibility are applied, such expenditure is not allowed in computing profits, because at the time none exists. However, if the expenses are such that they would have been allowable if they were incurred at a time when a trade did exist, the expenditure is treated as if it were incurred on the day on which, and taken into the calculations of the profit or loss for the first period in which, the trade is first carried on. Examples of the types of expenditure to which this relief applies include:

- Rent for business premises
- Rates, insurance, heating and lighting
- Bank charges and interest
- Incidental costs of obtaining qualifying loan finance
- Wages or other payments to employees
- Lease rentals on machinery and plant and office equipment
- Accountancy fees
- Advertising costs.

Expenditure on the formation of a company or other capital expenditure is not allowable. The cost of an advance purchase of trading stock does not qualify for relief in this way because it will be deductible in arriving at profits when trading begins.

Where expenditure is incurred on the appraisal of the trade, its viability and its markets, outlets, suppliers or customers, there may be difficulty obtaining relief on the basis that such appraisal expenditure would only be incurred in the period leading up to the commencement of trade because it is incurred with a view to deciding whether to trade at all. Thus, it is expenditure that would not be incurred after the trade has been commenced and does not meet the special deductibility test.

Capital allowances are due in the same way as allowances given for expenditure incurred in the first period of trading, except that there is no seven-year time limit on expenditure.

If a company pays interest (thus giving rise to a non-trading debit under the FA 1996 loan relationship rules), it may make an election to carry forward the debit so that it can be relieved in the first accounting period in which it trades. The election must be made within two years from the end of the period in which it arose (FA 1996, s 82).

3.3 EXPENDITURE

3.3 1 **General rules**

The guiding principle in computing business profits for income or corporation tax purposes is that expenditure cannot be deducted if:

(1) it falls within the scope of any of the specific prohibitions in the income or corporation tax rule; or
(2) it violates the rule of tax law under TA 1988 that profits or income are computed on:
　(a) the full amount of the tax year's profits (Schedule D Cases I and II; s 60(1));
　(b) the actual amount of income arising in the tax year (Case III; s 64(1));
　(c) the full amount of income arising in the tax year (Cases IV and V; s 65(1));
　(d) the full amount of profits or gains arising in the tax year (Case VI; s 69);
　(e) the full amount of profits, gains or income arising in the accounting period (corporation tax; s 70(1)).

For an item of revenue expenditure to be a proper deduction in computing the taxable profits of a trade, it must be properly deductible in the trade's accounts following ordinary commercial accounting principles provided that there is no specific statutory prohibition on such deduction. The principal statutory authority under which a deduction may be denied is TA 1988, s 74, which sets out restrictions on the items which may be deducted in computing profits under Schedule D Case I or II. In particular, it prohibits deduction in respect of the following

Disbursements or expenses not wholly and exclusively laid out or expended

The legislation requires the expenditure to be incurred 'wholly and exclusively for the purposes of the trade'. Consequently, expenses incurred partly for trade purposes and partly for personal reasons are not allowable. For example, the Revenue invoked TA 1988, s 74(1)(a) to disallow the cost of clothing in *Mallalieu v Drummond* (1983) 57 TC 330 and of meals incurred by a self-employed carpenter working away from home in *Caillebotte v Quinn* (1975) 50 TC 222.

Where an expense is incurred for mixed purposes, the whole amount is disallowed. However, where it can be shown that an *additional* cost was incurred wholly for business reasons, a deduction may be due. Consequently, if a trader pays his wife a salary which exceeds the real value of her services as an employee, it is normally only the excess which is disallowed.

Note that the requirement is that the expenditure is incurred wholly for the *purposes* of the trade. This implies that the test which must be satisfied is a subjective, rather than an objective, one. There is support for this in *Bentleys, Stokes & Lawless v Beeson* (1952) 33 TC 491, where it was held that if the activity is undertaken to both promote business and, say, entertain a friend, the requirement is not satisfied. If, however, the activity is solely to promote business, the requirement is met and the expenditure allowed. Note, however, that there is now a statutory disallowance for entertaining expenditure (see 3.3.2).

Unfortunately, more recent decisions by the courts have suggested that the proper test may be an objective one. In *Mallalieu v Drummond* (1983) 57 TC 330, in which a barrister claimed clothing expenses, it was held that she needed clothes to travel to work and to wear at work, and that the fact she had to wear a certain type of clothing (ie black dresses) did not amount to expenditure made wholly for trade purposes.

A similar interpretation lies behind the decision in *Mackinlay v Arthur Young McClelland Moores & Co* (1989) 62 TC 704, which concerned removal expenses borne by the firm for two partners who were relocated within the UK. The problem lies in whether it can be said a partner's removal costs are laid out only partly for partnership purposes, or exclusively. The answer must be ascertained by the motive for the move. Thus here it was held that as the partners had moved to be nearer the partnership business *and* to establish a private residence for themselves and their families, the expenditure could not treated as exclusively for the partnership's purposes.

Prima facie, terminal payments to employees on the cessation of a business cannot, on the authority of *CIR v Anglo Brewing Co Ltd* (1925) 12 TC 803, be deducted. Such payments relate to not carrying on the business! However, TA 1988, s 579 allows the deduction of statutory redundancy payments, In addition, TA 1988, s 90 enables payments in addition to statutory redundancy payments to be relieved to the extent that outgoings do not exceed three times the statutory sums. Section 90 also applies to partial discontinuances if the discontinued part of the business can be identified and the s 74(1)(a) test is otherwise satisfied.

Disbursements or expenses for domestic or private, as distinct from trade, purposes

Even if it were not disallowed under TA 1988, s 74(1)(a) as being not wholly and exclusively for business purposes, expenditure for domestic and private purposes is explicitly disallowable under s 74(1)(b).

Often such expenditure has a 'dual purpose'. The cost of nursing home treatment was disallowed even though the reason for the expenditure was the need for a private room from which to conduct business (*Murgatroyd v Evans-Jackson* (1966) 43 TC 581). Expenditure on ordinary clothing is not normally allowable (*Mallalieu v Drummond*, above). The costs of meals at regular partners' lunchtime meetings was disallowed, but expenditure on accommodation, food and drink at the annual weekend conference was allowed (*Watkis v Ashford, Sparkes and Harward* (1985) 58 TC 468). In *McKnight v Sheppard* (1999) 71 TC 419, legal expenses in defending charges brought by a professional regulatory body were allowed – despite the fact that the taxpayer's 'personal reputation was inevitably involved'. But contributions towards the removal expenses of a partner moved in the interests of the firm were not allowed in *Arthur Young McClelland Moores & Co*, above.

ESC A32 concerns goods taken by traders for personal consumption. *Sharkey v Wernher* (1955) 36 TC 275 established the principle that such a transfer should be treated as if it were a sale at market value. The Revenue takes a reasonably broad view in applying this principle. However, the case is not considered to apply to

(1) services rendered to the trader personally or to his household, the cost of which should be disallowed under s 74(1)(b);
(2) the value of meals provided for proprietors of hotels, boarding houses, restaurants etc and members of their families, also disallowed under s 74(1)(b);
(3) expenditure incurred by a trader on constructing an asset which is to be used as a fixed asset in the trade.

If an item of trading stock is disposed of otherwise than in due course of the trade, the amount to be brought into account as a trade receipt is that representing the item's market value at the date of its disposal, and not its cost (*Sharkey*, above). This applies where a trader takes goods from trading stock for his personal use or consumption, or disposes of them otherwise than by sale in the course of trade, but it does not apply to services rendered to the trader personally or to expenditure incurred on the construction of a fixed asset for use in the trade.

Example

A is a grocer. Before adjusting for the items noted below, A's accounts for the year ended 30 June 2000 show a profit of £30,800. It is ascertained that

(a) A has withdrawn from his trading stock goods which cost him £1,000, and which he would normally sell for £1,250 for consumption by himself and his family;
(b) an assistant has employed his spare time in:
  (i) constructing shop fittings estimated to be worth £2,450;
  (ii) repainting the shop front (value of work done estimated to be £500);
  (iii) decorating a bedroom (value of work done estimated to be £450).
  It is estimated that the cost of the assistant's services was (1) £1,100, (2) £200, and (3) £150. The materials involved have already been treated correctly in the accounts.

A's Schedule D Case I computation for the tax year to 30 June 2000 is as follows:

	£	£
Profit shown by accounts		30,800
Add: Market value of goods consumed	1,250	

Cost of assistant's time		
(i) capital – constructing shop fittings	1,100	
(ii) not trading – decorating bedroom	150	2,500
Adjusted profit		33,300

It is useful to bear in mind that the disposal of an asset by a taxpayer after he has withdrawn it from his trading stock may give rise to a chargeable gain or allowable loss, and that for this purpose a trader is treated as having acquired the asset for 'a consideration equal to the amount brought into the accounts of the trade in respect of it for tax purposes' (TCGA 1992, s 161).

Rent for the whole or a part of a dwelling house or domestic offices

If premises are partly used privately (eg a farmhouse, a shop with residential accommodation above), an allowance of not more than two-thirds of the rent is allowed unless the circumstances justify a higher proportion. In practice, council tax and day-to-day repairs are similarly apportioned. In *Thomas v Ingram* (1979) 52 TC 428, a freelance draughtsman's private earnings were minimal, and a claim for an allowance of 25% of the rates, heating and lighting expenses against income of £125 and £136 was reduced to £10. In *Mason v Tyson* (1980) 53 TC 333, the expenses of a flat used occasionally to enable a professional man to work late were not allowed.

Repair of premises and repairs or alterations of implements, utensils or articles

TA 1988, s 74(1)(d) prohibits any deduction 'beyond the sum actually expended' for repairs of premises, and the Revenue's contention that this debarred any allowance for such was rejected by the Special Commissioners in *Jenners Princes Street Edinburgh Ltd v CIR* 1998 Sp C 166. The Revenue now accepts that provisions properly made under FRS 12 are tax deductible unless there is an express rule to the contrary (eg provisions for capital expenditure).

Expenditure on repairs to plant, buildings, tools, utensils, office machinery, fixtures and fittings, etc may be deducted, but not expenditure upon the reconstruction of buildings even if undertaken in lieu of repairs, there being no provision for the allowance of a notional amount for repairs not done.

A sum set aside to meet the cost of renewals under a contractual obligation is not allowed if the renewals are not actually carried out (*Peter Merchant Ltd v Stedeford* (1948) 30 TC 496).

Disputes arise frequently with the Revenue with regard to repairs to business premises, and while the principle involved is relatively simple, its practical application may be more difficult. If expenses are incurred in erecting a new structure in its entirety so that a new capital asset is created, the expenses are clearly of a capital nature and are therefore not allowable deductions in arriving at trading profits. The replacement of an entirety (ie a distinguishable separate structure having no physical connection with any other part of an industrial plant) is a capital expenditure (*O'Grady v Bullcroft Main Collieries Ltd* (1932) 17 TC 93), but the renewal of a part of an existing structure is not (*Samuel Jones & Co (Devondale) Ltd v CIR* (1951) 32 TC 513). Expenses incurred in the maintenance or reconstruction of an existing asset are generally allowed as a revenue expense. However, there are borderline cases which depend on their own circumstances.

If repairs and improvements are mixed, there is no provision for an apportionment of the total expenditure between repairs and improvements.

Repairs accumulated before use in the business are not allowable if the expenditure is necessary to bring the asset up to standard. Such expenditure is capital and therefore is disallowed as a charge on the trade profits (*CIR v Law Shipping Co Ltd v CIR* (1923) 12 TC 621). Where the asset is capable of use before the expenditure is incurred, it is likely to be treated as a repair (*Odeon Associated Theatres Ltd v Jones* (1971) 48 TC 257). In this case, some importance was placed on the accounting treatment of the expenditure as a repair. This importance was clarified in *Heather v PE Consulting Group Ltd* (1972) 42 TC 293, in which the Court of Appeal made clear that whether expenditure is capital or revenue is a matter of fact for the court to decide.

Loss not connected with or arising out of the trade, profession or vocation

In *Strong & Co of Romsey Ltd v Woodifield* (1906) 5 TC 215, damages recovered by a guest injured by a falling chimney while staying at an inn were not allowed, on the grounds that the loss fell on the taxpayers in their capacity of 'householder' and not that of 'trader'.

Where a person holds an office and also carries on a profession, the expenses of the office not allowed for Schedule E purposes cannot be deducted from the Schedule D assessment in respect of profits of his profession, as these Schedules are mutually exclusive.

The writing-off of a bad debt cannot be disallowed under TA 1988, s 74(1)(a) because it is not a disbursement or expense. An alternative disallowance would be under s 74(1)(e) as loss not arising out of a trade. In *Sycamore plc and Maple Ltd v Fir* 1996 Sp C 104, the company had claimed a deduction for a bad debt for goods which it had supplied to a subsidiary. It had also made a loan to the subsidiary. The point at issue was whether payments made by the subsidiary should be credited to the loan account or should reduce the trade debt. The Special Commissioner held that the value of goods originally supplied to the subsidiary, and subsequently recovered, should be credited to the trade account and not to the loan account. The balance of the trade debt which was written off was allowable under s 74(1)(j). The loss on goods supplied while the subsidiary was making loan repayments was a loss 'connected with or arising out of the trade' and thus was not disallowed by s 74(1)(e).

Capital withdrawn from, or employed or intended to be employed in, the trade

Sums spent on assets of circulating capital may be capital within TA 1988, s 74(1)(f), equally with sums spent on assets which are fixed capital. In *European Investment Trust Co Ltd v Jackson* (1932) 18 TC 1, a finance company was financed, in part, by fluctuating advances from its parent company. Interest was paid on daily balances. It was held that the advances were of moneys employed or intended to be employed as capital in the company's trade. Accordingly, the interest was disallowed.

Capital expenditure is not a cost which may be deducted in arriving at profits for tax purposes. The generally accepted definition of capital expenditure was given in *Atherton v British Insulated and Helsby Cables Ltd* (1925) 10 TC 155, where it was held that:

> 'when an expenditure is made with a view to bringing into existence an asset or an advantage for the enduring benefit of a trade ... there is very good reason (in the absence of special circumstances leading to an opposite conclusion) for treating such an expenditure as properly attributable not to revenue but to capital.'

The definition in *Atherton* is most general; for example, the fact that expenditure is recurring expenditure rather than a 'once and for all' outlay does not mean that it is revenue expenditure. Thus:

> 'if the sum payable is not a revenue payment it cannot be made so by permitting it to be paid by annual instalments' (*Henriksen v Grafton Hotel Ltd* [(1942) 24 TC 453]). It was also held in that case that an enduring benefit need not be a long-term benefit; expenditure incurred in obtaining a liquor licence for three years was held to provide an enduring benefit which was capital in nature.'

Money spent on acquiring an asset to be used for the trade is a capital outlay, whether the asset is a building or something liable to be worn out, such as a machine. The purchase of goodwill is capital expenditure, even though there is no tangible asset. Similarly, extensive repairs which had to be carried out before a ship could be used for a company's trade are regarded as capital expenditure (*Law Shipping Co Ltd v CIR* (1923) 12 TC 621). However, in *Odeon Associated Theatres* (above), the company had acquired several theatres which, because of wartime restrictions, needed repair and redecoration. This had not affected the purchase price and did not restrict their use for public performances. *Law Shipping* was distinguished because the theatres could still be used, whereas the ship required a refit to make it seaworthy. A lump sum payment to secure release from an onerous liability, such as a lease at a high rent or a fixed rate loan, is also regarded as capital expenditure.

The Revenue can take this to extremes. In the November 1991 issue of *Tax Bulletin*, the Revenue stated that expenditure on a course attended by a proprietor is regarded as capital expenditure if he attends to acquire new expertise, knowledge or skills. In contrast, where the individual attends merely to update expertise which he already possesses, the expenditure is normally regarded as revenue expenditure.

Capital employed in improvements of premises occupied for trade purposes

No deduction is allowed for any capital employed in the improvement of premises occupied for trade purposes. It follows that a deduction can be allowed only for the sum actually expended on repairing the business premises. There have been many cases on the question whether what was done was repair work or amounted to rebuilding.

In *Margrett v Lowestoft Water and Gas Co* (1935) 19 TC 481, the company built a water tower and constructed a new reservoir. However, the new reservoir was on a different site from and replaced an old reservoir which was considered to be not worth repairing. It was twice the size of the old one and technically it was an improvement on the old reservoir. It was held that no part of the expenditure on the new reservoir was expenditure for repairs and that the whole of it was capital expenditure.

In *Samuel Jones & Co (Devondale) Ltd* (above), the cost of replacing an old factory chimney by a new one, which was not a significant improvement over the old one, was allowed, together with the cost of removing the old chimney. In *O'Grady v Bullcroft Main Collieries* (above), the cost of replacing a chimney by another of an improved type, and on a different site, was disallowed as being capital expenditure. The distinction being made here is that in the latter case the replacement was regarded as being of the 'entirety', while in the former the chimney was merely an inseparable part of an 'entirety', ie the factory.

In *Thomas Wilson (Keighley) Ltd v Emmerson* (1960) 39 TC 360, the roof of a three-storey building fell into disrepair and reconstruction became necessary. The building acquired a new top floor and roof which was much higher than the old roof. It was held that the expenditure on this work was capital expenditure and therefore not an allowable deduction in computing the company's profits.

In the context of *Lurcott v Wakely and Wheeler* [1911] 1 KB 905, it was held that:

'Repair is restoration by renewal or replacement of subsidiary parts of a whole. Renewal, as distinguished from repair, is reconstruction of the entirety, meaning by the entirety not necessarily the whole but substantially the whole subject matter under discussion.'

Interest which might have been made

No allowance can be given on interest on any of the amounts disallowed in the foregoing commentary.

Debts

A general provision against bad debts is not allowable, but provisions against specific debts are a proper deduction for tax purposes provided that it can be shown that the amount is a reasonable provision. The exceptions are as follows:

(i)   a bad debt;
(ii)   a debt or part of a debt released by the creditor wholly and exclusively for the purposes of his trade, profession or vocation as part of a relevant arrangement or compromise (voluntary arrangements, Insolvency Act 1986; compromise or arrangement, CA 1985, s 425); and
(iii)   a doubtful debt estimated to be bad, ie in the case of the debtor's bankruptcy or insolvency, except to the extent that any amount may reasonably be expected to be received on the debt.

A provision may be allowable even though the debt is subsequently collected: the key question is whether the provision was reasonable at the time the accounts were drawn up. If this test is satisfied, the provision is allowable and the amounts subsequently collected are brought into account as receipts for the year in which they are received.

The Revenue has explained its approach to provisions for bad or doubtful debts in the August 1994 issue of *Tax Bulletin*. Its interpretation is that a trader may be entitled to a deduction provided the following circumstances are satisfied:

(1)   the debt existed at the balance sheet date; or
(2)   before the accounts were finalised the trader or the company's directors discovered that the debtor's financial position at the balance sheet date was such that the debt was unlikely to be paid.

The Revenue states that a common example of this is where a debtor goes into administration or liquidation shortly after the balance sheet date and before the date on which the financial statements are approved by the trader. Its occurrence before the accounts were finalised normally sheds light on the debtor's financial position at the balance sheet date. If the period between that date and approval of the accounts is short, it is unlikely that a debtor would have gone from financial good health to insolvency in that period. In these circumstances it is normally reasonable for the trader to regard the debt as doubtful. The acceptable amount of provision depends on the information available.

The Revenue contrasts this with a situation where a debtor is an habitually slow payer and there are no grounds to believe his financial position has changed. Here the Revenue argues that the length of time that a debt has been outstanding is not in itself a sufficient reason to regard the debt as doubtful.

A general bad debt provision to cover contingent bad debts is not allowed. A provision for discounts on debtors' accounts may be allowed, if it is reasonable and on a consistent basis from year to year.

Average loss beyond actual amount of loss after adjustment

The prohibition of the deduction of any sum in respect of 'any average loss beyond the actual amount of loss after adjustment' applies to cases of marine and aviation risk where either there is no insurance, or the insurance is for less than the full value, or is 'free from average'. If the loss is fully covered by insurance, the question does not arise. A 'general average loss' occurs where any damage or loss has been properly and voluntarily incurred in relation to a ship or its cargo for its safety. This would apply, for example, if cargo was thrown overboard to lighten the ship during a storm. The rule allows those who do not suffer any loss in such circumstances to deduct as an expense adjusted average contributions paid, and those who do suffer loss to deduct only the amount reduced by the average contribution received.

Sums recoverable under insurance or contract of indemnity

Where a business can get back from an insurance company the money that it has paid out, there is no deduction due for the expenditure. The same treatment applies where a trader has been indemnified against particular cost.

Premiums for business purposes are normally allowable, including insurance of assets, against accidents to employees and against loss of profits, and premiums under mutual insurance schemes. Any corresponding recoveries are trading receipts (or set off against trading expenses – see TA 1988, s 74(1)(l)) or capital, according to the nature of the policy.

Premiums on policies in favour of the employer insuring against death or critical illness of key employees are generally allowable, and the proceeds of any such policies are treated as trading receipts.

Annuity or other annual payment (other than interest) payable out of profits

The combined effect of subss (m) and (p) (and, before 6 April 1997, subs (q), now repealed) of TA 1988, s 74(1) is to prohibit the deduction in computing profits of annuities, annual payments (other than interest), patent royalties, etc payable under deduction of tax at source. Subsection (m) applies only to amounts 'payable out of the profits'. Payments made before the profits can be ascertained are not payable out of the profits and therefore not within the s 74(1)(m) prohibition (see *Gresham Life Assurance v Styles* (1890) 3 TC 185). A company can deduct the amounts paid as an annual charge.

Interest paid to non-UK resident person at more than reasonable commercial rate

Interest payable to non-UK residents is deductible only to the extent that it is payable at a reasonable commercial rate and either:

(1) is paid under deduction of tax (TA 1988, s 349) – in this event the gross amount of the interest is deductible from profits (TA 1988, s 82(5)), or
(2) is contractually payable abroad (and is in fact so paid) by a UK resident sole trader or partnership either on a liability incurred for purposes of the foreign activities of the trade, etc or in a currency other than sterling.

There can be no deduction of interest if the recipient is a partner in the trade, or both payer and recipient are under common control.

Note that this does not apply for corporation tax. Also, there are anti-avoidance provisions for interest paid to a connected non-resident.

Royalties or other similar payments

(See also comments above with regard to TA 1988, s 74(1)(m)).

Certain annual payments (eg patent royalties) generally need to be paid net of income tax at the basic rate. The payments are not deductible in arriving at an unincorporated trader's profits which are assessable under Schedule D Case I or II, although they are allowed as a deduction for higher rate purposes. A company can deduct the amounts paid as an annual charge.

Note that s 74(1)(p) does not cover royalties paid to a non-UK resident for the user of a patent abroad.

3.3.2 Expenditure specifically disallowed

Entertaining and gifts to customers
(TA 1988, s 577)

Any expenses for entertaining customers or suppliers are disallowed. There used to be an exception for the cost of entertaining overseas customers, but this no longer applies. There is an exception which may apply where the entertaining is provided by an hotelier, restaurateur or by someone else who provides entertainment in the ordinary course of his trade. Staff entertainment is also an allowable expense, but the individual employee may be assessed on a benefit in kind.

The cost of gifts to customers, potential customers and potential intro-ducers is also disallowed unless the gift carries a conspicuous advertisement and is neither food, drink, tobacco or a voucher exchangeable for such goods, nor an item which costs more than £10 per recipient per year.

Illegal payments and fines
(TA 1988, s 577A)

There is a specific provision disallowing illegal payments such as bribes. This also covers payments made in response to threats, menaces, blackmail and other forms of extortion.

Fines and penalties for breach of the law have been disallowed since *CIR v Alexander von Glehn & Co Ltd* (1920) 12 TC 232, in which a company was refused a deduction for the costs of settling an action for breach of World War I regulations. The Revenue often invokes this case to disallow parking fines.

Lease rentals on expensive cars
(CAA 1990, s 35)

Where a trader uses a leased car or provides a motor car to an employee and the original cost was £12,000 or more, part of the lease rentals must be added back as a disallowable expense. The amount disallowed is the fol-lowing proportion of the lease rental:

$$\frac{1}{2} \times \frac{(\text{Cost of car} - £12,000)}{\text{Cost of car}}$$

Thus, if a car which cost £16,000 is leased for a rental of £2,400 pa, the amount disallowed is:

$$\frac{1}{2} \times \frac{(£16,000 - £12,000)}{£16,000} \times £2,400 = £300$$

This treatment does not apply to maintenance costs included in the lease rentals provided they are identified separately under the terms of the leasing agreement.

War risk premiums
(TA 1988, ss 586 and 587)

War damage insurance premiums are not allowed for tax purposes except for ships, aircraft or goods in transit. Premiums relating to the risk of war injuries to employees are disallowed, as are payments to employees in respect of war injuries.

3.3.3 **Expenditure specifically allowed**

Cost of raising business finance
(TA 1988, s 77)

There are often certain costs in raising long-term finance. For many years these costs were regarded as capital expenditure by the Revenue. A statutory deduction is now available provided certain conditions are satisfied, ie the costs must:

(1) be wholly and exclusively incurred in obtaining loan finance, providing security or repaying a loan;
(2) represent expenditure on professional fees, commissions, advertising, printing or other incidental expenses in relation to raising finance.

In some cases a deduction is available even though the attempt to raise business finance failed.

The Revenue view is that premiums paid on an insurance policy do not qualify, even though the policy may have been taken out at the lender's insistence.

Contributions to local enterprise agencies
(TA 1988, s 79)

Contributions made to an approved local enterprise agency are deductible.

Contributions to training and enterprise councils and local enterprise companies
(TA 1988, s 79A)

Contributions made to a training and enterprise council (in England and Wales) or a local enterprise company (in Scotland) are deductible.

Expenses connected with foreign trades, etc
(TA 1988, ss 80 and 81)

Travelling expenses incurred by a UK resident and domiciled taxpayer from his home to a place of work carried on entirely overseas, where he carries on a trade, profession or vocation, are allowable for tax purposes. The section parallels broadly TA 1988, s 193. This means that board and lodging overseas is allowed. If the taxpayer is working overseas for a continuous period of 60 days or more, up to two visits per tax year by his spouse and by his children aged 18 or under at the beginning of the outward journey are also deductible.

Where such a person has more than one trade carried on overseas and at least one is carried on wholly overseas, the expenses of business travel between those trades are deductible for tax purposes (apportioned between the respective trades).

Patent fees, etc and expenses
(TA 1988, s 83)

In computing a trade's profits, there may be deducted any fees paid or expenses incurred in obtaining the grant of a patent, an extension of the term of a patent, the registration of a design or trademark, an extension of the period for which the right in a registered design subsists or the renewal of registration of a trademark, or in connection with a rejected or abandoned application for a patent made for the purposes of the trade.

Gifts in kind to charities
(TA 1988, s 83A)

Relief applies to gifts to charities by a trader of machinery or plant which he manufactures or sells, or has used in his trade, and claimed capital allowances therefor. This is achieved by providing that no amount is required to be brought into the Schedule D Case I computation as trading receipts or into the capital allowances computation as disposal consideration.

Gifts to educational establishments
(TA 1988, s 84)

Relief applies to gifts by a trader of machinery or plant which he manufactures or sells, or has used in his trade, and claimed capital allowances. The relief is achieved by not requiring any credit, either as a trading receipt or in the capital allowances computations.

Costs of establishing share option or profit-sharing schemes: relief
(TA 1988, s 84A)

Relief is available for the cost of establishing an approved share option scheme or a profit-sharing scheme.

Payments to trustees of approved profit-sharing schemes
(TA 1988, s 85)

Payments by a company to trustees of an approved profit-sharing scheme are allowable deductions for computing the company's trading profits.

Costs of establishing employee share ownership trusts
(TA 1988, s 85A)

Relief is available for the cost of establishing a qualifying employee share ownership trust.

Employees seconded to charities and educational establishments
(TA 1988, s 86)

An employer can obtain a deduction for the salary costs of staff seconded to charities and educational establishments.

Payroll giving schemes: contributions to agent's expenses
(TA 1988, s 86A)

If an employer operates an approved payroll giving scheme (under TA 1988, s 202), any voluntary contributions to the agent for the expenses of a running scheme are deductible.

Taxable lease premiums
(TA 1988, s 87)

Where the payer of an amount treated as a premium paid under a lease (under TA 1988, ss 34 and 35) uses the property acquired for the purposes of his trade, he is given relief in addition to any rent paid under the lease terms. Relief is given each year on the fraction of the chargeable amount that year. Note, however, that the relief is not granted for a premium paid for the assignment of a lease, but an assignee takes over the unexpired relief of the assignor.

Example

B acquired on 30 September 1987 a leasehold interest in factory premises to be used for his trade. The term of the lease was 30 years, and B paid a premium of £40,000. Accounts are made up annually to 31 December. For each accounting year B can deduct £560 from his chargeable profits in respect of the premium, computed as follows:

	£
Premium paid	40,000
$Less: \dfrac{30-1}{50} \times 40{,}000$	23,200
Chargeable amount	16,800
Period of lease (30 years)	
$\dfrac{16{,}800}{30}$ = Annual deduction	£560

Improvement to lease

Where the cost of work carried out by a tenant is deemed to be a payment of a premium, it shall be disregarded for the above relief if a claim for capital allowances may be made for it. Otherwise, the lease premium is increased by the amount of the cost of the work.

Alteration of lease premium

Where an alteration is made to the amount of any lease premium, the original deduction must be recalculated.

Payments to Export Credits Guarantee Department
(TA 1988, s 88)

Payments to the Export Credits Guarantee Department can be deducted as a trading expense under Schedule D Case I or II.

Debts proving irrecoverable after event treated as discontinuance
(TA 1988, s 89)

If a trade is treated as discontinued under TA 1988, s 113 on a change in partners or if a company ceases to trade within TA 1988, s 337, future profits of the trade are reduced by any additional bad debts not previously provided for.

Additional payments to redundant employees
(TA 1988, s 90)

Redundancy or similar payments made to employees which would have been allowable had the business continued to trade are deemed to be paid as allowable expenses on the last day of business, so long as it does not exceed three times the redundancy or other payments as defined by TA 1988, s 580.

Under general Schedule D Case I and II rules, redundancy payments are normally an allowable deduction provided that they are laid out wholly and exclusively for business purposes and the payments are not of a capital nature.

Where such payments are made in the course of the discontinuance of a trade, they are not admissible as a deduction (*CIR v Anglo Brewing Co Ltd* (1925) 12 TC 803). However, TA 1988, s 579 provides a deduction for statutory redundancy payments, and s 90 gives relief for additional payments, inadmissible on the *Anglo Brewing* principle, up to three times the statutory payment made. See further 3.2.4(1)–(4).

Where the right to a tax deduction is dependent on s 90 or 579, relief is due for the period of account in which the payment is made. If the payment is made after the discontinuance of the business, it is regarded for tax relief purposes as if it was made on the last day on which the business was carried on.

Cemeteries
(TA 1988, s 91)

The cost of land used for graves is allowed as a trading expense when sold. The amounts expended on land and buildings are written off progressively, as they are likely to be of little use when the cemetery is full. This is achieved by applying to such costs the fraction:

$$\frac{\text{number of graves sold}}{\text{number of graves sold} + \text{number of spaces remaining at period end}}$$

The same principle is applied to crematoria with the computation based on 'memorial garden plots' instead of grave spaces.

Waste disposal: restoration payments
(TA 1988, s 91A)

Where, as a condition of planning permission, expenditure is incurred to restore a waste disposal site, such expenditure is an allowable expense of the trade.

Waste disposal: preparation expenditure
(TA 1988, ss 91B and 91BA)

If a trader incurs expenditure to prepare a site for waste disposal, tax relief is given for appropriate expenditure. This includes the cost of obtaining the licence; it does not include site acquisition costs nor expenditure qualifying for capital allowances. Pre-trading expenditure is allowed as if incurred on the first day of trading.

Where the whole of a site is transferred to a new operator and he holds the necessary licence, he will become entitled to allowances on the same basis as they were given to the original operator.

Mineral exploration and access
(TA 1988, s 91C)

Businesses that incur expenditure on mineral exploration and access are not entitled to an immediate 100% deduction for the intangible cost of drilling oil production wells. The expenditure does, however, qualify for mineral extraction capital allowances at 25% a year on the reducing balance basis.

Rents payable for electric line etc wayleaves
(TA 1988, s 120)

Rents for any easement in connection with electric, telegraphic or tele-phonic wires or cables are now made without deduction of tax and are therefore allowed as Schedule D Case I deductions in the normal way.

Schemes for rationalising industry
(TA 1988, ss 568–572)

Contributions made to certified schemes for rationalising industry and to statutory redundancy schemes are deductible.

Statutory redundancy payments
(TA 1988, s 579)

The net cost of statutory redundancy payments is an allowable cost and is treated as paid on the last day of business. Additional payments to redundant employees of up to three times the statutory amount are also deductible (TA 1988, s 90).

Training courses for employees
(TA 1988, ss 588 and 589)

Expenditure on a qualifying course undertaken by a current or former employee for the purpose of retraining him for future employment elsewhere is allowable. If the retraining conditions are not fulfilled (eg because the employee is retained in employment), the relief is withdrawn and PAYE recovered on the benefits. A course is a 'qualifying course' if:

(1) it provides a course of training designed to impart or improve skills or knowledge relevant to, and intended to be used in the course of, gainful employment (including self-employment) of any description; and
(2) the course is devoted entirely to the teaching and/or practical application of the skills or knowledge; and
(3) the duration of the course does not exceed one year; and
(4) all teaching and practical application forming part of the course takes place within the UK.

A course is not regarded as a 'qualifying course' in relation to a particular employee unless:

(a) he attends the course on a full-time or substantially full-time basis; and
(b) he is employed by the employer full time throughout the period of two years ending when he begins to undertake the course or, if it is earlier, when he ceases to be employed by that employer; and
(c) the opportunity to undertake the course, on similar terms as to payment or reimbursement of relevant expenses, is available either generally to holders or past holders of offices or employment under the employer or to a particular class or classes of such holders or past holders.

An employee must

(1) begin to undertake the course of training while he is employed by the employer or within one year after he ceases to be so employed; and

(2) cease to be employed by the employer not later than the end of two years beginning at the end of the qualifying course of training.

Where an employee undertakes a qualifying course, the relevant expenses consist of:

(a) fees for attendance;
(b) fees for any examination taken during or at the conclusion of the course;
(c) the cost of books which are essential for a person attending the course; and
(d) travelling expenses incurred wholly, exclusively and necessarily in attending the course.

Counselling services for employees
(TA 1988, ss 589A and 589B)

Expenditure on qualifying counselling services for redundant employees is allowable. Services are 'qualifying counselling' services if:

(1) their purpose is to enable the employee to adjust to the loss of job and/or to find a new job (including self-employment);
(2) they consist of advice and guidance, imparting or improving skills, or providing the use of office equipment or similar facilities (but financial counselling is not covered);
(3) the employee has been employed full time for two years;
(4) the services are available either generally or to that class of employees; and
(5) the services are provided in the UK; if provided partly abroad, the expense can be apportioned.

Related travelling expenses incurred wholly, exclusively and necessarily in obtaining the counselling services are also deductible.

Pools payments for football ground improvements
(FA 1990, s 126)

Football pools promoters can, in computing their trading profits, deduct payments made to the trustees of the Football Trust 1990. The trustees spend the money on capital works to improve spectators' safety and comfort at football grounds in accordance with the recommendations in Lord Justice Taylor's report on the Hillsborough disaster. Football clubs can claim capital allowances on their gross qualifying capital expenditure and do not have to deduct the contribution received from the trustees.

Expenditure on films
(F(No 2)A 1997, ss 41–43 and 48)

Preliminary expenditure on planning on a qualifying film up to the first day of shooting is deductible. However, this must not exceed 20% of the film's total budget. Abortive expenditure is allowed if the film would have been a qualifying film.

Expenditure on producing or acquiring a qualifying film may be written off as to one third in the period in which it is completed or acquired and one third in each of the following two years. For expenditure between 1 July 1997 and 2 July 2002, a 100% write off is available. Extensive guidance on the treatment of such expenditure is given in SPs 1/93 and 1/98.

Consideration for certain restrictive undertakings
(FA 1988, s 73)

Payments to past, present or future employees for restrictive undertakings, where the employee is assessable on the payment as an emolument of the employment (TA 1988, s 313), are deductible in calculating the employer's taxable profits.

Contributions to qualifying employee share ownership trust
(FA 1989, s 67)

Corporation tax relief is given where a UK-resident company makes a payment to the trustees of a trust which is a qualifying employee share ownership trust the purpose of which is to acquire and distribute shares in the founding company to employees.

Expenditure on security assets and services
(TA 1989, ss 112 and 113)

Where a special threat to an individual's personal physical security (or that of any member of his family or household) arises directly from his trade, profession or vocation (carried on by him alone, or in partnership), then the cost of certain assets and services of improving physical security is deductible. Security assets include equipment and structures (eg a wall), but exclude cars, ships, aircraft and dwellings (including associated grounds). The Revenue view is that only those persons who are at a special risk from terrorists, extremists and other similar groups qualify for relief.

Loan relationships
(FA 1996, ss 82 and 84)

Deficits on a company's trading loan relationships are deductible. Charges and expenses in connection with a loan relationship are also allowed.

3.4 RECEIPTS

3.4.1 Introduction

The initial assumption is that most receipts coming into the hands of a person carrying on a trade, etc 'arise' from the trade (TA 1988, s 18(1)), insofar as they relate to the disposal of trading stock or from the provision of services, etc. So far as concerns such receipts, the only open question may be one of timing (ie the period of account in which they should be recognised). However, receipts may arise otherwise than as consideration for the provision of goods and services. There are two main points at issue: Does the sum concerned arise from the trade at all? If it does, is it a capital or revenue item?

Although receipts may be excluded because they are not trading receipts of the particular business under review, it is possible that they arise from another, separate business or are otherwise assessable under Schedule D. If a receipt is of a capital nature, or arises out of an asset or rights of some description, it is possible that there may be a disposal giving rise to a chargeable gain or allowable loss (see Chapter 5).

There is a distinction to make between money received by a trader in that capacity (receipts arising from the trade) and that received in a personal capacity. Sums received in a personal capacity include an unsolicited sum in the nature of a testimonial or a solatium, albeit with compensatory elements (which would make it a voluntary payment and not taxable), or where the recipient has suffered personal injury (which would be compensation for personal injury and not taxable). Compensation for personal injuries should not be included in the Schedule D Case I or II computation, even if the sum is calculated by reference to the loss of income already sustained, or the loss of future earning power. Indeed, the courts, in calculating amounts referable to the loss of earnings, treat the compensation as if paid net of the tax liabilities that would have arisen had the individual not suffered injury and the consequent income loss (following *British Transport Commission v Gourley* [1955] 3 All ER 796). This treatment applies only to compensation for injuries suffered by the proprietor of a business. Compensation received to compensate a trader for an injury to an employee is taxable, as are payments to companies.

3.4.2 Items included as trading receipts

The adjustment of accounts for tax purposes may involve the addition of sums which are assessable as trading income, or which are dealt with in some special way, but which have not been credited in the trading/profit and loss accounts. Among the items which may be involved are the following:

(1) Sums recovered under insurance policies on items which are current assets (eg amounts recovered from the insurer of stock destroyed by fire must be included as a trading receipt).

(2) Compensation, in so far as it fills 'a hole in the profits' rather than a 'hole in the capital' (eg compensation received upon the cancellation of an agency agreement (*Anglo-Persian Oil Co Ltd v Dale* (1931) 16 TC 253)).

(3) Sums recovered under insurance policies on the lives of employees where the premiums were allowed against profits.

(4) Agricultural and similar subsidies, but not those on capital account (see Chapter 4 for effect on capital allowances).

(5) Where the author of a literary, dramatic, musical or artistic work assigns the copyright in the work, or grants an interest in the copyright by licence, and he has been engaged in the work for more than one year – payment is deemed to be received by instalments depending on the number of years for which he has been so engaged, as follows:

   (a) if less than two years, by two instalments – one half at the time of the first payment, and one half 12 months later;

   (b) if more than two years, by three instalments – one third at the time of the first payment, one third 12 months later, and one third 24 months later (TA 1988, s 534).

   This treatment also applies to public lending rights (s 537).

(6) Where the author of a literary, dramatic, musical or artistic work assigns the copyright in the work, or grants an interest in the copyright by licence more than ten years after first publication thereof, and

   (a) for a period of more than two years the payment is treated as though received by six instalments; or

   (b) if the period of grant or assignment is less than six years, by instalments of equal number to the number of years for which it is granted or assigned (s 536).

   This treatment also applies to public lending rights (s 537).

(7) Where the designer of a design in which design right exists assigns that right, or the author of a registered design assigns the right in the design, or grants an interest in the copyright by licence and if he has been engaged upon the creation of the design for more than one year – payment is deemed to be received by instalments depending on the number of years for which he has been so engaged, as follows:

   (a) if less than two years, by two instalments – one half at the time of the first payment, and one half 12 months later;

   (b) if more than two years, by three instalments – one third at the time of the first payment, one third 12 months later, and one third 24 months later (s 537A).

(8) If a trade is treated as discontinued under TA 1988, s 113 on a change in partners or if a company ceases to trade within s 337, future profits of the trade may be reduced by any additional bad debts not previously provided for (s 89).

(9) Trade debts previously allowed as a deduction for tax purposes are assessed if they are released otherwise than as part of a relevant arrangement or compromise (s 94).

(10) Rents received by the landlord of tied premises (eg public houses owned by brewers) which are let in the course of a trade are treated as trading receipts (and expenses relating to the premises are treated as trading expenses) (s 98).

3.4.3 Receipts excluded from trading profits

There are also items which should be excluded from trading profits:

(1) Dividends and interest received under deduction of tax should be excluded from the adjusted profit as they have already suffered tax. Such interest as is received gross is strictly assessable under Schedule D Case III, and should similarly be deducted.

(2) The letting of property is not an operation of trade so any rent received should normally be excluded and taken in under Schedule A in the normal way. Where property is leased for the purposes of the trade and then sublet, it is common practice to include small amounts of rent receivable as a trading receipt, and deduct the rent payable.

(3) Capital profits on the sale of fixed assets should be excluded as such a surplus is not assessable in the normal way, but should be taken into account in the capital allowances computation or in the computation of a chargeable gain or allowable loss.

(4) Where insurance moneys are quantified with reference to a capital asset's diminished value, and not with reference to loss of trading profits, they are not a revenue receipt.

(5) Any re-transfer from a reserve or provision which was disallowed at the time it was made would also not be taxable.

(6) Enterprise allowance payments (business start-up allowances) are taxable under Schedule D Case VI (TA 1988, s 127).

3.5 CAPITAL OR REVENUE?

There is no statutory definition of 'capital' or 'revenue'. It can, however, be stated as a general rule that a receipt which is connected with the fixed capital (ie property acquired for retention and employment in a business with a view to profit) of a trade is not a trading receipt. But an item connected with the circulating capital (ie property acquired or produced with a view to sale at a profit) should be included in trading profits.

Normally, this is not a difficult distinction to make. For example, in a manufacturing business the factory and machinery and plant are fixed capital which the trader uses long term for generating profits. Any disposal proceeds from the sale of such an asset would be a capital receipt. Stock in trade, debtors and cash, on the other hand, are the trade's circulating capital. There are, however, cases where it is not immediately clear whether a receipt is of a revenue (income) nature or of a capital nature. Here, it is necessary to look not only at the nature of the asset concerned, but also at transactions involving that asset in the context of the particular trade. Thus, in a manufacturing business, an item of plant or machinery would usually be regarded as a capital asset and a sum received on the disposal thereof would be a capital receipt. But if the plant and machinery was itself manufactured by the trader and sold by him, that sale would be a trading receipt. A capital asset need not be tangible (eg a building or plant and machinery): it can be intangible (eg a lease or goodwill).

A receipt in a lump sum does not necessarily mean that the item is a capital one. The lump sum has to be treated for its capital or revenue character in just the same way as if it were a series of sums. But an isolated lump sum, which is unlikely to recur, is a pointer towards its being a capital item, although of itself this test is not conclusive. A surer test is whether the lump sum was received as consideration of the trader surrendering an asset which was wholly or mainly the foundation of his source of income. The following have been held to be capital receipts:

(1) compensation received by a fireclay company from a railway company for leaving part of the fireclay unworked (*Glenboig Union Fireclay Co Ltd v CIR* (1922) 12 TC 427);

(2) sum received on cancellation of the company's future rights under comprehensive agreements for sharing profits (*Van den Berghs Ltd v Clark* (1935) 19 TC 390);

(3) sums received from traders for the installation of plant for carrying out the company's patented process for renovating motor tyres, the company agreeing not to introduce another plant, nor canvass for orders, within the trader's territory (*Margerison v Tyresoles Ltd* (1942) 25 TC 59);

(4) compensation for the loss of an agency by a ship-managing company, which derived almost all of its receipts from this agency (*Barr, Crombie & Co Ltd v CIR* (1945) 26 TC 406);

(5) lump sums received by the owners of vessels, for reconditioning and refitting the vessels when derequisitioned, in place of the Ministry's original undertaking to return the ships in good order (*CIR v West* (1950) 31 TC 402);

(6) a lump sum paid to a company as compensation for a change in the continuity clause in an annually renewed contract (*Sabine v Lookers Ltd* (1958) 38 TC 120); and

(7) a payment to an actor not to engage in any film for any other person for a period of 18 months (*Higgs v Olivier* (1952) 33 TC 136). However, such a payment will only be a capital receipt under this rule if the trading activities are greatly restricted (*White v G & M Davis (a firm)* (1979) 52 TC 597).

The following have been held to be revenue receipts:

(1) a lump sum received on making a new agreement for hiring out the company's track (*Greyhound Racing Association (Liverpool) Ltd v Cooper* (1936) 20 TC 373);

(2) a lump sum received for the cancellation of an agreement to pay commission (*Shove v Dura Manufacturing Co Ltd* (1941) 23 TC 779);

(3) compensation on termination of agency agreement received by a company having a number of such agreements (*Kelsall Parsons & Co Ltd v CIR* (1938) 21 TC 608);

(4) a lump sum received by a company on a contract for the purchase of certain chemicals being cancelled, which was held to have been received in the ordinary course of the business (*Bush, Beach and Gent Ltd v Road* (1939) 22 TC 519);

(5) a lump sum received by a building company from a landowner following the latter withdrawing plots from a building agreement made with the former (*Shadbolt v Salmon Estate (Kingsbury) Ltd* (1943) 25 TC 52);

(6) compensation to a colliery company where part of the colliery was requisitioned for opencast working (*Waterloo Main Colliery Co Ltd v CIR (No 1)* (1947) 29 TC 235);

(7) compensation under planning legislation received by a building company where consent to the development of some of the company's land had been refused by the local authority (*Johnson v Try (W S) Ltd* (1946) 27 TC 167);

(8) a lump sum paid to an author as compensation for the termination of his contract with a film company (*Household v Grimshaw* (1953) 34 TC 366);

(9) a grant under the EC Dairy Herd Conversion Scheme to refrain from marketing milk products for a period of four years (*CIR v Biggar* (1982) 56 TC 254);

(10) compensation for loss of an opportunity to extend a company business (*Creed v H&M Levinson* (1981) 54 TC 479);

(11) compensation for unremunerated work or loss of anticipated profits paid to a diamond broker who solicited the payment (*Rolfe v Nagel* (1981) 55 TC 585);

(12) compensation under the Criminal Injuries to Property (Compensation) Act (Northern Ireland) 1971 paid by the Northern Ireland Office for consequential loss (comprising loss of profits) where the recipient did not recommence trading (*Lang v Rice* (1984) 57 TC 80);

(13) compensation received by a tenant for its agent's negligence in failing to serve a counternotice opposing an excessive rent increase on its leased business premises (*Donald Fisher (Ealing) Ltd v Spencer* (1989) 63 TC 168); and

(14) a lump sum received on termination of an agreement between a consultant and a corporation, even though the terms of the termination

included restrictive covenants (*Consultant v Insp of Taxes* [1999] STC (SCD) 63).

So, what are the tests for distinguishing between capital and revenue expenditure? Such a test was put forward in *Vallambrosa Rubber Co Ltd v Farmer* (1910) 5 TC 529, where the distinction was drawn between expenditure which is made once and for all (capital) and expenditure which will recur year by year (revenue). However, in *Smith v Incorporated Council of Law Reporting for England and Wales* (1914) 6 TC 477, a lump sum paid to a reporter on his retirement was held to be a payment on revenue account. In *Hancock v General Reversionary and Investment Co Ltd* (1919) 7 TC 358, a sum which was paid for purchasing an annuity for the benefit of a retiring employee was also held to be a revenue expense. The test which has been most frequently resorted to is that applied in *British Insulated and Helsby Cables v Atherton* (1926) 10 TC 155:

> 'The true question is: what does the company get for its expenditure? If the answer be that it is something of an enduring character . . . then the expenditure is a capital expenditure.'

In *Pitt v Castle Hill Warehousing Co Ltd* (1974) 49 TC 638, a company constructed a new road to avoid disturbance to local residents and claimed the cost was a revenue expense to protect its trade. The High Court held it to be capital, as an asset with enduring qualities had been acquired:

> 'But when an expenditure is made, not only once and for all, but with a view to bringing into existence an asset or an advantage for the enduring benefit of a trade, I think that there is very good reason (in the absence of special circumstances leading to an opposite conclusion) for treating such an expenditure as properly attributable, not to revenue, but to capital.'

3.6 TRANSFER PRICING

TA 1988, s 770A and Sched 28AA govern the 'transfer pricing' regime for accounting periods and tax years ending after 30 June 1999. Their purpose is to bring about the result that would have occurred had arm's length pricing been employed, by increasing the taxable profit of one of the parties to the transaction and providing for the other party to claim a corresponding adjustment to its profit. These are complex provisions and outside the scope of this book.

3.7 CHARGE OR EXPENSE?

Interest, whether short or annual, incurred wholly and exclusively for business purposes, may be deducted as an expense in computing the trade's profit or loss for income tax purposes, subject to certain restrictions on the deduction of annual interest paid to a person not resident in the UK (TA 1988, s 82). Annual interest may also qualify as a charge on income under TA 1988, s 353 if it is paid on a loan for one of the purposes specified in ss 354 and 359–365. Where interest qualifies for relief both as a deduction in computing trading profits and as a charge on income, the trader can claim under either head, but not under both (s 368). Where the trader chooses to treat the interest as a charge on income, but it cannot be wholly relieved because of a deficiency of income in the year of assessment in which it is paid, the unallowed part of the interest may be carried forward to succeeding years in the same way as a trading loss (s 390).

For corporation tax purposes, annual interest paid by a company can only be deducted in computing the trading profit for tax purposes if it is paid in accordance with the FA 1996 loan relationship provisions (TA 1988, s 337A).

Charges on income, such as any annuities and other annual payments not in respect of loan relationships, are treated as a deduction from the total company profits.

4

CAPITAL ALLOWANCES

DAVID BERTRAM, CLAYFIELD PROFESSIONAL GUIDANCE LTD

The Capital Allowances Act 1990 (CAA 1990) contains the rules for capital allowances (ie deductions on account of 'depreciation') in connection with:

(1) industrial buildings and structures (ss 1–21);
(2) machinery and plant (ss 22–83);
(3) agricultural land and buildings (ss 122–133);
(4) mines, oil wells, etc (ss 98–121);
(5) dredging (s 134); and
(6) dwelling houses let on assured tenancies (ss 84–97).

Relief in tax credit form is given for expenditure on R&D by TA 1988, ss 82A, 82B and 837A, and FA 2000, ss 68 and 69 and Scheds 19–21. The provisions relating to allowances for expenditure on patents are contained in TA 1988, ss 520–529, and for know-how in ss 530–533. Allowances for expenditure on cemeteries and crematoria are dealt with in TA 1988, s 91.

Although usually thought of in connection with Schedule D Cases I and II, allowances also apply in other circumstances (eg an employee may in certain circumstances claim capital allowances against his Schedule E assessment, a person may undertake a Schedule A business receiving rents etc).

4.1 ALLOWABLE EXPENDITURE

Capital allowances are given for capital expenditure, which is excluded in arriving at the amount of profits for Cases I and II purposes. Once it is established that capital expenditure has been incurred, the nature of the expenditure must be identified and the rules followed for the type of expenditure concerned. If the expenditure does not fit into any category for which capital allowances are given, no relief is due.

CAA 1990, ss 51–59 provide relief for expenditure on machinery and plant which becomes a fixture in a building. This legislation reverses *Stokes v Costain Property Investment Ltd* (1984) 57 TC 688, where it was held that the lessee was not entitled to capital allowances on fixtures which become part of the building, since they belonged to the landlord. Thus, for expenditure incurred on building fixtures where a lease applies, an allowance is given to the lessee incurring the expenditure, even though in law the asset belongs to the landlord.

4.2 MANNER OF GRANTING RELIEF

Relief is given in two main ways: 'in taxing a trade', and 'by discharge or repayment of tax'. The manner of relief which is appropriate in a particular case depends on the circumstances in which the allowances fall to be due.

4.2.1 Allowances given in taxing a trade
(CAA 1990, ss 140, 142 and 144)

For individuals and partnerships, allowances and charges under the capital allowance rules are usually given by treating any allowance as a trading expense in that period, and by treating the amount of any such charge as a trading receipt in that period. Under self-assessment for individuals, the claim or charge is made via the income tax return. This also applies to professions, vocations and, in limited circumstances, employments and offices.

There are two restrictions on the use of first-year allowances by means of set off against general income which intended to circumvent various leasing schemes set up to obtain tax relief:

(1) There is no first-year allowance for expenditure incurred on machinery or plant for leasing in the course of a trade if:
   (a) when the expenditure was incurred the trade was carried on in partnership with a company (with or without other partners); or
   (b) a scheme was effected or arrangements were made (whether before or after that time) with a view to the trade being so carried on.
(2) There is no relief for a first-year allowance if:
   (a) the allowance is made under TA 1988, s 839 in connection with:
      (i) a trade which at the time when the expenditure was incurred was, or which has subsequently been, carried on in partnership or transferred to a connected person; or
      (ii) an asset which after that time has been transferred to a connected person or, at a price lower than market value, to any other person; and
   (b) a scheme has been effected or arrangements made (whether before or after that time) where the sole or main benefit that might be expected to accrue to the individual from the transaction was to obtain a reduction in tax liability by set off against general income under TA 1988, ss 380 and 381.

For corporation tax, a company's profits for any accounting period are adjusted usually by treating the allowance as a trading expense and any charge as a trading receipt in a relevant period. Here, claims for capital allowances can only be made by being included in a company tax return or an amended company tax return (FA 1998, Sched 18, para 10(2)); however, companies need not claim all of the allowances to which they are entitled (see *Elliss v BP Oil Northern Ireland Refinery Ltd* (1986) 57 TC 474).

4.2.2 Allowances given by discharge or repayment of tax
(CAA 1990, ss 61, 73, 141 and 145)

Allowances given 'by discharge or repayment of tax' are usually expressed to be available primarily against a specified source of income. Prior to 1995–96, allowances given to the lessor of an agricultural or industrial building, or property let under the assured tenancy scheme, were dealt with in this way; since then, such allowances are given in taxing a Schedule A business's profits. Allowances still given in this way are for expenditure on machinery or plant leased otherwise than by way of trade (CAA 1990, ss 61(1) and 73(2)).

These allowances are deducted from or set off against income of the specified class for the period concerned. If the allowance is greater than the income from the specified class for that period, the balance is deducted from or set off against income of that class for the next period, and so on for subsequent periods. These allowances can only be set against income from leasing machinery or plant: they cannot be set against other income.

When a lessor ceases to let the machinery or plant otherwise than in the course of a trade, a balancing charge may arise. For income tax, the charge is made under Schedule D Case VI; for corporation tax it is made as income from letting the machinery or plant.

The allowance for expenditure on machinery or plant leased otherwise than by way of trade is available primarily against income from letting machinery or plant generally. If the lessee does not use the machinery or plant for trade purposes, the allowances can only be set against income from the letting of that machinery and plant (CAA 1990, s 73(3)).

4.2.3 Renewals basis

As an alternative to claiming capital allowances, it is possible to claim the cost of replacements on the renewals basis (*Caledonian Railway v Banks* (1880) 1 TC 487). The cost of replacing implements, utensils and articles employed for trade purposes can be deducted in computing that trade's profits (TA 1988, s 74(1)(d)); this is taken to include loose tools. If expenditure on such items is claimed as a revenue deduction, they do not qualify for capital allowances. By ESC B1, a trader may claim a revenue deduction for the cost of replacing larger items of machinery and plant instead of claiming capital allowances (known as the 'renewals basis'). No allowance is given for the cost of the original asset, and when a replacement is acquired the allowance is restricted by excluding any part of the cost representing addition or improvement. No capital allowances can be given on any part of the replacement cost, even if some of it has been excluded from the renewals allowance. Expenditure on any improvement of the original assets is not allowed to be charged, although it may be claimed as a capital allowance. The renewals basis is very rarely used in practice.

4.3 OTHER ADMINISTRATIVE MATTERS

4.3.1 Writing-down allowances for agricultural buildings and dredging
(CAA 1990, s 146)

Over the years, writing-down allowances for agricultural buildings and dredging have been given by reference to fixed writing-down periods of 10, 25 or 50 years and, having been given on a straight-line basis, the effective percentage rates have been 10%, 4% or 2% a year.

From time to time, initial allowances have been given in the year of expenditure. However, there is an overall limitation on the allowance which can be given, in that the total writing-down allowances made, together with any initial allowance given, cannot exceed the total expenditure. This means that where an initial allowance has been given, the writing-down allowances will cease before the end of the full writing-down period.

4.3.2 Exclusion of double allowances
(CAA 1990, ss 147 and 148)

If an allowance is made for capital expenditure under one of the capital allowances categories, an allowance cannot also be made under any other category either for that expenditure or for any expenditure in relation to constructing, providing or acquiring any asset to the construction, provision or acquisition of which the original allowance related. It also follows that such expenditure cannot be taken into account in determining qualifying expenditure for any writing-down allowance, or balancing allowance or charge, under CAA 1990, s 24.

4.3.3 Non-UK resident companies
(CAA 1990, s 149)

For non-UK resident companies which are within the charge to corporation tax for one source of income and to income tax for another, in applying CAA 1990 allowances related to any source of income are given against income chargeable to the same tax as is chargeable on income from that source.

4.3.4 **Apportionment of consideration, and exchanges and surrenders of leasehold interests**
(CAA 1990, ss 150 and 151)

Often, several assets are disposed of in a single transaction (eg the sale of a building containing machinery and plant (such as lifts, roller shutters, air conditioning) on which machinery and plant capital allowances have been claimed, as well as industrial buildings allowances on the building as such). Part of the consideration may be attributed to land. In these circumstances, an apportionment of the consideration is needed. Thus, where property is sold together with other property, so much of the net proceeds of the sale of the whole property as, on a just apportionment, is properly attributable to the first-mentioned property is deemed to be the net proceeds of the sale of the first-mentioned property.

All the property which is sold under one bargain is deemed to be sold together, notwithstanding that separate prices are, or purport to be, either agreed for separate items of that property or that there are, or purport to be, separate sales of separate items of that property. The above also applies to other sale, insurance, salvage or compensation moneys as they apply in relation to the net proceeds of sales. Furthermore, it also applies to the exchange of any property and, for a leasehold interest, the surrender thereof for valuable consideration.

The Revenue does not challenge amounts apportioned to qualifying assets as too low unless they consider that something else is overvalued, assuming arm's length transaction.

Where, under any of the capital allowance rules (except those for machinery and plant), any sum must be apportioned and, at the time of apportionment, it appears that it is material to the tax liability (for whatever period) of two or more persons, any question arising over the manner in which the sum is apportioned is determined by the Commissioners, who determine the question as if it were an appeal. This also applies to the determination of any price, or of any sale, insurance, salvage or compensation moneys, made under CAA 1990, s 10D. The determination, under the machinery and plant allowance rules, or under CAA 1990, ss 152 and 157, of the price which property would have fetched if sold in the open market is similarly made by the Commissioners.

4.3.5 **Succession to trades etc**
(CAA 1990, s 152)

Where a person succeeds to any trade, etc previously carried on by another person and, under the rules applying to changes in the membership of partnerships (TA 1988, s 113) and on companies beginning or ceasing to trade (s 337), the trade is treated as discontinued, and the following procedure applies. Any property which, immediately before succession, was in use for the discontinued trade and, without being sold, is immediately after succession in use for the new trade, is under the industrial buildings, mineral extraction, agricultural buildings and dredging allowance rules treated as if it had been sold to the successor when succession takes place, and as if the net sale proceeds had been at the open market rate.

4.3.6 Subsidies, contributions etc
(CAA 1990, ss 153–155)

Most grants from the Crown or from any government or public or local authority, whether in the UK or elsewhere, are deducted from capital expenditure so that capital allowances are claimed only on the net amount borne by the taxpayer (*Stokes v Costain Property Investment Ltd* (1984) 57 TC 688). This does not apply to grants under the Industrial Development Act 1982, the Industry Act 1972 or equivalent Northern Ireland legislation. It was held in *McKinney v Hagans Caravans (Manufacturing) Ltd* [1997] STC 1023 that the International Fund for Ireland is a public authority. The write-off of government investment is not treated as expenditure met by the Crown (TA 1988, s 400).

In most cases, grants received from the Crown or from any government or public or local authority, whether in the UK or elsewhere, are deducted from the relevant expenditure before capital allowances are computed. By ESC B16, fire safety expenditure incurred directly by the lessor (as contrasted to making a contribution to the lessee) is allowed if similar expenditure by the tenant or licensee would qualify for relief. Under ESC B49, if a grant is subsequently repaid, the amount repaid can then be treated as expenditure on which capital allowances may be given. Grants from the Football Trust towards a club's capital expenditure do not reduce the amount qualifying for capital allowances if derived from pool betting duty (or grants therefrom) (FA 1990, s 126(4)).

This treatment does not apply to insurance proceeds or other compensation moneys payable for any asset which has been demolished, destroyed or put out of use.

A recipient of a contribution towards capital expenditure (eg an electricity supply or drainage scheme) met by someone other than the Crown or a government or public or local authority may be able to claim capital allowances on the full cost without any deduction on account of the contribution. This is conditional upon no deduction from profits or as capital allowances being available to the contributor. It is irrelevant whether the contributor is within the charge to tax.

A payment or benefit taken into account hereunder is not also charged to tax as a reverse premium under FA 1999, Sched 6.

Capital allowances are usually available if a contribution is made towards someone else's capital expenditure, but for the contributor's or his tenant's trade purposes. The expenditure must have been eligible for industrial buildings, mineral extraction or agricultural buildings allowances. No allowance is available if the contributor and recipient are connected persons (TA 1988, s 839). Contributions made to a sewerage authority in the UK for an asset used for treating trade effluents qualifies for capital allowances. However, this does not include the cost of connection to main drainage (*Bridge House (Reigate Hill) Ltd v Hinder* (1971) 47 TC 182). The Revenue has confirmed that a contribution by a farmer towards the cost of installing telephones at railway crossing points qualifies for capital allowances.

Capital allowances due to a contributor are calculated on the assumption that the relevant asset continues to be used for his trade, even though it is owned by another person. Where a contribution relates to a trade carried on by a tenant, the contributor is deemed to have let the machinery or plant to the tenant, entitling him to the allowance.

If the contributor transfers his trade, the remaining writing-down allowances for his contributions are made to the transferee.

Where, when the contribution was made, the trade is carried on by a tenant of land in which the contributor had an interest, a writing-down allowance is made for a chargeable period at the end of that period to a person entitled to the contributor's interest in that land. The residue of expenditure provisions used to calculate the writing-down allowance due to the purchaser of an industrial building does not apply to contributions, and the transferee continues to receive the contributor's writing-down allowances.

4.3.7 Meaning of 'sale, insurance, salvage or compensation moneys'
(CAA 1990, s 156)

This depends upon the nature of the event which gives rise to a balancing allowance or charge, as follows:

Event	*Meaning*
Sale of property	Net proceeds of sale.
The coming to an end of an interest in property on or by reason of the coming to an end of a foreign concession	Any compensation payable for that property.
Demolition or destruction of any property	Net amount received for remains of the property, together with any insurance moneys received for demolition or destruction and any other compensation of any description received in respect thereof, in so far as that compensation consists of capital sums

A building or structure ceases altogether to be used or machinery or plant is put out of use	Any compensation of any description received for that event, so far as that compensation consists of capital sums.
The bringing or coming to an end of a toll road concession	Any insurance moneys or other compensation received for any capital expenditure on the construction of the road in question, in so far as that compensation consists of capital sums.

These rules do not apply to machinery and plant allowances, for which a balancing allowance or charge is calculated by reference to the 'disposal value' brought into account (CAA 1988, s 26).

4.3.8 Sales between connected persons etc
(CAA 1990, ss 157 and 158)

The rules described here, which do not apply to machinery and plant allowances, apply to sales of any property in two circumstances. The first is where the buyer (or seller) is a body of persons over whom the seller (or buyer) has control, or both the seller and the buyer are bodies of persons and some other person has control over both of them, or the buyer and the seller are connected under TA 1988, s 839. The second is where it appears, with respect to the sale or to transactions of which the sale is one, that the sole or main benefit which otherwise might be expected to accrue to any or all of the parties was to obtain an allowance or deduction or a greater allowance or deduction, or to avoid or reduce a charge (other than under the machinery and plant rules). 'A body of persons' includes a partnership. These rules apply to a sale even though they may not, in strictness, be fully applicable because any party is non-UK resident.

Where the property is sold at a price other than at its open-market value, it is deemed to be sold for the price it would fetch in the open market.

Where a sale is one to which the common control test applies, but it is not made primarily to obtain a tax benefit, and the parties so elect within two years after the sale, then instead of the open-market value, the transaction is deemed to take place at capital allowances written-down value, if lower, for the market value.

The capital allowances written-down value depends on which set of capital allowances rules apply. For an industrial building or structure, a qualifying hotel or a commercial building or structure, it is the residue of the expenditure on its construction immediately before the sale (CAA 1990, s 8).

For an asset representing allowable R&D (prior to 2000–01 referred to as 'scientific research') expenditure of a capital nature made under CAA 1990, s 137, the allowance is nil. In any other case, the allowance is the amount of expenditure.

No election is possible unless both parties to it are entitled to capital allowances. Nor can an allowance be made if the buyer is a dual resident investing company.

4.3.9 Capital expenditure
(CA 1990, s 159)

Capital expenditure and capital sums incurred or received by a person do not include any expenditure or sum which is tax deductible from or included in the profits or gains of his trade, profession, office, employment or vocation or Schedule A business. Nor do they include any expenditure or sum in the case of which a deduction is made as an annual charge under TA 1988, s 348 or 349(1).

The following rules determine when capital expenditure (other than an additional VAT liability) is to be taken to be incurred. The basic rule is that an amount of capital expenditure is taken to be incurred on the date on which the obligation to pay that amount becomes unconditional (whether or not there is a later date on or before which the whole or any part of that amount must be paid).

If, under any agreement:

(1) as a result of the issue of a certificate or some other event, an obligation to pay an amount of capital expenditure on an asset becomes unconditional, and

(2) at a time before that obligation becomes unconditional, the asset becomes the property of or is otherwise under the contract attributed to the person having that obligation,

then, in a case where the obligation referred to in (1) becomes unconditional within one month following the end of a chargeable period, but the time referred to in (2) falls at or before the end of that chargeable period, the obligation is deemed to be unconditional immediately before the expiry of that period.

Where, under any agreement, the whole or any part of capital expenditure must be paid on (or not later than) a date which is more than four months after the date on which the obligation to pay that amount becomes unconditional, so much of that expenditure as must be so paid is taken to be incurred on the date on or before which it must be so paid.

In any case where:

(a) under any agreement, an obligation to pay an amount of capital expenditure becomes unconditional on a date earlier than that which accords with normal commercial usage, and

BUSINESS TAX & LAW HANDBOOK

(b) the sole or main benefit which otherwise might have been expected to be obtained from the obligation becoming unconditional on that earlier date is that the expenditure would be taken to be incurred in a chargeable period which is earlier than would otherwise have been the case,

capital expenditure is taken to be incurred on the date on or before which it must be paid; the four-month rule does not apply.

These rules are not applied if other capital allowance rules treat expenditure as incurred on a date which is later than that which would result from the application of those rules (ie under the assured tenancies, mineral extraction and agricultural buildings allowances rules).

4.3.10 Additional VAT liabilities and rebates
(CAA 1990, s 159A)

An additional VAT liability or rebate arising is regarded as incurred or made on the last day of the relevant VAT interval. 'The relevant VAT interval' for these purposes is the period within the VAT period of adjustment in which the increase or decrease in use which gave rise to the liability or rebate occurred.

An additional VAT liability or rebate is regarded as incurred or made at a determined time and, except for the purpose of determining the chargeable period (see below), any such liability or rebate is not treated as incurred or made otherwise than on the last day of the relevant VAT interval. The chargeable period is that:

(1) for which an allowance or charge under the capital allowance rules may be made for the liability or rebate, or
(2) in which the liability or rebate amount is to be brought into account in making such allowances or charges.

For the purpose of determining the chargeable period:

(a) where a VAT return is made to Customs & Excise for a period in which the liability or rebate is accounted for, the liability or rebate is regarded as incurred or made in the chargeable period, which includes the last day of the period to which that return relates; but
(b) if, before any such return is made, Customs & Excise assesses the liability or rebate as due or repayable, then, notwithstanding (a) above, the liability or rebate is regarded as incurred or made on the day on which that assessment is made; and
(c) if the additional VAT liability or rebate has not been accounted for on a VAT return, or assessed by Customs & Excise before the trade has been, or has been treated as, permanently discontinued, then, notwithstanding (a) and (b) above, the liability or rebate is regarded as incurred or made on the last day of the chargeable period related to the discontinuance.

Where, disregarding any additional VAT liability or rebate, any allowance or charge for any capital expenditure falls to be determined by reference to a proportion only of that expenditure or of what that allowance or charge would otherwise have been, then, to the extent that so much of any allowance or charge so made for any additional VAT liability or rebate by reference to that expenditure would not otherwise be so determined, it is so determined.

4.3.11 Periods of account
(CAA 1990, s 160)

Almost all the allowances granted or charges made under TA 1988 and CAA 1990 are dependent, as regards any particular chargeable period, upon either the occurrence of a specific event (eg capital expenditure incurred on industrial buildings or structures) or the fulfilment of a specific condition (eg ownership and use of machinery and plant) in what is termed the 'basis period' appropriate to that chargeable period. For income tax, the period of account is any period for which accounts of a trade, profession or vocation are made up.

Where two periods of account overlap, the period common to both is deemed to fall in the first period of account only; where there is an interval between two periods of account, the interval is deemed to be part of the first period of account. Where a period of account ('the original period') would otherwise be more than 18 months, that period is divided into as many separate periods of account as may be necessary to secure that none of those periods is of more than 12 months. The first period must begin with the commencement date of the original period, and each subsequent period commences on the anniversary.

For any other person to or on whom an allowance or charge falls to be made, 'period of account' means any tax year.

For corporation tax, capital allowances are given by reference to accounting periods.

4.4 TYPES OF ALLOWANCE

4.4.1 Initial allowance
(CAA 1990, s 1)

A 100% 'initial allowance' is available to a person who incurs capital expenditure on the construction of an industrial building or structure in an enterprise zone, occupied for the purposes of a trade carried on by either that person or lessees and licensees. It is a prerequisite of the allowance that the expenditure is incurred, or is incurred under a contract entered into, at a time when the building or structure site is in an enterprise zone (ie not more than ten years after the site was first included in the zone).

4.4.2 First-year allowance
(CAA 1990, s 22)

A first-year allowance is granted on capital expenditure incurred on new or second-hand machinery and plant. The allowance rates and the qualifying categories of expenditure have varied from time to time. The allowance is deducted from cost taken into account in calculating any writing-down allowances in subsequent years.

4.4.3 Writing-down allowance
(CAA 1990, ss 3 and 24)

The writing-down allowance is a percentage allowance which must be considered separately for the two main categories of allowances for expenditure on (i) industrial buildings and structures, and (ii) machinery and plant.

For industrial buildings, it is a percentage allowance given each year based on the cost of the building. It is only granted when the building is owned and in use as an industrial building on the last day of the basis period. It is given for a full year no matter for how short a period it has been so owned or used. For machinery and plant, the reducing balance method is used. The method is to apply a percentage allowance to the balance outstanding after deducting previous writing-down allowances. In both cases, the allowance rates and the qualifying categories of expenditure have varied from time to time.

Writing-down allowances for agricultural buildings etc and dredging have, for various dates of expenditure, been at straight-line rates of 10%, 4% or 2% a year. The total writing-down allowances made together with any initial allowance cannot exceed the overall expenditure.

4.4.4 Balancing allowance and charge
(CAA 1990, ss 4 and 24)

On the disposal of an asset that has received capital allowances, its value after deducting those allowances (the written-down value) is compared with proceeds. If the proceeds are less than its value as written down, a further 'balancing allowance' is given for the chargeable period in which the disposal occurred. If the proceeds are in excess of the written-down value, the allowances granted have been too great and so a 'balancing charge' is made for the same chargeable period as would a balancing allowance. Note that CGT may be applicable, in addition to balancing charges, where an asset is disposed of for more than its cost price.

4.5 INDUSTRIAL BUILDINGS AND STRUCTURES

4.5.1 Definitions

'Industrial building or structure'
(CAA 1990, s 18)

Allowances are only granted for expenditure on premises within the scope of an 'industrial building or structure' as defined by CAA 1990, s 18. To come within the definition, a building or structure must be in use for the purposes of a trade or undertaking within the following list:

(1) a trade carried on in a mill, factory or other similar premises;
(2) a transport, dock, inland navigation, water, sewerage, electricity or hydraulic power undertaking;
(3) a tunnel undertaking;
(4) a bridge undertaking;
(5) a toll road concession;
(6) a trade manufacturing or processing goods or materials; this includes maintenance or repair, but does not apply to the maintenance or repair of actual tools or equipment used in the process;
(7) a trade which consists in the storage of goods or materials:
    (a) to be used in the manufacture of other goods or materials; or
    (b) to be subjected, in course of a trade, to any process; or
    (c) having been manufactured, produced or subjected in the course of a trade to any process, not yet delivered to any purchaser; or
    (d) on their arrival in any part of the UK from a place outside the UK; or
(8) a trade which consists in the working of any mine, oil well or other source of mineral deposits, or of a foreign plantation; or
(9) a trade consisting of ploughing and/or cultivating land (other than land occupied by the person carrying on the trade) and/or doing any other agricultural operation on such land, and/or threshing another person's crops; or
(10) a trade which consists in the catching or taking of fish or shellfish.

Note that, in particular, the expression 'industrial building or structure' includes any building or structure provided for the welfare of workers employed in the trade or undertaking and in use for that purpose.

    An 'industrial building or structure' does not include one used as, or as part of, a dwelling house, retail shop, showroom, hotel or office or for any purpose ancillary to such purposes. This does not apply to the whole or part of such building or structure constructed for occupation by or for the welfare of persons employed at or in connection with a mine, oil well or other source of mineral deposits, or crop growing or harvesting a foreign plantation, where that building or structure will have little or no value once that trade has ceased (eg buildings on site).

Where a building or structure is used by more than one licensee of the same person, it is not an industrial building or structure unless each licensee uses it or that part of it to which his licence relates for trade purposes within the above list.

Where only part of a building or structure is industrial, and the capital expenditure incurred on the construction of the non-industrial part is not more than 25% of the total capital expenditure incurred, the whole is treated as an industrial building or structure. This also applies to qualifying hotels and to commercial buildings and structures. Where a lessee incurs expenditure on part of a building, the Revenue considers the part on which expenditure is incurred and, if it is in use for a qualifying trade, the expenditure qualifies for the allowance. If there is further expenditure on the non-qualifying part of a building which takes the total expenditure over the 25% limit, initial expenditure on the non-qualifying part ceases to qualify. The 25% limit also applies to buildings in enterprise zones.

A road on an industrial estate is treated as used for trade purposes if the buildings and structures on the estate are used wholly or mainly for such purposes. A 'building or structure' includes a part of, or an addition or extension of, a building or structure; 'structure' includes walls, bridges, dams, roads, culverts and tunnels.

'Qualifying trade' includes servicing and maintaining vehicles, but not the sale of cars, parts or vehicle hire. If a garage business carries on a trade of servicing and maintaining vehicles for the public it is carrying on a qualifying trade and the premises used (eg a repair bay or a repair workshop) wholly or mainly for this purpose qualify for industrial buildings allowance. Many garages carry on other trades such as the sale of cars or spare parts. However, these are not qualifying trades and the premises used for these purposes do not qualify. Some garages carry on a trade of hiring vehicles – again, this is not a qualifying trade and any premises used for this purpose (including a repair workshop used to maintain and service the hired vehicles) do not qualify.

Despite the specific nature of the definition, there have been several cases concerned with its meaning. Cases where buildings and structures were held to be industrial include: *Ellerker v Union Cold Storage Co Ltd, Thomas Borthwick & Sons v Compton* (1938) 22 TC 195 (cold-storage premises containing ice-making machinery within definition of a mill); *CIR v Leith Harbour & Docks Commissioners* (1941) 24 TC 118 (grain elevators at docks similar premises to a mill); *Lancashire Electric Power Co v Wilkinson* (1947) 28 TC 427 (power house of an electricity generating station a single industrial building (each internal division not to be treated as a separate building, some qualifying and some not)); *CIR v Lambhill Ironworks* (1950) 31 TC 393 (drawing office related to the industrial process); *Kilmarnock Equitable Cooperative Society Ltd v CIR* (1966) 42 TC 675 (building in which goods repackaged for retail sale); and *CIR v Saxone, Lilley & Skinner (Holdings) Ltd* (1967) 44 TC 122 (warehouse in which were stored finished goods manufactured by the taxpayer (even though bought-in goods were also stored there)).

Cases where buildings and structures were held not to be industrial include: *Dale v Johnson Brothers* (1951) 32 TC 487 (warehouse for imported goods of a trade (not a manufacturer)); *CIR v National Coal Board* (1957) 37 TC 264 (employee's house at a colliery capable of subsequent use by others); *Bourne v Norwich Crematorium Ltd* (1967) 44 TC 164 (crematorium); *Abbott Laboratories Ltd v Carmody* (1968) 44 TC 569 (administrative offices within industrial complex, but connected to manufacturing part of site by means of covered walkway); *Buckingham v Securitas Properties Ltd* (1979) 53 TC 292 (secure area for counting wages (by a security company)); *Vibroplant Ltd v Holland* (1981) 54 TC 658 (premises for maintenance of plant where business was plant hire); *Girobank plc v Clarke* (1997) 70 TC 387 (building used by bank for processing documents); *Bestway (Holdings) Ltd v Luff* (1998) 70 TC 512 (cash and carry wholesale supermarket warehouse); and *Sarsfield v Dixons Group plc* [1998] STC 938 (distribution warehouse within retail group).

Maintenance/repair businesses

The subjection of goods to a process includes repair or maintenance work on any goods or materials provided that the activity does not form part of a retail business, or does not form part of a trade which would itself not qualify premises for industrial buildings allowance (eg plant hire: see *Vibroplant Ltd v Holland*, above). Accordingly expenditure on buildings for such purposes qualifies for industrial buildings allowance.

Warehousing and storage

In the light of the decision in *Crusabridge Investments Ltd v Casings International Ltd* (1979) 54 TC 246, the Revenue practice is to grant allowance for buildings used for warehousing and storage by traders and wholesalers where the goods involved are to be used for an industrial process. The allowance is not extended to premises used for storage for retailing purposes.

'Qualifying hotels'
(CAA 1990, s 19)

A 'qualifying hotel' is an hotel the accommodation of which is in a building or buildings of a permanent nature and which meets the following conditions:

(1) it is open for at least four months (120 days) in April to October, and
(2) during the open season:
   (a) it has at least ten letting bedrooms available to the public generally and not normally in the same occupation for more than one month;

   (b) the sleeping accommodation offered at the hotel must consist
         wholly or mainly of letting bedrooms;
   (c) the services provided for guests normally include breakfast,
         evening meal, making beds and cleaning rooms.

The breakfast and evening meal condition is satisfied where the offering (as distinct from the provision) of these meals is a normal event in the hotel's carrying on of its business. It is not sufficient that they are available only on request (see SP 9/87).

There are special rules to determine when an hotel first becomes a qualifying hotel, but an hotel is not treated as complying with the requirements at any time in a chargeable period after it has ceased altogether to be used.

Also qualifying for the allowance is any building (whether or not on the same site as any other part of the hotel) which is provided by the person carrying on the hotel for the welfare of workers employed there and is in use for that purpose (eg separate sleeping quarters or games areas). Hostels occupied by workers fall within this criteria, but not flats or houses provided for individual workers.

Where a qualifying hotel is carried on by an individual, whether alone or in partnership, no allowance is given for any accommodation which, during the open season, is normally used as a dwelling by that person or any member of his family or household. However, there is no restriction of allowances by the general 25% rule (see CAA 1990, s 18(7)).

'The relevant interest'
(CAA 1990, s 20)

Ownership of 'the relevant interest' in an industrial building or structure is crucial. The relevant interest, in relation to expenditure incurred on its construction, is the interest in that building or structure to which the person who incurred the expenditure was entitled when he incurred it.

It may be that, when he incurs expenditure on construction, a person is entitled to two or more interests in the building or structure. If one of those interests is reversionary on all the others, that interest is the relevant interest.

An interest does not cease to be the relevant interest on the creation of any lease or other interest to which that interest is subject. Where the relevant interest is a leasehold interest and is extinguished by its surrender or on the person entitled to it acquiring the reversionary interest thereon, the interest into which that leasehold interest merges becomes the relevant interest.

For expenditure incurred on the construction of any road, a highway concession for the road is not treated as an interest in the road. Where, for expenditure incurred on its construction, the person who incurred the expenditure was not entitled to an interest in the road when he incurred the expenditure, but at that time entitled to a highway concession for the road, the relevant interest in relation to that expenditure is the highway concession itself.

Other interpretations
(CAA 1990, s 21)

Expenditure incurred on the construction of a building or structure does not include any cost of acquisition of, or of rights in or over, any land. A person who has incurred expenditure on construction is deemed to have had the same interest therein as he would have had if the construction had been completed at that time. Apportionment can be made to eliminate the value of any non-industrial parts of the site (eg land: *Bostock & others v Totham* (1997) 69 TC 356).

4.5.2 Initial allowances for buildings and structures in enterprise zones
(CAA 1990, s 1)

If a person incurs capital expenditure which fulfils the conditions for the chargeable period which is related to incurring the expenditure, there is made to him an 'initial allowance' equal to 100% of that expenditure. The conditions are that the expenditure is:

(1) on the construction of an industrial building or structure which is to be occupied for the purposes of a trade carried on either by that person or by a lessee occupying the building under a lease to which the relevant interest is reversionary, and

(2) incurred, or is incurred under a contract entered into, at a time when the site is in an enterprise zone, being within not more than ten years after it was first included in the zone. However, this does not include expenditure incurred under a contract entered into at a time when the site is in an enterprise zone if the expenditure is incurred more than 20 years after the site was first included in the zone (see CAA 1990, s 17A).

Expenditure on buildings includes VAT and any additional VAT (see 4.3.10). A person making a claim to an initial allowance may require such allowance to be reduced to a lesser, specified amount.

4.5.3 Writing-down allowances
(CA 1990, s 3)

A writing-down allowance is made to the person concerned at the end of a chargeable period where

(1) he is entitled to an interest in a building or structure, and
(2) it is an industrial building or structure, and
(3) that interest is the relevant interest in relation to the capital expenditure incurred on construction.

The writing-down allowance is a straight-line 4% (or, where the expenditure was incurred before 6 November 1962, a straight-line 2%) of the capital expenditure incurred on construction. For a chargeable period of less or more than a year, that fraction of 4% or 2% is reduced or increased proportionately.

Expenditure on buildings includes VAT and any additional VAT (see 4.3.10). A person entitled to a highway concession for a road is treated as having an interest in the road.

4.5.4 Balancing allowances and charges
(CAA 1990, s 4)

A 'balancing allowance' or a 'balancing charge' is made to or on the person entitled to the relevant interest immediately before the event concerned occurs, for the chargeable period related to that event. The circumstances in which this is made are where any capital expenditure has been incurred on construction, and any of the following events occurs while the building is an industrial building or structure, or after it has ceased to be one:

(1) the relevant interest in the building or structure is sold, or
(2) that interest, being one depending on the duration of a foreign concession, comes to an end when that concession ends, or
(3) a leasehold interest comes to an end otherwise than on the person entitled to it acquiring the interest which is reversionary on it, or
(4) the building or structure is demolished or destroyed, or ceases altogether to be used, or
(5) that interest, being a highway concession, is brought to or comes to an end, or
(6) any capital value is realised (CAA 1990, s 4A), or
(7) an additional VAT rebate for any of the capital expenditure is made to the person entitled to the relevant interest.

No balancing allowance or charge can be made more than 25 years (or, where the expenditure was incurred before 6 November 1962, 50 years) after the building or structure was first used.

If for any part of the relevant period the building or structure was neither industrial nor used for R&D (prior to 2000–01 referred to as 'scientific research'), the procedure described below applies.

No balancing charge or allowance is made on a sale if, being a sale without a change of control or between connected persons, the building or structure is treated as having been sold for a sum equal to the residue of the expenditure on its construction immediately before the sale (CAA 1990, s 158).

The following terms are used to arrive at the charge or allowance:

'The relevant period'

This is the period beginning at the time when the building or structure was first used for any purpose and ending with the sale (or other event giving rise to the balancing allowance or charge). If the building had already been used when acquired, the relevant period is the date of acquisition to the date of disposal.

'The capital expenditure'

This is the capital expenditure incurred, or deemed to have been incurred (see CAA 1990, s 10(1), 10A, 10B or 10C), on construction reduced by any balancing charge made in relation to that expenditure on receipt of an additional VAT rebate for any capital expenditure made to the person entitled to the relevant interest. Where the person to or on whom the balancing allowance or charge falls to be made is not the person who incurred that expenditure, the capital expenditure is the residue of that expenditure at the beginning of the relevant period. Where a building or structure is demolished, and the demolition gives or might give rise to a balancing allowance or charge to or on the person incurring the demolition cost, the net cost to him (ie the excess, if any, of the cost over any moneys received for the property's remains) is added to the residue, immediately before the demolition, of the expenditure incurred on the property's construction. If this applies to the net demolition cost, the cost or net cost is not treated as expenditure incurred for any other property by which that property is replaced.

'The allowances given'

This means all industrial buildings allowances, R&D (before 2000–01 referred to as 'scientific research') allowances, and mills, factories, etc allowances (FA 1937, s 15 and FA 1941, s 19) given to the taxpayer for expenditure on the building. In no case can the amount on which a balancing charge is made on a person for any expenditure on construction exceed the initial allowance amount, if any, made to him for that expenditure together with the amount of any of the above or exceptional depreciation allowances for that building or structure, made to him for chargeable periods which end on or before the date of the event giving rise to the charge reduced by the amounts (if any) on which balancing charges for the expenditure have been made on him for any such chargeable periods.

'The adjusted net cost'

This is, where there are no sale, insurance, salvage or compensation moneys, the capital expenditure or, where those moneys are less than that expenditure, the amount by which they are less. In both cases the net cost is reduced by the proportion to which the period of qualifying industrial usage bears to the relevant period. Note that in those cases where proceeds are greater than the capital expenditure, the net cost calculation is otiose, as the balancing charge is simply the allowances given.

'Research and development'

This is defined as 'activities that fall to be treated as research and development in accordance with normal accounting practice' (TA 1988, s 837A; FA 2000, s 68 and Sched 19, para 1). Prior to 2000–01 the reference is to 'scientific research activities'.

4.5.5 Realisation of capital value
(CAA 1990, s 4A)

Where any capital expenditure has been incurred on construction and, while it is or after it has ceased to be an industrial building or structure:

(1) an amount of capital value is paid which is attributable to an interest in land (the 'subordinate interest') to which the relevant interest in the building or structure is or will be subject, and
(2) the payment is made not more than seven years after the agreement relating to the capital expenditure was entered into or (if the agreement was conditional) the time when the agreement became unconditional,

capital value of that amount is realised on making the payment. Capital value is attributable to the subordinate interest if it is paid:

(a) in consideration of the grant of the subordinate interest,
(b) in lieu of any rent payable by the person entitled to the subordinate interest or in consideration of the assignment of such rent, or
(c) in consideration of the surrender of the subordinate interest or the variation or waiver of any of the terms on which it was granted.

For these purposes, 'capital value' means any capital sum and includes what would have been a capital sum if it had taken the form of a money payment ('payment' and 'paid' are interpreted accordingly), but does not include so much of any sum as corresponds to any amount of lease premium, etc treated as rent or Schedule D profits (TA 1988, s 34).
Where:

(1) no premium is given in consideration of the grant of the subordinate interest or any premium given is less than the amount which would have been given by way of premium if the transaction had been at arm's length, and
(2) no commercial rent is payable for the subordinate interest,

the capital value attributable to the subordinate interest is the amount which would have been given by way of premium if the transaction had been at arm's length (and not any premium actually given) paid on and in consideration of the grant of the interest.
Where:

(a) any rent payable for the subordinate interest is assigned, the subordinate interest is surrendered or any of the terms on which such interest was granted are varied or waived, but

(b) no value is given in consideration of the event concerned, or any such value is less than the amount that would have been given if the transaction had been at arm's length,

the capital value attributable to the subordinate interest is that amount (and not any value actually given) paid on and in consideration of the event concerned. Where any value given in lieu of any rent payable by the person entitled to such interest is less than the amount that would have been given if the transaction had been at arm's length, the capital value attributable to the subordinate interest is that amount (and not any value actually given) paid.

4.5.6 Restricting balancing allowances on sale
(CAA 1990, s 5)

An anti-avoidance provision restricts the availability of balancing allowances on a sale of an industrial building or structure where:

(1) the relevant interest in a building or structure is sold subject to a subordinate interest; and
(2) a balancing allowance would otherwise be made to the person who is entitled to the relevant interest immediately before the sale ('the relevant person') (CAA 1990, s 4) by virtue of the sale; and
(3) either:
  (a) the relevant person, the person to whom the relevant interest is sold and the grantee of the subordinate interest, or any two of them, are connected (TA 1988, s 839), or
  (b) it appears the transaction's sole or main purpose was to obtain an industrial buildings allowance.

In the calculation of any balancing allowance or charge (see CAA 1990, s 4), the net sale proceeds to the relevant person are increased by any actual premium receivable by him for the grant of the subordinate interest. Where no, or no commercial, rent is payable for such interest, the net proceeds are taken to be what those proceeds would have been if a commercial rent had been payable (increased by any actual premium, as above). The deemed net proceeds cannot be taken to be greater than such amount as would secure that no balancing allowance is made.

4.5.7 Enterprise zones
(CAA 1990, s 6)

The general rules for writing-down allowances and balancing allowances and charges (CAA 1990, ss 3–7) and the various supplementary provisions (CAA 1990, ss 8–21) apply:

(1) with the modifications specified below in relation to capital expenditure on construction of an industrial building or structure, and

(2) as so modified, also in relation to capital expenditure on the construction of a qualifying hotel or of a commercial building or structure as if it were an industrial building or structure,

in any case where the expenditure is incurred, or is incurred under a contract entered into, when the site is in an enterprise zone, not being more than ten years after it was first included in the zone. The most important modification is that a straight-line writing-down allowance of 25% is given (in place of the normal 4%).

The general rules which treat qualifying hotels as industrial buildings (CAA 1990, s 7) do not apply to capital expenditure on qualifying hotels within enterprise zones.

An industrial building or structure, qualifying hotel or commercial building or structure in an enterprise zone is regarded as continuing to be, or to be used as, a building or structure of that description notwithstanding that it has become one of another such description.

4.5.8 Other hotels
(CA 1990, s 7)

Capital expenditure on the construction of a qualifying hotel is eligible for industrial buildings allowance, as are costs of extending an hotel, provided that the building meets the requirements for a qualifying hotel after the expenditure.

After a building has ceased to be a qualifying hotel otherwise than on a chargeable event giving rise to a balancing allowance or charge (CAA 1990, s 4(1)), a period of two years elapses in which it is not a qualifying hotel and without the occurrence of any such event, the rules for writing-down allowances, balancing allowances and charges, and the various supplementary provisions apply as if:

(1) the relevant interest in the building had been sold at the end of that period; and

(2) the net proceeds of the sale were equal to the price which that interest would then have fetched if sold in the open market.

A building or structure is not deemed to cease altogether to be used by reason only that it falls temporarily out of use, and where, immediately before any period of temporary disuse, it is an industrial building or structure it is deemed to remain so during the period of temporary disuse (CAA 1990, s 15(1)). However, a building cannot be deemed to continue to be a qualifying hotel for more than two years after the end of the chargeable period in which it falls temporarily out of use.

4.5.9 Writing off expenditure and meaning of 'residue of expenditure'
(CAA 1990, s 8)

Any expenditure (including any additional VAT liability) incurred on construction is treated under the industrial buildings allowance as written off to the extent and as at the times specified below, and references to the residue of any such expenditure are construed accordingly.

Where a research and development (prior to 2000–01 referred to as 'scientific research') allowance is made for any chargeable period for the expenditure, the amount of that allowance is treated as written off:

(1) for an allowance for capital expenditure on research and development/scientific research (CAA 1990, s 137), as at the end of the chargeable period, and

(2) for an allowance on an asset used for research and development/scientific research (CAA 1990, s 138), as at the time when the asset ceases to belong to the person in question.

In other cases, where an event occurs giving rise to a balancing allowance or charge, the amount to be written off as at that time is taken into account in computing the residue of the expenditure immediately before that event.

If there is any period during which the building or structure has not been in use as an industrial one, then there is, in ascertaining the residue, treated as having been previously written off for that period amounts equal to writing-down allowances made for the chargeable periods concerned at such rate(s) as would have been appropriate having regard to any sale within the following description. Where the relevant interest in a building or structure in relation to any expenditure is sold and the sale gives rise to a balancing allowance or charge, the writing-down allowance for any chargeable period that ends after the sale is the residue of that expenditure immediately after the sale, reduced in proportion (if it is less than one) which the length of the chargeable period bears to the part unexpired at the date of the sale of the period of 25 years (or, where the expenditure was incurred before 6 November 1962, 50 years) beginning with the time when the building or structure was first used.

Where, on a sale, a balancing allowance is made for expenditure, there is written off as at the time of the sale the amount by which the expenditure before the sale exceeds the net sale proceeds. Where, on a sale, the adjusted net cost of the building or structure is less than the allowances given, a balancing charge is made for an amount equal to the shortfall.

With regard to a balancing allowance or charge on demolition costs, see 4.5.4 under 'The capital expenditure'. Where an additional VAT rebate is made on any of the expenditure, there is treated as written off at the time the rebate is made an amount equal to the rebate.

4.5.10 Manner of making allowances and charges
(CAA 1990, s 9)

Generally, an allowance or charge to which a person is entitled or liable under the industrial buildings allowance rules is made in taxing that person's trade (CAA 1990, ss 140(2) (income tax) and 144(2) (corporation tax)). If the interest of that person in the building or structure is subject to a lease at the relevant time, the above has effect as if any Schedule A business carried on by him were the trade in the taxing of which the allowance or charge is to be made. This also applies where the building or structure is used by a licensee of the person entitled to the relevant interest as if that interest were subject to a lease.

4.5.11 Purchasing buildings and structures
(CAA 1990, s 10)

Where expenditure is incurred on construction and, before the building or structure is used, the relevant interest in it is sold, the vendor is not entitled to any allowance. Instead, the person who buys that interest is deemed to have incurred, on the date when the purchase price becomes payable, expenditure on construction equal to that actual expenditure or to the net price paid by him for that interest, whichever is less.

Subject to CAA 1990, s 10B, the rule described below applies where:

(1) expenditure is incurred on construction by a developer with a view to sell, and
(2) after the building or structure has been used, he sells the relevant interest in it in the course of that trade.

The rule applies in relation to the person who buys the interest as if:

(a) the original expenditure had been his capital expenditure,
(b) all appropriate writing-down allowances had been made to the person incurring it, and
(c) all appropriate balancing allowances or charges had been made on the occasion of the sale.

Special provision for enterprise zones
(CAA 1990, s 10A)

The rule described here applies where:

(1) expenditure is incurred on construction (actual expenditure);
(2) some or all of that expenditure is incurred, or is incurred under a contract entered into, at a time when the site is in an enterprise zone, being a time not more than ten years after the site was first included in the zone; and
(3) before the building or structure is used, the relevant interest in it is sold.

Where this rule applies, the actual expenditure is left out of account under the rules for initial allowances, writing-down allowances, and balancing allowances and charges (CA 1990, ss 1–8). However, the person who buys the relevant interest is deemed for those purposes to have incurred, on the date when the purchase price becomes payable, expenditure on construction (deemed expenditure) equal to the actual expenditure or to the net price paid by him for that interest, whichever is less.

The deemed expenditure is regarded as comprising an enterprise zone element and a non-enterprise zone element. The enterprise zone element is treated (for the purpose of determining entitlement to allowances) as incurred when the site is in an enterprise zone.

Where the actual expenditure was incurred by a developer and, before the building or structure is used, he sells the relevant interest in it in the course of that trade or of that part of that trade, then:

(1) if that sale is the only sale of the relevant interest before the use, the purchaser incurs deemed expenditure (see above) equal to the net price paid by him for that interest; and

(2) in any other case, the purchaser incurs deemed expenditure equal to the price paid on that sale or to the net price paid by him for that interest, whichever is less.

However, this does not include expenditure incurred under a contract entered into when the site is in an enterprise zone if the expenditure is incurred more than 20 years after that site was first included in the enterprise zone (CAA 1990, s 17A).

Purchase in enterprise zones within two years of use
(CAA 1990, s 10B)

This rule applies:

(1) where expenditure is incurred on construction (actual expenditure);

(2) where some or all of that expenditure is incurred, or is incurred under a contract entered into, at a time when the site is in an enterprise zone, being a time not more than ten years after the site was first included in the zone; and

(3) whether or not there were any sales of the relevant interest in the building or structure before it was used, that interest is sold after it has been used but before the expiry of two years beginning with the date on which it was first used; and

(4) where that sale is the first such sale in that period.

Where this rule applies, any balancing allowance or charge which is made on the sale is so made. The residue of expenditure immediately after the sale (if any) is left out of account for the purposes of the industrial buildings allowance rules. The purchaser of the relevant interest under the rules relating to the initial allowances, writing-down allowances, balancing allowances and balancing charges incurs deemed expenditure of an amount determined as set out below. Finally, in relation to the deemed expenditure, the building or structure is treated for the purposes of those rules as not having been used before the sale date.

The deemed expenditure is regarded as comprising an enterprise zone element and a non-enterprise zone element. The deemed expenditure amount is the sum of these two elements.

Initial allowances where contracts entered into between October 1992 and November 1993
(CAA 1990, s 10C)

The are special rules for expenditure incurred under contracts entered into between October 1992 and November 1993, which take account of the 20% initial allowance given for such expenditure.

Arrangements affecting value of purchased interest
(CAA 1990, s 10D)

There are special rules to eliminate from expenditure to which the industrial buildings allowance would apply costs attributed to the provision of benefits associated with the purchase, such as rental guarantees.

4.5.12 Long leases
(CAA 1990, s 11)

Where expenditure has been incurred on construction and a long lease is granted out of the relevant interest in relation to that expenditure, the industrial buildings rules are, if the lessor and lessee so elect, applied as if:

(1) the grant of the lease were a sale of the relevant interest by the lessor to the lessee at the time when the lease takes effect;
(2) any capital sum paid by the lessee in consideration for the grant were the purchase price on the sale; and
(3) the interest out of which the lease is granted had at that time ceased to be, and the interest granted by the lease become, the relevant interest in relation to that expenditure.

A 'long lease' is one the duration of which (ascertained under the rules in TA 1988, s 38(1)–(4) and (6)) exceeds 50 years; any question whether a lease is a long lease is determined without regard to the special rule applying where, on the termination of a lease, a new one is granted (CAA 1990, s16(5)).

The election cannot be made where:

(1) the lessor and lessee are connected (TA 1988, s 839); or
(2) it appears that the sole or main benefit hoped to be gained is a balancing allowance (CAA 1990, s 4).

4.5.13 Expenditure on repair of buildings
(CAA 1990, s 12)

The industrial buildings allowance rules apply to capital expenditure incurred by a person on improvements or extensions to any part of a building or structure as if it were capital expenditure incurred by him in the construction for the first time of that part of it. Any expenditure incurred for trade purposes on such repairs is deemed to be capital expenditure if it is not expenditure which could be deducted in computing, for tax purposes, the trade's profits.

The Revenue has stated that where a building is demolished to erect a new building and demolition costs cannot be taken into account in calculating the balancing adjustment. However, they can be treated as part of the costs of constructing the new building.

4.5.14 Expenditure on sites for machinery and plant
(CAA 1990, s 13)

Where capital expenditure is incurred on preparing, cutting, tunnelling or levelling land to prepare it for the installation of machinery or plant, and otherwise no allowance could be made on that expenditure under the industrial buildings allowance or the machinery and plant rules, then as regards that expenditure, the machinery or plant is treated under the industrial buildings allowance rules as a building or structure (whether or not it would otherwise be so treated).

4.5.15 Sports pavilions
(CAA 1990, s 14)

Where a building or structure which is not an industrial building is occupied and used as a sports pavilion for the welfare of all or any of the workers employed in a trade, the rules apply to that building or structure as if it were an industrial building.

4.5.16 Temporary disuse
(CAA 1990, ss 15 and 15ZA)

A building or structure is not deemed to cease altogether to be used if it falls temporarily out of use. Where, immediately before any period of temporary disuse, it is used as an industrial building, it is deemed to remain so used during temporary disuse. The rule described below applies in certain cases where an allowance or charge falls to be made to or on a person in a period during which the building or structure is temporarily disused, but is deemed still to be an industrial building or structure.

If on the last occasion upon which an industrial building or structure was in use it was for the purposes of a trade which has since been permanently discontinued, or the relevant interest in it was subject to a lease since ended, the allowance or charge is made (CAA 1990, s 9) as if the relevant interest were subject to a lease at the relevant time.

If, in a case where this rule applies, a balancing charge falls to be made on a person and the industrial building or structure was last in use for trade purposes carried on by that person, but has permanently been discontinued, the same deductions may be made from the amount of the balancing charge as may be made under TA 1988, s 105 from post-cessation receipts (TA 1988, s 103 or 104(1)).

By ESC B19, where an industrial building used in a trade is sold after the trade ceases, unused trading losses are allowed to be set off against any balancing charge.

References here to the 'permanent discontinuance of a trade' do not include an event treated as a permanent discontinuance under TA 1988, s 113 (change in partnership membership) or 337(1) (change in persons carrying on trade; circumstances in which company treated as beginning or ceasing to carry on trade).

This rule applies where the building or structure is used by a licensee of the person entitled to the relevant interest as if that interest were subject to a lease.

4.5.17 Mining structures etc: balancing allowances carried back to earlier chargeable periods
(CAA 1990, s 17)

If for a trade which consists of or includes the working of a mine, oil well or other source of mineral deposits:

(1) a balancing allowance falls to be made under the industrial buildings allowance rules for the last chargeable period in which the trade is carried on, and

(2) the event giving rise to the allowance is the mine, oil well or other source ceasing to be worked or the coming to an end of a foreign concession, and

(3) the allowance is for expenditure on a building or structure which was constructed for occupation by, or for the welfare of, persons employed at, or in connection with the working of, the mine, oil well or other source, and

(4) full effect cannot be given to the allowance because of an insufficiency of profits for that chargeable period,

the person entitled to the allowance may claim that the balance of the allowance is given for the last preceding chargeable period, and so on up to a total of five years. The allowance cannot be given to a company so as to create or augment a loss, nor can a company claim any carry-back under TA 1988, s 393A(1). A claim for allowances to reduce the company's profits of its mining trade for the current period is given in priority to allowances under a claim under s 393A to carry back other losses from the following accounting period.

4.5.18 Special cases
(CAA 1990, s 16)

Where, with the lessor's consent, a lessee remains in possession after the termination of the lease without a new one being granted to him, that lease is deemed to continue so long as he remains in possession.

On the termination of a lease, where a new one is granted to the lessee under an option available to him under the terms of the first lease, the rules apply as if the second lease were a continuation of the first. Where the lessor pays any sum to the lessee for a building or structure comprised in the lease, the industrial buildings allowance rules apply as if the lease had come to an end by reason of the surrender thereof in consideration of the payment. If another lease is granted to a different lessee and, in connection with the transaction, that lessee pays a sum to the person who was the lessee under the first lease, the rules apply as if both leases were the same lease and there had been an assignment by the lessee under the first lease to the lessee under the second in consideration of the payment.

4.6 MACHINERY AND PLANT: GENERAL

4.6.1 What is machinery and plant?

There is no definition of 'machinery and plant' in the legislation, and consequently it has been left to the courts to decide what is and is not plant and machinery. The judgments referred to below give a reasonable indication of the areas to be considered. As such, the identification of 'machinery' should cause few problems. Machinery includes machines and their working parts (eg motor vehicles, lathes and computers). However, there has been a long line of cases about the meaning of 'plant'.

In *Yarmouth v France* (1887) 19 QBD 647, it was held that:

> 'In its ordinary sense [plant] includes whatever apparatus is used by a businessman for carrying on his business – not his stock-in-trade which he buys or makes for sale; but all goods and chattels, fixed or moveable, live or dead, which he keeps for permanent employment in his business.'

Thus it is clear that something which is not used for carrying on the business

BUSINESS TAX & LAW HANDBOOK

is not plant; furthermore, 'plant' excludes stock-in-trade. The case also shows that business premises are not plant.

The question of whether an item is 'apparatus used in carrying on a business' is sometimes called the 'functional test'. In *Benson v The Yard Arm Club Ltd* (1979) 53 TC 67, it was held that this test 'provides the criterion to be applied. Is the subject matter the apparatus or part of the apparatus employed in carrying on the activities of the business?' It is important to note that the test is whether the asset functions as apparatus used in carrying on the business activities. By contrast, an asset which functions as the business premises is not plant.

J Lyons and Co Ltd v Attorney General [1944] 1 All ER 477 was a war damage compensation case. The War Damage Act distinguished between buildings and plant. Here it was claimed that lamps destroyed by enemy action were plant and should qualify for compensation. It was, however, held that they did not qualify as plant; they were part of the general setting in which, and not apparatus with which, the business was carried on.

Other cases have developed the concept that there can be items which, although part of the setting, are not part of the business premises. Such items have been classified as plant, being part of the apparatus with which the trade was carried on. *Jarrold v John Good & Sons Ltd* (1962) 40 TC 681, concerned moveable partitions. The Commissioners had found as a fact that from commercial necessity the partitions had to possess mobility and flexibility for the day-to-day running of the business, and 'undoubtably' regarded them as plant. However, this does not mean that all moveable partitions are plant: the Revenue is likely to check whether they need to possess mobility as a matter of commercial necessity. It may also need to be demonstrated that they have in fact been moved. In *Leeds Permanent Building Society v Proctor* (1982) 56 TC 293 it was found that decorative screens used for window displays were plant, as their purpose was to attract attention and bring business to the Society.

In *CIR v Scottish & Newcastle Breweries Ltd* (1982) 55 TC 252, the issue was whether light fittings and wiring, and decorative items such as wall plaques, tapestries, murals, prints and sculptures, were plant. Held, the electric wiring was merely part of the fabric of the building, but all the other items constituted plant on the basis that their purpose was to create an ambience, an important function of the company's particular trade of running public houses. The light fittings and decorative items satisfied the functional test required of plant notwithstanding that they formed part of the setting within which the trade was carried on. Note, however, rare instances where, for example, a dry dock in *CIR v Barclay Curle* (1969) 45 TC 221 and a grain silo in *Schofield v Hall* (1974) 49 TC 538, despite being part of the fabric of the building, were held to be plant because they passed the functional test.

Wimpy International Ltd v Warland, Associated Restaurants Ltd v Warland (1988) 61 TC 51 set out the boundaries of the 'setting' test.

Following a programme of improvement and modernisation of their restaurants, Wimpy and Associated had claimed machinery or plant allowances on replacement shop fronts, floor and wall tiles, murals, lighting, water tanks, staircases and raised floors. Following *Scottish & Newcastle*, the Special Commissioners allowed items such as murals, decorative brickwork and wall panels, but disallowed the rest. Before the House of Lords, their decision was upheld with the exception of the light fittings. The case sets three tests, all of which fall within the category of 'functional', to be considered in deciding whether an item is plant:

(1) Is the item stock-in-trade?
(2) Is the item the business premises or part of them (the premises test)? An item used for carrying on the business is not plant if the business use is at the premises or the place on which the business is conducted.
(3) Is the item used for carrying on the business (the business use test)? An item may pass this test, but that is not sufficient to make it plant (eg if the business use is as stock-in-trade). The asset must be employed in carrying on the business. In *Wimpy*, as in *Scottish & Newcastle*, the lighting was to create atmosphere and to attract customers.

Not surprisingly, in view of the absence of a clear definition of 'machinery and plant', there have been a range of cases concerned with its meaning. 'Plant' has been held to include:

- A brewery dray-horse (*Yarmouth v France* (1887) 19 QBD 647), but not stallions kept at stud (*Earl of Derby v Aylmer* (1915) 6 TC 665)
- Loose tools, knives and lasts used by a shoe manufacturer (*Hinton v Maden & Ireland Ltd* (1959) 38 TC 391)
- Moveable (and frequently moved) office partitioning (*Jarrold v John Good & Sons Ltd*, above)
- A dry dock (*CIR v Barclay, Curle & Co Ltd*, above)
- A swimming pool (*Cooke v Beach Station Caravans Ltd* (1974) 45 TC 221)
- Grain silos holding grain and from which the grain could conveniently be delivered (*Schofield v R & H Hall Ltd*, above)
- Law books as 'chattels of a barrister's profession' (*Munby v Furlong* (1977) 50 TC 491)
- Light fittings and murals in a hotel (*Scottish & Newcastle Breweries*, above)
- Decorative screens in windows (*Leeds Permanent Building Society*, above).

The following associated payments also qualified as plant:

- Finance charges for an oil rig (*Ben-Odeco Ltd v Powlson* (1978) 52 TC 460)

- Option cancellation payments (*International Drilling Co Ltd v Bolton* (1982) 56 TC 449)
- The extra sterling cost of a foreign currency instalment purchase (*Van Arkadie v Sterling Coated Materials Ltd* (1982) 56 TC 479).

Assets held not to be plant include:

- Electric lighting in teashop part of the 'general setting' (*J Lyons and Co*, above)
- Prefabricated buildings (*St John's School v Ward* (1974) 49 TC 524; note, however, that plant in the buildings did not qualify because there were no records apportioning the cost between plant and buildings)
- A filling station canopy (*Dixon v Fitch's Garage Ltd* (1975) 50 TC 509; compare a later Irish case where the canopy played an essential role in advertising the station's presence in *O'Culachain v McMullan Brothers* (1990) 1 IR 363)
- A ship used as a floating restaurant (*Benson v Yard Arm Club Ltd* (1979) 53 TC 67)
- A football spectators' stand (*Brown v Burnley Football & Athletic Club Ltd* (1980) 53 TC 357)
- Suspended ceilings covering service piping etc (*Hampton v Forte Autogrill Ltd* (1980) 53 TC 691)
- Slide and overhead projectors to illustrate a vicar's sermons (*White v Higginbottom* (1982) 57 TC 283)
- An inflatable tennis court cover (*Thomas v Reynolds & Broomhead* (1987) 59 TC 502)
- Glasshouses at a garden centre (*Gray v Seymour's Garden Centre (Horticulture)* (1995) 67 TC 401; see also *Tax Bulletin* 5 (November 1992), p 46)
- Newly constructed putting greens on a golf course (*Family Golf Centres Ltd v Thorne* 1998 SpC 150).

Cases where an apportionment was made between allowable and non-allowable assets include:

- Wallpaper pattern books (*Rose & Co (Wallpapers & Paints) Ltd v Campbell* (1967) 44 TC 500)
- Certain electrical installations in a department store, but not all (*Cole Brothers Ltd v Phillips* (1982) 55 TC 188)
- Restaurant improvements to premises and light fittings for general illumination (not specific to the trade) (*Wimpy International*, above; compare the earlier decision in *J Lyons and Co Ltd*)
- Mezzanine storage platforms in warehouses (*Hunt v Henry Quick Ltd; King v Bridisco Ltd* (1992) 65 TC 108)
- The structure of an underground electricity substation to contain plant (*Bradley v London Electricity plc* (1996) 70 TC 155)
- A car wash site (*Attwood v Anduff Car Wash Ltd* (1997) 69 TC 575).

CAA 1990, Sched AA1 was enacted in order to restrict the area of dispute, and contains rules which exclude, from the meaning of machinery and plant, expenditure on a building or structure or on the acquisition of an interest in land.

The rules set out general categories of assets which do not qualify as plant, but in so far as not to disqualify particular items within those categories which the courts have held to be plant, the tables include specific exemptions to cover such items. These rules do not apply to the following items for which the machinery and plant allowances are provided by specific legislation:

- thermal insulation (CAA 1990, s 67)
- computer software (s 67A)
- films, tapes and discs (s 68);
- fire safety (s 69)
- safety at sports grounds (s 70)
- personal security (s 71).

In the comments set out below, 'structure' means a fixed structure of any kind, other than a building; and references to the provision of any building, structure or other asset include references to its construction or acquisition.

Note that any expenditure on a glasshouse constructed so that the required environment (ie air, heat, light, irrigation and temperature) for growing plants is provided automatically by means of devices which are an integral part of its structure *is* expenditure on machinery or plant.

Assets included in the expression 'building'

Expenditure on machinery or plant does not include any expenditure on a building. 'Building' includes any asset in the building which is incorporated into the building, or which, by reason of being moveable or otherwise, is not so incorporated, but is of a kind normally incorporated into buildings. In particular, it includes any asset in or in connection with the building included in any of the items in CAA 1990, Sched AA1, Table 1, col 1 or 2.

This general definition does not affect the question whether expenditure on any of the categories of expenditure below is expenditure on machinery or plant:

(1) any asset falling within Sched AA1, Table 1, col 2;
(2) any cold store;
(3) any caravan provided mainly for holiday lettings;
(4) any building provided for testing aircraft engines run within the building; or
(5) any moveable building intended to be moved in the course of the trade.

Assets included in 'building' under Sched AA1, Table 1, col 1 are:

A   Walls, floors, ceilings, doors, gates, shutters, windows and stairs.
B   Mains services and systems of water, electricity and gas.
C   Waste disposal systems.
D   Sewerage and drainage systems.
E   Shafts or other structures in which lifts, hoists, escalators and moving walkways are installed.
F   Fire safety systems.

Assets so included, but expenditure on which is unaffected by Sched AA1 (Table 1, col 2) are:

(1) Electrical systems (including lighting systems), cold water, gas and sewerage systems provided mainly to:
     (a) meet the trade's particular requirements, or
     (b) serve particular machinery or plant used for trade purposes.
(2) Space or water heating systems; powered systems of ventilation, air cooling or air purification; and any ceiling or floor comprised in such systems.
(3) Manufacturing or processing equipment; storage equipment, including cold rooms; display equipment; and counters, checkouts and similar equipment.
(4) Cookers, washing machines, dishwashers, refrigerators and similar equipment; washbasins, sinks, baths, showers, sanitary ware and similar equipment; and furniture and furnishings.
(5) Lifts, hoists, escalators and moving walkways.
(6) Sound insulation provided mainly to meet the trade's particular requirements.
(7) Computer, telecommunication and surveillance systems (including their wiring or other links).
(8) Refrigeration or cooling equipment.
(9) Sprinkler and other equipment for extinguishing or containing fire; fire alarm systems.
(10) Burglar alarm systems.
(11) Any machinery (including devices for providing motive power) not within any other item in col 2 (see below).
(12) Strong rooms in bank or building society premises; safes.
(13) Partition walls, where moveable and intended to be moved in the course of the trade.
(14) Decorative assets provided for public enjoyment in the hotel, restaurant or similar trades.
(15) Advertising hoardings; signs, displays and similar assets.
(16) Swimming pools (including diving boards, slides and structures on which such boards or slides are mounted).

An asset does not fall within col 2 if its principal purpose is to insulate or enclose the building's interior or provide an interior wall, a floor or a ceiling which (in each case) is intended to remain permanently in place.

The general definition set out above does not include any expenditure on provision of structures or other assets as listed below, or any works involving the alteration of land.

Structures and assets
(CAA 1990, Sched AA1, Table 2, col 1)

A   Any tunnel, bridge, viaduct, aqueduct, embankment or cutting.

B   Any way or hard standing, such as a pavement, road, railway or tramway, a park for vehicles or containers, or an airstrip or runway.

C   Any inland navigation, including a canal, basin or navigable river.

D   Any dam, reservoir or barrage (including sluices, gates, generators and other equipment associated with it).

E   Any dock, including
   (a) any harbour, wharf, pier, marina or jetty, and
   (b) any other structure in or at which vessels may be kept or merchandise or passengers may be shipped or unshipped.

F   Any dike, sea wall, weir or drainage ditch.

G   Any structure not within any other item in col 1. An industrial structure (ie anything (other than a building) which is or is to be an industrial building or structure, as defined in CAA 1990, s 18) is not within item G. Section 18, as it applies for these purposes, includes buildings or structures in use for the purposes of
   (a) gas undertakings (ie for the extraction, production, processing or distribution of gas), and
   (b) a trade which consists in the provision of telecommunication, television or radio services (note that this does not extend the definition of industrial building for industrial buildings allowance purposes).

Expenditure unaffected by Sched AA1
(CAA 1990, Sched AA1, Table 2, col 2)

The following categories of expenditure are unaffected by these rules:

(1) the alteration of land for the purpose only of installing machinery or plant;

(2) dry docks;

(3) any jetty or similar structure provided mainly to carry machinery or plant;

(4) pipelines or underground ducts or tunnels with a primary purpose of carrying utility conduits;

(5) towers provided to support floodlights;

(6) any reservoir incorporated into a water treatment works or on any service reservoir of treated water for supply within any housing estate or other particular locality;

(7) silos provided for temporary storage or on the provision of storage tanks;

(8) slurry pits or silage clamps;

(9) fish tanks or fish ponds;

(10) rails, sleepers and ballast for a railway or tramway;

(11) structures and other assets for providing the setting for any ride at an amusement park or exhibition; and

(12) fixed zoo cages.

Land

Expenditure on machinery or plant does not include that on the acquisition of any interest in land. This does not apply under the machinery and plant allowance rules to any asset which is so installed or otherwise fixed in or to any description of land as to become, in law, part of that land.

In the context of Sched AA1, 'land' includes land covered with water, and any estate, interest, easement, servitude or right in or over land (Interpretation Act 1978, Sched 1, as modified). Subject to that, 'interest in land' means:

(1) the fee simple estate in the land or an agreement to acquire that estate;

(2) in Scotland, the estate or interest of the proprietor of the *dominium utile* (or, in the case of property other than feudal property, of the owner) and any agreement to acquire such an estate or interest;

(3) any leasehold estate in, or in Scotland lease of, the land (whether in the nature of a headlease, sublease or underlease) and any agreement to acquire such an estate/lease;

(4) an easement or servitude or any agreement to acquire an easement or servitude; and

(5) a licence to occupy land.

4.6.2 Manner of making allowances and charges
(CAA 1990, s 73)

Any allowance or charge made to or on any person under the machinery and plant allowances rules is made to or on that person in taxing his trade. If it is a Schedule A business, the allowances and charge are made in taxing the business.

However, where any machinery and plant is first let by a lessor who is not classed as carrying on a trade, then, whether or not it is used for trade purposes carried on by the lessee (CAA 1990, s 61(1)), the allowance is made by way of discharge or repayment of tax, and available primarily against income from the letting of machinery or plant.

Where an allowance is made for any chargeable period for expenditure on machinery or plant which is not used for trade purposes carried on by the lessee, that allowance or a proportionate part thereof is available primarily against income from the letting of that machinery or plant only.

Effect is given to any charge made if it is a charge to income tax by making the charge under Schedule D Case VI, and corporation tax by treating the amount on which the charge is to be made as income from let machinery or plant.

4.6.3 Finance leases

Meaning of 'finance lease'
(CAA 1990, s 82A)

Under the machinery and plant rules, 'finance lease' means any arrangements by which machinery or plant is leased or otherwise made available by a lessor to a lessee, and the arrangements are such that, in cases where the lessor and persons connected (TA 1988, s 839) with him are all UK companies, the arrangements are, in accordance with normal accountancy practice, treated in the accounts of one or more of those companies as a finance lease or a loan.

Further restrictions on allowances
(CAA 1990, ss 75, 76 and 76A)

Where a person incurs capital expenditure on the purchase of machinery or plant, and:

(1) he and the seller are connected, or
(2) the machinery or plant continues to be used for trade purposes carried on by the seller, or
(3) it appears with respect to the sale, or to transactions of which the sale is one, that the sole or main benefit was to obtain a machinery and plant allowance,

the expenditure is ignored to the extent that it exceeds the amount brought in as proceeds of sale. There are similar restrictions on sale and leaseback transactions.

These provisions do not prevent allowances from being granted in transactions which are wholly commercial and designed to make a profit (*Barclays Mercantile Industrial Finance Ltd v Melluish* (1990) 63 TC 95). It is also provided that allowances are not restricted where the machinery or plant has not been used before the contract and the supply is made in the ordinary course of business.

The capital allowances available to lessors of machinery and plant which is sold and leased back under a finance lease are limited to the seller's notional written-down value for the machinery and plant. This prevents the sale of unused past allowances to a finance lessor. It does not prevent the sale of future allowances; nor does it affect the sale and leaseback immediately after new equipment has been delivered in order to remove the lessor's commercial risk over the provision of the equipment.

No allowance can be given to a lessor under a sale and leaseback under a finance lease if he has avoided any risk that the lessee will not meet his obligations.

Further information

These are complex anti-avoidance rules. An article in *Tax Bulletin* (June 1998), p 539, 'Capital Allowances on Finance Leases', explains how these rules operate.

4.6.4 Successions to trades: connected persons
(CAA 1990, s 77)

Where a person succeeds to a trade which was until then carried on by another person and the two persons are connected, each is within the charge to tax in the UK on the trade's profits, and the successor is not a dual resident investing company, those persons may jointly elect:

(1) in making allowances and charges under the machinery and plant allowance rules, for any machinery or plant which:
   (a) immediately before the succession took place, belonged to the predecessor and was in use for trade purposes; and
   (b) immediately after that time, belonged to the successor and was in use for those purposes,
   to treat (notwithstanding any actual sale or transfer) that machinery and plant as sold by the predecessor to the successor at a price which does not give rise to a balancing allowance or charge; and
(2) for allowances and charges to be made under the machinery and plant allowance rules to or on the successor as if everything done to or by the predecessor had been done to or by the successor.

For this purpose the predecessor and the successor are connected if:

(a) they are connected within the terms of TA 1988, s 839;
(b) one of them is a partnership and the other has the right to a share in it;
(c) one of them is a body corporate and the other has control over it;
(d) both are partnerships and some other person has the right to a share in both of them; or
(e) both are bodies corporate, or one is a partnership and the other a body corporate, and (in either case) some other person has control over both of them.

'Control' is construed in accordance with TA 1988, s 840. Any reference to the right to a share in a partnership is a reference to the right to a share of that partnership's assets or income.

CAA 1988, ss 38G (disposal value of long-life assets), 41(5) (writing-down allowances for leased assets and inexpensive cars) and 78(1) (successions to trades where no election made under s 77) do not apply in any case where an election is made as above.

4.6.5 Succession to trades where no election made under s 77
(CAA 1990, s 78)

Where a person succeeds to any trade which until then was carried on by another person and, by TA 1988, s 113 (changes in persons carrying on a trade) and/or s 337(1) (special rules for corporation tax) and for tax purposes, the trade is treated as discontinued, the cessation also applies to machinery and plant capital allowances. As a result, any property which, immediately before the succession takes place, was either in use or provided and available for use for the purposes of the discontinued trade and, without being sold, is, immediately after the succession takes place, either in use or provided and available for use for the purposes of the new trade is treated as if:

(1) it had been sold to the successor when the succession takes place, and
(2) the net sale proceeds had been the price which that property would have fetched if sold in the open market.

It is, however, further provided that no further first-year allowance can be made because of this.

Where a person succeeds to a trade as a beneficiary under the will or on the intestacy of a deceased person who carried on the trade and the beneficiary so elects, then, in relation to any machinery or plant which passes to him together with the trade, he can similarly elect to take over the deceased's written-down values. Note that where a surviving spouse succeeds to a deceased's business, the deceased's unrelieved capital allowances cannot be used by the survivor.

4.6.6 Effect of part trade use
(CAA 1990, s 79)

Allowances may be made to a person for expenditure on machinery or plant notwithstanding that it appears that it is partly for purposes other than those of a trade carried on by him. However, the allowance here is so much only of that that would fall to be made if the provision of the machinery or plant were wholly and exclusively for trade purposes as may be just and reasonable having regard to all the relevant circumstances of the case and, in particular, to the extent to which it appears that the machinery or plant is likely to be used for those other purposes.

Where a person carrying on a trade incurs capital expenditure on machinery or plant partly for 'actual trade' purposes and partly for other purposes, it is assumed for CAA 1990, ss 24 (writing-down allowances and balancing adjustments), 25 (qualifying expenditure) and 26 (disposal value) purposes that he incurred the expenditure wholly and exclusively for 'notional trade' purposes carried on by him separately from the actual trade and any other trade carried on by him.

A person who has incurred expenditure on machinery or plant for 'actual trade' purposes must bring the machinery or plant's disposal value into account by reason of it beginning in that chargeable period to be used partly, but not wholly, for purposes other than those of the actual trade. It is assumed for the purposes of ss 24–26 that he incurs capital expenditure equal to that disposal value on machinery or plant wholly and exclusively for 'notional trade' purposes (as above).

The allowance or charge under s 24 which, on the above assumptions, would fall to be made for any chargeable period for the notional trade:

(1) is reduced to such extent as may be just and reasonable, having particular regard to the extent to which the machinery or plant was used in that chargeable period otherwise than for actual trade purposes; and

(2) as so reduced, may be made for the actual trade.

In practice, these rules apply only to sole traders and partnerships (eg for cars which are used partly for private purposes). Furthermore, the Revenue has on occasion claimed that there should be an additional disallowance for more expensive cars, basing their argument on *GH Chambers (Northiam Farms) Ltd v Watmough* (1956) 36 TC 711. However, the Revenue is usually satisfied with the restrictions on capital allowances for expensive cars under CAA 1990, s 34.

So far as concerns assets (including cars) provided by companies to their directors or employees, the Revenue does not seek to restrict capital allowances unless there is a 'blatant incongruity' between the asset provided and the business requirements.

4.6.7 Effect of subsidies towards wear and tear
(CAA 1990, s 80)

The machinery and plant allowances system in effect gives tax relief for wear and tear (depreciation) suffered on machinery and plant over its useful life. However, allowances are not given to the extent that the wear and tear is covered by a subsidy towards the expenditure. This is achieved by reducing the amount of the capital expenditure on which allowances are given by the amount of the subsidy and giving allowances by reference only to the net expenditure actually borne by the claimant.

Where this would apply to a person's expenditure on machinery or plant, but the subsidy takes account of only part of the wear and tear, allowances are made for the expenditure, but the amount is reduced to such extent as may be just and reasonable having regard to all the relevant circumstances of the case. This is dealt with in broadly the same way as for assets which are used partly for a trade and partly for other purposes (see CAA 1990, s 79; see 4.6.7).

4.6.8 Effect of use after user not attracting capital allowances, or after receipt by way of gift
(CAA 1990, s 81)

Where a person brings into use, for trade purposes carried on by him, machinery or plant which belongs to him, having incurred capital expenditure on its provision, for purposes not qualifying for machinery and plant allowances, or brings into trade use machinery or plant which belongs to him as a result of a gift, he is deemed to acquire the machinery or plant at its open-market value at the time.

4.6.9 First-year allowances

Outline
(CAA 1990, s 22)

A person carrying on a trade who incurs capital expenditure on machinery or plant wholly and exclusively for trade purposes, and as a result of his incurring the expenditure the machinery or plant belongs to him at some time during the chargeable period related to incurring the expenditure, is entitled to a first-year allowance for any expenditure (and any additional VAT liability) which:

(1) was incurred between 1 November 1992 and 31 October 1993 – 40%;
(2) was incurred by a small or medium-sized enterprise after 1 July 1998 – 40% (this does not apply to expenditure on long-life assets (CAA 1990, ss 38A–38H);
(3) was incurred by a small or medium-sized enterprise between 2 July 1997 and 1 July 1998 for
   (a) expenditure on long-life assets – 12%; and
   (b) for any other expenditure – 50%;
(4) was certified to be expenditure qualifies for a regional development grant, or a grant under the Industrial Development (Northern Ireland) Order 1982, Part IV, and consists of the payment of sums on a project:
   (a) in an area which on 13 March 1984 was a development area under the Industrial Development Act 1982 or the 1982 NI Order; and
   (b) for which a written offer of financial assistance was made between 1 April 1980 and 13 March 1984 under either s 7 or 8 of the 1982 Act or by the Highlands and Islands Development Board – 100%;
(5) was certified by the Department of Economic Development in Northern Ireland to be expenditure qualifies for a grant under Part IV of the 1982 Order and consists of the payment of sums on a project:
   (a) in Northern Ireland; and
   (b) for which a written offer of financial assistance under art 7 or 8 of the 1982 Order between 1 April 1980 and 13 March 1984 or in

respect of which a written offer of financial assistance was made in that period by the Local Enterprise Development Unit – 100%;

(6) was incurred between 1 November 1992 and 31 October 1993 – 100%;

(7) was incurred by a small or medium-sized enterprise between 2 July 1997 and 1 July 1998 – 100%;

(8) is (or was) incurred in the special relief period (ie between 12 May 1998 and 11 May 2002) by a small or medium-sized enterprise on machinery or plant for use primarily in Northern Ireland – 40%. This does not apply to expenditure on long-life assets, an aircraft or hovercraft or a goods vehicle for trade purposes which consist primarily of the conveyance of goods, nor to unauthorised expenditure on machinery or plant for use primarily in:

 (a) agriculture, fishing or fish farming, or

 (b) any relevant activity carried out in relation to agricultural produce, fish or any fish product for the purpose of bringing it to market. Expenditure is unauthorised expenditure unless it is authorised by the Department of Agriculture for Northern Ireland; 'relevant activity' means transportation, storage, preparation, processing or packaging; and

(9) is (or was) incurred on information and communications technology by a small enterprise between 1 April 2000 and 31 March 2003 – 100%.

Expenditure on information and communications technology means expenditure on items within any of the classes set out below.

A. Computers and associated equipment

This class covers computers and:

(1) peripheral devices designed to be used by being connected to or inserted into them;

(2) equipment (including cabling) for use primarily to provide a data connection between:

 (a) one computer and another, or

 (b) a computer and a data communications network; and

(3) dedicated electrical systems for computers.

For this purpose, 'computer' does not include computerised control or management systems or other systems that are part of a larger system the principal function of which is not processing or storing information.

B. Other qualifying equipment

This class covers:

(1) wireless application protocol 'phones;

(2) third generation mobile 'phones;

(3) devices designed to be used by being connected to a television set that are capable of receiving and transmitting information from and to data networks; and

(4) other devices substantially similar to those within (1), (2) and (3) that are capable of receiving and transmitting information from and to data networks.

C. Software

This class covers the right to use or otherwise deal with software for the purposes of any equipment within Class A or B above. No first-year allowance can be made for any expenditure to which this class applies otherwise than by CAA 1990, s 22(3C) (expenditure by small or medium-sized enterprise between 2 July 1997 and 1 July 1998), (3CA) (expenditure in Northern Ireland in special relief period from 12 May 1998 to 11 May 2002), (3D) (expenditure on assets, other than long-life assets, by small or medium-sized enterprises after 1 July 1998) and (3E) (information and communications technology):

(1) if the chargeable period related to the expenditure's incurrence is also the chargeable period related to the trade's permanent discontinuance; or

(2) incurred on a motor car; or

(3) on machinery or plant for leasing, whether in the course of a trade or otherwise, unless it appears that it will be used for a qualifying purpose in the requisite period and will not at any time in that period be used for any other purpose (see CAA 1990, s 50 for points of interpretation). This does not apply to expenditure:

   (a) incurred at any time on machinery or plant which is to be an integral part of a building or structure if an initial allowance under the industrial buildings allowance rules (CAA 1990, s 1) would apply to expenditure incurred at that time on the construction of that building or structure;

   (b) on vehicles if they are provided wholly or mainly for use by a person receiving disability living allowance by virtue of entitlement to the mobility component, a mobility supplement, or any payment appearing to the Treasury to be of a similar kind and so specified by order;

   (c) incurred between 1 November 1992 and 31 October 1993 but, except as provided under the rules for joint lessees on new expenditure (CAA 1990, s 43) (expenditure incurred after 31 March 1986), no first-year allowance is given on machinery or plant for leasing if:

      (i) it appears that the expenditure relates to assets leased outside the UK (CAA 1990, s 42); or

      (ii) each of the following conditions is satisfied:
         – it is incurred after 13 April 1993;
         – it is expenditure which would prevent a first-year allowance being made; and
         – the lessee or a connected person (TA 1988, s 839) used the

111

machinery or plant for any purpose at any time before its provision for leasing.

This does not preclude a first-year allowance being made for expenditure incurred on machinery or plant fixed to a building or land of which the person who incurs it is the lessor and the circumstances are such that a transfer of his interest in the building/land would operate to transfer his interest in the machinery or plant.

Further restrictions apply to expenditure incurred on hire vehicles, certain sea-going ships (if incurred before 1 January 2011) and railway assets (again, before 1 January 2011). Also, first-year allowances do not apply if the transition rules on long-life assets under s 38H apply; where the provision of machinery and plant is connected with a change in the nature or conduct of a trade carried on by the person incurring the expenditure; and where the main aim of such change is to obtain a first-year allowance

Expenditure incurred on machinery or plant is not taken to be expenditure in Northern Ireland in the special relief period from 12 May 1998 to 11 May 2002 (s 22(3CA)) if:

(1) when it is incurred, the person incurring it intends the machinery or plant to be used partly outside Northern Ireland; and

(2) a main benefit is to obtain a first-year allowance, or a greater first-year allowance, for the part of the expenditure attributable to the intended outside use.

A claim for one or more first-year allowances to be made for any chargeable period may require that the amount, or aggregate amount, be reduced to an amount specified in the claim. No such claim can be made for expenditure on a ship for which 'free depreciation' is available (CAA 1990, ss 30–33F).

Expenditure of small or medium-sized enterprise
(CAA 1990, s 22A)

A small company for these purposes is one for which two or more of the following conditions are met:

(1) the turnover is not more than £2,800,000,

(2) the balance sheet total is not more than £1,400,000, and/or

(3) the number of employees is not more than 50,

and for a medium-sized company:

(1) the turnover is not more than £11,200,000,

(2) the balance sheet total is not more than £5,600,000, and/or

(3) the number of employees is not more than 250,

and neither is a part of a large group. A small group for these purposes is one for which two or more of the following conditions are met:

(1) the aggregate turnover is not more than £2.8m net or £3.36m gross,
(2) the aggregate balance sheet total is not more than £1m net or £1.68m gross, and/or
(3) the aggregate number of employees is not more than 50,

and for a medium-sized group:

(1) the aggregate turnover is not more than £11.2m net or £13.44m gross,
(2) the aggregate balance sheet total is not more than £5.6m net or £6.72m gross, and/or
(3) the aggregate number of employees is not more than 250.

'Capital expenditure' for these purposes is that incurred by a business for trade purposes (the 'first trade') carried on by it, where the first trade is carried on by a 'hypothetical company' which would qualify as small or medium-sized. A hypothetical company is one where:

(1) every trade, profession or vocation carried on by it is a part of the first trade;
(2) the company's financial years coincide with the business's chargeable periods; and
(3) its accounts for any relevant chargeable period were prepared in accordance with the CA 1985 requirements as if that period were a financial year of the company.

A company is a member of a large group when any expenditure is incurred if at that time it is either the parent undertaking of a group which does not qualify as small or medium-sized, or a subsidiary undertaking in relation to the parent.

If, when expenditure is incurred, arrangements exist which, having been given effect immediately before the incurrence, the company or its successor would have been a member of a large group, this rule applies as if the company was a member of a large group at that time.

A company is the successor of another if:

(1) it carries on a trade which, in whole or in part, the other company has ceased to carry on, and
(2) the circumstances are such that TA 1990, s 343 applies in relation to the two companies as the predecessor and the successor.

Where, otherwise, first-year allowances would apply to any expenditure incurred between 12 May 1998 and 11 May 2002 on machinery or plant for use in Northern Ireland, no such allowance is given if, at any relevant time:

(1) its use is one outside Northern Ireland; or
(2) it is held for use otherwise than primarily in Northern Ireland.

Withdrawal of first-year allowance on change of use
(CAA 1990, s 22B)

This rule applies to any expenditure (and any additional VAT liability) incurred in the special relief period (ie 12 May 1998 to 11 May 2002) by a small or medium-sized enterprise on machinery or plant for use primarily in Northern Ireland (CAA 1990, s 22(3CA) and (3CB)). Where a person who has made a return afterwards becomes aware that anything contained in it has become incorrect by reason of the operation of this section, he must within three months give notice to the Revenue of those amendments.

4.6.10 Writing-down allowances and balancing adjustments
(CAA 1990, s 24)

Where a person carrying on a trade has incurred capital expenditure (and any additional VAT liability) on machinery or plant wholly and exclusively for trade purposes, and as a result the machinery or plant belongs or has belonged to him, allowances and charges are made to and on him as described as follows.

For any chargeable period for which a person has qualifying expenditure which exceeds any disposal value to be brought into account, he can claim:

(1) unless during the chargeable period the trade is permanently discontinued, a writing-down allowance of 25% of the excess, or a proportionately reduced or increased percentage of it if the period is one of less or more than a year, or the trade has been carried on for part only of the period;

(2) if during the chargeable period the trade is permanently discontinued, a balancing allowance equal to the whole of the excess.

A claim for writing-down allowance can be made for a lesser amount.

For any chargeable period for which a person's qualifying expenditure is less than the disposal value which he is to bring into account, a balancing charge is made in the amount of the difference.

The disposal value brought into account by a person for any chargeable period is that of all machinery or plant:

(1) on which for trade purposes he incurred capital expenditure; and

(2) belonging to him at some time in the chargeable period; and

(3) for which one of the following events occurs:
  (a) it ceases to belong to him;
  (b) he permanently loses possession of it or (in the case of mineral exploration and access) abandons it at the site;
  (c) it ceases to exist (eg through destruction, dismantling);
  (d) it begins to be used wholly or partly for other than the trade's purposes; or
  (e) the trade is, or is deemed to have, permanently discontinued;
  and that is the first such event to occur.

This does not require a person to bring into account the disposal value of any machinery or plant which he disposes of by way of gift which raises a charge to Schedule E taxation.

For machinery or plant consisting of, or the right to use or otherwise deal with, computer software, the disposal value to be brought into account also includes that of all such machinery or plant:

(1) on which for trade purposes he has incurred capital expenditure (and any additional VAT);

(2) belonging to him at some time in the chargeable period;

(3) for which, in the chargeable period, he grants to another person a right to use or otherwise deal with the whole or part of the software in circumstances where the consideration in money for the grant constitutes (or if there were consideration in money for the grant would constitute) a capital sum; and

(4) for which, while the machinery or plant belongs or belonged to him, neither
  (a) the machinery or plant began to be used wholly or partly for purposes which are other than those of the trade, nor
  (b) the trade was, or is deemed to have, permanently discontinued,
  before such grant.

The disposal value includes, where relevant, any VAT rebate.

4.6.11 Qualifying expenditure
(CAA 1990, s 25)

A person's qualifying expenditure for a chargeable period is the aggregate of the following amounts:

(1) the balance remaining after deducting any first-year allowances made for capital expenditure incurred in that chargeable period or at any previous time, and not being expenditure:
  (a) which, or any part of which, has formed part of his qualifying expenditure for any previous chargeable period, or
  (b) for which a first-year allowance is or could (assuming a claim therefore) be made for the chargeable period in question; and

(2) if for the chargeable period immediately preceding that in question there was an excess of qualifying expenditure over disposal value, the balance of that excess after deducting any writing-down allowance made by reference thereto (this is sometimes referred to as the pool).

Where:

(a) a person carrying on a trade incurs capital expenditure on machinery or plant for trade purposes, and

(b) if a claim were made, a first-year allowance would be made for that expenditure for the chargeable period in which it was incurred, and

(c) no claim is made but, by notice given to the Revenue, the person so elects,

then, for writing-down allowances and balancing adjustments, that expenditure is not excluded from the capital expenditure.

Where:

(1) a person carrying on a trade has incurred capital expenditure on machinery or plant for trade purposes, and
(2) a first-year allowance falls to be made to that person for that expenditure (and a claim is made for that allowance), and
(3) for the chargeable period in which it was incurred, a reduced amount is claimed (CAA 1990, s 22(7) or, for ships, 30(1)(b)),

then, for writing-down allowances and balancing adjustments, the amount of expenditure for which no first-year allowances were claimed is added to the pool.

Where a first-year allowance is made for capital expenditure on machinery or plant, and in the chargeable period in which it was incurred the disposal value of that machinery or plant falls to be brought into account, that expenditure (for which a first-year allowance is or could (assuming a claim therefore) be made for that chargeable period) is not, for writing-down allowances and balancing adjustments, the capital expenditure.

Capital expenditure incurred by any person in any chargeable period on machinery or plant for leasing under a finance lease is brought into account so as to form part of that person's qualifying expenditure for that period, except to the extent of the part of the expenditure for that period which is proportionate to the part of the chargeable period falling after the time when the expenditure was incurred. This does not apply where, in the chargeable period in which the expenditure was incurred, the disposal value falls to be brought into account. Where only part of any capital expenditure may be included in a person's qualifying expenditure for any chargeable period, the remainder of it is included in his qualifying expenditure for the next following chargeable period.

4.6.12 Disposal value
(CAA 1990, s 26)

The disposal value depends on the event by reason of which it falls to be taken into account, as follows.

Where the sale of machinery or plant is at a price lower than open-market value, and otherwise than in circumstances such that:

(1) the buyer's original expenditure can be taken into account for machinery and plant allowances and the buyer is not a connected dual resident investing company (TA 1988 s 839), or
(2) there is a Schedule E tax charge,

the disposal value is equal to the price the machinery or plant would have fetched in the open market. If it is sold at open-market value, the disposal value equals the net sale proceeds together with any insurance moneys received by reason of any event affecting the sale price and, so far as it consists of capital sums, any other compensation received.

If the machinery or plant is demolished or destroyed, the disposal value equals the net amount received for its remains, together with any insurance moneys received for the demolition/destruction and, so far as it consists of capital sums, any other compensation received. If it is lost permanently (other than by demolition or destruction), the disposal value equals any insurance moneys received for the loss and, so far as it consists of capital sums, any other compensation received.

Where the trade is permanently discontinued before any of the above events occurs, the disposal value is the same as for those events.

If a right is granted to use or otherwise deal with computer software for no consideration or for a consideration in money lower than that which would have been given in the open market, and otherwise than in circumstances such that:

(1) the grantee's expenditure on acquiring the right can be taken into account in making machinery or plant, or under research and development, allowances and the grantee is not a dual resident investing company connected with the grantor (TA 1988, s 839), or

(2) there is Schedule E tax charge,

the disposal value equals the consideration in money which would have been given if the right had been granted in the open market. If such a right is granted for a consideration not, or not wholly, consisting in money, the disposal value equals the consideration in money which would have been given had the right been granted in the open market. Further, if a right is so granted and neither of the previous two events related to software applies, the disposal value equals the net consideration in money received by the grantor, together with any insurance moneys and other compensation received by him by reason of any event affecting the consideration.

If an additional VAT rebate is made for capital expenditure incurred on machinery or plant, the disposal value equals the rebate amount.

Where a deemed disposal of machinery or plant arises solely under a production-sharing agreement (CAA 1990, s 64A(2), (4) or (6)) and capital compensation is received by the contractor or participator, the disposal value equals the compensation amount. For such a deemed disposal where no compensation is received, the disposal value is nil.

Under any other event, the disposal value equals the price which the machinery or plant would have fetched if sold in the open market at that time.

The disposal value cannot exceed the capital expenditure incurred on machinery or plant for trade purposes reduced by the aggregate amount of any additional VAT rebates made for any of that capital expenditure. In deciding, for this purpose, whether the disposal value of computer software (or the right to use or otherwise deal with it) exceeds the capital expenditure incurred on its provision, the disposal value is taken to be increased by the amount of any disposal value which is taken into account on any previous grants to another person of a right to use or otherwise deal with the whole or part of the software in circumstances where the consideration in money for the grant constitutes (or if there were consideration in money for the grant would constitute) a capital sum.

If the event by reason of which a disposal value is to be brought into account is an additional VAT rebate made to a person, the capital expenditure is reduced (or further reduced) by the amount of any disposal value brought into account by that person for the machinery or plant by reason of any earlier event (other than the making of an additional VAT rebate).

Where a person acquired machinery or plant as a result of a transaction which was, or a series of transactions each of which was, between connected persons (TA 1988, s 839), the limit on disposal value to be taken into account is the capital expenditure on machinery or plant incurred by whichever party incurred the greatest expenditure.

4.6.13 Application to professions, employments, vocations etc
(CAA 1990, s 27)

The machinery and plant allowance rules apply to professions, employments, vocations and offices as they apply in relation to trades. In their application to an office or employment, such rules apply:

(1) only to machinery or plant which is necessarily provided for use in the performance of the duties thereof, and
(2) subject to the exemption from Schedule D Case I for foreign emoluments (TA 1988, s 198(2)).

Where the machinery or plant consists of a road vehicle or a cycle (Road Traffic Act 1988, s 192(1)), and capital expenditure incurred on its provision is incurred partly for work and partly for other purposes, the rules apply only to those provided for use in the performance of work duties (note the omission of the word 'necessarily').

In connection with writing-down allowances and balancing adjustments for an office or employment, where a person's qualifying expenditure consists of expenditure incurred on machinery for use in the performance of work duties the claim is restricted in proportion to use for that purpose, and excludes any private use.

If an employee claims mileage allowance under the fixed profit car scheme, he cannot also claim capital allowances.

4.6.14 Schedule A cases (including furnished holiday lettings)
(CA 1990, ss 28A and 29)

Where any person carries on a Schedule A business, it is treated as a trade for the machinery and plant allowance rules, and that trade is treated as one carried on separately from any other trade carried on by him.

Expenditure incurred in providing machinery or plant for use in a dwelling house is not treated as incurred for trade purposes. Where it is provided partly for use in a dwelling house and partly for other purposes, the expenditure incurred is apportioned accordingly.

The rules apply to the commercial letting of furnished holiday accommodation in the UK where a single trade is carried on separately from any other Schedule A business *and* any other trade. Where accommodation is let partly for holiday purposes and partly for other purposes, the expenditure incurred is apportioned accordingly.

No machinery and plant allowances are given if the 'rent-a-room' relief is claimed.

4.7 MACHINERY AND PLANT: SPECIAL CASES

4.7.1 Assets held in separate pools

All items of expenditure form part of the main pool of expenditure except the following:

- Ships
- Expensive motor cars (costing over £12,000)
- Short-life assets
- Certain leased assets
- Machinery or plant used only partly for business purposes
- Machinery or plant where a subsidy has been received.

4.7.2 Ships
(CAA 1990, ss 30–33F)

The treatment of ships is an exception to the normal machinery and plant allowance rules. The trader who incurs the expenditure can elect for postponement of the whole or part of the first-year allowance. The amount withheld can then be claimed in any subsequent periods without time limit. Thus, the shipowner is given 'free depreciation' which he may claim as and when it best suits his tax position. The term 'ship' is not defined in the legislation. However, it is generally understood to include 'every description of vessel used in navigation' (Merchant Shipping Act 11995, s313(1)). More specifically, a 'qualifying ship' is a ship of a seagoing kind, registered in any jurisdiction, with a gross tonnage of at least 100 tons (CAA 1990, s 33E).

A detailed account of the capital allowance provisions for ships is beyond the scope of this book. Readers are advised to seek specialist advice on this subject.

4.7.3 Expensive motor cars

Over the years, various rules have applied to expenditure on motor cars. Currently, the amount of writing-down allowance that is given where the expenditure exceeds £12,000 is restricted to £3,000.

Definition of 'motor car', etc
(CAA 1990, s 36)

A 'motor car' is any mechanically propelled road vehicle other than a vehicle:

(1) of a construction primarily suited for the conveyance of goods or burden of any description, or
(2) of a type not commonly used as a private vehicle and unsuitable to be so used, or
(3) provided wholly or mainly for hire to, or for the carriage of, members of the public in the ordinary course of a trade. This applies to a vehicle only if:
  (a) the following conditions are satisfied:
    (i) the number of consecutive days for which it is on hire to, or used for the carriage of, the same person will normally be less than 30; and
    (ii) the total number of days for which it is on hire to, or used for the carriage of, the same person in any 12-month period is normally less than 90; or
  (b) it is provided for hire to a person who will himself use it wholly or mainly for hire to, or the carriage of, members of the public in the ordinary course of a trade and in a manner complying with the conditions specified in (a) above.

This definition does not affect vehicles provided wholly or mainly for the use by persons receiving a disability living allowance being entitled to the mobility component, a mobility supplement or similar kind of payment.

Not surprisingly, there have been a number of cases where the question at issue was whether particular models of cars, or vehicles with particular modifications, could be classed as private type cars. Driving school cars fitted with dual controls are not private cars (*Bourne v Auto School of Motoring (Norwich) Ltd* (1964) 42 TC 217). Vans and minivans were held to be vehicles of a type commonly used as private vehicles and suitable so to be used in *Tapper v Eyre* (1967) 43 TC 720 and *Laing v CIR* (1967) 44 TC 681. However, subsequently, in *Roberts v Granada TV Rental Ltd* (1970) 46 TC 295, it was held that vans and minivans, licensed as goods vehicles and so used, were vehicles of a type not commonly used as private vehicles and unsuitable to be so used. It is accepted that Land Rovers are vehicles of a type not commonly used as private vehicles and unsuitable to be so used. However, this does not extend to Range Rovers, other four-wheel drive vehicles or estate cars.

Restriction of writing-down allowances, etc for expenditure on expensive cars
(CAA 1990, s 34)

Where capital expenditure exceeding £12,000 is incurred on a motor car for the purposes of a trade, the expenditure is segregated in a separate pool and the writing-down allowance is restricted to £3,000 for a full 12-month period (pro rata for shorter periods).

If the motor car is used partly for trade and partly for other purposes, or a subsidy which takes account of wear and tear because of trade use is paid to the person carrying on the trade, neither CAA 1990, s 79 (partial trade use) nor s 80 (effect of subsidies towards wear and tear) apply. Instead, the allowance or charge which would otherwise be given is reduced to such amount as would be just and reasonable. The Revenue has, on occasion, argued that there should be an additional disallowance for the more expensive cars to reflect the personal choice of vehicle, basing their argument on *GH Chambers (Northiam Farms) Ltd v Watmough* (1956) 36 TC 711 when part of the allowance due on a Bentley owned by a farmer was disallowed. This does, however, depend on the facts of the particular case. In practice the Revenue is usually satisfied with the restrictions on capital allowances for expensive cars under s 34.

So far as concerns expensive motor cars provided by companies to their directors or employees, the Revenue does not seek to restrict capital allowances unless there is a 'blatant incongruity' between the asset provided and the business requirements.

Contributions to expenditure, and hiring of cars
(CAA 1990, s 35)

Where capital expenditure exceeding £12,000 is incurred on a motor car and CAA 1990, s 154 (allowance for contributions to capital expenditure) applies, writing-down allowances may be made to a person as if a contribution made by him to the expenditure had been expenditure on a motor car for the purposes of a trade. However, the allowance cannot exceed an amount bearing to £3,000 the same proportion as that borne by the contribution to the

121

capital expenditure actually incurred on the provision of the motor car for a full year. This is reduced proportionately for shorter periods. This does not apply where the hiring is under a hire-purchase agreement under which there is an option to purchase exercisable on the payment of a sum equal to not more than 1% of the retail price of the motor car when new.

By ESC B28, where a reduction has been made as above, any subsequent rebate of hiring charges is a taxable receipt in the hands of the hirer. The rebate is reduced in the same proportion unless it exceeds the rent previously paid, in which case the excess is taxed without reduction.

Where, otherwise, the amount of any expenditure on the hiring of a motor car the retail price of which when new exceeds £12,000 would be allowed to be deducted in computing for tax purposes the profits of any trade, that amount is reduced in the proportion which £12,000, together with one half of the excess, bears to that retail price. Where this has operated to reduce any expenditure on the hiring of a motor car, and subsequently either any rebate (by whatever name called) of the rentals is made or any transaction occurs with regard to any rentals that fall within TA 1988, s 94 (debts deducted and subsequently released), then the amount otherwise taxable for the rebate or transaction is reduced in the same proportion as the expenditure on hiring was reduced.

4.7.4 Short-life assets
(CAA 1990, ss 37 and 38)

The short-life assets rules apply where:

(a) capital expenditure is incurred on machinery or plant wholly and exclusively for trade purposes;
(b) the machinery or plant is not an excluded asset (see below);
(c) the expenditure does not fall within any category of long-life assets (broadly machinery and plant with an anticipated useful economic life of at least 25 years); and
(d) the trader makes an irrevocable election requiring that specified items of machinery or plant be treated as short-life assets.

Where an election is made, it is assumed for all writing-down allowances and balancing adjustments purposes (CAA 1990, ss 24–26) that:

(1) the trader incurred such expenditure wholly and exclusively for trade purposes carried on by him separately and the expenditure is taken into a separate 'pool' ('the notional trade'); and
(2) the separate 'pool' is permanently discontinued when the short-life asset begins to be used wholly or partly for purposes other than those of the actual trade.

Any allowance or charge which, on the above assumptions, is given to the separate pool is made for that period for the actual trade.

A further balancing allowance may be made of an amount equal to any additional VAT liability for the chargeable period of the actual trade in which the liability was incurred (and the liability is not brought into account for any chargeable period for the notional trade ('the separate pool')).

If no disposal, etc has occurred before the fourth anniversary of the end of the chargeable period in which the capital expenditure concerned or, as the case may be, the first part of that expenditure was incurred, then:

(1) in the first chargeable period ending after that fourth anniversary the notional trade ('the separate pool') is treated as permanently discontinued, but no balancing allowance or charge is made to or on the trader; and

(2) the amount which otherwise would be the trader's qualifying expenditure for that chargeable period for the notional trade ('the separate pool') is added to his qualifying expenditure for that period for his actual trade.

If, at a time before the notional trade ('the separate pool') would otherwise be permanently discontinued for all writing-down allowance and balancing adjustment purposes, a short-life asset provided for leasing begins to be used otherwise than for a qualifying purpose (s 39) and the occasion of its being so used falls within the requisite period (s 40), then at that time:

(1) the notional trade ('the separate pool') is treated as permanently discontinued, but no balancing allowance or charge is made to or on the trader; and

(2) the amount which otherwise would be the trader's qualifying expenditure for the notional trade ('the separate pool') for the chargeable period in which the asset began to be so used is for all writing-down allowance and balancing adjustment purposes added to the trader's qualifying expenditure for that chargeable period for his actual trade.

If, at a time before the notional trade ('the separate pool') is permanently discontinued for all writing-down allowance and balancing adjustment purposes, the trader disposes of a short-life asset to a connected person (TA 1988, s 839):

(1) the disposal is treated as a sale of the short-life asset at a price equal to the amount of the trader's qualifying expenditure for the notional trade ('the separate pool') for the chargeable period related to the disposal;

(2) none of the further restrictions on allowances where the purchaser and the vendor are connected (CAA 1990, s 75) applies in relation to the disposal;

(3) immediately after acquisition, the connected person is taken to have made a short-life assets election (so that, in his hands, the machinery or plant is also a short-life asset); and

(4) in relation to the connected person, any reference to the fourth anniversary (see above) is a reference to the date which was that fourth anniversary in relation to the trader.

Where a short-life asset is disposed of at a price lower than at open-market value, the provision applies whereby the buyer's expenditure on acquisition can be taken into account in making machinery and plant or dredging allowances and the buyer is not a dual resident investing company connected with the seller unless an election is made as above.

The following are specifically excluded from being treated as short-life assets by CAA 1990, s 38:

(1) ships;

(2) motor cars;

(3) machinery or plant on lease (CAA 1990, s 61);

(4) machinery or plant where there is partial private use (s 79(2));

(5) machinery or plant where a subsidy has been paid towards wear and tear (CAA 1990, s 80 applies);

(6) machinery or plant brought into use for a purpose qualifying for machinery and plant allowances after having been used for a purpose not so qualifying, or having been received as a gift (s 81(1)(a) or (b));

(7) machinery or plant used for leasing, whether or not in the course of a trade, unless it appears that it will be used for a qualifying purpose in the requisite period and will not at any time be used for any other purpose (s 22(4)(c)), thereby precluding a first-year allowance being made for the expenditure incurred on it for leasing (not applied to expenditure after 26 July 1989);

(8) machinery or plant provided for leasing, except:

    (a) that which it appears will be used in the requisite period (s 40) for a qualifying purpose (s 39) and will not at any time in that period be used for any other purpose;

    (b) vehicles provided wholly or mainly for use by a person receiving the disability living allowance mobility component, a mobility supplement, or any payment appearing to the Treasury to be of a similar kind and so specified by order (applied to expenditure before 27 July 1989);

(9) machinery or plant leased to two or more persons jointly where the expenditure was after 31 March 1986 (s 43) (not applied to expenditure after 26 July 1989);

(10) machinery or plant leased to two or more persons jointly where the expenditure was before 1 April 1986 (s 45) so that no first-year allowance is due (not applied to expenditure after 26 July 1989);

(11) machinery or plant leased outside the UK (s 42) for which only a 10% writing-down allowance is due; and

(12) machinery or plant the expenditure on which is certified as being within a regional project (s 22(2), (3) or (3A)) and for which a first-year allowance continues to be available.

4.7.5 Long-life assets

Expenditure to which long-life asset rules apply
(CAA 1990, s 38A)

The rules described here apply to any capital expenditure incurred by a person on machinery or plant which is a long-life asset, as follows:

(1) for new machinery or plant, it is reasonable to expect that the machinery or plant will have a useful economic life of at least 25 years; or
(2) in any other case, it was reasonable, when the machinery or plant was new, to expect that it would have a useful economic life of at least 25 years.

The useful economic life of machinery or plant is the period which begins with the first occasion on which the machinery or plant is brought into use, and continues until the machinery or plant ceases to be used (whether or not by the person who first brought it into use and whether or not in a manner in which he used it) as a business fixed asset.

Where, the long-life asset rules apply to part only of the expenditure so incurred, the part which is a long-life asset and the part which is not are treated as separate assets and apportionments are made accordingly.

Expenditure to which the long-life asset rules do not apply
(CAA 1990, s 38B)

The long-life asset rules do not apply to expenditure:

(1) on machinery or plant which is a fixture in, or is provided for use in, a dwelling house, a retail shop (including any premises of a similar character where retail trade or business (including repair work) is carried on), a showroom, an hotel or an office, or for purposes ancillary to them;
(2) on a motor car (including hire cars);
(3) expenditure incurred before 1 January 2011 on certain sea-going ships and railway assets.

Exclusion rules where limit for individuals and partnerships not exceeded
(CAA 1990, s 38C)

The long-life asset rules do not apply to any expenditure incurred by an individual, or by a partnership of which all the members are individuals, unless that expenditure is:

(1) incurred in a chargeable period the relevant limit (see below) for which is exceeded for that individual or partnership; or

(2) not subject to that limit.

The relevant limit is exceeded if the total amount of capital expenditure incurred in that period by that individual or partnership is subject to the limit, and is or otherwise would be expenditure to which the long-life assets rules apply, exceeds the limit applying to that period. Expenditure incurred by an individual is subject to the relevant limit for a chargeable period if:

(a) it was incurred by him for the purposes of a trade or profession carried on by him;
(b) he devotes substantially the whole of his time in that chargeable period to carrying on that trade or profession; and
(c) the expenditure is not excluded from the operation of the limit.

Expenditure incurred by a partnership is subject to the relevant limit for a chargeable period if:

(1) it was incurred by the partnership for the purposes of a trade or profession carried on by it;
(2) at all times throughout that period at least half of partners are devoting substantially the whole of their time to carrying on that trade or profession; and
(3) the expenditure is not excluded from the operation of the limit.

Expenditure excluded from the operation of the relevant limit for a chargeable period is any which falls within any of the following categories:

(1) expenditure on a share in machinery or plant;
(2) contributions towards capital expenditure treated as such on the provision of machinery or plant (CAA 1990, s 154); and
(3) expenditure incurred on machinery or plant for leasing (whether or not in the course of a trade).

Currently, the relevant limit for a chargeable period of 12 months is £100,000. For a chargeable period which is not 12 months, the relevant limit is the amount given by a proportional reduction or, as the case may require, increase of £100,000.

Where, for any contract for the provision of machinery or plant, the capital expenditure which is or is to be incurred under that contract is or may fall to be treated as incurred in different chargeable periods, all of the expenditure falling to be incurred under that contract on that machinery or plant is treated as incurred in the first chargeable period in which any of it is incurred.

Exclusion rules where company's limit not exceeded
(CAA 1990, s 38D)

The long-life asset rules do not apply for corporation tax purposes to any expenditure by a company unless that expenditure is:

(1) incurred in a chargeable period the relevant limit (see below) for which is exceeded in relation to that company; or

(2) excluded from the operation of that limit.

The relevant limit is exceeded only if the total amount of capital expenditure which is:

(1) incurred by that company in that period,

(2) not excluded from the operation of that limit, and

(3) or otherwise would be, expenditure to which the long-life assets rules apply

exceeds the limit applying to that period. Currently, the limit applying to a chargeable period of 12 months is £100,000. The limit applying to a chargeable period of less than 12 months is the amount given by a proportional reduction of £100,000.

Where, in a chargeable period, a company has one or more associated companies, the limit applying to that period is the amount produced by:

(a) taking the limit, or the reduced limit for periods of less than 12 months, and

(b) dividing that amount by one plus the number of those companies.

TA 1988, s 13(4) and (5) identifies the companies that are to count as associated companies.

The categories of expenditure excluded from the operation of the relevant limit, and the provisions for contracts to provide machinery or plant where capital expenditure may fall to be treated as incurred in different chargeable periods, are the same as for individuals and partnerships.

Separate pools for expenditure
(CAA 1990, s 38E)

Where expenditure within the long-life asset rules has been incurred on machinery or plant wholly and exclusively for the trade purposes ('the actual trade'), the following rules apply for writing-down allowances and charges to be made for the actual trade.

It is assumed for all writing-down allowance and balancing adjustment purposes (CAA 1990, ss 24–26) that:

(1) the person carrying on the actual trade incurred such expenditure wholly and exclusively for trade purposes carried on by him separately from the actual trade and from any other trade he carries on or is assumed to carry on;

(2) the purposes for which the machinery or plant is used (whether wholly or partly) are the separate trade if they are of the actual trade, but not otherwise; and

(3) the separate trade is permanently discontinued if the actual trade is or is treated as permanently discontinued, but not otherwise.

Any writing-down allowance or balancing charge (s 24) which, on those assumptions, would fall to be made for any chargeable period for the separate trade is made for that period for the actual trade.

If a writing-down allowance falling to be made for any chargeable period ('the earlier period') for the actual trade is not claimed or is claimed for a reduced amount, then, in determining the writing-down allowance or charge which would fall to be made for any subsequent chargeable period for the separate trade, any allowance falling to be made for the separate trade for the earlier period is treated as not claimed or, as the case may require, as proportionately reduced.

Where there is more than one item of machinery or plant, and expenditure is incurred on machinery or plant wholly and exclusively for trade purposes, the rule described here applies as if the separate trade for which, in that person's case, each of those items is treated as used were the same separate trade.

Here, expenditure incurred on machinery or plant wholly and exclusively for trade purposes does not include a reference to any amount falling by CAA 1990, ss 31 (ships), 61 (machinery or plant on lease), 79 (partial trade use) or 80 (subsidies towards wear and tear) to be treated as incurred on machinery or plant wholly and exclusively for the purposes of the separate trade mentioned in that section.

Modifications applying to pools for long-life assets
(CAA 1990, s 38E)

Where the rules for writing-down allowances and balancing adjustments apply, in any of the cases mentioned below, to any expenditure on long-life assets, the writing-down allowance given is 6%. The cases are where:

(1) the rules for writing-down allowances and balancing adjustments are applied by CAA 1990, ss 31, 38E, 79 or 80 (see above); and
(2) the machinery or plant is on lease (s 61).

Where:

(a) any person entitled to do so has made a machinery and plant allowances claim for expenditure so incurred,
(b) that expenditure falls to be treated for the purposes of that claim as expenditure to which the long-life assets rules apply,
(c) at any time after making that claim, that or another person makes a machinery and plant allowances claim for any capital expenditure incurred at any time (including before the incurrence of expenditure to which the earlier claim relates) on the same machinery or plant,
(d) the expenditure to which the later claim relates would not otherwise be

treated for the purposes of the later claim as expenditure to which the rules apply, or

(e) the expenditure to which the later claim relates does not fall within (d) above by being expenditure excluded from the application of the rules (s 38B),

the long-life asset rules apply in relation to the later claim as if the expenditure to which it relates were such expenditure.

Disposal value of long-life assets
(CAA 1990, s 38F)

If, where the rules for writing-down allowances and balancing adjustments are applied by the modified rules for pools of long-life assets in relation to any expenditure incurred by a person ('the charged person'),

(1) an event occurs by reason of which a disposal value of that machinery or plant is to be brought into account by the charged person,

(2) the amount of the disposal value to be so brought into account would otherwise be less than the machinery or plant's notional written-down value, and

(3) the event is comprised in, or occurs under, any scheme or arrangement which has avoidance as its main object, or one of its main objects,

the long-life asset rules apply in relation to the charged person as if the disposal value to be brought into account were equal to the notional written-down value. Here, 'the notional written-down value' means the amount which, if it were the disposal value falling to be brought into account and on the assumptions set out below were made, would give rise to neither a balancing allowance nor a balancing charge for the chargeable period for which that disposal value is to be brought into account. The assumptions are that:

(1) expenditure on the machinery or plant was the only expenditure ever taken into account in determining the charged person's qualifying expenditure (CAA 1990, s 24);

(2) such expenditure was not, in the charged person's case, excluded from eligibility as long-life assets because the £100,000 limit was not exceeded (s 38C or 38D); and

(3) the full amount of every allowance to which the charged person was entitled for that expenditure had been made to him.

In this context, 'avoidance' means:

(a) obtaining, under the long-life asset rules for the charged person, an allowance or deduction or a greater allowance or deduction, or

(b) avoidance or reduction of a charge under those rules.

Note that this anti-avoidance provision does not apply to connected party transactions on a succession to trade where election is made (CAA 1990, s 77).

Transitional provisions
(CAA 1990, s 38G)

The long-life assets rules do not apply to any expenditure incurred before:

(1) 26 November 1996; or
(2) 1 January 2001 under a contract entered into before 26 November 1996.

The long-life assets rules do not apply to expenditure incurred by any person ('the purchaser') on the acquisition of any long-life asset from another person ('the seller') in a case where:

(a) the seller has made a machinery and plant allowances claim for expenditure incurred on that asset ('the seller's expenditure'),
(b) that claim is one which the seller was entitled to make,
(c) the seller's expenditure was not expenditure falling for the purposes of that claim to be treated as expenditure on long-life assets, and
(d) the seller's expenditure would have fallen to be so treated if one or more of the following assumptions were made.
   (i) expenditure falling within (a) or (b) above is not prevented from being expenditure on long-life assets;
   (ii) the seller's expenditure was not prevented by (b) above from being expenditure on long-life assets; and
   (iii) the long-life assets rules or, as the case may require, corresponding provisions applied for chargeable periods ending before 26 November 1996.

Here, expenditure incurred under a contract entered into before 26 November 1996 does not, for a contract varied at any time on or after that date, include a reference to so much of the expenditure incurred under that contract as exceeds the amount of the expenditure that would have been incurred if that contract had not been so varied.

4.7.6 Leased assets

Meaning of 'qualifying purpose'
(CAA 1990, s 39)

Machinery or plant on which a person ('the buyer') has incurred expenditure is used for a qualifying purpose at any time if at that time any of the following conditions is satisfied:

(1) the machinery or plant is leased to a lessee who uses it for trade purposes, otherwise than for leasing, and the buyer's expenditure was either:

(a) old expenditure and, disregarding CAA 1990, s 22(2), (3), (3B), (3C), (3CA) and (3E), a first-year allowance could have been made to the lessee, under s 22, if he had bought the machinery or plant at that time and had incurred capital expenditure in doing so, or

(b) new expenditure (broadly expenditure after 31 March 1986) and, had the lessee bought the machinery or plant at that time and had incurred new expenditure in doing so, that expenditure would have fallen to be included, in whole or in part, in the lessee's qualifying expenditure for any chargeable period for writing-down allowances and balancing adjustments (s 24(2)–(5));

(2) the buyer uses the machinery or plant for short-term leasing;

(3) the machinery or plant is leased to a lessee who uses it for short-term leasing and either is UK-resident or so uses it in the course of a trade carried on by him there; and/or

(4) the buyer uses the machinery or plant for trade purposes other than for leasing.

A ship is also used for a qualifying purpose at any time when it is let on charter in the course of a trade which consists of or includes operating ships if:

(1) the person carrying on the trade is UK-resident or carries on the trade there, and

(2) he is responsible as principal (or appoints another person to be responsible in his stead) for navigating and managing the ship throughout the charter period and for defraying all expenses in connection with the ship throughout that period or substantially all such expenses other than those directly incidental to a particular voyage or to the employment of the ship during that period.

This also applies, with the necessary modifications, to aircraft. However, it does not apply (if the main object, or one of the main objects, of letting the ship or aircraft on charter, or of a series of transactions of which the letting on charter was one, or of any of the transactions in such a series was to obtain:

(1) if it is old expenditure (broadly, prior to 1 April 1986), a first-year allowance, or

(2) if it is new expenditure (broadly, after 31 March 1986), a first-year allowance under CAA 1990, s 22(3B) (expenditure between 1 November 1992 and 31 October 1993), or a writing-down allowance of an amount unconstrained by the restriction of such allowances to 10% where the assets are leased outside the UK (s 42(2))

for expenditure incurred on a ship or aircraft, whether that expenditure was incurred by a UK-resident person carrying on the trade there.

A transport container is used for a qualifying purpose at any time when it is leased in the course of a trade carried on by a UK resident or someone who carries on the trade there if:

(1) the trade involves operating ships or aircraft and the container is at other times used by the trader for those purposes, or
(2) the container is leased under a succession of leases to different persons who, or most of whom, are not connected.

For any part of the requisite period for which the machinery or plant belongs to a person who incurred the expenditure, so long as it belongs to a person who:

(1) is connected with him, or
(2) acquired it from him as a result of one or more disposals on the occasion of which, or each of which, the trade carried on by the person making the disposal was treated as continuing by TA 1990, ss 113(2) (change in membership of partnership) or 114(1) (computation of profits and losses of partnerships involving companies),

that person is treated as the buyer.

Meaning of 'short-term leasing' and 'the requisite period'
(CAA 1990, s 40)

Here, 'short-term leasing' means leasing the machinery or plant normally let to the same person:

(1) for less than 30 consecutive days, with the total number of days not exceeding 90 within a 12-month period; or
(2) for less than 365 consecutive days to lessees for other than leasing purposes in the course of a trade, the aggregate leasing period does not exceed two years. However, if the actual period within which the aggregated two years' leasing occurs exceeds four years, they are treated as four consecutive years.

There are further rules for aggregate periods of leasing within the 'requisite period'. The requisite period begins with the date on which the machinery or plant is first brought into use by the person who incurred the expenditure, and is:

(1) four years for expenditure not falling within (2) below, or
(2) ten years for:
    (a) new expenditure (broadly, after 31 March 1986), or
    (b) old expenditure (broadly, prior to 1 April 1986) to which FA 1982, s 70(3) had effect;

except that where the machinery or plant ceases to belong to that person at any time before the end of those four or ten years, the requisite period ends at that time. Connected persons are treated as the same person. Where a number of items form the leased machinery or plant and a substantial number of those items are used during the leasing and are not separately identifiable, they may all be treated as used for short-term leasing.

Under CAA 1990, ss 31(2) (single ship trade) and 37(6) (discontinuance of notional short-life assets trade), the requisite period is restricted to four years.

Writing-down allowances etc for leased assets
(CAA 1990, s 40)

Where the rules for assets leased outside the UK (CAA 1990, s 42) apply to expenditure on machinery or plant for leasing in the course of a trade, the following rules have effect for the writing-down allowances and balancing charges made for the actual trade under CAA 1990, s 24.

For all writing-down allowance and balancing adjustment purposes, the assumptions listed in 4.7.4 regarding CAA 1990, ss 24–26 apply, except here the allowance or charge which, on those assumptions, would fall to be made for any chargeable period for the *separate* trade are made for that period for the *actual* trade.

If an allowance or charge made for any chargeable period for the actual trade is not claimed or is claimed in a reduced amount (s 24(3)) then, in determining the allowance or charge for any subsequent chargeable period for the separate trade, any allowance falling to be made for the actual trade's chargeable period is treated either as not claimed or as proportionately reduced.

Where the ss 24–26 rules apply to different, leased items of machinery and plant in the separate trade, these are treated as used in the same trade and thus the separate trade is not treated is permanently discontinued until all such items begin to be used wholly or partly for purposes other than those of the actual trade.

Where the rules are applied for expenditure incurred by a person providing machinery or plant for trade purposes, if it is disposed of by him to a connected person and the disposal is not on an occasion on which the trade is treated as continuing by TA 1990, ss 113(2) (change in membership of partnership), 114(1) (computation of profits and losses of partnerships involving companies) or 343(2) (company reconstructions without change of ownership), or CAA 1990, s 77(1) (successions to trades by connected persons):

(1) the disposal value to be brought into account for the separate trade is that equal to the price the machinery or plant would have fetched on the open market or, if less, the capital expenditure incurred or treated as incurred on the provision of the machinery or plant by the person disposing of it; and
(2) the person acquiring it is treated for machinery and plant allowance purposes as having incurred on its provision expenditure equal to that disposal value.

These rules do not apply to machinery or plant:

(1) in relation to which the writing-down allowance and balancing adjustment rules apply in accordance with CAA 1990, ss 34 (writing-down
allowances for expensive cars), 79 (partial trade use) or 80 (subsidies
towards wear and tear); or

(2) the expenditure on which is eligible for the long-life assets treatment.

Assets leased outside the UK
(CAA 1990, s 42)

In their application to such expenditure (except on long-life assets), the
writing-down allowance and balancing adjustment rules apply by reference
to a 10% writing-down allowance:

(1) in accordance with CAA 1990, ss 41 (writing-down allowances etc for
leased assets), 80 (wear and tear), or 34 (expensive motor cars), or

(2) with respect to any motor car to which the restriction on the allowability of leasing payments applies because of contributions towards its
capital expenditure (CAA 1990, s 35(1)) applies, or

(3) with respect to machinery or plant on lease (CAA 1990, s 61).

The following rule applies to expenditure on machinery or plant for leasing
where it is at any time in the requisite period used for the purpose of being
leased to a person who:

(a) is not UK-resident, and

(b) does not use the machinery or plant exclusively for earning such profits as are chargeable to tax as profits arising from a trade carried on in
the UK,

and where the leasing is neither short-term leasing nor the leasing of a ship,
aircraft or transport container which is used for a qualifying purpose (per
CAA 1990, s 39(6)–(9)). No balancing or writing-down allowances are
available for such expenditure if the circumstances are such that the machinery or plant is used otherwise than for a qualifying purpose and:

(1) there is a period of more than one year between the dates on which any
two consecutive payments become due under the lease; or

(2) any (other than periodical) payments are due under the lease or under
any agreement which might reasonably be construed as being collateral
to the lease; or

(3) disregarding variations made under the lease terms which are attributable to changes in:
    (a) corporation or income tax rate, or
    (b) capital allowances rate, or
    (c) any interest rate linked to interest rate changes applicable to inter-
    bank loans, or
    (d) the premiums charged for any insurance by a person who is not
    connected with the lessor or lessee,

any of the payments due under the lease or agreement referred to in (2), expressed as monthly amounts over the period for which that payment is due, is not the same as any other such payment expressed in the same way; or

(4) either the lease is expressed to be for a period exceeding 13 years or there is, in the lease or in a separate agreement, provision for extending or renewing it or for granting a new one so that the machinery or plant could be leased for a period exceeding 13 years; or

(5) at any time the lessor or a person connected with him will or may become entitled to receive from the lessee or any other person a payment, other than of insurance moneys, which is of an amount determined before the expiry of the lease and which is referable to a value of the machinery or plant at or after that expiry (whether or not the payment relates to a disposal of the machinery or plant).

In applying these rules to old expenditure, this is extended to include first-year allowances.

Where a balancing or writing-down allowance has been made for expenditure incurred in providing machinery or plant and, at any time in the requisite period, an event occurs such that there is no right to that allowance, an amount equal to any such allowance which has been given previously (less any excess reliefs previously recovered under CAA 1990, s 46) is, in relation to the person to whom the machinery or plant belongs immediately before that event occurred, treated as if it were a balancing charge to be made on him for the chargeable period in which the machinery or plant is used when that event occurs. For this purpose, the allowances that have been made for expenditure on any item of machinery or plant is determined as if that item were the only item of machinery or plant to which the rules applied.

The following rule applies where:

(1) any amount is treated as if it were a balancing charge, and

(2) the person on whom such charge is to be made acquired the machinery or plant as a result of a transaction (including a series of transactions) which was between connected persons, and

(3) a first-year, balancing or writing-down allowance for expenditure on that machinery or plant has been made to any of those persons,

(except in regard to (2) above in relation to a change of partnership membership (TA 1990, s 113(2)), computation of profits and losses of partnerships involving companies (s 114(1)) company reconstructions without change of ownership (s 343(2)) or successions to trades by connected persons applied on the occasion of the transaction or transactions (CAA 1990, s 77(1)), and except with regard to a leased ship, aircraft or transport container under CAA 1990, s 39(6)–(9)). In these circumstances:

(a) the procedure for recovery of a balancing or writing-down allowance is extended so that it applies to any allowance under (3) above;

(b) any consideration paid or received on the machinery or plant's disposal between connected persons is disregarded; and

(c) if a balancing allowance or charge is made for machinery or plant, there are made such adjustments of the relief falling to be taken into account under (a) above as are just and reasonable in the circumstances.

Where under (2) above, at any time in the requisite period, an event occurs such that there is no right to that allowance, an amount equal to any such allowance which has previously been given (less any excess reliefs previously recovered under CAA 1990, s 47) is, in relation to the person to whom the machinery or plant belongs immediately before that event occurred, treated as if it were a balancing charge to be made on him for the chargeable period in which the machinery or plant is used when that event occurs.

In applying these rules to any expenditure to which the first-year allowance rules apply under one or more of CAA 1990, s 22(3B), (3C), (3CA), (3D) and (3E), they are extended to include first-year allowances. References to an event occurring such that there is no right to that allowance include one that, if the restriction of balancing and writing-down allowances were extended to include first-year allowances, there would be no such right.

4.7.7 Fixtures

A 'fixture' means machinery or plant installed or otherwise fixed in or to a building or land so that it becomes part of that building or land. 'Fixture' includes, for example, a boiler and water-filled radiators.

An 'interest in land' is defined in 4.6.1; here, except for leased machinery or plant, reference in the special rules for fixtures to a lease is to a leasehold estate (in Scotland, lease) or agreement to acquire such estate/lease. In relation to an agreement, 'grant' shall be construed accordingly. 'Relevant land' means the building or land of which a fixture becomes a part.

If an interest in land is conveyed or assigned by way of security and subject to a right of redemption, then, so long as such a right subsists, the interest held by the creditor is treated under the special rules for fixtures as held by the person having that right.

Any reference in the special rules for fixtures to a person entitled to an allowance for any capital expenditure incurred on a fixture is to a case where that person is:

(1) for any chargeable period, entitled to a first-year allowance for that expenditure; or

(2) entitled to have that expenditure taken into account in determining his qualifying expenditure for a chargeable period for

(a) an entitlement to a writing-down or balancing allowance (CAA 1990, s 24(2)),
(b) a reduced claim for a writing-down allowance (s 24(3)),
(c) a balancing charge (whether or not an allowance is made to him for that period) (s 24(5)),
and any reference to a chargeable period for which a person is so entitled is to:
(i) the chargeable period referred to in (1) or (2) above; or
(ii) any chargeable period subsequent to that in (2) above, but not later than that in which he would be required (disregarding s 24(7) (additional VAT)) to bring the fixture's disposal value into account for the purposes mentioned in (2).

References in the special rules to making a claim for an allowance for any expenditure include:

(1) making a return in which the expenditure is taken into account, as expenditure on a fixture, in determining a person's qualifying expenditure for s 24 purposes, and
(2) giving notice of any amendment of a return as provides for that expenditure to be taken into account.

Where a person who has made a return becomes aware that anything contained in that return has, after being made, become incorrect by reason of:

(1) making an election to use alternative apportionment under CAA 1990, s 59B, or
(2) operating, in his case:
    (a) s 56A(1) (restriction on duplicate allowances),
    (b) s 56B(1) (fixtures on which a former owner had an allowance), or
    (c) s 59C(3) (election to use alternative apportionment),

he must, within three months of first becoming so aware, give notice to the Revenue of the amendments that are necessitated in his return.

Where any question arises over whether any machinery or plant has become, in law, part of a building or land and it is material with respect to the tax liability (for whatever period) of two or more persons, the Special Commissioners will determine the question as if it were an appeal, except that in these circumstances all those persons are entitled to appear and be heard by, or make written representations to, the Special Commissioners.

Nothing in the special rules affects any person's entitlement to an allowance for contributions to capital expenditure (CAA 1990, s 154).

The capital allowances provisions for fixtures can be found in CAA 1990, ss 52–59C. Because of space restrictions, a detailed discussion of these rules is beyond the scope of this book, and readers are referred to these sections.

4.8 MISCELLANEOUS PROVISIONS

4.8.1 Machinery and plant on hire-purchase etc
(CAA 1990, ss 60 and 60A)

Where a person carrying on a trade incurs capital expenditure on machinery or plant under a hire-purchase or similar contract whereby he will or may become the owner of the machinery or plant on the performance of the contract, the machinery or plant is treated under the machinery and plant allowance rules as belonging to him so that he is entitled to writing-down allowances, etc under those rules. These rules do not apply where the capital expenditure was incurred on the provision of the machinery or plant for leasing under a finance lease.

4.8.2 Machinery and plant on lease
(CAA 1990 s 62)

Where machinery or plant is first let by any person otherwise than in the course of a trade, then, whether or not it is used for the purposes of a trade carried on by the lessee, the capital expenditure incurred by the lessor in providing the machinery or plant is treated under the machinery and plant allowance rules as having been incurred in providing it for the purposes of a notional trade (a 'separate pool') begun to be carried on by him, separately from any other trade which he may carry on, at the commencement of the letting.

When the lessor permanently ceases to let the machinery or plant otherwise than in the course of a trade, it is treated under the machinery and plant allowance rules as being used wholly for purposes other than those of the separate trade referred to above.

This does not apply to machinery or plant let for use in a dwelling-house.

Where an allowance falling to be made for any chargeable period as above is for expenditure on the provision of machinery or plant which for the whole or any part of that period is not used for the purposes of a trade carried on by the lessee, relief therefor by discharge or repayment of tax (relief by carry-back under CAA 1990, s 145(3)) does not apply to that allowance or, as the case may require, to a proportionate part of it. In this case TA 1988, s 403 (group relief) also does not apply.

Here, 'lease' includes an agreement for a lease where the term to be covered by the lease has begun, and any tenancy, but does not include a mortgage. 'Lessee' and other cognate expressions shall be construed accordingly.

4.8.3 Treatment of demolition costs
(CAA 1990, ss 62 and 62A)

Where any machinery or plant which is in use for the purposes of a trade is demolished, then, if the person carrying on the trade replaces the machinery or plant by other machinery or plant, the net cost to him of the demolition is treated under the machinery and plant allowance rules as expenditure incurred by him on the provision of that other machinery or plant. If he does not replace the machinery or plant, the qualifying expenditure for the chargeable period related to the demolition is treated under CAA 1990, ss 24 (writing-down allowances and balancing adjustments) and 25 (qualifying expenditure) as increased by the net cost to him of the demolition.

The net cost of such demolition is the excess of the demolition cost over any moneys received for the remains of the machinery or plant.

4.8.4 Partnership using property of a partner
(CAA 1990, s 65)

In taxing a trade carried on in partnership, the same allowances, deductions and charges are allowed or made under the machinery and plant allowance rules for machinery or plant used for the purposes of that trade but belonging to one or more of the partners. This does not apply to partnership property as would be allowed or made if the machinery or plant had belonged to all the partners and been partnership property and everything done by or to any of the partners in relation thereto had been done by or to all the partners. This does not include use under a letting by the partner(s) to their partnership or to use in consideration of making to the partner(s) in question of any payment which may be deducted in computing the profits of the trade.

4.8.5 Building alterations connected with installation of machinery or plant
(CAA 1990, s 66)

Where there is capital expenditure on alterations to an existing building incidental to the installation of machinery or plant for trade purposes, the machinery and plant allowance rules apply as if that expenditure were on the provision of that machinery or plant and as if the works representing that expenditure formed part of that machinery or plant.

4.8.6 Expenditure on thermal insulation
(CAA 1990, s 67)

If a person carrying on a trade has incurred expenditure in adding any insulation against loss of heat to any industrial building or structure (CAA 1990, s 18) occupied by him for the purposes of that trade, the machinery and plant allowance rules apply as if the expenditure were capital expenditure incurred on the provision of machinery or plant for such purposes, and as if the machinery or plant had, as a result of his incurring the expenditure, belonged to him, and as if the disposal value of the machinery or plant were nil.

Where the letting of an industrial building or structure by any person is deemed, as a Schedule A business, to be in the course of a trade, the above rule applies as if that person occupied that building or structure for the purpose of that trade throughout the period for which it is let by him.

4.8.7 Computer software
(CAA 1990, s 67A)

If a person carrying on a trade incurs capital expenditure in acquiring for trade purposes a right to use or otherwise deal with computer software, then, under the machinery and plant allowance rules:

(1) the right and the software to which it relates is treated as machinery or plant;
(2) that machinery or plant is treated as provided for trade purposes; and
(3) so long as he is entitled to the right, that machinery or plant is treated as belonging to him.

In any case where:

(1) a person carrying on a trade incurs capital expenditure on the provision of computer software for trade purposes, and
(2) in consequence of his incurring that expenditure, the computer software belongs to him, but
(3) the computer software does not constitute machinery or plant,

then under the machinery and plant allowance rules the computer software is treated as machinery or plant.

4.8.8 Exclusion of certain expenditure relating to films, tapes and discs
(CAA 1990, s 68)

Expenditure incurred on the production or acquisition of a film, tape or disc is regarded as expenditure of a revenue nature, subject to any election as described below. Here, any reference to a film, tape or disc is to the master negative, master tape or master audio disc of a film (F(No 2)A 1992, s 43), including any rights in the film (or its soundtrack) that are held or acquired with the master negative, tape or audio disc.

In computing the profits or gains accruing to any person from a trade or business which consists of or includes the exploitation of a film, tape or disc, expenditure of a revenue nature (whether as above or otherwise) which is incurred on its production or acquisition is allocated to relevant periods as below. Here 'relevant period' means a period for which the trade or business accounts are made up.

The amount of expenditure which is allocated to any relevant period is such as is just and reasonable, having regard to:

(1) the amount of that expenditure which remains unallocated at the beginning of that period;
(2) the proportion which the estimated value of the film, tape or disc which is realised in that period (whether by way of income or otherwise) bears to the aggregate of the value so realised and its estimated remaining value at the end of that period; and
(3) the need to bring the whole of the expenditure into account over the time during which the value of the film, tape or disc is expected to be realised.

In addition, if a claim is made, there is also allocated to that period so much of the unallocated expenditure as is specified in the claim and does not exceed the difference between the amount allocated to that period as above, and the value of the film, tape or disc which is realised in that period (whether by way of income or otherwise). 'The unallocated expenditure' for any relevant period is that expenditure which is not allocated to that period, and which has not been allocated to any earlier relevant period.

To the extent that a deduction has been made for any expenditure for a relevant period for production or acquisition expenditure (F(No 2)A 1992, s 42), no allocation of that expenditure can also be made under the above rules.

The rules do not apply to the profits of a trade in which the film, tape or disc constitutes trading stock, as defined in TA 1990, s 100(2).

Sums received from the disposal of the film, tape or disc are regarded as receipts of a revenue nature (if they would not be so regarded otherwise), and include:

(1) sums received from the disposal of any interest or right in or over the film, tape or disc, including an interest or right created by the disposal; and
(2) insurance or compensation moneys and other moneys of a like nature which are derived from the film, tape or disc.

These rules do not apply to expenditure in relation to which an election is made and which is incurred by a person who carries on a trade or business which consists of or includes the exploitation of films, tapes or discs; and on the production or acquisition of a film, tape or disc which is certified as a qualifying film, tape or disc and the value of which is expected to be realisable over a period of not less than two years.

An election may not be made for expenditure on a film, tape or disc if a claim has been made for any preliminary expenditure (F(No 2)A 1992, s 41) or for production or acquisition expenditure (s 42).

4.8.9 Expenditure on fire safety
(CAA 1990, s 69)

Machinery and plant allowances are given for expenditure by a trader in taking steps specified in a notice served on him by the fire authority under the Fire Precautions Act 1971, s 5(4) for premises used by him for trade purposes, and for which no other deduction could be made in computing the profits arising from it.

Allowances are also given for expenditure in taking, for any premises used for trade purposes, steps specified by the fire authority on an application for a fire certificate under the Fire Precautions Act 1971 for those premises, as steps that would have to be taken in order to satisfy the authority as required in s 5(4), being steps which might have been, but were not, specified in a notice thereunder. This also applies to steps which, as a result of making an order under s 10 of the 1971 Act prohibiting or restricting the use of the premises, had to be taken to enable the premises to be used without contravention of the order.

4.8.10 Expenditure on safety at sports grounds
(CAA 1990, s 70)

Machinery and plant allowances are given for expenditure on safety at sports grounds used for trade purposes or for any regulated stand at a sports ground so used being expenditure on steps necessary for compliance with the terms and conditions of a safety certificate which has been issued. Relief is also available for expenditure on steps specified by the local authority for the area in which the sports ground is situated, being steps the taking of which would be taken into account by them in deciding what terms and conditions to include in a safety certificate to be issued for the sports ground or stand or lead to the amendment or replacement of a safety certificate issued for it.

The expenditure is specified in the Safety of Sports Grounds Act 1975.

4.8.11 Security
(CAA 1990, ss 71 and 72)

The machinery and plant allowance rules are applied where:

(1) an individual, or a partnership of individuals, carries on a trade, profession or vocation;
(2) expenditure is incurred by the individual or partnership in connection with the provision for or use by the individual, or any of the individuals, of a security asset;
(3) no sum relating to the expenditure could be deducted in computing the profits of the trade, profession or vocation under Schedule D Case I or II; and

(4) apart from this rule, neither of CAA 1990, s 24(1)(a) nor (b) (or both) would apply.

This only applies if the asset is provided or used to meet a 'special' threat to the individual's personal physical security, and arises wholly or mainly by virtue of the particular trade, profession or vocation concerned. Furthermore, the person incurring the expenditure must have, as his sole object in doing so, the meeting of that threat, and must intend that the asset is to be used solely to improve personal physical security.

Where, apart from the absence of an intention that the asset is to be used solely to improve personal physical security, the above rule would apply, and the person incurring the expenditure intends the asset to be used partly to improve personal physical security, the rule is nevertheless applied, but only so as to treat the appropriate proportion of such expenditure as capital so incurred. The 'appropriate proportion' is such proportion of that expenditure as is attributable to the intention of the person incurring it that the asset is to be used to improve personal physical security.

A security asset is an asset which improves personal security, but this does not apply to cars, ships or an aircraft, nor to a dwelling or grounds appurtenant to a dwelling. However, an asset includes equipment and structures (eg a wall).

If the person incurring the expenditure intends the asset to be used solely to improve personal physical security, but there is another use which is incidental to improving it, that other use is ignored. The fact that an asset improves the personal physical security of any member of an individual's family or household, as well as that of the individual, does not disapply the relief.

It is immaterial whether the asset becomes affixed to land (whether constituting a dwelling or otherwise).

4.9 AGRICULTURAL BUILDINGS ETC

4.9.1 Interpretation
(CAA 1990, s 133)

Under the agricultural buildings allowance the following definitions apply:

- 'agricultural land': land, houses or other buildings in the UK occupied wholly or mainly for the purposes of husbandry;
- 'agricultural income': income chargeable under Schedule A in respect of agricultural land or under Schedule D in respect of farming or market gardening in the UK;
- 'husbandry': any method of intensive rearing of livestock or fish on a commercial basis for human consumption;

- 'expenditure under an existing contract': under the agricultural buildings allowance rules, expenditure consisting of the payment of sums under a contract entered into before 14 March 1984 by the person incurring the expenditure.

Any reference in agricultural buildings allowance rules to a writing-down allowance is to an allowance under CAA 1990, s 123 (see 4.9.2). But any reference to expenditure incurred on the construction of a building does not include any expenditure incurred on the acquisition of, or of rights in or over, any land.

The sum paid on the sale of the relevant interest in, or the receipt of, insurance, salvage or compensation moneys payable for, a building, fence or other works is deemed to be reduced by an amount equal to so much of it as, on a just apportionment, is attributable to assets representing expenditure other than in respect of which an allowance can be made under the agricultural buildings allowance rules.

Any transfer of the relevant interest (in relation to any s 123 expenditure) otherwise than by way of sale is treated as a sale of the interest for a price other than that which it would have fetched on the open market. If CAA 1990, s 157 would not otherwise have effect in relation to a transfer treated as a sale, that section applies in relation to it as if it were a sale between connected persons (s 157(1)(a)).

4.9.2 Allowances for expenditure incurred after 31 March 1986
(CAA 1990, s 123)

If a person having a major interest in any agricultural land has incurred or incurs any capital expenditure on the construction of farmhouses, farm buildings, cottages, fences or other works, writing-down allowances of an aggregate amount equal to that expenditure are made to him during a 25-year period beginning on the first day of the chargeable period related to the incurring of the expenditure.

Growers' glasshouses, with certain exceptions, qualify for allowance under the agricultural buildings allowances rules. Capital expenditure on construction includes improvements, non-allowable repairs, demolition costs preliminary to replacing a building and architects' fees. The Revenue has stated that 'works' include drainage and sewerage works, water and electricity installations, walls, shelter belts of trees, glasshouses on market garden land and the reclamation of former agricultural land. Farm shops may qualify for agricultural buildings allowance.

4.9.3 Expenditure qualifying for allowances
(CAA 1990, s 124)

No expenditure is taken into account for writing-down allowance purposes unless it is incurred for husbandry on the agricultural land in question, and where:

(1) the expenditure is on a farmhouse, one-third only of the expenditure is taken into account or, if the farmhouse accommodation and amenities are out of due relation to the nature and extent of the farm, such proportion not greater than one-third as may be just,
(2) expenditure is incurred on any asset other than a farmhouse to serve partly husbandry and partly other purposes, such apportionment of the expenditure is made for writing-down allowances as may be just.

In any case where:

(a) capital expenditure is incurred on the construction of any building, fence or other works, but
(b) when the building, fence or other works come to be used they are not used for husbandry,

the expenditure is left out of account for writing-down allowances and, accordingly, any writing-down allowance made for s 123 expenditure is withdrawn.

4.9.4 Initial allowances: contracts entered into between October 1992 and November 1993
(CAA 1990, ss 124A and 124B)

If a person having a major interest in any agricultural land incurs any expenditure to which this rule applies, an initial allowance equal to 20% of the amount of that expenditure is made to him for the chargeable period related to the incurring of the expenditure. This rule applies to any s 123 capital expenditure incurred under a contract which is:

(1) entered into either:
    (a) from 1 November 1992 to 31 October 1993, or
    (b) to secure that obligations under a contract entered into in that period are complied with; but
(2) not entered into to secure that obligations under a contract entered into before the beginning of that period are complied with.

No s 123 expenditure is taken into account for any initial allowance purposes unless it is incurred for husbandry on that agricultural land. Likewise, no initial allowance is made for s 123 expenditure unless the building, fence or other works is or is to be first used for husbandry before 1 December 1995. The apportionment rules for expenditure incurred on a farmhouse or any asset (other than a farmhouse) which is to serve partly husbandry and partly other purposes are the same as for 4.9.3. In a case where:

(1) any expenditure is incurred on the construction of any building, fence or other works, and
(2) either:
    (a) when those works come to be used they are not used for husbandry, or
    (b) they have not come to be so used by the end of 31 December 1994,

the expenditure is left out of account for initial allowances purposes and, accordingly, any initial allowance made for the expenditure is withdrawn.

A person making a claim may require the initial allowance to be reduced to a specified amount.

Where an initial allowance is made for any chargeable period for expenditure on the construction of a building, fence or other works, a writing-down allowance for that expenditure is made for the same chargeable period only if such works have come to be used for husbandry before the end of that period.

4.9.5 Meaning of 'major interest' and 'the relevant interest'
(CAA 1990, s 125)

In the agricultural buildings allowance rules, a 'major interest' in land means:

(1) the fee simple estate in the land or an agreement to acquire that estate;
(2) in Scotland, the estate or interest of the proprietor of the *dominium utile* (or, for property other than feudal property, of the owner) and any agreement to acquire such an estate or interest; and
(3) a lease.

'The relevant interest' means, in relation to any capital expenditure on the construction of farmhouses, farm buildings, cottages, fences or other works, the major interest in the agricultural land concerned to which the person who incurred the expenditure was entitled when he incurred it.

Where, when he incurs capital expenditure on construction, a person is entitled to two or more major interests in the agricultural land concerned, and one of those interests is one which is in reversion on all the others, that is the relevant interest.

A major interest does not cease to be the relevant interest for agricultural buildings allowance rules purposes by reason of the creation of any lease (or other interest) to which the interest is subject. Where the relevant interest is a lease which is extinguished:

(1) by reason of its surrender, or
(2) on the person entitled to it acquiring the reversionary interest

then, unless a new lease of that land is granted to take effect on the former lease's extinguishment, the interest into which that lease merges becomes the relevant interest.

4.9.6 Transfers of relevant interest
(CAA 1990, s 126)

In any case where:

(1) if the former owner continued to be the owner of the relevant interest in any land, he would be entitled to an allowance under the agricultural buildings allowance rules for any expenditure, and
(2) the new owner acquires the relevant interest in the whole or part of that land (whether by transfer, by operation of law or otherwise),

the former owner is not entitled to an allowance for any chargeable period of his after that related to the acquisition and the new owner is entitled to allowances for the chargeable period of his related to the acquisition and for subsequent chargeable periods falling within the writing-down period. If, in such a case, the date of acquisition occurs during a chargeable period of the former owner, he is entitled:

(a) to the whole of any initial allowance for the chargeable period related to the acquisition; but
(b) only to an appropriate proportion of any writing-down allowance for the chargeable period so related.

Similarly, if the acquisition date occurs during a chargeable period of the new owner, he is entitled only to an appropriate proportion of any writing-down allowance for the chargeable period (of his) related to the acquisition.

Where the new owner acquires the relevant interest in part only of the land, the above applies to so much only of the allowance as is properly referable to that part of the land as if it were a separate allowance.

The matter of a major lease affected by the creation of a lease and the extinguishment of a lease is as listed under 4.9.5. In this event, if the person who owns the interest into which the lease is merged is not the same as the person who owned the lease, the relevant interest is treated as acquired by the owner of the interest into which the lease is merged.

Where the relevant interest is a lease which comes to an end and the merger does not apply, then:

(1) if a new lease is granted to a person who makes any payment to the out-going lessee for assets representing the expenditure, the new lease is treated as the same interest as the former lease and, accordingly, the relevant interest is treated as acquired by the incoming lessee; and
(2) if a new lease is granted to the person who was the lessee under the former lease, the new lease is treated as the same interest as the former lease; and

(3) in any other case, the former lease and the interest of the person who was the landlord under it is treated as the same interest and, accordingly, the relevant interest is treated as acquired by that person.

If the total allowances (including any initial allowance) which otherwise would fall to be made for any expenditure during the writing-down period appropriate to it would be less than the amount of that expenditure, then, for the chargeable period in which that writing-down period ends, the allowance in respect of that expenditure is increased to such amount as will secure that the total of the allowances equals the amount of that expenditure.

4.9.7 Buildings etc bought unused
(CAA 1990, s 127)

This rule applies where any capital expenditure is incurred on construction works (as above) and, before such works come to be used, the relevant interest is sold. Where this rule applies:

(1) the expenditure is left out of account for agricultural buildings allowance rules purposes and, accordingly, any writing-down allowance made for the expenditure is withdrawn;
(2) CAA 1990, s 126 (transfers of relevant interest) does not apply; and
(3) the person who buys the relevant interest is treated as having incurred, on the date when the purchase price becomes payable, the capital expenditure on construction works. This expenditure is whichever is the lesser of:
   (a) the net price paid by the person for the purchase of the relevant interest; and
   (b) the capital expenditure on construction works.

The capital expenditure on construction works includes neither expenditure which, being on a farmhouse or assets only partially used, is disregarded for writing-down allowance purposes (CAA 1990, s 124(1)); nor expenditure some or all of which is expenditure under contracts entered into between 1 November 1992 and 31 October 1993 (s 124A). Accordingly, any expenditure which is treated as incurred in the acquisition of the relevant interest is treated as incurred on a farmhouse or partially used assets.

Where the relevant interest is sold more than once in circumstances where any capital expenditure is incurred on construction works and, before works come to be used, the relevant interest is sold, the above rules apply only to the last of those sales.

4.9.8 Purchases of buildings and structures: cases involving initial allowances
(CAA 1990, s 127A)

This rule applies where:

(1) there is capital expenditure on construction works ('the actual expenditure') which is not expenditure which is disregarded for writing-down allowance purposes under CAA 1990, s 124(1) (see 4.9.7);

(2) some or all of the actual expenditure is expenditure under contracts entered into between 1 November 1992 and 31 October 1993 (s 124A), or would be such expenditure if it were capital expenditure; and

(3) before the works come to be used, the relevant interest is sold.

Where the relevant interest is sold under a contract entered into from 1 November 1992 to 31 October 1993 by a person who:

(a) carries on a trade which consists, in whole or in part, in the construction of buildings or structures with a view to their sale; and

(b) has been entitled to that interest since before 1 November 1992, CAA 1990, s 124A(2), which provides the expenditure in the above period is eligible for a 20% initial allowance,

any capital expenditure on construction works incurred under a contract entered into either before 1 November 1993 or for the purpose of securing that obligations under a contract entered into before that date are complied with. Where this rule applies

(1) the actual expenditure is left out of account and, accordingly, any initial or writing-down allowance made for the actual expenditure is withdrawn; and

(2) CAA 1990, s 126 (transfers of the relevant interest) does not apply; and

(3) the person who buys the relevant interest is treated as having incurred, on the date the purchase price becomes payable, capital expenditure on construction works ('the deemed expenditure'); and

(4) the deemed expenditure is treated as incurred for husbandry on that agricultural land.

The deemed expenditure is whichever is the lesser of the net price paid for the purchase of the relevant interest and the actual expenditure, and is regarded as comprising 'a section 124A element' (expenditure from 1 November 1992 to 31 October 1993) and a residual element. The section 124A element is calculated in accordance with the formula:

$$A \times \frac{B}{C}$$

where

A = the deemed expenditure;
B = so much of the actual expenditure as is expenditure from 1 November 1992 to 31 October 1993 or that would be such expenditure if it were capital expenditure; and
C = the actual expenditure.

The residual element of the deemed expenditure is so much (if any) of the deemed expenditure as does not comprise the section 124A element.

Notwithstanding that the person who buys the relevant interest is treated as having incurred the deemed expenditure:

(1) the section 124A element is treated for the purpose only of determining entitlement to allowances as expenditure from 1 November 1992 to 31 October 1993; and
(2) the residual element is treated for that purpose as expenditure which is not such expenditure.

Where the relevant interest is sold more than once before the works are used, the above has effect only in relation to the last of those sales.

4.9.9 Balancing allowances and charges
(CAA 1990, s 129)

If, in respect of any capital expenditure on construction works, a balancing event occurs in a chargeable period and, otherwise, a person would be entitled to an allowance under the agricultural buildings allowance rules for that expenditure for the chargeable period related to that event, no such allowance is made. However, a balancing allowance or balancing charge is, in the circumstances mentioned below, made for that period to or on the person entitled to the relevant interest immediately before that event occurs.

In relation to any expenditure, the amount of any balancing allowance or charge is determined in accordance with the following provisions by reference to:

(1) the residue of that expenditure (ie the amount of that expenditure falling to be taken into account for any allowances less the aggregate of any such allowances made for it (whether or not to the person to or on whom the allowance or charge is to be made)); and
(2) any sale, insurance, salvage or compensation moneys related to the event which gives rise to the balancing allowance or balancing charge.

If s 124(1) applies (see 4.9.7), and only a portion of any expenditure falls to be taken into account for allowances, any reference below to sale, insurance, salvage or compensation moneys is a reference only to the like portion of those moneys.

Where there are no such moneys, or where the residue of the expenditure immediately before the balancing event exceeds those moneys, a balancing allowance is made of an amount equal to that residue or to the excess of it over those moneys. If such moneys exceed the residue immediately before the event, a balancing charge shall be made on an amount equal to that excess.

In no case can the amount on which a balancing charge is made on any person exceed that of the allowances made to him for the expenditure before the balancing event. If a balancing event relates to:

(a) the acquisition of the relevant interest in part only of the land in which it subsisted at the time the expenditure was incurred, or

(b) only part of the building, fence or other works on the construction of which the expenditure was incurred,

the above rules apply to so much of the expenditure as is properly attributable to the part of the works concerned, as if it were an item of expenditure separate from the rest.

4.9.10 Balancing events
(CAA 1990, s 129)

In relation to original expenditure for which, other than balancing allowances and charges (s 128), the former owner would be entitled to an allowance, the following are balancing events under the agricultural buildings allowance rules:

(1) the acquisition of the relevant interest by the new owner (s 126); and

(2) where any works on the construction of which the expenditure was incurred is demolished, destroyed or otherwise ceases to exist as such.

Such an event is not a balancing event unless an election is made for it.

Where, during the writing-down period applicable to the original expenditure, a balancing event arises under s 126, the amount of any writing-down allowances to which the new owner is entitled for chargeable periods which end after the balancing event is determined as if:

(a) that part of the writing-down period applicable to the original expenditure which falls after the balancing event were itself the writing-down period in which the allowances were to be made; and

(b) the allowances were in respect of expenditure equal to the residue of the original expenditure (ie the amount of that expenditure falling to be taken into account for any allowances less the aggregate of any such allowances made for it (whether or not to the person to or on whom the allowance or charge is to be made) (s 128(2)(a)) immediately before the balancing event less the amount of any balancing allowance made to the former owner or, as the case may be, plus the amount on which any balancing charge was made on him by reason of the balancing event.

An election is made where the event is:

(1) the acquisition under s 126, jointly by the former owner and the new owner; and

(2) the demolition, destruction or otherwise ceasing to exist as such of any works on the construction of which the expenditure was incurred, by the former owner.

No election can be made if any person by whom that election should be made is not within the charge to UK tax; and no election may be made under s 126 if it appears that the sole or main benefit of that acquisition, or with respect to transactions of which that acquisition is one (and apart from sales between connected persons under s 157), might have been expected to accrue to any party an allowance, or a greater allowance, under the agricultural buildings allowance rules.

4.9.11 Restriction of balancing allowances on sale of buildings
(CAA 1990, s 130)

Where:

(1) the relevant interest in a building is sold subject to a subordinate interest; and

(2) a balancing allowance under s 128 would otherwise be made to the former owner by virtue of the sale; and

(3) either:
 (a) the former owner, the person to whom the relevant interest is sold and the grantee of the subordinate interest, or any two of them, are connected (TA 1988, s 839), or
 (b) it appears with respect to the sale or to the grant of the subordinate interest, or to transactions including the sale or grant, that the sole or main benefit was to obtain an allowance,

for the purposes of balancing allowances and charges, the net proceeds to the former owner of the sale:

(1) are taken to be increased by an amount equal to any premium receivable by him for the grant of the subordinate interest; and

(2) where no, or no commercial, rent is payable for the subordinate interest, are what those proceeds would have been if a commercial rent had been payable and the relevant interest had been sold in the open market (increased by any actual premium receivable by him for the grant of the subordinate interest);

but the net proceeds of sale cannot be taken to be greater than such amount as will secure that no balancing allowance is made.

Where this operates in relation to a sale to deny or reduce a balancing allowance for any expenditure, s 129(3) applies if that balancing allowance had been made or, as the case may be, had not been reduced.

In this rule:

- 'subordinate interest' means any interest in or right over the building (whether granted by the former owner or by somebody else);
- 'premium' includes any capital consideration except so much of any sum as corresponds to an amount of rent or profits falling to be computed by reference to that sum under TA 1988, s 34 (premium treated as rent or Schedule D profits);
- 'capital consideration' means consideration which consists of a capital sum or would be a capital sum if it had taken the form of a money payment;
- 'rent' includes any consideration which is not capital consideration; and
- 'commercial rent' means such rent as may reasonably be expected to have been required in respect of the subordinate interest (having regard to any premium payable for the grant of the interest) if the transaction had been at arm's length.

Where the terms on which a subordinate interest is granted are varied before the sale of the relevant interest, any capital consideration for the variation is treated as a premium for the grant of the interest. The question whether any and, if so, what rent is payable in respect of the interest is determined by reference to the terms as in force immediately before the sale.

4.9.12 Manner of making allowances and charges
(CAA 1990, s 132)

An allowance or charge to which a person is entitled or is liable under the agricultural buildings allowance rules is made in taxing that person's trade (ss 140(2) (income tax) and 144(2) (corporation tax)). In the case of an allowance or charge made to a person for a chargeable period in which he is not carrying on a trade, this applies:

(1) as if any Schedule A business carried on by that person at that time were the trade in the taxing of which the allowance or charge is to be made; or

(2) where that person is not carrying on such a business at that time, as if he were carrying on such a business and the business were the trade in the taxing of which the allowance or charge is to be made.

4.10 ALLOWANCES FOR EXPENDITURE ON DREDGING
(CAA 1990, ss 134 and 135)

A detailed account of capital allowance rules for dredging activities is beyond the scope of this book. Generally, however, the writing-down period for expenditure on dredging is 25 years or, if the expenditure was incurred before 6 November 1962, 50 years beginning with the first relevant chargeable period. Readers should refer to the legislation and/or seek specialist advice for further details on this subject.

4.11 RESEARCH AND DEVELOPMENT

4.11.1 Meaning of 'research and development'
(TA 1988, ss 837A, 837B; CAA 1990, s 139)

Research and development (R&D) comprises activities that are treated as such following normal accounting practice for the accounts of companies incorporated in a part of the UK. This ensures that normal accounting practice has the same meaning as UK GAAP (Generally Accepted Accounting Practice in the UK). Thus, the definition of 'research and development' in SSAP 13 is included in the statutory definition.

However, this can be altered by regulations made by the Treasury to exclude certain activities from the definition, and to include other activities. These regulations are made by reference to guidelines issued by the Secretary of State for Trade and Industry which clarify the definition to be imported into the legislation.

Unless otherwise expressly provided, 'oil and gas exploration and appraisal' is not included within R&D. This is because, although this exploration and appraisal is not within the accounting definition of 'research and development', it has been accepted as qualifying for scientific research allowances in the past. A new definition of such exploration and appraisal is included to allow it to qualify as R&D

Oil and gas exploration and appraisal activities are those carried out in the search for petroleum in any area, or in ascertaining the extent or characteristics of any petroleum-bearing area, or the reserves of petroleum in such an area, so as to determine whether the petroleum is suitable for commercial exploitation.

References to expenditure incurred on R&D do not include expenditure incurred in the acquisition of rights in, or arising out of, R&D, but include all expenditure incurred for the prosecution, or the provision of facilities for the prosecution, of R&D.

References to R&D related to a trade include any R&D:

(1) which may lead to or facilitate an extension of that trade; or
(2) of a medical nature which has a special relation to the welfare of workers employed in that trade.

The same expenditure cannot be taken into account for any R&D allowance purposes for more than one trade.

4.11.2 Allowances for capital expenditure
(CAA 1990, s 137)

Where a person incurs expenditure (and any additional VAT) of a capital nature on R&D:

(1) while carrying on a trade, which is related to that trade and directly undertaken by him or on his behalf, or
(2) directly undertaken by him or on his behalf, and thereafter sets up and commences a trade connected with that R&D,

a deduction equal to the whole of the expenditure is allowed in taxing the trade for the relevant chargeable period. No allowance is made for expenditure on the acquisition of, or of rights in or over, any land except in so far as, on a just apportionment, that expenditure is referable to the acquisition of, or of rights in or over, or of machinery or plant which forms part of, a building or other structure already constructed on that land.

Expenditure on the provision of a dwelling is not R&D expenditure; but where part of a building is used for R&D and part consists of a dwelling and, disregarding any additional VAT liability or rebate, the just apportionment of capital expenditure on the construction or acquisition of the dwelling is not more than one-quarter of that of the whole building, the whole building is treated as used for R&D.

The relevant chargeable period is the chargeable period in which the expenditure was incurred. If it was incurred before the trade was set up and commenced, it is the chargeable period beginning with that setting-up and commencement.

4.11.3 Allowances for revenue expenditure
(TA 1988, s 82A)

Where a person carrying on a trade incurs revenue expenditure on R&D related to that trade, and which is undertaken directly by him or on his behalf, the expenditure incurred may be deducted as an expense in computing the trade's profits for tax purposes.

4.11.4 Payments to research associations, universities etc
(CAA 1990, s 82B)

Expenditure falling into either of the following categories may be deducted as an expense in computing a trade's profits for tax purposes. These are the payment of any sum to:

(a) an approved association the object of which is to undertake scientific research related to the class of trade to which the trade belongs, or

(b) be used for such scientific research to any approved university, college research institute or other similar institution.

4.11.5 Assets ceasing to belong to traders
(CAA 1990, s 138)

The following rules apply where an asset representing allowable R&D expenditure of a capital nature incurred by the person carrying on a trade ceases to belong to him ('the relevant event'). If the relevant event occurs in or after the chargeable period for which an allowance for the expenditure (and any additional VAT) is made (CAA 1990, s 137), then:

(1) the sum by which the aggregate of the asset's disposal value and the amount of the allowance exceeds the expenditure amount, or

(2) the amount of the allowance if it is less than that sum,

are treated as a trading receipt of the trade accruing at the time of the relevant event or, if such event occurs on or after the date on which the trade is permanently discontinued, accruing immediately before the discontinuance.

If the relevant event occurs before the chargeable period for which an allowance for expenditure would be so made, that allowance is not made, but, if the asset's disposal value is less than the expenditure, a deduction equal to the difference is allowed in taxing the trade for the chargeable period in which the relevant event occurs.

In any case where:

(a) a person carrying on a trade has incurred allowable R&D expenditure of a capital nature (s 137(a) or (b)), and

(b) an additional VAT rebate relating to that expenditure is made to him at any time before the relevant event occurs in relation to the asset in question,

then, unless that rebate is brought into account to make allowances and charges under the industrial buildings or the machinery and plant allowance rules, an amount equal to the rebate is treated as a trading receipt of the trade accruing for the chargeable period related to making the rebate or, if the rebate is made on or after the date on which the trade is permanently discontinued, accruing immediately before the discontinuance.

An asset's disposal value depends on the nature of the relevant event, and

(1) if that event is the actual sale of the asset at a price not lower than that which it would have fetched in the open market, equals the proceeds of that sale;

(2) if that event is the deemed sale of the asset, equals the deemed proceeds of sale; and

(3) in any other event, equals the price which the asset would have fetched if sold in the open market.

Where an asset is destroyed, it is treated as if it had been sold immediately before its destruction. Any insurance moneys or other compensation of any description received by the person carrying on the trade in respect of the destruction, and any moneys received by him for the remains of the asset, are treated as if they were proceeds of that sale. Where this rule applies on the demolition of an asset:

(a) the cost of demolition to the person carrying on the trade is added to the expenditure represented by the asset, and

(b) if by reason of that addition, the aggregate of the asset's disposal value and the amount of the allowance is less than the amount of the expenditure represented by the asset, then, unless prior to its demolition the asset had begun to be used for purposes other than R&D related to the trade, a deduction equal to the difference is allowed in taxing the trade for the chargeable period in which the asset is treated as having been sold or for the last chargeable period before discontinuance.

No amount can be charged under this rule on any relevant event if that event gives rise to a balancing charge under the industrial buildings or the machinery and plant allowance rules.

4.11.6 Entitlement to R&D relief
(FA 2000, Sched 20, paras 1–12)

Small and medium-sized companies can deduct 150% of their qualifying R&D expenditure when computing their profits. Companies in profit reduce the cash cost of their qualifying R&D by 30% if they are taxed at the current small companies rate. Companies not in profit can take the relief up front as a cash payment by surrendering their R&D losses in return for payment of an R&D tax credit equal to 24% of the cash cost of the qualifying R&D. Companies that are carrying on R&D, but have not yet started trading for tax purposes, are also able to benefit from this measure.

There is an overriding rule that, to qualify for the relief, the company must be a small or medium-sized enterprise for the accounting period and its annualised qualifying R&D expenditure deductible in that period must not be less than £25,000.

In this context a 'small or medium-sized enterprise' is defined in European Commission Recommendation 96/280/EC of 3 April 1996 as enterprises which:

(1) have fewer than 250 employees, and
(2) have either:
    (a) an annual turnover not exceeding Euro 40m (about £25m), or
    (b) an annual balance sheet total not exceeding Euro 27m (about £17m) and

(3) are not owned as to 25% or more of the capital or the voting rights by one or more enterprises falling outside the definition in (1) and (2). This threshold may be exceeded if:

    (a) the enterprise is held by public investment corporations, venture capital companies or institutional investors, provided no control is exercised either individually or jointly, or

    (b) the capital is spread in such a way that it is not possible to determine who holds it and if the enterprise declares that it can legitimately presume that it is not owned as to 25% or more by one enterprise or jointly by several enterprises falling outside the definition in (1) and (2).

There is an overriding requirement that all of the following conditions must be satisfied for expenditure to qualify as R&D expenditure on which a company may claim R&D tax relief:

(a) the expenditure must not be of a capital nature;

(b) the expenditure must be attributable to relevant R&D undertaken directly by the company or on its behalf;

(c) the expenditure must be incurred on staffing costs, or on consumable stores, or be qualifying expenditure on subcontracted R&D;

(d) any intellectual property created as a result of the R&D to which the expenditure is attributable is, or will be, vested in the company (whether alone or with other persons);

(e) the expenditure must not be incurred by the company in carrying on activities contracted out to the company by any person; and

(f) the expenditure must not be subsidised.

'Relevant research and development', in relation to a company, means R&D related to a trade carried on by the company, or from which it is intended that a trade to be carried on by it will be derived. R&D which is 'related to a trade carried on by the company' includes R&D which may lead to or facilitate an extension of that trade, and R&D of a medical nature which has a special relation to the welfare of workers employed in that trade.

The 'staffing costs' that can qualify for R&D tax reliefs comprise the following:

(1) the emoluments paid by the company to company directors or employees, including all salaries, wages, perquisites and profits (excluding benefits in kind);

(2) the secondary Class 1 NICs paid by the company (excluding NICs on excluded benefits in kind); and

(3) the contributions paid by the company to any pension fund (TA 1988, s 231A(4)) operated for the benefit of company directors or employees.

A company's staffing costs attributable to relevant R&D are those paid to or for directors or employees directly and actively engaged in such R&D. Persons who provide purely 'support' services are not treated as directly and actively engaged in R&D. Therefore, staff peripheral to or remote from the R&D activity (eg central pay-roll, clerical, secretarial and administrative services) are excluded; however, staff directly engaged in carrying on the R&D, including ancillary staff employed in a dedicated R&D facility such as technicians, maintenance, clerical and security staff, are included.

Where a director or employee is partly engaged directly and actively in relevant R&D, the following rules apply:

(1) if the time he spends so engaged is less than 20% of his total working time, none of the staffing costs relating to him are treated as attributable to relevant R&D;

(2) if the time he spends so engaged is more than 80% of his total working time, the whole of the staffing costs relating to him are treated as attributable to relevant R&D;

(3) in any other case, an appropriate proportion of the staffing costs relating to him is treated as attributable to relevant R&D.

Expenditure on consumable stores is expenditure that would be treated as such following normal accounting practice. Such expenditure is attributable to relevant R&D if the stores are employed directly in that R&D.

'Intellectual property' means:

(1) any industrial information or techniques likely to assist in:
   (a) the manufacture or processing of goods or materials, or
   (b) the working of a mine, oil well or other source of mineral deposits or the winning of access to it, or
   (c) the carrying out of any agricultural, forestry or fishing operations;

(2) any patent, trade mark, registered design, copyright, design right or plant breeder's right, and any corresponding or similar rights under the law of a country outside the UK.

A company's expenditure is treated as subsidised in the following circumstances:

(a) if a notified state aid is or has been obtained for the whole or part of the expenditure, or any other expenditure (whenever incurred) attributable to the same R&D project – here, no expenditure on the R&D project can qualify for tax relief;

(b) to the extent that a grant or subsidy (other than a notified state aid) is obtained for the expenditure;

(c) to the extent that it is otherwise met directly or indirectly by any person other than the company.

Here, 'notified state aid' is a state aid (other than R&D tax reliefs or R&D tax credit) notified to and approved by the European Commission. Any grant towards an R&D project out of government or public funds, or from the Commission itself, would normally fall into this category. A notified state aid, grant, subsidy or payment that is not allocated purely for R&D expenditure is apportioned accordingly.

Subcontracted R&D

A company incurs expenditure on subcontracted R&D if it makes a 'sub-contractor payment' to a subcontractor for relevant R&D contracted out by the company to that subcontractor. Whether R&D tax reliefs can be claimed in such circumstances depends on whether the parties are connected under TA 1988, s 839, and whether the actual expenditure is incurred by the sub-contractor in carrying out the subcontracted R&D.

The subcontractor must have brought the whole of the subcontractor payment and all of its relevant expenditure into account in its profit or loss for a relevant period, in accordance with normal accounting principles. The amount of the company's qualifying expenditure on subcontracted R&D is the lower of the amount of the particular subcontractor payment and the subcontractor's relevant expenditure. 'Relevant expenditure' is defined here as revenue expenditure (ie not expenditure of a capital nature) which is not subsidised expenditure incurred by the subcontractor on staffing costs and consumable stores in carrying out the subcontracted work represented by the company's subcontractor payment.

A 'relevant period' is defined as a period for which the subcontractor draws up accounts ending not more than 12 months after the end of the accounting period of the company in which the company recognises the subcontractor payment as a deduction brought into account in accordance with normal accounting principles. Any necessary apportionment of expenditure of the company or the subcontractor is made on a just and reasonable basis.

A company and a subcontractor who are not connected may elect jointly for the connected persons' treatment to be applied to subcontractor payments. This election, which once made is irrevocable, must be made for all subcontractor payments paid under the same contract or other arrangement.

Where the company and subcontractor are not connected, and no election for connected persons treatment has been made, and a company makes a subcontractor payment, 65% of the subcontractor payment amount is treated as qualifying expenditure on subcontracted R&D.

4.11.7 Manner of giving effect to relief
(FA 2000, Sched 20, paras 13–20)

Where a company is entitled to R&D tax reliefs for an accounting period, is carrying on a trade in that period, and has qualifying R&D expenditure that is allowable as a deduction in computing for tax purposes the trade's profits for that period, it may (on making a claim) treat that qualifying

R&D expenditure as if it were an amount equal to 150% of the actual amount.

The rule described here applies to pre-trading qualifying R&D expenditure. It has effect where a company is entitled to R&D tax reliefs for an accounting period, and has incurred qualifying R&D expenditure in that accounting period which meets the following test. It must be shown that it is not allowable as a deduction in computing, for tax purposes, the profits of a trade that was carried on by it at the time the expenditure was incurred, but that it would have been so allowable had the company, at that time, been carrying on a trade consisting of the activities in relation to which the expenditure was incurred.

Companies that are carrying on R&D, but not as part of a taxable trade, can gain the immediate benefit of R&D tax reliefs by electing to treat 150% of the deductible qualifying R&D expenditure as if it were a trading loss of the period. The loss can then be used under the normal provisions for trading losses (eg by offset against investment income which the company may be earning on its capital). Where such an election is made for an accounting period, TA 1988, s 401 (relief for pre-trading expenditure) cannot also apply to that qualifying R&D expenditure.

A company can claim an R&D tax credit for an accounting period in which it has a 'surrenderable loss'. In this context, a company has a surrenderable loss in an accounting period in two circumstances:

(1) if it is entitled to R&D tax reliefs for that accounting period, is carrying on a trade in that accounting period, has qualifying R&D expenditure which is allowable in computing, for tax purposes, the profits of the trade for that period and has made a claim to treat the expenditure as increased to 150% of the actual amount of the expenditure, and has made a trading loss in that trade and for that period; or

(2) if it is entitled to R&D tax reliefs for an accounting period, has incurred qualifying R&D expenditure which, being incurred before the trade commenced, the company has elected to be treated as if it had incurred a trading loss in that accounting period equal to 150% of the actual amount of the expenditure.

The surrenderable loss amount for claiming an R&D tax credit is equal to the lower of so much of that trading loss as is unrelieved, or 150% of the related qualifying R&D expenditure.

The amount of a trading loss that is 'unrelieved' is the amount of that loss reduced by the following amounts:

(a) any relief that was or could have been obtained by the company making a claim under TA 1988, s 393A(1)(a) to set the loss against profits of whatever description of the same accounting period;

(b) any other relief obtained by the company for the loss, including relief under s 393A(1)(b) to set the losses against profits of an earlier accounting period;

(c) any loss surrendered under s 403(1) to group or consortium members; and

(d) amounts surrendered as group relief are also excluded.

No account is taken of any losses brought forward from earlier accounting periods under s 393(1), or carried back from later accounting periods under s 393A(1)(b), being taken into account when computing the surrenderable amount.

The amount of the R&D tax credit payable in relation to a surrenderable loss is 16% of qualifying R&D expenditure which corresponds to 24% of the corresponding R&D expenditure. It is, however, subject to a 'cap' and cannot exceed the 'total amount of the companies PAYE and NICs liabilities' for payment periods within the accounting period. The effect of this rule is to allow companies that are carrying out R&D, but which are not in profit, to receive the benefit of R&D tax reliefs earlier than would otherwise be the case.

For the above purpose the amount of the company's PAYE liabilities for a payment period is the total income tax for which the company is required to account to the Revenue for that period under the PAYE regulations, disregarding any deduction the company is authorised to make in relation to the working families' and disabled person's tax credit.

The amount of the company's Class 1 NICs is the total amount for which the company is required to account to the Revenue for that period, disregarding any deduction the company is authorised to make in relation to payments of statutory sick pay, statutory maternity pay, and working families' and disabled person's tax credit.

The amounts of PAYE and NICs taken into account are for the whole company, and are not limited to the liabilities in relation to staff directly carrying on the R&D.

The amount of loss that can be carried forward where a claim is made under TA 1988, s 393 for trading losses to be relieved against future trading profits is restricted where there is a claim for an R&D tax credit. In such a case, the company's trading loss for a period for which it claims an R&D tax credit is treated as reduced by the amount of the loss surrendered.

The amount of the loss surrendered is defined. Where the maximum amount of R&D tax credit was claimed, it is the whole of the surrenderable loss for that period. Where less than the maximum amount was claimed, it is a corresponding proportion of the surrenderable loss for that period. The 'maximum amount' is (at the time of writing) 16% of the amount of the surrenderable loss for the period.

A payment of the R&D tax credit is not treated as income of the company for any tax purpose and is exempt from tax.

The rules providing relief for R&D expenditure do not apply to expenditure incurred before 1 April 2000. Furthermore, the pre-trading rules in TA 1988, s 401 are prevented from treating expenditure made before 1 April 2000 as qualifying R&D expenditure if the trade in relation to which the R&D is carried out commences after that date.

4.12 MINERAL EXTRACTION

A detailed account of the capital allowance rules for mineral extraction activities is beyond the scope of this book. Readers should refer to the legislation and/or seek specialist advice for further details on this subject.

4.13 DWELLING HOUSES LET ON ASSURED TENANCIES

A form of capital allowances was available for expenditure incurred before 1 April 1992 on the construction of dwelling houses let under the assured tenancy scheme. A writing-down allowance of 4% (straight line) is available. The allowance, the rules of which were similar to those for industrial buildings, was only available to companies.

5

MAIN PRINCIPLES OF CAPITAL GAINS TAX

DAVID BERTRAM, CLAYFIELD PROFESSIONAL GUIDANCE LTD

5.1 BASIC OUTLINE OF CAPITAL GAINS TAX
(TA 1988, s 6; TCGA 1992, s 1)

An individual's capital gains are assessed for a tax year. The due date for payment of tax is 31 January following the tax year concerned (ie for 2000–01 payment is due on 31 January 2002). A company's capital gains are included in its 'profits' and corporation tax is charged thereon for the accounting period concerned.

5.1.1 Annual exemption
(TCGA 1992, s 3)

An individual is entitled to an annual exemption, as follows:

	£
2000–01	7,200
1999–00	7,100
1998–99	6,800
1997–98	6,500
1996–97	6,300
1995–96	6,000

A company is not entitled to an annual exemption.

5.1.2 No gain/loss on spouse transactions
(TCGA 1992, s 58)

There is no chargeable gain on any assets transferred from one spouse to the other, whether by gift or sale. The asset is treated as passing across on a no gain/no loss basis, with the recipient acquiring it at his spouse's cost plus indexation up to 5 April 1998 (see 5.5.5 on indexation relief). The only exception to this rule is where the couple is separated on a permanent basis.

5.1.3 Losses
(TCGA 1992, ss 16 and 18)

Capital losses are, broadly, computed in the same way as capital gains. The normal rule is that capital losses cannot be off-set against a person's income but may be carried forward against capital gains of future years. However, losses arising from transactions involving connected persons may only be set against gains arising from transactions with the same person. Brought forward losses do not need to be set against gains which are covered by the annual exemption. Current year losses must be set against capital gains before using the annual exemption.

Save that companies are not entitled to an annual exemption, losses suffered by companies are dealt with in a similar way.

An individual can obtain relief for trading losses, insofar as not relieved against other income sources for the tax year, against capital gains of that tax year or against income and capital gains of the previous tax year.

5.1.4 Rate of tax for individuals
(TCGA 1992, s 4)

Once an individual's gains for a tax year have been computed (net of any losses), the annual exemption is deducted. The balance is then added to the individual's taxable income and the CGT is normally ascertained by working out the additional income tax which would be payable if the capital gains had been taxable income.

5.1.5 Rate of tax for companies
(TCGA 1992, ss 6, 8, 13 and 13AA)

A company's chargeable gains are taxed as part of its overall profits, with no differentiation from its income. The full rate of corporation tax on its gains for the financial year 2000–01 (beginning on 1 April 2000) is 30% (full rate) or 20% (small companies rate). There is a 10% starting rate for very small companies. See further at 20.2.

5.2 WHO IS SUBJECT TO CAPITAL GAINS TAX?
(TCGA 1992, ss 2, 10, 10A and 12)

An individual's residence and domicile status may have a crucial bearing on his liability to CGT. He can be liable only if he is resident or ordinarily resident for the year in which relevant disposals take place. Residence and ordinary residence are determined in the same way as for income tax. Where a non-resident and non-ordinarily resident person has been carrying on a trade or profession through a branch or agency in the UK, CGT may be charged on a disposal of assets used in that branch despite the fact that the person would normally be outside the charge on capital gains.

An individual who is resident (or ordinarily resident) and domiciled in the UK is subject to CGT on gains realised both in this country and abroad. By contrast an individual who is not domiciled in the UK is charged tax on gains from foreign assets only if the proceeds are brought into this country (or, as the legislation puts it, the gains are 'remitted' to the UK).

For a fuller discussion of residence and domicile, see *Allied Dunbar Tax Handbook 2000–01*, Chapters 21 and 22.

A company is subject to tax on its capital gains if it is resident here or if the gains arise from disposals of assets used in a UK branch or agency (see 20.1.1).

5.3 WHAT ASSETS ARE CHARGEABLE ASSETS?

5.3.1 Assets within scope of CGT
(TCGA 1992, s 21)

Gains on virtually all types of assets are potentially subject to CGT, subject to certain stated exceptions under TCGA 1992, s 21(1) including:

(a) options, debts and incorporeal property generally, and
(b) any currency other than sterling, and
(c) any form of property created by the person disposing of it, or otherwise coming to be owned without being acquired.

Examples of 'assets' in this context include:

(1) An employer's rights under a contract of service with an employee as in *O'Brien v Benson's Hosiery (Holdings) Ltd* (1979) 53 TC 241 in which the employee made a payment to the employer to secure his release from his employment contract.
(2) Compensation received by a UK resident for property confiscated in 1940 when Latvia was annexed by the USSR. Property which she had held in her own right was categorised under TCGA 1992, s 22(1)(a) (capital sums received by way of compensation for any kind of damage or injury to assets or for the loss, destruction or dissipation of assets or for any depreciation or risk of depreciation of an asset). Property which had been held by her late mother was categorised under s 21(1)(a) (options, debts and incorporeal property generally) (see *Davenport v Chilver* (1983) 57 TC 661).
(3) A payment for an unfettered right to pursue trading activities was, in effect, a capital sum derived from an asset, namely goodwill (*Kirby v Thorn EMI plc* (1987) 60 TC 519).
(4) An arrangement for the future allotment of shares against an advance

payment was held to be a disposal of incorporeal rights in *Cleveley's Investment Trust Co v CIR (No 1)* (1971) 47 TC 300.

(5) A right to receive deferred consideration on an earlier sale (*Marren v Ingles* (1980) 54 TC 76; *Marson v Marriage* (1980) 54 TC 54).

In some circumstances, transactions have been held to comprise the disposal of two or more assets, as follows:

(a) On the disposal of a business, a lease of a shop and the goodwill of the business were separate assets (*Butler v Evans* (1980) 53 TC 558).

(b) The disposal of a milk quota under EU regulations is separate from the land to which it relates (*Cottle v Coldicott* (1995) SpC 40, following *R v Ministry of Agriculture Fisheries and Food, ex p Bostock* (1994) 1 ECR 955).

(c) The sale of land and the grant of a mortgage in a case where part of the purchase consideration was left outstanding by way of loan from the vendor to the purchaser were separate transactions so that the disposal proceeds for the sale of the land was the gross consideration passing (ie the cash paid plus the amount left on loan) and a set-off producing a lower (net) figure was not possible (*Coren v Keithley* (1972) 48 TC 370).

(d) The sale of shares and the accompanying waiver of a debt were separate transactions (*EV Booth (Holdings) Ltd v Buckwell* (1980) 53 TC 425)

In some cases it is necessary to apportion consideration between various elements in a transaction (*Neely v Rourke* [1988] STC 216).

The asset does not have to be transferable or capable of being assigned. The term 'any form of property' is all embracing. For example, the courts have held that CGT was due on an employer's right to compensation from an employee who wished to be released from his service agreement. In another case, the right to compensation in respect of property expropriated by the USSR in 1940 was held to be a form of property and therefore an asset for CGT purposes. Similarly, the High Court held in *Zim Properties Ltd v Procter* [1985] STC 90 that the right to bring an action before the courts constitutes an asset which can be turned to account by the potential litigant negotiating a compromise and receiving a lump sum.

The conclusion therefore is that virtually all forms of property which can yield a capital sum are subject to CGT unless they are specifically exempt.

5.3.2 What assets are specifically exempt?

The following are the main categories of exempt assets which are relevant in the context of this book.

(1) Chattels which are wasting assets (TCGA 1992, s 44).

(2) Chattels where the sale consideration is less than £6,000 (TCGA 1992, s 262). There may be some marginal relief where more than £6,000 is received.

(3) Foreign currency acquired for personal expenditure outside the UK (TCGA 1992, s 269). This includes money spent on the purchase or maintenance of any property situated outside the UK.

(4) Compensation or damages for wrong or injury suffered in a profession or vocation (TCGA 1992, s 51).

(5) Debts (TCGA 1992, s 251).

(6) Gilt-edged securities and qualifying corporate bonds and any options to acquire or dispose of such investments (TCGA 1992, s 115). A qualifying corporate bond is a loan stock which is not convertible and is not a deep discount or a deep gain security.

(7) Shares held by an individual in ISAs and personal equity plans (TCGA 1992, s 151).

(8) Shares issued under the Enterprise Investment Scheme provided the EIS relief has not been withdrawn (FA 1994, s 135 and Sched 14).

(9) Shares held by an individual in a Venture Capital Trust (TA 1988, s 842 and Sched 28).

(10) Sale by an individual of his principal private residence.

(11) Motor cars (unless not suitable or commonly used for the carriage of passengers) (TCGA 1992, s 263). Also veteran and vintage cars.

(12) Woodlands ((TCGA 1992, s 250).

(13) Gifts to charities (TCGA 1992, s 257).

No gain is assessable where an asset is exempt. Unfortunately, it follows that no relief is normally given for losses (losses on a disposal of shares in an EIS are an exception to this general rule).

5.4 WHICH TYPES OF TRANSACTION MAY PRODUCE A CHARGEABLE GAIN?

The most obvious type of disposal is an outright sale with immediate settlement, but there are many other transactions which count as a disposal for CGT purposes, as discussed in 5.4.1–5.4.8 below. The liability to CGT is determined by the tax year or accounting period in which the date of disposal falls.

5.4.1 Outright sale
(TCGA 1992, s 28)

The date of disposal is the day on which the unconditional contract is entered into, which may, of course, be different from the date that the property is conveyed or transferred, or when the vendor receives payment (s 28(1)). Where payment is made by instalments, it may be possible to pay CGT over a period of up to eight years if the Revenue is satisfied that hardship would otherwise result (TCGA 1992, s 280).

The Revenue operates a concession where a purchaser defaults and the vendor takes back the asset in satisfaction of the sums due to him (see ESC D18). The disposal is effectively treated as if it has never happened.

5.4.2 Conditional sale

A conditional sale is a contract which does not take effect until a stated condition is satisfied or an option is exercised (s 28(2)).

Example – Conditional sale

A agrees to purchase *B*'s shares in XYZ Ltd provided the local authority grants planning permission over land owned by XYZ Ltd by April 2001. Under this type of agreement, *B* remains the legal owner of his shares until the condition is satisfied. If the local authority does not in fact grant planning permission, *A* is under no obligation to buy *B*'s shares.

The date of disposal under such contracts is the day that the condition is satisfied and the contract becomes unconditional, eg in this example, the date planning permission is granted.

5.4.3 Exercise of an option
(TCGA 1992, s 144)

A 'call' option is a legally binding agreement between the owner of an asset and a third party under which the owner agrees to sell the asset if the other party decides to exercise his option. The purchase price payable upon the exercise of the option is normally fixed at the outset; this constitutes one of the terms of the option. A 'put' option is one where the other party agrees to buy the asset if the owner decides to exercise an option requiring him to do so.

The grant of either type of option does not constitute a disposal of the asset concerned. This happens only when the option is exercised; the day on which this happens is the date of disposal. In some cases, payment is made for the option to be granted. This is treated as a disposal of a separate asset unless the option is subsequently exercised.

5.4.4 Exchange of property

An agreement to exchange an asset for another is a disposal of the old asset and an acquisition of the new asset. If there is any cash adjustment, this must also be brought into account. For example, if *A* exchanges his holding in EF plc for *B*'s shareholding in GH plc, *A* is treated as if he has disposed of the EF plc shares for the market value of the GH plc shares at the time of the exchange. This type of transaction commonly occurs where an individual transfers portfolio investments to a unit trust in return for units.

Exception for certain share exchanges
(TCGA 1992, s 136–138)

There is an important exception to the rule that an exchange constitutes a disposal which may apply where a shareholder takes securities offered to him on a company takeover. Provided the conditions set out below are satisfied, the exchange does not count as a disposal and the securities issued by the acquiring company are deemed to have been derived from the original shares, with the shareholder carrying forward his original acquisition value.

The conditions to be satisfied are that the share exchange is a bona fide commercial transaction and not part of a tax avoidance scheme and either:

(a) the acquiring company secures 25% or more of the target company's ordinary share capital; or
(b) the offer which is made would result in the offeror obtaining control of the target company, if it were to be accepted.

It is possible to obtain advance clearance from the Revenue that the requirements of s 136 are satisfied. A written application should be sent to the Revenue's specialist division and the Revenue has 30 days in which to give clearance or come back for further information. The Revenue, once clearance has been given, cannot subsequently go back on this unless it can show that the information supplied by the taxpayer was incorrect or incomplete.

Example – Exchange of shares on company takeover

B holds 1,000 shares in XYZ plc which he acquired in 1985 for £9,000. Another company, ABC plc, makes a take-over bid and offers all XYZ shareholders a share exchange whereby they receive one ABC share (worth £30 each) for every two XYZ shares that they own. The offer document confirms that agreement has been obtained from the Revenue that TCGA 1992, s 136 applies.

If *B* accepts, he will receive 500 ABC shares worth £15,000. However, he will be deemed to have acquired them in 1985 for £9,000. No disposal is deemed to have occurred on the share exchange.

Professional advice should be taken if the securities offered by way of the share exchange include qualifying corporate bonds (see 5.3.2).

5.4.5 Compulsory acquisition of assets
(TCGA 1992, ss 22 and 246)

The transfer of land to, for example, a local authority exercising its compulsory purchase powers is a disposal for CGT purposes. In some cases, once the compulsory purchase order has been served, contracts are drawn up and the land is transferred under the contract. In such a case, the rules in relation to outright sales and conditional sales apply.

Where the compulsory purchase order is disputed, the date of disposal is the date on which compensation for the acquisition is agreed or otherwise determined. Variations on appeal are disregarded for this purpose.

5.4.6 Sums payable as compensation or proceeds under an insurance policy
(TCGA 1992, s 22)

An asset (for example a building) may be destroyed or damaged and a capital sum is received as compensation for this. In such cases, the asset is deemed to have been disposed of at the date that the capital sum is received. Similarly, where a capital sum is received from an insurance policy following such damage the receipt of the insurance money is treated as constituting a disposal.

5.4.7 Gifts
(TCGA 1992, ss 17, 165 and 260)

A gift is treated as a disposal at market value (except where it is from one spouse to the other). It was once possible for assets to be transferred at cost, but this general form of hold-over relief was abolished by FA 1989. In some cases the capital gains may still be held over, such as where the gift involves business property or is a chargeable transfer for IHT purposes (see 23.10 on lifetime gifts to discretionary trusts).

A gift is normally a 'bargain not at arm's length' which is treated in the same way as a transaction between connected persons.

5.4.8 Asset destroyed or becoming of negligible value
(TCGA 1992, s 24)

The total destruction or entire loss of an asset constitutes a disposal. This could be physical destruction (eg by fire) or legal/financial destruction (eg bankruptcy or winding-up). The legislation also permits a person to elect that he should be treated as having disposed of an asset which has become of negligible value. Normally, a capital loss arises on such an occasion.

'Negligible value' is interpreted by the Revenue as meaning considerably less than small. For example, the Revenue will only agree that shares, loan stock and other securities are of negligible value on being satisfied that the owner is unlikely to recover anything other than a nominal amount on the liquidation of the company. The mere fact that shares have been suspended or de-listed by the Stock Exchange is not regarded as sufficient.

The legislation provides that a disposal is deemed to take place in the year during which the inspector agrees that the asset has become of negligible value. A claim takes effect up to two tax years prior to the claim provided that the asset was of negligible value in the prior year.

5.5 COMPUTATION OF CAPITAL GAINS

5.5.1 Amount to be brought in as disposal value

Market value
(TGCA 1992, s 17)

The general rule is that market value must be used unless the transaction is a bargain at arm's length. In the straightforward situation where a contract is entered into with a third party on a commercial basis, the disposal proceeds are the actual sale proceeds. An individual is not penalised because he has made a bad bargain and sold an asset for less than it is really worth. However, if the bargain is not at arm's length and the individual deliberately sells the asset for an amount which is less than its true value, the legislation requires market value to be substituted. If the disposal is to a connected person such as a relative or the trustee of a family settlement or a family company, there is an automatic assumption that the bargain is not at arm's length and market value will always be substituted for the actual sale proceeds if the two amounts are different.

The two main exceptions to the above are transactions between spouses and gifts to charities and similar bodies. In both of these circumstances, the person making the disposal is deemed to sell at a figure which produces a no gain/no loss situation.

Contingent liabilities
(TCGA 1992, s 49)

There may be occasions where the contract requires part of the proceeds to be returned at some time in the future. This is known as a sale with 'contingent liabilities'. For example, suppose a vendor receives £150,000 for the disposal of a plot of land, but is under an obligation to return £60,000 in certain circumstances. Is the capital gain charged on sale proceeds of £150,000 or £90,000? In fact, TCGA 1992, s 49 provides that in these circumstances the capital gain must be computed in the first instance without any deduction for the contingent liability. However, if and when the vendor is required to refund part of the sale proceeds because the contingent liability has become an actual liability, the CGT assessment is adjusted accordingly.

Contingent consideration
(TCGA 1992, s 48)

In a similar way, it is possible that the contract may provide that additional sums may be payable if certain conditions are satisfied in the future. If it is possible to put a value on the further amount of consideration which is 'contingent' (ie which is payable only if certain conditions are satisfied) the full amount which may be received is brought into account at the date of disposal without any discount. If the conditions are not in fact satisfied, so that the further amounts are never received, an adjustment is made when that becomes clear.

The position is different where the contingent consideration cannot be ascertained at the date of disposal (this is normally the situation where the contingent consideration may vary and is not a fixed amount). Basically, the legislation requires that the market value of the right to receive the future consideration should be regarded as the disposal proceeds (*Marren v Ingles* (1980) 54 TC 76). The difference between this amount and the amount eventually received forms a *separate* CGT computation for the year in which the final amount of the actual contingent consideration is determined. The treatment of contingent consideration, especially variable contingent consideration, is complex. It normally arises in relation either to land or shares in private companies. This is an area where it is essential to take professional advice.

Adjustment for amounts charged as income or deducted from income
(TCGA 1992, ss 37 and 39)

In some cases the disposal of an asset by an individual may give rise to an income tax charge. Where this happens, the amount which is charged as income is deducted from the sale proceeds and only the balance is brought into account for CGT purposes. This commonly arises where a private company buys back its own shares from an individual or trustee shareholders and the transaction is treated as a distribution (see 20.5). Unfortunately, the Revenue does not accept that this applies where a corporate shareholder has shares bought back by the company in which it has invested.

Amounts deducted in arriving at amounts chargeable to income tax cannot also be taken into account in the computation of capital gains.

5.5.2 What costs are allowable?
(TCGA 1992, s 38)

Certain specific types of expenditure

The legislation permits a limited range of expenses to be deducted in computing capital gains and losses. TCGA 1992, s 38(1) states:

'... the sums allowable as a deduction from the consideration in the computation of the gain accruing to a person on the disposal of an asset shall be restricted to –

(a) the amount or value of the consideration, in money or money's worth, given by him or on his behalf wholly and exclusively for the acquisition of the asset, together with the incidental costs to him of the acquisition or, if the asset was not acquired by him, any expenditure wholly and exclusively incurred by him in providing the asset,

(b) the amount of any expenditure wholly and exclusively incurred on the asset by him or on his behalf for the purpose of enhancing the value of the asset, being expenditure reflected in the state or nature of the asset at the time of the disposal, and any expenditure wholly and exclusively incurred by him in establishing, preserving or defending his title to, or to a right over, the asset,

(c) the incidental costs to him of making the disposal.

Incidental costs of acquisition

These are limited to:

(1) fees, commission or remuneration paid to a surveyor, valuer, auctioneer, accountant, agent or legal adviser;
(2) transfer/conveyancing charges (including stamp duty); and
(3) advertising to find a seller.

Enhancement expenditure

The legislation permits a deduction to be claimed for expenditure incurred to enhance the value of the asset provided that such expenditure is reflected in the state or nature of the asset at the time of disposal. The latter condition excludes relief for improvements which have worn out by the time the asset is disposed of. Certain grey areas are worth mentioning:

(1) Initial expenditure by way of repairs to newly acquired property which is let may be allowable if no relief has been given in computing Schedule A income.
(2) Expenditure means money or money's worth. It does not include the value of personal labour or skill.

Incidental costs of disposals

The following expenses may be deductible:

(1) Fees, commission or remuneration for the professional services of a surveyor, valuer, auctioneer, accountant, agent or legal adviser.
(2) Transfer/conveyancing charges (including stamp duty).
(3) Advertising to find a buyer.

(4) Any other costs reasonably incurred in making any valuation or apportionment for CGT purposes, including in particular expenses reasonably incurred in ascertaining market value where this is required. Professional costs incurred in getting a valuation agreed with the Revenue are not allowable.

Part disposals
(TCGA 1992, s 42)

Where a person disposes of part of an asset, the cost is apportioned between the part disposed of and the part retained according to the formula [A ÷ (A + B)] where A is the consideration received or deemed to have been received and B is the market value of the part retained.

Example – Part disposals

B holds 1,000 shares in XYZ Ltd which cost him £10,000. The company is taken over and he receives cash of £5,000 and convertible loan stock issued by the acquiring company worth £15,000 (assume that in this particular case no capital gain arises in respect of the loan stock because it is issued on the occasion of a takeover and the necessary Revenue clearances have been obtained). B's acquisition value is apportioned as follows:

$$£10,000 \times \frac{5,000}{5,000 + 15,000} = £2,500$$

ie the proportion of acquisition value which relates to the part sold.

£7,500 is treated as the acquisition value of the part retained, ie it is taken into account in computing any gain or loss as and when the loan stock is sold.

Special rules may apply where shares are sold out of a shareholding which includes shares held on 31 March 1982 and shares acquired after that date.

Small capital receipts
(TCGA 1992, s 122)

There are occasions where the formula [A ÷ (A + B)] does not have to be used, and the amount received is simply deducted from the owner's acquisition value. The most common situation of this is where a shareholder sells his entitlement under a rights issue, normally on a nil paid basis. Provided that the amount received is small as compared with the value of the asset, the receipt can be deducted from the owner's acquisition value. 'Small' in this context is interpreted by the Revenue as an amount not exceeding 5% of the market value or £3,000, whichever is the lesser.

Capital sums applied in restoring assets
(TCGA 1992, s 23)

Under normal circumstances, an asset is regarded as having been disposed of for CGT purposes if it is lost or destroyed. However, where a capital sum is received from such an asset (eg the proceeds of an insurance policy), the owner may claim that the asset is not treated as disposed of if at least 95% of the capital sum is spent in restoring the asset.

5.5.3 Assets held at 31 March 1982
(TCGA 1992, s 35 & Scheds 2–3)

This applies only to companies, and to individuals to establish 'frozen' indexation up to 5 April 1998.

The general rule is that where assets were held at 31 March 1982, it is to be assumed that the assets were sold on that date and immediately re-acquired at their market value at that time. This is known as 'rebasing'. The original cost still applies in certain circumstances as the rebasing rule is subject to the following qualifications:

(1) Where the gain since March 1982 is smaller than that measured by reference to original cost (or vice versa), the chargeable gain is confined to that figure.
(2) Where a loss has arisen, the allowable loss is the smaller of the loss measured by reference to original cost and the loss measured by reference to the 31 March 1982 value.
(3) Where a gain arises when one has regard to original cost, but a loss arises when one takes the 31 March 1982 value (or vice versa), the position is regarded as no gain/no loss.

However, even these qualifications are ignored if a universal rebasing election has been made.

5.5.4 Other acquisition values

Assets acquired via inheritance or from family trust
(TCGA 1992, ss 62 and 71)

Where a person inherits an asset, he is generally deemed to have acquired it for its market value at the date of the testator's death (ie probate value). There is one exception to this. It is possible to claim a form of relief from IHT where quoted securities have gone down in value after the person has died. Where such relief has been claimed, a corresponding adjustment is made so that the person taking the assets concerned is deemed to have acquired them not at probate value, but at the value actually brought into account for IHT purposes after taking account of the fall in value.

Where assets have been acquired from a trust, the beneficiary's acquisition value is normally the market value at the time that the asset is transferred to him. However, the acquisition value may be lower than this where the trustees have claimed hold-over relief either under the general hold-over relief provisions which prevailed up to 5 April 1989, or under the more restrictive provisions which have applied subsequently.

5.5.5 Indexation
(TA 1992, ss 53–57)

This now only applies to companies, and to individuals to establish 'frozen' indexation up to 5 April 1998.

A company which makes a capital gain is allowed to deduct not only its actual acquisition value, but also a proportion which represents the increase in the RPI between the month of acquisition and the month of disposal. The formula used is $[(RD - RI) \div RI]$ where:

RD = retail prices index in month of disposal
RI = retail prices index for March 1982 or month in which expenditure incurred, whichever is the later.

Example – Indexation

A acquired shares in X plc on 1 June 1991 for £20,000. He sells them in January 1997 for £30,000. The gain before indexation is £10,000. Indexation relief is as follows:

$$\text{Cost £20,000} \times \frac{\text{RPI for January 1997} - \text{RPI for June 1991}}{\text{RPI for June 1991}}$$

That is $£20,000 \times \dfrac{157.5 - 134.1}{134.1}$ or $£20,000 \times 0.174 = £3,480$

The chargeable gain is £6,520.

Restriction to indexation relief
(TCGA 1992, s 55(2A))

Indexation relief may only reduce or extinguish a gain; it cannot convert a gain into a loss or increase a loss.

5.6 TAPER RELIEF

5.6.1 Overview

The effect of taper relief (TCGA 1992, s 2A) is that the amount on which CGT is levied, on non-corporate taxpayers, is reduced by a percentage that varies according to the length of time (up to ten years) that an asset is held. A different scale of percentages applies to gains on the disposal of business assets and non-business assets. Also for business assets, there is an extension to the general definition which applies for assets acquired before 17 March 1998. The period for which the asset has been held after 5 April 1998 is, for disposals in 1998–99 and 1999–2000, notionally extended by a 'bonus' year.

For disposals of business assets made after 5 April 2000, the maximum relief is obtained after four complete years. However, the 'bonus' year given for business assets held on 17 March 1998 is not available for disposals of business assets made after 5 April 2000.

Indexation allowance (TCGA 1992, s 53) is frozen as at April 1998 for expenditure prior to that date, and does not apply at all for later expenditure. Indexation remains available for disposals by companies, to whom taper relief does not apply.

5.6.2 How taper relief is given
(TCGA 1992, s 2A)

Taper relief is given as an adjustment to the amount otherwise chargeable to CGT for the tax year concerned. This is the amount by which a person's chargeable gains for a tax year exceeds the aggregate of any allowable losses arising in that tax year and any unrelieved allowable losses brought forward from earlier tax years (TCGA 1992, s 2(2)). Where there is such an excess, taper relief is available if the excess is, or includes the whole or a part of any chargeable gain that is, eligible for taper relief. CGT is then chargeable only on a reduced amount which is found by taking the amount otherwise chargeable to CGT and recomputing the reduced amount as follows:

(1) taper relief is applied to so much of every chargeable gain as is eligible for the relief which is represented within the excess;
(2) the reduced amounts of each such gain are then aggregated;
(3) to this aggregate is then added the full amount of any gain, represented in the excess, but not eligible for taper relief.

It is necessary to establish whether the asset on which a chargeable gain has arisen is a business asset or a non-business asset. For a disposal of a business asset a chargeable gain is eligible for taper relief after a qualifying holding period of at least one year. If the gain arises on the disposal of a non-business asset the qualifying holding period must be of at least three years.

Taper relief is then calculated by reference to a table appropriate to business or non-business assets, as the case may be, and is applied on the basis of a percentage of the gain given by the relevant table to business or non-business assets, as the case may be, for the number of whole years in the qualifying holding period of that asset.

The qualifying holding period for an asset is, broadly, the period for

Table 5.1

Gains on disposals of non-business assets		Gains on disposals of business assets	
Number of whole years in qualifying holding period	Percentage of gain chargeable	Number of whole years in qualifying holding period	Percentage of gain chargeable
–	–	1	87.5
–	–	2	75
3	95	3	50
4	90	4 or more	25
5	85		
6	80		
7	75		
8	70		
9	65		
10 or more	60		

which that asset had been held at the time of its disposal. More specifically, the qualifying holding period starts on 6 April 1998, or on the actual date of acquisition, whichever is later, and ends with the disposal of the asset concerned.

Where taper relief applies to the whole or any part of a gain on the disposal of a business or non-business asset, that relief is given by multiplying the amount of the gain or part of a gain by the percentage given by Table 5.1 for the number of whole years in the qualifying holding period of that asset (TCGA 1992, s 2A(4) and (5), as amended by FA 2000, s 66(2)).

The extent to which the whole or any part of a gain on the disposal of a business or non-business asset is treated as represented in the excess referred to above is found by taking the deductions made to give effect to taper relief as set against chargeable gains in such order as results in the largest reduction of the amount otherwise chargeable to CGT. The first step is to identify the extent to which the chargeable gains for the year exceed the current and brought forward losses. The rules allow the individual concerned to allocate the particular gains of the year to the excess (as contrasted with being covered by allowable losses) on the basis which produces the result most favourable to him. Losses carried back, from the year of an individual's death, for up to three years are treated in the same way as brought forward losses for the purposes of taper relief. They are deducted before taper relief so that taper relief only applies to reduce the net gains after allowing the losses brought back.

The qualifying holding period of an asset depends on whether it is a business asset or a non-business asset. There are several possibilities:

(1) If the asset is a business asset, the qualifying holding period is the period after 5 April 1998 for which the asset had been held at the time of its disposal.

(2) In the case of a non-business asset, where:
   (a) the time (under TCGA 1992, Sched A1, para 2) when the asset is taken to have been acquired by the person making the disposal is a time before 17 March 1998, and
   (b) there is no period which (under Sched A1, para 11 (change of activity by the company) or 12 (share subject to value shifting)) does not count for the purposes of taper relief
   the qualifying period is the period after 5 April 1998 for which the asset has been held at the time of its disposal plus a 'bonus' year.

(3) For any other non-business asset, the qualifying holding period is the period after 5 April 1998 for which the asset had been held at the time of its disposal.

(TCGA 1992, s 2A(8) as inserted by FA 2000, s 66(3).)

Note that where Sched A1, para 11 or 12 applies to deny taper relief for some part of the period of ownership of a non-business asset (ie where the asset is a holding of shares in a non-trading company where there has been either a relevant change in that company's activities or a relevant shift of value involving those shares), there is a double penalty. In addition to a reduction in the qualifying holding period being reduced (Sched A1, para 2(4)), the 'bonus year' is also withdrawn. Schedule A1, para 10 (periods of limited exposure to fluctuations in value) can also reduce the qualifying holding period, but in that case the bonus year is not forfeited.

Where the period after 5 April 1998 for which an asset had been held at the time of its disposal includes any period which, under Sched A1, para 10, 11 or 12, is a period that does not count for the purposes of taper relief:

(a) the asset's qualifying holding period is reduced by the length of any period that does not count; and
(b) any period that does not count:
   (i) is left out of account in computing the period of ten years ending with the time of the asset's disposal; and
   (ii) is assumed not to be comprised in the asset's relevant period of ownership.

(Sched A1, para 2(4).)

In the context of the Enterprise Investment Scheme, the qualifying holding period of the original shares for the purposes of taper relief is the period beginning with the date of issue of the original shares and ending with the date of the relevant disposal (TCGA 1992, Sched 5BA, para 3). This is subject to adjustment if there are periods that do not count for taper relief purposes.

Schedule A1 provides more detailed rules for applying taper relief.

Example – Where there is only one asset disposal

Alex acquired a business asset on 1 August 1998 for £50,000 and sold it on 1 September 2000 for £90,000. It is held as a business asset throughout the whole of that period. He realises a gain of £40,000.

There are two whole years between the dates of acquisition and disposal. The asset has been a business asset throughout the whole of this period, so only 75% of the gain remains chargeable to CGT. In this case there are no losses available for offset arising in the same tax year or brought forward from an earlier tax year. Thus the gain chargeable to CGT (subject to the annual exempt amount) is £30,000.

Example – Where there are losses to take into account

Simon realises gains on two separate assets in the same tax year

Asset 1: Gain before taper relief is £21,000
The period for which the asset has been held (the taper period) is three years
The asset is held as a business asset throughout.

Asset 2: Gain before taper relief is £15,000
The period for which the asset has been held (the taper period) is eight years
The asset is held as a non-business asset throughout.

Asset 3: Loss (no taper relief available on losses) is £9,000.

The loss is set against the gain which qualifies for the least taper relief so that the maximum taper relief applies against the gain which qualifies for the largest reduction. The loss is therefore set against the gain on Asset 2 as it qualifies for reduction only to 70% of the untapered amount, whereas the gain on Asset 1 will be reduced to 50%.

So, of the net gain on Asset 2 of £6,000 (£15,000 – losses of £9,000), 70% is chargeable (ie £4,200).

Asset 1:	Gain	21,000
	Taper (business asset): three years = 55%	10,500
Asset 2	Gain	15,000
	Less loss on Asset 3	(9,000)
		6,000
	Taper (non-business asset): eight years = 70%	4,200
	Gains chargeable (subject to annual exempt amount)	15,750

The following points are worth noting:

(1) Except in relation to companies, indexation ceased to run on 6 April 1998. The new scheme is advantageous to persons whose assets have a

comparatively low acquisition cost (eg shares in newly formed companies). In their case the taper relief reduces the amount chargeable to a percentage of the gain. Under indexation, the gain was reduced only by a percentage of the acquisition cost.

(2) For acquisitions after 6 April 1998 the qualifying holding period runs from when the asset is first acquired. This is of considerable importance if the asset's value is disproportionately enhanced by subsequent allowable expenditure. No adjustment to taper relief is made for subsequent expenditure.

(3) Losses are not tapered. Care is needed to ensure that sufficient untapered gains or gains qualifying only for a smaller amount of taper relief are realised in a tax year where the taxpayer has allowable losses.

(4) Taper relief does not apply to gains realised by companies (because TCGA 1992, s 2(2) only applies to CGT, and s 2A applies only where there are net gains chargeable to CGT).

(5) Indexation continues to apply to companies. Furthermore, indexation continues to apply to the gains of non-resident close companies apportioned to participators under TCGA 1992, s 13.

(6) Changes in the rules for shares and other assets to qualify as business assets took effect for periods of ownership from 6 April 2000. As a result, some shares and other assets might be treated as non-business assets for periods of ownership up to 5 April 2000 but as business assets after 5 April 2000. The gain on disposal is apportioned between a gain on a business asset and a gain on a non-business asset.

Example – Apportionment between gains on business and non-business assets

On 6 October 2003, Russell sold shares he had owned since before 17 March 1998. He realised a gain of £132,000. Thus there are five whole years in the qualifying holding period which is used for determining taper relief from 6 April 1998 to 6 October 2003. Non-business (but not business) assets qualify for the bonus year.

The relevant period of ownership which is used for apportionment of gains on business and non-business assets is from 6 April 1998 to 6 October 2003. Here, the shares are non-business assets up to 6 April 2000 and, because of the change in the definition of business assets, are business assets from 6 April 2000 to the date of disposal.

The gain on the disposal is divided between the relevant periods of ownership that the shares had been non-business and business assets respectively. An apportionment of the relevant period of ownership of five years and six months (66 months in total) is made on the following basis:

Two years as a non-business asset:	$^{24}/_{66}$ months
Three years and six months as a business asset:	$^{42}/_{66}$ months
As a non-business asset: $\quad ^{24}/_{66} \times 132,000$	£48,000
As a business asset: $\qquad ^{42}/_{66} \times 132,000$	£84,000

The non-business asset gain is entitled to five years' non-business taper relief (plus the bonus year).

The business asset gain is entitled to five years' business asset taper relief appropriate to three complete years (with no bonus year).

Non-business asset gain:	£48,000 × 80%	38,400
Business asset gain:	£84,000 × 50%	42,000
CGT due on		80,400

5.6.3 Definitions of general application to taper relief rules

Period for which asset held and relevant period of ownership
(TCGA 1992, Sched A1, para 2)

When an asset is disposed of after 5 April 1998, the period of ownership is taken as measured down to the time of its disposal. It is taken as the period for which the asset had been held at the time of its disposal which:

- begins with whichever is the later of 6 April 1998 and the time when the asset concerned was acquired by the person making the disposal; and
- ends with the time of the disposal on which the gain accrued.

This rule applies equally to business and to non-business assets. Taper relief is, however, given only for the 'relevant period of ownership'. This is whichever is the shorter of:

- the period after 5 April 1998 for which the asset had been held at the time of its disposal; and
- the period of ten years then ending.

Certain matters are disregarded in determining whether a person is treated for this purpose as having acquired an asset. The matters concerned are:

(1) the death of a person entitled to an interest in settled property (as against trustees) insofar as it treats the asset concerned as acquired at a date before 6 April 1965 (TCGA 1992, s 73(1)(b));
(2) employee trusts (s 239(2)(b));
(3) gifts to charities (s 257(2)(b)); and
(4) gifts to housing associations (s 259(2)(b)).

Where the period after 5 April 1998 for which an asset had been held at the time of its disposal includes any period which does not count for the purposes of taper relief, then certain adjustments are required. The periods concerned are:

(1) periods of limited exposure to fluctuations in value (Sched A1, para 10);
(2) periods of share ownership where there has been a change of activity by a company (para 11); and
(3) periods of ownership affected by value shifting (para 12).

The adjustments required are:

(1) reduce the qualifying holding period of the asset by the length of the period, or by the aggregate of the lengths of such periods;
(2) leave such period(s) concerned out of account in computing the period of ten years ending at the time of the asset's disposal; and
(3) assume that such periods are not comprised in the asset's relevant period of ownership.

These rules are modified in the following circumstances (Sched A1, para 5):

- options (Sched A1, para 13);
- assets derived from other assets (para 14);
- assets transferred between spouses (para 15);
- postponed gains (para 16);
- property settled by a company (para 17);
- assets acquired in the reconstruction of mutual businesses, etc (para 18); and
- ancillary trust funds (para 19).

Relevant period of ownership
(TCGA 1992, Sched A1, para 2)

The 'relevant period of ownership' is a period, within the period of ownership, being whichever is the shorter of the period after 5 April 1998 for which the asset had been held at the time of its disposal and the period of ten years then ending.

5.6.4 Business or non-business assets

Basic rule
(TCGA 1992, Sched A1, para 3)

The basic rule is that a chargeable gain accruing to any person on the disposal of any asset is a gain on the disposal of a business asset if that asset was a business asset throughout its relevant period of ownership. This is, however, subject to a number of modifications to deal with particular circumstances.

Suppose, for example, that a person realises a chargeable gain on the disposal of an asset which has not been a business asset throughout its relevant period of ownership, but *has* been a business asset for periods comprising *part* of its relevant period of ownership. In such event, a proportional part of that gain is treated as a gain on the disposal of a business asset, with the remainder treated as a gain on the disposal of a non-business asset.

A slightly different treatment is applied where, under the above rules, there is a gain on the disposal of a business asset and also, on the same disposal, a gain on the disposal of a non-business asset. In such a case the two gains are treated for taper relief as separate gains on separate disposals of separate assets. However, the periods after 5 April 1998 for which each of the assets is treated as having been held at the time of their disposal is the same and is determined without reference to the length of the relevant period of ownership and the periods throughout which an asset is taken to have been a business asset.

5.6.5 Conditions for shares to qualify as business assets
(TCGA 1992, Sched A1, para 4(1)–(5))

There is a number of rules which apply in particular circumstances, and set out the rules for determining, in those particular circumstances, whether a disposal of shares or of an interest in shares in a company (here referred to as the 'relevant company') can be treated as a disposal of the underlying business assets.

Disposal by an individual

The asset is treated as a business asset if, at the time of the disposal, the relevant company is a qualifying company by reference to that individual.

Disposal by the trustees of a settlement

The asset is treated as a business asset if, at the time of the disposal, the relevant company is a qualifying company by reference to those trustees.

Disposal by an individual's personal representatives

The asset is treated as a business asset if, at the time of the disposal:

(1) the relevant company is a trading company or the holding company of a trading group; and
(2) not less than 25% of the voting rights in that company are exercisable by the deceased's personal representatives.

Disposal by a legatee

A special rule applies where the disposal is made by an individual who acquired the asset as a legatee (under TCGA 1992, s 64) at which time the asset was represented by shares in a company which would, at that time, have been a qualifying company by reference to that individual. In such a case the asset is treated as a business asset at that time if, at that time, it was held by the deceased's personal representatives.

5.6.6 Conditions for other assets to qualify as business assets
(TCGA 1992, Sched A1, para 5(1)–(5))

The following rules apply to determine whether, prior to its disposal, an asset other than shares, or an interest in shares, is a business asset.

Disposals by individuals

The asset is treated as a business asset if, at the time of the disposal, it was being used, wholly or partly, for any one or more of the following purposes:

(1) a trade carried on at that time by that individual or by a partnership of which he was at that time a member;
(2) any trade carried on by a company which at that time was a qualifying company by reference to that individual;
(3) any trade carried on by a company which at that time was a member of a trading group the holding company of which was at that time a qualifying company by reference to that individual;
(4) any qualifying office or employment to which that individual was at that time required to devote substantially the whole of his time; and/or
(5) any other office or employment provided that it was an office or employment with a trading company in relation to which that individual was, at that time, a full-time working officer or employee.

Disposal by the trustees of a settlement

The asset is treated as a business asset if, at the time of the disposal, it was being used, wholly or partly, for any one or more of the following purposes:

(1) a trade carried on at the time by the settlement trustees;
(2) a trade carried on at that time by an eligible beneficiary or by a partnership of which an eligible beneficiary was at that time a member;
(3) any trade carried on by a company which at that time was a qualifying company by reference to the settlement trustees or an eligible beneficiary;
(4) any trade carried on by a company which at that time was a member of a trading group the holding company of which was at that time a qualifying company by reference to the settlement trustees or an eligible beneficiary;
(5) any qualifying office or employment to which an eligible beneficiary was at that time required to devote substantially the whole of his time; and/or
(6) any office or employment provided that it was an office or employment with a trading company in relation to which an eligible beneficiary was, at that time, a full-time working officer or employee.

Disposal by an individual's personal representatives

The asset is treated as a business asset if, at the time of the disposal, it was being used, wholly or partly, for any one or more of the following purposes:

(1) a trade carried on by the deceased's personal representatives;
(2) any trade carried on by a company which at that time was a qualifying company by reference to the deceased's personal representatives; and/or
(3) any trade carried on by a company which at that time was a member of a trading group the holding company of which was at that time a qualifying company by reference to the deceased's personal representatives.

Disposal by a legatee

A special rule applies where the disposal is made by an individual who acquired the asset as a legatee (under TCGA 1992, s 64) at which time the asset does not qualify as a business asset under the rules applying for individuals but, being held by personal representatives of the deceased, is being used wholly or partly for a purpose within the rules for personal representatives. In such a case the asset is treated as a business asset at that time if, at that time, it was so held and used by the personal representatives.

5.6.7 Companies which are qualifying companies
(TCGA 1992, Sched A1, para 6(1)–(3))

The following rules are applied to determine whether a company is a qualifying company.

By reference to an individual

A company is a qualifying company by reference to an individual at any time when the following conditions are satisfied:

(1) it is a trading company or the holding company of a trading group, and
(2) one or more of the following conditions is met:
    (a) it is unlisted;
    (b) the individual is an officer or employee of the company, or of a company having a relevant connection with it; or
    (c) the voting rights in the company are exercisable, as to not less than 5%, by the individual.

By reference to the trustees of a settlement

A company is a qualifying company by reference to the trustees of a settlement at any time when:

(1) it was a trading company or the holding company of a trading group, and

(2) one or more of the following conditions is met:
   (a) it is unlisted;
   (b) an eligible beneficiary is an officer or employee of the company, or of a company having a relevant connection with it; or
   (c) the voting rights in the company are exercisable, as to not less than 5%, by the trustees.

By reference to an individual's personal representative

A company is taken to have been a qualifying company by reference to an individual's personal representatives at any time when:

(1) the company was a trading company or the holding company of a trading group, and
(2) one or more of the following conditions was met:
   (a) the company was unlisted; or
   (b) the voting rights in the company were exercisable, as to not less than 5%, by the personal representatives.

In the above cases, prior to 6 April 2000, the voting rights test was applied as to not less than 25%.

5.6.8 Persons who are eligible beneficiaries
(TCGA 1992, Sched A1, para 7)

An eligible beneficiary, in relation to an asset comprised in a settlement and a time, is any individual having at that time *a relevant interest in possession* under the settlement in either:

- the whole of the settled property; or
- a part of the settled property that is or includes that asset.

For this purpose 'relevant interest in possession', in relation to property comprised in a settlement, means any interest in possession under that settlement other than:

- a right under that settlement to receive an annuity; or
- a fixed-term entitlement; here, 'fixed-term entitlement', in relation to property comprised in a settlement, means any interest under that settlement which is limited to a term that is fixed and is not a term at the end of which the person with that interest will become entitled to the property.

5.6.9 Cases where there are non-qualifying beneficiaries
(TCGA 1992, Sched A1, para 8)

A further rule applies to a disposal of an asset by the trustees of a settlement where the asset's relevant period of ownership is or includes a period throughout which:

- the asset was a business asset by reference to one or more eligible beneficiaries;
- the asset would not otherwise have been a business asset; and
- there is a non-qualifying part of the relevant income, or there would be if there were any relevant income for that period.

This is referred to as a 'a sharing period'.

The period throughout which the asset disposed of is to be taken to have been a business asset is determined as if the relevant fraction of every sharing period were a period throughout which the asset was not a business asset. Here, 'the relevant fraction', in relation to any sharing period, is the fraction which represents the proportion of relevant income for that period which is, or (if there were such income) would be, a non-qualifying part of that income. Where a sharing period is a period in which such proportion has been different at different times, a separate relevant fraction has to be determined for, and applied to, each part of that period for which there is a different proportion. The non-qualifying part of any relevant income for any period is so much of that income for that period as is or, as the case may be, would be income to which:

- no eligible beneficiary has any entitlement; or
- a non-qualifying eligible beneficiary has an entitlement.

A 'non-qualifying eligible beneficiary', in relation to a period, means an eligible beneficiary who is not a beneficiary by reference to whom (if he were the only beneficiary) the asset disposed of would be a business asset throughout that period. 'Relevant income' is income from the part of the settled property comprising the asset disposed of.

5.6.10 Cases where an asset is used at the same time for different purposes
(TCGA 1992, Sched A1, para 9)

There is a special rule which applies to a disposal by any person of an asset where the asset's relevant period of ownership is or includes a period ('a mixed-use period') throughout which the asset was:

- a business asset by reference to the conditions for other assets to qualify as business assets (Sched A1, para 5(2)–(5)); but
- at the same time, being put to a non-qualifying use.

The period throughout which the asset disposed of is to be taken to have been a business asset is determined as if the relevant fraction of every mixed-use period were a period throughout which the asset was not a business asset. Here, 'the relevant fraction', in relation to any mixed-use period, means the fraction which represents the proportion of the use of the asset during that period that was a non-qualifying use.

A special rule applies in circumstances where both of the rules for cases where there are non-qualifying beneficiaries (Sched A1, para 8) apply to cases where an asset is used at the same time for different purposes. In such event, the rules for cases where there are non-qualifying beneficiaries take precedence. Further reductions in the period for which the asset disposed of is taken to have been a business asset are made only in respect of the relevant part of any non-qualifying use. In this context, the relevant part of any non-qualifying use is the proportion of that use which is not a use to which a non-qualifying part of any relevant income is attributable.

The following rule applies where a mixed-use period is a period in which:

(1) the proportion of the use of the asset during that period that was a non-qualifying use has been different at different times, or

(2) where different attributions have to be made for different parts of the period because both of the rules for cases where there are non-qualifying beneficiaries apply to cases where an asset is used at the same time for different purposes.

In such cases, a separate relevant fraction has to be determined for, and applied to, each part of the period for which there is a different proportion or attribution.

Under these rules, 'non-qualifying use', in relation to an asset, means any use of the asset for purposes which are not purposes for which the asset would fall to be treated as a business asset at the time of its use.

The non-qualifying part of any relevant income for any period is so much of that income for that period as is or, as the case may be, would be income to which:

- no eligible beneficiary has any entitlement; or
- a non-qualifying eligible beneficiary has an entitlement.

'Relevant income' is income from the part of the settled property comprising the asset disposed of.

5.6.11 Anti-avoidance measures

In order to prevent manipulation of the taper relief rules so as to gain a tax advantage, or to mitigate the effect of the rules, a number of anti-avoidance measures are built into the legislation. The areas concerned are:

- periods of limited exposure to fluctuations (TCGA 1992, Sched A1, para 10);
- periods of share ownership where there is a change of activity by the company (para 11);
- periods of share ownership where there is value shifting (para 12);
- special rules where property is settled by a company (para 17).

5.6.12 Miscellaneous special rules

There are rules to deal with a number of special situations:

- Options (TCGA 1992, Sched A1, para 13);
- Further rules for assets derived from other assets (para 14);
- Assets transferred between spouses (para 15);
- Postponed gains (para 16);
- Assets acquired in the reconstruction of mutual businesses (para 18);
- Ancillary trust funds (para 19);
- General rule for settlements (para 20); and
- General rule for apportionments (para 21).

5.7 SOME SPECIAL PROBLEM AREAS

5.7.1 Land and buildings

The basic principles apply in computing gains on land and buildings as they do for other assets. However, there are certain complications which regularly arise in practice.

Expenditure on improvements

Where a property is disposed of, bear in mind that the acquisition cost includes allowable enhancement expenditure only if the expenditure is reflected in the state of the property at the date of disposal. Thus, beware of a situation where property has a high cost but much of the enhancement expenditure relates to additions or improvements which have been worn out, or which have themselves been replaced.

Disallowed initial repairs

The reverse situation often applies where a property is acquired in a very poor state of repair. Expenditure incurred in bringing it into a fit condition is often disallowed. Such repairs are treated as capital expenditure. Where this has happened, the amount disallowed in computing trading profits or Schedule A income can be treated as enhancement expenditure for CGT purposes.

Past expenditure qualified for capital allowances

A trader's expenditure on a building may include sums which have qualified for capital allowances, eg expenditure on installing a lift or carrying out structural work so that a computer can be installed. Such expenditure can be allowed for CGT purposes provided it does not mean that there is a loss.

Leases with less than 50 years to run
(TCGA 1992, s 240 & Sched 8)

Another aspect to bear in mind is that the interest in the property which is being disposed of may be a lease which has less than 50 years to run and is therefore regarded as a wasting asset. Where a person disposes of such an asset, his acquisition value is restricted according to specific rules which effectively write off the cost of a wasting asset over the period of its life.

Example – Disposal of a short lease

A Ltd purchased a 20-year lease in 1985 for £100,000. In 1995 it disposes of the lease for £100,000. However, this is not a no gain/no loss situation as the proper calculation is as follows:

	£	£
Disposal proceeds		100,000
Original cost of lease	100,000	
Reduced by $\dfrac{72.770 - 46.695}{72.770}$ =	(35,832)	
		(64,168)
Gain before indexation		35,832

The figures of 72.770 and 46.695 for 20 and ten-year leases are contained in the table in TCGA 1992, Sched 8.

Time apportionment and land held before 6 April 1965
(TCGA 1992, s 35 & Sched 2)

Where a person has owned land or buildings since a date prior to 6 April 1965, it may be possible for any capital gain to be computed on the time apportionment basis. This is not possible if the person has made a universal rebasing election (see 5.5.3) or if the land or buildings have development value when they are sold.

The time apportionment basis operates on the assumption that appreciation has occurred at an even rate over the total period of ownership. Because CGT was first introduced on 6 April 1965, the chargeable gain is computed as follows:

$$\text{Overall gain} \times \frac{\text{Period since 6 April 1965 – date of disposal}}{\text{Total period of ownership}}$$

Example – Where time apportionment basis is beneficial

B Ltd sells an agricultural property in March 2001 for £510,000. It was originally acquired in April 1945 for £10,000. Its value at 31 March 1982 was £150,000. Ignoring indexation, the time apportionment basis produces the following result:

$$£500,000 \times \frac{\text{6 April 1965 – March 2001 (36 years)}}{\text{6 April 1945 – March 2001 (56 years)}} = £321,429$$

This compares with a gain of £350,000 before indexation if the gain is measured by reference to the 31 March 1982 value.

5.7.2 Unquoted shares

A valuation may be required where a shareholder makes a gift or there is some other disposal which is not a bargain at arm's length and the transaction is treated as a disposal at market value (see 5.5.1). A valuation may also be required at 31 March 1982 where this value may be deducted instead of original cost in computing the person's capital gain (see 5.5.3). In both these situations, it is generally necessary to negotiate with the Revenue's Shares Valuation Division. This division operates according to long established rules which have been upheld by court decisions.

Valuation of minority shareholdings

It must not be assumed that the value of a 10% shareholding is the same as 10% of the value of the company as a whole. A firm distinction is drawn between a 51% or greater shareholding which carries control and a minority shareholding. The Revenue's normal view is that the underlying assets are irrelevant when valuing a small minority shareholding and what matters is the dividend history and the extent to which an investor could reasonably expect the past level of dividends to be maintained in the future.

General principles

One aspect to be borne in mind is that the definition of market value for capital gains purposes is the value for the person who acquires the asset. In this regard, the valuation may differ from that used for IHT purposes (see 23.3.3). Thus, if an individual makes a gift out of his 51% shareholding of shares which add up to 17% of the company's share capital, the disposal is normally deemed to take place at a consideration equal to the market value of a 17% shareholding.

Special rules where series of connected disposals made
(TCGA 1992, ss 19 and 20)

There are anti-avoidance provisions designed to prevent a person achieving an advantage by making several separate disposals to connected persons. Basically, the anti-avoidance provisions apply where a person makes several gifts or other disposals to connected persons within a six-year period and the value of the property given away in stages is more, when valued at a totality, than the combined value of the separate gifts.

Example – How a series of gifts may be dealt with

A made five separate gifts of shares in B Ltd to his son. Assume that an 11% shareholding in B Ltd is worth only £20,000 whereas a 55% controlling shareholding has a value of £300,000.

Where the Revenue is able to apply the anti-avoidance legislation, the transactions are linked and the individual is assessed as if he had made a disposal on each occasion on a part of the overall value. Thus, *A* would be deemed to have made five separate disposals on the basis that the deemed disposal proceeds on each occasion amounted to £60,000 (ie ⅕ of the value of a 55% shareholding).

Valuing shareholdings at 31 March 1982

When valuing shares it is not normally appropriate to have regard to shares held by a connected person. Thus, if a husband and wife each held 30% of the shares in a company at 31 March 1982, each shareholding should be valued on the basis of a 30% minority shareholding, even though when taken together the husband and wife would have control. However, the Revenue operates an extra statutory concession so that if a husband and wife held 30% each at 31 March 1982, but one spouse later transferred all his or her shares to the other, the 31 March 1982 value may then be based on the rights etc attaching to a 60% shareholding.

The Revenue also has a concession which deals with the converse situation. Suppose that an individual had 51% of the shares in his private company at 31 March 1982, and his wife had 9%. If he gave 21% of his shareholding to his wife with a view to equalising their shareholdings, there could be a disadvantage in that the combined value of the two 30% shareholdings might not equate to the value of a 51% and a 9% shareholding. In these circumstances, the Revenue allows the individual's wife to claim that the 21% shareholding given to her by her husband should have a 31 March 1982 value based on it being part of a 51% controlling shareholding.

Time apportionment basis

The time apportionment method of computing gains (mentioned in 5.7.1) also applies to shares in an unquoted company.

5.7.3 Foreign property

Gains should be computed in sterling

Where a foreign property or shares in a foreign company are disposed of, it is not correct to calculate the gain or loss in foreign currency terms and then convert that into sterling at the time of disposal. Instead, the following formula should be used:

Disposal proceeds converted into sterling at the rates prevailing at the time of the disposal
Less Acquisition cost of 31 March 1982 value converted into sterling at the exchange rate prevailing at that time
Equals Gain before indexation.

Borrowings in foreign currency

Often an individual or partnership has financed the acquisition of a foreign property with a foreign currency loan and the foreign currency appreciates against sterling. When a disposal of the property takes place, and the loan is redeemed, the extra cost of repaying the loan is not allowable in computing the capital gain on the disposal of the asset.

Example – Gain on foreign property

A financed the purchase of a warehouse in Germany by borrowing the full purchase price of DM 4m. At that time, the sterling equivalent was £1m (DM 4 = £1). When *A* sells the warehouse for DM 6m, the exchange rate is DM 2.50 = £1.

Overall, *A*'s profit after repaying his loan is DM 2m ie £800,000 when one looks at the exchange rate at the time of disposal. However, for tax purposes, the transaction is broken down as follows:

	£
Sale proceeds (DM 6m converted at DM 2.50 = £1)	2,400,000
Cost (DM 4m converted at DM 4 = £1)	1,000,000
Capital gain before indexation	1,400,000
Extra cost in sterling terms of repaying loan	(600,000)

A will be taxed on his gain of £1.4m (less indexation relief) with no relief for the currency loss on repaying his borrowings.

A currency loss of this nature is also not normally allowable in computing an unincorporated trader's profits although special rules now apply for companies (see 20.11 on Forex).

5.7.4 Foreign currency
(TCGA 1992, s 252)

This is regarded as a chargeable asset and a gain (or loss) may arise when the currency is disposed of. Such a disposal may take the form of the foreign currency being spent, or being converted into another foreign currency, or converted into sterling. In each of these situations, the sterling equivalent of the foreign currency at the date of disposal is compared with the sterling equivalent at the date of acquisition.

The one circumstance where foreign currency is an exempt asset is where it was acquired for an individual's personal expenditure abroad.

6

CAPITAL GAINS TAX AND BUSINESS TRANSACTIONS

DAVID BERTRAM, CLAYFIELD PROFESSIONAL GUIDANCE LTD

This chapter focuses on the CGT aspects of various business transactions.

6.1 LOANS TO PRIVATE BUSINESSES

A person may make a loan to a sole trader or partnership (an 'unincorporated business') or to a private company, or he may give a guarantee to a bank etc which makes a loan to a business. CGT loss relief may be available if a loan has to be written off or a person is required to make a payment under a bank guarantee that he has given.

6.1.1 Loans to unincorporated businesses
(TCGA 1992, s 253)

A CGT loss may be deemed to arise if the Revenue is satisfied that a loan has become irrecoverable. There are various conditions which must be fulfilled:

(1) The borrower must not be the lender's spouse.
(2) The borrower must be resident in the UK.
(3) The borrower must have used the loan wholly for the purposes of a trade carried on by him. The trade must not have been a trade which consists of (or includes) lending money.

When a claim is submitted, the inspector of taxes must satisfy himself that any outstanding amount of the loan is irrecoverable and that the lender has not assigned his right to recover the loan. Strictly speaking, relief is due only when a claim is made and admitted but, in practice, the Revenue permits claims to be made within two years of a tax year provided the other conditions were satisfied at the end of that year of assessment (ESC D36).

6.1.2 Loans to companies
(TCGA 1992, s 253)

Similar provisions apply where a person has made a loan to a company which proves to be irrecoverable. The principal conditions which need to be satisfied are:

(1) the company must be UK resident; and
(2) it must be a trading company.

No relief is due where a company makes a loss on a loan to another company in the same group unless the loan is a debt on security (ie a debenture which is capable of being transferred).

6.1.3 Payments under loan guarantees
(TCGA 1992, s 253(4))

Instead of lending money to a relative or friend or his private company, an individual may have given a guarantee to a bank etc. Similarly, a director of a company may have had to give personal guarantees for bank loans to his company.

Where the borrower cannot repay the loan, the bank calls on the guarantor to pay the amount due. In these circumstances, the guarantor may be able to claim a CGT loss under TCGA 1992, s 253 as if he had made a loan which was irrecoverable. The following conditions must be satisfied to claim such relief:

(1) payment has been made under a guarantee;
(2) the payment should arise from a formal calling in of the guarantee – a voluntary payment attracts no relief;
(3) the original loan met the requirements listed in 6.1.1;
(4) the amount paid under the guarantee cannot be recovered either from the borrower or from a co-guarantor.

Where a company has guaranteed another UK company's borrowings and the money has been used for the borrower's trade, a payment under the guarantee may qualify under s 253. This still applies even if the guarantor and borrower are members of the same group of companies.

6.2 LOSSES ON UNQUOTED SHARES
(TA 1988, s 574)

6.2.1 Special relief for subscribers

From time to time, an individual may invest in a private company, either as a working director/shareholder or perhaps as a 'passive' investor with a minority shareholding. Investments may also be made in companies which, whilst they are public companies as defined by the Companies Act 1985, are not quoted companies.

A loss may arise on a disposal of shares in such a company. If the investor acquired existing shares by purchasing them, the loss is a normal CGT loss and the only way in which it can be relieved is by its being set against capital gains. However, if the individual acquired his shares by *subscribing* for new shares, it may be possible to obtain income tax relief for the loss. Subject to certain conditions, the capital loss may be off-set against the individual's income for the year in which the loss is realised. The following conditions must be satisfied:

(1) The loss must arise from one of the following:
  (a) a sale made at arm's length for full consideration (this rules out a sale to a connected person); or
  (b) a disposal which takes place when the company is wound up; or
  (c) a deemed disposal where the shares have become of negligible value.
(2) There are conditions which relate to the company itself, in particular:
  (a) The company must have been resident in the United Kingdom throughout the period from its incorporation until the date of the individual's disposal of shares.
  (b) The company must not have been a quoted company at any time during the individual's period of ownership. The fact that any class of shares has had a Stock Exchange quote rules out relief under TA 1988, s 574 even though the loss may have arisen on a class of share which did not have a quote.
  (c) The company must be a trading company, or the holding company of a trading group, at the date of disposal or it must have ceased to have been a trading company not more than three years prior to the date of disposal and it must not have been an investment company since that date.
  (d) The company's trade must not have consisted wholly or mainly of dealing in shares, securities, land, trades or commodity futures.
  (e) The company's trade must have been carried on on a commercial basis.

6.2.2 Relief also available for subscriber's spouse

The spouse of a person who subscribed for shares may also claim relief under TA 1988, s 574 where he has acquired the shares in question through an *inter vivos* transfer from his spouse. However, shares which are acquired on the death of a spouse do not entitle the widower/widow to s 574 relief on a subsequent disposal.

6.2.3 Nature of relief

The loss is calculated according to normal CGT principles. If the loss is eligible for relief under TA 1988, s 574, the individual may elect within two years for the loss to be set against his taxable income. The loss may be set either against the individual's taxable income for the year of the loss, or his taxable income for the preceding year. Either claim may be made independently of the other. Where an individual has losses which are available for relief under s 574 and he is also entitled to relief for trading losses (see 18.6), he can choose which losses should be relieved in priority to the other.

Any part of the capital loss which cannot be relieved under s 574 can be carried forward for set-off against capital gains in the normal way.

6.2.4 Similar relief for companies
(TA 1988, s 573)

There is a similar relief for investment companies (see 20.8.5) which realise capital losses. Once again, the shares need to have been acquired by subscription. The shares must not be in a subsidiary company or in an associated company (see 20.2.6).

Once again, the investment company's capital loss must be computed on ordinary CGT principles. If relief is required under TA 1988, s 573, an election must be submitted to the Revenue within two years of the end of the company's accounting period in which the loss is realised. The loss may then be set against the company's income and other profits for that year. If the loss exceeds the company's profits for that period, the excess is carried back and set against profits of the preceding accounting period. Any balance can then be carried forward and set against the investment company's capital gains.

6.3 ROLL-OVER RELIEF

6.3.1 Basic principles
(TCGA 1992, s 152(1) and (2))

Relief may be available where a person disposes of an asset which is used by him in a trade (or in certain circumstances, an asset which is used by his family company) and re-invests in replacement assets used for business purposes. This relief is termed 'roll-over' relief. The gain is said to be rolled over in that it is not charged to tax, but is deducted from the person's acquisition cost of the new assets.

Example – Roll-over relief

A sells a farm for £450,000. His capital gain is £200,000. He starts up a new business and invests £500,000 in a warehouse.

By claiming roll-over relief, A avoids having to pay tax on the gain of £200,000. The acquisition cost of his warehouse is reduced as follows:

	£
Actual cost	500,000
Less rolled-over gain	(200,000)
Deemed acquisition cost	300,000

The relief is really a form of deferment since a larger gain will arise on a subsequent disposal of the replacement asset.

6.3.2 Conditions which need to be satisfied
(TCGA 1992, s 155)

There must be a relevant disposal, although this need not be a sale and could, for example, be a gift or an exchange of assets. The asset that has been disposed of must have been used in a business and must have fallen into one of the following categories:

Class 1	Head A: Land and buildings
	Head B: Fixed plant and machinery
Class 2	Ships, aircraft and hovercraft
Class 3	Satellites, space-stations and spacecraft
Class 4	Goodwill
Class 5	Milk and potato quotas
Class 6	Ewe and suckler cow premium quotas
Class 7	Fish quotas
Class 8	Lloyd's syndicate rights ('capacity').

The replacement assets must also fall into one of these categories, but not necessarily the same category as the asset which has been sold. Moreover, the asset can be used for a completely different trade. It is not possible to claim roll-over relief on the disposal of shares in a family company, nor is it possible to claim it for expenditure on such shares on the basis that this is replacement expenditure.

The replacement assets must normally be acquired within a period starting one year before the date of the disposal of the original asset and ending three years after the date of disposal. The time limit can be extended (at the Revenue's discretion) if the acquisition of replacement assets within three years was not possible because of circumstances outside the person's control.

Example – Full relief available only where all sale proceeds reinvested
(TCGA 1992, ss 152(3)–(11) and 154)

> Using the same figures as above, *A* sells his farm for £450,000, making the same capital gain of £200,000. He starts up a new business but invests only £400,000 in the new warehouse. The part of the £450,000 disposal consideration for the farm which is not applied in acquiring the warehouse is £50,000. This is less than the gain which arose on the disposal of the farm and the balance of the gain may be rolled-over. The acquisition value of the warehouse is reduced by £150,000.

6.3.3 Old assets not used for business throughout ownership

If the old asset was not used for business throughout the period of ownership, TCGA 1990, s 152(7) applies as if a part of the asset used for the purposes of the trade was a separate asset to that which had not been wholly used for the purposes of the trade.

Example – Old assets

> In April 2000, *B* sells a hotel for a gain, after indexation has been calculated, of £50,000. It had originally been bought in April 1992 but was at first let out as an investment. It was used by *B* for a trade carried on by him only from April 1984. The amount of gain which can be rolled over into the purchase of a new asset is calculated as follows:
>
> $$\text{Chargeable gain £50,000} \times \frac{\text{period of trading use of old asset}}{\text{period of ownership}}$$
>
> This equals £50,000 × ⅘ = £37,500. The balance of £12,500 (£50,000 – £37,500) is a chargeable gain.

6.3.4 Treatment where replacement assets are wasting assets
(TCGA 1992, s 154)

The roll-over relief is modified where the replacement expenditure consists of the purchase of a wasting asset (an asset with an expected useful life of less than 50 years) or an asset which will become a wasting asset within ten years. Plant and machinery is always considered to have a useful life of less than 50 years. Furthermore, the acquisition of a lease with less than 60 years to run will also constitute the acquisition of a wasting asset. Rather paradoxically, the goodwill of a business is not regarded as a wasting asset.

The capital gain in these circumstances is not deferred indefinitely, but becomes chargeable on the first of the following occasions:

(1) the disposal of the replacement asset; or
(2) the asset ceasing to be used in the business; or
(3) the expiry of ten years.

Examples – Roll-over relief on wasting assets

> (1) *B* sells a factory and re-invests in a 59-year lease of a warehouse which he uses in his business. In the sixth year the warehouse is let as an investment property. The rolled-over gain would become chargeable in year six.
> (2) *C* also rolls over into a 59-year lease. He is still using the property after ten years, but because it has become a wasting asset within that period, the rolled-over gain becomes chargeable in year ten.

6.3.5 Reinvestment in non-wasting assets
(TCGA 1992, s 154(5))

If a person acquires new non-wasting replacement assets during the ten years, the capital gain which was originally rolled over into the purchase of the wasting assets can be transferred to the new replacement assets. Assume in example (1) above that *B* had bought the goodwill of a business in year five. He could transfer his roll-over relief claim to the new asset. No gain would then become chargeable in year six when he lets the warehouse.

6.3.6 Replacement asset must be brought into use

Temperley v Visibell Ltd [1974] STC 64 concerned a company which purchased land to build a factory. In the event, planning permission was refused and the factory was never built. It was held that the intention to use an asset for the trade was not sufficient and the expenditure on the land did not qualify for roll-over relief.

However, where the replacement asset is not brought into use right away, roll-over relief may still be available if the following conditions are satisfied:

(a) the trader proposes to incur capital expenditure for the purpose of enhancing its value;
(b) any work arising from such capital expenditure begins as soon as possible after acquisition, and is completed within a reasonable time;
(c) on completion of the work the asset is taken into use for the purpose of the trade and for no other purpose; and
(d) the asset is not let or used for any non-trading purpose in the period between acquisition and the time it is taken into use for the purpose of the trade.

6.3.7 Acquisition of freehold

The Revenue used to deny roll-over relief where a trader acquired a further interest in an asset already used by him for his trade, eg where a tenant farmer bought the freehold. ESC D25 now provides relief as if the expenditure were on a new asset.

6.3.8 Roll-over relief for partners

Where the asset which is disposed of is owned by a partnership, part of the gain belongs to each partner (see 6.5) and it is up to him whether he claims roll-over relief. Because the replacement asset need not be used by the disponor in the same trade, an individual partner may roll-over by incurring expenditure on his own account whereas other partners may choose not to do so.

Roll-over relief can be secured where the replacement assets are used by a partnership in which the owner is a partner (SP D11).

6.3.9 Assets used by an individual's personal trading company
(TCGA 1992, s 157)

Relief can also be obtained where an individual disposes of a property etc which is used by his 'personal trading company', but only if the replacement asset is acquired by him and is used by the same company. A company is an individual's personal trading company if he personally owns at least 5% of the voting shares. The individual need not be a director of the company – indeed he need not even be employed by it. Also, roll-over relief is not lost because he has charged the company rent.

6.3.10 Assets owned by employee or office-holder
(TCGA 1992, s 158)

An employee or office-holder may claim roll-over relief where he disposes of an asset used in the employment. This condition may apply, for example, to a sub-postmaster who has an 'office' for tax purposes, but who generally owns the sub-post office premises. For further details, see SP5/86.

There are circumstances where these provisions mean that a director of a family company who has sold an asset used by one company, and bought new assets used by another family company, is entitled to roll-over relief. However, this is a difficult area where professional advice is essential.

6.4 HOLD-OVER RELIEF FOR GIFTS OF BUSINESS PROPERTY
(TCGA 1992, s 165)

Under the legislation which applied up to 5 April 1989, a UK-resident individual could transfer any asset to another UK-resident person on a no gain/no loss basis by claiming hold-over relief.

Example – Hold-over relief

B transferred shares in X plc to her brother C in 1988. They were both resident in the United Kingdom. B's shares were worth £29,000 and her capital gain would normally have been £13,000. By claiming hold-over relief, B could avoid having a chargeable gain of £13,000. C's acquisition value was then taken as:

£

Market value at acquisition	29,000
Less held-over capital gain	(13,000)
	16,000

In 1989, the Chancellor abolished the hold-over relief for gifts in general. However, the same type of hold-over relief can still be claimed on gifts of business property and shares in unquoted trading companies.

6.4.1 Definition of business property
(TCGA 1992, s 165(2))

Business property is defined for these purposes as:

(1) an asset used by the transferor in a trade, profession or vocation;
(2) an asset used by the transferor's personal company in a trade;
(3) an asset used for a trade by a subsidiary of the transferor's family company;
(4) agricultural land which qualifies for IHT agricultural property relief (see 23.9).

Where an asset has been used for non-qualifying purposes for part of the person's period of ownership, only a corresponding part of any capital gain may be held over.

Example – Restriction on hold-over relief

A Ltd acquired a property in March 1985 for £190,000. In 2000 it is worth £480,000. Take indexation as 84%.

To begin with, A Ltd rented it out as an investment and occupied it for its business only for the period from April 1993 to March 2000. If A Ltd transfers the property by way of a gift, its capital gain will be:

	£	£
Market value		480,000
Less cost	190,000	
Indexation	160,000	
		(350,000)
		130,000

The maximum part of the gain which may be held over is as follows:

$$\frac{\text{April 1993 to March 2000}}{\text{March 1985 to March 2000}} = \frac{7}{15}$$

Thus only £50,000 of the gain may be held over.

6.4.2 Hold-over relief on shares

The definition of business property also includes:

(1) unquoted shares in a trading company; and
(2) quoted shares if the company concerned is the transferor's personal company (it is very unusual for this condition to be satisfied).

A similar restriction to that illustrated in the example in 6.4.1 may apply on a transfer of shares in an unquoted trading company if that company holds investments or other chargeable assets which are not business assets. The restriction is based on the following formula:

$$\frac{\text{Chargeable assets used in the business}}{\text{Total chargeable assets}}$$

Example – Restriction on hold-over relief

B gives his son his shares in X Ltd. The balance sheet of X Ltd shows assets as follows:

	£
Stock	100,000
Factory	500,000
Investments	500,000
Cash	200,000

> Only half of B's capital gain may be held over, ie $\dfrac{\text{Value of factory}}{\text{Factory and investments}}$

6.4.3 Hold-over relief not available on certain gifts

The legislation provides that hold-over relief is available only if the recipient of the transfer is either UK-resident or ordinarily resident. Moreover, hold-over relief is not available if the recipient is dual resident, and the relevant double taxation agreement has the effect of treating him as if he were not resident in the UK.

Hold-over relief is also precluded where an individual etc transfers an asset to a UK-resident company which is controlled by persons who are neither UK-resident nor ordinarily resident.

6.4.4 Hold-over relief for transactions which are chargeable transfers for IHT purposes
(TCGA 1992, s 260)

There is a completely separate provision which provides hold-over relief where the disposal is a chargeable transfer for IHT purposes and the recipient is UK-resident or ordinarily resident. The main circumstance where this may apply is where assets are transferred by way of gift etc to a discretionary trust (see 23.10).

Where a transfer of assets comes within both ss 165 and 260 of TCGA 1992, s 260 takes priority. Note that where hold-over relief is available under s 260 on a disposal which is a chargeable transfer for IHT purposes, there is no restriction as in 6.4.1 or 6.4.2 because the asset has not been used for business for the whole of the person's period of ownership, or the property includes non-business assets.

6.4.5 Clawback of hold-over relief
(TCGA 1992, s 168)

Hold-over relief is clawed back if the recipient of the gift etc ceases to be resident within six years. The held-over gain is deemed to arise immediately before he ceases to be resident and, if the individual concerned fails to pay the resultant CGT, the transferor can be held liable.

There is one circumstance where the emigration of the recipient does not give rise to a chargeable gain. If the individual is required to work abroad because of his employment, and he returns to the UK within three years still owning the asset, the temporary 'emigration' does not count for these purposes.

6.4.6 Practical aspects

In strictness, an individual's capital gain should be formally agreed even though it is held-over. However, if both the transferor and transferee agree, it can be left in abeyance, to be ascertained only as and when the transferee makes a chargeable disposal. See SP 8/92.

6.5 PARTNERS AND CAPITAL GAINS

The way in which CGT affects partnership transactions can at times be complex. The Revenue's practice is set out in SP D12 but this is extremely technical and to understand its implications professional advice should be sought. The following paragraphs describe some key aspects.

6.5.1 Partnership's acquisition value

Although individual partners' entitlement to profits may vary from time to time, the partnership's acquisition value for the firm's chargeable assets is not affected unless there are cash payments from one partner to another to acquire a greater interest in the firm or unless assets are revalued as part of the arrangements for changes in profit-sharing.

6.5.2 Assets held by firm at 31 March 1982

The partnership may make a universal rebasing election for the values at 31 March 1982 to be used instead of cost. This is quite separate from the individual partners' position in relation to their personal assets when a disposal of an asset takes place. There may be partners who were not in the partnership at 31 March 1982, but this does not affect the computation of the gain.

6.5.3 Partnership gains divisible among partners

Where a partnership asset is sold at a capital gain (or loss), the gain is divided among the partners in accordance with their profit-sharing ratios. Each partner is personally assessable on his share of the gain. The partner's actual CGT liability depends on his own situation, ie whether he has other gains for the year, has available losses, can claim roll-over relief or is entitled to retirement relief (see 6.7).

6.5.4 Revaluations

Problems may arise where a partnership has substantial assets which are chargeable assets for CGT purposes and which are worth more than their book value (ie the value at which they are shown in the firm's accounts). A revaluation to bring their book value into line with their market value can produce a liability for individual partners if there is a reduction in their profit-sharing ratios. This commonly happens when existing partners retire or new partners are introduced.

There is no such problem where partners leave or come in and there is no revaluation of assets. In such a case, the remaining or incoming partners normally take over the outgoing partners' acquisition values for the firm's asset.

Example – Retirement of partner

A is a partner in a five partner firm and is entitled to 20% of the profits. He retires and his colleagues then share profits on the basis of 25% each. As part of the arrangements for his retirement, the book value of the firm's office block is increased from £150,000 to its current value of £750,000. The surplus is credited to each partner's account so that *A* is credited with £120,000.

A is treated as if he has realised a gain on the disposal of a one-fifth share of the building. This would be based on the £120,000. The remaining four partners are not treated as having made a disposal. Indeed, they each have made an acquisition of a 5% interest in the building for an outlay of £30,000.

Example – Introduction of new partner

B and *C* are partners. Their premises are included in their firm's balance sheet at £200,000 (original cost), but are actually worth £500,000. *B* and *C* agree to admit *D* as an equal partner in return for his paying in new capital into the firm of £700,000. They revalue the premises before admitting *D* as a partner, and the surplus of £300,000 is credited to their accounts. In this case, *B* and *C* are each regarded as having made a disposal of a one-sixth interest in the premises. This is because *D*'s new capital goes into the firm as a whole. After coming in, he effectively owns one-third of all the assets (and is responsible for one-third of the liabilities). The former partners' ownership of the premises has been reduced from 50% to a one-third interest.

Example – Change of partners with no assets revaluation

A and *B* are in partnership. They own premises which have a book value of £94,000 (equal to cost in 1980). *A* retires and is replaced by *C*. The premises are not revalued. Later the premises are sold for £244,000. *B* and *C* are assessed on their share of the gain.

The gain is computed by reference to the original cost (£94,000) or the premises' market value at 31 March 1982, *not* their value at the time that *C* became a partner.

This does *not* apply where the partners are connected persons (perhaps because they are relatives), or where cash payments are made to acquire an interest in the firm. In either of these categories you should seek specialist advice.

6.5.5 Partner leaves after roll-over relief secured on purchase of new asset by firm

A capital gain may arise for a partner on his leaving the firm, even though he receives no consideration from his former partners in return for giving up his interest in the firm beyond being paid out his capital account. Take a situation where there are five partners sharing profits and losses equally. One partner leaves and the remaining four continue. The balance sheet shows the partnership premises as having a cost of £500,000. However, on closer examination, it transpires that some years ago the former partnership premises were disposed of, realising a capital gain of £280,000. Roll-over relief was obtained against this capital gain by reference to the purchase of the current partnership premises.

The Revenue takes the view that the outgoing partner is deemed to have realised a capital gain as follows:

	£
⅕ share in partnership premises (deemed proceeds)	100,000
Less cost (⅕ of cost as adjusted for roll-over relief)	(44,000)
Gain before indexation	56,000

The four continuing partners' base value for CGT purposes is increased by £25,000 each.

6.6 RETIREMENT RELIEF – GENERAL PROVISIONS
(TCGA 1992, s 163)

Where an individual is aged at least 50 and he satisfies the necessary conditions for a period of ten years, he may be entitled to total exemption for the gain up to a lower threshold, plus one-half of the gain up to a higher threshold.

6.6.1 The amount available for relief
(TCGA 1992, Sched 6, para 13)

Retirement relief is being phased out over the tax years 1999–2000 to 2002–03. The thresholds are being reduced progressively over those tax years as set out below (FA 1998, s 140).

Year	Full relief (£)	Partial relief (£)
1998–99	250,000	1,000,000
1999–00	200,000	800,000
2000–01	150,000	600,000
2001–02	100,000	400,000
2002–03	50,000	200,000

On a qualifying disposal by an individual the amount available for relief is

- so much of the gains qualifying for relief as do not exceed the appropriate percentage of £250,000; and
- one half of so much of those gains as exceed the appropriate percentage of £250,000 but do not exceed that percentage of £1,000,000.

'The appropriate percentage' is a percentage tapered according to the length of the qualifying period which is appropriate to the disposal on a scale rising arithmetically from 10% where that period is precisely one year to 100% where it is ten years. Full retirement relief is thus available only where the individual has been in business for a period of at least ten years ending with the disposal. The relief is not determined by the period of ownership of particular assets.

Example

> *B*, who has been a sole trader manufacturing widgets since 1994, acquired factory premises in 1996 for £100,000. These are now worth £800,000. If *B* sold his business in September 2000, and all of the capital gains realised relate to the premises, he will qualify for retirement relief as follows:
>
> | | | £ | £ |
> |---|---|---:|---:|
> | Capital gains on premises | | | 800,000 |
> | Indexation (say) | | | (80,000) |
> | | | | 720,000 |
> | Retirement relief: | $\frac{6}{10} \times 150,000$ | 90,000 | (90,000) |
> | | $\frac{6}{10} \times 600,000$ | 360,000 | |
> | | *less* relief at full rate | (150,000) | |
> | | | 300,000 | |
> | | $\times 50\%$ | | (150,000) |
> | Chargeable gain | | | 480,000 |
>
> If *B* had started the business in 1987 the relief would be:
>
> | | | £ | £ |
> |---|---|---:|---:|
> | Capital gains on premises | | | 800,000 |
> | Indexation (say) | | | (80,000) |
> | | | | 720,000 |
> | Retirement relief | | | (150,000) |
> | | | 600,000 | |
> | | *less* relief at full rate | (150,000) | |
> | | | 450,000 | |
> | | $\times 50\%$ | | (225,000) |
> | Chargeable gain | | | 345,000 |

Trustees' disposals are treated as disposals by the qualifying beneficiary. If, on the same day, there is both a trustees' disposal and a material disposal of business assets by the qualifying beneficiary, the amount available for relief is applied to the beneficiary's own disposal in priority to the trustees' disposal.

6.6.2 Date of disposal for retirement relief

Although the date of disposal for CGT purposes is generally the date that contracts are exchanged, or the point in time that a conditional contract becomes unconditional, the Revenue operates a concession for retirement relief purposes. The key date here is the date that the contract is completed.

Example – Retirement relief by reference to completion date

> *A* is aged 49 and 10 months when he enters into a contract to sell his hotel business. However, the sale is actually completed three months later, just after he has attained age 50. Because of ESC D31, *A* will normally be given retirement relief.

6.6.3 Retirement through ill health
(TCGA 1992, s 164(1)(b))

The legislation provides that retirement relief is also available to an individual who is below age 50 but is required to dispose of his business because ill health makes it impossible for him to carry on. In practice, the Revenue requires claimants to provide a medical certificate, signed by a qualified medical practitioner (whether or not the claimant's own general practitioner). The Board itself takes advice from the Regional Medical Service of the Department of Health, and in some cases a further medical examination by the regional medical officer is required.

The Revenue has made it clear that retirement relief will *not* be given to someone aged below 50 where he has ceased work because of the ill health of someone else, for example his spouse.

6.6.4 Conditions to be satisfied for ten years if full relief to be available
(TCGA 1992, s 163(4))

The full relief is given only if the individual has satisfied various requirements for a period of ten years but some relief is due provided the qualifying period is at least 12 months. A period is a qualifying period if the individual was in business as a sole trader or partner or he was a full-time officer (eg a director) or employee of a personal trading company. The definition of a personal trading company is the same as in 6.3.8, ie the individual must have at least 5% of the voting rights. Separate periods during which an individual satisfied one of these requirements can normally be aggregated provided there is not an interval between them of more than two years.

For specific requirements in relation to disposals by sole traders, partners and full-time directors and employees of personal trading companies, see 6.7 and 6.8 respectively.

6.6.5 Retirement relief for trustees
(TCGA 1992, s 164(3))

There are certain circumstances where the sale by trustees of family settlements of business property or shares can attract retirement relief. This is an area where professional advice should be taken, but in essence the trustees may be able to utilise unused relief available to a beneficiary (normally a life tenant) who uses land etc which is owned by the trustees for a trade carried on by him. Similarly retirement relief may be due to trustees who hold shares in a company where the beneficiary is a full-time director or employee.

6.7 RETIREMENT RELIEF AND UNINCORPORATED TRADERS

The sale of a business may be broken down for tax purposes into the disposal of distinct assets (ie goodwill and buildings, plant and equipment, stock debtors and cash). The CGT position must be looked at separately for each asset.

6.7.1 Retirement relief for sole traders

The legislation requires that a capital gain should arise on the disposal of a business or part of a business. There have been several cases concerning farmers where the individual concerned has disposed of part of his land. In each of these cases, the courts have held that retirement relief was not due since the asset disposed of was used in the business rather than part of the business itself. A similar point arises if a sole trader sells a warehouse or office block, but continues in business.

In practice, the Revenue resists relief for farmers unless the disposal concerns at least 50% or more of the total area being farmed.

6.7.2 Retirement relief for partners

A gain may attract retirement relief where it arises on a disposal which takes place on the introduction of a new partner or on some other change in profit-sharing ratios combined with a revaluation of partnership assets (see 6.5.4).

In some cases, a partner may own an asset which is used by his firm.

Retirement relief is available to cover a gain arising from the disposal of such an asset provided the following conditions are satisfied:

(1) The disposal of the asset must take place as part of the individual's withdrawal from participation in the business carried on by the partnership.

(2) Immediately before the disposal (or the cessation of the business) the asset must have been used for the purposes of the partnership business.

(3) During the whole or part of the period in which the asset has been in the ownership of the individual, the asset must have been used for the purposes of:
(a) the business; or
(b) another business carried on by the individual or by a partnership of which the individual concerned was a member.

The amount of retirement relief on the disposal may be restricted where the partner has charged his firm a commercial rent for use of the property.

Example – Restriction on retirement relief where partner has charged rent

> A is a partner in a four partner firm, and he takes a 25% share of profits. He owns the offices used by the firm and charges a market rent of £10,000 per annum.
>
> The Revenue ignores the rent that A effectively bears himself, but in this situation only 25% of any capital gain realised on the sale of the offices would qualify for retirement relief. If A had charged only £5,000 (ie less than the market rent of £10,000) the proportion of the gain eligible for retirement relief would be
>
> $$\frac{10,000 - 3750}{10,000} \quad \text{ie} \quad \frac{5}{8}$$

6.8 RETIREMENT RELIEF AND FULL-TIME DIRECTORS AND EMPLOYEES
(TCGA 1992, ss 163–164)

This section focuses on the way in which the capital gain on the sale of shares in a personal trading company (see 6.3.8) and assets owned privately by the shareholder may qualify for retirement relief.

6.8.1 Full-time working directors and managers

To qualify for retirement relief, it is sufficient for an individual to work for the company on a full-time basis in a managerial or technical capacity.

There is no statutory definition of what full-time means in this context. In practice, it is understood that the Revenue accepts that a director whose normal working week is 30 hours (excluding meal breaks) qualifies for relief. A person is required to devote more or less the whole of his time if that is what his job and service contract involve. Absence through illness does not normally prejudice entitlement to the relief.

In some cases, the individual will be working full-time for a group of related companies. Relief is available where a person is required to devote more or less the whole of his time to the service of a commercial association of companies which carry on businesses and which are of a nature that the business of a company and the associated companies taken together may be reasonably considered to make up a single composite undertaking.

This is an area where professional advice may be required in the light of the circumstances of the particular case.

A director who has retired from full-time employment, but who continues to spend an average of at least ten hours per week in the conduct and management of the company's business, may qualify for relief. However, his entitlement is based on the period of full-time service which he had up to the date of his retirement.

6.8.2 Possible restriction of retirement relief

Where a company has investments as well as business interests, the gain which may attract retirement relief is restricted to the proportion of the gain determined by the following fraction:

$$\frac{\text{Chargeable assets used for business purposes}}{\text{Total chargeable assets}}$$

Where a company has disposed of business assets within six months of a disposal of shares, the individual may elect for the restriction to be computed by reference to the position if the company had not sold the assets concerned.

Example of restriction

D holds all the shares in X Ltd. The balance sheet of X Ltd shows the following assets:

	£
Cash at bank	100,000
Gilts	400,000
Quoted shares	500,000
Factory	1,000,000
	2,000,000

The normal approach would be to treat only a proportion of any gain as qualifying for retirement relief. The proportion would be:

$$\frac{1,000,000}{1,500,000} \quad \text{ie} \quad \frac{\text{(Business assets)}}{\text{(chargeable assets)}}$$

215

The cash and the gilts are not chargeable assets and are therefore left out of the equation altogether.

However, it may be that the company has a chargeable asset which does not feature in the balance sheet (goodwill) and the inclusion of this business asset at its market value may increase the proportion of the gain which qualifies for retirement relief.

6.8.3 Sale of premises etc used by company

An individual who has been a full-time director or employee may own property or some other assets which are used by his personal trading company. Retirement relief may be claimed in respect of a disposal of such assets provided the following conditions are satisfied:

(1) the disposal of the asset must take place as part of the withdrawal of the individual concerned from participation in the business carried on by the company; and

(2) the asset must be in use for the purposes of the company's business at the time of the disposal or it must have been so used at the time that the company's business ceased; and

(3) the asset must have been used in the whole or part of the period in which the individual has owned it for the purposes of:
   (a) the business carried on by the company; or
   (b) another business carried on by the individual or by a partnership of which the individual was a member; or
   (c) another business carried on by the individual's personal trading company.

Relief is restricted where the individual has charged rent. If a full market rent has been charged, no retirement relief is due whatsoever. If the rent is half of the market rent, half of the gain on the disposal of the property may be eligible for retirement relief.

7

OUTLINE OF VAT

DAVID BERTRAM, CLAYFIELD PROFESSIONAL GUIDANCE LTD

Value added tax was introduced by FA 1972 and became operational on 1 April 1973 when it replaced purchase tax and selective employment tax. In concept, it is a simple tax, although various exclusions from a VAT charge and the EU influence have resulted in a simple concept becoming one of the most complicated taxes of all time.

7.1 INTRODUCTION

Part of the EU philosophy is the harmonisation of taxing statutes, particularly those that affect cross-border trading activities. For example, customs duty is an EU tax and is payable when goods enter the EU. It is charged at the same rate when or wherever the goods enter the Community.

Once customs duty is paid the goods are in free circulation and can move freely between member states without the payment of any further duty or being subject to customs' controls. The legislative authority for customs duty is found in EU Regulations which, once agreed by the EU Commission, have immediate direct effect in each member state.

The harmonisation of VAT has been the subject of much discussion by the EU Commission, which has resulted in the introduction of transitional rules with effect from 1 January 1993, commonly referred to as the Single Market Legislation. The rules implement a degree of harmonisation on the VAT accounting requirements of the movement of goods between member states. The ultimate legal authority for VAT is a number of EU VAT directives, which must be reflected in the national legislation of each member state. To that extent, directives have direct effect. For example, if the national law is not in accordance with a directive and thereby disadvantages the taxpayer, the taxpayer can argue his case in the national court, which must recognise the directive. The ultimate right of appeal lies to the European Court of Justice.

The administration of VAT was given to HM Customs and Excise, which introduced a completely new system of tax enforcement to the majority of businesses and the accounting profession. Customs, which is steeped in the history of duty enforcement, brought with it its practical approach to controlling the taxpayer. For the first time, many businesses and their professional advisers had to justify, face to face with the enforcement agencies (the VAT control officer), what had been declared in the VAT return and the amounts shown in the annual accounts.

In principle, for the majority of businesses VAT is not a tax on profits. It is a tax on the consumer that is collected in stages throughout the business chain and is collected, eventually, by the business person supplying the consumer (ie an individual or a business which is not registered for VAT). If a business fails to charge and account for VAT correctly, it must account for both the VAT and any penalties from its own resources and thereby, by default, VAT becomes a charge on profits. Put simply, the business person is a tax collector.

Within the EU, neutrality is achieved by means of an exemption or zero-rating of goods to other member states and taxing 'acquisitions' in the member state of destination. The VAT paid by the final consumer in any country is therefore the same whether he obtains the goods from his own country or from another EU country.

Example – How the VAT system works

A retailer sells goods for £1,000 excluding VAT and therefore adds £175 (at a UK VAT rate of 17.5%). The retailer pays his supplier £750 plus VAT of £131.25. He has to pay VAT charged on the sale to Customs but is entitled to deduct the VAT paid to his suppliers. Hence the net payment to Customs is £43.75.

7.2 LEGAL AUTHORITIES

There is no single piece of legislation covering the administration and collection of VAT. The VAT legislation is described briefly below.

7.2.1 The VAT Act 1994 (VATA 1994)

This is a consolidation Act which brings together VATA 1983 and subsequent Finance Acts amending the original legislation. VATA 1994 deals with the administration of the tax and provides for certain aspects to be dealt with by delegated legislation.

7.2.2 Statutory instruments (SIs)

There are various SIs which deal with particular aspects of VAT administration. The most notable is the Value Added Tax Regulations 1995 (SI No 2518) which deals with a wide range of administrative procedures which must be complied with (eg tax invoices, when they should be issued and the details required to be shown; how to recover VAT when a VAT-registered person is not entitled to a full recovery of VAT paid to its suppliers; special VAT accounting procedures for particular transactions, etc).

7.2.3 Treasury orders

Certain Treasury orders describe, among other things, what is or is not chargeable to VAT and also give legal authority to certain organisations able to recover VAT which would otherwise be irrecoverable. Occasionally, Treasury orders are published in the *London Gazette*.

7.2.4 Customs notices and leaflets

The general principle is that VAT public notices are not part of the law. Certain notices, however, are published pursuant to VATA 1994 and SIs and, thereby, *are* part of the law. As such they have the same status as an Act of Parliament and are legally binding upon the taxpayer. For example, Notice 700 (General Guide) is principally Customs' interpretation of the law, but the section dealing with the maintenance of accounting records is part of the law, as is the Public Notice on the special VAT Retail Schemes (Notice 727).

Customs' leaflets are not strictly part of the law but certain leaflets, which explain the commissioners' requirements for particular types of transactions, are, in practical terms, legally binding. This applies to relatively few of the leaflets, the vast majority being simply the commissioners' interpretation of the law.

7.2.5 EC directives

All VAT law stems from the EC Sixth VAT Directive which has direct effect in all member states through respective national laws. Other directives deal with specific aspects such as that which, on 1 January 1993, introduced VAT harmonisation in the single market and others which provide the right to recover VAT incurred in other countries.

7.3 BASIC PRINCIPLES

The basic rule is that VAT is chargeable on the taxable supply of any goods or services in the UK when supplied by a taxable person 'in the course or furtherance of any business'.

7.3.1 Supplies

The application of VAT differs depending on whether there is a supply of goods or of services. A supply of goods is where legal title to the whole property is, or is to be, transferred to another person. This includes, for example, the transfer of title in land by means of a freehold sale or a lease exceeding 21 years. Anything which is not a supply of goods which is done for a consideration is a supply of services and, therefore, subject to the VAT regime. A VAT charge only arises where consideration is present and, accordingly, a free supply of services is outside the scope of VAT. Care is required, because what may appear to be free is not necessarily so in real terms and a hidden VAT liability could arise. By Treasury Order, any transaction can be deemed to be a supply of goods and not a supply of services (or vice versa). Examples of supplies of goods which may not be self evident are as follows:

(1) The application to another person's goods of a treatment or process which produces goods (eg the making of a suit by a tailor from the cloth provided by his customer is a supply of goods and not a supply of tailoring services).
(2) The supply of any form of power, heat, refrigeration or ventilation.

A supply is subject to VAT at the standard rate unless the VAT legislation provides for specific relief. VATA 1994 provides for two forms of relief:

(1) Zero rating under s 30 and specified in Sched 8 to the Act.
(2) Exemption under s 31 and specified in Sched 9 to the Act.

Taxable

These are supplies that are subject to VAT at either the zero or the standard (currently 17.5%) rate. Supplies of fuel and power are taxable at 5% when supplied for domestic use or for use for a charity otherwise than in the course or furtherance of a business.

Zero-rated supplies

The zero-rated supplies are exports of goods to places outside the EU (VATA 1994, s 30) and the 16 groups listed in VATA 1994, Sched 8:

(1) Food for human consumption
(2) Sewerage services and water (but not bottled water)
(3) Books, etc
(4) Talking books for the blind and handicapped, and wireless sets for the blind
(5) Construction and sales of new dwellings
(6) Approved alteration of protected buildings
(7) International services·
(8) Transport
(9) Caravans and houseboats
(10) Gold

(11) Bank notes
(12) Drugs, medicines, aids for the handicapped etc
(13) Imports, exports etc
(14) Charities (certain supplies to or by charities)
(15) Protective and young children's clothing and footwear.

Exempt

These are supplies that are exempt from VAT by statute, ie those listed in VATA 1994, Sched 9. Exemption and zero-rating must not be confused because the overall effect on a business is totally different. Zero-rating gives entitlement to recover VAT on underlying costs whereas exemption does not (see 7.4.5). The main headings under Sched 9 are:

(1) Land (with some exceptions)
(2) Insurance
(3) Postal services
(4) Betting, gaming and lotteries
(5) Finance
(6) Education (when provided by eligible bodies); this heading also includes supplies by youth clubs
(7) Health and welfare
(8) Burial and cremation
(9) Trade unions and professional bodies
(10) Sports competitions and physical education
(11) Works of art etc (in limited circumstances)
(12) Fund-raising events by charities and other qualifying bodies
(13) Cultural services
(14) Supplies of goods where input tax cannot be recovered
(15) Investment gold.

Outside the scope

Certain supplies or business activities are 'outside the scope' of VAT. This includes an employee's services to an employer but can also include what, on the face of it, are the organisation's normal trading activities. For example, the supply of goods that are situated outside the UK, although part of the UK business activities, are outside the scope of UK VAT. Similarly, with effect from 1 January 1993, certain services that are either physically performed or are to be received outside the UK are deemed to have been supplied outside the UK and, therefore, outside the scope of UK VAT.

Generally speaking, an organisation's 'outside the scope' activities do not permit the recovery of VAT on related costs. The exception to this general principle is where a VAT-registered person supplies goods or services outside the UK that would be subject to VAT if made in the UK. There are also special arrangements for certain services which are exempt in the UK but the recipient belongs outside the EU.

7.3.2 Business
(VATA 1994, s 94)

A supply for VAT purposes must be made in the course or furtherance of any business. As with supply, the word 'business' has not been defined in the legislation but has been interpreted to have a very wide meaning and covers all organisations that carry on activities in a businesslike way. There are directions in the legislation of what the term encompasses and excludes, eg:

- Business includes any trade, profession or vocation.
- Any act done in the furtherance of a business's termination or disposition, whether or not in connection with its reorganisation or winding-up, is regarded as a supply in the course or furtherance of a business.
- A body is *not* treated as carrying on a business if its objects are in the public domain and are of a political, religious, philanthropic, philosophical or patriotic nature, and a subscription by members only entitles the member to participate in the management or receive reports on its activities.

In *C & E Commissioners v Apple and Pear Development Council* [1984] STC 296 the decision included the following definition of business:

> 'a business for the purpose of Value Added Tax requires the carrying on of an occupation, function or activity which includes the making of some supplies recognised for Value Added Tax purposes.'

A number of organisations which do not consider themselves to be carrying on a business (such as clubs and associations, charities etc) have to conform with the VAT legislation and, where appropriate, register and account for VAT on their business income.

If it can be demonstrated that the activity is purely and simply a hobby, there is no requirement to charge VAT on any resulting income. An employee's services to an employer in return for a salary meets the 'supply of services' definition but the law specifically provides that such services are not in the course or furtherance of a business and, therefore, are outside the scope of VAT.

Charities

There is no automatic relief from VAT for supplies either to or made by charities. If a charity is carrying on a business activity it is required to register and account for VAT on its business income the same as any commercial organisation. Normally a business activity is one which is concerned with the making of taxable supplies for a consideration. The following is a guide to the business and non-business position of the more common activities of charities.

Non-business activities include:

- Donations, legacies and other voluntary contributions from the public.
- Voluntary services performed free of charge.

Business activities include:

- Grants which are the consideration for services rendered, where a benefit is provided to the grantor.
- Sales of donated goods, but in certain circumstances such sales are relieved of VAT by zero rating.
- Hiring out charity run buildings.

Several income sources could be business or non-business depending on the circumstances. The most common area of difficulty is sponsorship. If a sponsor receives nothing in return for his sponsorship, the donation is outside the scope of VAT. If the contribution is made on condition that the sponsor is promoted or receives some benefit, it is the consideration for a taxable supply.

There is relief from VAT by means of zero rating for certain supplies to charities. These are mainly in the health and welfare area but also include:

- The supply of an advertisement on television or in a newspaper, periodical or journal for educational or fund-raising purposes. The relief has recently been extended to job recruitment advertisements provided the advert publicises the charity objectives.
- The supply of a new building and an extension to an existing building which is otherwise standard rated provided the building is intended solely for use for a relevant residential or relevant charitable (ie non-business) purpose.
- Supplies in the course of constructing a building for use as above.

Clubs and associations
(VATA 1994, s 94(2)(a))

Many local clubs and associations, usually formed by local residents, consider they are not carrying on a business, but this is incorrect. The law specifically provides that the provision of benefits to members in return for a subscription or other payment is a business activity. Similarly certain trade and professional organisations consider they are not in business or qualify for exemption as professional associations and there is no requirement to register for VAT. Such organisations generally provide other benefits to their members and, possibly, non-members which are not within the exemption and, therefore, there may be a liability to register.

Admission to premises
(VATA 1994, s 94(2)(b))

The admission, for payment, of persons to any premises is a business activity. Any person carrying on such an activity is required to register and account for VAT if such income exceeds the registration threshold. To avoid the risk of penalties all clubs, associations, charities and similar organisations should review their activities to ensure that they meet their VAT obligations at the correct time.

7.3.3 Taxable person

In addition to considering the words 'supply' and 'business', it is necessary to consider the meaning of 'taxable person' since VAT is not chargeable on supplies made by non-taxable persons. A taxable person is one who is or is liable to be registered for VAT. In other words, it is not possible to avoid VAT by failing to register. Registration is considered in 7.4.1 below.

'Taxable person' is also defined by art 4 of the EC Sixth Directive as 'any person who independently carries out in any place any economic activity'. 'Economic activity' includes all activities of producers, traders and persons supplying services (including mining and agricultural activities) and professionals' activities. The exploitation of tangible or intangible property to obtain income therefrom on a continuing basis is also considered an economic activity.

7.3.4 Consideration

VAT is chargeable on the consideration provided for a supply. Consideration is important as supplies of services for no consideration are not taxable supplies and therefore outside the scope for VAT.

7.4 PRACTICAL IMPLICATIONS

The administration of VAT is by a system of registration, accounting and the submission of regular returns by the taxpayer and control verification visits by Customs.

7.4.1 Registration

Registration is required where a business or any other organisation makes taxable supplies over a pre-determined limit. The limits, based on gross turnover, are increased each year generally in line with inflation.

It is the person who is registered, not the business activity. Once registered, all business activities must be reflected in the VAT accounting records: for example a VAT-registered sole proprietor carrying on several businesses must include the turnover from all his businesses in his VAT accounts. A company is a separate entity from the individuals who own it and must be registered separately. For VAT purposes, a partnership is a separate entity to the persons who are partners in it.

From 1 April 2000 registration is required when one of the following two conditions is satisfied:

(1) When, at the end of any month, the gross taxable turnover during the previous 12 months, on a rolling basis, exceeds £52,000. Such a liability must be notified within 30 days and registration is effective from the first day of the month following the month in which a liability to notify arose. For example, where taxable turnover in the 12 months to 31 January was, say, £55,000, notification must be made within 30 days and registration is effective from 1 March. VAT has to be accounted for on all income received after 1 March, whether or not it refers to invoices issued on or before 28 February. There is no VAT liability for income received prior to the effective date of registration.

(2) As soon as there are reasonable grounds to believe the value of taxable supplies to be made during the following 30 days will exceed £52,000. Registration is due immediately and will be effective from the beginning of the period.

It is only *taxable* turnover (ie goods or services liable to VAT at either the zero or standard rate) that is taken into consideration when determining whether there is a liability to register. Income which is exempt and outside the scope of VAT is ignored. Supplies of goods which are capital assets of the business are disregarded for the purpose of the registration thresholds, with the exception of standard-rated supplies of interests in land.

Note that self supplies, imported services and acquisitions from the EU all need to be taken into account when determining whether registration is necessary.

Voluntary registration

There is an entitlement to register voluntarily for VAT even if the taxable turnover is below the VAT registration limits. This could be an advantage to an expanding or small business as VAT on costs are recoverable and this, providing the charging of VAT on supplies does not reduce demand for the product, increases profitability. Similarly businesses based in the UK which do not make any supplies there, but make what would be taxable supplies overseas, are entitled to register and are thereby able to recover VAT on UK costs.

Intending registration

A person is eligible to register for VAT even though he is not yet making taxable supplies. The *Merseyside Cablevision Ltd* case (MAN/85/327; [1987] 3 CMLR 290) has affected radically the rules relating to intending registration. Prior to FA 1988, a person who satisfied Customs that he intended to make taxable supplies from a specified date and would be liable to be registered when he commenced to make taxable supplies could request to be registered and Customs could, subject to such conditions as it thought fit to impose, register him from a date as agreed between them. However, these terms were *ultra vires* the provisions contained in VATA 1983, Sched 1, para 5. This provided taxpayers with a right to registration where the taxpayer is carrying on a business, and there is an intention to make taxable supplies in the course or furtherance of that business.

There appears to be no time limit between the dates on which intending registration takes effect and the first taxable supply is made. Normally this is a matter of several months or perhaps one or two years, as stocks are bought in and premises are prepared.

Applicants for intending registration must satisfy Customs that there is an intention to make taxable supplies. This could mean submitting documentation (ie contracts or purchase invoices).

Group registration

Incorporated companies under common control with a belonging in the UK may register as a group and if so are treated as a single unit. The main advantage of group treatment is any supplies from one member of the group to another are disregarded for VAT purposes. One company is nominated as representative member and any supplies made by or to the group are treated as being made to or by the representative member. However, each company within the group is jointly and severally liable for any tax due from the representative member. Only one VAT return need be completed showing the consolidated figures for all members of the VAT group.

There are two main conditions for entry into a VAT group:

- *Residence*   To meet this test the company must be UK resident (ie belonging) although a non-UK-resident company may become a member of a VAT group provided it has an established place of business in the UK which would constitute a belonging.
- *Control*   All companies in a group must be under the control of the same person or persons. This control can be exercised by a company (which need not be a member of the group itself), an individual or a partnership.

Customs uses the definition of control set out in the Companies Act 1985. Control is held to exist:

- where a company holds the majority voting rights in another;
- where the company is a member of the other company and has the right to appoint or remove the majority of its board of directors;
- where one company has the right to exercise a dominant influence over the other company either by provision in the memorandum or articles of association or by virtue of a control contract;
- where a company is a member of another and, by reason of an agreement with the other members, controls a majority of voting rights in the company.

For an individual or individuals to be considered to have control they must have the same control as if they were a holding company and the rules were applied as above.

In *CCE v Kingfisher plc* [1994] STC 63, the effect of a VAT group registration under s 29 of VATA 1983 (now VATA 1994, s 43) was considered. The Commissioners contended that the effect of group registration was merely to provide a simplified accounting procedure whereby supplies of goods and services intra group were disregarded for VAT purposes, but that group registration did not create a single taxable person. The VAT tribunal decided that the purpose of group registration was to enable the group to be treated as if it were a single body corporate, the different member companies being no more than different departments. On an appeal by the Commissioners to the High Court, the tribunal decision was upheld.

Customs has specific authority to deny entry into a group registration where it considers it necessary to protect the Revenue. Customs has fuller powers to restrict changes in VAT groups, including preventing the removal of a member from the group and its complete disbandment. This is as a direct result of the tribunal's decision in *Thorn Materials Supply Ltd & Thorn Resources Ltd* (LON194/1996A and 1987A) which highlighted a simple loophole to avoid VAT. These powers have been further strengthened in FA 1997.

A VAT group registration may not be identical to an accounting group. Companies within an accounting group, which are not members of a VAT group, must account for VAT on supplies to each other as if they were unconnected.

Applications for group registration should be submitted at least 90 days before the intended date of the registration coming into effect.

7.4.2 Deregistration

A registered person, or one who has become liable to be registered, only ceases to be liable to be registered if at any time Customs is satisfied that:

- he has ceased to make taxable supplies;
- the value of taxable supplies in the period of one year then beginning will not exceed specified limits; the current limit is £50,000.

It is a requirement that a person who ceases to make or intends to make taxable supplies must notify Customs within 30 days of the date on which he does so or forms the intention to do so. Notification must be in writing and state the date on which the registered person ceased to make or have the intention of making taxable supplies.

One of the consequences of deregistration is that, subject to certain exceptions, tax must be accounted for on any goods forming part of the business assets which were on hand at the close of business or on the last day of registration. The exceptions include where:

(1) the business is transferred as a going concern to another taxable person;
(2) a taxable person has died, become bankrupt or incapacitated and the business is carried on by another person who is treated as the taxable person;
(3) the tax involved is not more than £250.

In addition, the provisions do not apply to any goods where the taxable person can show that no credit for input tax had been allowed for the supply of goods.

7.4.3 Accounting for VAT

It is a requirement for all taxpayers to maintain a VAT account. The VAT Regulations 1995 (SI No 2518), regs 31–39 set down specifically what is to be included in the account. Separate accounts should be maintained for each tax period, known as prescribed accounting periods, and each account should be split into two portions – tax payable and tax allowable. The tax payable portion should include a total of output tax due for that prescribed accounting period, a total of output tax due on acquisitions from other member states, and corrections and adjustments to the tax payable. The tax allowable portion should include a total of the input tax allowable to the taxable person for that prescribed accounting period including the total allowable for acquisitions from other member states and corrections and adjustments.

VAT returns have to be submitted on a regular basis. Each VAT-registered person is normally allocated a three-monthly VAT accounting period, but it is possible to request a particular VAT period (for example to coincide with the business's financial year). It is also possible to request monthly returns if the business regularly recovers VAT from Customs. There is also a scheme whereby it is possible to make annual returns (see 7.7.4).

The largest VAT-registered businesses (ie those which normally pay more than £2m annually to Customs) are required to make monthly payments on account with a balancing payment when the three-monthly VAT return is submitted. The actual monthly payments are calculated by reference to the VAT liability of a reference year.

Returns must be submitted with full payment by the end of the month following the end of the VAT accounting period (the due date). A failure to submit returns and make full payment by the due date is subject to penalties (see 7.8.2). Taxpayers who make regular payments can apply to use the Credit Transfer Scheme which allows a further seven days for payment.

Where a registered person has failed to make a return for a period or where the return appears to be incomplete or incorrect, Customs is empowered to make an assessment of the amount due and notify it to the registered person. The assessment is usually produced automatically by the VAT Central Unit and estimates the amount based on the taxpayer's previous VAT return history. Where the assessed amount is lower than the actual liability, a further assessment is issued when this fact is discovered, usually by the local VAT control officer.

7.4.4 Output VAT

The VAT chargeable on supplies (known as output tax) made during a period must be declared on the return which is provided automatically each period by Customs. Output VAT is due on all supplies made (normally invoices issued during the period), irrespective of whether the invoices have been paid for. There are special schemes available to ease this particular requirement for certain business classes as explained below. In addition, VAT is due on all money received for supplies made during the period and for which a tax invoice has not been issued (eg scrap sales, vending machine income, emptying telephone boxes, staff canteen sales, and certain deductions from salaries for supplies to staff).

For businesses which do not issue tax invoices, such as retailers, VAT is due on the gross taxable income received during the VAT period.

Tax invoices

A registered taxable person making a standard-rated taxable supply to another taxable person must provide him with a tax invoice. The issue of invoices for zero-rated supplies and for supplies to customers who are not taxable persons is optional. A tax invoice must, unless Customs agrees otherwise, be issued within 30 days after the basic tax point (see below), the time the VAT is due.

The invoices are often addressed to the person who is going to pay them and not to whom the goods and services are supplied. It is important to be aware that this may cause problems as only the person receiving goods or services can recover VAT on the invoice.

The details to be shown on a tax invoice are the:

(1) identifying number;
(2) date of supply (ie tax point);
(3) date of issue;
(4) supplier's name, address and registration number;

(5) name and address of the person to whom the goods or services are supplied;
(6) type of supply;
(7) description;
(8) for each description, quantity or extent of services, rate of tax and amount payable excluding tax;
(9) gross amount payable;
(10) rate of any cash discount offered;
(11) amount of tax chargeable at each rate; and
(12) total amount of tax chargeable.

Tax points

The output tax on a supply of goods or services becomes chargeable at a definite time, called the tax point. The rate of tax charged is the rate in force on the tax point, and the supply must be accounted for on the VAT return which covers the prescribed accounting period in which the tax point occurs. The tax point is also important for recovery of VAT because it determines when a claim for VAT may be made. Particular rules are laid down which determine the tax point in a wide variety of circumstances. Many of the rules are, in principle, common to both supplies of goods and services.

The basic tax point is when VAT becomes due and chargeable and is generally determined at the time:

(1) goods are removed by or made available to the customer;
(2) services are performed (ie completed).

The basic tax point for both goods and services may be overridden by the issue of a tax invoice or the receipt of payment in either of the following circumstances:

(1) Where a tax invoice is issued or payment is received before the basic tax point, this earlier date is taken as the tax point.
(2) Where a tax invoice is issued within 14 days after the basic tax point, the date of the invoice is taken as the tax point. Customs has discretion to allow a longer period than 14 days if requested.

The question of whether the receipt of a payment constitutes a tax point has been considered in various court cases. In *C&E Commrs v Faith Construction* [1989] STC 539 the Court of Appeal held that the word should take its ordinary meaning, so that if the customer's liability has been discharged, and the recipient is left without any right to sue for payment, then a payment has been received, even if that payment is regarded as fettered.

In *C&E Commrs v Moonrakers Guest House Ltd* [1992] STC 544, the High Court held deposits for rooms were taxable when received, even if the booking was subsequently cancelled with the deposit forfeited if the room was not re-let. By contrast, in *Richmond Theatre Management Ltd* the VAT

Tribunal decided that the tax point for advance ticket sales was when the performance in question ended. This was because the monies received were said to be held in trust for the customer and were refundable if the performance did not take place or the customer was refused admission. This decision was later overturned by the High Court (((1995) *The Times*, 1 February) which ruled that the customers had allowed the company to make whatever use it wished of the ticket money. Therefore output tax was due at the time of payment.

Note that there are special arrangements which apply to the supply of continuous or periodic services. The tax point is the earlier of the date of issue of a tax invoice or the date a payment is received.

Bad debt relief

There have been a number of amendments to the VAT bad debt relief scheme. These changes take effect from a variety of dates.

If a supply is made after 26 November 1996, and the debtor has not paid the supplier within six months, the unpaid supplier can make a claim for bad debt relief (it is not necessary to show that the customer is formally insolvent, merely that he has not paid). At the same time, the debtor ceases to have the right to claim input tax credit on the supply which he has received but not yet paid for, and must repay the input tax claimed to Customs. If, later, the debtor makes payment to his supplier, then the debtor's input tax claim is restored. However, the supplier must now repay the bad debt relief which he has received.

From 17 December 1996, the six-month period for a claim for bad debt relief is measured from the time when payment for the supply is due (and not from the date of the supply).

From 19 March 1997 it is not necessary for the goods to have passed from the supplier to the customer before the supplier can make a claim for bad debt relief. This is useful if the supplier claims reservation of title (*Romalpa* clause).

From 1 May 1997, if a business is transferred as a going concern and the purchaser takes over the seller's VAT registration (on Form VAT 68), the purchaser takes over the seller's entitlement to bad debt relief. He also has an obligation to repay any bad debt relief if payment is subsequently received from the debtor.

7.4.5 **VAT recovery**

VAT-registered businesses may offset any VAT paid to suppliers (known as input tax) against the output tax declared, subject to the following conditions:

(1) Goods or services have been *supplied to* and have been, or will be, used by the business to make taxable supplies.

(2) Documentary evidence of the supply received (ie a tax invoice to the business by the supplier) is retained. If there is no tax invoice or other documentary evidence, the VAT officer may refuse claims for input tax, although Customs has discretion to accept alternative evidence.

Supplies of zero-rated goods or services are taxable supplies with an entitlement to recover VAT on related costs; there is no such entitlement for exempt supplies. In addition VAT is not recoverable as input tax on goods or services received by the VAT-registered person which are used for a non-business activity or for private use, or are certainly outside the scope transactions. Many people believe that because a VAT-registered business pays an invoice, there is an entitlement to recover the VAT shown on the invoice. This is not correct and to do so may give rise to penalties.

The recovery of VAT by businesses which make both taxable and exempt supplies is described at 7.4.6.

Subject to certain exceptions, VAT on the purchase of a motor car or on business entertainment expenses is not recoverable as input tax (VAT (Cars) Order 1992 (SI No 3122) and VAT (Input Tax) Order 1992 (SI No 3222)). Note that a question has been raised of whether the UK is correct in blocking VAT recovery on cars, and the law may be altered.

Motor cars

'Motor car' is defined as a vehicle usually used on public roads with three or more wheels which either:

(1) is constructed solely for the carriage of passengers; or
(2) has roofed accommodation fitted with, or constructed or adapted for the fitting of, windows to the rear of the driver.

The definition is wide and a number of semi-commercial vehicles fall within the definition, eg Land Rovers (see *C&E Commrs v Jeynes t/a Midland International (Hire) Caterers* [1984] STC 30).

VAT is normally recoverable on the acquisition of a motor car where it is:

(1) leased or hired (not a lease purchase);
(2) acquired unused specifically to be sold;
(3) acquired to convert it into a vehicle which is not a motor car;
(4) unused and supplied to a person whose only taxable supply is the hire of motor cars to other taxable persons whose business is predominately the provision of motor cars to disabled persons in respect of a mobility allowance.

In addition, VAT is recoverable on the purchase of motor cars by the following businesses:

(1) self-drive hire companies providing the hiring is to the same person (which may be a company) and is less than 30 consecutive days on any one occasion and 90 days total pa;
(2) driving schools;
(3) taxi firms;
(4) companies leasing cars to any of the above businesses.

With effect from 1 August 1995, recovery of VAT is allowed on cars purchased wholly for business use. If a car is made available for private use, recovery of input tax remains blocked. The relief generally applies to car leasing companies. Taxpayers leasing cars where there is an element of private use are restricted to a 50% recovery of VAT on the leasing charges. The UK has applied for a derogation from the European Commission to restrict recovery.

Business entertainment

Business entertainment is not regarded as including staff entertainment, but problems may arise where costs of staff entertainment arise incidentally from the provision of entertainment for clients. Staff entertainment does not include entertainment of self-employed representatives and therefore the VAT is non-recoverable (see *C&E Commrs v Shaklee International* [1981] STC 776).

There are a number of occasions where VAT on promotional activities is classified as business entertaining and the VAT non-recoverable. It includes for example the cost of a box at a racecourse, entertainment at trade fairs, exhibitions etc, subscriptions to squash clubs etc, entertaining shareholders, and entertainment by market research companies who invite people for group discussions.

There are two conflicting court decisions on business entertainment. In each case the issue was whether, where the supply in question was used partly for business entertainment and partly for normal use, the whole of the input tax should be excluded from credit, or whether an apportionment was permissible. In *C&E Commrs v Plant Repair and Services (South Wales) Ltd* [1994] STC 232 it was decided that once it was shown that goods or services were used or to be used for business entertainment purposes, the input tax on the entire supply was non-recoverable. In *Thorn EMI plc v C&E Commrs* [1994] STC 469 the opposite conclusion was reached. It was held that a system of proportional deduction was in order where goods and services were used in part for business use and in part for business entertainment. This decision was upheld in the High Court where the previous ruling in *Plant Repair and Services,* above, was also overturned.

7.4.6 Partial exemption

A business that makes both exempt and taxable supplies is known as partially exempt and is generally unable to recover all VAT paid to its suppliers. However, if the VAT on costs relating, directly and indirectly, to the exempt activities (known as exempt input tax) is below prescribed limits, all the VAT is recoverable in full. The current limits for VAT years commencing on or after 1 December 1994 are that exempt input tax must not exceed £625 per month on average in the VAT year (which ends 31 March, 30 April or 31 May depending on the business's VAT return period). In addition, this exempt input tax must also represent less than 50% of the total input tax incurred by a business on all its purchases and expenses for the period. If these limits should be exceeded in any VAT year, *all* the relevant VAT is irrecoverable.

There are other minor limits that apply in particular circumstances and certain exempt supplies may be ignored. The rules are complex and it is advisable to obtain professional advice. Full details may be found in the VAT Regulations 1995 (SI No 2518), regs 99–109 and Customs VAT Notice 706.

Input tax which can be directly attributable to taxable supplies can be recovered in full. Input tax wholly attributable to exempt supplies is not recoverable. The purpose of a partial exemption method is to allocate such input tax as cannot be directly related in either taxable or exempt supplies, in a fair and reasonable proportion. The method, known as the standard method, allocates input tax on the basis of a ratio of the value of taxable supplies to the value of total supplies, rounded up to the nearest whole number. This method can be used without obtaining permission from Customs.

The use of any other method requires Customs' agreement. Customs normally approves any method which produces a fair and reasonable result. Other methods available include using a ratio of exempt input tax to total input tax, a ratio of staff generating taxable income to staff generating exempt income, or a ratio of the number of taxable transactions to exempt transactions.

7.5 IMPORTS, EXPORTS AND SINGLE MARKET

The term imports and exports refers only to goods entering or leaving the UK from or to a place outside the EU.

7.5.1 Imports of goods from outside EU

VAT is due upon the importation of all goods into the UK which would bear VAT if supplied within the UK. The VAT may be paid on importation in one of three ways:

(1) via a deferment facility arranged with Customs;
(2) by arrangement with the clearing/shipping agent;
(3) payment in cash or a banker's draft.

The recovery of VAT paid is determined by the same considerations as would apply to any purchase made in the UK. The evidence required to support input tax deduction on importation is form C79. This is issued by Customs as a certificate detailing the amounts of VAT paid or deferred on importations within the previous calendar month.

7.5.2 Export of goods outside EU

In general, the export of goods from the UK is zero rated. However, to satisfy Customs that zero rating is appropriate it is necessary to hold some evidence that the goods have been exported. An overseas address on a sales invoice is insufficient.

Customs requires supporting evidence in the form of commercial documentation. If this is not available within three months of the date of zero rating the supply, Customs states that the supply is to be treated as standard rated, and VAT accounted for on the relevant VAT return.

7.5.3 Transactions within the single market

With effect from 1 January 1993, supplies to and from EU member states are not regarded as imports (known as acquisitions) or exports (known as supplies). Businesses must maintain records of all movements of goods and make returns for statistical and control purposes.

No VAT is charged on goods arriving from other EU countries where the UK business's VAT registration number is quoted on the invoice. The recipient of the goods must account for VAT on his next VAT return as if he had supplied them. He must calculate the VAT which would have been payable and include the amount with his normal output tax. The same amount may also be recovered as input tax, subject to the normal rules and restrictions on recovery. If the UK VAT number is not quoted, the supplier charges VAT at source.

Supplies of goods to other EU countries are zero rated, provided that the customer's VAT registration number is shown on the sales invoice. If the customer's number is not shown, VAT must be charged at the rate which would be applicable if the goods had been supplied in the UK. Persons selling goods to other EU member states must submit an aggregate sales list within 42 days of the end of each period. This must show, for each quarter, the value of goods supplied to each EU customer together with each customer's VAT registration number.

There is a requirement to furnish more detailed information, known as 'intrastat' returns, for acquisitions (known as arrivals) and supplies (known as despatches). The returns must be furnished when the threshold for arrivals or despatches is exceeded. Currently the threshold for both is £150,000. Returns are required monthly and should be lodged within ten working days following the end of the month. The information required on the intrastat is extensive, and reference should be made to Customs Notice 60. Note that intrastat relates only to goods, not services.

7.6 ANTI-AVOIDANCE MEASURES

7.6.1 Business splitting

Where a business activity is divided among a number of legal entities (eg a series of partnerships with a partner common to all) and the reason for the division is to avoid having to account for VAT, Customs may issue a direction informing all the businesses that they are registered as a single unit and that VAT must be accounted for on all taxable income. The direction can only be from a current or future date.

Rules of similar purpose apply to groups of companies (especially if there is a foreign branch, or overseas company involved).

7.6.2 Sales to connected parties

Where a VAT-registered business supplies goods or services at below market value to a connected party which is not entitled to a full recovery of input tax, Customs may direct, within three years following the supply, that the open market value is used.

7.6.3 Self supplies, etc

Prior to 31 March 1995, in certain circumstances, an output VAT charge arises on normal business activities which are not supplies made to third parties, ie on business expenditure (usually referred to as 'self supplies'). The value of such self supplies is taken into consideration when determining a liability to register for VAT; the more important ones are described below. The reasons behind this liability are both anti-avoidance and to reduce possible trade distortion.

Buildings

Where a business constructs, or has constructed, on its own land a new commercial building of a value exceeding £100,000 and the building is used for exempt supplies (eg as a head office of a partially exempt business, an exempt lease or as a doctor's surgery) there is an output VAT liability. The value is the total construction costs plus the value of the land. Note that the self supply on buildings was repealed with effect from 1 March 1995, but there are transitional arrangements for buildings uncompleted at this date.

Stationery

If an exempt, or partially exempt, business prints its own stationery there is an output VAT liability on the total printing cost (including all overheads). If the in-house printing costs of an otherwise exempt business exceed the VAT registration threshold there is a liability to register and account for VAT on such costs.

Reverse charges

Certain professional and intellectual services purchased from overseas persons give rise to an output tax liability on the recipient. The services are deemed to be both supplied by and received by the UK organisation, ie there is an output tax liability and the VAT may also be recovered under the normal rules (restricted if partially exempt). The services include royalty and/or licence payments; financial, insurance, advertising, legal, accountancy and consultancy services; and the hire of staff or equipment. A full list is contained in VATA 1994, Sched 5.

7.6.4 Transfer of a business

Where a business's assets are transferred to another person who intends to use them to carry on the same kind of business as the vendor, the transaction is not subject to a VAT charge. However, where a VAT group which is partially exempt (ie not entitled to a full recovery of input tax) acquires assets in these circumstances, there is a deemed taxable supply by the VAT group and output tax must be accounted for on the VAT group's return. The corresponding input tax is restricted by whatever method has been agreed with the local VAT office.

7.7 SPECIAL SCHEMES

There are a number of special schemes which are either designed to simplify VAT accounting or reduce the VAT liability.

7.7.1 Retail schemes

These schemes are used by retailers, ie those in trade classification Groups 24 (Retail Division) and 28 (Miscellaneous Services). Generally this means those who deal direct with the public on a cash basis and who do not normally issue tax invoices.

7.7.2 Second-hand schemes

There are a number of special second-hand schemes which provide for VAT to be charged on the profit, if any, as opposed to the full selling price. Schemes are available for:

(1) cars;
(2) motor cycles;
(3) caravans/motor caravans;
(4) works of art, antiques and collector's items;
(5) boats and outboard motors;
(6) electronic organs;
(7) aircraft;
(8) firearms; and
(9) horses and ponies.

Special stock recording and detailed records including invoices are required. The scheme was extended from June 1995 to cover virtually all second-hand goods, works of art, antiques and collectors' items except precious metals and gemstones. It is recognised that dealers in low value, high volume goods will have difficulty maintaining the detailed records required. A simplified method of VAT accounts has therefore been introduced, known as 'global accounting'. Under the system 'eligible businesses' (those who cannot maintain the detailed records) are able to account for VAT on the difference between the total of purchases and sales in each tax period rather than on individual items. This scheme can only be used for eligible second-hand goods which have a purchase price of less than £500 per item.

7.7.3 Cash accounting

The general principle is that VAT must be accounted for on all tax invoices issued whether or not the customer/client has paid for the supply. Businesses that cannot use the retail scheme, and whose annual turnover is less than £350,000 (excluding VAT), may use the cash accounting scheme, provided certain conditions are satisfied. The conditions are laid down in regulations as described in Customs Notice 731, which in this respect has the force of law. Output VAT is not due until payment has been received but, similarly, input tax on purchases/expenses cannot be recovered until the supplier has been paid and a receipt obtained.

7.7.4 Annual accounting

To avoid having to submit returns quarterly, businesses with an annual turnover not exceeding £300,000 (excluding VAT) may be authorised, in writing, by Customs to use the annual accounting scheme. Nine payments, based on the previous year's VAT liability, are made by direct debit and a final, balancing payment is made with the VAT return at the end of the second month following the allocated VAT year.

7.7.5 Tour operators' margin scheme

This scheme must be used by any VAT-registered business which supplies packaged travel/accommodation services. As the name implies, VAT is accountable on the margin, if any, on the package's taxable element. Special record keeping and an annual calculation is required.

7.7.6 Agricultural flat rate scheme

Under this scheme, farmers and other agricultural businesses need not register and submit VAT returns to recover VAT on overhead expenses, etc. Instead, the farmer charges VAT at a nominal 4% on all his supplies which he retains (in lieu of input tax) and which the recipient is entitled to recover as input tax under the normal rules. The scheme requires Customs authorisation and is not applicable to all farmers. Farmers who would benefit by more than £3,000 compared to being VAT-registered are not entitled to join the scheme.

7.8 ENFORCEMENT PROCEDURES

7.8.1 VAT visits

Customs regularly visits VAT-registered businesses to verify the returns submitted. Its powers are extensive and include the rights to see any documents, accounts, etc relating to the business activities and to inspect (but not search) the business premises. The frequency of visit depends upon a number of factors such as the business's size, types of business activity and compliance history. Visits can range from half a day every few years for smaller businesses to several weeks a year for multi-nationals.

Where errors are discovered, the visiting officer raises an assessment for VAT previously under-declared and, where appropriate, imposes a penalty and interest charges (see 7.8.2). It is advisable, therefore, to have all assessments independently reviewed. Customs collects over £1,000m by way of additional assessments from approximately 450,000 visits each year, but most visits do not result in assessments being issued. If the accounting records are well kept and independently reviewed regularly no problem should arise at the visit.

7.8.2 Penalties

There are a number of penalty provisions which Customs may impose automatically, and arbitrarily, for a failure to comply with the many complex VAT regulations. These were introduced with the view to improving compliance and reducing the amount of VAT outstanding at any one time.

Late registration
(VATA 1994, s 67(1))

Failure to notify a liability to register at the correct time (see 7.4.1) results in Customs imposing a financial penalty. From 1 January 1995 the penalty is a percentage of the net tax due between the date notification was required and the actual date of notification, as follows:

- Belatedness not exceeding nine months: 5%.
- Belatedness exceeding nine months but not exceeding 18 months: 10%.
- Belatedness exceeding 18 months: 15%.

A penalty is not imposed (or is withdrawn) where there is a reasonable excuse for the late notification. What amounts to a reasonable excuse is constantly explored by VAT tribunals. In *G Davies* (LON/86/174 (2126)) it was held that an understandable error in determining the liability of supplies was a reasonable excuse.

Ignorance (see *Neal v C&E Commrs* [1988] STC 131), overwork or the reliance on another person are not normally reasonable excuses. Appeals have succeeded where, on the facts of a particular case, an appellant took reasonable steps to notify (*S Zoweni (t/a The Paper Shop*) (1986) VATTR 133).

Late returns
(FA 1994, s 59)

If one payment is submitted late in any 12-month period, Customs notifies the VAT-registered person that payments submitted late during the following 12 months are subject to a default surcharge. If a payment is submitted late during the 12-month surcharge period, a 2% penalty is imposed and the surcharge period extended for a further 12 months. The surcharge rises for each successive late payment to 5% and by increments of 5% to a maximum of 15%. If payments are submitted by the due dates for 12 months, the business is removed from the default surcharge regime and the cycle starts again. The surcharge is waived if it is assessable at the lower rates and is below a minimum amount (ie £200).

A default surcharge is not imposed until after Customs has issued a Surcharge Liability Notice (SLN). There have been several tribunal hearings on this subject and where the taxpayer has been able to demonstrate that he never received an SLN, the surcharge has been withdrawn.

A default surcharge does not apply if a taxpayer has a reasonable excuse for late submission or payment. It is difficult to satisfy this requirement. The tribunal has accepted that the last minute breakdown of the computer, the unforeseen sickness of the person preparing the return at the time it was due or other such catastrophes constitute a reasonable excuse. If a taxpayer can demonstrate that the return and payment were posted in reasonably sufficient time to reach Customs by the due date, there is a reasonable excuse and a default surcharge is not imposed. Posting the return on the last day of the month, however, results in a default occurring.

Insufficiency of funds is not a reasonable excuse. However, in *C&E Commrs v Steptoe* [1992] STC 727, the Court of Appeal confirmed that where lack of funds was due to an unforeseeable inescapable misfortune, beyond the taxpayer's control, insufficiency of funds was a reasonable excuse for non-payment of VAT. The taxpayer had one major customer who was persistently slow in paying invoices.

Misdeclaration penalty

(FA 1985, s 14)

If a VAT officer discovers an under-declaration which exceeds specified limits, he assesses a serious misdeclaration penalty of 15% of the additional VAT assessed. The penalty, which is based on each individual period (ie it is not cumulative), is imposed where the additional VAT assessed exceeds the lesser of:

(1) £1m; and
(2) 30% of the gross amount of tax due for the appropriate return period.

The gross amount of tax is the total combined input tax and output tax for the period. Prior to the aforementioned date, the basis applied was the true amount of tax, ie the amount payable or repayable. The old basis continues to apply for failure to render VAT return cases where the taxpayer fails to notify the Commissioners within 30 days that an assessment issued centrally is lower than the true liability.

Reasonable excuse

A penalty is not imposed where a taxpayer can establish a reasonable excuse to the satisfaction of Customs or on appeal to a VAT tribunal. In addition, a penalty can be mitigated down to an amount (including nil) by Customs or, on appeal, a tribunal.

In *Clean Car Co Ltd* (90/1381 (5965)) the chairman tried to provide objective guidelines for when an appellant has a reasonable excuse. It was

241

stated that the correct test was whether the taxpayer's actions would have been a reasonable action had it been done by a reasonable trader, conscious of, and intending to comply with, his tax obligations, but having the experience and other relevant attributes of a taxpayer and placed in the taxpayer's actual situation at the relevant time.

Voluntary disclosure

A penalty is not imposed where an error is notified to Customs at a time when a taxpayer has no reason to believe his affairs are being looked into. This condition was imposed very strictly by Customs, but they have since been persuaded that the strict application is creating a disincentive to disclose errors. Under a revised code of practice, errors discovered after a visit date has been arranged, including those disclosed at the start of a visit, and in some cases during and after a visit, are normally accepted as voluntary disclosures.

Tax which would have been lost

This is the amount of understatement of output tax or overstatement of input tax. For prescribed accounting periods beginning prior to 1 June 1994, where for any period there was an understatement of output tax or an overstatement of input tax, allowance for the error could be made in determining the lost tax for the prescribed accounting period concerned. This was as a result of a decision in *C&E Commrs v Peninsular and Oriental Steam Navigation Co C/A 1993* [1994] STC 259.

However, following this case, the VAT legislation was amended to prevent the offsetting against an under-declaration of over-declarations arising in other periods. The change is not retrospective, ie it only has effect for prescribed accounting periods beginning after 1 June 1994. For periods prior to this date, the old legislation remains in force and thus errors discovered in previous periods can be offset.

Interest
(FA 1994, s 74)

An interest charge is imposed on assessments for additional tax issued by VAT visiting officers. The interest rate is the prescribed rate as enacted by Treasury order and is not deductible for income or corporation tax. However, Customs has stated that interest may not be imposed where there is no overall loss of revenue eg where a supplier has failed to charge VAT to a customer who would have been entitled to recover the VAT charge. Customs has indicated that each case is decided on its merits, but that officers have been made aware of the need to consider whether there has been a loss of revenue.

Other penalties

There are a number of other penalty provisions such as failure to maintain or produce records, unauthorised issue of a tax invoice (by non-registered persons), and persistent incorrect returns. There are, in fact, over 60 regulatory offences which could give rise to a penalty.

7.9 FRAUD

In VAT law there are two forms of fraud: civil and criminal.

7.9.1 Civil
(FA 1994, s 60)

If, after an investigation, Customs is satisfied there has been an element of dishonesty, it may seek to impose a civil fraud penalty of 100% of the tax involved. If there has been full co-operation by the taxpayer, Customs, or (on appeal) a VAT tribunal, may reduce the penalty by whatever percentage is considered reasonable. In a civil fraud investigation, Customs has only to prove on a balance of probabilities that a fraud had been committed to impose a penalty.

7.9.2 Criminal
(VATA 1994, s 72)

The more serious cases are dealt with under criminal law with penalties of up to three times the VAT involved, or imprisonment, or both. In these cases Customs must use the criminal rules of evidence, etc and prove beyond reasonable doubt that a fraud has been committed deliberately.

7.10 APPEALS

7.10.1 VAT tribunals

There is a right of appeal to an independent VAT tribunal on a number of matters including:

(1) assessments which are considered to be incorrect or not issued to the Commissioners' best judgement;
(2) liability rulings by Customs in respect of a specified supply;
(3) penalties, other than the interest charged for errors, if there is a reasonable excuse for the error; the law does not define 'reasonable excuse' but does state the insufficiency of funds or the reliance on another is *not* one;
(4) the amount of the reduction, if any, of a penalty for a civil fraud where the taxpayer considers he has provided full co-operation with the investigating officers.

The details of appeal procedures are outside the scope of this book. However, the procedure for lodging an appeal to a VAT tribunal (which must be made within 30 days of the appealable event) is straightforward. It is prudent to obtain professional advice before doing so and it is advisable to be represented at the tribunal hearing, which in many ways resembles a court hearing although less formal.

A VAT tribunal decision may be appealed to a higher court on a point of law and, in limited circumstances, an appeal may be referred to the European Court of Justice for a ruling.

7.10.2 Departmental reviews

Many disputes are settled by negotiations with Customs by formally requesting a departmental review of the disputed ruling/assessment within the 30-day time limit. This allows discussions to continue without the loss of the right to appeal to an independent VAT tribunal. Commissioners, if requested, usually review an assessment after the 30-day limit has expired and will, where appropriate, reduce the amount assessed. In certain circumstances it is also possible to make an application to a VAT tribunal to hear a case that is out of time. It is prudent to take professional advice before lodging an appeal.

8

STAMP DUTY AND BUSINESS TRANSACTIONS

Stamp duty is a tax payable on the processing of documents; it is not paid directly on transactions, unlike most taxes. It is paid when documents are written and signed in connection with transactions. Stamp duty is one of the oldest of UK taxes and is governed broadly by the Stamp Act 1891. The Act sets out the basis of stamp duty charge and itemises by process of scheduling the various types of document which can attract a stamp duty charge.

It is important to note that UK documents (or indeed non-UK documents which relate to something done inside the UK) cannot be used as evidence in court (except in proceedings of a criminal nature) unless they have been properly stamped in accordance within the terms of the Stamp Act 1891. Similarly, documents which have to be registered in an official register or entered in statutory books must carry a stamp signifying that the appropriate level of duty has been paid.

Stamp duty reserve tax (SDRT) is payable on certain undertakings, 'agreements' or 'deals' effecting the transfer of chargeable securities. Such agreements need not be effected in writing as SDRT is not a documentary tax or duty. Where a transfer is made between the parties to an agreement of this sort, a document is effected to evidence it and the transfer is then duly stamped; the SDRT paid is deducted from the amount then due.

8.1 DOCUMENTS LIABLE TO DUTY

Stamp duty was first introduced in 1694 and the law has not been redrafted since the Stamp Act of 1891. Numerous amendments have however been made (to block loopholes or to grant new reliefs) and the result is legislation which is archaic, exceptionally complex and difficult to follow, and in which the detailed exceptions are more important than the broad general rules. For example, the scheme of the legislation is not to impose duty on documents implementing the sale of certain types of property, but to impose duty on all documents implementing the sale of *any* type of property and then to provide a series of exceptions.

The practical effect of this legislation is to impose stamp duty on documents implementing:

(a) the sale of shares and other securities;
(b) the sale of freehold land and buildings and the grant or assignment of leases;
(c) the sale of certain types of business property, such as goodwill and patent rights.

This is not a comprehensive list but it does include all the charges likely to be incurred by a business proprietor.

Stamp duty is charged only on sales and not (since 1985) on gifts. Nor is any duty payable when assets are put into trust. However, a sale is defined to include the exchange of property for shares or securities, or the exchange of one block of shares for another. Stamp duty is either charged at a fixed rate (eg 50p) or as a percentage of the value (ie ad valorem duty).

A document should be presented for stamping within 30 days of execution (ie signature). Late stamping attracts a substantial financial penalty (see 8.2).

8.1.1 Sale of shares or other securities

Stamp duty is charged on documents transferring ownership of shares (in both quoted and private companies), debentures, unit trust units and other securities. The rate of duty is 0.5%, rounded up to the next 50p (for example, the duty on a sale for £325 would be £2). British Government stocks ('gilts') and stocks issued by certain international bodies (such as the EC) are exempt from duty. The stamp duty is borne by the purchaser and is shown as a disbursement on the broker's contract note. It counts as part of the cost of the holding for CGT purposes.

Where one block of shares is exchanged for another, the transaction is treated as two sales, so both participants must pay the usual duty. In certain circumstances it is possible for shares to be sold without a stampable document being created. This most commonly happens where a block of shares, traded on the London Stock Exchange, changes hands several times in the space of a few days. In such circumstances, SDRT is charged on the transaction. The SDRT is equal in amount to the stamp duty that would otherwise have been paid and so, from the purchaser's point of view, it is immaterial which tax is paid.

For some years now, the Government and the Inland Revenue have been intent upon the abolition of the charges to stamp duty on trades in stocks and shares as and when the Stock Exchange introduces its so-called 'paperless trading system'. There have been several attempts to introduce such a system over the last 15 years, beginning with TAURUS in 1991 and CREST in 1996.

For instruments executed on or after 1 October 1999, under FA 1999, s 112 (see below) the rate of duty is 0.5% of the consideration, rounded up to the nearest multiple of £5.

8.1.2 Sale of freehold land and buildings

From 28 March 2000 the rates of stamp duty are as follows:

Transactions of value over £500,000	4%
Transactions of value between £250,000 and £500,000	3%
Transactions of value between £60,000 and £250,000	1%

Property transactions (except shares and marketable securities) are free of stamp duty if the total consideration is less than £60,000.

Under FA 1999, s 112, for documents executed after 30 September 1999, the old charging provisions under which the amount of duty otherwise due was rounded up to a multiple of between 50p and £12 have been changed. For documents executed after that date stamp duty is charged in multiples of £5 in all cases.

Stamp duty is payable by reference to the actual consideration which passes and has no relationship to the actual value of the asset which is the subject of the transaction. Although some gifts were taxable at one stage, these are now mainly exempt from stamp duty.

Some contracts for property sales are subjected to ad valorem stamp duty. This occurs where there is no immediate conveyance or transfer by way of sale. Where such properties are later transferred by way of sale or conveyance covered by a document, no additional stamp duty is chargeable on that subsequent document.

If a contract includes stampable and non-stampable property (eg movable goods which normally pass by simple delivery), it is necessary for an apportionment to be made of the purchase price in order to arrive at the appropriate level of duty.

8.1.3 Sale and grant of a lease

The stamp duty payable on an assignment of an existing lease is calculated in exactly the same way as for freehold property. It is the capital sum paid for the lease that determines the amount of stamp duty; the amount of rent payable under the lease is irrelevant.

Where a new lease is granted, and a premium is paid, it must carry stamp duty at the appropriate ad valorem rate as if it were a transfer of conveyance on sale. Lease duty is also chargeable on the average rent payable over the length of the lease.

For short leases of up to seven years (or for an indefinite term), the threshold for stamp duty on the granting of a lease is £5,000. This threshold applies to the annual rent charge so if the rent is less than £5,000 pa and there is no premium the lease does not need to be stamped.

8.1.4 Stamp duty and VAT

Sales and rentals of some commercial property may be subject to VAT. In such cases, stamp duty is charged on the VAT-*inclusive* sale price, premium and/or rent. Moreover, in certain circumstances the landlord may have the right to add VAT to the rent at a later date: again, the VAT-inclusive figure must be taken (see SP11/91).

8.1.5 Sub-sales
(Stamp Act 1891, s 58)

Where a person

(a) has entered into a contract to purchase a property and
(b) enters into a sale contract before the original contract has been completed,

and the property is then conveyed to the new purchaser, only the second contract generally attracts ad valorem duty. The original purchase contract is not subject to stamp duty. Thus, if A enters into a contract to buy a property for £1m, and then enters into a sub-sale for £1.5m to B, stamp duty is payable by B only on the conveyance arising out of the contract for sale for £1.5m.

FA 1984 introduced some restrictions; specialist legal advice should therefore be taken.

8.1.6 Sale of contract

If a purchaser who holds the benefit of a contract which has not been completed sells the benefit of his contract to a third party who then completes the purchase, the transaction is treated in a similar way to a sub-sale. Thus if the contract is for the purchase of a property for £1m, and A sells that contract to B for £500,000, B pays ad valorem duty each on the £500,000 purchase price of the contract and on completing the purchase. Overall he pays 4% of £1.5m.

8.1.7 Sale of goodwill and other business assets

The types of property which may be included in arriving at a business's value for stamp duty purposes include book debts, plant and machinery and stock in trade, goodwill, and copyrights, patents and trade marks. The way in which a contract is drafted may have stamp duty consequences and the advice of an experienced solicitor should be sought. Having said this, the normal position is as follows:

(1) The usual arrangement for book debts is for the purchaser to collect them as agent for the vendor as this means that ownership remains with the person selling the business and so no stamp duty is payable on

them. Unless documentation is defective, no stamp duty should be payable on the transfer of plant and machinery and stock in trade as legal title can pass by delivery and the purchaser can therefore acquire a good title without a stampable document. The rate of duty on goodwill, copyrights, patents and trade marks is the same as for land and buildings.

(2) Exemption is available where the value of the transaction does not exceed £60,000, but the sale of a business as a going concern counts as a single transaction. Therefore, if a shopkeeper sells his shop premises for £50,000 and his goodwill for £20,000, the value of the transaction is £70,000 and exemption is not available.

Because the stamp duty definition of a sale includes an exchange of property for shares, the incorporation of a sole trader's or partnership business is treated as a sale of that business in exchange for shares in the new company. Stamp duty is charged according to the value of the shares received by the proprietor or the partners which will, effectively, be an amount equal to the value of the business as a going concern (discussed in greater detail at 8.3.7).

8.1.8 Partnerships

A partnership deed or agreement is not normally liable for stamp duty but special rules may apply for a limited partnership (see 17.2).

Where a person joins a partnership, ad valorem stamp duty is payable on any document transferring an interest in the firm to him from an existing partner on the basis that the document is a conveyance. On the other hand, the contribution of new partnership capital gives rise to no such charge unless an existing partner withdraws capital at the same time (in which case the document for the transaction is regarded as a conveyance which attracts ad valorem duty).

The dissolution of a partnership and the division of the firm's assets do not normally attract ad valorem duty. The exception is if an individual partner takes a greater proportion of certain assets and makes a cash adjustment for this; it is then effectively a type of sale.

8.1.9 Trade marks

Stamp duty is payable on instruments concerning trade marks which are either exclusive non-revocable licences or assignments. The Trade Marks Act 1994, s 61 specifically exempts from the ambit of stamp duty, instruments relating to a Community trade mark, registered under the Community trade mark system, or an international trade mark, being a trade mark which is entitled to protection in the UK under the Madrid Protocol. Fees are payable for registration, but there will be no imposition of stamp duty.

8.2 SANCTIONS WHERE DUTY IS NOT PAID

As a general rule, the Revenue cannot enforce the payment of stamp duty by taking court proceedings (although it can enforce the payment of SDRT). Nevertheless, a number of effective sanctions do exist, which mean that in practice it is usually best to ensure that a stampable document is indeed stamped:

(1) Although the Revenue cannot take civil proceedings to enforce payment of stamp duty, it can prosecute a purchaser or lessee who fails to produce for stamping a conveyance of freehold land, or the grant or transfer of a lease for seven years or more. The maximum fine is £1,000.
(2) HM Land Registry will not accept any document which is not duly stamped and it is very unwise not to register a purchase of land or a lease for a term exceeding 21 years at the Registry.
(3) A transfer of shares or debentures cannot be registered unless the transfer document has been properly stamped. (Any purported registration by the company is simply not valid in law.)
(4) An unstamped document will not be accepted in any court proceedings.

8.2.1 Interest and penalties

For documents executed after 30 September 1999, a new interest regime for late payment applies, with interest incurred on stamp duty that is not paid within 30 days of a document's execution. It starts to accrue from the date that the stamp duty was due until it is paid. This applies wherever execution has taken place; therefore, documents executed overseas after 30 September 1999 are brought into the interest regime immediately if the document later has to be brought into the UK and stamped. If such document is stamped within 30 days of being brought into the UK, although a penalty is not charged, it appears that interest is chargeable from the date of execution.

The amount of interest paid depends on the duty and how late the payment is. A standard rate of interest is applied in working out the charge. The amount of interest is rounded down where necessary to a multiple of £5, but no interest is payable unless the calculated amount is at least £25.

Interest paid is not allowable against corporation tax or income tax and nor do interest added repayments enter into computing profits under those taxes.

Interest is also added to repayments of overpaid stamp duty and runs from 30 days after execution of the document, or from the date of payment of the duty if later. The current rates of interest on late paid and overpaid stamp duty and SDRT (from 6 February 2000) are 8.5% on tax due and 4% on tax rebates. For documents executed after 30 September 1999 penalties apply to all documents submitted for stamping more than 30 days after the document was executed (or in the case of documents executed abroad, over 30 days after the document is first brought into the UK).

There is a maximum penalty of £300 (or the amount of duty if it is less) on documents submitted up to one year late and £300 (or the amount of duty if it is more) for documents submitted later than that. No penalty is charged if there is a reasonable excuse for delay, and all penalties are open to mitigation.

All stamp duty penalties for administrative offences are £300, or £3,000 where the case is one of fraud.

8.3 AVOIDING OR REDUCING DUTY

8.3.1 Sale of shares or other securities

The opportunities to avoid or mitigate duty are circumscribed by the rule that a company may not register a transfer of shares or debentures unless the transfer document has been duly stamped. Beneficial ownership may, of course, be transferred without any change in the registered owner of the shares (eg where the shares are registered in the name of a nominee company).

8.3.2 Depositary receipts

From 25 August 1999, no SDRT is payable on UK depository receipts in foreign securities. This exemption is made by the Stamp Duty Reserve Tax (UK Depository Interests in Foreign Securities) Regulations 1999 (SI No 2383) under FA 1999, s 119.

Otherwise, there is a charge to SDRT under FA 1986, s 93 on the issue of a depository receipt for chargeable securities. The rate is the same as that applicable to stamp duty on bearer securities (ie 1.5%). There is no SDRT charge when a depository receipt changes hands (FA 1986, s 99(6)).

A depository receipt is defined by FA 1986, s 99(7) as an instrument acknowledging both:

(1) that a person holds stocks or shares or evidence of the right to receive them; and
(2) that another person is entitled to the rights, whether expressed as units or otherwise, in or in relation to stocks or shares of the same kind, including the right to receive such stocks and shares (or evidence of the right to receive them from the person mentioned above).

There are three occasions of charge under FA 1986, s 93(1):

(1) the chargeable securities are transferred to the nominee of the person whose business is or includes issuing depository receipts (usually a bank);
(2) the chargeable securities are issued to the nominee; and
(3) the securities are appropriated by such a person towards the eventual satisfaction of the entitlement of the holder of the receipts to receive chargeable securities.

8.3.3 **Company reconstructions**
(FA 1986, s 75)

There is a limited statutory relief for the stamp duty payable on the documentation arising out of certain company reconstructions and mergers without change of ownership: this is an area in which proper professional advice is essential. The basic conditions for relief are that:

(a) the acquiring company issues shares to all the shareholders of the target company;
(b) no other consideration passes other than the assumption or discharge by the acquiring company of liabilities of the target company; and
(c) both companies must be incorporated in the UK.

Furthermore, relief is due only where the following further conditions are satisfied.

(i) The acquisition is effected for bona fide commercial reasons and does not form part of a scheme or arrangement of which the main purposes, or one of the main purposes, is avoidance of liability to stamp duty, income tax, corporation tax or capital gains tax.
(ii) After the acquisition has been made, each shareholder of the target company will be a shareholder of the acquiring company.
(iii) After the acquisition has been made, the proportion of the acquiring company's shares held by any shareholder is the same as the proportion of shares originally held in the target company.

The Stamp Office has indicated that it will regard the requirement of the reconstruction to be effected for bona fide commercial reasons as being satisfied where clearance has been granted under TCGA 1992, s 138 (see 5.4.4).

The procedure for claiming s 75 relief is set out below.

(1) A claim should be made in a letter signed by a responsible officer of the acquiring company eg the secretary or a director or the company's professional advisers.
(2) The letter should include the following information and be accompanied by:
    (a) the name, registered number and authorised and issued capital of the acquiring company at the relevant date;
    (b) the name, registered number and authorised and issued capital of the acquired company at the relevant date;
    (c) details of and the reason for the reconstruction;
    (d) details of the consideration and how it was satisfied;
    (e) whether an application for clearance under TCGA 1992, s 138 or 139 has been made to the Revenue and a copy of any application for clearance together with copies of any correspondence with the Revenue;

(f) confirmation that the shares in the acquiring company have been issued to the acquired company's registered shareholders and that their names have been entered on the acquiring company's register of members;

(g) a copy of the certificate of incorporation of all relevant companies and all changes of names;

(h) particulars of the acquired company's register of members immediately prior to the transaction;

(i) particulars of the acquired company's register of members immediately after the transaction for which relief is claimed;

(j) a copy of the agreement or offer document; and

(k) a copy of the instruments of transfer.

(3) A completed Adjudication Application Form (ADJ 467) stating any related adjudication references known should be sent with the claim to:

The Controller of Stamps (Adjudication Section)
West Block
Barrington Road
Worthing
West Sussex BN12 4SF

8.3.4 Loan stock

Where a person takes loan stock as consideration for the sale of an asset, such acquisition does not normally attract duty unless:

(a) the loan capital carries a right of conversion into shares or other securities or to the acquisition of shares or other securities; or

(b) the rate of interest exceeds a reasonable commercial return on the capital's nominal amount; or

(c) the amount of interest is determined to any extent by reference to the results of, or any part of, a business or to the value of any property; or

(d) there is a right to be repaid more than the nominal amount of the loan and that amount is not reasonably comparable with what is generally repayable (in respect of a similar capital's nominal amount) under the terms of issue of loan capital in the Official List of The Stock Exchange.

Any transfer of loan capital which does not come within these exemptions is chargeable at the rate of 0.5% ad valorem.

8.3.5 Sale of land and buildings

One widely used way of mitigating stamp duty was closed by FA 1994. If two owners exchange houses, stamp duty is now payable on the market value of the properties as well as on any cash adjustment. Prior to 8 December 1993, stamp duty was payable only on the cash element in the consideration and even this attracted duty only if it exceeded £60,000.

253

The Stamp Office has agreed that where the documents are correctly drafted the ad valorem charge can be limited to one property. It appears that if a person transfers property A to another person on the basis that the sale consideration is £x and this is to be satisfied by the other person transferring property B, 1% stamp duty is payable on property A and the transfer of property B attracts only 50p stamp duty. However, very careful drafting is required in cases where there is a cash adjustment rather than a straightforward exchange with no other consideration passing between the parties.

Stamp duty is not charged on that part of the agreed purchase price which is allocated to items such as fixtures and fittings which are left in the property. This is because ownership of such items is transferred not by the conveyance, but by delivery.

To reduce duty, purchasers are sometimes tempted to apportion an unrealistically high percentage of the agreed overall price to the contents – especially where this brings the price allocated to the house itself below the threshold and so avoids duty altogether. The Stamp Office is, of course, alive to this temptation and will refuse to stamp a conveyance if the valuations used cannot be justified.

A suggestion sometimes put forward is that a person can buy the site and then contract separately with the builder for him to carry out the building work. Certainly, if the buyer buys a building plot and then contracts with an unrelated third party for the construction of a house, stamp duty is payable only on the 'site value' price actually paid. *Prudential Assurance Co Ltd v IRC* [1993] 1 WLR 211 indicates that this still applies even if the buyer buys a plot from the builder and then commissions him to construct a building on that site *provided* that the site is conveyed to the purchaser before a substantial start is made on the building work.

Where a long lease at a substantial rent is proposed, it is sometimes possible to save duty by splitting the period between two shorter leases; eg instead of a 50-year lease with stamp duty of 12% of the annual rent (see 8.1.3), at the outset sign two leases, one for 20 years and the second for 30 years (commencing on the expiry of the first), with the duty on each lease then being only 2% of the annual rent. For legal reasons, the first lease must be 21 years or less and so counts as a short lease which cannot be registered at the Land Registry.

8.3.6 Sale of business assets

In general, the ownership of buildings and goodwill can only be transferred by a written document and so duty must be paid. There are however three ways of avoiding or reducing duty, though all three are usually only practicable where vendor and purchaser trust each other completely.

(1) Stamp duty is payable on a *conveyance* of freehold land although the *contract* is sufficient to transfer beneficial ownership to the purchaser. Therefore, if vendor and purchaser sign and exchange contracts, but

never 'complete' by conveyance, no duty is payable. This was upheld by the courts in 1889 and the Government has never blocked the loophole. The drawback is that, without a stamped conveyance, the purchase cannot be registered at the Land Registry, and this is why this device is only to be recommended where vendor and purchaser trust each other completely (eg on a sale to a connected company or a sale within a family).

(2) The second method is simply not to stamp the documentation. Though failing to stamp a conveyance or the grant or assignment of a lease is a punishable offence (see 8.2), the only sanction against failure to stamp a transfer of goodwill is the double charge if it later needs to be stamped out of time.

(3) Where substantial amounts of money are at stake, advantage may be taken of the rule that a document executed (signed) outside the UK need not be stamped until it is brought into the UK. (The document may be stamped without interest or penalty provided it is presented at a Stamp Office within 30 days of being brought to the UK, as required under the Stamp Act 1891, s 15.) The usual procedure is to take a day trip to Jersey or Guernsey, sign the documents, and leave them in a local safe deposit or bank vault.

8.3.7 Transfer of a business to a company

Stamp duty is payable where a sole trader's or partnership business is incorporated because the trader or the partnership is treated as having sold the business in exchange for shares in the new company (see 8.1.7). Where the successor company is a limited company, its proprietors must produce to the Registrar of Companies a properly stamped copy of the contract by which the business was sold to the company. It is therefore necessary to pay stamp duty on assets which did not pass by delivery. However, a stamped contract is not required where a business is transferred to an unlimited company (see 19.1.2); it is possible to transfer a business to an unlimited company by means of an unstamped contract (for example, one kept outside the UK) and then to re-register that company as a limited company.

8.3.8 Intra-group transfers

Statutory exemption from stamp duty applies, subject to conditions, where property is transferred from one member of a group of companies to another. For this purpose, a 'group' consists of a holding company and its 75% subsidiaries. The holding company need not be a UK company. A subsidiary is a 75% subsidiary only if the parent company owns, directly or indirectly, 75% of the subsidiary's ordinary share capital. Until May 1995, the requirement was that the subsidiary should be a 90% subsidiary, but the test was by reference to the nominal value of issued share capital of all classes, not just ordinary shares.

Section 27(3) of FA 1967 provides that, to obtain the relief, the transferee company must provide confirmation that the document giving rise to the intra-group transfer was not executed in pursuance of or in connection with an arrangement whereunder:

(a) the consideration, or any part of the consideration, for the conveyance or transfer was to be provided or received, directly or indirectly, by a person other than a body corporate which at the time of the execution of the instrument was associated with either the transferor or the transferee; or

(b) the said interest was previously transferred or conveyed, directly or indirectly, by such a person; or

(c) the transferor and the transferee were to cease to be associated by reason of a change in the percentage of the issued share capital of the transferee in the beneficial ownership of the transferor or a third body corporate.

In order to prevent manipulation of group structures to exploit the inter-company relief the stamp duty provisions are fully aligned with the membership requirements for corporation tax so that only companies that qualify as a group for corporation tax purposes can benefit from stamp duty relief.

8.4 EXEMPT INSTRUMENTS

Some documents are completely exempt from stamp duty provided that an appropriate certificate is signed and endorsed at the time of the execution of the instrument. The relevant instruments (as far as companies are concerned) include (under the Stamp Duty (Exempt Instruments) Regulations 1987 (SI No 516)):

(1) property vesting in a trust where new trustees are appointed or where a trustee retires;

(2) conveyances by a liquidator to a shareholder in satisfaction of the shareholder's rights in a winding-up;

(3) the grant of a service contract for money or money's worth; and

(4) the grant of easements over land.

Most of the other exempt instruments are concerned with the death of individuals or with the transfer of property by individuals.

The Stamp Office provides a recommended form of words to accompany a document where it is claimed that an exempt instrument is being effected. If such a certificate is effected, there is no requirement to send the documents to the Stamp Office for adjudication.

Declarations of trust of life policies are, since 1 October 1999, exempt (Stamp Duty (Exempt Instruments) (Amendment) Regulations 1999 (SI No 2539)).

9

CONTRACT LAW

RICHARD LAWSON, LAWMARK

This chapter covers the main general principles of contract law. A detailed study of contract law is beyond the scope of this book.

In any binding contract there are three major components:

(a) an offer which is made by one party and accepted by the other;
(b) an intention to be legally bound by both parties; and
(c) consideration.

9.1 OFFER

For an offer to be capable of being accepted, and leading to a binding contract, an intention must be shown, on the part of the party making the offer, to be legally bound if the offer is accepted. It may be made to an individual person or to a group of people. It may be expressly made in words or by conduct. Sometimes a party may be bound by his offer even if he can later show that he did not intend to make it to the person who accepted it; it is the impression given to the person who accepted it that is important and account is taken of whether a reasonable man in the circumstances would also have had the same view.

9.1.1 Invitation to treat

It is not uncommon for parties to enter into preliminary discussions prior to a contract being made which include requests for information. These are known as invitations to treat, which generally invite an offer and are sometimes confused with an offer.

For example, in *Harvey v Facey* [1893] AC 552 the plaintiff sent a telegram to the defendant saying 'will you sell us Bumper Hall Pen? Telegraph us lowest cash price'. The court decided that no contract had been formed. This telegram was a request for information which the defendant had supplied in their telegram and not an offer.

Generally speaking, a display of goods on which is indicated the price of those goods for sale, in either a shop window or inside a store, is an invitation to treat. If the customer decides to buy some goods then the action by him to take the goods to the cash till is the offer to buy which can be accepted by the shop owner or his employee.

9.1.2 Advertisements

A newspaper advertisement may show certain goods for sale at certain prices. This is not an offer capable of acceptance. Furthermore, it has been held that circulation of a price list by a wine merchant is merely an invitation to treat (see *Partridge v Crittinden* [1968] 1 WLR 1204). However, there are some circumstances where the advertisement could only be held to relate to one matter and to a certain individual or party of individuals and then it may be an offer. In *Carlill v Carbolic Smoke Ball Co Ltd* [1893] 1 QB 256 the advertisement stated that anyone who purchased a carbolic smoke ball, used it in accordance with the instructions and then suffered from flu would receive £100 from the company. The court held that this was an offer which the defendants had shown themselves to be legally bound by and which was capable of acceptance. Their intention to be bound was confirmed in that they had deposited £1,000 with their bankers to show their sincerity.

In *Wood v Letrik Ltd* (1932) *The Times*, 12, 13 January, an advertisement for an electric comb said: 'What is your trouble? Is it grey hair? In 10 days not a grey hair left. £500 guarantee'. Mr Wood used the comb without success and claimed the £500. Rowlatt J held that:

> '"guarantee" was about as emphatic a word in a contract as one could well imagine. When people read the word "guarantee" they understand that the person using it was offering to bind himself to be responsible for the happening, continuance or existence of a certain state of facts.'

In *Fordy v Harwood* (unreported, Court of Appeal, 30 March 1999), a kit replica car had been advertised as 'absolutely mint', with 'all the right bits and does it go!'. The High Court had held that these statements were no more than puffs which were not intended to give rise to any legal obligation. As for the statement that the replica kit was 'absolutely mint', the Court of Appeal noted that the appearance of the car was obvious to anyone looking at it. It was not a museum piece and was intended to be driven as a normal car. As for the claim that the car had 'all the right bits', the Court of Appeal disagreed with the High Court and held that, while the words no doubt meant that the car had all the authentic component parts and fittings, they would also mean that the right bits had been installed as such, which, in this case, they had not.

9.1.3 Termination of offer

Generally an offer may be terminated at any time before it is accepted. The revocation of an offer must be communicated to the offeree. This need not be done by the offeror himself so long as the offeree knows it has been terminated.

9.1.4 Rejection and counter offers

Where an offer is rejected it is terminated and therefore cannot be accepted. Where an offer is made on new terms which were not contained in the original offer, it may be a rejection accompanied by a counter offer. In *Hyde v Wrench* (1840) 3 Beav 334 *A* offered to sell a farm to *B* for £1,000. *B* replied, offering to buy it for £950. *A* rejected the counter offer so *B* tried to accept *A*'s original offer. It was held that no contract had been made since *B*'s rejection and counter offer terminated *A*'s original offer.

However, in some cases the communication from the offeree may not be regarded as a counter offer but merely a request for more information. An objective test then has to be applied to determine whether a communication is sufficient to be regarded as a counter offer.

In *Norfolk County Council v Dencora Properties* (unreported, 1996, *The Buyer*, Issue 1), a contract for a lease gave a right to terminate 'before 25 March'. The tenant had asked if this meant that notice could be given at any time, so long as not given before that date. The tenant said that this was a mere request for information, but the court held that it was a counter offer. Its effect was 'to sweep the offer . . . off the negotiating table so that it was no longer there to accept'. The landlord found the terms of the tenant's proposals 'not acceptable' and this in turn meant that the counter offer had been rejected.

In *Society of Lloyd's v Twinn* (unreported, 23 March 2000), the claimant had served bankruptcy petitions, and the registrar made bankruptcy orders, against accepting Names for unpaid sums said to be due from them under the claimant's Reconstruction and Renewal plans. The High Court allowed the Names' appeals on the ground that the registrar had been wrong to hold that they were accepting Names, since their purported acceptance was in fact a counter offer. The Court of Appeal reversed the High Court decision, holding the Names had effected an acceptance by executing acceptance forms. The covering letter which stated that they had no means to pay the finality amounts was an attempt to obtain concessions. The Names were accepting even though they could not pay: there was an effective acceptance and not a counter offer.

9.1.5 Lapse of time

An offer which expressly states that it will last for a specified period of time cannot be accepted once that time has passed. Where the offer is not limited in time, then it only lapses after whatever period of time is considered reasonable in the circumstances.

In *Ramsgate Victoria Hotel Co v Montefiore* (1866) LR 1 Exch 109, the defendant applied to the company for shares and paid a deposit. Five months later, the company sent him an acceptance by issuing a letter of allotment and requesting the balance due on the shares. He refused to pay, contending that his offer had expired. The court upheld his argument. His offer was for a reasonable time only and five months was deemed unreasonable.

In *Chemco Leasing v Rediffusion* [1987] 1 FTLR 201, an offer was made in January to assume certain liabilities; the offer was accepted in November. The court held that, since about four months was a reasonable time for the offer to run, it had lapsed by the time of the purported acceptance which had, therefore, no effect.

9.2 ACCEPTANCE

Acceptance of an offer must be final and unqualified and it must be communicated to the offeror. An acknowledgement of the offer is not acceptance of it. Acceptance may be made by conduct, eg where *A* offers to send goods, sends them to *B* and *B* then uses them, *B*'s conduct can be regarded as acceptance.

Where the parties carry on lengthy negotiations it may be difficult to say when exactly an offer is made and accepted. Parties may in fact not agree that an offer has been made and accepted. In these circumstances, a court considers all negotiations and looks to the parties' intentions to establish whether an agreement exists. There may be correspondence between the parties after an offer has been made but before acceptance. Careful examination must be made to determine whether such communication can be regarded as an acceptance or whether it is an attempt to vary terms or introduce new ones.

In *Manatee Towing Co v Oceanbulk Maritime SA* (unreported, 18 May 1999), the High Court laid down the following principles:

(1) The court's task is to review what the parties said and did, and from the material to infer whether the parties' objective intentions as expressed to each other were to enter into a mutually binding contract.

(2) When a contract by telex or correspondence is alleged, the court will look at the correspondence as a whole and not merely at one or two documents picked out from a connected sequence.

(3) Where the parties have not reached agreement on terms which they regard as essential to a binding agreement, it follows that there can be no binding agreement until they do agree on those terms. At the same time, the parties may, by words and conduct, make it clear that they do intend to be bound, even though there are other terms yet to be agreed, even terms which may often or usually be agreed before a binding contract is made. The more important the term, the less likely that the parties will leave it for future decision, but there is no legal obstacle in the way of parties agreeing immediately to be bound and leaving important matters for later agreement.

(4) Though the parties might have reached agreement on all the terms of the proposed contract, they might still intend the agreement not to

become binding until some further condition is fulfilled. This is the ordinary 'subject to contract' case. Alternatively, the intention may be that the agreement does not become binding until some further term is agreed. Conversely, they may agree to be bound immediately, even though there are further terms to be agreed or some formality to be fulfilled.

(5) The court must always bear in mind the subject-matter with which it is dealing. The relevant principles of the law of contract are of universal application, but the proper inference to draw may differ widely according to the facts of any particular case.

(6) The courts recognise that business terminology and practice may differ from one market to the next. See also *Pagnan SpA v Feed Products Ltd* [1987] 2 Lloyd's Rep 601.

It is common business practice for one party to wish a contract to be governed by his standard trading conditions. An offer by him may include a statement that both parties should be bound by these terms. The other party's reaction to this determines whether he is bound by these terms.

This can often give rise to what is sometimes called 'the battle of the forms' when each side presents its own terms and conditions as providing the basis of the contract. The basic rule is that the person who is the last to present his terms and conditions is the one who succeeds in having them incorporated into the contract (*Butler Machine Tool Co v Ex-Cell-o Corp* [1979] 1 All ER 963; see also *Albright & Wilson UK Ltd v Biachem Ltd* (unreported, 12 April 2000), which concerns a sequence of five contracts sent by fax and the confusion of which company's terms and conditions applied).

9.2.1 Cross offers

Where each party concerned makes an offer to the other which mirrors the other's offer, there can be no contract even though the offer is identical. What one party must do on receipt of the other's offer is to contact him and confirm acceptance.

9.2.2 Communication of acceptance

This must be made to the offeror, otherwise no contract exists. The communication need not be made by the offeree. However the third party who communicates the acceptance (eg an agent) must have the authority to do so from the offeree.

An exception to communicating acceptance to the offeror arises where acceptance is by conduct. For example, a tenant may be regarded as accepting an offer of new tenancy by remaining in the property.

9.2.3 Method of acceptance

There is no set method of acceptance, although the offeror may indicate that acceptance can only be made in a certain way; if so, that requirement must be adhered to. Acceptance by an alternative method (eg orally where the offer states that acceptance must be in writing) may not bind the offeror.

The offeror cannot impose acceptance where the offeree is silent. This principle was laid down in *Felthouse v Bindley* (1862) 11 CBNS 869. Where, however, the offeree himself indicates that the offer is to be taken as accepted if there is no indication to the contrary, that can amount to acceptance (*Re Selectmove* [1995] 2 All ER 531).

9.2.4 Acceptance by post

Acceptance by post is effective when the letter is posted, not when the letter is received. If it is not received by the offeror it may still be deemed effective acceptance. Nevertheless, the offeree may have difficulty proving that he had posted the acceptance.

If the circumstances of the negotiations make it clear that an acceptance must reach the other party, this is what must happen (*Holwell Securities Ltd v Hughes* [1974] 1 All ER 161).

Acceptance by post takes priority over the withdrawal of an offer which may have been posted before the acceptance was, but had not reached the offeree when the acceptance was posted. This is an exception to the general rule that an offer may be withdrawn at any time before the offeror is notified of an acceptance.

9.2.5 Contract to make a contract

In certain cases the parties may have agreed in principle but not sorted out the contract details. Whether a contract exists depends on the terms still left to be agreed. However, it is possible for the parties to be bound by contract to make a contract. This is not the same as an agreement to negotiate because that is too uncertain. See *Courtney & Fairburn Ltd v Tolaini Bros (Hotels) Ltd* [1975] 1 All ER 716, and *Walford v Miles* [1992] 2 AC 128.

9.2.6 Certainty of terms

Where the terms are vague or uncertain they cannot be binding. This does not necessarily mean that there is no contract since a court may, if it considers it appropriate, merely delete the ambiguous words from the contract (see 9.7.4).

9.2.7 Contractual intention

The parties must have intended to create legal relations. It is not necessary generally to produce evidence to show this: it will normally be inferred. However, where one party alleges that this requirement does not exist, then it is for him to show that it does not.

9.3 CONSIDERATION

A contract is not binding unless it is either made as a deed or supported by some 'consideration'. 'Consideration' is the value by which one party suffers a detriment (promisee) or the other gains (promisor). For example, *A*'s payment to *B* is in consideration of *B*'s promise to deliver the goods to *A*.

The court does not generally concern itself whether adequate consideration has been given – whether a person has paid too little or too much does not affect the contract's validity but it might give rise to a claim by that person against the other. An exception to this general rule would occur where a party may have exercised undue influence on the other to enter the contract and the contract may therefore be regarded as being one-sided (see 9.6).

Consideration may be nominal; for example, a contract in which *A* agrees to buy a valuable business for only £1 is just as valid as if he were to agree to pay £10,000. However, a consideration must be real in that it must have some value in the eyes of the law.

Where a contract is made but the performance of it is utterly impossible, so long as both parties are unaware of that fact the consideration is still likely to be effective.

9.3.1 Past consideration

It is often said that consideration for a promise is given in return for the promise itself. If the act or agreement not to do an act, regarded as a consideration, has already been carried out before the 'promise' is made and independently of it, then it is regarded as being 'past consideration'. In these circumstances the contract is not enforceable.

Where, for example, an employer promises to make a payment to an ex-employee for his past services, the contract is unenforceable unless, perhaps, the ex-employee agreed not to work for a competitor for a certain period after leaving (ie the consideration is his promise not to work for the competitor).

There is an exception to the general rule for past consideration; there is consideration where an act is performed before a promise made where three conditions are satisfied:

(1) the act must be done at the request of the person making the promise;
(2) it must be understood that the payment would be made; and
(3) the payment must in any event be legally recoverable.

The Limitation Act 1980 qualifies the rules relating to past consideration, providing that where a person acknowledges a debt in writing and signs the acknowledgement, the debt is deemed to accrue on that date and no earlier date. This extends the period of limitation and enables a party to sue at a later date than he would otherwise have been able to on a debt. However, where a debt has become statutorily barred, the right to sue is lost and the later acknowledgement cannot revive it.

9.3.2 Agreement not to sue

Where a creditor *A* agrees not to sue *B* in return for a promise by *B* to pay interest or additional interest on the sum involved, the promise by *A* is valid consideration. The agreement may be for a limited period of time (perhaps to allow *B* time to pay) or it may be final and perhaps incorporated in a settlement.

The agreement or forebearance to sue may be implied from a person's actions (eg where a party does not sue even though he has stated to the other to whom he owes the money that he will). However, the forebearance must be accompanied by a promise from the debtor for it to be a consideration.

9.3.3 Promising to perform existing obligations

Generally, a person cannot provide consideration by promising to do something that he is already legally obliged to do. However, where he promises to do more than he is legally obliged to do (eg a police force providing a greater degree of protection than it thinks reasonably necessary in the circumstances) then this may be good consideration.

Nevertheless, there are situations where one party's legal obligation to perform something for another can be regarded as consideration to a third party. In *Scotson v Pegg* (1861) 6 H&N 295, *B* contracted with *A* to deliver coal to *B* or to *B*'s order. *B* then ordered *A* to deliver the coal to *C* who promised to unload it. *A* sued *C* for failure to unload. It was held that *A*'s delivery was good consideration for *C*'s promise even though he was contractually bound by his contract with *B* to deliver to *C*.

It has been held that the principle that a promise to perform an existing obligation can amount to good consideration where there were practical benefits to the party receiving the performance is confined to cases where the obligation involved a supply of goods or services. The principle cannot be extended to an obligation to make a payment (eg a tax payment: *Re Selectmove* [1995] 2 All ER 531).

9.4 MISTAKE

The traditional way of dealing with the effect of mistake on a contract is to ask whether the mistake is one which falls into any of the categories dealt with below.

9.4.1 Common mistake

If the parties have made the same mistake about a fundamental element of the contract, the court may find it void. For example, if two parties agree to supply and purchase goods but, unknown to them, the goods do not exist when the contract is made, the court may declare it void. In deciding whether the contract should be made void in these circumstances, the court first has to be sure that neither party had accepted responsibility for the goods' existence. That is, could a term be implied into the contract which encompassed that obligation? In the majority of disputes this is usually the case. In *Associated Japanese Bank (International) v Credit du Nord SA* [1988] 3 All ER 902, the court emphasised that the rules on mistake were for exceptional circumstances, so mistake is not an excuse to get out of a bad bargain. Consequently, a mistake regarding the quality of the contract's subject-matter will not affect the contract's validity.

In *Leaf v International Galleries* [1950] 1 All ER 693, Leaf bought a painting believed by both parties to be by John Constable from the defendant. Five years later, Leaf discovered it was not by Constable. The court held the contract was unaffected: both parties had made the mistake, so the contract remained valid.

Where a common mistake is not sufficiently fundamental to render the contract void at common law, equity may hold that the contract is voidable in order to achieve a fair result. In *Solle v Butcher* [1950] 1 KB 671, both parties to a lease thought that the recently refurbished flat was no longer subject to the Rent Acts and agreed a rent of £250 a year. However, they were mistaken, and the maximum rent under the Acts, at that time, was £140. The tenant claimed repayment of the excess rent and the landlord served notice on the lessee. The Court of Appeal held the mistake was not sufficiently fundamental for the contract to be void; however, it was voidable in equity. The tenant had the choice of giving up the lease or accepting a new one at an increased maximum rent under the Rent Acts.

9.4.2 Mutual mistake

This involves situations where the parties are at cross purposes. For example, *A*, when buying a house, thinks the carpets are included in the sale, but *B*, the seller, believes they are excluded. The sale goes ahead, then the mistake is discovered. Clearly there is no consensus, but rarely is the contract held to be void at common law. Usually, the court resolves the contract in favour of one party by deciding what a reasonable onlooker would understand the terms of the contract to be. In *Smith v Hughes* (1871) LR 6 QB 597, a racehorse owner, after inspecting a sample, bought 'last season's' oats instead of 'this season's', and they were of no use to him. He claimed the contract was void for mistake. The seller had not misrepresented the oats as being last season's; neither was he aware of the buyer's impression. The court held that, taking an objective view, there was a valid contract. The buyer had been careless and merely misled himself as to the type of oats.

If, however, from the reasonable onlooker's standpoint, the parties have clearly failed to reach any agreement, the contract will be void for mistake. This is exemplified in *Raffles v Whichelhaus* (1864) 2 H&C 906. The parties agreed, in London, on a contract of sale for a cargo of cotton 'Ex Peerless from Bombay'. There were, in fact, two ships called *Peerless* sailing from Bombay with cotton, one departing in October, the other in December. The buyer intended to buy the October shipment, the seller intended to sell the December shipment. It was held there was no agreement, offer and acceptance did not coincide, and the contract was void for mistake.

9.4.3 Unilateral mistake

A unilateral mistake arises when only one party is mistaken and the other is aware of it. This may arise in two situations: a mistake regarding the contract terms or regarding a party's identity. In *Harthog v Colin Shields* [1939] 3 All ER 566, the defendants offered to sell animal skins and negotiated a price per skin, as was the trade custom. Subsequently, the contract was concluded mistakenly at a price per pound, which the plaintiffs accepted. They were prevented from enforcing the deal on the basis that they must have been aware of the defendants' mistake.

For the contract to be void at common law, the unilateral mistake must be fundamental to the nature of the contract and it must induce the innocent party to enter into it. In *Cundy v Lindsay* (1877–78) 3 AC 459, a fraudster called Blenkarn wrote to Cundy ordering goods, giving his address as 37 Wood Street and signing his name so that it appeared to be Blenkiron & Co, a respectable business with whom Cundy had traded on previous occasions and whose offices were at 123 Wood Street. Cundy sent the goods to Blenkiron at No 37 and Blenkarn sold them on to Lindsay. Cundy sued Lindsay to recover the goods' value, claiming the contract was void for mistake. The court held that the contract was void. Cundy intended only to contract with Blenkiron and no title passed to Blenkarn.

If, however, the parties deal face to face rather than by letter or telephone, it is more likely that the contract will be voidable for fraudulent misrepresentation. In *Lewis v Avery* [1971] 3 All ER 907, the plaintiff advertised his car for sale. A person falsely claiming to be the actor Richard Green came to buy it. A deal was agreed and the 'actor' signed a cheque, showing a pass for Pinewood Studios as proof of identity. Lewis accepted the cheque, which was dishonoured when presented at the bank. Meantime, the fraudster sold the car to Avery, who bought it in good faith with no knowledge of the fraud.

If the contract between Lewis and the fake Green was void for mistake, then Green never had title to the car and therefore neither did Avery. Lewis would get his car back and Avery would bear the loss. If, on the other hand, the contract between Lewis and Green was voidable for fraudulent misrepresentation, then Green did have good title to the car which he had passed on to Avery before Lewis avoided the contract. In that case, Lewis would bear the loss. The Court of Appeal found that the contract was not void for mistake because the evidence showed that Lewis intended to sell the car to the person who turned up at his house.

9.4.4 *Non est factum*

Where a party has been misled into signing or executing a document which is substantially different to that which he intended to sign or execute, is he bound by it? To be successful in getting a transaction set aside, a person must be able to show that the document he thought he was signing was markedly different from the one that he actually did sign. He must have made a fundamental mistake in the character and effect of the document.

Where a person signs a document in blank and hands it to another to complete the blanks and finalise the transaction, he may be able to rely on this doctrine. However, where the details which are completed are not what the signatory believed they would be, but nevertheless they do not change the transaction's subject, then the contract is unlikely to be set aside.

A person trying to have the contract set aside must show that he acted carefully (eg that he was not negligent in any way). The standard to be applied to his actions would be that of a reasonably prudent person.

9.5 MISREPRESENTATION

There are basically three types of misrepresentation: negligent, fraudulent and innocent. Misrepresentation arises from a statement of fact as opposed to a statement of opinion, intention or law. If a statement of opinion later turns out to be unfounded it is not usually enough to have a transaction set aside. However, it is enough where a statement of opinion is clearly intended to be relied on, the same way the statement of fact would be. For example, in *Smith v Land and House Property Corp* (1884) 28 ChD 7, the vendor, during a sale of property, described a tenant as 'a most desirable tenant' when he knew that the tenant was substantially in arrears with the rent. In these circumstances the purchaser was not bound by his contract with the vendor.

It is not always easy to distinguish between statement of fact and statement of the law, although it is important to do so because, whereas the former constitutes representation, the latter does not.

To successfully claim misrepresentation, a party must be able to show that it was reasonable for him to rely on the other's statements, rather than to rely on his own judgement.

9.5.1 Non-disclosure

This does not generally lead to misrepresentation. Exceptions occur where a certain special relationship exists between the parties.

It is possible to be liable for misrepresentation as a result of a party's conduct. For example, a person who goes into a restaurant and sits down and orders a meal is representing that he has the ability to pay.

If A makes a representation to B which is true at the time he made it but which later becomes untrue, and he does not communicate this to B prior to the contract being entered into, A's failure to tell B of the changes amounts to misrepresentation.

9.5.2 Constructive notice

In *Barclays Bank v O'Brien* [1992] 4 All ER 983 the defendant wanted to borrow money from the bank which insisted on security. The security was provided by a charge over property jointly owned by the defendant and his wife, and the bank required her to enter the charge also. The wife gave her consent as a result of a misrepresentation made to her by her husband and under undue influence exerted by the husband on her. The court held that in circumstances where a close relationship arises and the wife's position is not as favourable financially as the husband's, then the bank has constructive notice of the misrepresentation unless it has taken reasonable steps to satisfy itself that the wife entered into the transaction freely and with full knowledge of the facts.

A misrepresentation may be made to a group of persons. However, a plaintiff will only be successful if he can show that he is within the group of people who might be regarded as likely to rely on the misrepresentation.

The misrepresentation must have induced a person to enter the contract. Where an estate agent's particulars misrepresented the size of a garage and the buyer had himself examined the property on two occasions, the misrepresentation was held not to have induced the plaintiff to enter the contract.

The person who makes a misrepresentation does not have to intend that the other party will rely on the misrepresentation; it is usually sufficient to show that he should have realised that the other party would be likely to.

9.5.3 Damages for misrepresentation

Damages can be recovered as a result of misrepresentation. The extent of damages claimed depends largely on the type of misrepresentation.

Fraudulent misrepresentation

A wronged person may rescind the contract, claim damages or do both. Fraud has been described as being a false representation '[which] has been made (1) knowingly or (2) without belief in its truth or (3) recklessly as to whether or not this is true or false' (*Hartelid v Sawyer & McCockin Real Estate Ltd* [1977] WLR 481). The damages will compensate for the actual loss resulting from the fraud (*Smith New Court Securities Ltd v Scrimegour Vickers Ltd* [1994] 4 All ER 225).

It is sufficient if the maker of the statement suspects that it is inaccurate without actually knowing it to be false. It is not necessary to show that his motive is dishonest.

Negligent misrepresentation

Negligent misrepresentation is a statement made in the belief that it is true, but with no reasonable grounds for that belief. There are two paths open to a party misled by a negligent statement to gain compensation. First, since the decision in *Hedley Byrne and Co Ltd v Heller and Partners Ltd* [1964] AC 465, it is possible to take action in tort for negligent misstatement, and provided the claimant can prove a special relationship with the defendant and therefore reliance on the defendant's skill, compensatory damages will be payable. Secondly, the innocent party may rescind the contract and claim damages under the Misrepresentation Act 1967. Under the Act, it is the defendant who must prove that he had reasonable grounds for making the statement, whereas in tort it is the claimant who must prove that the defendant was negligent.

In *Howard Marine and Dredging Co Ltd v A Ogden & Sons (Excavations) Ltd* [1978] QB 574, the plaintiffs hired two barges from the defendants. The barges' carrying capacity was crucial and the defendants misrepresented the sizes, basing their information on facts from Lloyd's Register, which were wrong; however, they could have checked with the barge owners. The court was not sure whether there was a duty of care in negligence, but under the Misrepresentation Act the defendants failed to prove that they had not been negligent.

Innocent misrepresentation

A statement made in the belief that it is true, and with reasonable grounds for that belief, is an innocent misrepresentation. The remedy is rescission of the contract, but under the Misrepresentation Act 1967, s 2(2) the court may instead award damages. In *Government of Zanzibar v British Aerospace (Lancaster House) Ltd* (unreported, 26 January 2000), it was held that, under s 2(2), if the claimant had lost the right to rescind, he also lost the right to damages.

9.5.4 Other matters

Where a party after discovering a misrepresentation does something to suggest that he does not want to rescind the contract, then he is prevented from doing so. Such actions include allowing a period of time to lapse after the contract was made.

A party cannot contract out of his liability for misrepresentation or any appropriate remedy unless it satisfies the test of reasonableness (see 9.8.4).

9.6 DURESS AND UNDUE INFLUENCE

9.6.1 Duress

Contracts may be alleged to have been entered into as a result of duress on the part of one party. The duress must be such that it prevents the person who complains of it from having a free will to enter the contract voluntarily. The effect of duress is to render a contract void (ie unenforceable) or voidable (ie a party complaining of duress has a choice of whether to affirm the contract or avoid it).

Duress is a combination of pressure and the lack of freedom to choose. Pressure is commonplace in commercial transactions and so long as the party being 'pushed' is not forced to enter without freedom of choice, then it is considered perfectly proper and an everyday commercial activity.

Duress may be exerted on a person through threats of violence or actual threat and imprisonment; on goods (ie unlawful detention of a person's goods, or a threat to detain them); or by 'economic duress'.

Duress administered to a person renders the contract void in serious cases and voidable in others. So far as duress to goods is concerned, a person who handed over money as a result of actual or threat of detention of goods can recover that money from the other party.

Economic duress

One party may exert economic pressure on the other which is such that the latter has no realistic choice but to enter the contract on the terms required by the first party. In *North Ocean Shipping Co Ltd v Hyundai Construction Co Ltd* [1979] QB 705 the shipbuilders who were building a ship threatened, without justification, to terminate the contract unless the other party agreed to increase the price for the work they were doing. The plaintiffs needed the ship urgently and reluctantly agreed. Although they stated that they reserved their rights, at no later stage did they raise any objections. They continued to make stage payments to the shipbuilders and eventually took delivery of the ship. The court decided that economic duress had been used by the shipbuilders and therefore the plaintiffs would have been entitled to refuse to pay 10% and to enforce the original contract if they so wished. However, under the circumstances they were regarded as affirming the new price terms. They should have raised further objections not only throughout the contract when the stage payments were made but more particularly at the time of expected delivery.

In *Universe Tankships Inc of Monrovia v International Transport Workers' Federation and Laughton (The Universe Sentinel)* [1983] AC 366, the plaintiff's ship was 'blacked' by a trade union. In order to secure its release, the plaintiff paid a sum of money into the union's welfare fund. The House of Lords held the agreement was vitiated by economic duress. Lords Scarman and Diplock concluded that economic duress may arise where there is an intentional submission to the inevitable and that the pressure used to secure such submission was illegitimate in that there was suppression of the will of the victim.

In *Atlas Express Ltd v Kafco (Importers and Distributors) Ltd* [1989] 1 All ER 641, the plaintiffs, a firm of road hauliers, contracted with the defendants to deliver cartons of basketware to branches of Woolworth. Prior to entering into the contract, a manager of the plaintiffs estimated that each load would comprise between 400 and 600 cartons. On this basis he agreed a contract rate of £1.10 per carton. The first load fell well below his estimations, comprising only 200 cartons. The manager then stated they would be unable to transport any more loads unless the defendants agreed to a minimum price of £440 per load. The defendants, a small concern which was heavily dependent on their contract with Woolworth, were unable to find another carrier willing to transport their goods and so they agreed reluctantly to pay the minimum charge. They later refused to pay that charge and, when sued, claimed economic duress as a defence. The court held that where a defendant had no alternative but to accept revised terms that were detrimental to its interests, this amounted to economic duress that vitiated the apparent consent to the renegotiated terms.

CTN Cash and Carry Ltd v Gallaher Ltd [1994] 4 All ER 714 illustrates the limits of economic duress. CTN bought cigarettes from G under a long-standing contract, with each purchase a separate transaction. G regularly gave credit to CTN. A consignment of cigarettes worth £17,000 due to be delivered was stolen from a warehouse and there was a disagreement about which party bore the risk. It later became clear that the risk was with G, but before this a representative of G made it clear that if CTN did not pay the £17,000, all credit facilities would be withdrawn. CTN decided that paying was the lesser of two evils. They later sought to recover on the grounds that they had only paid as a result of economic duress. The court did not uphold the claim. It was accepted that the threat to remove credit facilities was coercive, but not improper. The defendants were using the threat as a means of getting money they believed was due to them and not as a means of extorting money they knew not to be due.

Where one person owes another money, the former may offer a lower amount than he actually owes, forcing the other to accept it where perhaps his financial circumstances are such that he has no choice. Such an agreement cannot be forced upon him and he should be entitled to recover the balance he is actually owed (*D and C Builders Ltd v Rees* [1966] 2 QB 617; *Ferguson v Davies* (unreported, 21 November 1996). As mentioned above, not all threats can be considered to be duress as some may be commercially legitimate. There seems to be no doubt that where the threat is one to commit an act which is unlawful, it is considered to be duress. However, a threat by a party to break a contract where it can be shown that that threat did not force the other party to enter into the contract may not be considered to be duress. Furthermore, a threat not to supply goods unless a higher price is paid is not duress if it can be shown that the other party could have bought a plentiful supply of those goods elsewhere. Therefore, where the threat to do something is lawful but is clearly in excess of that which is regarded as commercially acceptable, it is held to be duress. In *Hughes SA v Peter Cremer GmbH & Co* (unreported, 21 October 1988), it was held that the 'minimum basic test of subjective causation in economic duress ought to be a "but for" test. Good or bad faith [is] also relevant, but not decisive'.

A situation could occur where a party has a right to bring a prosecution lawfully but threatens another party with a prosecution unless that other party enters a contract or agrees to more certain terms. This may be regarded as being duress as a threat amounts to excessive pressure which is not acceptable. Furthermore a court will not condone a situation where a party agrees to anything being done on the basis that a prosecution may be stifled.

In a threat to issue civil proceedings (ie where a party threatens to sue unless the other party agrees to certain clauses) a court will not interfere where a party is in fact threatening to enforce its legal right.

Where a person can show that the other party entered into a contract irrespective of the duress then a contract will be valid. However, it is the person accused of duress who is responsible for showing that the other would have entered the contract anyway.

What is the effect of duress?

The person who is subjected to the duress can normally choose whether he affirms or avoids the contract. If duress has occurred and he has taken no steps to set aside the contract, he may be held to have affirmed it.

9.6.2 Undue influence

This is an equitable doctrine which arose to deal with the situation where donations and gifts are allegedly made as a result of one party exerting unreasonable pressure on another. The basic principle arose to prevent one person profiting from his own fraud or wrongful act. A presumption of undue influence arises where the transaction is manifestly disadvantageous to the person who has been influenced.

Where a special relationship exists (eg with a parent and child or solicitor and client), undue influence is likely to be presumed. Therefore, where one party is shown to be disadvantaged, the presumption arises. Family arrangements are treated far more leniently than, say, a relationship between solicitor and client. However, where a parent has exercised undue influence over a child, the transaction is likely to be set aside.

To rebutt the presumption of undue influence, a party must show that the donor was acting independently of any influence from the donee. Perhaps the best way of showing this is to show that he had received independent advice from a third party. That advice must be such that an honest and competent adviser would give if acting solely in the interests of the donor.

A contract made under undue influence is voidable, and not void. Therefore the party influenced has the right to decide whether to affirm or avoid the contract. However, he may lose the right to set aside the contract if he does something to affirm the contract in any way or leaves matters for such a substantial period of time that he may be deemed to have acquiesced and therefore be bound by the transaction.

In a number of more recent cases, particularly concerning the husband and wife relationship, the wife has been persuaded to enter some surety contract or guarantee with a bank or similar creditor on the basis of undue influence or misrepresentation not by the creditor, but by a third party (ie the husband). In *Barclays Bank plc v O'Brien* (below), the Court of Appeal created a special class of surety which would apply mainly to wives, but also to other cohabitees.

Whether the bank/creditor is bound by the wrongdoings of the husband (the principal debtor), and thereby unable to enforce security against the wife (the guarantor), depends on whether the bank/creditor had actual or constructive notice of the wife's equitable right to have the surety agreement set aside on the basis of undue influence or misrepresentation. The informality of the dealings between a wife and husband means that there is a higher likelihood of the husband misrepresenting the liability of the contract to the wife in order to secure her agreement to the undertaking. Thus where the bank/creditor is aware that the transaction is manifestly disadvantageous to the wife, and there is a substantial risk of the husband using undue influence or misrepresentation, then the bank/creditor is put on notice. In which case, the creditor/bank should explain to the wife privately the implications of the transaction and advise her to take independent advice. If this is not done, and if there was undue influence or misrepresentation, the creditor will be unable to enforce the security free of the wife's interest.

In *National Westminster Bank v Morgan* [1985] 1 All ER 821, Mr and Mrs Morgan jointly owned the family home. Mrs Morgan agreed to sign a remortgage of the house in favour of the bank to prevent the original mortgagee repossessing the house because of mortgage arrears due to Mr Morgan's business problems. The bank manager visited Mr and Mrs Morgan and she made it clear she had little confidence in her husband's business. The manager, in good faith but incorrectly, told her that the mortgage only secured liabilities in respect of the house. In fact, it covered all Mr Morgan's debts to the bank. When the loan was not repaid the bank sought to repossess the home. Mrs Morgan pleaded undue influence. The House of Lords found no undue influence. The relationship between Mrs Morgan and the bank was an ordinary one: no relationship of trust existed and so there was no onus on the bank to advise her to take independent advice. Neither was the transaction manifestly disadvantageous to her: indeed, it helped her to keep her home.

In *Barclays Bank plc v O'Brien* [1994] 1 AC 180, Mr O'Brien wanted to increase the overdraft facilities for his business. The bank agreed to a loan of £120,000 provided it was secured by his house, which he owned jointly with his wife. He told her that the loan was only £60,000. The bank manager gave instructions that both Mr and Mrs O'Brien should be advised on the nature of the transaction and to take independent advice. These instructions were not complied with and the wife and husband signed the documents without reading them. The business later collapsed and the issue of whether Mrs O'Brien was bound by the contract arose when the bank took proceedings to repossess the house. The Court of Appeal held the bank was aware that the parties were husband and wife, and as such were put on notice as to the circumstances in which the wife would have been asked to sign the surety. The bank failed to warn her of the risks she ran in entering into the surety contract or as to her potential liability in respect of her husband's debts. Furthermore, the bank had not properly advised her to seek independent advice. On this basis the bank was fixed with constructive notice of the misrepresentation made by the husband to induce his wife into the contract, and therefore the wife was entitled to have the legal charge set aside.

The principles are not confined to married couples. They extend to cohabitees and any situation where the creditor is aware that the surety places a confidence and trust in the principal debtor. In *Avon Finance Co Ltd v Bridger* [1985] 2 All ER 281, a son persuaded his parents to act as surety for his debts by means of a misrepresentation. It was held that the surety was unenforceable by the finance company, *inter alia* because the company had knowledge of the trust the parents reposed in their son with regard to their financial dealings.

In *Lloyds Bank v Bundy* [1974] 3 All ER 757, the plaintiff and his son both used the same bank. The son's business ran into difficulties and the father was asked to guarantee his son's overdraft, putting up his farm as security. He did this and when the son could not pay, the bank sought to repossess the farm. The father claimed the contract should be set aside on the grounds of undue influence. He had banked with that branch for many years and had placed total trust in them, yet the bank had not warned him of the possible consequences of the guarantee. The Court of Appeal held that the presumption of undue influence does not usually arise between a bank and its customers, and thus it would usually have to be proved, but the facts in this case did raise the presumption. There was a relationship of trust and the bank was unable to rebut the presumption.

See further *CIBC Mortgages plc v Pitt* [1993] 4 All ER 433, in which the House of Lords made it clear that the directions in *O'Brien* need only be followed if the lender knows that the transaction is manifestly disadvantageous to the wife.

9.7 TERMS OF CONTRACT

Assuming that it can be established that a contract has been made, it is important to know what terms of a contract have been agreed upon and are therefore binding on the parties concerned.

Not all contracts are expressed in writing – some may be oral or may have terms which are partly oral or partly in writing. Generally, a party is bound by the terms of an agreement if he has agreed to them being incorporated in writing.

Prior to a contract being agreed, representations may be made by one party to encourage the other to enter into the contract. These representations are not usually considered to be the terms of a contract.

9.7.1 Standard form of contract and incorporation of terms

A party may be keen to show that the terms of agreement are those contained in a pre-prepared standard contract form, perhaps in a ticket or enclosed with a letter containing an offer. These standard terms are very often handed to a person at the time a contract is made. The question of whether the terms are then incorporated into the contract is an important one since the standard form of contract frequently tends to impose obligations on the parties and contains clauses which purport to exclude or limit liability in many situations so far as the party who prepared the conditions is concerned.

The conditions must be brought to the notice of the party who receives them either before or at the time the contract is made. If not, they cannot be incorporated into the contract. In *Olley v Marlborough Court* [1949] 1 KB 532, a person who checked into a hotel found that some of his property had been stolen. He sued the hotel which placed reliance on a notice which disclaimed liability for any lost or stolen article but which was on the back of his bedroom door. On arriving at the hotel when he had signed the hotel register, there had been no mention of any exemption clauses. The court held that the notice was ineffective since it had not been brought to his attention until after the contract had been made.

The conditions must be contained in a document which it would be reasonable for the receiving party to expect to contain conditions. For example, conditions contained on a deck chair hire ticket or a parking ticket issued by an automatic machine from a car park are ineffective for bringing attention to the party receiving it (*Chapleton v Barry UDC* [1940] 1 KB 532; *Thornton v Shoe Lane Parking Ltd* [1971] 2 QB 163).

It is common that two parties engaged in trade enter into several contracts with each other. Where it can be shown that the parties intended that the conditions which had been used in previous contracts should continue to be used throughout the course of dealing between the parties, then those conditions are likely to be effective in the most recent agreement. See, for example, *Henry Kendall & Sons v William Lillico & Sons* [1968] 2 All ER 444, which concerned verbal contracts followed by 'sold notes' which contained an exclusion clause which the recipient was aware of but had never read. Held, the recipients' readiness to be bound by the printed conditions, despite not having read them, meant they had accepted them. Thus, the general conditions became part of the oral contract. Contrast the findings in *McCutcheon v MacBrayne* [1964] 1 All ER 430, where the plaintiff's agent, who had dealt with the defendants on a number of occasions, sometimes signed a risk note containing the relevant exclusion clauses and sometimes did not. Held, it is the consistency of a course of conduct which gives rise to the implication that in similar circumstances a similar contractual result will follow. When the conduct is not consistent, there is no reason why it should still produce an invariable contractual result. See also *Hollier v Rambler Motors Ltd* [1972] 2 QB 71; *Knight Machinery (Holdings) v Rennie* [1995] SLT 166; and *Petrotrade Inc v Texaco Ltd* (unreported, 21 December 1999).

Similarly, conditions used in a particular trade or business may be incorporated where both parties are in the same trade and are aware that those conditions are used, even when they do not actually refer to them in the contract between themselves (*British Crane Hire Corp v Ipswich Plant Hire* [1975] QB 303).

It is not essential that the party receiving the conditions should have read them. In order for the other party to rely on them being incorporated, he must be able to show that the person receiving the document knew that there was writing or printed matter on the document and that it contained or referred to the conditions on which he intends to rely. The party intending to rely on the conditions must take reasonable steps to give notice to the other party of the conditions. If the receiving party knew that there was writing or printed matter on the document and sufficient steps were taken to give him notice of the conditions, then even if he did not actually know that it contained conditions, he is still likely to be bound by the contract's terms.

The steps to be taken to give reasonable notice of the conditions depends on the facts of each case. It is not always necessary for a set of conditions to be sent to the person concerned; it may be sufficient that the party seeking to rely on them had made specific mention of any pre-contract documents.

If the term on which a party intends to rely is considered onerous, then he must show that he has taken reasonable steps to bring the effect of that clause to the other party's attention. What a party must do depends on the fact of each case, but the court would have to be satisfied that clear steps were taken to draw the effect of that clause to the other party's attention before it is allowed to be incorporated (*Interfoto Picture Library Ltd v Stilleto Visual Programmes Ltd* [1988] 1 All ER 348; *AEG (UK) Ltd v Logic Resources Ltd* (*The Buyer*, December 1995).

If one party intends to rely on printed notices to bring to the other party's attention certain clauses they must be in a clearly visible place and they must be brought to the party's attention prior to entering into the contract.

9.7.2 What if each party wants to contract on its own terms?

A common situation is where *A* sends to *B* an offer, perhaps asking for supply of goods and/or services, and indicates in that letter that he intends to be bound by his own standard terms and conditions, a copy of which will be enclosed with the letter. *B* then replies, indicating that the order is accepted but that he intends to trade on his own terms only. Whose terms are incorporated into the contract? In the example described, neither of the parties' terms are incorporated. *B*'s reply to the order is regarded as a counter offer and not an acceptance.

If after having received *B*'s counter offer, *A* confirms the order, this may be regarded as being his acceptance to *B*'s counter offer and the contract is governed by *B*'s standard terms. The terms must satisfy all the rules relating to incorporation, such as reasonable notice. If these are satisfied, the terms are likely to govern the contract.

There is relatively little case law on this specific area. What often happens is that each party writes to the other indicating that he intends to contract only on his own standard terms. At some stage a contract is made and the difficulty is determining whose conditions apply. It is often described as the 'battle of the forms'.

The general principle that has arisen is known as the 'last shot' doctrine: in other words, a court looks into the communication between the parties and tries to establish at which point one set of conditions was unconditionally accepted by the other party (*Butler Machine Tool Co Ltd v Ex-Cell-o Corp (England) Ltd* [1979] 1 WLR 401). However, subsequent case law has placed slight variations on the principle, and in *British Steel Corp v Cleveland Bridge & Engineering* [1984] 1 All ER 504 the court found it impossible to identify an offer which had been accepted. Even though the goods had been delivered and 'accepted' by the receiving party, it was clear that party would never have agreed to the seller's standard terms. In that case the court found that no contract was concluded.

See also *Chichester Joinery v John Mowlem* (1987) 42 BLR 100, in which numerous terms and conditions were referred to in correspondence regarding a subcontract, and where it was held, distinguishing *Butler Machine Tool*, under such circumstances that counter offers had been made, and that the subcontractor's counter offer had 'killed' the defendant's previous counter offer.

It is important therefore that any party who intends to contract on his own standard terms should ensure that *all* correspondence and contractual documents contain a copy of, or reference to, his standard terms.

9.7.3 Conditions and warranties

Once it is established that a certain term has been incorporated into a contract, it is important to know whether that term will be classified as a condition or a warranty. A *condition* is an essential stipulation of the contract in which one party guarantees to the other that it is true or that certain promises will be fulfilled. Breach of the condition permits the innocent party, if he wishes, to treat himself as being free from any obligation to be bound by the contract and claim damages for any loss he sustains as a result. A *warranty* is a term of the contract which is not regarded as so essential as a condition. Breach of a warranty does not allow a person to treat the contract as discharged but to claim damages only – even if he has suffered no prejudice by the breach.

Furthermore, certain terms may not be clearly defined as either a condition or a warranty; this third category is often referred to as an intermediate term. The consequence of the breach of that term simply depends on the nature of the breach itself. If the breach is a minor one, it can be remedied by an award of damages. If it is so important or fundamental it affects the whole contract, the contract must be regarded as discharged (*Hong Kong Fir Shipping Co Ltd v Kawasaki Kisen Kaisha Ltd* [1962] 2 QB 26). Some terms are categorised automatically as warranties and conditions (see Chapter 10).

9.7.4 Meaning and construction of term

It is important that the terms on which the party intends to rely can be easily understood. Therefore where any technical or unusual words are incorporated into a contract, there should be a clear explanation of their meaning to avoid any ambiguity. If there is ambiguity a court may delete that part of the contract or, if the majority of the contract is not clearly intelligible, all of it.

The court looks at the whole context of an agreement to establish the meaning of any particular term or clause. It is not open to a court to alter the words used or to impose a meaning that it believes the parties ought to have included, unless it is clear that that is actually what the parties had intended. In other words, a court will not rewrite the terms of a contract.

The modern approach to the interpretation of contract terms has been stated as follows in *Investors Compensation Scheme Ltd v West Bromwich Building Society; Alford v West Bromwich Building Society* [1998] 1 All ER 98:

(1) Interpretation is the ascertainment of the meaning which the document would convey to a reasonable person having all the background knowledge which would reasonably have been available to the parties in the situation in which they were at the time of the contract.

(2) The background, subject to the requirement that it should have been reasonably available to the parties and to the exception to be mentioned next, includes absolutely anything which would have affected the way in which the language of the document would have been understood by a reasonable man.

(3) The law excludes from the admissible background the previous negotiations of the parties and their declarations of subjective intent. They are admissible only in an action for rectification. The law makes this distinction for reasons of practical policy and, in this respect only, legal interpretation differs from the way we would interpret utterances in ordinary life. The boundaries of this exception are in some respects unclear. But this is not the occasion on which to explore them.

(4) The meaning which a document (or any other utterance) would convey to a reasonable man is not the same thing as the meaning of its words. The meaning of words is a matter of dictionaries and grammars; the meaning of the document is what the parties using those words against the relevant background would reasonably have been understood to mean. The background may not merely enable the reasonable man to choose between the possible meanings of words which are ambiguous but even (as occasionally happens in ordinary life) to conclude that the parties must, for whatever reason, have used the wrong words or syntax.

(5) The 'rule' that words should be given their 'natural and ordinary meaning' reflects the common sense proposition that we do not easily accept that people have made linguistic mistakes, particularly in formal documents. On the other hand, if one would nevertheless conclude from the background that something must have gone wrong with the language, the law does not require judges to attribute to the parties an intention which they plainly could not have had.

This statement was adopted by Morritt LJ in *WRM Group v Wood* (unreported, 21 November 1997) and approved by Thomas J in *Kumar v AGF Insurance Ltd and others* [1998] 4 All ER 788.

9.7.5 Extrinsic evidence

In an ideal world all the terms which affect a contract will be supported by written evidence in the contract itself.

One party may wish to adduce evidence which is extrinsic to the written contract on the basis that the written terms themselves do not clearly show all the points which were agreed between the parties. If after hearing the evidence a court determines that terms additional to those contained in the document were agreed upon and were intended by the parties to be incorporated into the contract, that contract will consist partly of the terms of the document and partly those outside it. If, however, the court finds that the document is a complete record of the contract, it will reject the extrinsic evidence produced. This latter situation is known as the 'parol evidence rule'. Therefore, where a document appears to be a complete contract, a party will have great difficulty convincing a court that further terms outside the agreement were intended to be incorporated into the contract.

Where certain contracts must by law be evidenced in writing, then any extrinsic oral evidence is likely to be excluded.

9.7.6 Collateral contracts

In certain circumstances, although the party intended to be bound by all the terms in a written document, there may be a collateral contract of agreement outside the main agreement which gives efficacy to matters on which the main contract may be silent. This collateral agreement may be oral. A court may determine that it does have effect and that it runs alongside the main contract.

Although the parol evidence rule stipulates that no extrinsic evidence can be included to affect the main written agreement, there are some exceptions to that rule:

(1) Evidence adduced to determine the written agreement's validity or effectiveness.
(2) Evidence used to determine the agreement's true nature.
(3) Evidence to interpret or explain parts of the written agreement.
(4) Evidence of custom or trade usage.

9.7.7 Implied term

Although it is always hoped that any terms incorporated into the contract are expressed either in writing or openly agreed between the parties before the contract is made, it is possible that terms are implied into the contract. This is particularly so in certain types of contracts (eg sale of goods, landlord and tenant, and employment).

Terms implied into the contract do not necessarily reflect the party's intention, although this is possible. Certain contracts might be silent about particular aspects of the contract. However the court does not imply a meaning simply because it improves the contract. It must be a necessity.

Certain statutes imposed implied terms or a term may be implied from general usage or custom in any particular trade or activity. Similarly, evidence of a previous course of dealing between the parties may give rise to certain terms being implied into the contract.

Where however there is an express term which clearly contradicts that which might be considered to be customary in the circumstances then the general rule is that the express terms will prevail.

9.8 EXEMPTION AND EXCLUSION CLAUSES

It is common for parties to want to exclude or limit their liability in the terms of any contract they enter into. Furthermore, they may want to provide time limits in which the other party can lodge a claim.

Exclusion clauses are generally construed strictly. The court takes into account the circumstances of the case and tries to give effect to what they believe to be the parties' intentions. The words must therefore be clear and unambiguous. Where a clause is ambiguous a court infers whichever meaning favours the party against whom the clause is intended to operate, to the detriment of the party seeking to rely on it. This principle is known as 'contra preferendum'.

Where an exclusion clause is drafted so widely that, if interpreted literally, it defeats the main purpose of the contract, the court attempts to interpret it to reflect the parties' intentions.

9.8.1 Liability for negligence

It is possible to exclude or restrict a party's liability for negligence, but the parties must ensure that the words are clear and it is made certain that they intended to exclude such liability (*Smith v Smith Wales Switchgear* [1978] 1 WLR 165). However, it is not possible, in most cases, to exclude liability for death or personal injury (see 9.8.4).

9.8.2 Burden of proof

This is placed upon the person who intends to rely on the exemption or exclusion clause. He must show that the clause covers the liability that he intends to restrict or exclude. If he satisfies a court of this, the other party will try to convince the court that the loss or damage that arose emanated from an act or omission which falls outside the scope of the clause.

9.8.3 Exemption clause from third party

A third party (ie one that is not a party to the contract) cannot at common law rely on an exemption clause contained in the contract; the exemption clause is intended to apply to the relationship *vis-à-vis* the parties to the contract (*Scruttons Ltd v Midland Silicones Ltd* [1962] AC 446). However, a situation could arise, say, where the duty of care owed by *A* to *B* arises as a result of a contract between *B* and *C*. An exemption clause in the contract between *B* and *C* which purports to exclude or restrict liability may be regarded as applying to any liability attaching to *A*. The condition that must be proven is that it was the intention of all the parties that such a clause should apply to *A*'s liability.

The position described above has been affected considerably by the Contracts (Rights of Third Parties) Act 1999 (see 9.11.1).

9.8.4 Statutory control and exemption clauses

Unfair Contract Terms Act 1977

The Act seeks to control terms contained in the contract (and also non-contractual notices which seek to exclude or restrict liability in tort) where those terms purport to exclude or restrict liability. The Act may make the clause concerned ineffective or it may mean that the clause must satisfy the requirement of reasonableness to be effective.

Dealing as a consumer

The Act draws a distinction between situations where a party deals as a consumer and where he does not. There are three conditions to be satisfied for the party to be regarded as dealing as a consumer:

(1) he must not make the contract in the course of the business or hold himself out as doing so;
(2) the other party must make a contract in the course of a business; and
(3) the goods must be of a type ordinarily supplied for private use or consumption.

An illustration to this rule arose in *R & B Customs Brokers Co Ltd v United Dominions Trust Ltd* [1988] 1 WLR 321. The court held that a freight forwarding company dealt as a consumer when it entered into an agreement with a finance company for the purchase of a motor vehicle which was for a director's personal and business use. The decision was made on the basis that the company had not held itself out as making the contract in the course of a business.

Section 3 of the Act applies to a contract where one of the parties deals as a consumer or on the other party's written standard terms of business. No definition is provided in the Act for the meaning of 'written standard terms', presumably because these can be easily recognised in the instant case. It has been held that a contract can be on written standard terms even if some of those terms have been negotiated individually (*McCrone v Boots Farm Sales* [1981] SLT 103; *The Salvage Association v CAP Financial Services Ltd* [1995] FSR 654). The party cannot by reference to any contract term, except in so far as the term satisfies the test of reasonableness, exclude or restrict any liability in respect of his breach of contract, or claim that he is entitled to render a contractual performance which is substantially different from that which is reasonably expected of him, or render no performance at all for all or some of his contractual obligations.

Section 4 states that a person who deals with a consumer cannot by way of any contract term be made to indemnify another person in respect of any liability for negligence or breach of contract, except in so far as the contract term satisfies the test of reasonableness. Indemnities given by people who do not deal as a consumer are not affected by this section.

Liability for negligence

Section 2 prevents a person excluding or restricting his liability (arising from business liability) for death or personal injury resulting from negligence. Any such clause is totally ineffective. Nor can he exclude or restrict his liability for any other loss or damages which arise out of his negligence unless the term satisfies the test of reasonableness.

Consumer guarantees

Section 5 states that any clause which attempts to exclude or restrict business liability for loss or damage resulting from the negligence of the manufacturer or distributor of any goods is ineffective. 'Goods' for the purpose of this section are those ordinarily supplied for private use or consumption. The loss or damage must arise from the goods being defective whilst in use by a person other than exclusively for business.

'Business liability' is defined by s 1 as applying to liabilities for breach of any obligations which arise from something which occurs in the course of a person's business or from the occupation of premises used for business purposes.

Sale, supply and hire purchase

Section 6 prevents the person who sells or lets out his goods under hire-purchase agreements from excluding or restricting liability for any of the undertakings as to title implied by the Sale of Goods Act 1979, s 12 or the Supply of Goods (Implied Terms) Act 1973, s 8. Furthermore, s 6 also provides that the terms implied by those enactments as to description, quality and fitness for purpose cannot be excluded where the other party deals as a consumer. The use of an exclusion clause seeking to avoid these provisions in a consumer contract is also rendered a criminal offence by the Consumer Transactions (Restrictions on Statements) Order 1977 (SI No 1813). If that party deals as a business, those provisions can be excluded subject to the reasonableness requirement.

Section 7 applies to other contracts such as those for hire of goods or work and materials.

As against a consumer, liability in respect of description, quality or fitness cannot be excluded. Against a business, such provisions can be excluded subject to the reasonableness requirement. Terms relating to title implied by the Supply of Goods and Services Act 1982 cannot be excluded regardless of whether the other party is a consumer or business. Where a term seeks to exclude terms as to title which are not implied by that Act, it is valid only if reasonable, again regardless of the other contracting party's status.

Reasonableness test

To be effective, many of the clauses governed by the Act must satisfy the test of reasonableness. To satisfy the test, s 11 states that 'the term shall have been a fair and reasonable one to be included having regard to the circumstances which were, or ought reasonably to have been, known to or in the contemplation of the parties when the contract was made'. The reasonableness of the term is determined at the time when the contract was made; therefore any facts not known at that time are likely to be irrelevant in determining whether a clause is reasonable.

Schedule 2 lays down guidelines (which are not exhaustive) to assist in determining whether a clause satisfies the test. The guidelines apply to contracts dealing with the sale of goods and hire purchase, and contracts for the supply of goods, but they are often regarded as being of general use in assisting to determine whether a clause is reasonable (see eg *Flamar Interocean v Denmac* [1990] 1 Lloyd's Rep 434; *St Albans City and District Council v ICL Ltd* [1995] FSR 686). The guidelines are as follows:

(a) the strength of the bargaining positions of the parties relative to each other, taking into account . . . alternative means by which the customers requirements could have been met;

(b) whether the customer received an inducement to agree to the term, or in accepting it had an opportunity of entering into a similar contract with other persons, but without having to accept a similar term;

(c) whether the customer knew or ought reasonably to have known of the existence and extent of the term (having regard . . . to any custom of the trade and any previous course of dealing between the parties);

(d) where the term excludes or restricts any relevant liability if some condition is not complied with, whether it was reasonable at the time of the contract to expect that compliance with that condition would be practicable;

(e) whether the goods were manufactured, processed or adapted to the special order of the customer.

Limiting liability

Section 11 provides that where a person, by use of a contract term, seeks to restrict liability to a specified sum and the question arises whether that term satisfies the test of reasonableness, then consideration must be given (without ignoring the guidelines listed above) to:

(1) the resources that he could expect to be available to him to meet the liability if it arises, and
(2) how far it was open to him to cover himself by insurance.

A court must determine whether a clause is reasonable. It cannot re-write the term, nor can it delete words to render what it believes is an 'unreasonable' term, reasonable.

Exceptions

Certain contracts are not affected by ss 2–4 of the 1977 Act (Sched 1). They relate to contracts for insurance: creation or transfer of an interest in land, patents, trademarks and copyright; formation or dissolution of a company or the rights or obligations of its members; and any contract relating to creation or transfer of rights in securities. For illustrative cases on the scope of those exclusions, see *Micklefield v SAC Technology* [1990] 1 WLR 1002, and *Electricity Supply Nominees Ltd v IAF Group plc* [1993] 1 WLR 1059.

Schedule 1 qualifies the Act's effect on any contract of marine salvage or towage, a charter party, and for the carriage of goods by a ship or hovercraft. It further qualifies any contract of employment in that any attempt to exclude liability for negligence will not be effective unless it favours an employee.

Misrepresentation

Section 8 of the 1977 Act provides that where a term or clause attempts to exclude or restrict any liability of or any remedy available to a party arising from a misrepresentation, then that term or clause has no effect in so far as it satisfies the test of reasonableness in s 11.

Unfair Terms in Consumer Contracts Regulations 1999

These regulations (SI No 2083) implement the EC Directive 93/13/EC. The Directive attempts to harmonise for all member states the laws on safeguarding the consumer with regard to unfair terms in contracts. They repealed the Unfair Terms in Consumer Contracts Regulations and came into force on 1 October 1999.

The Regulations do not affect the provisions of the Unfair Contract Terms Act 1977; nor do they apply to non-consumer contracts. Therefore in some circumstances a party only has the choice of an action under the 1977 Act.

The Regulations prohibit the use of unfair terms in consumer contracts, whether oral or written. They apply to any term or contract concluded between a seller or supplier and a consumer where the term has not been individually negotiated (ie where it has been drafted in advance and a consumer has not been able to influence the term's content).

Whereas the 1977 Act applies only to specific types of clauses, the Regulations apply to all clauses of a contract which are not individually negotiated.

Plain intelligible language

Regulation 6 provides that terms must be drafted in plain intelligible language. If there is any doubt about the meaning of a written term, the interpretation which is most favourable to a consumer prevails. By using plain intelligible language, contract provisions relating to definition of the subject matter, the price or remuneration are not subject to any test. However, these may be factors which must be taken into account in considering whether another term is fair.

The Regulations require that any term satisfies the test of 'fairness' (unlike the 1977 Act's test of reasonableness). If a term is regarded as unfair then it is not binding on a consumer. However, the Regulations stipulate that although one term may be ineffective, where the balance of the contract can continue without that term, it shall be binding on the parties.

What is unfair?

Under reg 5, 'an unfair term is one which contrary to the requirement of good faith causes a significant imbalance in the parties' rights and obligations under the contract to the detriment of the consumer'. When assessing the unfair nature of a term, the following must according to reg. 6 be considered:

(1) the nature of the goods and services to which the contract applies;
(2) all the circumstances at the time the contract was concluded; and
(3) all other terms of the contract or of another contract on which that contract may be dependent.

Schedule 2 to the Regulations lists 17 terms which it is stated *may* be unfair. The list, although lengthy, is not exhaustive, and includes the following:

(1) inappropriately excluding or limiting the consumer's legal rights;
(2) irrevocably binding the consumer to terms with which he had no real opportunity of becoming acquainted before the conclusion of the contract;
(3) obliging the consumer to fulfil his obligations where the seller/supplier does not perform his;

(4) enabling the seller/supplier to alter the contract's terms unilaterally without a valid reason specified in the contract.

In *Director General of Fair Trading v First National Bank plc* [2000] 2 All ER 759, the Director General of Fair Trading sought an injunction against the continued use of a clause which sought to claim all outstanding moneys owed, along with legal costs, charges and expenses, in the event of late payment of instalments. The complaint regarded the operation of the clause should the courts extend the time for repayment, which would make interest at the contractual rate *and* accrued unpaid interest at the date of judgment payable. The Director General maintained that the average consumer was unlikely to notice the effects of such a clause in these circumstances. The High Court held the clause to be reasonable, but this was reversed by the Court of Appeal.

The examples are guidelines only; each term must be assessed on its own merits. It is always possible for a listed term to be fair in the specific circumstances of any one case.

Complaints to qualifying bodies

The reg 11(1) provisions are new to the 1999 Regulations. Where a qualifying body notifies the Director General in writing that it agrees to consider a complaint that any contract term drawn up for general use is unfair, that body is obliged to consider that complaint. It is then obliged to give reasons for any decision whether to apply for an injunction and, in so deciding, to take account of any undertaking which might be forthcoming.

The relevant qualifying bodies are the Data Protection Registrar, the Director General of Gas and Electricity Management (along with the Northern Ireland counterpart), the Director General of Telecommunications, the Director General of Water Services, the Rail Regulator, every weights and measures authority in Great Britain, and the Department of Enterprise, Trade and Investment. There is nothing in the Regulations to restrict these bodies to terms arising in their own field of interest, though this is no doubt how it will operate in practice. While the Director General of Fair Trading must be notified by a qualifying body of intended action, the former has no powers to stay any action.

The OFT has signed certain agreements with the Consumers' Association, the Department of Enterprise, Trade and Investment, the Office of Telecommunications and with LACOTS (the Local Authority Co-ordinating Committee on Food and Trading Standards).

Application for an injunction

Regulation 12(1) gives the Director General of Fair Trading and any of the above qualifying bodies, and also the Consumers' Association, the power to apply for an injunction, including an interim injunction, against any person appearing to be using, or recommending, an unfair term drawn up for general use in consumer contracts.

Before a qualifying body applies for an injunction, reg 12(2) requires it to notify the Director General in writing at least 14 days before the date on which the application is made, beginning with the date on which such notification is given. The Director General can, however, consent to a shorter period of notice.

Regulation 12(3) provides that the court may grant an injunction on such terms as it thinks fit, and reg 12(4) further provides that the injunction may relate not only to the use of a particular contract term drawn up for general use, but to any similar term, or term having like effect, used or recommended by any person.

Obtaining documents and information

Regulation 13 gives extensive powers to the Director General and the qualifying bodies (but not the Consumers' Association) to obtain documents and information. Regulation 13(3) gives such parties the right to require any person to supply:

(1) a copy of any document which that person has used or recommended at the time when notice is given as a pre-formulated standard consumer contract; and

(2) information about the use or recommendation by that person of that or any other document in dealings with consumers.

Regulation 13(4) states that these powers are to be exercised by a written notice which may specify the way and the time within which the notice is to be complied with. It also provides that any such notice can be varied or revoked by a subsequent written notice. Regulation 13(6) provides for the court, when approached by the party issuing the notice, to make such order as it thinks fit in the event of non-compliance. Regulation 13(5) states that nothing in these provisions can compel any person to supply a document or information which he would be entitled to refuse to produce or give in civil proceedings.

Notification of undertakings and orders

Regulation 14 requires qualifying bodies to notify the Director General of any undertakings it has obtained under regs 10 and 11. The qualifying body is also required to give the Director General written notice of the outcome of any application made for an injunction, and of the terms of any undertaking given to, or order made, by the court. Such body must also give the Director General written notice of the outcome of an application made to enforce any previous court order.

Dissemination of information on the Regulations

The 1999 Regulations require the Director General to arrange for the publication, in such form and manner as he considers appropriate, of any:

(1) undertaking or order notified by a qualifying body;

(2) undertaking given as to the continued use of a term which the Director General considers unfair in consumer contracts;

(3) application made by him for an injunction and of the terms of any undertakings given to, or order made by, the court;

(4) application made by him to enforce a previous court order.

Regulation 14(2) obliges the Director General to inform any person, on request made in whatever form, whether a particular term covered by the Regulations has been the subject of an undertaking given or notified to him by a qualifying body, or the subject of a court order made on application by or as notified to him by such body. When responding, the Director General is to provide the person making the request with details of the undertaking, or a copy of the order, together with a copy of any amendments which the person giving the undertaking has agreed to make to the term in question. It would appear that, only when providing such a copy, this is the only time when the Director General's response must be in writing.

Regulation 14(3) provides that the Director General may (not must) arrange for the dissemination in such form and manner as he considers appropriate of such information and advice as to the operation of the Regulations as may appear to him expedient to give to the public and to all persons likely to be affected by the Regulations.

9.9 BREACH OF CONTRACT

There are many ways in which a contract can come to an end other than by way of the parties discharging their obligations and promises under the contract's terms. However, perhaps one of the most important is by breach of contract.

A breach of contract generally gives rise to a cause of action for the person who has been aggrieved. This does not mean that whenever there is a breach, the aggrieved person is entitled to treat himself as discharged from any further obligation to accept the other party's performance of his contractual duty or any attempt to perform them. However, the aggrieved party usually prefers this course of action, although in some situations he may wish to treat the contract as continuing. Furthermore, he may decide to waive his rights to treat the contract as discharged, except for the other party's performance even though it is defective, and instead sue for damages.

9.9.1 Affirming the contract

The aggrieved party may treat the contract as continuing, in which case he is said to have 'affirmed' the contract. Affirmation may be express or implied if, with knowledge of the breach and knowledge of his right to choose between the alternatives open to him, he does some unequivocal act which suggests that he intends to go on with the contract regardless of the breach. Nevertheless, by affirming the contract the aggrieved party does not lose his right to claim damages for loss he suffered due to the breach.

An aggrieved party may lose his right to treat the contract as repudiated if he conducts himself in such a way that the other party believes that he does not intend to exercise his right. The aggrieved party must have shown unequivocal representation in either words or conduct that he does not intend to do so. Furthermore, it must be shown that the aggrieved party knew of the circumstances giving rise to the breach and of his right to treat the contract as repudiated. Another condition that must be satisfied is that the party who claims that the other has waived his right has relied to such an extent on the action which he regards as being the waiver, that it is unjust not to allow the contract to continue. The facts of each case decide whether a court accepts that an aggrieved party waived his right.

9.9.2 Repudiation must be accepted

Where an aggrieved party decides to treat himself as discharged of his obligation under the contract, he must accept repudiation. Otherwise, the contract continues to exist. In other words, he must indicate to the other party that he considers that that party is in breach and that he intends to treat the contract as repudiated. Once acceptance has been communicated, it cannot then be withdrawn. Therefore, if the parties decide to resume the contract's performance, the contract is regarded as renewed, even if the terms are the same.

9.9.3 What if both parties are in breach?

The effect of this depends on the order of the breaches by each party. If party A admits the breach and party B follows with an act which is also a breach of contract, then if party B informs A that he intends to treat the contract as repudiated on the basis of party A's breach, failure to perform does not give rise to a breach of contract to A.

If both parties commit a breach of contract simultaneously, it is suggested that neither party is entitled to treat the contract as repudiated.

9.9.4 Anticipatory breach

If one party indicates to the other that he intends to do or not do something which leads a reasonable person to believe that the party does not intend to fulfil his obligations under the contract, this could be regarded as an 'anticipatory breach' of the contract. In these circumstances, the 'aggrieved' party may indicate to the other that he 'accepts' the repudiation and sue for damages immediately, or he may wait and see whether the breach does occur and then sue for damages.

9.10 FRUSTRATION

Despite the best intention of both parties to the contract, an event may occur once the contract is entered into which makes it physically or commercially impossible for the contract to be performed. The principles of frustration were illustrated in *Taylor v Caldwell* (1863) 32 LJQB 164, in which the defendants had agreed to allow the plaintiffs to use a music hall for concerts on four specified nights. Before the first night, but after the contract was made, the music hall was completely destroyed by fire. The defendants were sued but the court held that they were not liable in damages to the plaintiffs. It is not necessary that physical destruction of any subject matter has to take place but merely that an event occurs outside the control of either party and is such that it brings the contract to an immediate end.

A court which is asked to determine whether contracts have been frustrated will try to determine whether the contract's terms are wide enough to enable the contract to continue in the new situation; if it is not, the contract must be regarded as frustrated.

9.10.1 Delay

It is not always easy to determine whether an unexpected delay in the performance of a contractual duty gives rise to the contract being frustrated. To amount to frustration, the delay must be unexpected and abnormal in that its effect or length would not be reasonable for the contracting parties to have contemplated it occurring. Much depends on the length of the delay in relation to the nature of the contract and the effect which the delay causes upon the contractual duty. If the delay is held to be within the commercial risks undertaken by the party to the contract, the court will hold that there is no frustration.

9.10.2 Sale of goods

The Sale of Goods Act 1979 makes provision where a certain set of circumstances gives rise to the contract being frustrated. Section 7 provides: 'Where there is an agreement to sell specific goods and subsequently the goods, without any fault on the part of the seller or buyer, perish before the risk passes to the buyer, the agreement is avoided.' Apart from this particular set of circumstances, the normal rule relating to frustration applies where it is claimed that an agreement to sell goods has been frustrated.

9.10.3 Consequences of frustration

The common law rules, to deal with the consequences of frustration, can be found in three court rulings: *Chandler v Webster* [1904] 1 KB 493 (a room was booked to view Coronation procession which did not take place; held, even though the contract had been frustrated, the lessee could not recover the advance payment and remained liable for the balance); *Krell v Henry* [1903] 2 KB 740 (loss to be borne by the debtor if the obligation to pay did not mature until after the discharge of the contract); and *Fibrosa Spolka Akcyjna v Fairbairn Lawson Combe Barbour Ltd* [1943] AC 32 (contract frustrated by the outbreak of war, where the request for the return of an advance payment was refused because of the considerable amount of work already done; held, the money could be recovered as there had been a total failure of consideration). Note that the ruling in *Fibrosa* applies only in the case of a total failure of consideration. It does not permit the recovery of an advance payment if the consideration has only partly failed (ie if the payer has received even a small benefit for his payment). However, while the payee may be compelled to repay the money on the ground that the payer has received no benefit, he may himself, in partial performance, have incurred expenses for which he has no redress.

While the position was considerably affected by the Law Reform (Frustrated Contracts) Act 1943, the Act does not apply to contracts to which s 7 of the Sale of Goods Act applies (see 9.10.2), nor to any other contract for the sale or the sale and delivery of goods, where the contract is frustrated because the goods have perished. In such cases, the common law rules continue to apply.

Section 1(2) of the Act provides that all sums which have been paid or are payable in pursuance of the contract before the time of the frustration shall, in the case of sums actually paid, be recoverable and, in the case of sums payable, cease to be payable. There is a proviso that where the party to whom the sums were paid or are payable incurred expenses before the time of frustration, in performance of the contract, then a court may allow him to retain, or recover, a sum up to the level of the expenses incurred.

Benefit acquired under the contract

Section 1(3) states that where a party has, by reason of any performance of another party under the terms of the contract, obtained a valuable benefit (other than a payment of money) before the contract is frustrated, then a sum can be recovered from him which should not exceed the value of the benefit and should be such a figure as the court thinks fit, having regard to all the circumstances. The 'benefit' is the product of the services supplied, but it might be the services themselves. It is up to the court to place a value on the benefit received. This is not always easy since a small service may result in something of great value to the receiving party, or a substantial service may produce something of little value.

The court must take into account the amount of any expenses incurred, if any, by the party who benefited, including any sum that he paid to any other party and the effect, in relation to the benefit, of the circumstances giving rise to the frustration. In effect, the court must first identify the 'valuable benefit', then place a value upon it, and finally consider the award of a just sum, which cannot be greater in value than the actual benefit obtained.

Severing part of the contract

Section 2(4) provides that a court can sever any part of a contract that it believes is severable and treat it as if it were a separate contract which had not been frustrated. The rest of the contract is therefore regarded as frustrated. The Act has no effect upon the part of the contract which can be regarded as being completely performed.

Excluding the Act

Under s 2(3), if it is clear that the parties have anticipated that the frustrating event might occur and have provided for what should happen in the event that it did occur, the Act does not apply. However, where the circumstances are so unusual and the effect so serious that they fall outside the clauses' intention, the Act may not have been excluded.

Where the parties intend to make provision in the event that the contract is frustrated, they must make it very clear what the alternative consequences of frustration are. Otherwise, it is likely that the common law rule will apply which may be detrimental to, for example, the paying party.

Exclusion

Certain types of contract are excluded from the Act and these include charter parties, contracts for the carriage of goods by sea, for insurance and for the sale of specific perishable goods, whether or not the risk passes to the buyer before the date of perishing.

9.11 PRIVITY OF CONTRACT

The general rule is that only the parties to a contract incur rights and obligations under it. This is illustrated by *Dunlop Pneumatic Tyre Co v Selfridge & Co* [1915] AC 847. The plaintiff supplied tyres to a wholesaler on condition that, if the wholesaler supplied any retailer, the retailer must promise not to sell the tyres to the public below a minimum price. The wholesaler supplied the defendant with tyres on that condition and with an agreement that, should they sell the tyres at a discount, the defendant must pay the plaintiff £5 per tyre sold at discount. The defendant sold the tyres to the public at a discount and the plaintiff sued to recover £5 per tyre. The House of Lords decided that there was a contract between the plaintiff and the wholesaler and another contract between the wholesaler and the defendant retailer, but none between the plaintiff and defendant. Thus the plaintiff could not recover damages under the agreement between the wholesaler and the defendant because it was not privy to that contract.

This means that no third party can sue or be sued on a contract, even if the contract is made for their benefit. In *Tweddle v Atkinson* (1861) 1 B&S 393, the plaintiff was engaged to be married to the defendant's daughter. His father and prospective father-in-law made a contract which provided that each of them would give a certain sum of money to the plaintiff when the marriage took place. The father-in-law died before making the payment and the plaintiff sued his estate. The court held that even though the contract expressly provided that the plaintiff was to be entitled to enforce it, he could not do so in law.

In *Beswick v Beswick* [1967] 2 All ER 1197, a coal merchant agreed to transfer his business to his nephew on condition that his nephew paid him a pension and, after his death, would pay his widow a weekly annuity. The uncle died and only one payment was made. The widow, as her husband's administratrix, sued for an order of specific performance. She was granted the order, only because of her position as administratrix. If she had sued as an intended beneficiary she would have been unsuccessful because she was not party to the contract. A party to a contract which is for the benefit of a third party can enforce it, but the damages recovered will only be nominal because a plaintiff can only recover damages for losses they have suffered. Remedies other than damages may be available.

If the contract is for the benefit of a third party and the contracting party then, in certain situations, damages may be awarded for their losses. This was the decision in *Jackson v Horizon Holidays* [1975] 3 All ER 92. In *Woodar Investment Development Ltd v Wimpey Construction UK Ltd* [1980] 1 All ER 571, however, the House of Lords confirmed that the principle stated by Lord Denning in *Jackson* was not of general application but confined to the special facts in that case.

9.11.1 Contracts (Rights of Third Parties Act) 1999

This Act reforms the common law rule of privity of contract and provides for circumstances in which a third party is to have a right to enforce a contract term effectively where the contracting parties intend this to be so.

9.11.2 Right of third party to enforce

There are effectively two requirements for a third party to have the right to enforce a contract under the Act. These are contained in the Contracts (Rights of Third Parties) Act 1999, s 1(1)–(3), as follows:

(1) either:
   (a) where the contract expressly provides that they should have that right, or
   (b) if the contract expressly confers a benefit on them and they are identified expressly (unless it appears on a true construction of the contract that the contracting parties did not intend the third party to have the right of enforcement); and
(2) they must be identified in the contract by name, class or description and do not even have to be in existence at the time the contract is made. This allows those making contracts to confer benefits on eg unborn children, a future spouse or a company that has not yet been incorporated.

The contract can state that the right of enforcement may be limited (ie the contract may provide that a third party can only enforce the contract by way of arbitration, and not litigation). All usual remedies for breach of contract will be available to a third party with the right to enforce (1999 Act, s 1(5)). As well as being able to enforce a term made for their benefit, s 1(6) makes it clear that a third party can take advantage of an exclusion or limitation clause in the contract. Should there be any doubt about whether a contract confers a benefit on a third party, a contractor can, by a term in the contract, expressly exclude a third party from any benefit.

9.11.3 Variation and rescission of contract

Once a third party has a right to enforce a term under the Act, the contracting parties cannot cancel or vary the original contract terms so as to affect that right without the third party's consent (1999 Act, s 2(1)). This is provided where either the:

(1) third party has communicated his assent to the term to the promisor (the party to the contract against whom the term is enforceable by the third party);
(2) promisor is aware that the third party has relied on the term; or
(3) promisor can reasonably be expected to have foreseen that the third party would rely on it and the third party has done so.

The Act restricts this third party right in the following ways:

(a) if the contract states expressly that it can by agreement be rescinded or varied without the third party's consent, then s 2(1) will not apply (s 2(3));

(b) if the contract states expressly that the third party's consent is to be required in circumstances different to those which are set out in s 2(1), this subsection will not apply; and

(c) a court or arbitral tribunal may dispense with the need for third party consent if the third party cannot be found to give his consent, if he is mentally incapable of giving consent, or if there is no proof that he relied on the term (s 2(4) and (5)).

9.11.4 Defences etc available to promisor

A promisor (the party to the contract against whom the term is enforceable by the third party) has various defences or set-offs available to him if a third party brings a claim against him.

First, he can rely on a defence or set-off which arises out of the contract and is relevant to the term being enforced and which would have been available to him had the claim been brought by the promisee (the party to the contract by whom the term is enforceable against the promisor) (1999 Act, s 3(2)). The explanatory notes to the Act set out illustrations of how the rule might work in practice, as follows:

(1) A third party can no more enforce a void, discharged or unenforceable contract than a promisee could.

(2) P1 (the promisor) and P2 (the promisee) contract that P2 will sell goods to P1, who will pay the contract price to P3 (the third party). In breach of contract, P2 delivers goods that are not of the standard contracted for. In an action for the price by P3 (just as in an action for the price by P2), P1 is entitled to reduce or extinguish the price by reason of the damages for breach of contract.

Secondly, he can rely on a defence or set-off if an express contract term provides for it to be available to him in a claim brought by a third party and if it would have been available to him had the claim been brought by the promisee (who is the party to the contract by whom the term is enforceable against the promisor) (1999 Act, s 3(3)). The explanatory notes to the Act illustrate how the rule might work in practice with one example: P1 and P2 contract that P1 will pay P3 if P2 transfers his car to P1. P2 owes P1 money under a wholly unrelated contract. P1 and P2 agree to an express term in the contract which provides that P1 can raise against a claim by P3 regarding any matter which would have given P1 a defence or set-off to a claim by P2.

Thirdly, he can rely on a defence or set-off, or make any counterclaim not arising from the contract if this would have been possible had the third party been a party to the contract (ie specific to the third party and unavailable to the promisor in an action by the promisee) (1999 Act, s 3(4)). The explanatory notes to the Act set out illustrations of how the rule might work in practice, as follows:

(a) P1 contracts with P2 to pay P3 £1,000. P3 already owes P1 £600. P1 has a set-off to P3's claim so that P1 is only bound to pay P3 £400.

(b) P3 induced P1 to enter into the contract with P2 by misrepresentation, but P2 has no actual or constructive notice of that misrepresentation. P1 may have a defence (or a counterclaim for damages) against P3 which would not have been available had the action been brought by P2.

The first and third defences or set-offs above are subject to any express term of the contract which narrows the defences or set-offs, or counterclaims available (s 3(5)).

9.12 DAMAGES

In the event of a breach of contract, damages are assessed according to the rules laid down in *Hadley v Baxendale* (1854) 9 Ex 341. This states that damages are recoverable for all the losses which flow as a natural result of the breach. Further damages are recoverable for losses not so flowing if, given the circumstances prevailing at the time the contract was made, these were contemplated by the contract breaker as a probable result of the breach. In appropriate cases, the innocent party can seek an injunction, to prevent the breach, or specific performance, to order the contract to be performed.

10

SALE OF GOODS

RICHARD LAWSON, LAWMARK

The law of contract for sale of goods was consolidated in the Sale of Goods Act 1979, as amended by the Sale and Supply of Goods Act 1994. Provisions relating to contracts for work and materials exist in the Supply of Goods and Services Act 1982. Agreements of hire purchase, condition of sale and credit sale are governed by the Consumer Credit Act 1974 and the Supply of Goods (Implied Terms) Act 1973.

10.1 TERMS IMPLIED INTO A SALE OF GOODS CONTRACT

Section 12 of the 1979 Act states that there is an implied term on the seller's part that he has a right to sell the goods and, in an agreement to sell, that he has a right to sell the goods at a time when the property is to pass. Furthermore, in a contract for sale (other than that in which the seller intends to transfer only such title as he or a third person may have (and which is governed by s 12(3)–(5)) there is also an implied term in s 12(2) that:

(a)   the goods are free, and will remain free until the time when the property is to pass, from any charge or encumbrance not disclosed or known to the buyer before the contract is made, and

(b)   the buyer will enjoy quiet possession of the goods except so far as it may be disturbed by the owner or other person entitled to the benefit of any charge or encumbrance so disclosed or known.

This implied term is regarded as a condition and therefore if it is breached the buyer can treat the contract as repudiated and claim damages. Alternatively, he may affirm the contract and also claim damages. Under s 12(2), these obligations are warranties and give rise to no more than a claim for damages.

The exclusion of the provisions of s 12 is prohibited by s 6 of the Unfair Contract Terms Act 1977.

10.2 DESCRIPTION

Section 13 of the 1979 Act provides that where there is a contract for the sale of goods by description there is an implied term that the goods will correspond with this description. Furthermore, if the sale is by sample as well as by description it is not sufficient that the bulk of the goods corresponds with the sample if the goods do not also correspond with the description. Care must be taken to ensure that the description is as accurate as possible.

In *Arcos Ltd v Ronaasen & Son* [1933] AC 470, the contract was for wooden staves which were to be ½″ thick. About 5% of the staves delivered corresponded to this measurement, the remainder being ⁹⁄₁₆″. All the staves were suitable for the buyer's purpose. The House of Lords ruled that there had been a breach of s 13. The court held that when buyers 'descend to minute measurements' ½″ does not mean about ½″, though it did add: 'No doubt there may be microscopic deviations which businessmen and therefore the courts will ignore.'

10.3 FITNESS FOR PURPOSE AND QUALITY

10.3.1 Fitness for purpose

Section 14 states that where a buyer expressly or impliedly makes known to

(1) the seller who sold him the goods in the course of business, or
(2) the credit broker who had previously sold the goods to the seller, where the buyer is paying all or part of the goods' purchase price in instalments,

the particular purpose for buying the goods, there is an implied condition that the goods are reasonably suited to that purpose. This applies whether or not the goods are commonly supplied for such purpose, but not if the buyer does not, or it is unreasonable for him to, rely on the seller's or credit broker's skill or judgement. A credit broker is defined by s 61(1) as

> a person who acts in the course of a business of credit brokerage carried on by him, that is a business of effecting introductions of individuals desiring to obtain credit –
>
> (a) to persons carrying on any business so far as it relates to the provision of credit, or
> (b) to other persons engaged in credit brokerage.

Where the buyer is required to make the purpose of goods known, he is not required to make it known expressly. For example, where an article can only be for one particular purpose, then it is unnecessary for the buyer to make it clear that he wants the article for that purpose. Where the goods may be used for several purposes it may be necessary, but not definitely, to indicate the intended purpose.

The seller must prove that the buyer did not rely on his judgement. If the seller informs the buyer that he has no knowledge or expertise of the goods being bought or the buyer has more knowledge of the goods than the seller, the buyer cannot make a successful claim against the seller that the goods were not fit for their purpose.

The duty to provide goods which are reasonably fit for their purpose is strict and a party cannot successfully defend a claim by showing that he took all reasonable care. However, a seller is not liable where the goods are used by the buyer for purposes which are outside the range of the purposes which the seller could reasonably foresee.

Where a buyer purchases goods there is no breach of the implied term where failure of the goods to meet the intended purpose arises from an abnormal feature or idiosyncrasy, not disclosed to the seller, in the buyer or in the circumstances of the goods' use by the buyer, irrespective of whether the buyer was himself aware of the abnormal feature or idiosyncrasy (*Griffiths v Peter Conway Ltd* [1939] 1 All ER 685; *Slater v Finning Ltd* [1996] 3 All ER 398).

10.3.2 Quality

The requirement that the quality of the goods sold should be of 'merchantable' quality as required by s 14 of the 1979 Act was amended by the 1994 Act. Section 14 (as amended) now provides that where a seller sells goods in the course of a business, there is an implied term that the goods supplied are of 'satisfactory' quality.

Goods are of satisfactory quality if they meet the standard that a reasonable person would regard as satisfactory, taking into account any description of the goods, the price (if relevant) and all other relevant circumstances. The 1979 Act states that the quality of the goods includes their state and condition, and suggests that some of the things that must be taken into account when considering the quality are:

  (i) the fitness for all the purposes for which goods of the kind in question are commonly supplied;
 (ii) appearance and finish;
(iii) being free from minor defects;
 (iv) safety; and
  (v) durability.

This does not apply where the unsatisfactory nature of the goods is specifically drawn to the buyer's attention, or where the buyer examines the goods, but only as regards defects which that examination ought to reveal. This provision applies only if there is an examination: it does not apply if the buyer was offered the chance to examine and rejected it.

10.4 SALE BY SAMPLE

Section 15 of the 1979 Act applies where by purchasing the bulk of the goods the buyer can place his reliance on examination of a sample. It must be clear that the parties intended that the sample, which is exhibited to the buyer at the time of sale, is a sample of the goods which the buyer is purchasing. Section 15 states that the bulk *must* correspond with the sample in quality and the buyer must have a reasonable opportunity of comparing the bulk with the sample before he is deemed to have accepted the goods.

Further, s 15 (as amended) states that the goods will be free from any defect which might make their quality unsatisfactory, which might not be apparent on reasonable examination of the sample.

10.5 EXCLUSION OF TERMS IMPLIED BY SS 13–15 OF THE 1979 ACT

Where the buyer is a consumer, as defined in the Unfair Contract Terms Act 1977, the seller cannot exclude or restrict his liability by reference to any contract terms imposed by ss 13–15. It is a criminal offence to employ any such exclusion or restriction in a consumer contract by virtue of the Consumer Transactions (Restrictions on Statements) Order 1976 (SI No 1813). If the exclusion or restriction clause appears in a contract with a business, the clause will be valid if it can be shown to be reasonable.

10.6 BREACH OF AN IMPLIED TERM

The terms implied by ss 13–15 of the 1979 Act are conditions and as such an aggrieved party is normally entitled to treat the contract as repudiated and reject the goods. However, the 1994 Act made an important amendment for non-consumers; where the breach on the part of the seller is so slight that it is unreasonable for him to reject the goods, 'the breach is not to be treated as a breach of condition but may be treated as a breach of warranty'. The aggrieved party can claim damages only. This provision only applies unless a contrary intention appears, or is to be implied, from the contract.

10.7 STIPULATIONS OF TIME

Section 10 of the 1979 Act provides that unless a contrary intention appears from the contract's terms, stipulation of time of payment is not deemed to be of the essence of a contract of sale. Whether any other stipulation of time is of the essence of the contract depends on the terms of the contract itself.

In other words, late payment does not give rise to an action for damages. However the Act further provides that a court has the power to award interest. Late payment can, however, give a right to interest under the provisions of the Late Payment of Commercial Debts (Interest) Act 1998.

10.8 CONTRACTS SIMILAR TO CONTRACTS OF SALE

The terms as to title, description, fitness for purpose and satisfactory quality implied into contracts for hire purchase, supplying work and materials or for hiring goods, and the provisions as to excluding or restricting these terms, are essentially identical to the terms provided in the Sale of Goods Act (Supply of Goods (Implied Terms) Act 1973; Supply of Goods and Services Act 1982). Under the terms of the latter, those who provide a service must provide it with reasonable care and skill.

10.9 CONSUMER PROTECTION

10.9.1 Cancellation rights

The Consumer Credit Act 1974 enables a buyer who is a consumer to cancel a contract for sale of goods where that contract is within the definition of a consumer credit or hire agreement within the Act. The agreement itself may be generally defined as a credit agreement where the buyer is not a corporate body and where the credit provided or the amount of the rental does not exceed £25,000 (other than an exempt agreement), or one which is financed wholly or partially by a loan under a regulated agreement connected with arrangements made between the lender and the seller. The Act stipulates when the right of cancellation arises and how it should be exercised. There is generally a 'cooling off' period which starts when the buyer receives a statutory copy of the credit agreement, so that the consumer is free to decide whether he wishes to enter the contract.

Further provisions exist to protect the consumer from the effects of any contract which arises as a result of 'cold calling' (ie where a consumer receives an unexpected visit from the seller and/or his employees). The Consumer Protection (Cancellation of Contracts Concluded Away from Business Premises) Regulations 1987 (SI No 2117) allow a 'cooling off' period which permits cancellation and the return of any money to the consumer. The Regulations do not apply to contracts for the supply of food, drink and other goods which are for current consumption, certain contracts concluded on the basis of a trader's catalogue, contracts which do not require the consumer to make total payments exceeding £35, and contracts cancellable by virtue of the Consumer Credit Act 1974.

Rights of cancellation are also provided under the Timeshare Act 1992 and by the Consumer Protection (Distance Selling) Regulations 2000 (SI No 2334).

10.9.2 Product liability: Consumer Protection Act 1987

The Act imposes liability on manufacturers and certain other people for death, personal injury and physical damage to property which arises from defective products. The liability imposed does not depend upon proof of negligence and (subject to certain defences) is therefore a strict liability.

The plaintiff must show that the injury or damage suffered was caused by the product and that the product was defective. Once these conditions are satisfied the manufacturer or other person is likely to be liable unless he comes within the defences provided for by the Act. The products covered are virtually all goods.

The following people can be held jointly and severally liable:

(1) the manufacturer of the finished product;
(2) the manufacturer of any part of the product which is defective;
(3) any person who permitted his name or logo to be placed on the product and thereby held himself out to be a producer;
(4) the importer of the product into the EU;
(5) the supplier of the product who may be unable to trace the product back to its manufacturer.

10.9.3 General product safety

Under the1987 Act provisions, and the General Product Safety Regulations 1994 (SI No 2328), a criminal offence can arise if unsafe goods are placed on the market. In addition, under the 1987 Act provisions, a number of safety regulations have been enacted setting out standards for various goods. Details of the current list of regulations can be obtained from the Department of Trade and Industry, Consumer Safety Unit, Victoria St, London SW1H 0ET.

The 1987 Act also provides for prohibition notices and notices to warn. These are notices issued by the Secretary of State for Trade and Industry which, respectively, serve a notice on a party banning the supply by him of goods considered to be unsafe; and on a party requiring him to give notice that he has supplied goods which are considered unsafe.

Defence

Section 4 of the 1987 Act sets out six defences which are available, notwithstanding the strict liability imposed. A person is afforded a defence if he can show that:

(1) the defect is attributable to compliance with any requirement imposed by or under any enactment or with any EU obligation; or
(2) he did not at any time supply the product to another; or

303

(3) the supply of that product by him was otherwise than in the course of his business and that he is not caught within the definition of identifiable people who should be liable; or

(4) the defect complained of did not exist in the product at the relevant time (ie it arose after the time when he supplied the product); or

(5) the state of the technical and scientific knowledge at the time of the supply was such that he would not be able to discover the defect (sometimes known as the 'state of the art' defence); or

(6) the defect was contained in a product which eventually became comprised in a final product and was fully attributable to the final product's design or due to compliance with the requirements made by the final product's producer.

It is also possible for the person being sued to rely on a claim for contributory negligence on the part of the person complaining of the damage.

In *Worsley v Tambrands Ltd* (1999) 96(48) LSG 40, the claimant brought an action against the defendant tampon manufacturer claiming damages for personal injuries suffered as a result of toxic shock syndrome after inserting a regular tampon, a type she had used since age 15. She contended that the warnings on the packet were defective. Held, the box gave unambiguous instructions to read the detailed leaflet inside, and the leaflet was true and accurate. The claim therefore failed.

In *Richardson v LRC Products Ltd* (unreported, 2 February 2000), the claimant had given birth to a baby despite using a condom. She brought an action against the defendant on the basis that ozone damage to the rubber condom's surface while still in the factory had caused it to split. Held, on consideration of the expert evidence, that method of contraception had never been claimed to be 100% effective, the condoms were manufactured to the required standard, and sufficient warnings had been given of the chance of them splitting. The claim failed.

10.10 PASSING OF PROPERTY AND RISK

Sections 16–20 of the Sale of Goods Act 1979 contain the rules governing the passing of property, in goods sold, from the seller to the buyer. All provisions of ss 16–20 can be varied and in most cases the parties, whether buyer or seller, will want to vary them by way of specific terms in the contract. Section 16 refers to unascertained goods (eg '50 kilograms of flour') and provides that no property in the goods transfers to the buyer unless and until the goods are actually ascertained.

Section 17 provides that for specific or ascertained goods, the property is transferred to the buyer at such time as the parties intend it to be transferred. In other words consideration must be given to the contract's terms, the parties' conduct and the general circumstances of the case.

Section 18 sets out various rules for ascertaining the parties' intention for the time when the property in the goods is to pass to the buyer, in the absence of any contrary intention by the party. They can therefore be excluded by reference to terms in the contract.

Section 19 states that where there is a contract for sale of specific goods (or where goods are subsequently appropriated to the contract) the seller may reserve the right of the goods' disposal until certain conditions are fulfilled. In those circumstances the property in the goods does not pass to the buyer until these conditions are fulfilled.

10.10.1 'Romalpa' clauses; retention of title

This type of clause puts the seller in a more favourable position than he would normally be if the buyer is unable to pay. Under the 1979 Act the property in specific goods passes to the buyer when the contract is made, irrespective of the time of payment or delivery. Consequently, a seller is advised to include a clause stipulating that he retains property in the goods supplied until he receives payment. The principle arose as a result of *Aluminium Industrie Vaassen BV v Romalpa Aluminium Ltd* [1976] 1 WLR 676. Such a clause is beneficial to the seller if, for example, the buyer goes into liquidation.

Five broad categories of clause have emerged:

(1) *Simple clause* – retaining ownership in the goods supplied under the contract until they are paid for.
(2) *Current account clause* (sometimes called 'all liabilities' or 'all monies') – retaining ownership in the goods until they are paid for, plus all other sums due from the buyer are paid (ie for goods or services supplied under separate contracts). This means that where a supplier makes regular deliveries, the property in goods in earlier deliveries is retained long after they have been paid for, so long as any part of the price on later deliveries is unpaid. The buyer, if continually enjoying credit periods, never gets to own any goods supplied.
(3) *Extended clause* – claiming ownership against both the buyer and any sub-buyers to whom the goods are sold.
(4) *Proceeds clause* – retaining ownership in the goods and claiming the proceeds of any resale.
(5) *Products clause* – retaining ownership in the goods supplied and in any new product into which the goods are incorporated.

Where the buyer is a company, the CA 1985, ss 395 and 396 (as amended by the CA 1989) arguably apply. These sections provide that certain classes of charge are void against a liquidator or administrator and any creditor of the company unless registered. Where the buyer is an individual or partnership, a trustee in bankruptcy may argue that the clause is in effect a bill of sale which is void unless registered pursuant to the Bills of Sale Act 1878.

A charge is defined as any form of security interest (fixed or floating) over property, other than an interest arising by operation of law. It is now settled, following *Clough Mill Ltd v Martin* [1984] 3 All ER 982, that a 'simple' reservation of title clause does not create a charge and therefore does not require registration. However, 'proceeds' and 'products' clauses are clearly within the ambit.

10.10.2 Passing of the risk

Section 20 of the 1979 Act states that unless it is otherwise agreed in the contract, the goods remain at the seller's risk until the property in them is transferred to the buyer. Then the goods are at the buyer's risk, whether or not delivery has been made.

10.11 DELIVERY AND ACCEPTANCE

10.11.1 Delivery

Detailed rules for delivery of goods are contained in the Sale of Goods Act 1979. Section 29 deals with the place and time of delivery, goods which may be in possession of a third person and expenses incurred in connection with the delivery. Section 30 sets out what might be regarded as a defective, insufficient or excessive delivery. It has been affected by the Sale and Supply of Goods Act 1994 to the extent that s 30(4) (the buyer's right to reject part of the delivery of goods, some which satisfy the contract description) is repealed. Furthermore, a new provision is inserted for situations in which there is a shortfall or excess in the delivery.

Where there is a shortfall the buyer can either reject the delivery, recover the price paid and sue for any loss suffered, or he can accept the quantity delivered, paying for this at the contract rate and recovering any additional money paid; he can also claim damages for breach. Where there is an excess, the buyer can either:

(1) reject the whole of the goods delivered; or
(2) select the correct quantity and reject the rest; or
(3) accept the whole delivery and pay for the excess at the contract rate.

A new provision, inserted by the 1994 Act, states that a buyer who does not deal as a consumer is not entitled to reject the goods where there is a shortfall or an excess if it is so slight that it would be unreasonable for him to do so. The seller must show that a shortfall or excess is so slight that it is unreasonable for the buyer to reject the delivery.

Section 31 deals with delivery by way of instalment (for example, it stipulates when the buyer is not bound to accept delivery by instalments). Section 32 sets out the rules for where delivery is made to a carrier; s 33 makes a buyer take responsibility for the risk of any deterioration in the goods where a seller has agreed to deliver at his own risk to a place other than where they are sold.

All the above rules referred to can be altered by the party by reference to terms of the contract; close consideration should be given to this.

10.11.2 Acceptance

The general rules of acceptance are that where a buyer accepts the goods, he cannot repudiate the contract at a later stage. Therefore any rights he may have had with regard to a breach of condition would then have to be treated as a breach of warranty and would entitle him to claim for damages only.

Section 34(2) of the 1979 Act states that when a seller attempts to deliver goods he must allow the buyer, if requested, a reasonable opportunity of examining them to ascertain whether they conform with the contract and, if appropriate, to compare the bulk of the delivery with the sample. Section 35 (as amended) states that the buyer is deemed to have accepted the goods (except as provided below) when:

(1) he intimates to the seller that he has accepted them;
(2) the goods are delivered to him and he does any act which is inconsistent with the ownership of the seller; or
(3) after a reasonable period of time has passed, he retains the goods without intimating to the seller that he has rejected them.

When considering whether a 'reasonable' time has passed, consideration must be given to whether the buyer has had a reasonable opportunity to examine the goods.

If the buyer has not previously examined the goods, then he is not deemed to have accepted them when they are delivered unless he has a reasonable opportunity to examine them as specified in s 34(2) (see above). Furthermore, where the buyer deals as a consumer, he cannot lose his right to have a reasonable opportunity of examining the goods. Any attempt by the seller to persuade him to contract out of this right will be ineffective.

A buyer is not deemed to have accepted goods merely because he asks for or agrees to them being repaired or where the goods are delivered to another person under a subsale.

In *AC Daniels & Co Ltd v Jungwoo Logic* (unreported, 14 April 2000), the claimant had ordered from the defendant an injection mould for the claimant's plastic medical waste bins. However, the mould had to be returned to the defendant nine times because of faults. The claimant finally rejected the mould and turned to another supplier, and brought an action for repayment of fees and damages for breach of contract against the defendants. Held, the claimant had not accepted the mould and the rejection was effective.

Where the contract relates to the making of one or more commercial units, and a buyer accepts any goods included in a unit, he is deemed to have accepted all the goods comprised in that unit.

A right of 'partial rejection' was introduced by the 1994 Act. Where the buyer has the right to reject goods by virtue of the seller's breach which affects some or all of the goods, but he accepts some of the goods including all those unaffected by the breach, he is not regarded as losing his rights to reject the rest. The rule also applies where the buyer is faced with an instalment of goods rather than the entire delivery. Goods are 'affected by a breach' if, as a result of the breach, they do not conform with the contract. The right to partial rejection can be amended or deleted by agreement in the contract.

Section 36 provides that where goods are delivered to the buyer and he refuses to accept them, having the right to do so, he is not bound to return them to the seller; it is sufficient if he intimates to the seller that he refuses to accept them. However, he cannot exercise a lien over the goods to obtain repayment from the seller.

Where the buyer refuses to take delivery within a reasonable time from a request by the seller that he should take delivery, s 37 makes him liable to the seller for any loss which is occasioned by his neglect or refusal to take delivery and also for a reasonable charge for the care and custody of the goods.

10.12 SALES BY A NON-OWNER

The fundamental principle is that no-one can transfer a better title to property than he has. So, for example, if the seller has stolen the goods, obtained them by deception or has them under a hire-purchase agreement (whereby ownership remains with the creditor until all instalments have been paid), then the true owner should be able to recover those goods. The rule also covers less obvious situations where the seller has a defective title, or where some other person has a limited interest in the goods (eg where the seller has obtained goods subject to a reservation of title clause (see 10.10.1)), where the goods have been used as security for a loan, or some other charge or encumbrance exists to give a third party rights over the goods.

In such situations the seller will be in breach of the Sale of Goods Act 1979, s 12, the implied condition that the seller has a right to sell and the implied warranty that the buyer will obtain goods free from encumbrances (see 10.1). The buyer will therefore have a claim against the seller for a refund and/or damages. Such a claim may prove fruitless if the seller is a thief who promptly disappears having sold the goods. Unless one of the exceptions to the rule applies, then the true owner can recover the goods. The owner may also have a claim against the seller in the tort of conversion (ie a person without authority dealing with goods intending to assert a right to them inconsistent with his right).

10.12.1 Exceptions to the rule

These exceptions give protection to innocent parties who buy in good faith without notice of the lack of title:

(1) The seller may have the owner's authority or consent to sell (eg if acting as an agent: Sale of Goods Act 1979, s 21(1)).

(2) Where an agent has the status of a 'factor' or 'mercantile agent', he need not have the owner's authority to sell. A mercantile agent is one whose customary business is to be entrusted with goods in order to sell or otherwise dispose of them. If he has possession of goods (or documents of title) but is instructed not to sell, but nevertheless does so, then he passes on good title (1979 Act, s 21(2)).

(3) The owner may represent by his words or conduct that the seller is the owner or has the authority to sell (ie by giving that impression to the buyer). The owner is then 'estopped' (ie he cannot deny the authority of the seller to sell: 1979 Act, s 21(1)).

(4) The seller has a 'voidable title' which the true owner has failed to avoid at the time of sale (eg if the seller paid the owner by a cheque which is dishonoured, and the owner fails to take steps to reclaim the goods before they are resold: 1979 Act, s 23).

(5) A person may have sold goods but remain in possession of them. Property (title) has legally passed to the buyer, but nevertheless if the seller then resells to someone else, that second buyer gets good title (1979 Act, s 24).

(6) A buyer may have obtained possession of the goods with the seller's consent, but the property has not passed (as with a reservation of title clause). If he then resells he can pass on a good title to the subsequent buyer (1979 Act, s 25).

(7) A special exception applies to motor vehicles sold when under hire-purchase or conditional sale agreements. Generally a person who acquires goods under such agreements cannot pass on title because ownership does not pass until he has paid all the instalments and, for hire-purchase, exercised the option to purchase (sometimes requiring an additional payment). The Hire Purchase Act 1964, Pt III, however, makes an exception for a private purchaser of a motor vehicle (as opposed to a trader) who, subject to certain provisos, will obtain a good title.

10.13 REMEDIES OF THE SELLER

An unpaid seller normally sues the buyer for the price of the goods or for damages for non-acceptance of them. Section 39 of the 1979 Act provides that notwithstanding the property in the goods may have passed to the buyer, the unpaid seller of the goods has a lien on the goods or right to withhold the price while he is still in possession of them. Furthermore, where the buyer becomes insolvent, the seller has a right to stop the goods in transit after he has parted possession with them. The Act also gives him a right of resale as defined by s 48. The unpaid seller must be regarded as being in possession of the goods to exercise his right of lien (ie he must retain general control of them).

Section 43 states that the unpaid seller may lose his right of lien or of retention when he delivers the goods to a carrier to transport them to the buyer without reserving the right of the goods' disposal or by his agent lawfully obtaining possession of the goods or by waiving his lien (eg by agreeing to a subsale or when making a new arrangement with the buyer which is inconsistent with his right to a lien). The lien may also be lost if the seller refuses to deliver the goods on some ground other than the buyer's failure to pay. However, an unpaid seller does not waive his lien when he obtains judgment for the price. Only when judgment is satisfied can his lien be defeated.

Where the property and goods do not pass to the buyer, the seller is likely to seek remedy in an action for damages for non-acceptance under s 50 for consequential losses or expenses under s 54 or 37.

Section 50 states that the measure of damages is 'the estimated loss directly and naturally resulting, in the ordinary course of events, from the buyer's breach'. Where there is an available market for the goods in question, the measure of damages is likely to be the difference between the contract price and the market price at the time, if there is one, when the goods ought to have been accepted.

10.14 REMEDIES OF THE BUYER

10.14.1 Damages for non-delivery

Section 51 states that where the seller wrongfully neglects or refuses to deliver the goods, the buyer may maintain an action for damages. The measure of damages is the estimated loss directly and naturally resulting in the ordinary course of events from the seller's breach. Where there is an available market for the goods, the measure of damage is similar to that contained in s 50 (see 10.13 above).

Where the loss suffered by the buyer does not result directly and naturally in the ordinary course of things from the breach, he can recover for such loss only if the seller, given what he knew or should have known when the contract was made, contemplated such loss as the probable result of the breach (s 55; *Hadley v Baxendale* (1854) 9 Ex 341).

10.14.2 Damages for delay in delivery

Where there is a delay in delivery, the buyer may still accept delivery. If he suffers consequential losses such as additional expenses or loss of profit, he is entitled to sue the seller for such sum which would put him in the financial position he would have been in had the seller made delivery on the expected day.

10.14.3 Damages for defective quality

The buyer may have an action for damages for breach of warranty under s 53 of the Act. He may be entitled to claim damages for diminution in the goods' market value, and for the cost of adaptations or of substituted goods.

Where a buyer, despite having received defective goods, can nevertheless sell the goods to a sub-buyer, his damages should not be reduced by taking the subsale into account. He can rely on the normal measure of damages.

Other items of damage a buyer may wish to claim for are loss of profits under a subsale, wasted expenses; possible fines imposed from the buyer because the goods are defective; and any compensation he may have to pay to a third party because of the defect.

This is subject to the proviso that the relevant head of damage was contemplated by the seller as a probable consequence of breach (*Re Hall and Pim's Arbitration* [1928] All ER Rep 763).

10.14.4 Other remedies of the buyer

Rejection of goods

Where the seller breaches a condition of the contract, the buyer may choose to treat it as terminated, reject the goods and sue the seller for damages (see also 10.11.2 regarding partial rejection). However where there is a breach of a condition, and the buyer is not a consumer and normally has the right to reject the goods under ss 13–15 of the Sale of Goods Act 1979, but the breach is so slight that it would be unreasonable for him to reject them, then that breach cannot be treated as a breach of condition but may be treated as a breach of warranty. This prevents a non-consumer buyer from objecting to goods in those circumstances. He is entitled to a claim for damages.

The seller must show that the breach is slight. This provision can be deleted or amended by an appropriate clause in the contract.

Recovery of money paid to the seller

Section 54 states that nothing in the Act shall affect the buyer's right to recover money paid, whether or not consideration for the payment of it has failed.

Specific performance

The buyer may wish to insist on the performance being carried out by the seller. Section 52 provides that a court may direct that this should happen. It is always within the court's discretion whether such an order is made. It is not lightly made where the goods are likely to be of an ordinary type and where similar goods could be obtained elsewhere.

Other claims the buyer may wish to make include an application for an injunction, perhaps to prevent the seller from disposing of the goods else-where; a declaration from the court of the buyer's position as against his legal rights against the seller; or he may issue proceedings against the seller claiming damages for his wrongful interference with the goods.

BUSINESS PREMISES

NICHOLAS MARSHALL, SOLICITOR, PARTNER, MARSHALL HATCHICK

11.1 INTRODUCTION

Even in these days of virtual reality and e-commerce, most businesses need premises. Leasehold premises provide greater flexibility and less capital commitment and so are more attractive for most businesses than freehold premises. This chapter accordingly also looks at various aspects of lease-hold premises. We assume a direct landlord/tenant relationship. There are further complications involving eg underleases and various parties who may be involved apart from the landlord and the tenant and space does not permit these to be dealt with here. In all cases the reader should seek specialist professional advice.

The statutory framework for business tenancies in England and Wales is contained largely in the Landlord and Tenant Act 1954 (the 1954 Act), Part II of which has remained on the statute book for nearly 50 years in large part untouched. The case-law on business tenancies is significant, largely because of the large sums of money which can be involved, the major impact on a business which can result from problems with its premises, and the contrasting commercial pressures of boom and recession.

11.2 WHAT IS A PROTECTED BUSINESS TENANCY?

It is important for a tenant to establish whether a tenancy of business premises is 'protected' under the 1954 Act. Broadly, if protected, the tenant will be entitled to remain in the premises and to call for a new lease on expiry. Subject to certain exceptions as set out below, the 1954 Act applies to 'any tenancy where the property comprised in the tenancy is or includes premises which are occupied by the tenant and are so occupied for the purposes of a business carried on by him or for those and other purposes' (s 23(1)).

11.2.1 Tenancy

There must be a 'tenancy'. This is distinct from a 'licence' to occupy land. The leading case is *Street v Mountford* [1985] AC 809 which (although it is a judgment in respect of residential accommodation) sets out the tests which are clearly applicable to commercial premises. This case is regarded as a watershed in the development of the lease/licence distinction. It came at a time when there was an increased tendency (in both residential and commercial premises) for contracts to be entered into purporting to be a 'licence to occupy' rather than a tenancy, and thereby avoiding the statutory protection that would otherwise be available to the tenant.

Street v Mountford established that a tenancy, as opposed to a licence, is created where there is:

- exclusive possession of the premises;
- a fixed or periodic term; and
- the payment of rent and/or a premium.

The principal test for distinguishing between a lease and licence in business tenancies is that of 'exclusive possession', which is a question of fact in each case to be determined on the evidence. Today, in many cases most landlords would regard it as too risky to attempt to grant a licence: the fear is that if challenged the court would look behind the form of the document, or the veneer of its title, and construe the existence of a lease where the landlord had not intended this. Accordingly landlords will use other means to ensure that the tenant will not obtain statutory protection, eg by granting a lease for a term which does not exceed six months or by contracting outside the 1954 Act (see below).

Care must be taken over the six-month exception: for example, if a second term of six months or less is granted which follows on from a previous term and the total of the two exceeds 12 months, then the second term will be protected (1954 Act, s 43(3)).

A 'tenancy at will' is excluded from the 1954 Act. This can be created expressly or by implication of law. A tenancy at will is a popular method of letting business premises by a landlord for an undefined term. Such a tenancy will also often arise when a contracted out tenancy comes to an end and the tenant remains in occupation temporarily.

A tenancy at will is a purely personal relationship which can be determined by either party at any time, although the court would look carefully at any such tenancy to discover whether it is a true tenancy at will, or whether it is in fact periodic or for a term certain. If it is correctly drafted the tenant will not have the benefit of statutory protection.

There are some tenancies which, by their nature, are excluded from the 1954 Act, such as an agricultural tenancy, a tenancy created by a mining lease and a service tenancy. Nor does it apply, as we have seen, to a tenancy granted for a term certain which cannot exceed six months unless the tenant has been in occupation for a period which, together with any period during which any predecessor in the carrying on of the business carried on by the tenant was in occupation, exceeds 12 months (s 43(3)).

11.2.2 Premises

It is for the benefit of both the landlord and the tenant that the precise extent of the premises comprised in the tenancy is clearly defined. If not, dispute could arise over whether certain parts of the building are within the tenancy, and therefore within the scope of the tenant's liability to repair them. In extreme circumstances, the tenancy can be void for uncertainty and therefore unenforceable.

This is particularly the case where a tenant is taking a suite or floor of offices in a block. Does the tenancy include the kitchen, the toilets or the boiler or are these the landlord's responsibility in terms of cleaning and maintenance? It is insufficient to say merely that the 'interior' of the premises is demised: the fabric of the building from the glass in the windows to the structural beams or girders should be described and allocated clearly to either the landlord or the tenant. A well-drawn plan should also be attached to the lease, but this will often only be to identify the property leased – its precise extent being described in words.

The lease should provide clear details of the tenant's rights or 'easements', eg the right to use the kitchen and toilets not leased to the tenant and to use the common parts of the building or the estate.

11.2.3 Occupied by the tenant

Only an occupying business tenant is protected by the 1954 Act. If the business tenant only occupies part of the premises that are let to him, then statutory protection applies only to that part. Usually there are no difficulties in establishing whether a tenant does occupy the premises, but problems can arise (eg where there is seasonal occupation of premises such as holiday resorts, occupation by the tenant is normally presumed during the out-of-season months provided occupation is resumed each season). In *Hancock and Willis v GMS Syndicate Ltd* [1982] 265 EG 473, a firm of solicitors acquired additional accommodation and let out the basement and ground floor of their original building under a licence and used the remainder of the building for the storage of files and for the occasional lunch. The court held that this was insufficient and the 'thread of continuity' had been broken for the purposes of business use. Therefore the tenant lost security under the 1954 Act.

The question of occupation by the tenant is also relevant in cases involving termination of leases by the tenant at the end of the term (see below). This has been an uncertain area of law in recent years, although the situation is now judicially more certain. Great care is needed on this point.

11.2.4 For the purposes of a business

In order to attract the statutory protection, business premises must be occupied 'for the purposes of a business . . . or for those and other purposes' and therefore it is necessary to consider whether what is being carried on at the premises falls within the meaning of a 'business'.

In s 23(2) of the 1954 Act, 'business' is defined as a trade, profession or employment and also includes any activity carried on by a body of persons whether corporate or incorporate. This wide interpretation was held soon after the Act came into being to cover a tennis club in *Addiscombe Garden Estates Ltd v Crabbe* [1958] 1 KB 513, but was held in *Abernethit v AM & J Klieman Ltd* [1970] 1 QB 10 not to cover a Sunday school. According to Harman LJ, to apply the 1954 Act to a Sunday school would be to fall into 'the pond of absurdity'. Quite so (although whether the waters of the pond of pomposity were undisturbed by his Lordship's turn of phrase is for the reader to judge). In this case the loft of a house was used for the Sunday school at an unspecified hour every Sunday on a regular basis. It will be a question of fact for the court to resolve in each case.

Problems do arise with mixed residential/business uses. The tenant must show that the business is a 'significant purpose' of the tenant's occupation of the building. It is a question of law whether the tenant occupies the premises for the purposes of a business carried on by him. In *Royal Life Savings Society v Page* [1978] 1 WLR 1329, a doctor who had consulting rooms in Harley Street, but who occasionally saw patients at his rented home with the landlord's consent, was held to be not protected under the 1954 Act. This is to be contrasted with *Cheryl Investments Ltd v Saldanha* [1978] 1 WLR 1329, where an accountant used his flat for the purposes of a seafood importers without his landlord's knowledge and was held to occupy the premises for the purposes of the 1954 Act. The more common situation is a single lease of a shop, with a flat above; this will generally fall squarely in the ambit of the 1954 Act, even if the area of the flat exceeds that of the shop.

11.2.5 'Contracting out' of 1954 Act

The letting of business premises 'outside the 1954 Act' has become increasingly popular in recent years where the landlord is unwilling to commit itself in times of economic uncertainty to any long-term commitment. We have seen that the licence to occupy route is potentially unsafe and the only certain way of excluding security on leases of more than six months is to contract out of the 1954 Act.

The parties cannot contract out of the 1954 Act without the authority of a court order, which will only be provided where the court is satisfied that both the parties, in particular the tenant, have taken (or have been provided with the opportunity to take) legal advice. The order must be obtained before the lease is entered into.

Although the tenant will not have a statutory right to call for a renewal of the lease in these circumstances, the 'upside' for the tenant of a contracted out lease is that he can usually negotiate a more favourable rent than if security had been on offer, and also less onerous repairing obligations. The tenant should be in a position to ensure that the repair obligations are limited to internal decoration and/or repair only and for the shorter terms may only be required to hand the premises back in no worse a state of condition than they were at the beginning of the term, as endorsed by an agreed schedule of condition, preferably with photographs. Schedules of condition are often over-used, however: they are really only of use in very short-term leases as the longer the term, the more impractical it generally is for the tenant to repair to the standard of the schedule only.

11.3 PRIVITY AND CONTINUING LIABILITY

In contrast to a recessionary background where a tenant is able to demand a short-term lease in more buoyant economic circumstances, it is the landlord who often has the upper hand and bargaining power. The landlord will seek high quality tenants who are willing and able to take full repairing and insuring (FRI) leases, maybe for a term of 20 years. Such tenants are said to be a 'good covenant'.

It is clear that any tenant wishing to take on such a long-term contract needs to consider extremely carefully whether it is willing to take on such a potentially onerous liability. Even if the tenant assigns the lease during the term, that may not be an end of its liabilities. Unless the position has been changed by agreement in the lease (which was none), a tenant under a lease signed before 1 January 1996 would always ultimately be liable to the landlord even after assignment of the lease, if the assignee defaulted.

Example

In 1967 Mr and Mrs A took a lease on a small industrial unit at a relatively low rent for 21 years. The business prospered and in 1977, after the rent had increased on review comfortably in line with inflation, Mr and Mrs A sold their business which provided them with sufficient funds to buy a bungalow by the coast and to invest a lump sum in the bank on which to live on. In 1987, after two more rent reviews the company that took over the lease of the premises from Mr and Mrs A went into liquidation owing £50,000 in rent and service charges to the landlord. The landlord exercised its right to pursue Mr and Mrs A as the original tenants for the rent arrears: after all, they had signed a lease for 21 years. The capital that they had saved was insufficient to cover the debt and they were forced to sell the bungalow and to take rented accommodation to raise the funds to satisfy the debt. They would still have been liable, as original tenants, no matter how many times the lease had been assigned.

Many (mainly tenants) would say this is iniquitous; others (mainly landlords) would say that when a lease is taken for 21 years it means exactly that and the tenant should not be able to walk away from the contract. After many years of political lobbying by pressure groups on both sides, the law was changed with effect from 1 January 1996. The Landlord and Tenant (Covenants) Act 1995 had the effect of abolishing privity of contract (the legal doctrine under which original tenants were liable for the whole term) in the case of new leases. Although an ongoing tenant may be required to guarantee the performance of the party taking over the lease (ie its immediate assignee), the liability cannot extend beyond that second assignment (if both assignments are lawful). Such a guarantee is called an 'authorised guarantee agreement' (AGA) and is likely to apply in the case of most first assignments of business leases. The onus is still on the original tenant to find a good assignee that is likely to fulfil its obligations. The original tenant is concerned to ensure not only that the first assignee's references are sufficiently strong to prevent the landlord from being able to withhold its consent (which will probably be required), but also that he will be able to pay the rent and generally be a good tenant.

In the case of insolvency of the first assignee and eventual disclaimer by its liquidator, the original tenant may be required to take up a new lease on the same terms and for the same duration as the original lease.

There is a provision in the 1995 Act that relates to both new and existing leases. A landlord who wishes to pursue the original tenant or guarantor must serve a default notice under s 17 of the 1995 Act notifying him of the potential claim for what is called a fixed charge (ie rent, service charge, liquidated damages and interest) within six months of the current tenant's default. Arrears accrued more than six months prior to a default notice will not be recoverable from the original tenant or guarantor.

Once the former tenant or guarantor has received a default notice, he is entitled to take some control over the problem by paying the arrears and other sums demanded in full and calling upon the landlord to grant to him an overriding lease of the premises. This places the former tenant/guarantor in a contractual position between the landlord and the defaulting tenant. The terms of the overriding lease will include all the provisions of the defaulted lease with the exception of any personal covenants given by the defaulter.

Once in possession of the overriding lease, the former tenant/guarantor can then take proceedings against the defaulting tenant to recover the arrears discharged by him under the default notice. If he fails, the former tenant/guarantor will be entitled to recover possession of the premises to enable him to relet or possibly retain for his own use.

The 1995 Act also has the effect of amending s 19(1) of the Landlord and Tenant Act 1927 in relation to assignment of commercial leases. Effectively, in exchange for the above changes which improve the tenant's position, landlords have been able to exercise more control over who the lease is assigned to. Landlords can now specify in advance the circumstances in which consent to an assignment can be withheld or any conditions subject to which consent can be granted. If the provision is worded so that if there is no subjective element, the landlord is deemed to be acting reasonably if the agreed terms are adhered to. For example, if there is a requirement that any assignee must be able to produce the most recent set of accounts showing net profits before tax of at least three times the passing rent, then this would be acceptable. Alternatively, if the circumstances or conditions are to be determined by an independent third party or by the landlord who is required to act reasonably, this will also be acceptable.

11.4 COVENANT STRENGTH

The strength of the tenant's covenant is all important to the landlord. The businessman offering his company as a tenant, whether on taking a new lease or on taking an assignment of an existing lease, may not provide sufficient comfort for the landlord.

The landlord will be concerned about how the quality of the tenant's covenant is to affect the value of its investment. A tenant which is a company listed on the Stock Exchange is likely to enhance the value of the freehold.

Where the tenant's covenant is not strong enough (eg a start-up company or an individual of limited means) the landlord would generally require some security to persuade it to accept the prospective tenant.

11.4.1 Personal guarantees

It is a provision in many commercial leases that on assignment the landlord can require two directors of any assignee company to provide personal guarantees. References should be taken up for the directors or any prospective guarantors. A landlord would normally require two guarantors providing joint and several liability, ie each guarantor can be held responsible for the defaulting tenant's total debt if the landlord chooses. In the past, over-confident businessmen have sometimes provided personal guarantees without a second thought, only subsequently to have to pay the price (often of bankruptcy) for their optimism. As in the case of any previous tenants who may still be liable, a landlord will not hesitate to pursue guarantors where there is any chance of recovery of the tenant's indebtedness.

Under the 1995 Act, the guarantors under the AGA are released when the guaranteed tenant is released. Previously (unless released by the landlord or as stated otherwise in the lease) the guarantee subsisted for as long as the term itself.

11.4.2 Security deposit

The landlord may require deposit of a lump sum as security, generally representing three or six months' rent. This sum is placed on bank deposit (with interest normally accruing to the tenant) and a deed drawn up between the landlord and tenant records in what circumstances the landlord is entitled to withdraw funds.

The tenant will be required by the deposit deed to repay any sums withdrawn, but the drawback from the landlord's point of view is that once the fund has been used up and assuming the arrears persist, there is no guarantee that any excess sums will be recovered. At least in these circumstances the landlord will have had time to consider his options and, in the case of an empty building and an insolvent tenant, have an opportunity of seeking a new tenant.

The problem for a tenant, of course, particularly in the case of a new business venture, is the immediate tying-up of capital which provides no benefit to the start-up company except nominal interest. The protection of the director of the new company from the risks of providing personal guarantees usually makes it worthwhile. It may be possible for the tenant to negotiate repayment of the fund in certain circumstances (eg after three years of net profits of the tenant company exceeding an agreed multiple of the annual rent). The deed should state that upon expiry or lawful assignment of the lease, the fund will be returned to the tenant.

11.4.3 Bank guarantees

Less common now than previously, bank guarantees are usually an expensive option for a tenant as banks generally now require both deposit of assets to cover the amount of the guarantee and payment of a procuration or arrangement fee.

11.4.4 Break clause

Inclusion of a break clause provision enables the landlord to determine the lease before its expiry, should it wish to be rid of the tenant for any reason. The tenant should obviously beware here as, assuming the tenant's rights to renewal of the lease under the 1954 Act are excluded (see below), the tenant will be vulnerable to being evicted or financially exploited by the landlord. This brings us to the increasingly common, and often problematic, question of a tenant-only break clause.

This provides the tenant with an opportunity to determine the lease, normally on a fixed date (eg the first or some subsequent rent review date). The tenant has the peace of mind of knowing that if the business does not work out he has an opportunity to terminate the lease on the relevant date. The only items that the tenant has to worry about are to ensure that

(1) sufficient care is taken in serving notice at the right time and on the right person in accordance with the provisions of the break clause in the lease; and

(2) there are no subsisting breaches of covenant at the time of service of such notice and until termination of the lease.

If the landlord is reluctant to accept the tenant's notice, then the landlord will take every opportunity to keep the tenant 'on the hook'. A landlord may, for example, argue that because of a subsisting (albeit minor) breach of covenant, it is not obliged to accept the notice. The tenant should take care to ensure that the rent is paid on the due date and that at the very least the repair covenant has been complied with if he has any intention of exercising the break provision.

It was held in *Trane (UK) Ltd v Provident Mutual Life Assurance* (1995) 03 EG that the requirement in a lease that the tenant had to observe the tenant's covenants up to the intended termination date had the effect of being what is called a 'condition precedent'. Accordingly, any subsisting breach, however minor, would prevent the break clause from being exercised.

In *Trane*, the tenant attempted to exercise a ten-year break option in a 25-year lease of industrial premises. The problem was that the tenant was in breach of its repairing obligations, albeit a minor breach. Because of this, the tenant was held not to be entitled to determine the lease. No building is ever going to be in perfect condition at a particular moment. The covenant to repair in this context according to Cooke J was 'to take all proper steps to repair the building once out of repair and to do so with all proper speed and in a reasonable time'. It follows that if a tenant is contemplating exercising a break clause, he should instruct his surveyor to prepare a schedule of condition beforehand so that any such problems can be remedied prior to service of the notice and the premises maintained thereafter.

11.5 RENT REVIEWS

Except in the case of short-term leases of about five years or less, it is likely that there will be provision for the rent to be reviewed from time to time. The purpose of a rent review is to ensure that the landlord continues to receive a market rent for the premises and not simply the historical rent that was fixed at the beginning of the term. Rent reviews are usually fixed by reference to the open market, but there are other alternatives.

11.5.1 Open market rent reviews

An open market 'rent review' amounts to a reappraisal of the rent for the same premises on the assumption that a willing landlord wishes to grant to a willing tenant the premises in good condition for the original length of term or otherwise the unexpired length of term. The formula for rent reviews differs from one lease to the next and often depends on the drafting preferences of the landlord's solicitors. Of course, care does have to be taken by the tenant's solicitor to ensure that the landlord does not have an unfair advantage at the negotiating table on rent review. A large amount of law has evolved, largely as a result of judicial decisions, in this field.

Example – Typical scenario of a rent review

> The lease provides for a rent review on 29 September. The landlord is required to serve a notice of intention to review the rent not more than six months and not less than three months before the review date. In his notice the landlord, having taken the advice of his surveyor, suggests an increase to £X to take effect from the rent review date. The tenant acknowledges receipt of the notice but suggests a far smaller rental increase from the current rent of £Y. The lease provides that if one month after service of the notice of intention to review the rent, no rent has been agreed between the landlord and tenant, then either party may refer the matter to either an expert or an arbitrator as stated in the rent review formula. In this case the negotiations between the landlord and tenant are unproductive and their respective surveyors are brought in to endeavour to negotiate an agreement.

A starting point for surveyors is often 'comparables' – ie rents agreed on other comparable properties at around the relevant time. This is easier in a shopping parade or business park than with restaurants or hotels. The parties should give careful consideration to the wording of the rent review clause and in particular the factors or circumstances to be assumed and disregarded. The review procedure and the negotiation of the rent operate as if a notional or hypothetical lease was being granted and there are certain assumptions behind that hypothetical lease. For example, it may be required to assume the premises are 'fit' and 'available for immediate occupation and use' and that improvements carried out at the expense of the tenant are disregarded when assessing the rent. On occasions the landlord may agree to a substantial rent-free period at the beginning of the lease in exchange for a higher rental figure, in order to retain/enhance the building's investment value. This practice can have a major impact on rent reviews, as has been shown by a number of cases to have come before the courts in recent years. The landlord will wish to disregard all such rent-free periods or other inducements at each rent review, in order to perpetuate what might be an artificially high rent. A well-advised tenant will wish to restrict any such disregard to rent-free periods granted to compensate the tenant for fitting out the premises.

Despite efforts by The Law Society and the RICS to introduce model forms of rent review, these are not widely used and therefore it is dangerous to assume that any two different leases have identical rent review clauses.

A cornerstone of the rent review formula has been that reviews are usually 'upwards only'. Accordingly, even in the time of falling rents, if a landlord called for a review the rent would not fall. As in the case of the recession causing the misery of negative equity for homeowners, so have upwards-only rent reviews resulted in premises being over rented where there is no possibility that the passing rent can fall to the market rent on review. If the premises are surplus to requirements then an assignment of that lease becomes virtually impossible unless there are substantial induce-ments such as rent-free periods and reverse premiums. The tenant may also find that any opportunity for underletting at less than the passing rent is pro-hibited by the terms of the lease and therefore the landlord can reasonably withhold its consent to any underletting on this basis. Although properly advised, there may be ways around this for a tenant.

11.5.2 Turnover rents

Rents linked to the turnover of the tenant's business are an alternative to market rents. This is now not uncommon, eg in shopping precincts and also hotels and restaurants. In this case the landlord is able to monitor each retailer's turnover and the rent that is paid is calculated by reference to that turnover. If the tenant suffers, then so does the landlord, and the landlord may feel it incumbent on it to see what it can do to help that tenant's trad-ing. For example, a landlord decided to improve a 1960s shopping precinct by providing a covered area for pedestrians at one end of the precinct where it was previously exposed to the elements. The effect of this was to secure and in some cases improve the turnover of those shops within the covered area while those outside the covered area began to suffer. As a result of this the landlord extended the covering to all the shops in the precinct for mutual benefit. Another advantage from the tenant's point of view is the saving on professional fees. It follows that the involvement of the professional adviser is likely to be minimal where negotiation is largely unnecessary.

It is worth noting that reference is made to 'turnover' rather than 'profit'. Turnover may be perceived to increase simply as the rate of VAT goes up, whereas this may not have a similar effect upon profits. In *Tucker v Granada Motorways Services Ltd* [1977] 3 All ER 865, the Minister of Transport granted a lease to a tenant of a motorway service area. The tenant paid a fixed rent together with an additional variable rent based on the tak-ings from the petrol station and catering services. The gross takings included the tobacco duty payable on cigarettes, cigars, etc. Accordingly, when tobacco duty rose so did the tenant's rent, even though its profit remained the same. Therefore, it is important that advice is taken on the def-inition of 'turnover'. For the tenant, as far as possible this should be linked to the profit of the business, although opportunities for abuse and difficulty in policing may cause landlords to resist this.

11.5.3 Index-linked rents

One advantage of index linking is that both the landlord and the tenant can monitor the rent relatively easily. As in the case of an open market rent review, it is often the case that the review date is fixed by reference to an anniversary and, if the formula in the lease is correctly worded, then the new rent will reflect the rate of inflation rather than property values. Although index linking is cheap to operate for the landlord and tenant, it may well not reflect the reality of market conditions. If the tenant is in a depressed area where there is a number of empty units around him this would work in his favour in an open market rent review, but would have no influence on the RPI. For a unit situated in an affluent and popular area, the converse would be the case. Index linking is not recommended for anything but short- to medium-term leases.

11.5.4 Fixed increases

For shorter leases of anything up to three or five years the parties may agree to fixed increases, perhaps on an annual basis, and so expose each party to a certain degree of risk. As in the case of a home buyer locking himself into a fixed-rate mortgage, it is likely that one of the two parties may regret such a commitment at some stage in the lease.

11.6 DURING THE LEASE

The heads of terms are now set out in a lease. The lease has been completed and the tenant is in occupation. We now look at some aspects of the landlord/tenant relationship during the term of the lease.

11.6.1 Implied and express covenants

A lease or tenancy agreement is a contract between the landlord and the tenant, and various express obligations, mainly of the tenant, but some of the landlord too, are set out in the document. Alongside the express obligations on each party in the lease are various implied obligations, but well-advised parties will prefer to set out matters expressly, rather than rely on the often rather 'grey areas' which can be encountered with implied obligations.

It is likely that the bulk of the lease will be made up of the 'tenant's covenants' requiring in particular the rent to be paid on certain days and for the tenant to acknowledge certain obligations and responsibilities. Five of the more important areas of liability which the tenant will incur are considered below: rent payment, repair, alterations, user and 'alienation'.

11.6.2 Payment of rent

Generally this will be quarterly in advance and most modern leases will specify that the tenant must pay by direct debit/standing order if the landlord requires. Interest will be payable on rent not paid on time. Importantly, particularly in a multi-occupied building with service charges where there is most potential for landlord/tenant dispute, the lease will probably require payment *without deduction or set-off*. Put simply, if for example the tenant has a claim against the landlord for inadequate services which the landlord is required to provide, then the tenant may not deduct rent to cover this. The landlord is able to pursue the tenant, by various means, for payment of the outstanding rent without regard to the tenant's claim in respect of service charge.

11.6.3 Repair

The tenant's repair responsibility generally applies either to the whole building or, in the case where the lease is for part only of a building, merely the interior. As a general rule, the longer the lease, the greater the repair responsibility on the tenant. The lease may state that the tenant is required 'to keep the demised premises in good and substantial repair'. The definition of 'demised premises' is important here and will show whether the repair responsibility is full repairing or simply internal. There is also likely to be a requirement on the tenant to decorate the demised premises on fixed dates. It is possible the tenant's liability has been limited by providing for amendments in the repair covenant (eg by reference to a schedule of condition).

If the tenant neglects his duties, the landlord is entitled to seek a remedy against the tenant. Modern leases generally provide the landlord with the power to enter the premises to carry out these works at the tenant's cost. The landlord's claim would be for a debt against the tenant. A case in the Court of Appeal in 1997, *Jarvis v Harris*, resolved an uncertainty which previously surrounded this important point: it is now clear that if the landlord is prepared to risk incurring the cost of repairing the premises where the tenant is in breach of covenant, then that cost will be reasonable as a straightforward debt due from the tenant to the landlord. This assumes that the lease contains the appropriate express provisions, as most leases do.

The alternative of suing for damages or for an order requiring the tenant to comply with its covenant is more complex. For example, if the lease was granted for seven years or more (and at the time of service of the landlord's notice of dilapidations or a notice under s 145 of the Law of Property Act 1925 there are three or more years of that term unexpired), the tenant is entitled to the protection provided by the Leasehold Property (Repairs) Act 19310. In this case, leave of court is required before the landlord can enforce a right to damages or forfeiture and the onus is on the landlord to establish a ground to secure leave of the court. Such lease can only be granted in certain specified grounds and will generally not be given unless the breach of covenant is very substantial.

11.6.4 Alterations

It is common for a lease to provide that no alterations can be carried out to the premises except internal alterations which require the landlord's consent. In this case there is an 'absolute' covenant against external alterations, building of extensions etc and a 'qualified' covenant against internal alterations. In the case of the absolute prohibition, this does not prevent the tenant from asking the landlord for consent. The landlord is entitled to refuse permission and is not under any obligation to justify its refusal. Equally, the landlord may agree to the alteration (which would be evidenced by a suitable licence) on the basis of receipt of an appropriate premium.

If the tenant wished eg to erect internal partitioning, then the landlord would not be able to withhold his consent unreasonably. This is the case whether or not words such as 'such consent not to be unreasonably withheld' are included, as by virtue of s 19(2) of the Landlord and Tenant Act 1927 that qualification is deemed to apply in any event. The 1927 Act provides that not only cannot the landlord unreasonably withhold his consent, but also that the landlord cannot demand a premium for doing so, apart from a reasonable sum 'in respect of any damage to or diminution in the value of the premises' or any legal or other expenses incurred in providing its consent. Again this would be evidenced by a licence to alter. Typically the licence will provide that the tenant must comply with all planning and any other statutory obligations in carrying out the alterations and reserve the right in favour of the landlord to require the tenant to reinstate the premises to their previous condition at the end of the term.

11.6.5 User

User covenants are either expressed positively (eg only 'to use the demised premises as . . .') or negatively ('not to use the demised premises except as . . . and for no other purpose'). The user may express specific terms and refer to the proposed use of that tenant, or express broad terms and, for example, refer to the most recent Use Classes order. As in the case of alterations there may be an absolute restriction against change of use or a qualified restriction. In this case, however, there is no statutory implication that consent is not to be unreasonably withheld. However, if the landlord does grant his consent, the conditions which the landlord is entitled to impose on the tenant are limited by s 19(3) of the 1927 Act. Should the landlord decide to withhold consent, then there is little more the tenant can do. In the event of breach of this covenant the landlord is entitled to apply to the court for an injunction to stop an unauthorised use where it is clear that damages are not an adequate remedy.

11.6.6 Alienation

The two most important ways in which a tenant can dispose of all or part of its interest under a lease are assignment and underletting.

Assignment

It is possible to assign part only of a lease, but this is unusual, gives rise to various problems, and the lease generally prohibits this.

Assignment of the whole of the premises will generally be permitted, and the terms on which this can happen are likely to depend on whether the lease was completed before or after 1 January 1996 (ie whether the Landlord and Tenant Covenants Act 1995 applies). The circumstances in which the tenant can assign, and the conditions of any assignment, are likely to be more stringent in the case of post-1996 leases, namely to compensate the landlord for the fact that the tenant will be released from further liability on the occasion of the second lawful assignment.

Subletting

Creating a sublease leaves the landlord/tenant relationship in place and creates a third interest below that of the tenant, namely the subtenant. The tenant's liability to the landlord is thereby unaffected, but this arrangement provides more flexibility: the tenant can sublet the property for a temporary period with a view to its regaining possession at a later date when it is anticipated that the business will again require the premises. That in turn raises the question of whether the subtenant will be entitled to the protection of the 1954 Act, thereby depriving the tenant of the right to resume occupation. The tenant generally will be entitled to resist any application for a new tenancy on the grounds that he needs the premises for his own use, but in this situation it is better to contract the sublease outside the security of tenure provisions in the 1954 Act (see 11.2.5); this will avoid the subtenant making any application for a new lease in the first place.

A further aspect of flexibility provided by the subletting route is the facility, subject to the terms of the lease, to be able to sublet part, if the configuration of the building is such that a part can be sublet conveniently (eg if a tenant takes a lease of two floors of an office building the lease might permit a sublease of part as long as that part comprises the whole of either of the floors). Again, it would be advisable for the sublease to be contracted outside the 1954 Act and it is probable that the landlord will also require this by means of a provision in the lease. The landlord's concern will be to prevent the indefinite fragmentation of occupation which could arise if a subtenant part became entitled to renew the sublease. Arrangements such as this tend to be of relatively short-term duration.

Where a landlord has other premises in the area, it will be concerned to ensure that the rent on any sublease, of whole or part, is at the higher of the market level at the time, or the passing rent payable under the lease. There are two reasons for this. First, any underletting at less than market rent would adversely affect the landlord's position as regards rent reviews or lease renewals in respect of both the premises themselves and other premises owned nearby – the lower rent on the sublease could be quoted as a comparable by other tenants in order to justify a lower rent. Secondly, in the event of premature termination of the headlease, in certain circumstances the landlord could be left with a subtenancy in place at lower rent.

Accordingly, alienation clauses generally contain detailed and complex provisions to protect the landlord from various adverse consequences which could arise as a result of assignment or underletting, while at the same time giving the tenant the requisite freedom and flexibility which it will need if it is to enter into a lease for anything other than a very short term.

11.7 EXPIRY OF THE LEASE

We now look at the position on the expiry of the contractual term of a lease within the 1954 Act. Where the tenant does *not* have security (eg a lease which is excluded from the 1954 Act by court order), the tenant is *not* entitled to remain in occupation beyond the expiry of the contractual term. This is not always so under the 1954 Act. The assumption is made in this part of the chapter that the tenant wishes to remain in occupation.

11.7.1 Right to renew

A tenant protected under the 1954 Act has an automatic right to renew his tenancy at the current market rent. As long as the tenancy meets the definition referred to in s 23(1) of the 1954 Act (see 11.2), then until statutory notices are served by either the landlord or the tenant, the lease continues indefinitely. This assumes that the premises continue to be occupied by the tenant for business purposes (see 11.7.6). In this case the tenant is 'holding over'. While the tenant is holding over, the terms of the expired contractual tenancy continue as before.

If the tenant is no longer in occupation for business purposes then he will have no automatic right to renew the lease.

At a time of falling rents, it may well suit the landlord to 'overlook' serving any notice to determine the lease. If it is likely that on a renewal the market rent will be less than the passing rent under the current lease, there may be no point for the landlord to determine the lease. It follows that at a time of rental growth, a landlord may suffer significant losses in rental income if he fails to serve his notice in good time. At a time when the commercial property market is relatively stagnant there is often a stand-off between landlords and tenants in many business premises. The landlord is not confident that it will be able to negotiate any increase in the rent on renewal and the tenant is equally not inclined to commit himself to a new lease during times of uncertainty. In the meantime, the lease continues on the same terms.

11.7.2 The landlord's notice

Under s 25(1) of the 1954 Act, 'The landlord may terminate a tenancy . . . by a notice given to the tenant in the prescribed form specifying the date at which the tenancy is to come to an end'. The date specified in the notice must be not less than six months and not more than 12 months from the date the notice is issued.

Example – Landlord's notice

If a lease is due to expire on 25 December 2000 and the landlord wishes it to be determined on that date, a notice must be served before 24 June 2000 and after 25 December 1999. If the matter was overlooked, a notice could be served, say, in August 2000, citing the date for determination as 1 March 2001 (ie at least six months ahead). In the meantime the tenant continues paying the rent at the current rate, but the landlord has lost the right to receive a higher rent (assuming a rising market) for the period from December 2000 to March 2001.

11.7.3 Tenant's response to landlord's notice

A notice served by the landlord under s 25 will state that within two months after the date of the notice the tenant must advise the landlord in writing whether at the date of termination he is willing to give up possession of the property. If the tenant wishes to renew but does nothing to respond to the s 25 notice within the two months, the tenant will lose all rights to renew. It is essential upon receipt of any notice under the 1954 Act that a tenant takes legal advice. Within four months from the date of the landlord's notice the tenant must commence proceedings in the court for a new tenancy unless a new lease has been granted in the interim. If the tenant fails to do so, he will lose all rights of renewal under the 1954 Act. Where the landlord and the tenant have taken all the correct steps and proceedings have commenced, then the terms of the new lease are a matter of negotiation. Failing agreement, the court will take such decisions as it thinks best not only whether a tenancy shall be granted, but also with regard to the terms of a tenancy.

11.7.4 Tenant's request for a new tenancy

It is possible for the tenant to take the initiative which in the days of the rising market was called a 'pre-emptive strike'. If a tenant is certain he wishes to renew (particularly in a situation where the market rent is likely to be less than the passing rent), the tenant has power to terminate the contractual tenancy. A tenant is entitled to serve a notice under s 26 of the 1954 Act which, as in the case of s 25, may be served not more than 12 months and not less than six months before the date of termination. The tenant has to propose the terms of the new lease (eg rent, length of term, etc), and a s 26 notice cannot be served if the landlord has already served a s 25 notice. Within two months of the date of the tenant's notice the landlord must give notice to the tenant whether it will oppose an application to the court for the grant of a new tenancy. If the landlord does oppose, then the grounds for such a position must be stated. Any ground referred to is significant in that it determines whether any compensation is payable to the tenant (see 11.7.7) and the landlord may not be able to subsequently claim the benefit of other grounds not stated in the original notice.

If the landlord fails to respond to the notice within the two-month period, it cannot prevent the grant of a new lease on the basis of the statutory grounds of opposition.

11.7.5 Application to court for new tenancy

Under s 24(1) of the 1954 Act:

> 'the tenant . . . may apply to the court for a new tenancy –
>
> (a) if the landlord has given notice under [s 25 of this Act] to terminate the tenancy, or
> (b) if the tenant has made a request for a new tenancy in accordance with section 26 of this Act.'

The application should be made not less than two months and not more than four months after the giving of either of the above notices. It is essential that these time periods are adhered to as failure to do so could mean that a tenant will lose the premises it needs for its business.

In the majority of cases the court procedure goes no further than the issue of the application to preserve the tenant's right to a new lease. Often the summons issued by the court provides for a date to be fixed to enable negotiations to continue between the parties. This is assuming that the landlord is happy for the renewal to take place. However, the landlord can oppose the application.

11.7.6 Landlord's opposition to renewal

There are seven specified grounds under which a landlord can oppose an application to renew, which are set out in s 30(1) of the Act as follows.

Disrepair
(1954 Act, s 30(1)(a))

'The tenant ought not to be granted a new tenancy in view of the state of repair' because of a breach of the tenant's obligations under his lease. It was held in *Lyons v Central Commercial Properties London Ltd* [1958] 1 WLR 869 that 'the neglect of repair to which the section refers should be substantial'. A court has a discretion to consider the seriousness of the breach, the tenant's overall conduct and the reasons for the breach which has arisen.

Rent arrears
(1954 Act, s 30(1)(b))

'The tenant ought not to be granted a new tenancy in view of his persistent delay in paying rent . . .' Again the court must exercise its discretion in deciding whether this ground has been established. If the court feels that the landlord should not be required to experience the problems and expense of recovering the rent if the lease were renewed, then the landlord's application may well be granted.

Breaches of other obligations
(1954 Act, s 30(1)(c))

'The tenant ought not to be granted a new tenancy in view of other substantial breaches by him of his obligations under the current tenancy, or for any other reason connected with the tenant's use or management of the holding.' This provides a wider ground for the landlord to oppose renewal in that, for example, it could include breaches of planning regulations. The question that the court asks is whether the landlord's interest has been prejudiced by the breach.

Alternative accommodation
(1954 Act, s 30(1)(d))

'The landlord has offered and is willing to provide or secure the provision of alternative accommodation for the tenant . . .' The alternative accommodation must be available on terms that are reasonable, having regard to the provisions of the current tenancy and to all other relevant circumstances. This ground is rarely cited and there are few reported cases.

Uneconomic subletting
(1954 Act, s 30(1)(e))

'Where the current tenancy was created by the sub-letting of part [and] that the aggregate of the rents reasonably obtainable on separate lettings of the holding and the remainder of that property would be substantially less than the rent reasonably obtainable on a letting of that property as a whole.' This is not a common ground and is a purely financial one. It is only open to the 'competent landlord' if he is a superior landlord and is not available to the immediate landlord. The court will agree to this ground if the landlord, by letting the tenanted premises together with the rest of the property in the head lease as a single unit, could expect more rent than by letting the individual units separately.

Demolition or reconstruction
(1954 Act, s 30(1)(f))

'The landlord intends to demolish or reconstruct the premises comprised in the holding or a substantial part of those premises or to carry out substantial work of construction on the holding or part thereof and it could not reasonably do so without obtaining possession of the holding.' This is a common ground for opposition by a landlord. Its intention to carry out these works must be genuine and settled, and established by the date of the hearing. Considerable case-law exists for whether the landlord had the necessary intention (eg it is often recommended that a landlord which is also a company passes a formal board resolution referring to the intention to demolish or reconstruct the premises). The landlord also needs to show a legal and financial ability to proceed (ie legal in the sense of planning consent and financial in the sense of either having the finance or being able to raise it). Contractors' tenders should be obtained and made available to the court as further evidence of intention to proceed with the work.

Own occupation
(1954 Act, s 30(1)(g))

'On the termination of the current tenancy the landlord intends to occupy the holding for the purposes, or partly for the purposes, of a business to be carried on by him therein or as his residence.' There is 'a five-year rule' to be satisfied, namely that the landlord cannot rely on this ground if his interest was purchased or created within five years ending with the termination of the current tenancy. If the landlord itself granted the tenancy then the five-year rule does not apply. The landlord will have the same problems in establishing 'intention' as under s 30(1)(f) above. The landlord's occupation does not have to be immediate upon the termination of the lease, so long as it is within a reasonable time after the end of the term; nor does the landlord have to occupy all of the premises – a substantial part normally will be sufficient. Note that this ground can also be used if the landlord wishes to occupy the premises as his own residence, although there are few if any reported cases on this. The writer had a case where, acting for the tenant in receipt of a notice under this ground, the landlord wished to use the subject premises not 'as his residence' but as part of his residence. Could he rely on the ground? The case was settled before going to court and so the question remained open.

11.7.7 Compensation

Compensation for non-renewal

Where the landlord is successful in denying the tenant a new lease on one of the last three grounds referred to above (ie uneconomic subletting, demolition and reconstruction, or owner occupation), compensation is payable to the tenant.

The amount of compensation is based on the rateable value of the holding multiplied by an 'appropriate multiplier' as prescribed by the Secretary of State for the Environment made by statutory instrument. The rateable value is ascertained at the date of the service of the s 25 or s 26 notice so that the multiplier is *one*, except in a case in which the tenant elects to be paid compensation by reference to the rateable value of the holding on 31 March 1990, in which case the multiplier is *eight*. The tenant will make this election if the holding includes a residential element, but cannot do otherwise.

The compensation is doubled if for the 14 years ending with the date of termination of the current tenancy all or part of the premises have been occupied for business purposes and on any change of occupier each is a successor to his predecessor's business. Any agreement in the lease to exclude or reduce compensation where the occupation for carrying on the business has lasted for five years prior to the date when a tenant is to quit is void under s 38(2) of the 1954 Act.

Compensation for improvements

A tenant is rarely entitled to compensation for any improvements he has carried out unless specific provisions have been written into the documentation. There is machinery in the Landlord and Tenant Act 1927 for statutory compensation, but this is impractical, cumbersome and rarely used.

Tenant's notice to determine

Until recently it was thought that a tenant could not walk away from his obligations under a lease simply by giving up possession and surrendering the keys to the landlord at the end of the term. It was thought that the tenant must give three months' notice to the landlord and that the lease would continue if he did not do so. The decision of the Court of Appeal in *Esselte v Pearl Assurance plc* [1997] 02 EG 124 has thrown a lifeline to tenants.

If the lease is contracted out of the 1954 Act, then neither party is required to serve notice and the lease will determine on the contractual expiry date.

In other cases, whether or not a landlord has served a s 25 notice (and provided the tenant has been in occupation under the tenancy for at least one month) he can give not less than three months' notice to end the lease on its contractual expiry date (1954 Act, s 27). A s 27 notice cannot be served after a tenant's request for a new tenancy has been served on the landlord unless the procedure under the s 26 notice has been followed by formal discontinuance through the court.

If there is less than three months to go before the contractual expiry date, a tenant can still serve notice under s 27(2) of the 1954 Act by giving not less than three months' notice to expire on a quarter day *after* its contractual expiry date. The notice under s 27(2) may be served before the contractual expiry date (in anticipation of the lease being continued under the Act) or after the contractual expiry date.

Example – Notice to determine less than three months before contractual expiry date

Where the contractual expiry date is 25 December 1998, the tenant can serve a s 27(1) notice to expire on 25 December 1998, on any day up to 24 September 1998. After that day, the earliest date that the lease can be determined using s 27(2) is the following quarter day, namely 25 March 1999.

12

EMPLOYMENT LAW

RICHARD LAWSON, LAWMARK

12.1 INTRODUCTION

Over recent years domestic employment law has undergone a metamorphosis with the result that a considerable body of law now exists governing the relationship between an employer and its workforce. EU legislation and ECJ decisions have had an increasing influence on domestic employment law and this trend is set to continue. Over a similar period the number of disputes coming before employment tribunals has risen steadily.

It is therefore important for employers to be aware of this complex body of law that governs all employment relationship aspects from recruitment to termination (and in some instances beyond). This chapter concentrates on the areas governing the individual employment relationship as they affect the rights and obligations between employer and employee. It does not attempt to deal with collective employment law except where this affects individual employment law in such areas as redundancy and transfer of undertakings.

12.2 THE IMPACT OF EU LAW

EU law has had a profound effect on UK employment law and the rights afforded to individual employees. It is therefore important to have an understanding of the way EU law operates and impacts upon both employers and employees in the UK.

Much of the law affecting UK employers has been implemented to give effect to EU legislation. Indeed, in certain circumstances, employees may be able to rely directly upon the provisions of EU law to enforce rights, where they would have no claim under UK law. The main sources of EU law are:

- *The provisions of the Treaty of Rome 1957* One of the most important provisions of the Treaty in the employment law field is art 119 which provides that men and women should receive equal pay for equal work (see 12.23 below).

- *Legislation in the form of directives*   Directives take the form of instructions to countries that are EU members (including the UK) to pass national legislation, by a specified date, to implement each directive's provisions.

Certain provisions of EU law have what is known as 'direct effect'. This means that individuals can rely directly on directly-effective EU law in the UK courts. In order for direct effect to be established the provision of EU law must be unconditional, clear and precise. The most important directly-effective provision of EU law is art 119.

In contrast to art 119, directives do not have general direct effect and therefore cannot generally be relied upon by individuals directly in UK courts. However, directives have direct effect where the individual seeking to rely on directive's terms is employed by the State, or by a body that is 'an emanation of the State', in effect public sector employees. However, in contrast to public sector employees, those employed in the private sector are unable to rely on a directive's provisions. However, they may have a claim against the UK government for its failure to implement fully the provisions of any directive into national legislation by the specified date. See *Francovich v Italian Republic* [1992] IRLR 84.

Furthermore, it has been held that the national courts must, as far as is possible, interpret national law in the light of the wording and purpose of any relevant EU directive. This is the case whether the national law was passed before or after the adoption of the directive. This is known as 'the purposive approach'. However, this approach should only be adopted where the national legislation can be interpreted consistently with the directive without distorting the meaning of the domestic legislation itself.

Some of the most important provisions in the context of employment law are:

(1) Equal pay – art 119 and the Equal Pay Directive.
(2) Sex discrimination – Equal Treatment Directive.
(3) Transfer of undertakings – Acquired Rights Directive.
(4) Maternity rights – Pregnant Workers Directive.
(5) Contracts of employment – Proof of Employment Directive.

The importance of EU law in the field of UK employment law cannot be understated. Throughout this chapter references are made to relevant EU provisions, where appropriate.

12.3 EMPLOYING THE WORKER: THE WORKER'S STATUS

Before the employment relationship commences, the most fundamental question to be considered by the employer is whether the worker is to be an employee. Is the worker to be employed under a contract of service (ie an employee) or a contract for services (an independent contractor)? This distinction is extremely important as it forms the basis of the relationship between the parties and the rights and obligations of both parties arise from it. In practice, the vast majority of workers are employees, but in certain circumstances the employer may not feel this is appropriate. Some of the important consequences of the distinction, by which the employer can make a reasoned decision on the employee's status, are listed below:

Employee rights

- Written Statement of Terms and conditions of employment
- Protection against unfair dismissal
- Entitlement to redundancy pay
- Statutory minimum notice entitlement or agreed contractual notice
- Right to statutory sick pay
- Maternity rights, including statutory maternity pay entitlement
- Not to be discriminated against on grounds of sex, race or disability
- Not to be discriminated against on grounds of membership or non-membership of a trade union
- Time off for trade union activities
- Medical suspension payment entitlement
- Guarantee payment entitlement
- Equal pay
- Protection in connection with a transfer of an undertaking
- Right to be consulted on health and safety issues.

Employee obligations

- To work in accordance with the employer's instructions
- To work with due diligence
- To pay income tax through PAYE
- To pay employee NI contributions.

Self-employed – rights

- Entitlement to contractual benefits
- Not to be discriminated against on grounds of sex, race or disability
- Where appropriate to work within a safe system of work and place.

Self-employed obligations

- To work with due skill and diligence
- To pay own tax under Schedule D
- To pay self-employed NI contributions.

The obligations and consequently the costs placed upon an employer are far greater in relation to an employee. However, balanced against this is the high level of control that an employer has over an employee.

12.3.1 Distinguishing between contract of service and contract for services

Once the employer reaches a decision on the worker's status, it is important to ensure that the status that is intended is actually achieved, as it can be seen from above, a number of factors such as tax and NI obligations and statutory employment protection flow from the definition of the relationship. The mere description of the relationship by the parties as being one of employer/employee or employer/independent contractor is not decisive. The label put on the relationship is not conclusive and over the years the courts have developed a number of tests in an attempt to ascertain the true nature of employment relationships.

The tests

Mutuality of obligation

This is one of the more recent tests and was first expounded by the courts in *Nethermere (St Neots) Ltd v Gardiner* [1984] IRLR 240, where it was stated that for there to be a contract of service there must be 'an irreducible minimum of obligation on each side'. There must be an obligation on the employer to provide work for the employee and on the employee to perform such work for the employer. Without this element there could not be a contract of service.

The control test

This was the first test developed by the courts and looked at the level of control exercised by the employer over the worker, not only about the particular work that the worker was required to do but also whether the employer controlled how and when the work should be done. The greater the control the more likely that the worker was to be an employee. This test however was not sufficient when dealing with more skilled workers, such as, for example, brain surgeons, and the courts therefore developed what is known as the integration test.

The integration test

This test was set out by Denning LJ in *Stevenson, Jordan & Harrison Ltd v McDonald and Evans* [1952] 1 TLR 101 and looks at whether the worker is an integral part of the business. The closer the connection between the worker and the business the more likely the worker was to be an employee, whereas an independent contractor was more likely to be merely an accessory to the business.

The multiple test

The case of *Ready Mixed Concrete (South East) Ltd v Minister of Pensions and National Insurance* [1968] 2 QB 497 stated that a contract of service existed if:

(1) The worker agrees, in consideration of a wage or other remuneration, to provide his own work and skill in the performance of some service for his master.
(2) He agrees expressly or impliedly that in performance of the service he is sufficiently subject to the control of the other to make him a master.
(3) All the other provisions of the contract are consistent with it being a contract of service. It is important to note that an obligation to work subject to the other party's control was not to be the overriding factor, if all the other provisions of the contract were inconsistent with a contract of service. Therefore, it was important to look at the relationship as a whole and not isolated factors.

Subsequently, in *Market Investigations Ltd v Minister of Social Security* [1969] 2 QB 173 it was again reiterated that control was not the decisive test and that the most important question to ask was whether 'a person was in business on his own account'.

It was stated in *Hall (Inspector of Taxes) v Lorimar* [1994] 1 All ER 250 that the question of whether a person is in business on his own account, though often helpful in distinguishing between a contract of service and a contract for services, might be of little assistance in the case of a person carrying on a business or profession. In such cases the traditional distinction between an employee and an independent contractor should be borne in mind, namely, the extent to which the individual is dependent or independent of a particular paymaster for the financial exploitation of his talents.

The overview approach

It must be emphasised that there is 'no single path to a correct decision'. As the *Ready Mixed Concrete* and *Market Investigations* decisions show, although control is still an important factor, each case will turn on its own facts. Factors which are important will be:

(1) degree of control;
(2) the chance of profit and the risk of loss;
(3) method and payment of tax;
(4) exclusivity of service;
(5) intention of the parties;
(6) integration of the worker into the business;
(7) the employer's right to suspend and/or dismiss;
(8) whether the worker provides his own equipment;
(9) whether the worker is free to hire his own helpers.

When deciding to take on a worker as an independent contractor, it is essential that legal advice is sought to ensure that the way that the relationship is structured is one of employer/independent contractor. Failing to correctly define the relationship can have financial implications. For example, the Inland Revenue has wide ranging powers to recover tax from an employer who has failed to make the appropriate deductions through the PAYE system as he incorrectly thought that his worker was an independent contractor and therefore responsible for his own tax and national insurance contributions. In doubtful cases, it is always advisable to seek prior clearance from the Revenue as regards the tax treatment.

12.4 THE EMPLOYEE

In many instances, employers may wish to employ employees on a part time, temporary or seasonal basis. Particular matters should be borne in mind when engaging such employees.

12.4.1 Temporary employees

First, it is important to note that where temporary employees obtain the necessary two years' continuous employment, they will attain statutory employment protection rights. There are essentially two types of temporary employees.

First, those that are commonly known as 'temps' who are employed through an employment agency which charges its client a fee from which it pays the temp directly. In this instance the employment agency is to be treated as the primary employer and the agency's client as a secondary or quasi employer. It is unlikely that a claim for unfair dismissal or a redundancy payment in these circumstances would be successful against the secondary employer, and an employee should pursue the primary employer.

Secondly, there are temporary employees who are employed for a certain fixed period. If at the time of employing the temporary employee, the employer informs him that his employment is temporary and is to be terminated on the first employee resuming work, then such termination is likely to be a fair reason for some other substantial reason. The tribunal would then go on to consider whether the employer acted reasonably as defined by s 98(4) and (6) of the Employment Rights Act 1996 (ERA). See 12.11 below.

Under ERA, s 106, where an employer employs a temporary replacement to cover an employee who is absent because of pregnancy, childbirth or medical suspension, if at the time of employing the temporary replacement the employer informs the employee in writing that his employment will be terminated on the resumption of work by the other employee, then such a dismissal is deemed to be fair for some other substantial reason and, as above, the tribunal will go on to assess reasonableness in accordance with s 57(3).

12.4.2 Seasonal employees

These are employees who are taken on for a limited period of time, to cover, for example, busy periods in the tourism industry for the summer months. Seasonal employees, subject to the necessary qualifying conditions, are entitled to all the normal employment protection rights. Accordingly, their contracts can only be terminated on the employer providing them with the statutory minimum notice requirement (if there is not a longer contractual period).

There is one particular area of concern which employers should bear in mind when engaging seasonal employees. If the period between seasons of work is short and the particular worker is habitually re-engaged then continuity of employment may be preserved in accordance with the rules dealing with absence due to temporary cessation of work (see 12.9.2 below). This is obviously important with a view to the employee gaining statutory employment protection rights, especially the right to claim unfair dismissal and a redundancy payment.

12.4.3 Part-time employees

Although until 1995 part-time employees' rights to employment protection were limited, now part-time employees enjoy the same rights as full-time employees.

12.4.4 Directors

Directors are not automatically employees of a company. However, a director who is paid a salary and devotes his whole time and attention to the business of the company, will normally work under a contract of employment and be an employee.

A director's contract must be approved by the company's board and under the Companies Act 1985, s 319 a company is prohibited from entering into a contract with a director which it cannot terminate by notice (or can only terminate in specified circumstances) for a period exceeding five years, unless the term has been approved by a resolution of the company in general meeting. Any term not so approved is void and is deemed to be replaced by a term entitling the company to terminate on reasonable notice.

For a fuller discussion of the role of directors, see 19.5 below.

12.5 THE CONTRACT OF EMPLOYMENT

The contract of employment governs the relationship between the employer and the employee. Although in practice a single document is referred to as 'the contract of employment' in reality the contract need not be in writing but can be oral. Indeed a contract can, and in most instances does, include terms expressly agreed between the parties, implied terms, terms implied by custom and practice or arrangement and terms incorporated into a contract from other documents such as collective agreements (where a collective agreement contains terms appropriate for incorporation into an individual contract).

12.5.1 The terms of the contract

Express terms

These are terms which the parties specifically agree upon between themselves.

Implied terms

Frequently many terms of a contract of employment are left unspecified, but nevertheless are implied into the contract. This occurs where implied terms are necessary to give effect to the contract or if such terms are customary in a particular trade or are a usual arrangement for a particular employer. There are terms which are commonly implied into a contract and which affect both the employer and employee. A number of these are listed below.

Employers' duties

To maintain the relationship of mutual trust and confidence There is a duty on an employer not to destroy the trust and confidence that exists in an employment relationship. Breach of this implied term may entitle the employee to treat himself as having been constructively dismissed (see 12.11.1 below) and bring a claim for unfair dismissal as a result of a fundamental breach of a term of the contract by the employer.

To safeguard the employee's health and safety An employer owes a duty to all his employees to safeguard their health and safety. This includes a duty to provide safe equipment and a safe system of work. For a fuller discussion on health and safety and the employer's duties, see Chapter 15.

To terminate the contract on reasonable notice This term is implied where there is no express agreement between the parties. The contract can be terminated by either party on reasonable notice and what is deemed to be reasonable depends upon the particular employment circumstances. Such an implied notice term applies to both employer and employee.

To provide work In general terms, provided the employer fully remunerates his employee, it is not a breach of contract for the employer not to provide work. However, a term to provide work for an employee is implied where, for example, the level of remuneration is dependent upon the amount of work done or where an employee has particular skills which will deteriorate through lack of use.

Employee duties

Fidelity   An employee is under a duty to act faithfully on behalf of his employer and to act in the interests of his employer's business. For example, the employee must be honest and not steal from his employer. It is also a breach of the implied duty of fidelity for an employee to compete with his employer's business whilst still employed. However, where an employee merely takes steps in his own time to compete at the end of the employment relationship there would not be a breach of the implied contractual duty of fidelity (*Ixora Trading Inc v Jones* [1990] FSR 251).

Obedience   It is an implied term of the contract that an employee obeys his employer's lawful orders; and not to do so is a breach of the contract. However, such a duty extends only to lawful orders – it is not a breach to disobey an unlawful order.

To work with due diligence and care   An employee is under a duty to take reasonable care when performing tasks for his employer. Where an employee fails to take reasonable care in the performance of his duties the employer may be vicariously liable for his employee's lack of care (see Chapter 15).

Not to use or disclose trade secrets or confidential information   Another breach of the implied duty of fidelity is for an employee to use or disclose to third parties confidential information of his employer during employment. However, in the absence of an express term in the contract, on termination of employment the implied duty is not as extensive as during employment and only extends to information which is not merely confidential but which can be described as a trade secret. The circumstances of each case have to be assessed in deciding whether any information amounts to a trade secret, but in *Faccenda Chicken Ltd v Fowler* [1986] ICR 297 a number of factors were stressed to be important in deciding whether the implied duty of fidelity applied to confidential information after the termination of employment. These factors were as follows:

(1) The nature of the employment – Did the employee work in a business (or part of a business) where he regularly handled sensitive information?
(2) The nature of the information – Was the information such as to be so highly confidential as to amount to a trade secret?
(3) Did the employer impress upon the employee the confidential nature of the information? What was the employer's attitude?
(4) Could the particular information be easily isolated from other information which the employee was free to use or disclose?

Whilst the employment relationship subsists the implied duties on employees are wide ranging. However, on termination of employment apart from the implied duty not to disclose trade secrets an employee is free to set up a competing business and in theory to solicit customers and employees of his former employer. Therefore, in many cases employers will wish to incorporate into employment contracts express covenants restricting an employee's activities on termination.

12.6 THE DOCTRINE OF RESTRAINT OF TRADE

Express covenants in a contract of employment restricting an employee's activities after termination of employment are governed by the doctrine of restraint of trade. Such covenants are *prima facie* void on public policy grounds.

To be valid this type of covenant must be reasonable in both the interests of the parties and of the public (*Nordenfelt v Maxim Nordenfelt* [1894] AC 535). A covenant will only be upheld to the extent that it is reasonably required for the protection of the employer's legitimate interests. A protectable interest must first be established and then the clause must be limited to what is reasonably necessary to protect that interest.

Restraint of trade covenants fall into two main categories.

12.6.1 Non-competition covenants

Although any attempt by an employer to prevent a former employee from competing against him by inserting into that employee's contract a blanket non-competition covenant after termination will not be upheld by the courts, an employer is free to seek to uphold a covenant restricting an employee from working for a trade rival. Such a covenant is likely to be upheld provided it is limited to a reasonable period of time (*Littlewoods Organisation Ltd v Harris* [1977] 1 WLR 1472). A reasonable period of time is likely in most circumstances to be one not exceeding one year after termination.

Employers can also seek to prohibit a former employee from working in the same business as that for which he worked for his former employer within a specific geographical area and for a specific period of time. Such clauses are extremely restrictive and are only upheld by the courts where the employer can show that he has a large concentration of customers within a particular area that it is necessary for him to protect. If the employer can show this, the covenant is still only reasonable to the extent that the area it seeks to cover is limited and that the covenant runs only for a certain length of time. It is important to remember that a valid covenant covering a particular radius in one part of the country may not be valid covering the same radius in another area. Contrast a highly populated urban area with a rural area with a low population level (*Scorer v Seymour-Johns* [1966] 3 All ER 347, CA).

12.6.2 Non-solicitation covenants

Such a covenant will seek to restrict the former employee from soliciting his former employer's customers or clients. Again such covenants must be reasonable in relation to the time that they run and should be limited to those customers with which the former employee dealt with.

Furthermore, it was standard practice for employers to include a covenant in contracts prohibiting the poaching of fellow employees. However, following the Court of Appeal decision in *Hanover Insurance Brokers Ltd v Schapiro* [1994] IRLR 82, such covenants are generally unenforceable. In order to try and enforce such a covenant, it should be limited to very senior employees or those employees who have a particular expertise that it is necessary for the employer to protect and should only cover individuals who were employees at the same time as the departing employee.

Also, covenants were frequently specified to apply however the contract was terminated. Again, recently, this has been held to be too wide and covenants are only enforceable if a contract is terminated lawfully (*Living Design (Home Improvements) Ltd v Davidson* [1994] IRLR 69).

The drafting of restrictive covenants is extremely tricky and legal advice should be sought on every occasion. The above is only a brief summary of the relevant law and failure to carefully consider with appropriate advice when drafting covenants may result in them being unenforceable, because they are too wide in nature.

In certain circumstances the courts are willing to sever an unenforceable covenant or part of a covenant providing that what remains makes sense without the need for modifying the wording and that the sense of the contract itself is not altered. However, it is far preferable to insert into a contract a correctly drafted limited covenant which is likely to be upheld by the courts than to seek reliance on a widely drafted covenant which will fail and cannot at a later stage be altered.

If an employer, after termination of an employee's contract, wishes to rely upon any express covenants contained within that contract there are two remedies available:

(1) *An injunction.* This is the usual and most effective remedy by an employer seeking to enforce a term of the employment contract. An application for an injunction can be made once evidence of any breach has come to light and a successful application will result in the employee being restrained from breaching any of the terms of the covenant.

(2) *Damages.* An employer can also bring a claim against his employee for damages for breach of contract or breach of confidence. In such cases the employer, in order to recover damages, has to show that he has incurred a loss. There is also a potential claim against the employee's new employer for inducing the breach of contract, if the new employer was aware of the employee's breach.

12.6.3 Intellectual property rights

A complex body of law exists to deal with intellectual property rights that arise during the course of the employment relationship. This legislation governs copyright, patent and design rights.

The right of copyright is governed by the Copyright, Designs and Patents Act 1988. Section 11(2) of the Act states that, subject to contrary agreement, the first owner of any copyright in a work made by an employee during the course of his employment is his employer.

The Patents Act 1977 governs the protection of an original invention capable of industrial application by means of a patent. Section 39 of that Act states that an invention made by an employee belongs to his employer if:

(1) it was made in the course of the employee's normal duties; or
(2) it arises out of duties specifically assigned to him, in circumstances where an invention might reasonably be expected to result from the performance of those duties; or
(3) it was made in the course of the employee's duties and at that time the employee had, because of the nature of his duties and the particular responsibilities arising from them, a special obligation to further the interest of his employer's undertaking.

Further, s 40 of the 1977 Act states that in certain circumstances, where a patent is granted in relation to an invention made by an employee, but which belongs to an employer, and the patent is of outstanding benefit to the employer, compensation may be payable to the employee. The object of the compensation is to award the employee with a fair share of the benefit that the employer has derived or can be reasonably expected to derive from the patent.

Finally, s 42 of the 1977 Act states that any attempt by an employer to diminish the employee's rights in relation to inventions is unenforceable.

The Copyright, Designs and Patents Act 1988 introduced for the first time a design right. Section 215(3) of the 1988 Act states that where a design is created by an employee in the course of his employment, the employer is the first owner of the design right.

12.7 WRITTEN PARTICULARS OF EMPLOYMENT

A contract of employment contains both express and implied terms and need not be set out in writing (see 12.5).

However, under s 1 of the ERA an employer is now under a duty to provide each employee (whose employment is to continue for more than one month) with a written statement of certain terms and conditions of his contract of employment within two months of the commencement of employment. This new provision, however, does not apply to an employee whose employment had begun with the employer prior to the date when the provision came into force (30 November 1993). However, such employees have a right to ask for a statement in the new form either before or within three months of termination of employment and the employer must comply with the request within two months of such request being made.

The written statement must contain the following specific information.

(1) The names of both the employer and the employee.
(2) The date employment began.
(3) The date continuous employment began (if applicable).
(4) The employee's job title or a brief description of the job.
(5) The place or places of work.
(6) The scale or rate of remuneration together with payment intervals and the method of calculating remuneration.
(7) The hours of work.
(8) Holiday entitlement (including public holidays) and holiday pay containing sufficient information to enable an employee to calculate entitlement to accrued holiday pay on termination of employment.

These details must be provided in a single document that is known as the principal statement. Further additional information which must be provided must include:

(1) Terms and conditions for sickness, injury and sick pay.
(2) Pensions.
(3) Length of notice required from both employer and employee to terminate the contract.
(4) Where the employment is not intended to be permanent, the period for which it is expected to continue, or if for a fixed term the date when that term will end.
(5) Details of any collective agreements which directly affect the terms and conditions of the employment.
(6) Disciplinary rules and procedures, together with details of a person to whom an employee can appeal against any disciplinary decision.
(7) Details of a person whom an employee can approach seeking redress of any grievance relating to his employment.

These further provisions may be contained in other documentation which either the employee has reasonable opportunity of reading in the course of his employment or which are made reasonably accessible to him in some other way.

Where there are no provisions relating to any of the matters listed above, this fact must be stated in the written statement.

12.7.1 Changes to statement of terms and conditions of employment

Where there is a change to any of the terms contained in the written statement, the employer is under an obligation at the earliest opportunity, and in any event not later than one month after the change, to provide the employee with a written statement containing particulars of the change. It is important for the employer when altering an employee's contractual terms to remember that as a general rule this should only be done with the employee's consent. A unilateral variation by the employer will constitute a breach of contract and may give rise to unfair dismissal claims (see 12.11 and in particular 12.11.10).

It was held in *Cantor Fitzgerald International v Callaghan* [1999] 2 All ER 411 that where an employer unilaterally reduced his employee's pay or diminished the value of his salary package, the entire foundation of the contract of employment was undermined; thus, an emphatic denial by the employer of his obligation to pay the agreed salary or wage, or a determined resolution not to comply with his contractual obligations in relation to pay and remuneration, would normally be regarded as repudiatory. Similarly, where an employer imposed an apparently slight change on a reluctant employee by economic pressure, the employer would be entitled to treat the contract of employment as discharged by the employer's breach.

The House of Lords held in *Carmichael v National Power plc* [1999] 4 All ER 897 that, unless it appeared from the terms of documents, or from what was done or said at the time or subsequently, that the parties intended those documents to form an exclusive memorial of their relationship, it was not appropriate to determine the nature of that relationship solely by reference to the documents. Moreover, the question whether the parties intended a document or documents to be the exclusive record of the terms of their agreement was a question of fact.

12.7.2 Employees working overseas

Where an employee is required to work outside the UK for a period of more than one month, the employer must provide details of the period for which the employee has to work outside the UK, the currency in which he will be paid, details of any additional remuneration and benefit and any conditions that relate to his return to the UK.

12.7.3 Unlawful terms

A contract must not contain any term which is unlawful or contrary to public policy, for example, contracts entered into knowingly with a view to defrauding the Revenue or contracts for an immoral purpose.

12.7.4 Remedies for failure to provide written particulars

If an employee has not been provided with a written statement under ERA, s 1, or if the written statement provided raises a query as to certain terms or conditions that should have been included or referred to in it, the employee can make a complaint to an employment tribunal. Where there is no express or implied agreement concerning a particular term, a tribunal, if it considers the complaint well founded, will state the particulars which should have been given and the employer is then deemed to have provided a statement containing such particulars. Thereafter, if the employer has been in breach of any of those terms, the employee can bring an appropriate action against the employer. There is no right to claim compensation for failure on the part of an employer to provide a written statement.

A claim before the tribunal can be brought by any employee who has more than 13 weeks' continuous employment. Where the employment has been terminated, the complaint must be brought within three months of the date of the termination of the employment or within such further period as the tribunal considers reasonable where it was not reasonably practicable for the employee to bring the application within the three-month time limit.

Therefore, an employer is under a duty to provide a minimum statement of certain terms of employment. However, although the written minimum statement is relied upon in many cases, there is benefit to be obtained by the employer in providing a more detailed contract of employment. The employer can make provision for such matters as restraint of trade clauses (the importance of which is noted at 12.6 above) and any other special rules which that particular type of business may require.

Furthermore, under ERA, s 13 it is unlawful for an employer to make deductions from an employee's wages unless such deduction is required or permitted by a statutory or contractual provision, or the worker has given his prior written consent to the deduction. Therefore, incorporation into the contract of a term entitling the employer to make deductions from an employee's wages in certain circumstances ensures that the employer does not breach the Wages Act provisions (see 12.19 below).

Finally, as a matter of good practice, an employer should ensure that his employees sign a copy of their contract of employment to prove receipt.

12.8 WORK PERMITS AND IMMIGRATION MATTERS

12.8.1 Introduction

Decisions upon immigration are referred to the Home Office, but the position concerning work permits vests with the Department for Education and Employment (DfEE). If DfEE refuses to grant the permit there is no formal appeal against this decision (other than possibly requiring a judicial review of such decision where appropriate).

An EU citizen is permitted to enter the UK without first obtaining leave of the Home Office as this is guaranteed by the Treaty of Rome (see further EC Council Regulation 1612/68 and various directives under the Treaty). If a non-EU citizen is employed by an entity from a member state and that entity is carrying out a project in the UK it is probably also sufficient.

The rules regarding the issue of work permits are contained in Parts 5 and 6 of the Immigration Rules HC395 (statement of changes in Immigration Rules). If a person requires a work permit under rule 128 he must also:

(a) 'not be of an age which puts him outside the limits of employment';
(b) be 'capable of undertaking the employment specified on the work permit';
(c) 'not intend to take employment except as specified in his work permit';
(d) be 'able to maintain and accommodate himself and any dependants adequately without recourse to public funds';
(e) if the work permit is for 12 months or less show an intention to leave the UK at the end of the approved employment.

A maximum period of time a person can remain within the UK is four years (but this can be renewed).

There are special categories and considerations applicable to post-graduate doctors and dentists, working holidaymakers, seamen, seasonal workers at agricultural camps, training and work experience persons, representatives of newspapers, journalists, news agencies and broadcasting organisations etc, sole representatives of foreign firms, diplomats and their servants, ministers of religion, overseas government employees, airport operational ground staff or working for an airline.

12.8.2 Employer's duty

Section 8 of the Asylum and Immigration Act 1996 makes it an offence to employ individuals who do not have permission to live and work in the UK. An employer found guilty is liable to a fine not exceeding £5,000 for each illegal employee. It is a defence for an employer to show that before the employment began, relevant documentation was inspected, eg:

- National insurance documentation
- The employee's birth certificate or passport
- A certificate of registration or naturalisation as a British citizen
- Documentation evidencing citizenship of an EEA country (these being the EU states, Norway, Iceland and Liechtenstein).

12.8.3 DfEE requirements

Initially a potential employer must fill out a Form WP1 which should be filed as promptly as possible. An application should be made within six months before the relevant employee is required in the UK or in the case of renewal within three months before a leave expires. No application can be made by the potential employee.

Normally permits are restricted to posts requiring degree level or professional qualifications (normally with a minimum of two years' post-qualification experience). When a work permit has been issued it is the employer who becomes responsible for paying the employee and ensuring the correct tax and NICs are dealt with. An employer is required to ensure that the terms and conditions relating to such employment are equal to those UK employees doing a similar job.

12.8.4 Form WP1

This is divided into two parts. In the case of senior positions only the first part requires to be completed (eg a senior post in an international company with respect to an existing overseas employee, a board level appointment where there is no suitable alternative candidate, a post essential to investment creating jobs and capital in the UK or those occupations where there is an acute shortage nationally). This part of the form requires the following details to be included:

(a) name of proposed employer (within the UK) and proposed employee;
(b) details of job offered, period required for work permit, duties of the job and details of pay and working hours;
(c) employee's qualifications and employment record; and
(d) reasons for recruiting outside the EU and evidence which shows that there is no suitable candidate within the EU (eg details of recruitment methods, adverts etc).

Part 2 of the form needs to be completed for any other category. For such people the test is more exacting:

(1) Evidence must be shown that the need to recruit outside the EU cannot be extinguished by training an existing employee or transfer from within the EU and that the job cannot be filled by an EU worker.
(2) For key workers (ie those having technical specialist skills, knowledge or experience not readily available in the EU) evidence needs to be shown of what makes him uniquely qualified to do the job, how the business's success depends upon such recruitment and why such unique skills are essential for the job.

Employers need to supply:

(a) proof of the relevant applicant's qualification together with original references taken over the preceding two years;
(b) copies of all advertisements;
(c) if the person is in the UK and not in approved employment, his passport, the application, a copy of the employer's audited accounts and the

latest annual report (this is unnecessary if an application has been made within the preceding four-year period).

With reference to the advertisement, it needs to specify the nature of the post and should have been advertised within the last six months before the application was made in a quality newspaper with national or EU circulation or alternatively in trade journals. In the case of key worker posts suitable adverts should also have been placed in each EU country.

Separate forms are provided for entertainers and sports people (WP3) and for applications made under the Training and Work Expansion Scheme (WPR).

12.8.5 Extending a work permit

This is available so long as the work permit has not lapsed and the applicant can show that his own circumstances have not changed to take him outside the requirements of rule 128 (see 12.8.1) and that he has the DfEE's permission to remain in employment. If the Secretary of State is not satisfied that this exists he may refuse to renew the permit.

Under rule 134 a work permit holder may stay in the UK indefinitely if he has spent a continuous period of four years there with a work permit and has complied with all requirements throughout this period and he is still required for the relevant employment. All applications for extension of work permits should be made on a Form WP5 and the applicant's passport needs to be sent in at the same time as the application is made. An application should not be made earlier than three months before the permit expires but must be made before it does so.

Indefinite leave to remain is not automatic and must be applied for after four years' continuous service. The required criteria enabling the employer to obtain a work permit for that employee must continue to exist.

12.8.6 Sole representatives

The provisions in the rules are aimed at overseas companies with no UK branch or subsidiary and which wish to appoint a sole representative there. Such an employee must:

(a) have been recruited and taken on as an employee outside the UK as a representative of the firm which has its headquarters and principal place of business outside the UK and has no branch, subsidiary or other representative there;

(b) have full authority to make operational decisions on behalf of the overseas company and establish and operate a registered branch or wholly owned subsidiary in the UK;

(c) be engaged full time in this capacity and not be a majority shareholder of that company; and

(d) maintain and accommodate himself independently and adequately without recourse to public funds and hold a valid UK entry clearance in this capacity.

The period normally granted is not more than 12 months, but this can be extended if the same conditions still apply. Any such extension can be up to three years and after four years have been completed then indefinite leave can be applied for (see 12.8.5). In making an application, information concerning the following must be supplied:

(a) the time and effort the representative puts into his business;
(b) what has been achieved and what can be expected to be achieved by him; and
(c) the role he plays in the overall commercial activity of the company he represents.

To show a good case the sole representative must show that there is continuous time and effort in acting for the overseas company and that his role is more than that of just a distributor or sales agent. In particular he must have authority to take operational decisions.

There are special rules applying to those people wishing to enter or remain in the UK as independent businessmen or self-employed people, investors, and creative artists; the first two categories are dealt with here.

12.8.7 Businessmen and self-employed persons

The rules require that a person intending to establish a new business must show that he will:

(a) be bringing to the country sufficient funds of his own to establish that business, and
(b) create full-time employment for at least two people already settled in the UK (rule 203).

In addition he must provide a written statement of terms under which he is to take over or join the business, audit accounts for the business in previous years and evidence that the business will result in the increase of employment as already mentioned.

Finance

The businessman is required to have no less than £200,000 of his own money under his control and disposable within the UK (this must be held in his own name and not in the form of a trust or other investment vehicle but does not need to be lodged with a UK financial institution) and he must show that he will be investing this in his business. The business must produce sufficient funds to maintain and accommodate him and any of his dependants without recourse to employment (other than his work for the business) or public funds. He must show that he is actively involved full time in the promotion and management of the business. Rule 201 contains a number of other rules of importance:

(1) His financial investment should be proportional to the interest in the business.
(2) He must have either controlling or equal interest in the business and any partnership or directorship must not amount to disguised employment.
(3) He must bear his share of liabilities.
(4) There must be a genuine need for his investment and services in the UK.
(5) He must not need to supplement his business activities by taking or seeking employment within the UK other than for work in the business concerned.
(6) He must hold a valid UK entry clearance.

Under rule 204 the DfEE has a discretion to grant permission for a person to enter the UK for up to 12 months if he is trying to establish a business on the basis that he does not take employment. The rules provide a definition of the word 'business' as being an enterprise involving a sole trader, partnership or company registered in the UK. Before trying to obtain entry in the UK an applicant must have an entry clearance. The rules' intention is that the applicant should be the controller of a business and not a sham or substitute for someone else. The business should not result in disguised employment for the individual. In one case (*Pritpol Singh* [1972] Imm AR 154) an individual received no share of profits, could be removed from the board at any time and received a salary. It was held that the arrangement was a sham and in reality the individual was an employee.

In the case of family money there needs to be an unfettered control and an ability to dispose of it in such manner as the applicant decides. In particular it has been established that an applicant cannot set up a business on borrowed money over which he has no control or ability to service a loan and the provisions are not satisfied where an applicant merely inherits a business worth in excess of £200,000 which is already established in the UK. Money invested in a freehold property may be difficult to sell and may be able to be used for other purposes so is not acceptable under this head. The rule is that the money must be immediately available for investment and the Home Office normally expects money to be invested within 12 months of admission. Where a business incurs liabilities in the ordinary course, the individual must be able to meet these.

Where a person is taking over or joining an existing business audited accounts for the business for the previous years and evidence that his services and investment will result in an increase of employment by at least two full-time employees need to be shown. The showing of accounts and employment of employees is mandatory and the mere creation of self-employment is not sufficient (*Seyed v Secretary of State for the Home*

Department [1987] Imm AR 303, IAT). The evidence required to be given is the employment as a result of the investment.

A person intending to establish a new business in the UK must show that he is bringing sufficient monies of his own into this country to do so and that that investment will create at least two full-time jobs. There are various concessions relating to particular categories of people (for example lawyers, barristers and consultants in overseas law practices coming to England do not need to invest £200,000 provided he/they can show a bona fide purpose etc).

Entrance into the UK is normally limited to a comparatively short period of time (eg one year), but extensions are available. Normally, in order to justify an extension there must be evidence that investment has been made and employees engaged and that the requirements referred to above have all been satisfied. Where extensions have been granted which in some cases exceed four continuous years a person may apply for permanent settlement.

For nationals of Poland and Hungary there are EC association agreements which facilitate the establishment of a business.

12.8.8 The investor

Where an investor wishes to enter the UK he must show that he:

(a) has under his control and disposable within the UK an amount of no less than £1m;
(b) intends to invest not less than £750,000 of his capital within the UK by the purchase of UK bonds, share capital or loan capital in active and trading UK registered companies (excluding property investment and the investment by the applicant in bank or building society deposits, etc);
(c) wants to make the UK his main home;
(d) can maintain and accommodate himself, his dependants, etc without recourse to employment or public funds; and
(e) holds UK entry clearance.

Normally an investor is allowed to enter the UK for a period up to 12 months provided he can satisfy the above requirements. So long as those requirements remain constant he is able to apply for an extension and for indefinite leave to remain after he has spent a continuous period of four years there.

12.8.9 The future

The DfEE have recently announced that some major changes are to be made to the grant of work permits. Further announcements are expected over an approximately 12-month period commencing September 2000.

12.9 CONTINUITY OF EMPLOYMENT

A number of statutory employment protection rights are dependent upon the employee having worked continuously under a contract of employment for a minimum period of time.

The main statutory employment rights which are subject to a qualifying period of continuous employment are as follows:

Right	*Qualifying period*
Redundancy payment	Two years
Unfair dismissal	One year
Statement of written reasons for dismissal	Two years
The right to up to 40 weeks' maternity leave	One year
Statutory maternity pay	26 weeks before the beginning of the 14th week before the expected week of confinement
Written particulars of employment	Two months
Minimum notice period	One month
Guarantee payment	One month ending with the day before the workless day or more than three months if engaged on a fixed term or specific task contract for three months or less
Medical suspension payment	One month ending on the day before suspension begins or more than three months if engaged on a fixed term or specific task contract for three months or less

An employee's period of continuous employment is determined on a week by week basis, although it is the total number of calendar months or years of employment attained that is important for qualifying periods or statutory rights. The period begins with the day on which the employee actually commences work and ends on the day that is to be ascertained in accordance with the appropriate rules. In most cases this will be the last day the employee works. Once an employee has commenced work there is, subject to contrary evidence, a presumption that employment is continuous. Therefore, it is important to look at the rules for calculating what weeks count towards a period of continuous employment and under what circumstances continuity will be broken.

12.9.1 Weeks which count

The ERA set out detailed rules regarding what weeks counted in calculating an employee's period of continuous employment. Continuous employment is calculated in the same way for part-time and full-time employees, irrespective of hours worked.

Any week during which an employee's relations with his employer are governed by a contract of employment count in calculating continuity.

12.9.2 Periods where no contract of employment exists

Periods in which there is no contract of employment may nevertheless count as periods of employment for continuous employment purposes. The situations in which continuity of employment are preserved are set out below. If in any week the employee is for the whole or the part of that week:

(1) incapable of work in consequence of illness or injury, a period of not more than 26 weeks under this provision counts in preserved continuity;
(2) absent from work on account of a temporary cessation of work, this covers the situation where an employee is habitually re-engaged by an employer and the periods of no employment in between are relatively short;
(3) absent from work in circumstances such that, by arrangement or custom, he is regarded as continuing in the employment of his employer for all or any purpose, this would cover such instances as where an employee is absent on unpaid leave;
(4) absent from work wholly or partly because of pregnancy or childbirth, and furthermore in relation to the right to return to work after absence for pregnancy or childbirth, if an employee exercises her right to return in accordance with ERA, s 71 (see 12.14.4 below), all weeks during that period of absence count in calculating continuity.

Further instances in which continuity is preserved are as follows:

(1) Under ERA, ss 94 (unfair dismissal) and 193 (redundancy payment) when employment is terminated in a situation where notice should have been given, but was not, and as a result the employee did not attain the qualifying condition of two years' service for claims for unfair dismissal or a redundancy payment, the employee's employment is treated as continuing until the expiry of the statutory minimum notice period that that employee would have been entitled to.
(2) Section 210(5) of ERA applies to preserve continuity of employment where an employee's contract of employment is renewed or he is re-engaged under a new contract of employment in pursuance of an offer made by his employer before the ending of his employment under a previous contract or within four weeks thereafter.
(3) An employee who is dismissed and then reinstated or re-engaged

pursuant to an industrial tribunal award or by a settlement through ACAS has continuity preserved, notwithstanding the period between dismissal and reinstatement.

(4) On the transfer of a trade or business from one person to another, the period of employment of an employee with the transferor company counts as a period of employment with the transferee company and consequently continuity of employment is preserved (see 12.25 below).

(5) If an employee's employment is transferred to another employer who at the time the employee enters his employment is an 'associated' employer of the former employer, again that employee's continuity of employment is preserved. Employers are treated as associated if one is a company of which the other (directly or indirectly) has control, or if both are companies of which a third person (directly or indirectly) has control.

12.9.3 Weeks which do not count but which do not break continuity

Certain weeks do not count in the calculation of continuous employment, but do not operate so as to break continuity. Where an employee's period of employment includes intervals which do not count in calculating continuity, but which do not break it, the commencement of the employee's continuous employment is treated as having been postponed by the number of days which do not count. Circumstances where these rules apply are:

(1) any week during which an employee takes part in a strike or is absent from work because of a lock-out;

(2) any week during which an employee is employed overseas.

This applies only in calculating the qualifying period and amount for redundancy payment purposes.

12.9.4 Statutory maternity pay (SMP)

For the purposes of calculating entitlement to SMP, continuous employment is defined in Statutory Maternity Pay (General) Regulations 1986 (SI No 1069), Part III. The definition is, however, much the same as discussed above.

12.10 WORKING TIME

The Working Time Regulations 1998 (SI No 1833), as amended by the Working Time Regulations 1999 (SI No 3372), provide as follows.

12.10.1 Weekly limits

Workers have the right not to work more than an average of 48 hours in any seven-day period. The average is calculated, normally, using a 17-week period of assessment, but this can be extended to 26 weeks if the workers are covered by derogations of up to 12 months by a collective and/or workforce agreement between employer and works. 'Working time' means the time when a worker is working and at his employer's disposal and carrying out his activities or duties.

12.10.2 Night work

Night workers have the right not to be required to work more than an average of eight hours in any 24-hour period. The standard averaging period is again 17 weeks, but can be extended by the derogations or by an agreement between employer and workers. If the work involves special hazards or heavy physical or mental strain, the eight-hour limit is absolute.

Adult night workers have the right to a free health assessment (and a young worker to a health and capacities assessment) before being required to perform night work, and periodically thereafter. All night workers are entitled to be transferred to day work if a registered medical practitioner has advised that the worker is suffering health problems associated with night work and if there is suitable day work available.

12.10.3 Daily rest periods

Adult workers are entitled to 11 hours of consecutive rest in each 24-hour period. Young workers are entitled to 12 hours of consecutive rest in each 24-hour period unless periods of work are split up over the day or are of short duration.

12.10.4 Weekly rest periods

Adult workers are entitled to an uninterrupted rest period of not less than 24 hours in each seven-day period. This may be averaged over a two-week period. Young workers are entitled to two days of rest in each week. This cannot be averaged over a two-week period, but can be reduced to 36 hours where justified by 'technical or organisation reasons'.

12.10.5 Rest breaks

Adult workers who work more than six hours in any day are entitled to a rest break. The length of the rest break may be determined by a collective or workforce agreement. If, however, there is no agreement, the worker's break must be at least 20 minutes long. Young workers are entitled to a minimum 30-minute rest break if they work for longer than 4½ hours.

12.10.6 Paid annual leave

Subject to the exclusion identified below, workers have the right to four weeks' annual leave. The annual leave cannot be paid in lieu except in the event of termination.

12.10.7 Qualifications

The Regulations apply to workers over the minimum school-leaving age. The definition of 'worker' covers those with a contract of employment plus a wider group who undertake work under other forms of contract (eg agency and temporary workers, freelancers, etc). To qualify for the rights relating to night work, the worker's daily working time must include at least three hours of night time (generally 11 pm to 6 am).

To qualify for the right to paid annual leave, the worker must have continuous employment of not less than 13 weeks.

To qualify as a 'young worker' for the purposes of the Regulations, the worker must be over the minimum school-leaving age but under 18.

12.10.8 Specific exclusions

In specified circumstances workers will not have the rights they would otherwise have in respect of rest breaks, daily rest, weekly rest and night work. The specified circumstances include workers engaged in security and surveillance activities, activities involving the need for continuity of service of production (such as dock work, hospital services, the provision of utilities, civil protection services, agriculture) and where there is a foreseeable surge of activity such as in tourism. Workers will, however, be entitled to compensatory rest of an equivalent period or where this is not possible appropriate protection.

Workers whose working time is not measured or predetermined, or who can themselves determine the duration of their working time, are excepted from provisions of the Regulations relating to weekly working time, night work, rest periods and breaks. Where a worker's working time is partly measured, predetermined or determined by the worker and partly not, the provisions relating to weekly working time and to that part of the night work will only apply in relation to that part of the worker's work which is measured, predetermined or cannot be determined by the worker himself.

Shift workers are excluded from taking their entitlements to daily or weekly rest where this is impossible. There is a similar exception for those engaged in activities involving periods of work split up over the day. In both cases, the workers will be entitled to compensatory rest.

The maximum weekly working time limit and the entitlements in respect of night work will not apply to domestic servants employed in a private household.

Workers' entitlements under the provisions in relation to night work, rest breaks, daily rest and/or weekly rest may be modified or excluded by a collective agreement and/or a workforce agreement. A workforce agreement is one reached between the employer and workers the terms and conditions of which are not determined by reference to a collective agreement or their representatives. Compensatory rest must be given if there is any such modification/exclusion.

The maximum weekly working hours limit will not apply in respect of workers who enter into an individual voluntary arrangement with their employer that the limit will not apply. Any such agreement must be terminable upon notice (maximum of three months, but in default of express provision, seven days).

12.10.9 Remedies

Complaint may be made to an employment tribunal where there has been a failure to provide paid annual leave, rest breaks, daily rest or weekly rest. The complaint must be brought within three months of the act or omission complained of unless the tribunal considers it was not reasonably practicable to do so. The tribunal may make a declaration that the complaint is well founded and award compensation.

Note also that there are additional restrictions on the working time of children (essentially 12- to 18-year-olds) which are contained in the Children and Young Persons Act 1993, as amended by s 2 of the Children (Protection) at Work Regulations 1998 (SI No 276).

12.11 UNFAIR DISMISSAL

Sections 94–110 of ERA concern the right of an employee, subject to certain qualifying conditions, not to be unfairly dismissed by his employer. An affected employee may bring a claim of unfair dismissal before an industrial tribunal. If the claim is successful, the tribunal may order the employer to reinstate or re-engage the employee and/or to pay compensation.

The interpretation of the law of unfair dismissal has resulted in substantial case law, but many decisions can only be explained on their own specific facts. However, the decisions do give guidance and reference has been made to leading cases in particular areas of unfair dismissal law.

12.11.1 The basis of a claim

Pre-conditions

In order for the employee to be able to bring a claim for unfair dismissal before a tribunal he must first show that he was employed by the employer under a contract of employment; that he was dismissed by the employer; and that he has attained the necessary two-year period of continuous employment.

Certain employees are excluded from bringing a claim, for example when the employee is over the normal retirement age in the particular employment in question; or he is working abroad; or he has been dismissed in connection with a lock-out or strike. The burden of proof rests with the employee to show that he satisfies the necessary qualifying conditions.

Dismissal by the employer

Sections 95 and 136 of ERA state that an employee is to be treated as having been dismissed if and only if:

(1) the contract under which he is employed by the employer is terminated by the employer with or without notice; or

(2) where under that contract he is employed for a fixed term and that term expires without being renewed under the same contract; or

(3) the employee terminates that contract with or without notice, in circumstances in which he is entitled to terminate the contract without notice by reason of the employer's conduct (what is known as 'constructive dismissal').

Termination by the employer

It is important to note that once an employer gives notice of dismissal to an employee, as a general rule this cannot be withdrawn without the employee's consent. Likewise, the same principle applies to notice of resignation given by the employee.

Expiry of a fixed term contract

The expiry of a fixed term contract which is not renewed by the employer is a dismissal for unfair dismissal purposes. However, under ERA, s 197 an employer and employee can agree in writing to exclude the employee's right to claim unfair dismissal arising out of the non-renewal of the contract where the employee is employed under a fixed term of one year or more. If it is intended to exclude such rights, provision should be made in the contract of employment itself.

It was held in *BBC v Kelly-Phillips* [1998] 2 All ER 845 that the reference to a contract for a fixed term included a contract which had been varied by an extension of the term under the same contract.

Constructive dismissal

Constructive dismissal occurs where an employer has committed a repudiatory breach of the employee's contract of employment, which entitles the employee to resign. The leading case in this area is the Court of Appeal decision in *Western Excavating (ECC) Ltd v Sharp* [1978] IRLR 27. There must be an intention by the employer to break one or more of the essential terms of the employee's employment. It is not sufficient that the employer has merely acted unreasonably.

The repudiatory breach by the employer need not be of an express term of the contract, but could be a breach of an implied term such as that of mutual trust and confidence (see 12.5.1 above). Examples of actions by an employer which may justify an employee claiming constructive dismissal are a unilateral reduction in an employee's pay or a substantial change in the nature of the employee's job.

It is important that an employee must not affirm the breach of contract by his employer by delaying his resignation for a substantial period of time or by doing some other act which is inconsistent with his acceptance of the breach.

12.11.2 Qualifying period

An employee must have been continuously employed for a period of at least two years at the effective date of termination (EDT) to be able to bring a claim for unfair dismissal. The period of continuous employment is calculated from the date of commencement to the effective date of termination. The two-year period of qualification was lowered to one year with effect from 1 June 1999 by the Unfair Dismissal and Statement of Reasons for Dismissal (Variation of Qualifying Period) Order 1999 (SI No 1436). The reduction takes effect in all cases where the EDT falls on or after that date. The EDT is defined in ERA, s 97(1) as:

(1) where an employee's employment is terminated by notice, either by the employer or the employee himself, the date on which that notice expires;

(2) where an employee's employment is terminated without notice, the date on which that termination takes effect;

(3) where an employee is employed under a fixed term contract which expires without the term being renewed, the date on which that term expires.

In most instances the EDT is the date on which the employee finishes work. However, where an employee is dismissed without notice or with notice that is less than the statutory minimum, the EDT is the date on which the minimum statutory notice would have expired if it had been given (see 12.9.2

above). Accordingly, an employee who is dismissed without notice one week short of attaining one year's continuous employment is nevertheless, under the operation of this rule, deemed as having one year's continuous employment and therefore is entitled to bring a claim for unfair dismissal.

12.11.3 The reasons for dismissal

Once the employee has established that he has been dismissed and that he satisfies the other qualifying conditions, the burden of proof switches to the employer to show:

(1) the reason or the principal reason for the dismissal; and
(2) that reason was one of the *prima facie* fair reasons set out in ERA, s 98.

Section 98 sets out the following *prima facie* fair reasons for dismissal:

(1) a reason related to the capability or qualifications of the employee to carry out the particular job which he was employed to do;
(2) a reason relating to the employee's conduct;
(3) the employee's redundancy;
(4) that the employee could not continue in his position without contravening a duty or restriction imposed by or under an enactment;
(5) some other substantial reason of a kind such as to justify the dismissal of an employee holding the position which that employee held.

12.11.4 Fairness – has the employer acted reasonably?

If the employer has established one of the *prima facie* fair reasons set out in ERA, s 98, the tribunal will then go on to consider the question of whether the dismissal was fair or unfair in all the circumstances of the particular case (having regard to equity and the substantial merits of the case). The question is whether the employer acted reasonably in treating the reason for dismissal as a sufficient reason for dismissing the employee.

The burden of proof does not rest on either party, but it is for the tribunal to be satisfied that the employer acted reasonably when dismissing the employee. A leading case on this point is *Iceland Frozen Foods Ltd v Jones* (1982) IRLR 439, in which the EAT stated that it was the function of an employment tribunal to determine whether in the particular circumstances of each case the decision by the employer to dismiss the employee fell within the band of reasonable responses which a reasonable employer might have adopted. If the dismissal falls within the band, then it is fair; if it does not, then it is unfair. It is not for the tribunal, in judging whether the employer acted reasonably, to substitute for the employer's decision what they believe the right course of action should have been. In many instances one employer might have dismissed whereas another might have taken some other form of disciplinary action, but either decision could fall within the band of reasonable responses.

It is also for an employer, to show that he has acted reasonably, to have adopted fair procedures when taking a decision to dismiss an employee. Until the House of Lords' decision in *Polkey v AE Dayton Services Ltd* [1988] ICR 142, it was believed that if the employer had adopted an unfair procedure in dismissing an employee, but established that if he adopted a fair procedure, the employee would still have been dismissed, then that dismissal could still be fair. However, in *Polkey* the House of Lords held that this was the wrong approach and that fair procedures must be followed regardless of whether or not a failure to do so would in fact not affect the ultimate outcome.

12.11.5 Automatically unfair dismissals

Certain dismissals are deemed to be automatically unfair and are not subject to the reasonableness tests set out in ERA, s 98(4). Also in certain cases, an employee may be able to bring a complaint despite the fact that he does not satisfy the necessary qualifying condition regarding continuous employment:

Trade union related dismissals

It is automatically unfair for an employer to dismiss an employee for either:

(1) being or proposing to become a member of an independent trade union; or
(2) refusing to join or remain a member of a trade union; or
(3) taking part or proposing to take part in union related activities at an appropriate time, ie outside working hours or within working hours if agreed with the employer.

An employee can bring a claim under this heading irrespective of the fact that he may not have two years' continuous service or that he may be over the age of 65 or the normal retiring age in his employment. In such a case, the burden of proof rests upon the employee to show that the reason for the dismissal was union related. However, if he does satisfy the necessary qualifying conditions, it is for the employer to prove the reason for dismissal in the usual way.

Maternity related dismissals

Under ERA, s 99(1), it is automatically unfair for an employer to dismiss any woman irrespective of her hours of work or length of service if the sole or principal reason for her dismissal is that she was pregnant or was for any other maternity related reason. For further discussion, see 12.14.7 below.

Health and safety related dismissals

Section 100 of ERA now makes it automatically unfair for an employer to dismiss an employee for certain health and safety reasons. Again, no qualifying period of employment is required.

Assertion of statutory rights

Under ERA, s 104, it is automatically unfair to dismiss an employee if the reason or principal reason for the dismissal was the allegation by an employee that his employer had infringed a statutory right or that the employee had brought proceedings to enforce a particular right. The relevant statutory rights include, for example, claims made under ERA, s 13 (protection of wages) and claims to a written statement of terms under ERA, s 1. Again, no qualifying period of employment is required.

Spent convictions

Where under the Rehabilitation of Offenders Act 1974 a conviction has been spent, it is automatically unfair for an employer to dismiss an employee for failure to disclose such a spent conviction.

Transfer of undertaking related dismissals

It is automatically unfair to dismiss an employee where that dismissal is for a reason connected with the transfer of an undertaking unless such dismissal can be justified as being for an ETO reason entailing changes in the workforce (see 12.25 below).

Redundancy – unfair reasons for selection

It is automatically unfair for an employee to be selected for redundancy because he is a trade union member or has refused to become one, or an employee is selected for redundancy because she is pregnant; or where the employee is selected for redundancy in breach of an agreed practice or customary arrangement.

Sunday working

The Sunday Trading Act 1994 provides that if a protected shop worker is dismissed or selected for redundancy, and the reason or principal reason was a refusal to work on a Sunday, or the worker opted out of such work, the dismissal will be unfair. No service qualification is required for an unfair dismissal claim to be brought in such a case.

Whistleblowing

Under the ERA, as amended by the Public Interest (Disclosure) Act 1998, the dismissal of an employee because, or principally because, he made a protected disclosure is automatically unfair. There is no qualifying period nor upper age limit.

12.11.6 Grounds for dismissal

Capability

Capability is defined as being assessed by reference to skill, aptitude, health or any other physical or mental quality. Capability falls into two classes: (1) the inability of an employee to carry out his particular job to the required standard (ie incompetence), and (2) ill health.

Incompetence

In incompetency cases it is important for the employer to show:

(a) what was required of the employee;
(b) that the employee was aware of what was required; and
(c) that he fell short of the required standard.

Complaints about an employee's incompetence must relate to 'work of the kind which he was employed by the employer to do'. Therefore, in certain circumstances a single act of incompetence or negligence may be sufficient to justify dismissal in some cases. For example, in *Alidair Ltd v Taylor* [1978] ICR 445 an airline pilot who landed his aircraft negligently so as to put the lives of his passengers at risk was fairly dismissed by his employer in view of his gross incompetence and the potentially calamitous consequences that his actions could have had.

However, most incompetency cases involve a number of relatively minor incidents, which taken in isolation are relatively unimportant but which accumulated over a sufficient period of time may constitute a reason for dismissal. In cases of this kind, it is important for an employer to adopt a fair procedure in dealing with the employee and such procedure should include the following steps:

(1) Where an employee falls short of the required standards, the employer should arrange a meeting with him (and his representative) at which he should be informed of the areas in which he is falling short of those standards and the time period during which his performance must improve. The employee should also be told that if the required improvement does not occur, he will receive a formal written warning and that if after that time further improvement is not seen, the ultimate sanction of dismissal may be considered.

(2) If no improvement is apparent, the employee should be called to a

second meeting, together with his representative, at which he should be warned of the areas in which he has failed to improve and he should be given the opportunity to explain why there has been no improvement. The employee should be given a formal written warning. At the conclusion of that meeting he should be informed that he will be given a further period in which to improve, but that if there is no substantial improvement within that time then such failure will result in his dismissal.

(3) When no further improvement occurs, a third meeting should be called at which the employer should be given the opportunity to state his case and notice of dismissal will be given. The employee should then be given the opportunity to appeal against the decision to dismiss him.

In certain circumstances, the employer should consider further training for the employee. If the employee can show that the reason for his incompetence is that the employer failed to provide adequate training or adequate tools to perform the task satisfactorily, then a dismissal may well be unfair. The provision of further training and supervision is particularly important where an employee has been recently promoted. Furthermore, an employer should consider whether he has other work available to which the employee would be better suited.

Whether an employer follows all the procedural steps outlined above depends upon the circumstances of each particular case. In the case of a senior employee, he should reasonably be expected to be aware of the standards that are required of him and therefore several warnings may not be appropriate. However, it is advisable that, except in cases of clear gross incompetence, warnings should always be provided.

Illness

Frustration   Where ill health may make future performance of the employment contract impossible, the contract may be frustrated and there will be no dismissal of the employee. However, frustration of a contract is rare in these circumstances. For a discussion of the law relating to frustration of contracts, see 12.13.1 below.

Long-term sickness   As it is not normally difficult to show that the reason for dismissal was ill health, attention is generally focused on whether the employer acted reasonably in treating ill health absenteeism as sufficient grounds for dismissal. Therefore, of primary importance is the adoption by the employer of a fair procedure.

Before dismissing an employee for ill health the employer should be aware of the current medical position. With the employee's consent, he should obtain a report from the employee's doctor and in many circumstances also have the employee examined, with his consent, by the employer's own doctor.

In *Spencer v Paragon Wallpapers Ltd* [1976] IRLR 373 and *East Lindsey District Council v Daubney* [1977] ICR 566 various principles were set out which would indicate a fair procedure had been adopted in relation to the dismissal of an employee on ill health grounds. The employer having informed himself of the employee's medical condition should consider the following factors:

(1) The nature of the illness.
(2) The likelihood of the illness recurring.
(3) The requirements of his business and the need for the job to be done. Is it essential, because of the nature of the job, that the position needs to be filled quickly, or can the remaining employees cover the work for a period of time?
(4) The employee's past sickness record.
(5) Whether there is an alternative position within the company which would be more suitable to the employee.

Also throughout the period of illness the employer should consult with the employee on a regular basis. Failure to consult with the employee will in most cases render a dismissal unfair.

Persistent short-term absenteeism   In cases where there is persistent short-term absenteeism due to unrelated illnesses, a medical examination may not be appropriate. In such circumstances the employee should be told what level of attendance he is expected to attain and be warned that if there is no improvement within a set period, this may result in his dismissal. The situation should then be monitored for a period of time (*International Sports Co Ltd v Thompson* [1980] IRLR 340).

Misconduct

Cases of misconduct fall into two categories: first single acts of misconduct not sufficient by themselves to justify dismissal, and secondly gross misconduct which may entitle an employer to dismiss an employee summarily (without notice). Examples of categories of gross misconduct would include theft, fraud, deliberate falsification of records, fighting, serious incapability through alcohol, being under the influence of illegal drugs, serious negligence which causes loss, damage or injury and serious acts of insubordination. Whereas any of the above examples may justify summary dismissal, in contrast a one-off incident of bad timekeeping would not.

It was stated in *British Home Stores Ltd v Burchell* [1980] ICR 303 that where an employer dismisses an employee for misconduct, the employer must establish that he had a belief that the employee was guilty of misconduct. Furthermore, the employer must have had reasonable grounds for that belief, and that in forming that reasonable belief he had carried out a reasonable investigation into all the circumstances of the matter.

Accordingly, it can be seen that the burden of proof in such cases is not as high as the burden of proof of reasonable doubt in a criminal court.

Therefore, if an employer has a reasonable belief that one of a number of employees is guilty of dishonesty and following a full and proper investigation into the matter it cannot identify the particular employee responsible, it may be reasonable for the employer to dismiss all those who could have been responsible (*Frames Snooker Centre v Boyce* [1992] IRLR 472).

Furthermore, in cases where an employee is arrested by the police and criminal charges are pending, an employer does not have to wait for the outcome of the criminal case before deciding what action to take. If the employer carries out his own investigation and as a result dismisses the employee for dishonesty, such dismissal may be held to be reasonable, even if the employee is subsequently acquitted at trial.

The conduct for which an employee is dismissed usually relates to his behaviour during his employment. However, in certain instances behaviour outside of employment may affect his continued employment. For example, a teacher who has a conviction for indecent assault on a child, even though such conviction was for an offence outside his normal working hours, may be unsuitable to continue on his employment.

12.11.7 Dismissal procedures

Even in cases of serious misconduct, it is important that employers follow a fair procedure when dealing with cases of misconduct by employees. Failure to follow a fair procedure is likely to result in the dismissal being unfair. It is therefore important for all employers to have properly set out disciplinary procedures.

Two publications by ACAS set out certain steps which should be included in fair disciplinary procedures. These two publications are the ACAS 1977 Code of Practice on Disciplinary Practice and Procedures in Work and the 1987 Advisory Handbook *Discipline at Work*.

Paragraph 10 of the 1977 Code states that procedures should:

(1) Be in writing.
(2) Specify to whom they apply.
(3) Provide for matters to be dealt with quickly.
(4) Indicate the disciplinary actions which may be taken.
(5) Specify the levels of management which have the authority to take the various forms of disciplinary action, ensuring that immediate superiors do not normally have the power to dismiss without reference to senior management.
(6) Provide for individuals to be informed of the complaints against them and to be given an opportunity to state their case before decisions are reached.
(7) Give individuals the right to be accompanied by a trade union representative or by a fellow employee of their choice.
(8) Ensure that, except for gross misconduct, no employees are dismissed for a first breach of discipline.

(9) Ensure that disciplinary action is not taken until the case has been carefully investigated.

(10) Ensure that individuals are given an explanation for any penalty imposed.

(11) Provide for a right of appeal and specify the procedure to be followed.

When a matter of misconduct arises, the incident should be fully investigated immediately and witness statements taken if appropriate. Where witness statements are taken and these are the main evidence which are relied upon in taking disciplinary action against an employee it is appropriate for copies of the statements to be provided to the employee in question.

In cases of suspected serious misconduct, an employer should consider a brief period of suspension with pay. However, it is important to note that unless there is express provision in an employer's disciplinary procedures which are incorporated into a contract of employment, the employer does not have the right to suspend an employee. In the absence of this being an express term of the contract, any suspension is a fundamental breach of the contract of employment by the employer which entitles the employee to resign and claim constructive dismissal.

Before a disciplinary decision is taken, a hearing should be held at which the employee is given an opportunity to state his case. He should be given the opportunity of having a fellow employee or trade union representative present at the meeting.

An employer, before deciding on the appropriate penalty, must take account of the employee's record and any other relevant factors. It is good practice for an employer to adjourn the hearing to consider a case before giving his decision. Once a decision has been made, this should be notified to the employee in writing and the employee should be informed of his right of appeal. The letter should state how the appeal should be made and to whom. Any appeal should be conducted by a member of senior management who has not been involved in the previous decision or investigation.

It is essential that records are kept of all disciplinary proceedings and copies of letters are retained on an employee's personnel file as this will be important evidence should an unfair dismissal claim be made to an industrial tribunal.

12.11.8 Redundancy

Where the reason or the principal reason for an employee's dismissal is redundancy it may be unfair in two circumstances.

First, a dismissal is automatically unfair if the circumstances constituting the redundancy applied equally to one or more employees in the same undertaking who held positions similar to that held by the dismissed employee and who have not been dismissed by the employer, and the reason for the selection for dismissal was either

(i) trade union related,
(ii) health and safety related,
(iii) related to an assertion by him of his statutory rights,
(iv) maternity related, or
(v) he was selected in contravention of a customary arrangement or agreed redundancy procedure and there were no special reasons justifying a departure from that arrangement or procedure.

Secondly, where the dismissal is not automatically unfair under the above principle, it may be still be unfair in that it does not fulfil the reasonableness tests contained in ERA, s 98(4). For example, the failure to consult may render a dismissal unfair (see 12.12.3 below).

In *Williams v Compair Maxam Ltd* [1982] ICR 156 the EAT sought to lay down certain principles on which a fair selection procedure for redundancy should be based. These principles were laid down in a case where there was a recognised trade union, but are generally accepted as good practice (although failure to follow all the steps would not necessarily render a dismissal unfair). The employer should:

(1) give as much warning as possible of impending redundancies to enable the employees concerned or the recognised trade union (if appropriate) to take early steps to inform themselves of the relevant facts, consider possible alternative solutions and, if necessary, find alternative employment;
(2) consult the recognised trade union (if appropriate) of the best means by which the desired result can be achieved fairly and with as little hardship to the employees as possible;
(3) seek to establish criteria for selection which so far as possible do not depend solely upon the opinion of the person making the selection, but can be objectively checked against such matters as attendance record, efficiency at the job, experience or length of service;
(4) ensure that the selection is made fairly in accordance with those criteria;
(5) see whether instead of dismissing an employee he can offer him alternative employment.

However, these principles should now be considered in the light of TULR(C)A, s 188, which imposes more onerous consultation duties upon an employer (see 12.12.3 below).

It is important to emphasise that the necessity for consultation before redundancy notices are sent out is extremely important. Consultation must take place with both the affected employees and also the recognised trade union (if relevant). It would be very rare for a redundancy dismissal to be held to be fair where there has been no consultation.

12.11.9 Contravention of any enactment – illegality

If an employee is dismissed by his employer because the employee could not continue to work in the position he held without breaking the law, such dismissal will be for a *prima facie* fair reason. This must be a matter of fact; it is not enough that the employer genuinely believes that he would be breaking the law by continuing to employ the employee.

The employer must still act reasonably in all the circumstances, having regard to the size and administrative resources of his organisation. An employer should arrange a meeting at which the employee should be informed of the situation and invited to express his views. In appropriate cases an employer should consider whether it or an associated company has a suitable vacancy which the employee can be offered instead.

A common example of a fair dismissal under this head would be where it is an integral part of an employee's job to drive a motor vehicle and he has been disqualified from holding a valid licence.

12.11.10 Some other substantial reason

Section 98 of ERA provides a 'catch all' potentially fair reason for dismissal which is for 'some other substantial reason of a kind such as to justify the dismissal of an employee holding the position which that employee held'. The employer is required to show only that the other substantial reason for dismissal was a potentially fair one. Once the reason has been established, the industrial tribunal must then decide whether the employer acted reasonably under s 98(4) in dismissing for that reason.

The most common example of a *prima facie* fair dismissal falling within this category is where an employer has had to undergo a necessary reorganisation of his business. This may apply in cases, for example, where as a result of the reorganisation he has had to alter his employees' terms and conditions of employment. Usually such alteration would be a fundamental breach of the contract of employment entitling the employee to resign and claim constructive dismissal. However, if the employer can show that it was *prima facie* fair because of the necessity of the business reorganisation, then the tribunal will go on to consider whether the employer had acted reasonably in accordance with all the circumstances under s 98(4).

12.11.11 Remedies

Procedure

Where an employee considers that he has been unfairly dismissed, providing that he satisfies the necessary qualifying conditions, he should present a claim for unfair dismissal to an employment tribunal within three months of the effective date of termination. The tribunal has a discretion to allow a complaint outside the three-month time limit if it considers that it was not reasonably practicable for the employee to bring the claim within the appropriate time limit.

Tribunal awards

If a tribunal considers that an employee has been unfairly dismissed, it must then decide which remedy is appropriate. There are three basic remedies available, as follows:

Reinstatement

This is an order that the employer should treat the employee in all respects as if he had not been dismissed. If the tribunal makes a reinstatement order the employee is entitled not only to be restored to his previous position with the company, but also to an amount equal to the salary he would have received had he continued to be employed, together with any benefits he would have been entitled to (eg Christmas bonus, wage increase). The tribunal in making such an order must spell out the relevant terms and conditions which apply to the employee and the date by which reinstatement is to take effect.

Re-engagement

This is an order that the employee be re-engaged by the employer (or the employer's successor or an associated employer) in employment that is comparable to that from which he was dismissed or in other suitable employment. If the tribunal makes such an order it must state the employer's identity, the nature of the employment, the rate of pay, the amount of arrears of pay which the employee is entitled to and other benefits and privileges which must be restored to the employee, and the date on which the re-engagement order is to take effect.

Reinstatement and re-engagement

In considering whether to make both orders, the tribunal must consider a number of factors including whether the employee wishes to be reinstated and whether it is practicable for an employer to comply with an order for reinstatement or re-engagement. In most instances such orders are not appropriate because the working relationship has broken down so completely that it is not practicable to expect the employer and the employee to work together again.

Additional tribunal award

If a reinstatement or re-engagement order is made by an industrial tribunal and an employer fails to comply with it this may result in the employee being given an additional award, unless the employer can show that it was not reasonably practicable for him to comply with the order. The additional award is normally an amount between 26 and 52 weeks' pay. A week's pay is subject to the statutory limit of £230. The award may exceed these limits, where necessary, to enable the award to fully compensate for the loss suffered from the date the employee was dismissed to the date he should have been reinstated.

Compensation

Compensation for unfair dismissal has two elements: a basic award and a compensatory award.

Basic award

The basic award is calculated in the same way as a redundancy payment and is dependent upon the employee's gross weekly pay, length of service and age at the date of termination. The amount of a week's pay is subject to a statutory maximum of £230 and the maximum number of years to be taken into account is 20.

The number of complete years of continuous employment are taken into account in calculating the basic award. Consequently, the employee receives:

(1) One and a half week's pay for each full year of employment in which the employee was not below the age of 41.
(2) One week's pay for each full year of employment in which the employee was not aged below 22.
(3) Half a week's pay for each year of employment not falling within (1) or (2) above.

Consequently the maximum basic award is $20 \times 1\frac{1}{2} \times 230 = £6,900$.

The basic award may be reduced in four circumstances:

(a) where the employee's conduct before dismissal or before being given notice of dismissal was such that it was just and equitable to reduce the award;
(b) where the employee has already received a redundancy payment in relation to the same dismissal;
(c) the employee has unreasonably refused an offer of reinstatement;
(d) the employee is aged 64 on his effective date of termination, in which case the basic award is reduced by $\frac{1}{12}$ for each whole month during which the employee has been employed since his 64th birthday.

Compensatory award

The compensatory award is intended to restore the employee to the position which he had prior to his dismissal. The amount of compensation is such sum as the tribunal considers just and equitable in all the circumstances, having regard to the loss sustained by the employee as a consequence of the dismissal where that loss can be attributed to action taken by the employer. The maximum award as laid down by the Employment Relations Act 1999 is £50,000.

In assessing the compensatory award the main heads of compensation (see *Norton Tool Co Ltd v Tewson* [1972] ICR 501) are:

(1) *Loss of earnings* from the date of dismissal to the date of the tribunal hearing. This figure is calculated net of tax and NI contributions, and any payment in lieu of notice that the employee received is taken into account. Also, if an employee has found a new job, his earnings in that new employment are also taken into account.

(2) *Future loss of earnings.* If an employee is still unemployed at the date of the hearing, or is earning less than he previously earned, the tribunal will award a sum for future loss of earnings for such period as it considers reasonable.

(3) *Loss of benefits in kind.* These would include such things as loss of company car, medical insurance and free or subsidised accommodation. In calculating the loss suffered by an employee as a result of losing such benefits, the correct approach in calculating the loss is the cost to the employee in replacing the lost benefits.

In calculating the loss of benefit of using a company car, reference can be made to AA guidelines. See *Shore v Downs Surgical plc* [1984] ICR 532.

(4) *Loss of pension rights.*

(5) *Loss of statutory rights.* The tribunal awards a nominal figure for loss of the protection from unfair dismissal or the right to a redundancy payment for the first one or two years of any new employment. The usual figure awarded in this respect is £200.

(6) Expenses reasonably incurred as a result of the dismissal. In *Leech v Berger Jonsen and Nicholson Ltd* [1972] IRLR 58, expenses incurred in looking for new employment were a recoverable loss.

A tribunal may also award compensation for loss of the accrued right to the statutory minimum period of notice.

Reduction of the compensatory award

A tribunal may reduce the level of any compensatory award for the following reasons:

(1) *Contributory fault.* Where a tribunal finds that an employee has to any extent caused or contributed to his own dismissal by his actions it reduces the amount of the compensatory award by such proportion as it considers just and equitable (see *W Devis & Sons Ltd v Atkins* [1977] ICR 662). In rare cases the reduction may be as much as 100%.

(2) *Where the employee has failed to take reasonable steps to mitigate his loss.* The employee is under a duty to mitigate his loss. He should therefore take all reasonable steps to find alternative employment. If he does not do so, this may be taken into account in reducing the compensatory award. It is important to note that an employee is not obliged to accept the first job offered irrespective of pay and conditions.

(3) *Where the tribunal considers a reduction just and equitable.* The tribunal has the power to reduce the compensatory award to reflect

general considerations of fairness. The cases where tribunals may decide that it is just and equitable to reduce compensation under this head can be divided roughly into two groups:

(a) where, by the time of the hearing, the employer can show that the employee is guilty of misconduct which would have merited dismissal, even if the employer did not know about that misconduct at the time of the dismissal; and

(b) where the employee could have been fairly dismissed at a later date or if the employer had followed a fair procedure. See *Chaplin v HJ Rawlinson Ltd* [1991] ICR 553.

Additional award

If a tribunal makes an award for reinstatement or re-engagement but the employee is not reinstated or re-engaged, in breach of the order, the tribunal will make a basic and a compensatory award. In these circumstances, the normal maximum of £50,000 may be exceeded, if necessary, to ensure that the award fully reflects the terms of the original order relating to loss of pay and benefits with which the employer failed to comply. Unless the employer can show that it was not practicable to comply with the order, or except in the case of dismissal relating to Sunday trading or for trade union activities, it will also make an additional award of an amount not less than 26 and not more than 52 weeks' pay. The current maximum weekly pay is £230. Thus, the normal maximum award is a basic award of £6,900 and a compensatory award of not more than £11,960, making a grand total of £68,340.

Where sex, race or disability discrimination is involved, the total amount of compensation may be unlimited. Where an employee is unfairly dismissed because that employee made a protected disclosure, the compensatory award for unfair dismissal is unlimited (ERA, s 124(1A), as amended by the Public Interest Disclosure (Compensation) Regulations 1999 (SI No 1548)). These Regulations were made pursuant to ERA, s 127B.

Trade union and health and safety dismissals

Where dismissal is to be regarded as automatically unfair when it relates to trade union and health and safety related matters, and the employee is not reinstated or re-engaged, the award will consist of a basic award (calculated as above), a compensatory award (unlimited in relation to dismissal related to health and safety reasons) and an additional award (see above).

Index linking

Under the Employment Relations Act 1999, s 34, the limit on a week's pay is index-linked to the retail prices index for September each year, and shall, depending on whether the RPI is higher or lower, be increased or decreased by a percentage equivalent to the rise or reduction in the index. The resulting figure will then be rounded up to the nearest £10. The Employment Rights (Increase of Limits) Order 1999 (SI No 3375) provides for the first such indexation to take effect from 1 February 2000. This reflects the increase in the RPI between September 1998 and September 1999.

Under s 34, the compensatory award of up to £50,000 (for dismissals where the effective date of termination falls on or after 25 October 1999 – the old £12,000 limit applies for dismissals where the EDT falls before that date) is index-linked to the RPI index for September each year, and shall, depending on whether the RPI is higher or lower, be increased or reduced by a percentage equivalent to the rise or reduction in the index. The resulting figure will then be rounded up to the nearest £100.

The recoupment provisions

If an employee who has brought a claim for unfair dismissal has received unemployment benefit, job seekers allowance or income support between the date of his dismissal and the employment tribunal hearing, the employer may be ordered by the Department of Employment, in a recoupment notice, to pay part of the compensation awarded not to the employee but to the Department of Employment or DSS so that the benefit money can be recovered.

Interest on tribunal awards

Employment tribunal compensation awards now carry interest which starts to run 42 days after the tribunal's written decision is sent to the parties.

12.11.12 Settlement

An employer may wish to settle a claim for unfair dismissal rather than proceed to a hearing. In order for any agreement that is reached with the employer to be binding it must be in one of the following forms:

(1) An agreement reached through the auspices of an ACAS conciliation officer. Once a complaint of unfair dismissal has been presented, an ACAS conciliation officer is appointed to the case to conciliate between the employer and the employee (or their representatives) to establish whether a settlement is possible. Any agreement to settle should be recorded in writing and on a form designed for the purpose (form COT3). Once the COT3 has been signed by both parties and the settlement sum paid, an employee is then precluded from bringing any further claims to an industrial tribunal.

(2) Compromise agreement. Under ERA, s 203, an unfair dismissal claim may be settled if the conditions governing a statutory compromise agreement are fulfilled. The most important of these conditions are that the agreement must be in writing and the employee must have

received independent legal advice from a qualified lawyer as to the terms and effects of the proposed agreement and, in particular, its effect on the employee's ability to pursue his rights before an industrial tribunal. If the conditions are not fully satisfied, the employee will not be precluded from bringing further claims. The following claims can also be settled by means of a compromise agreement:

- itemised pay statements
- guarantee payments
- medical suspension pay
- time off for public duties
- time off for training while under redundancy notice
- time off for ante-natal care
- written reasons for dismissal
- unlawful deduction from pay under the ERA 1996
- sex discrimination
- race discrimination
- equal pay
- rights not to suffer a detriment in health and safety cases
- rights to alternative work and pay in maternity suspension cases.

12.12 REDUNDANCY

An employee who is dismissed by his employer in certain circumstances is entitled to a redundancy payment as set out in ERA, s 139(1). To qualify for a redundancy payment an employee must satisfy certain qualifying conditions.

12.12.1 Qualifying conditions

To be entitled to a redundancy payment, a person must be:

(a) An employee Only employees are entitled to redundancy payments. The burden is upon the person applying for the payment to show that he is an employee. He must have been continuously employed for a period of two years ending with the relevant date. The relevant date is defined in the same way as the effective date of termination for unfair dismissal purposes. However, for redundancy purposes an employee is not entitled to count any period of employment before his 18th birthday in calculating his period of continuous employment.

Also, as for unfair dismissal purposes, where an employee has been dismissed with no notice or less than the statutory minimum period of notice, the relevant date for the purpose of calculating continuous employment is extended to the date upon which the statutory minimum notice would have expired had it been given (see 12.9.2 above).

(b)   Dismissed   The employee must have been dismissed. The statutory definition of dismissal for redundancy payment purposes is the same as that for unfair dismissal (see 12.11.1 above). The employee must have been dismissed by reason of redundancy. Section 139(1) of ERA contains the definition of redundancy and provides that an employee who is dismissed shall be taken to have been dismissed by reason of redundancy if the dismissal is attributable wholly or mainly to:

'(a)   the fact that his employer has ceased, or intends to cease, to carry on the business for the purposes of which the employee was employed by him or has ceased or intends to cease to carry on that business in the place where the employee was so employed; or

(b)   the fact that the requirements of that business for employees to carry out work of a particular kind in the place where he was so employed have ceased or diminished or are expected to cease or diminish.'

Sub-paragraph (a) covers the situation in which the place of business where the employee could be required to work under his contract is shut. Therefore, where the contract contained a mobility clause entitling the employer to transfer an employee, it was thought that the employer could invoke the mobility clause to transfer the employee from the workplace which had closed down to one where there was work. If the employee refused, he could then be dismissed for misconduct and a redundancy payment avoided.

However, following the EAT decision in *Bass Leisure Ltd v Thomas* [1994] IRLR 104, this approach has been doubted. It was held that an employee's place of work is not wherever an employer can require him to work under his contract. A factual enquiry should be undertaken to ascertain where the employee's true place of work is and if work has ceased there, and the employee is dismissed, he is redundant and can claim a redundancy payment. The exception would be when the new location represents suitable alternative employment which the employee unreasonably refuses (see (g) below).

Sub-paragraph (b) refers to circumstances of a reduction in the business requirements for employees to carry out work of a particular kind, (ie the employer has a surplus of labour). It is important to note that there is no requirement for the work to reduce, but only a requirement that the number of employees carrying out that particular work can be reduced. This would be the case where an employer ascertains that there is over-manning.

(c)   Below retirement age   To claim a redundancy payment the employee must be below the age of 65 or the normal retiring age in the business in which he is employed. For employees over the age of 64 the amount of any redundancy payment payable is reduced by $\frac{1}{12}$ for each month by which his age exceeds 64.

(d)   Not ordinarily working outside Great Britain

(e)   Must not have contracted out of his rights to claim a redundancy payment   Where an employee is employed under a fixed term contract for a minimum of two years and he has agreed in writing to contract out of his right to a redundancy payment, then he is dismissed on the expiry of that fixed term without it being renewed, and he is not entitled to a redundancy payment.

(f)   Eligible   Certain employees such as civil servants and other public employees are specifically excluded from the right to a redundancy payment.

(g)   Redundant without an offer of suitable alternative employment   An employee who has been offered employment either on the same terms and conditions as he previously enjoyed or has been offered suitable alternative employment and he has in either case unreasonably refused the new offer of employment, loses his right to a redundancy payment. The offer of alternative employment must be made by his original employer or an associated employer before his previous employment comes to an end and must start immediately upon the ending of his previous employment or within four weeks thereof.

Where the terms and conditions of the new contract differ wholly or partly from those which the employee previously enjoyed, then he is entitled to a statutory trial period of four weeks, which can be extended by mutual agreement, in which to decide whether the alternative employment is suitable.

Where the employee accepts the offer of alternative employment there is no redundancy situation. However, he may reject the new offer of employment if it is not suitable and, provided the rejection is reasonable, he is entitled to a redundancy payment.

12.12.2 The redundancy selection process

Once an employer has decided that a redundancy situation exists he must then implement that redundancy. It is important that when implementing a redundancy an employer adopts a fair procedure. Failure to do so can result in an employee who satisfies the necessary qualifying conditions bringing a claim for unfair dismissal.

An unfair dismissal may result where an employer has selected an employee or employees for redundancy in contravention of a customary arrangement or agreed selection procedure. Where such an arrangement or procedure exists the employer must adhere to it. Furthermore, an employer must not select an employee for redundancy for an inadmissible reason such as his membership of or participation in the affairs of a trade union. In these circumstances a selection for redundancy is automatically unfair.

Where there is no customary arrangement or agreed procedure, the employer is free to use his own selection criteria, which must be reasonable and properly applied. One of the standard criteria for selection is that known as 'last in, first out', but other factors which may also be considered are the type of skills of an employee for which there is a continuing employment need and the suitability of individual employees to perform those tasks; the employee's competence, and his past conduct.

12.12.3 Consultation and notification requirements

The Collective Redundancies and Transfer of Undertakings (Protection of Employment) (Amendment) Regulations 1995 (SI No 2587) require an employer proposing to make 20 or more employees redundant to consult recognised trade unions, or any appropriate representatives elected by the employees, about ways of avoiding the dismissals, reducing the numbers to be dismissed and mitigating the consequences of the dismissals.

Failure to consult could lead to a claim for compensation known as a 'protective award', where the affected employees are compensated by ordering the employer to make payments for the protected period, or any portion of it for which they have not been paid. The amount of award is what the employment tribunal considers reasonable taking into account the seriousness of the breach and will be up to:

(1) 90 days where 90 days' minimum notice should have been given;
(2) 30 days where 30 days' minimum notice should have been given;
(3) 28 days in any other case.

The period of the award begins on the date on which the first dismissals take place or the date of the award, whichever is the earlier. This is known as the 'protected period'. Consultation must be undertaken 'with a view to reaching agreement'.

Notification should be delivered in writing to each of the appropriate representatives or, in the case of trade union representatives, by post to the union's head office. The appropriate representatives must be given access to the employees being made redundant and be provided with appropriate accommodation and other facilities.

The definition of 'redundancy', for the purposes of trade union consultation and Department of Trade and Industry notification only, is a 'dismissal for a reason not related to the individual concerned or for a number of reasons all of which are not so related'.

12.12.4 Redundancy checklist

The following is a checklist that an employer should consider before implementing any redundancies:

(1) Once the decision to make redundancies has been made the employer should first consult with any recognised trade union representatives,

bearing in mind the appropriate time limits, and should provide them with all the appropriate information. Where there is no recognised trade union, the employer should consult with the individual employees.

(2) He should notify the Department of Employment where appropriate, again bearing in mind the appropriate time limit.

(3) Having decided on the numbers to be made redundant he should invite volunteers for redundancy.

(4) He should then establish the selection criteria with the agreement (if possible) of the recognised union. He should consider whether the numbers of employees to be made redundant can be reduced and should also consider whether there is any suitable alternative employment within the company or associated company for the affected employees.

(5) He should consult with the individual affected employees.

(6) He should then send out the notices of dismissal informing the employees of their impending redundancies. He should allow the affected employees time off to look for other employment.

12.12.5 Claim for a redundancy payment

The claim for a redundancy payment must be made within six months of the relevant date by either submitting a claim in writing to the employer claiming a redundancy payment, or by bringing a claim for a redundancy payment to the employment tribunal, or by submitting an unfair dismissal complaint. If a claim is not brought within six months the tribunal has a limited discretion to allow a claim to be brought within a further six months.

12.12.6 Calculation of the redundancy payment

The redundancy payment is calculated along similar lines to that of the basic award for unfair dismissal purposes. It is therefore calculated by multiplying one week's gross pay (subject to the statutory maximum of £230) by a factor depending upon the employee's age and the number of completed years of service (subject to the statutory maximum of 20 years). Therefore:

(1) for every year during the whole of which the employee is aged 41 or over – a multiplier of one and a half;

(2) for every year during the whole of which the employee is aged between 22 and 40 – a multiplier of one;

(3) for every year during the whole of which the employee is aged between 18 and 21 – a multiplier of one half.

The employer should give the employee a statement showing how the redundancy payment has been calculated.

Finally, it should be remembered that in addition to any statutory redundancy payment, an employee may be entitled to a contractual redundancy payment under his contract of employment and will also be entitled to work out his notice period or be paid in lieu of notice.

12.12.7 Rights on insolvency of an employer

The ERA insolvency provisions apply when a company has become legally insolvent. This can mean liquidation, receivership, an administration order or voluntary arrangement approved by the court or bankruptcy. If the company merely ceases trading, these provisions may not apply.

When an employer becomes insolvent, the following payments owed to his employees will be regarded as preferential debts:

- Arrears of wages or salary
- Guarantee payments
- Remuneration for suspension on medical grounds
- Time-off payments
- Remuneration under a protective award.

Employees can apply to the Redundancy Payments Office of the Department of Trade and Industry covering the employer's area. If satisfied that the employer is insolvent and the employees are entitled to the payments, the Department will make the following payments, for a period of up to eight weeks, out of the National Insurance Fund. Note that there is a statutory limit on the amount for any one week of £230.

(1) Any arrears of pay up to eight weeks (includes guarantee payments, remuneration for suspension on medical grounds, time-off payments, remuneration under a protective award): up to £1,840.
(2) Any money due to employees who have received notice (maximum 12 weeks' statutory notice after 12 years' service): £2,760 maximum.
(3) Holiday pay up to six weeks: £1,380 maximum.
(4) Basic compensation for unfair dismissal: £6,900 maximum (calculated in the same way as a redundancy payment: see above).
(5) Reimbursement of fees, etc paid by apprentices.

Provision is also made for the payment of unpaid contributions to occupational pension schemes out of the National Insurance Fund, and for liability to statutory maternity pay and statutory sick pay to be met by the President of the Board of Trade.

12.13 TERMINATION OF EMPLOYMENT

There are three kinds of claim potentially available to an employee on termination of his contract of employment:

(1) unfair dismissal;
(2) a redundancy payment; and

(3) a claim for damages for wrongful dismissal derived from the common law relating to contract.

12.13.1 Lawful methods of termination

A claim for wrongful dismissal arises where an employer has terminated an employee's employment in breach of the employee's contract. However, a claim for wrongful dismissal does not arise where the contract is terminated in accordance with one of five common law methods:

By agreement

An employer and employee may agree to terminate the contract of employment and thereby release each other from their obligations. However, any agreement is void if it purports to exclude the rights conferred on all employees by employment protection legislation (eg unfair dismissal/ redundancy).

By effluxion of time

A fixed term contract or a contract to perform a specified task automatically terminates at the end of the term or when the task is completed.

By notice

A contract of employment usually contains an express term setting out the notice period. Where, however, the contract fails to specify a notice period then the contract is deemed to be terminable by either party giving reasonable notice. What amounts to reasonable notice depends on the particular circumstances of the employment concerned. Such factors which are taken into account in deciding what is a reasonable notice period are: the type of job; the employee's status; the period by which the employee's pay is calculated; and any custom or practice which is established in the industry or profession.

Whatever period of notice is specified it must not be less than the statutory minimum period of notice laid down by ERA, s 86. This states that where an employee is continuously employed for at least one month but less than two years he is entitled to one week's notice. Thereafter he is entitled to one week's notice for each complete year of employment up to a maximum of 12 weeks' notice, after 12 years' employment.

Following repudiatory breach

Following a repudiatory breach of the employment contract an employee can be dismissed immediately without notice. This is known as summary dismissal. Typical examples of conduct which may entitle an employer to dismiss summarily include theft by an employee of his employer's property and gross insubordination.

Frustration

A contract is frustrated where its performance becomes impossible or substantially different from that which the parties envisaged at the time of entering into the agreement by reason of an unforeseen event which has occurred and which is not the fault of either party. Where the contract is held to be frustrated, there is no dismissal and therefore there can be no claim for wrongful dismissal, unfair dismissal or a redundancy payment. The question of whether a contract has been frustrated most frequently occurs in the cases of illness and imprisonment, although it must be said that the doctrine of frustration is not frequently applied in illness cases.

12.13.2 Written reasons for dismissal

Under ERA, s 92 an employee is entitled to be provided by his employer, within 14 days of his request, with written reasons for his dismissal. The statement giving the written reasons is admissible in evidence at any proceedings and it is therefore important that the statement is consistent with the employer's case before an employment tribunal. An employee must have two years' continuous employment to be entitled to written reasons for dismissal.

Where a request for written reasons for dismissal has been made by an employee and the employer has failed to comply, an employee can bring a claim to a tribunal on the grounds that his employer has unreasonably failed to provide written reasons for his dismissal or that the reasons given are inadequate or untrue. The claim must be brought within three months from the effective date of termination of the employment. This period can be extended if the tribunal is satisfied that it was not reasonably practicable to bring the claim within that period.

If the tribunal finds the claim well founded it may make a declaration as to what it believes the employer's reasons were for dismissing the employee, and will award a sum equal to the amount of two weeks' pay (not subject to the statutory maximum of £230 per week).

12.13.3 Wrongful dismissal

Where an employer dismisses an employee in breach of his contractual or statutory obligations to give that employee notice or any other contractual obligation, it may become liable to pay the employee damages for breach of contract. Examples of actions by an employer which can lead to a claim for damages for wrongful dismissal are as follows:

(1) Where an employer terminates an employee's contract without proper notice, either contractual or statutory.

(2) Where an employer terminates a fixed term contract before the expiry of the term. However, it is usual to make provision in a fixed term contract for earlier termination by including a provision that the contract may be terminated by either side giving a specified period of notice.

(3) A claim for wrongful dismissal can arise when an employer is found to have repudiated the contract in breach of one of the fundamental contractual obligations. Repudiation occurs where an employer, by his conduct, displays an intention not to be bound by the contract. For example, where an employer insists on imposing new terms and conditions on an employee without that employee's consent, this can amount to a breach of a fundamental term of the contract entitling the employee to treat the contract as discharged and then sue his employer for wrongful dismissal for breach of contract.

(4) Disciplinary procedures may form part of a contract of employment. If an employer dismisses an employee without following contractual disciplinary procedures this may amount to a serious breach of contract (*Boyo v Lambeth LBC* [1994] ICR 727, CA).

12.13.4 Damages for wrongful dismissal

Once an employee has established that he has been dismissed in breach of contract or without being given the proper statutory minimum period of notice, he must then show that he has suffered loss as a result of the breach by the employer.

The employee's remedy for his employer's breach of contract is damages, the aim of which is to place the employee in the same situation he would have been in if the contract had been properly performed. The amount of damages that an employee receives is based upon the amount of pay and other fringe benefits (such as company car, pension and medical insurance) that he would have been entitled to had the employer complied with his contractual and statutory obligations. Therefore, the courts cannot award compensation beyond the time when the contract could have been brought to an end by the employer in accordance with its terms. For example, in the case of a fixed term contract where the fixed term is for a period of five years and the contract is brought to an end after three years, the employee is entitled to compensation for pay and fringe benefits for the unexpired two-year term.

As stated, an award of damages is based upon contractual entitlements. Therefore benefits that are merely discretionary should be excluded from a damages calculation (*Lavarack v Woods of Colchester Ltd* [1967] 1 QB 278).

Where an employer has dismissed an employee in breach of the disciplinary procedures laid down in the contract of employment, the level of damages are based on the length of time it would have taken for the employment to be terminated lawfully by the employer if he had followed the correct disciplinary procedures.

12.13.5 Mitigation

An employee must take all reasonable steps to mitigate his loss by seeking other employment. If he fails to take such steps his level of damages may be reduced accordingly. If the employee finds alternative employment then such payments that he receives are taken into account in reducing the level of any compensation that he may be entitled to. Furthermore, statutory benefits received are taken into account in assessing damages.

12.13.6 Accelerated receipt

A further deduction in the level of compensation may be made under this heading. This is particularly relevant where an employee on a long fixed term contract is wrongfully dismissed after the contract has run only a short period of time. For example, where an employee is employed under a five-year fixed term contract and is dismissed after only one year then he is entitled to receive his pay for the further four remaining years. However, by awarding such a large lump sum which could be invested to produce an income, the employee is actually better off than he would have been if the contract had been properly performed. Therefore, as the courts do not allow an employee to make a profit, a deduction is made to account for the employee receiving the money in advance, and having the opportunity to benefit by investment.

12.13.7 Interest

Interest may be awarded on the damages from the date when the cause of action arose to the date of judgment, or in the case of payment made before that date, the date of payment.

12.13.8 Payment in lieu of notice

An employer who intends to dismiss an employee may in certain circumstances consider it desirable that the employee should not work out his notice period. The employer pays that employee in lieu of notice instead.

There has been considerable case law over recent years concerning whether a payment in lieu of notice is taxable. Where the contract of employment expressly provides that an employer may pay an employee in lieu of notice then such a right constitutes an 'emolument' of the employment and therefore is subject to deduction for tax and national insurance in the normal way.

However, where there is no express contractual provision for payment in lieu of notice, then it can be said that a payment in lieu of notice is compensation for loss of office and therefore as not paid in connection with the contract of employment, it is not subject to tax and national insurance and can be paid gross.

If a non-contractual payment in lieu of notice is held to be compensation, it is tax free. However, it may in any event be subject to tax under the rules regarding payments on loss of office (commonly known as 'golden handshakes'). These rules provide that where the total amount paid to an employee on the termination of his employment (including any redundancy payment) exceeds £30,000, then the balance above £30,000 is taxable.

Should an employer include an express right to pay in lieu of notice in an employee's contract?

Where there is an express right to pay in lieu of notice, then any such payment will be fully taxable. Furthermore, where there is an express payment in lieu clause, and an employer dismisses an employee by making a payment in lieu, it was held in *Abrahams v Performing Right Society* (1995) *The Independent*, 25 May that the employee is not under a duty to mitigate his loss (see 12.13.5 above). The employee is therefore entitled to be paid for the whole of his notice period. This is because a payment in lieu is not treated as a claim for damages (as the employer has the express right to lawfully terminate by making a payment in lieu), but is rather a debt due under the contract. Therefore, where the employee is under a long notice period or on a fixed term contract where there is a lengthy period of the contract still unexpired, the amount due may be substantial, where there is no duty on the employee to mitigate.

However, an express payment in lieu clause is extremely important where an employee is subject to restrictive covenants. Where an employer dismisses an employee by making a payment in lieu, he is in breach of contract unless the contract expressly allows termination with a payment in lieu. If not, the breach by the employer prohibits him from enforcing clauses in the contract intended to survive termination, such as restrictive covenants (see *General Billposting Co Ltd v Atkinson* [1909] AC 118).

12.13.9 Wrongful dismissal claims – procedure

Actions for wrongful dismissal have to be brought in the county court or High Court or employment tribunals. The tribunals have a limited jurisdiction to hear breach of contract claims, but the maximum that a tribunal can award in respect any one claim or any number of claims relating to the same contract is £25,000.

Where an employee would have met the necessary service qualification to claim unfair dismissal, but for the fact that his employment was terminated prematurely by the employer's failure to follow a contractual disciplinary procedure, the EAT has held that damages awarded for wrongful dismissal can include a sum to compensate the employee for the loss of the right to complain of unfair dismissal (*Raspin v United News Shops Ltd* [1999] IRLR 9).

A breach of contract claim is brought by presenting an Originating Application to an employment tribunal within three months of the effective date of termination of the contract.

There is therefore now a dual procedure available to employees in bringing breach of contract claims. It may be that employees will still bring breach of contract claims in the county court as they will be entitled to their costs from the employer should they be successful, whereas they will not if the claim is in an employment tribunal.

12.14 MATERNITY RIGHTS

This is an extremely complex area of the law and it is possible to give here only an outline of the rights protecting pregnant employees. Not only is the law relating to statutory maternity leave and maternity pay relevant, but also the law relating to sex discrimination and equal pay. Furthermore, individual employees' own terms and conditions of employment may be more favourable than the statutory minimum protection.

12.14.1 Time off for ante-natal care

An employee who is pregnant and who, on the advice of a registered medical practitioner, registered midwife or registered health visitor, has made an appointment to attend at any place for the purpose of receiving ante-natal care, has the right not to be unreasonably refused time off during her working hours to enable her to keep the appointment. The employee also has the right to be paid for that period of absence at the appropriate hourly rate. There is no minimum qualifying period for employees to attain this right.

An example where an employer can reasonably refuse to allow an employee time off to attend an ante-natal class could be in respect of a part-time employee who could be expected to attend when not at work. Where an employer has unreasonably refused an employee time off for ante-natal care or where he has failed to pay the employee the amount due to her while attending the ante-natal appointment, the employee may present a complaint to an industrial tribunal. If the complaint is well founded the tribunal will make a declaration to that effect and can order the employer to pay to the employee the amount of money which would have been due under the statutory provisions.

12.14.2 Maternity leave

All women expecting a baby have the right to 18 weeks' statutory maternity leave. This right applies to all women irrespective of their length of service or the number of hours they work each week. Furthermore, employees who have more than one year's continuous employment can delay their return to work for up to 29 weeks after the beginning of the week in which their baby was born.

During the 18-week maternity leave period all employment rights other than 'remuneration' must be preserved. There is no statutory definition of remuneration and its scope is uncertain, but it is obvious that it covers the normal wage, commission and bonus payments, if these are contractual.

To identify the maternity leave period the employer must have regard to two sets of rules governing both its start date and when it ends. The commencement of the maternity leave period is usually within the particular woman's control as it is the date on which she notifies her employer as the date she wishes her maternity leave to begin. This date must not be before the eleventh week before the expected week of childbirth (EWC). A woman is not, however, free to choose the start date of her maternity leave where she is absent from work wholly or partly because of pregnancy or childbirth after the beginning of the sixth week before the EWC. In this instance the maternity leave period is triggered on the first day of absence.

Additional maternity leave

The rules as to extended or additional maternity leave are governed by the Maternity and Parental Leave etc Regulations 1999 (SI No 3312) and the ERA, as amended by the Employment Relations Act 1999. Women who have at least two years' continuous service at the beginning of the 11th week before the EWC are entitled to take extended maternity leave. This gives them the right to return to work up to 29 weeks after the baby is born.

12.14.3 Notice requirements

To qualify for the basic maternity leave period of 18 weeks, the employee must:

(1) as required by the employer, produce a doctor's or midwife's certificate stating the expected week of confinement;
(2) notify the employer at least 21 days before her absence begins, or as soon as is reasonably practicable, that she is pregnant, and of her expected week of childbirth (or if it has occurred, the date when it occurred); and
(3) notify the employer of the date when she intends the maternity leave to begin or, where maternity leave has been triggered automatically, details of the event which caused it to begin (this information is to be given only if the employer requests).

In the case of additional maternity leave, the employee must:

(a) have continuous employment for at least one year immediately before the beginning of the 11th week before the expected week of the confinement, unless dismissed because of pregnancy before that time where, but for the dismissal, she would have been so employed;

(b) produce, if requested by the employer, a doctor's or midwife's certificate giving the expected week of confinement; and

(c) at least 21 days before the employee wishes to start her leave, notify the employer of her pregnancy; the expected week of confinement; and when she wishes to start her leave. There is no requirement for her to state that she wishes to take additional maternity leave, the presumption being that she will unless she notifies her intention to return early.

Where the employee has not been in touch to notify the date of birth, the employer may write to her not earlier than 21 days before the end of the ordinary maternity leave seeking confirmation of the date of birth and of her intention to return. The employee must respond within 21 days of receiving the request. The employer must then confirm the last possible date by which she must return. Where the employee fails to respond to the employer's request for confirmation within the time limit, the employer can take appropriate disciplinary action.

12.14.4 The right to return to work

An employee has the right:

(1) to return to work with her former employee at any time before the end of the period of 29 weeks beginning with the week in which the date of confinement falls; and

(2) on her return, to be employed on terms and conditions not less favourable than those which would have been applicable if she had not been absent; or

(3) if she is not able to return to work by reason of redundancy, to be offered alternative employment (where there is a suitable vacancy) under a new contract, involving suitable work on not substantially less favourable conditions.

12.14.5 Statutory maternity pay (SMP)

Most women are entitled to SMP during their maternity leave. This benefit is administered and paid directly to eligible employees by their employers. The following is a brief summary of the complex SMP provisions; for greater detail reference should be made to the appropriate DSS leaflet NI257, *Employers Guide to Statutory Maternity Pay*.

Eligibility

To be eligible for SMP an employee must:

(1) be pregnant and have ceased work wholly or partly because of pregnancy or childbirth;

(2) must have 26 weeks' continuous employment ending with the immediately preceding week before the EWC;

(3) must have reached or given birth before reaching the eleventh week before the EWC;

(4) must have normal weekly earnings of at not less than the current lower earnings limit on which Class 1 NICs is payable. The current limit is £67 per week in the eight weeks preceding the fourteenth week before the EWC.

Period and rate of payment

SMP is payable for 18 weeks. Therefore if a woman returns to work at the end of her 18-week statutory maternity leave period, no further SMP is payable.

The maternity pay period starts no earlier than 11 weeks before the EWC, or if a woman works beyond this then the week following the week in which she stops work. Where, however, a woman is absent from work wholly or partly because of pregnancy or confinement in the six weeks before her EWC then the maternity pay period commences in the week on which that day falls.

For the first six weeks of the maternity pay period, SMP is payable at 90% of the employee's normal weekly earnings. Thereafter, SMP is payable at the rate of £60.20.

Recovery of SMP by the employer

An employer can recover up to 92% of SMP paid by making appropriate equivalent deductions from its NI contributions. A 'small employer', defined as one whose total NICs for the qualifying tax year do not exceed £20,000, may recover the full amount of SMP and an additional sum equal to 7% of the SMP he has paid. All forms of compensation are paid by making deductions from Class 1 NICs.

12.14.6 Maternity allowance

Maternity allowance is a state benefit payable to a pregnant woman who does not satisfy the eligibility criteria for SMP. In order to qualify the pregnant woman must satisfy the following conditions:

- She must be pregnant at the start of the 11th week before the EWC or have given birth prior to that date.
- She must have been employed or self-employed for at least 26 out of the 66 weeks immediately before the EWC.
- She must have paid Class 1 or Class 2 NICs for at least 26 weeks of the 66 weeks immediately before the EWC. In respect of Class 1 NICs

these should be paid by the employee and not just the employer and not have been payable at the reduced rate (ie on table letters B, E or G).

The rates payable are as follows:

– £60.20 pw, if the woman was employed into her qualifying week.
– £52.25 pw if the woman was not employed or was self-employed in her qualifying week.

The Chancellor of the Exchequer intends to relax the qualifying rules to enable maternity allowance to be paid to all women expecting a baby on or after 20 August 2000, earning £30 a week or more and less than the lower earnings limit.

Self-employed women will become entitled to the higher rate of the allowance where their expected week of confinement is on or after 20 August 2000.

Maternity allowance is not taxable and not treated as earnings for NICs purposes. A woman is entitled to a national insurance credit for each week that the allowance is payable.

12.14.7 Protection from dismissal on the grounds of pregnancy or maternity related reasons

Under ERA, s 99, it is automatically unfair for an employer to dismiss any woman, irrespective of her hours of work or length of service, if the sole or principal reason for her dismissal is one of the following:

(1) That she is pregnant or is dismissed for any other reason connected with her pregnancy.
(2) She is dismissed at any time during her 14-week maternity leave period and the sole or principal reason for that dismissal is that she has given birth or is for any other reason connected with her having given birth.
(3) She is dismissed at the end of her maternity leave period and the sole or principal reason for her dismissal is that she was away from work during her maternity leave period, or that she had the benefit of her usual terms and conditions (excluding remuneration) during her maternity leave period.
(4) She is dismissed because she has given birth or for any other reason connected with her having given birth within four weeks of the end of her maternity leave period. The woman must submit a medical certificate during her maternity leave period which states that she will be incapable of work at the end of her maternity leave period by reason of ill health. Also at the date of the dismissal the incapability must continue and the certificate must remain current.
(5) The sole or principal reason for her dismissal is a requirement or recommendation to suspend her on health and safety grounds.

(6) She is made redundant during her maternity leave period and is not offered a suitable alternative available vacancy.

The new s 60 gives women greatly increased rights to protection from dismissal on the grounds of pregnancy or for a reason related to pregnancy. A claim under s 60 must be brought within three months of the dismissal or such other period as the tribunal considers reasonable if it was not reasonably practicable to bring the claim within three months.

12.14.8 The right to return to work and dismissal

If at the end of a woman's extended maternity leave (ie up to 29 weeks after the week of the birth) an employer refuses to allow the woman to return to work there will be a deemed dismissal under ERA, s 96 on the date that she had notified her employer that she wished to return to work. The employer then has to establish that the reason why the woman was not permitted to return fell within one of the *prima facie* fair reasons for dismissal contained in ERA, s 98. If the tribunal considers that the dismissal was for one of the maternity related reasons set out in ERA, s 96, the dismissal is automatically unfair.

There are two situations in which a woman will in any event lose her right to return to work after extended maternity absence. These are:

(1) If her employer can show that it has fewer than six employees and it was not reasonably practicable for it to allow the woman back or to offer her suitable and appropriate alternative work.
(2) If the employer can show that it was not reasonably practicable for a reason other than redundancy to give her her old job back, and he offered her suitable and appropriate alternative work which she has either accepted or unreasonably refused.

It should be noted that the onus lies on the employer to show that there was no suitable and appropriate alternative work.

12.14.9 Redundancy and maternity dismissal protection

Where a redundancy situation arises during a woman's maternity leave, the employer is entitled to make that woman redundant provided that the reason for her redundancy is not a maternity related one. However, the employer is under a duty to offer the woman any suitable and appropriate alternative work which is available, failing which the redundancy related dismissal is automatically unfair. Again, the obligation is on the employer to show that there was no suitable and appropriate alternative work. Where this is the case, the woman is nevertheless entitled to a redundancy payment, providing of course she has the necessary two years' continuous employment.

Also, even if the woman does not have the right to claim that the redundancy was for a s 60 reason and therefore automatically unfair, if she has the one year's continuous employment she may nevertheless bring an 'ordinary' unfair dismissal complaint on the grounds that her selection for redundancy was unfair.

12.14.10 Written reasons for dismissal

Where a woman is dismissed while she is pregnant or where the dismissal ends her maternity leave period, she is automatically entitled to written reasons for her dismissal, irrespective of her hours of work or length of service.

Dismissal will be automatically unfair for any of the following reasons:

(1) The reason or principal reason for dismissal is that she is pregnant or for any other reason connected with her pregnancy.
(2) Her maternity leave period (MLP) is ended by the dismissal and the reason or principal reason for her dismissal is that she has given birth to a child or any other reason connected with her having given birth to a child.
(3) The reason or principal reason for her dismissal, where her contract of employment was terminated at the end of her MLP, is that she took, or availed herself of the benefits of, maternity leave.
(4) The reason or principal reason for her dismissal is that she has given birth to a child or any other reason connected with her having given birth to a child where both:
    (a) before the end of her MLP she gave to her employer a certificate from a registered medical practitioner stating that, by reason of disease or bodily or mental disablement, she would be incapable of work after the end of that period; and
    (b) her contract of employment was terminated within the four-week period following the end of her MLP in circumstances where she continued to be incapable of work and the certificate relating to her incapacity remained current.
(5) The reason or principal reason for her dismissal is a health and safety requirement or recommendation.
(6) Her MLP is ended by the dismissal, and the reason or principal reason for her dismissal is that she is redundant, and she has not been offered available suitable alternative employment.

Any of the reasons for dismissal set out above are inadmissible and do not require the individual to satisfy any qualifying service conditions.

12.14.11 Maternity protection and health and safety

Employers are under a general duty to take reasonable care for the health and safety of their employees. These duties are laid down both in common law and in statute; for a fuller discussion on an employer's health and safety obligations in general see Chapter 15. Employers should also make reference to guidelines issued by the HSE.

Under ERA, s 99 it is automatically unfair for an employee to be dismissed if the reason for doing so was a requirement or recommendation to suspend that employee on health and safety grounds, irrespective of the employee's hours or length of service. As a result of the implementation of the Pregnant Workers Directive by the Management of Health & Safety at Work (Amendment) Regulations 1994, further stringent obligations are laid upon employers in relation to the health and safety of new or expectant mothers in their employment.

Under these amended regulations an employer, whose workforce includes women of child-bearing age, is under an obligation to carry out risk assessments in relation to that risk group. Where any risks are identified, an employer must take preventative or protective measures to avoid those risks. If these measures will not be effective in avoiding such risks, then the employer must alter the woman's working conditions or hours of work. Furthermore, if this alteration is not reasonable or still does not avoid the risks, then the employer must offer the woman any suitable alternative work which is available. If no alternative work is available, the woman must be suspended from work on full pay.

Where there is suitable alternative work available, and the employer fails to offer it to the affected employee, she has the right to bring a complaint to an employment tribunal. Such a claim must be brought within three months beginning with the first day of the suspension or if this was not reasonably practicable within such time as the tribunal considers reasonably practicable. Where the complaint is upheld the tribunal can award such compensation as it considers just and equitable.

Where a woman is suspended on the grounds that there is no suitable alternative work and the employer fails to pay her her full remuneration during the suspension period, again she can bring a complaint to an industrial tribunal within three months, or such further period as the tribunal considers is reasonably practicable.

If a pregnant woman works nights and it is necessary for her to be moved off night work for health and safety reasons, the employer must ensure that this is done.

There are further specific regulations which place obligations upon employers in relation to pregnant workers. Employers are advised to contact their local Health & Safety Office for advice if they have any queries as to their obligations in this respect.

In *Day v T Pickles Farms Ltd* [1999] IRLR 217, the EAT confirmed that the duty to carry out a risk assessment under reg 13A arises as soon as a female of childbearing age enters the workforce, not just when an existing employee becomes pregnant or is breast-feeding. If this is not done at the start of employment, an employee may, depending on the facts of the case, be able to argue that she has been subjected to a detriment by the employer's failure in this respect. If an employee suffers such detriment, this could amount to unlawful direct discrimination under the SDA.

The EAT also held that the requirement to notify the employer in writing of the fact of pregnancy under the Management of Health and Safety at Work Regulations could potentially be fulfilled by the employee providing the employer with a series of doctor's sick notes indicating the fact that she was pregnant. The employer would then have to prove that the doctor's certificates did not amount to written notification of pregnancy.

12.14.12 Maternity rights and inter-relationship with sex discrimination law

Although the dismissal of a woman for pregnancy or for a pregnancy related reason is automatically unfair under ERA, s 99, a woman may also be able to obtain a remedy under the Sex Discrimination Act where she is either refused employment or treated unfavourably as a result of her pregnancy. As there is no statutory cap on the amount of compensation for sex discrimination – from a compensation point of view it may well be desirable to bring a claim under the Sex Discrimination Act rather than under s 99 where the statutory limit on unfair dismissal compensation applies. There is no limit on orders under the Sex Discrimination Act.

Until recently, it was established law that where a pregnant employee was treated unfavourably, she had to show that she was treated less favourably for a reason connected with her pregnancy than a man would have been treated in such circumstances if he had been ill. In *Webb v EMO Air Cargo Ltd (No 2)* [1995] 4 All ER 577, the House of Lords held that the terms of the test of unlawful discrimination set out in the SDA were to be construed in accordance with the ruling of the ECJ on the Equal Treatment Directive as meaning that, in a case where a woman was engaged for an indefinite period, the fact that the reason why she should be temporarily unavailable for work at a time when, to her knowledge, her services would be particularly required, pregnancy was a circumstance relevant to her case, being a circumstance which could not be present in the case of the hypothetical man. It did not, however, follow that pregnancy would be a relevant circumstance in the situation where the woman was denied employment for a fixed period in the future during the whole of which her pregnancy would make her unavailable for work, nor in a situation where after engagement for such a period the discovery of her pregnancy led to the cancellation of the engagement.

12.15 PARENTAL LEAVE

The UK has adopted the Parental Leave Directive (96/34/EC) through the Employment Relations Act 1999 and the Maternity and Parental Leave

Regulations 1999 (SI No 3312). The Regulations add to the existing rights for natural mothers and give rights for the first time to fathers and adoptive parents. An employee must have been continuously employed for a period of not less than one year.

The parental rights are only in relation to unpaid leave. If an employee is entitled to paternity or parental leave under their terms and conditions of employment then the employee can choose the more generous option, but the statutory entitlement will be reduced *pro rata*. Therefore, if a company paternity scheme allows one week's paid leave to fathers then an employee can take that week as paid leave but will only be entitled to 12 weeks' parental leave under the Regulations.

12.15.1 Amount of leave

The basic entitlement is to 13 weeks' unpaid leave per child (therefore 26 weeks for twins). The leave can be taken any time before the fifth birthday or the fifth anniversary of the placement of the child for adoption with the employee, with three exceptions:

(1) In the case of an adopted child, if the child's 18th birthday falls before the fifth anniversary of the placement then entitlement to parental leave ends on the 18th birthday.
(2) If the child (natural or adopted) is entitled to a disability living allowance then parental leave can be taken anytime up to the child's 18th birthday.
(3) If any leave requested by an employee is postponed by the employer in accordance with the Regulations to a date after entitlement would otherwise have expired, then that leave may still be taken.

12.15.2 Workforce agreements and default provisions

The specific provisions governing the parental leave scheme for a particular organisation can be contained in a workforce agreement or collective agreement. The requirements for the creation of a workforce agreement are set out in Sched 1 to the Regulations. The agreement should cover:

- Conditions relating to providing evidence of entitlement
- Notice to be given by the employee
- Postponement of leave requested by an employee
- Minimum periods of leave
- Maximum annual leave.

Where there is no agreement in force, the default provisions contained in Sched 2 to the Regulations will apply.

12.15.3 Protection of employees on parental leave

The ERA, as amended, provides that an employee on parental leave is protected from suffering any detriment through the action or deliberate inaction of the employer. An employee can also claim automatic unfair dismissal if the reason for dismissal was connected with the employee taking parental leave.

An employee taking parental leave of less than four weeks is entitled to return to the same job. An employee taking parental leave of more than four weeks (in a single continuous period) is entitled to return to the same job or a similar job if it is not reasonably practicable to return to the original job. The alternative similar job must be suitable and appropriate to the employee's circumstances and on terms not less favourable than the original job.

Parental leave is included for the purposes of calculating continuous employment.

12.15.4 Right to time off to deal with family emergencies

The Parental Leave Directive also included rights for employees to unpaid leave to deal with emergencies involving dependants. The ERA has been amended by the insertion of a new s 57A to give this right in the UK. An employee is entitled to take a reasonable amount of time off during working hours in order to take action necessary:

(1) to provide assistance on an occasion when a dependant falls ill, gives birth, or is injured or assaulted;
(2) to make arrangements for the provision of care for a dependant who is ill or injured;
(3) in consequence of the death of a dependant;
(4) because of the unexpected disruption or termination of arrangements for the care of a dependant;
(5) to deal with an incident which involves a child of the employee and which occurs unexpectedly in a period during which an educational establishment, which the child attends, is responsible for him.

There is no statutory right to payment for the time off and any payment is to be determined by the contract of employment.

12.16 STATUTORY SICK PAY (SSP)

Where an employee is absent from work due to sickness he may be entitled to:

(1) contractual sick pay as set out in his written statement of terms and conditions of employment;
(2) SSP.

There are numerous regulations governing this complex area, but the main provisions are contained in the Social Security Contributions and Benefits Act 1992 and the Statutory Sick Pay Act 1994.

12.16.1 Qualifications for SSP

The main requirements for an employee to be entitled to SSP are that he must:

(1) have four or more consecutive qualifying days of sickness;
(2) notify his absence to his employer;
(3) supply evidence of his incapacity for work. This is usually agreed between the employer and employee and normally involves a self-certification by the employee for periods of absence of four to seven days and thereafter a doctor's certificate.

The following groups are specifically excluded:

(1) Pensioners.
(2) Employees on short-term contracts of three months or less. (However, employers should note that a series of short-term contracts would be likely to create an entitlement.)
(3) Employees whose average earnings are lower than the point at which NICs become payable, ie the lower earnings level (£67 pw for 2000–01).
(4) Those receiving a sickness or invalidity benefit or maternity allowance in the 57 days preceding the first day of sickness.
(5) Employees who have not yet started work.
(6) Any employee affected by a trade dispute at his workplace, unless the employee was:
   (a) sick before the dispute began, or
   (b) able to prove that he was not participating in, or directly interested in the dispute.
(7) An employee who had already received 28 weeks of SSP and had stopped getting SSP less than eight weeks before.
(8) An employee who becomes sick while entitled to maternity allowance or statutory maternity pay, or falls sick with a pregnancy-related illness on or after the start of the sixth week before the week in which the baby is due.
(9) An employee who is in legal custody

12.16.2 The period of payment

As mentioned above an employee is only entitled to SSP once he has been absent for four or more qualifying days. This period is known as a period of incapacity for work. SSP is therefore payable on the fourth qualifying day and thereafter until either the employee has reached his full entitlement of 28 weeks' SSP or returns to work. An employer's liability to pay SSP ends once the employee has received 28 weeks' SSP during a three-year period.

Once the employee's entitlement to SSP has terminated, if the employee is still sick, he will then be entitled to incapacity benefit.

12.16.3 The amount payable

Employees who earn less than the lower weekly earnings limit for NI liability (£67 for 2000–01) are not entitled to SSP. There is one rate of SSP (£60.20 for 2000–01) payable to all qualifying employees.

An employer is entitled to recover any amount by which the payments of SSP made by him in any month exceed 13% of the amount of the employer's liabilities for NICs payments in respect of that month.

Where an employee also has a contractual right to sick pay, an employer is well advised to include within an employee's written statement of terms and conditions that he is only entitled to contractual sick pay as is appropriate to top up wages to the normal level of remuneration after payment of SSP or any sickness benefit received afterwards.

An employer is obliged to keep minimum information on record for SSP purposes for at least three years. Furthermore, when an employee leaves in certain circumstances an employer is under a duty to issue the employee with a 'leaver's statement'.

The SSP rules and regulations are extremely complex and failure to comply with them can amount to a criminal offence. This section is only a summary of some of the more important rules relating to SSP. When dealing with these complicated issues employers should refer to DSS booklets on SSP and seek legal advice.

12.17 FURTHER STATUTORY PAYMENTS TO EMPLOYEES

12.17.1 Medical suspension payment

Where an employee is suspended from work on medical grounds in compliance with any law or regulation concerning workers' health and safety, that employee may be entitled to be paid by his employer during each week of the period of suspension for a maximum of 26 weeks. To claim such a payment the employee must have been continuously employed for a period of one month ending with the day before that on which the suspension begins.

It should be noted that an employee who is employed either:

(1) under a contract for a fixed term of three months or less, or
(2) under a contract made in contemplation of the performance of a specific task which is not expected to last for more than three months,

is not entitled to a medical suspension payment unless he has been continuously employed for a period of more than three months ending with the day before the day on which the suspension begins. An employee is not entitled to such a payment where either he is absent from work because of illness during the period where such a payment would be due or is offered suitable alternative work which he unreasonably refused to perform.

If an employer fails to pay a medical suspension payment where due, an employee can bring a claim to an employment tribunal within three months of the date on which the claim for a payment was made, or within such further reasonable period, if the tribunal considers it not reasonably practicable to bring the claim within the three-month time limit. If the complaint is well founded, the tribunal will make an order for the employer to pay the employee the amount considered to be due.

12.17.2 Guarantee payments

Where an employee, on any day which in accordance with his contract of employment he is normally required to work, is not provided with work by his employer by reason of either:

(1) a diminution in the requirements of the employer's business for work of the kind which the employee is employed to do, or
(2) any other occurrence affecting the normal working of the employer's business in relation to work of the kind which the employee is employed to do,

that employee may, subject to certain exceptions, be entitled to a guarantee payment. The qualifying conditions are the same as those for a medical suspension payment. An employee is not entitled to a guarantee payment where the employer's failure to provide work is as a result of a strike, lock-out or other industrial action, not necessarily involving the employee concerned.

An employee is not entitled to a guarantee payment for a workless day if his employer has offered to provide alternative work for that day which is suitable in all the circumstances and the employee has unreasonably refused the offer or he does not comply with reasonable requirements imposed by his employer with a view to ensuring that his services are available.

Amount of payment

There are detailed rules governing the calculation of guarantee payments. However, at present the maximum amount of any guarantee payment is £16.10 per day at the time of writing and such payment cannot exceed five days in any period of three months.

Where an employer fails to make payment to an employee, that employee may present a claim to an employment tribunal. The time limit for presenting the claim is the same as for a medical suspension payment. If the tribunal finds the complaint well founded, it will order the employer to pay the amount of the guarantee payment to the employee that is found to be due.

12.18 ITEMISED PAY STATEMENTS

An employee is, subject to certain statutory exceptions, entitled to a written pay statement from his employer detailing:

(1) the gross amount of salary;
(2) the amount of any variable or fixed deductions from that amount and the reasons for which they are made; this can however be done under a separate statement of fixed deductions;
(3) the net amount of wages;
(4) where parts of the net amount are paid in different ways, the amount and method of each part payment.

If an employer does not provide an employee with a pay statement, the employee can apply to an employment tribunal and the tribunal can make a declaration concerning the particulars to be included in any statement. Furthermore, where the tribunal finds that any unnotified deductions have been made from the employee's pay, during the period of 13 weeks immediately preceding the date of the application made by the employee, the tribunal may award a sum not exceeding the amount of the unnotified deductions during that period.

An application can be brought at any time whilst employment continues or within three months after the termination of employment. The tribunal does not have the power to extend the time limit in any circumstances.

12.19 WAGES: PAYMENT AND DEDUCTIONS

The payment of wages is governed by an individual's contract of employment. If there is no express term governing how wages are to be paid, then payment is determined by an implied term and such implied term is likely to be that which is customary for the payment of wages in a particular industry.

12.19.1 Deduction from wages

Under the ERA, s 13 an employer is not entitled to deduct sums from an employee's wages unless either:

(1) such deduction is required or permitted by a statutory or contractual provision; or
(2) the worker has given his prior written consent to the deduction.

Therefore, if in certain circumstances an employer wishes to make deductions from an employee's wages, the right for him to do so should, for the sake of clarity, be in writing and contained within the contract, a copy of which should be given to the employee.

It is important to note that the provisions of the ERA apply not only to employees, but also to persons working under a contract for services. The following deductions are excluded from the operation of the provisions:

(1) deductions made to reimburse an employer for any overpayment of wages or expenses;
(2) deductions made pursuant to any statutory disciplinary proceedings;
(3) statutory payments due to a public authority;
(4) sums payable to third parties, made either pursuant to a contractual term to which the worker has agreed in writing or to which he has otherwise given his previous written agreement or consent (the most common example of this would be trade union dues);
(5) deductions made as a result of participation in a strike or other industrial action;
(6) deductions made for the purpose of satisfying a court or tribunal order for the payment of an amount by a worker to his employer; this requires the worker's prior written agreement or consent.

The definition of wages for ERA purposes includes all sums payable to a worker in connection with his employment including any fees, bonuses, commission and holiday pay or other emoluments referable to his employment.

There are however a number of payments that are specifically excluded from the wages definition and these include advances under loan agreements or by way of an advance of wages; payments for expenses incurred in carrying out employment; payments by way of pension, allowance or gratuity in connection with the worker's retirement or as compensation for loss of office; any payment in relation to the worker's redundancy; or any payment otherwise than in the worker's capacity as a worker.

12.19.2 Retail workers

Special rules regarding wage deductions apply to retail workers. The employer of such a worker cannot deduct wages for cash shortages or stock deficiencies that amount to more than one-tenth of the worker's gross wages payable on a particular pay day. An employer must make any deduction below that limit not more than 12 months after the date on which he discovered the shortage or deficiency or ought reasonably to have discovered it.

The employer of a retail worker cannot receive any payment from the worker on account of a cash shortage or stock deficiency unless he has:

(1) notified the worker in writing of his total liability in respect of that shortage or deficiency, and
(2) made a demand for payment which is both in writing and on a pay day.

The demand must be made not earlier than the first pay day after the date of the written notification and not later than 12 months after the date when the employer discovered the shortage or deficiency or ought reasonably to have done so. As stated above, the amount demanded must not exceed one-tenth of the worker's gross wages payable on the particular pay day.

The restriction of deductions to one-tenth of gross wages does not apply to deductions from a final wages payment.

12.19.3 Worker's remedy for unlawful deduction

The worker's remedy is by way of complaint to an employment tribunal. The complaint must be brought within three months of the date of the deduction, or within such further period if it was not reasonably practicable for the complaint to be brought within the time limit. If the tribunal finds that the complaint is well founded, a declaration is made to that effect and the employer is ordered to repay to the worker the amount of the deduction.

It is important for employers to note that where sums have been wrongfully deducted and they have been ordered by a tribunal to repay such sums to an employee, the employer cannot at a later stage seek to recover those same sums by lawful means, even if the sums were properly owing to the employer. It is therefore important for employers to ensure that they deduct money correctly on the first occasion to ensure that any sums owing to them will be recovered.

12.20 THE MINIMUM WAGE

The provisions as to the minimum wage are governed by the National Minimum Wage Act 1998 and the National Minimum Wage Regulations 1999 (SI No 584). A person qualifies for the national minimum wage (NMW) if they are an individual who:

(1) is a worker;
(2) is working or ordinarily works in the UK under their contract subject to condition (3) below being satisfied, such a worker will be entitled to the NMW when temporarily working outside the UK; and
(3) has attained the age of 18.

The coverage of the 1998 Act extends beyond an employee and also covers a worker who has entered into, works or has worked under a contract, whether express or implied, whereby the worker undertakes to do or perform personally any work or services for another party to the contract whose status is not by virtue of the contract that of a client or customer of any profession or business undertaking carried on by the worker. The 1998 Act may cover agency workers, homeworkers, teleworkers, and casual and temporary workers, but will not cover self-employed persons.

A worker's length of employment or the country in which his employer is based does not affect his entitlement to the NMW.

A worker who has not yet reached age 18 does not qualify for the NMW. For workers over 18, there are at the time of writing three different rates of the NMW: £3.70; or £3.20 for workers aged 18–21 and for accredited trainees.

12.21 SEX AND RACE DISCRIMINATION

Discrimination on the grounds of sex or marital status is made unlawful by the Sex Discrimination Act 1975 (SDA); discrimination on racial grounds is unlawful under the Race Relations Act 1976 (RRA). Both Acts make discrimination unlawful in every stage of employment, from recruitment to dismissal. Furthermore, the Acts apply to self-employed workers as well as employees. (Disability discrimination is dealt with at 12.22 below.)

The scope of the SDA has been extended by the Sex Discrimination (Gender Reassignment) Regulations 1999 (SI No 1102). By virtue of these Regulations, s 2A of the Act makes it unlawful to discriminate against a person and treat him or her less favourably than others on the grounds that he or she intends to undergo, is undergoing or has undergone gender reassignment (ie sex change).

In *Smith v Gardner Merchant Ltd* [1998] 3 All ER 852, the Court of Appeal held that, for the purposes of the Sex Discriminaiton Act, there was a difference between discrimination on the ground of sex and discrimination on the ground of sexual orientation, and a person's orientation was not an aspect of his or her sex. It was still possible, however, for discrimination based on a man's homosexuality to be discrimination against him as a man if the same would not have been directed against a homosexual woman.

12.21.1 Recruitment

Discrimination can occur in recruitment in a number of ways – either in the arrangements that an employer makes for determining who should be offered employment (ie job specifications), or in the terms on which an employer offers employment, or by the employer directly refusing or omitting to offer employment. For example, a question at interview to a female employee as to whether she has any plans to start a family could amount to sex discrimination.

It is important for employers to ensure that any of their staff who are involved in conducting job interviews should be aware of the potential pitfalls. The Equal Opportunities Commission (EOC) has issued a Code of Practice for the elimination of discrimination on the grounds of sex and marriage through the promotion of equality of opportunity in employment. In recruitment situations, it suggests that the following considerations should be borne in mind:

(1) Applications from both men and women should be processed in the same way.
(2) There should not be separate lists of male and female applicants, or those that are married and those that are single.
(3) Any questions asked at interview should relate to the requirements of the job.
(4) Questions about plans for marriage or family intentions are liable to be interpreted as discriminatory.
(5) There should be proper training of staff involved in conducting interviews so that potential discriminatory questions can be avoided.
(6) Records should be kept showing the reasons why particular applicants were or were not appointed. Such records could prove to be important evidence if queries ever arose.

Once employment has commenced, discrimination can occur in a number of ways, either in the terms of the employment afforded to an employee or the denial or limited provision afforded to an employee regarding access to promotional opportunities, training facilities or any other benefits or by subjecting a person to any detriment, or by dismissing them.

12.21.2 Types of discrimination

Discrimination can occur in three ways: directly, indirectly, or by victimisation. In ascertaining whether there has been discrimination, the position of the person alleging discrimination is compared with someone of similar ability and qualifications in a similar situation. In all circumstances 'like will be compared with like'.

12.21.3 Direct discrimination

Direct discrimination occurs where a person is treated less favourably than another on the grounds of sex, marital status or racial grounds. It is important to note that the employer's intentions are irrelevant. Therefore, even if the employer feels that he is acting in the best interests of the person concerned, if that person is treated less favourably by the employer, then there is direct discrimination. The test is simply one of whether the treatment was less favourable. In *R v Birmingham City Council, ex p EOC* [1989] IRLR 173, HL denying girls the same number of places in selective secondary education as boys amounted to direct discrimination. It was not necessary to show that selective education was more desirable than non-selective education.

12.21.4 Indirect discrimination

Indirect discrimination occurs where an employer applies a requirement or condition which applies equally to all persons, but:

(1) the proportion of women, married persons or persons of a particular race who can comply with that condition is considerably smaller than the proportion of men, unmarried persons or persons not within that race; and

(2) the employer cannot show that condition to be justifiable irrespective of the sex, marital status or race of the person to whom it is applied; and

(3) the requirement is to that person's detriment because he or she cannot comply with it.

In considering whether an employer has indirectly discriminated against an employee, it is necessary to consider carefully the different concepts involved in the above definition of indirect discrimination.

First, a requirement or condition imposed by the employer must operate as a bar preventing the employee concerned from obtaining what is sought. For example, in *Home Office v Holmes* [1984] IRLR 299 an obligation on an employee to work full time was held to be a requirement for the purposes of the definition of indirect discrimination.

Secondly, when deciding whether the requirement or condition has had a disproportionate impact on one particular sex or racial group, it is necessary to define the appropriate pool for comparing members of one sex or racial group with members of the other sex or another racial group. The choice of the appropriate pool for comparison is a question of fact for an employment tribunal and will turn on the particular circumstances of each case. However, the Court of Appeal in *Jones v University of Manchester* [1993] IRLR 218 indicated that any pool for comparison should be defined broadly, so as to cover all men and women to whom the employer applied or would apply the requirement.

In deciding whether a particular employee 'can comply' with a requirement or condition, the question is not whether the employee is physically able to comply but whether he can in practice comply, having regard to custom and usual behaviour. For example, in *Mandla v Lee* [1983] IRLR 209 the House of Lords rejected an argument that Sikh employees could comply with a prohibition on wearing turbans, as in accordance with custom and cultural conditions they could not comply, although theoretically they could have done.

Thirdly, the requirement or condition must be shown to operate to the particular employee's detriment because he cannot comply with it. This is an objective test and it would be sufficient for the employee concerned to show that he could not comply with the requirement or condition at the time when his claim arises.

The test of justifiability

Even when the above requirements are satisfied, an employer may still avoid liability for indirect discrimination if it can show that the requirement or condition was justifiable irrespective of sex or race.

The question of whether a particular discriminatory condition is justifiable depends upon an objective test. The correct approach was stated by the ECJ in *Bilka-Kaufhaus GmbH v Weber von Hartz* [1987] ICR 110. The employer in order to justify a discriminatory practice must put forward objective economic grounds relating to the management of the business. The practice must also be necessary and in proportion to the objectives pursued by the employer. It is a matter for determination by an employment tribunal on the facts of each case when striking a balance between the requirement's discriminatory effect and what are the employer's reasonable needs. For example, in *Singh v Rowntree Mackintosh Ltd* [1979] ICR 554, the employer imposed the rule that none of his employees could have beards. This condition effectively excluded Sikhs from employment at the company and Mr Singh complained of indirect discrimination. The tribunal held that indeed the condition was discriminatory, but that it was justifiable on the grounds of hygiene.

Two examples where an employer has been held to indirectly discriminate against an employee are as follows:

(1) A refusal by an employer to allow a request from an employee returning from maternity leave to work on a part-time basis after the birth of her baby amounted to indirect sex discrimination, even though the employee had worked on a full-time basis prior to maternity leave. The employer could not justify the requirement of full-time work as it needed only to have made a relatively minor adjustment within the organisation of its department to accommodate the employee's request for part-time work (*Guthrie v Royal Bank of Scotland* (Case No 31796/86), 10 March 1987).

(2) A blanket mobility clause imposed on all staff may amount to indirect sex discrimination as it is likely to have a disproportionate adverse effect on women. This is because women tend to earn less than their husbands and a higher proportion of women than men would find it impossible to relocate as their husbands, the main breadwinners, could not realistically give up their jobs (*Meade-Hill & The National Union of Civil and Public Servants v The British Council* (1995) *The Times*, 7 April).

12.21.5 Victimisation

It is also unlawful for an employer to treat any person less favourably than another due to the fact that that person brings proceedings, gives evidence or information or takes or threatens to take any action, or makes any allegation concerning his employer with reference to either the SDA, the Disability Discrimination Act (see 12.22), the RRA or the Equal Pay Act 1970.

12.21.6 Genuine occupational qualification

An employer also has a defence to an allegation of sex or race discrimination where he can show that the discrimination is as a result of a genuine occupational qualification. Therefore, if the defence can be established, an employer can discriminate in relation to advertisements, interviewing procedures and in job offers. Once the employment relationship has been established, again if the defence is available, an employer can refuse individual opportunities for promotion, training or transfer.

In the context of sex discrimination, a genuine occupational qualification can be established where, for example, the essential nature of the job calls for a man for reasons of physiology. This does not relate to physical strength or stamina but would, for example, apply in the case of an employer seeking male models or in the case of theatrical performances, for reasons of authenticity, male actors. It can also be a genuine occupational qualification where the need for the job to be held by a man is important in order to preserve decency or privacy.

In the context of race discrimination, an example of a genuine occupational qualification would be where for reasons of authenticity an employer may require members of only one race (eg Indian waiters in an Indian restaurant).

12.21.7 Liability for discriminatory acts

Both the individual concerned and his employer are liable for discriminatory acts carried out by an employee during the course of his employment, whether or not those acts are done with the employer's knowledge or approval. However, an employer does have a defence to vicarious liability where he can show that he has taken such steps as were reasonably practicable to prevent an employee from doing such acts during the course of his employment. It is therefore important for an employer to be seen to be proactive in this field. If allegations of discriminatory acts are brought to his attention he should deal with these immediately.

12.21.8 Remedies

An individual who is alleging sex or race discrimination can bring a complaint to an employment tribunal. Such complaint must be brought within three months of the discriminatory act. However, a tribunal can consider an application out of time if it considers that it is just and equitable to do so.

If the complaint is well founded, the tribunal can make a declaration declaring the complainant's and the employer's rights in relation to the act of discrimination which has been complained about. For example, the declaration can state that certain training facilities should be made available to an employee. Furthermore, an award of compensation can be made. The amount of compensation awarded may include a sum for injury to feelings which results from the employee's knowledge that it was a discriminatory act which brought about the employer's action. Until *Marshall v Southampton & South West Hampshire Regional Health Authority (No 2)* [1993] IRLR 445, there was a maximum limit of £11,000 on the amount of compensation recoverable in discrimination cases. However, this case held that it was inconsistent with EU law (ie the Equal Treatment Directive) for there to be a limit on compensation when this bore no relation to the loss that had actually been suffered. Following this decision, the UK government enacted amending legislation so that the maximum limit has now been removed for both sex and race discrimination cases. Furthermore, as a result of *Marshall (No 2)*, the relevant amendments have been consolidated in the Industrial Tribunals (Interest on Awards in Discrimination Cases) Regulations 1996 (SI No 2803) to give a tribunal power to award interest on compensation.

Finally, a tribunal can make a recommendation that the employer within a specified period of time takes such action as appears to be practicable for the purpose of obviating or reducing the adverse effect on the complainant of any act of discrimination to which the complaint relates.

12.21.9 The role of the Equal Opportunities Commission and the Commission for Racial Equality

The Commissions are both extremely active in the fields of sex and race discrimination. They have the power to carry out formal investigations and as a result of those investigations serve non-discrimination orders on employers. Such an order is made if a Commission is satisfied that an employer has committed or is committing a discriminatory act or maintaining a discriminatory practice. The terms of the non-discrimination notice require the employer to cease committing such acts and institute any necessary changes in any of its practices to avoid any discriminatory effects. If this order is not complied with, it can be enforced in a county court. The Commissions also adopt a proactive role in advising individuals about their rights in relation to discriminatory matters. Where appropriate, they can support individuals in claims against an employer.

Where a person has brought a claim for discrimination to an employment tribunal, they can serve on the employer concerned a questionnaire that has been compiled by the Commissions. If then an employer does not answer the questions on the questionnaire or provides inadequate answers, its replies can be taken into account in the tribunal proceedings and a tribunal has the discretion to draw adverse inferences from them.

The field of potential discriminatory acts is very wide and extends from recruitment right through training, promotion, transfer, redundancy selection procedures through to dismissal. In all cases an employer should consider carefully whether action that it proposes to take could have a potential discriminatory effect. Legal advice is important in this area and should certainly be sought, for instance before the placing of job advertisements in local or national newspapers.

12.22 DISCRIMINATION ON GROUNDS OF DISABILITY

The Disability Discrimination Act 1995 (DDA) made it unlawful for employers (with certain exceptions (see 12.22.5)) to discriminate against those with disabilities.

The key elements of the DDA that are relevant to employers are that:

(a) it is now unlawful to discriminate against current or prospective employees with disabilities because of a reason relating to that disability; and

(b) the DDA obliges employers to make reasonable adjustments if their employment arrangements or premises place the disabled employee or disabled applicant at a substantial disadvantage.

As with the RRA and SDA there is no qualifying period of employment before a claim may be presented and that the tribunals are able to award unlimited compensation for discrimination.

12.22.1 Definition of 'disability'

The definition of 'disability' is particularly wide and goes beyond those who are registered as disabled to include all persons who have a 'physical or mental impairment which has a substantial and long-term adverse effect on [that person's] ability to carry out normal day-to-day activities'.

The meaning of 'mental' or 'physical' impairment is intentionally not specifically defined by the DDA so that the Act is able to potentially cover all physical and mental impairments. However, certain conditions are excluded from the DDA by virtue of reg 4 of the Disability Discrimination (Meaning of Disability) Regulations 1996 (SI No 1455). Excluded conditions include kleptomania, pyromania, a tendency to physical or sexual abuse of other persons, exhibitionism, voyeurism, hay fever and addiction to alcohol, nicotine or other drugs.

To be a substantial and long-term condition, it must either:

(a) have lasted at least 12 months;
(b) be likely to last at least 12 months; or
(c) be likely to last for the rest of the lifetime of that person.

To affect normal day-to-day activities the condition must affect at least one of the following activities:

- Mobility
- Manual dexterity
- Physical co-ordination
- Continence
- Ability to lift, carry or otherwise move everyday objects
- Speech, hearing and sight
- Memory or ability to concentrate, learn or understand perception of the risk of physical danger

- Severe disfigurement is also treated as having a substantial and long-term adverse effect on the person's ability to carry out normal day-to-day activities.

12.22.2 Types of discrimination

As opposed to the SDA and the RRA, which cover three types of discrimination (direct, indirect and victimisation) the DDA only defines discrimination as (1) direct discrimination (s 5) and (2) victimisation (s 55).

It was held in *Clark v TDG Ltd* [1999] 2 All ER 977 that, having regard to the provisions of the DDA, a disabled person was treated less favourably than others if the reason for the treatment did not or would not apply to others. Since that test was not based on the fact of disability, a tribunal was not required to compare the treatment of the disabled person and others in similar circumstances, but had simply to identify others to whom the reason for the treatment did not or would not apply.

Direct discrimination is defined in a similar way to that of the RRA and SDA (see 12.21.3) as is victimisation (see 12.21.5). However, the DDA has also introduced a new obligation on an employer that is specific to the realms of disability discrimination. This is the employer's duty to make reasonable adjustments in order to accommodate the disabled person (s 6).

12.22.3 Employer's duty to make reasonable adjustments

Under DDA, s 6(1) the employer is required to take such steps as are reasonable in all the circumstances to prevent the disabled person from being placed at a substantial disadvantage compared to others. Examples of steps that an employer would be expected to take are, for example, altering premises (such as providing ramps and widening doorways for wheelchair access), altering working hours or allocating certain duties to another person. The list of steps that an employer may be expected to take is not exhaustive but an employer is only expected to make such adjustments that are reasonable in the circumstances.

In determining whether an action is reasonable in the circumstances s 6(4) provides that an employer should consider:

A. The extent to which taking the step would prevent the effect in question;
B. The extent to which it is practicable for the employer to take the step;
C. The financial and other costs which would be incurred by the employer in taking the step and the extent to which taking it would disrupt any of its activities;
D. The extent of the employer's financial or other resources;
E. The availability to the employer of financial or other assistance with respect to taking the step.

Note that the duty to make reasonable adjustments does not mean an employer has to act in anticipation of employing persons with disabilities.

The employer only has to make the adjustments if he employs or is considering employing a disabled person.

12.22.4 Remedies

The remedies under the DDA are similar to those available for SDA and RRA claims (see 12.13.8).

12.22.5 Exemptions

Certain employers are exempt from the requirements of the DDA. The main exemption is for employers who employ less than 15 people. However, note that DDA, s 68(1) classifies apprentices and self-employed workers as employees.

Also beyond the realms of the Act are partners. Although employees of a partnership that has more than 15 employees will be protected by the DDA, the partners themselves are not given such protection.

Other exemptions include police officers, persons working in the armed forces, firefighters and prison officers.

12.22.6 The Disability Code

The Disability Code explains in more detail the operation of the DDA, gives practical examples of the circumstances which employers may find themselves in, and the actions they must take in order to avoid liability under the Act. Section 51 provides that the Code does not impose specific legal duties, but it is admissible as evidence in any proceedings under the Act, and the tribunal or court must take it into account where it is relevant in deciding a question arising in proceedings.

12.22.7 The Disability Commission

The DDA provided for the establishment of a National Disability Council. A major criticism of this body was that it was purely advisory, lacking the power to investigate discrimination and enforce the DDA provisions. The Disability Rights Commission Act 1999, establishes a Disability Rights Commission to replace the Council. Its functions are broadly comparable to those of the EOC and the CRE. Its general functions are to:

- work towards the equalisation of opportunities for disabled persons;
- take such steps as it considers appropriate with a view to encouraging good practice in the treatment of disabled persons; and
- keep under review the working of the DDA.

In addition to its general functions, the Commission has a number of specific functions. These include undertaking formal investigations; issuing non-discrimination notices; entering into agreements in lieu of enforcement action; providing assistance in relation to proceedings under the DDA; facilitating conciliation in relation to disputes under the DDA; and the preparation and issue of codes of practice.

12.23 EQUAL PAY

The Equal Pay Act 1970, as amended, sets out the domestic provisions underpinning a woman's right to equal pay to that of a man (or vice versa) for like work or work rated as equivalent or work of equal value. EU law is also very important in this area, especially art 119 of the EC Treaty which sets out the principle that men and women are entitled to equal pay for equal work. Article 119 can be enforced directly by individuals in the UK courts. There is also the Equal Pay Directive 1975 (75/117/EEC) which can be used as an aid in construing domestic law, where this falls short of EC law requirements. The Directive prohibits discrimination between men and women when it comes to levels of pay for the same work or work of equal value.

It is important to note that, in line with the SDA and the RRA, the Equal Pay Act 1970 applies to the self-employed as well as employees.

All complaints regarding discrimination in contractual pay or benefits should be brought under the Equal Pay Act and not the SDA.

The Equal Pay Act deems an equality clause to be included in a woman's contract, where it is not incorporated expressly. Such a clause operates so that if a term in a woman's contract is less favourable to her than a similar term in a man's contract, then the appropriate term in the woman's contract is modified so as to make it as favourable as the term in the man's contract. Also, if a woman's contract does not include a beneficial term which is within a man's contract, then again the woman's contract is modified to include that term. The equality clause applies not only to pay but to all terms and conditions of employment.

The EOC has issued a Code of Practice on Equal Pay.

The Act has been extended to workers posted to Great Britain by an undertaking established in an EU member state under certain circumstances to perform at least part of their work in Great Britain, even if their work is performed mainly outside Great Britain.

12.23.1 Like work

A woman is treated as employed on like work to that of a man if her work is the same or of a broadly similar nature to that of a man's, and any differences in the work are not of practical importance in relation to the performance of her contract. As to what amounts to a difference of practical importance, this depends upon the facts of each particular case, but regard will be had to the nature, extent and the frequency with which such differences occur in practice. However, if the difference is merely incidental to the main employment, such difference is not of practical importance.

12.23.2 Work rated as equivalent

A woman can claim equal pay even if not employed on like work if, after a job evaluation study has been carried out, the woman's job has been rated as equivalent to a man's in terms of the demand made on the worker. There are various headings for evaluation within such a scheme such as effort, skill and decision. All job evaluation schemes must be carried out on an objective basis and if as a result of the scheme the woman's work has been rated as equivalent, the woman is entitled to equal pay. If, however, the work has not been rated as equivalent, her case for equal pay may fail. However, a woman may challenge a job evaluation scheme if it is discriminatory in itself.

12.23.3 Work of equal value

Even if a woman is not employed on like work or work that has been rated as equivalent under a job evaluation scheme, she may now claim equal pay if her work is of equal value to that of a man's. Equal value is assessed in relation to the demands placed upon a worker under headings such as effort, skill and responsibility. It is important to note that a claim can still be brought under this heading even if a man is paid the same as a woman for doing like work, but there is another man doing a different job who is paid more but the work is deemed to be of equal value.

12.23.4 The comparator

The basis of any claim for equal pay is that of a comparison between a man and a woman (or vice versa). The comparator must be a person of the opposite sex employed in the same employment (or in the employment of an associated employer) at the same place of work, or at another place if there are common terms and conditions of employment observed at the different places of work. Also, under art 119 of the EC Treaty a comparison can be made with a previous employee who has subsequently left the employment.

In *Preston v Wolverhampton Healthcare NHS Trust* (ECJ, 16 May 2000), a question arose in relation to the operation of the Equal Pay Act. Section 2(4) required proceedings to be brought within a period of six months following the cessation of the employment. The claimants said that such provisions were incompatible with EU law because they made it excessively difficult to exercise the rights conferred by art 119 and because they were more restrictive than other UK provisions relating to discrimination. The ECJ held that the procedural rule in s 2(4) was not contrary to EU law so long as the limitation period was not less favourable for actions based on EU law than for those based on domestic law. The principle of equivalence required a comparison not between an action under art 119 and one under the 1970 Act, but an objective consideration of the purpose and essential characteristics of allegedly similar domestic actions in the field of employment law.

12.23.5 The material factor defence

Even if a woman has succeeded in showing that she is entitled to equal pay as she is performing either like work, work rated as equivalent or work of equal value, it is possible for an employer to justify the difference between the man's and the woman's contract by showing that the variation is genuinely due to a material factor which is not the difference in sex. In *Rainey v The Greater Glasgow Health Board* [1987] ICR 129 it was held that in establishing the material factor defence, the material difference need not be restricted to the personal qualities of the employee and the relevant comparator, but can extend to other factors such as market forces.

In *Barry v Midland Bank* [1998] 1 All ER 805, the Court of Appeal, in a ruling upheld by the House of Lords, ruled that the defence had been made out when the amount paid out under a voluntary redundancy scheme depended on the number of completed years' service, and on the employee's pay at the date of termination of the employment. The main objective of the scheme was to cushion employees against unemployment and job loss, and to compensate them for loss of job and loyalty to the bank. The Court of Appeal held such an objective was legitimate and non-discriminatory and did not fail to take into account to a significant effect the full service of an employee or to meet its objectives. Furthermore, the form of the scheme was both appropriate and reasonably necessary, since basing the award on the pay at termination of the employment was not a mere matter of convenience but was designed to promote the scheme's primary objective. It followed that any discrimination was because of a genuine material factor other than the difference of sex.

In *Glasgow City Council v Marshall* [2000] 1 All ER 641, the claimants, seven women and one man, worked as instructors at special schools. They were paid less than teachers at these schools. They brought an action under the 1970 Act, contending that they did like work to that done by teachers of the opposite sex in the same schools and that, accordingly, they were entitled to the same pay as their respective male and female comparators. The defendants explained that the pay disparity was because, for historical reasons, teachers and instructors were paid according to two different nationally agreed pay scales. The House of Lords ruled that the defendants had identified the factor which had caused the pay disparity, and no one questioned the genuineness of that explanation or suggested that the pay disparity was tainted with sex discrimination. The employers had therefore made out the material factor defence.

12.23.6 Remedies

Any claim under the Equal Pay Act 1970 must be brought before an employment tribunal. If the claim is successful, the woman is entitled to the insertion of an equality clause into her contract of employment which then entitles her to be paid at the same rate as that of her male comparator. The woman is also entitled to recover arrears of wages for up to two years before the commencement of proceedings. Employment tribunals also have a discretion to award interest on the amount of any award of compensation; this to be calculated with effect from the date of the discriminatory act. Even if equality has been achieved at the time of the application, arrears of pay may be awarded for any inequality that existed during the preceding two years.

12.23.7 Pension schemes

Pension schemes now come within the definition of pay for the purposes of legislation relating to equal pay for men and women. This was confirmed in the ECJ in the ruling relating to *Bilka-Kaufhaus GmbH v Karin Weber von Hartz* [1986] 5 ECR 1607. The employer must, therefore, not discriminate on grounds of sex, in any aspect of the scheme, including the conditions for joining the scheme, the level and type of benefits available and their timing. This applies to all benefits in respect of periods of employment from 17 May 1990, which was the date of the ruling in the ECJ on the *Barber v Guardian Royal Exchange Assurance Group* [1990] IRLR 240. This ruling states that sex discrimination in occupational scheme benefits is unlawful.

The equality requirements that are now largely incorporated in the Pensions Act 1995. Section 62 specifies that the equal treatment rule applies both to the terms on which employees join the scheme, and how they are treated once they have joined. This requirement is broad, and outlaws both direct and indirect discrimination. Thus, although it remains possible for the employer to determine the categories of employees eligible to join the scheme, and to provide different benefits for different categories, this must not be on a basis which unfairly differentiates between the sexes. For example, it is not permitted to discriminate on the basis of the number of hours worked, if to do so would result in one sex being disproportionately favoured in comparison with the other. This would be regarded as indirect discrimination.

Where equalisation of benefits has not been fully applied under a scheme from that date, levelling up applies, ie the benefits for the disadvantaged sex must be increased to the level available to the advantaged sex.

In *Preston v Wolverhampton Healthcare NHS Trust* (see 12.23.4), it was held that EU law precluded a national rule of procedure which had the effect of requiring a claim for membership of an occupational pension scheme to be brought within six months of the end of each contract of employment to which the claim related where there had been a stable employment relationship resulting from a succession of short-term contracts concluded at regular intervals in respect of the same employment to which the same pension scheme applied.

The tribunal may make an award equal to the difference in pay between that of the claimant and the equal or equivalent employee for a period of up to two years before the date of the complaint to it.

12.24 INSOLVENCY OF EMPLOYER

On an employer becoming insolvent, it is likely that a number, if not all, of the employees will have outstanding claims. Under the Insolvency Act 1986 certain claims by employees are treated as preferential debts. However, in many cases there will be insufficient funds to meet even those preferential debts and consequently an employee may be left in an unsatisfactory position. However, employees now have the right to make an application to the Secretary of State for Employment for payments from the National Insurance Fund under the ERA. These debts include:

(1) Up to eight weeks' arrears of pay. For these purposes, pay includes a guarantee payment, a medical suspension payment, remuneration under a protective award and any payment for time off from work which is permitted by statute.
(2) A payment in respect of the statutory minimum period of notice.
(3) Up to six weeks holiday pay relating to the previous 12 months.
(4) A basic award for unfair dismissal.

There is a statutory limit (£230 per week at the time of writing) that is payable in respect of each debt.

12.24.1 Redundancy payments

An employee can also make a claim under the ERA against the National Insurance Fund where he claims that his employer is liable to pay him a redundancy payment and that his employer is insolvent and that the whole or part of his redundancy payment remains unpaid.

12.24.2 Occupational pension schemes

The Secretary of State, acting under the Employment Protection (Consolidation) Act 1978, may also make payments out of the National Insurance Fund into an occupational pension scheme, where an employer has become insolvent and at the time of the insolvency there were unpaid relevant contributions that had to be paid by the employer into the scheme.

12.24.3 Statutory sick pay

Where the employer is insolvent, the Secretary of State is liable to pay SSP in respect of every day of incapacity for work (see SI 1982 No 894).

12.24.4 Statutory maternity pay

Where the employer is insolvent, the Secretary of State is liable to pay SMP as from the week in which the employer first becomes insolvent until the end of the maternity pay period (see SI 1986 No 1960).

12.24.5 Remedy

Where an employee has applied for payment from the National Insurance Fund and his application has been refused, he may under the ERA present a complaint to an employment tribunal either that the Secretary of State has failed to make any payment or that the amount of any payment made is less than the amount that should have been paid. The complaint should be brought within three months of the date on which the Secretary of State's decision is given to the employee, or if the tribunal considers that it was not reasonably practicable to bring a complaint within that time, within such further period as is considered reasonable.

If the complaint is well founded, a declaration is made to that effect and the amount that is due from the Fund is stated.

12.25 THE TRANSFER OF UNDERTAKINGS (PROTECTION OF EMPLOYMENT) REGULATIONS 1981 (TUPE)

The TUPE Regulations, which implement the Acquired Rights Directive (EEC) 77/187, are designed to protect the rights of employees on a change of employer, whether such change results from a takeover or merger or a contracting out situation. The UK courts when construing the TUPE Regulations adopt a purposive approach in line with the Acquired Rights Directive and ECJ decisions (see 12.2 above).

12.25.1 Application

The Regulations apply whenever there is a transfer from one person to another of an undertaking or part of an undertaking which is situated in the UK immediately before the transfer. For there to be a relevant transfer there must be a transfer of an undertaking or part of an undertaking as a 'going concern'.

It was originally thought that, therefore, the TUPE Regulations only applied to undertakings which were commercial ventures. However, following the case of *Dr Sophie Redmond Stichting v Bartol* [1992] IRLR 366 the exclusion of undertakings that were not in the nature of a commercial venture from the operation of the TUPE Regulations was contrary to the Acquired Rights Directive. Accordingly, the Regulations were amended by the Trade Union Reform and Employment Rights Act 1993 so that this inconsistency with the Directive was removed.

In deciding whether there has been a transfer to which the Regulations will apply, the ECJ in *Spijkers v Gebroeders Benedik Abbatoir CV* [1986] 2 CMLR 296 stated that the important question is whether the entity retains its identity after the transfer. Is there a separate identifiable economic entity which is transferred and which is continued after the transfer by the new employer in substantially the same manner?

In answering this question, the circumstances of each particular case should be examined, but a number of useful guidelines are:

(a) the type of undertaking in question;
(b) whether tangible assets, such as buildings and stock, transfer;
(c) whether goodwill transfers;
(d) whether customers transfer;
(e) whether there is an intention to transfer employees;
(f) whether there is any suspension in the carrying on of the activities, and if so for what period of time;
(g) the degree of similarity of the activities carried on before and after the transfer.

There has been considerable litigation as to whether there is a transfer of an undertaking to which the Regulations apply when a service which has previously been carried on 'in house' is 'outsourced' to an external contractor or when a new contractor takes over the provision of those services from the previous contractor. Case law indicates that such circumstances can amount to a transfer falling within the ambit of the Regulations (see *Rask v ISS Kantineservice (A/S)* [1993] IRLR 133 (the contracting-out of an in-house catering service to a private contractor); *Kenny v South Manchester College* [1993] IRLR 265 (contracting-out of the provision of prison education services); and *Dines v Initial Health Care Services Ltd* [1994] IRLR 336 (change of contractor for the provision of hospital cleaning services after competitive tendering)).

The law relating to transfers is constantly developing and will cover many scenarios. There can be a transfer to which the Regulations apply even where there is no transfer of assets or customers. For example in *Kenny v South Manchester College* [1993] IRLR 265, on the College successfully tendering to provide prison education services, there was a relevant transfer for the purposes of the Regulations, despite the fact that the premises, books and other items required to provide the education services would remain the property of the Home Office or the local education authority. Nevertheless, the Regulations applied as the education department in the prison was a clearly identifiable entity and would continue after the transfer in substantially the same manner as it did beforehand.

Furthermore, in *Schmidt v Spar Und Leuhkasse Der Fruheren* [1994] IRLR 303, it was confirmed that the Acquired Rights Directive, and as a consequence TUPE, can apply to a business or operation carried on by just one person.

However, the test laid down in *Spijkers* (of whether there is a separate economic entity which is in existence after the transfer, carrying on the same economic or similar activity as it carried on prior to the transfer) will be the decisive criterion in deciding whether there has been a transfer to which TUPE applies. In *Isles of Scilly Council v Brintel Helicopters Ltd* [1995] IRLR 6, it was stated that the question of retention of identity could be supplemented by enquiring whether the job previously done by the employee was still in existence after the transfer.

In this context, it is important to note that TUPE only applies to a transfer from one legal person to another. Therefore, the Regulations will not apply where there is merely a change in ownership by way of share transfer.

There have also been a number of recent developments that affect the application of TUPE. *Süzen* [1997] IRLR 255 has transformed the general approach to transfers. This case involved the transfer of a school cleaning contract from one contractor to another. The employer who won the contract dismissed its employees and the question arose whether the transfer of the cleaning activity to a new contractor equated to the transfer of an undertaking.

The case was referred to the ECJ which held that a transfer of activities does not, in itself, constitute a transfer of undertaking.

This ruling has since been accepted by the Court of Appeal in *Betts v Brintel Helicopters Ltd* [1997] IRLR 361, in which the court drew a distinction between labour intensive activities and other types of activities. The court suggested that with labour intensive activities, if the activity continued with 'substantially the same staff after the alleged transfer the court may well conclude that the undertaking was transferred . . .'. This effectively takes the ruling in *Süzen* one step further, as where an undertaking is transferred with 'substantially the same staff' as before the transfer then there may very well have been a transfer regulated by TUPE. We have yet to see how case-law in this area develops, and although employers may see these decisions as a way of avoiding TUPE it must be remembered that all of the circumstances of the transfer should be considered before concluding that a transfer is not regulated by TUPE.

These matters were considered afresh by the Court of Appeal in *ECM (Vehicle Delivery Service) Ltd v Cox* [1999] 4 All ER 669. It was held that, to determine whether an undertaking had continued and retained its identity in different hands, a tribunal has to consider all the facts characterising the transaction in question. In carrying out that exercise, the tribunal had to take account of the similarity of the pre- and post-transfer activities, the type of undertaking concerned and whether the majority of employees had been taken over by the new employer to enable it to carry on the activities of the undertaking on a regular basis. A transferee's failure to appoint any former employees of the transferor, however, did not point conclusively against a transfer, and a tribunal was entitled to take into account the reason for that failure. (The facts of the case are complex, and the reader is advised to turn to the report for full details.) The Court of Appeal upheld the decision, distinguishing *Süzen* in that the present case was not one of the loss of a contract with one customer being said to amount to a transfer; and distinguishing *Bett* as being of the loss of a contract for one location being said to be a transfer of an undertaking.

12.25.2 Operation

The most important consequence of a transfer to which the Regulations apply is contained in reg 5 which provides that those employees employed in the undertaking immediately before it is transferred are transferred to the new employer (the transferee) on the same terms and conditions of employment that they enjoyed with their previous employer (the transferor). Subject to certain limited exceptions, all the transferor's rights, powers, duties and liabilities under or in connection with the contract of any transferring employee are transferred to the transferee. Furthermore, anything done by the transferor in respect of a transferring employee is deemed to have been done by the transferee. Accordingly, the transferee inherits:

(1) all existing contractual terms, both express and implied;
(2) liabilities for past breaches of contract;
(3) statutory liabilities such as unfair dismissal compensation, redundancy payments and claims for compensation under discrimination legislation;
(4) continuous employment with the transferor;
(5) tortious liability, such as liability for personal injuries.

However, the transferee does not inherit criminal liability and liabilities relating to the provisions of occupational pension schemes which relate to old age, invalidity or survivor's benefits. In *Walden Engineering Co Ltd v Warrener* [1993] IRLR 420, an argument that transferring employees should be entitled to equivalent pension benefits after the transfer was specifically rejected.

In *British Fuels Ltd v Baxendale* [1998] 4 All ER 609, the question arose whether dismissals of employees prior to the transfer of an undertaking, including a trade or business, were nullities so that, on the transfer, the employees were entitled to retain the benefit of the terms and conditions of their previous employment despite their dismissal by their old employer and re-engagement by the new employer on different terms. The House of Lords ruled that the dismissals were not nullities, nor was there an automatic obligation on the transferee's part to continue to employ the employees who had been dismissed. The court also held that, although on a transfer the employee's rights against the previous employer are enforceable against the transferee, and cannot be amended by the transfer itself, there can be a variation of the terms of the contract for reasons which are not due to the transfer either on or after the transfer of the undertaking.

In *The Chancellor, Master and Scholars of the University of Oxford v Humphreys* [2000] 1 All ER 996, the House of Lords held that the Regulations did not extinguish the right of action of an employee who had objected to a transfer of his employment contract on the grounds of a detrimental change in working conditions. It was rather the case that, in such circumstances, the Regulations preserved an employee's common law rights to sue for dismissal in accordance with the provisions of the Acquired Rights Directive. The House also held that the right to terminate and sue for constructive dismissal preserved by the Regulations had to be asserted against the transferor, and not against the transferee. The remedy against the transferor was not transferred. In *Martin v Lancashire County Council* (2000) *The Times*, 26 May, the Court of Appeal held that when an undertaking was transferred under TUPE, a transferor's liability in tort to an employee in respect of a personal injury which had accrued before the transfer would be transferred to the transferee. Where the transferor had effected an employer's liability policy, the transferor's right of indemnity under that policy would also be transferred to the transferee by virtue of the Regulations.

12.25.3 'Immediately before the transfer'

An employee only transfers to the transferee company if he is employed by the transferor 'immediately before the transfer'. Until the House of Lords' decision in *Lister v Forth Dry Dock and Engineering Co Ltd (in Receivership)* [1989] IRLR 161, there had been considerable case law regarding the meaning of the phrase 'immediately before'. If a transferor was to dismiss certain employees, for example, three hours before a transfer would this avoid the application of the Regulations?

The House of Lords, in *Lister*, adopted a purposive approach in construing reg 5 of the TUPE Regulations and stated that it referred not only to a person employed immediately before the transfer, but also to an individual 'who would have been so employed if he had not been unfairly dismissed for a reason that was connected with the transfer which was not an economic, technical or organisational reason entailing changes in the workforce' (see 12.25.4). Therefore, if the transferor dismisses employees prior to a transfer, but for reasons connected with it, the TUPE Regulations will bite.

12.25.4 Unfair dismissals and business transfers

Regulation 8 provides that a dismissal, the reason or principal reason for which is the transfer or a reason connected with it, is automatically unfair whether the dismissal occurs before or after the transfer. However, reg 8(2) provides a defence for an employer where the dismissal is because of an 'economic, technical or organisational reason entailing changes in the workforce of either the transferor or the transferee before or after the transfer'. Where the dismissal can be shown to be for such an 'ETO reason' this does not make the dismissal automatically fair, but the tribunal will go on to consider whether the dismissal was fair and reasonable in all the circumstances in accordance with the reasonableness tests under EP(C)A, s 57(3).

Under the Regulations an employee must bring a claim for unfair dismissal within three months of the date he was dismissed.

A dismissed employee may also have claims for a redundancy payment or wrongful dismissal.

12.25.5 What amounts to an ETO reason?

An employer can establish a defence to a transfer related dismissal if it can show that it was for an ETO reason entailing changes in the workforce. In *Wheeler v Patel* [1987] ICR 631, it was stated that an economic reason must relate to the conduct of the business itself. Therefore, a dismissal which is made to facilitate a transfer or which is made at the request of the transferee does not amount to a relevant economic reason.

The ETO reason must also entail 'a change in the workforce'. In *Berriman v Delabok Slate Ltd* [1985] ICR 546, this phrase was held to mean a change in the number of employees or a change in the functions that the employees are required to perform. It does not cover the situation where an employer merely dismisses those employees who do not agree to changes in their terms and conditions of employment. Therefore, where an employer seeks to harmonise the terms and conditions of the transferring workforce with those of its present employees, any such attempt at harmonisation is connected with the transfer and does not amount to an ETO defence. However, where a number of employees are not required by the transferee, and in a non-transfer situation would be deemed to be redundant, then the ETO defence should apply.

12.25.6 Redundancy payments

Where an employee is automatically transferred to the transferee in accordance with the Regulations, he is not dismissed by the transferor and therefore is not entitled to a redundancy payment. However, where an employee is either dismissed by the transferor before the transfer for a genuine redundancy reason or where following the transfer, the transferee dismisses the employee for a genuine redundancy reason, the employee is still entitled to a redundancy payment, even though the dismissal is for an ETO reason connected with the transfer.

12.25.7 Avoiding the Regulations

Regulation 12 provides that any agreement that attempts to exclude or limit the operation of the Regulations is invalid. However, in any transfer documentation, it is usual for the transferor and the transferee to agree certain warranties and indemnities that provide who is liable for payment of any sums deemed to be payable as a consequence of any transfer related dismissal, or any liability that may transfer as a result of the operation of the Regulations.

From an employee's point of view, following *Katsikas v Konstantinidis* [1993] IRLR 179, an employee cannot be forced to transfer to a new employer against his will. Accordingly, following amendments to reg 5 by TURERA, an employee's contract is not transferred if the employee informs either the transferor or the transferee that he objects to becoming employed by the transferee. However, it is unlikely that an employee would exercise this right to object as the Regulations further provide that if an employee exercises his right to object, then his contract of employment is automatically terminated and he is not treated as having been dismissed by the transferor and therefore is not be entitled to any compensation.

12.25.8 Collective agreements and trade union recognition

Regulation 6 provides that any collective agreement which has been made between a transferor and a trade union which is recognised by the transferor, and which applies to transferring employees, continues to have effect after the transfer as if made by the transferee with the relevant trade union. However, the effect of this regulation is minimal as collective agreements are unenforceable unless the contrary is stated in the agreement itself.

Furthermore, reg 9 provides that where, after a transfer, the undertaking transferred retains an identity distinct from the remainder of the transferee's undertaking, any trade union which the transferor recognised with regard to the transferring employees is deemed to be recognised also by the transferee.

12.25.9 Provision of information and consultation with trade unions

The 1981 Regulations, as amended by the Collective Redundancies and Transfer of Undertakings (Protection of Employment) (Amendment) Regulations 1999 (SI No 1925), apply to business transfers completed for redundancies on or after 1 November 1999. An employer must inform the appropriate representatives of any employees who may be affected by the transfer or any measures taken in connection with it of:

(1) the fact that the transfer is to take place, approximately when it will occur and the reasons for it;

(2) the legal, economic and social implications of the transfer for the affected employee;
(3) whether he expects to 'take measures' in relation to those employees in connection with the transfer, and if so what measures; and
(4) if the employer is the transferor, whether or not the transferee expects to 'take measures' in relation to any employees it is taking over and, if so, what measures.

Such information must be given to the representatives long enough before the transfer to enable consultations to take place.

The 'appropriate representative', where a union has been recognised, is a union representative. Where no union is recognised, elected representatives are to be consulted. If affected employees fail to elect representatives within a reasonable time of being asked to do so, the employer must give the employees the required information individually. Requirements are laid down for the election process, such as ballots being in secret and principles of fairness being observed.

If there are special circumstances which render it not reasonably practicable for the employer to comply with the above duties, he must take all such steps as are reasonable in the circumstances.

In the event of a breach of these duties, a tribunal may make a declaration to that effect and award compensation of up to 13 weeks' pay for each affected employee mentioned in the award.

12.25.10 References

An employer is under no legal duty to provide a reference for an employee (*Gallear v J F Watson & Son Ltd* [1979] IRLR 306). However, where an employer agrees to provide a reference, it should exercise great care when compiling that reference.

In *Spring v Guardian Assurance* [1994] IRLR 460, the House of Lords held that employers owe a duty of care to employees in respect of the preparation of a reference. Whilst, when providing a reference to a prospective employer, the former employer does so for the benefit of that person, it also does so to assist the employee who has to rely on his former employer to exercise due skill and care. The implication of this decision is that it is now far easier for employees to challenge references given by a former employer if they can show that the employer has not taken all reasonable care in compiling a reference.

An employee may also have actions in defamation or malicious falsehood where his previous employer provides an inaccurate reference. However, these claims are far more difficult to prove and are not very common.

Furthermore, when an employer supplies a reference to a prospective employer, he will owe that employer a duty to exercise a reasonable degree of care and skill to ensure that the reference is accurate and not misleading (see *Hedley Byrne and Co Ltd v Heller and Partners Ltd* [1963] AC 465).

Consequently, if the prospective employer suffers loss as a result of its reliance on an inaccurate reference, the old employer may be held liable to pay damages on account of its negligence, if the mistake was due to carelessness.

An employer, when providing a reference, may therefore include a disclaimer of any liability arising out of a result of a potential new employer relying on the reference. However, any such disclaimer is subject to the provisions of the Unfair Contract Terms Act 1977 and of the Unfair Terms in Consumer Contracts Regulations 1999 (SI No 2083), and will only be enforceable if the disclaimer is reasonable or, respectively, fair.

13

TAX AND EMPLOYEE COMPENSATION

In this chapter, we deal with an employer's obligations to operate PAYE and national insurance contributions and we also cover the tax treatment of benefits in kind and other forms of employee compensation.

13.1 SCHEDULE E

13.1.1 Scope of Schedule E
(TA 1988, ss 19 and 192)

The basic rule of Schedule E is that income tax is charged on the emoluments of an office or employment on emoluments which fall under one or more than one of the following Cases:

Case I: Any emoluments for any tax year in which the person holding the office or employment is resident and ordinarily resident in the UK (excepting the emoluments of a person not domiciled in the UK from an office or employment under any person, resident outside, and not resident in, the UK).

Case II: Any emoluments for duties performed in the UK, for any tax year in which the person holding the office or employment is not resident (or, if resident, not ordinarily resident) in the UK (excepting the emoluments of a person not domiciled in the UK from an office or employment under any person, resident outside, and not resident in, the UK).

Case III: Any emoluments for any tax year in which the person holding the office or employment is resident in the UK (whether or not ordinarily resident there) so far as the emoluments are received in the UK.

There are rules to identify the tax year to which to relate emoluments received before an employment starts, or after employment has ceased.

Schedule E is also chargeable directly by other provisions of TA 1988 (eg gains from share options (TA 1988, s 135)). Such charges are outside the three Cases described above.

430

13.1.2 Assessment of employee earnings
(TA 1988, ss 202A and 202B)

Income tax is charged under Schedule E Cases I and II on the full amount of the emoluments (wherever received) from the employment in a tax year from the office or employment concerned (s 202A(1)). Under Case III, income tax is charged on the full amount of the emoluments received in the UK in a tax year from the office or employment concerned. This applies whether the emoluments are for that year or for some other year of assessment, and whether or not that office or employment is held at the time the emoluments are received or (as the case may be) received in the UK (s 202A(2)).

There are rules to be followed to ascertain when emoluments are treated as received (taking the earlier or earliest time in a case where more than one rule applies):

(1) the time when payment is made of or on account of the emoluments;
(2) the time when a person becomes entitled to payment of or on account of the emoluments;
(3) where the emoluments are from an office or employment with a company, the holder of the office or employment is a director of the company and sums on account of the emoluments are credited in the company's accounts or records, the time when sums on account of the emoluments are so credited; any fetter on the right to draw the sums is disregarded;
(4) where the emoluments are from an office or employment with a company, the holder of the office or employment is a director of the company and the amount of the emoluments for a period is determined before the period ends, the time when the period ends;
(5) where the emoluments are from an office or employment with a company, the holder of the office or employment is a director of the company and the amount of the emoluments for a period is not known until the amount is determined after the period has ended, the time when the amount is determined.

Rules (3)–(5) above apply to all of a director's emoluments whether or not the office or employment is that of director. They also apply if the holder of the office or employment is a director of the company at any time in the tax year of assessment in which the time there mentioned falls.

A 'director' is, in relation to a company whose affairs are managed by:

(1) a board of directors, a member of that board,
(2) a single director, that director, and
(3) the members themselves, a member of the company.

'Director' in relation to a company also includes any person in accordance with whose directions or instructions the company's directors are accustomed to act. However, this does not apply where the company's directors only act on advice given by him in a professional capacity.

There are special rules dealing with the time of receipt for vouchers, living accommodation, expenses and benefits in kind (in particular cars made available for private use, car fuel provided, beneficial loan arrangements, employee shareholdings and director's tax paid by the employer). For non-cash vouchers, credit tokens and cash vouchers taxable under PAYE, see 13.2.9. Living accommodation provided for the employee (s 145(1)) is treated as received for the period for which it is provided.

In all of the following cases, the benefits concerned (for employees earning more than £8,500 and directors) are treated under TA 1988 as received in the tax year concerned at the amount of their cash equivalent for that year:

- General charging provision (s 154(1))
- Cars available for private use (s 157(1))
- Car fuel (s 158(1))
- Beneficial loan arrangements (s 160(1))
- Loans written off (s 160(2))
- Disposal of employee shares in excess of market value (s 162(6))
- Directors' tax paid by employer (s 164).

If emoluments take the form of a benefit not consisting of money, and the special rules set out above do not apply, the emoluments are treated as received at the time when the benefit is provided.

Amounts deducted in arriving at pay
(TA 1988, s 202)

Contributions made by an employee to an approved retirement benefit scheme and contributions of unlimited amount to a payroll giving scheme ('give as you earn') are deducted from an individual's salary in arriving at taxable pay for the purposes of both PAYE and Schedule E. A 10% supplement is added by the Government on donations made between 6 April 2000 and 5 April 2003.

Note that NICs are based on pay *before* such amounts are deducted (see 13.17 below).

The point in time at which PAYE should be applied can, in certain circumstances, be earlier than the date of actual payment.

13.2 PAYE

13.2.1 Introduction
(TA 1988, s 203)

When an employer makes a payment of any income assessable under Schedule E, PAYE is deducted or repaid by the person making the payment. There are detailed regulations dealing with the assessment, charge, collection and recovery of income tax deducted, under PAYE, from income assessable under Schedule E (see Income Tax (Employments) Regulations 1993 (SI No 744)). The deductions of income tax made under these Regulations are at the basic or other rate(s) in such cases or classes of cases as are provided for by the Regulations.

Tax tables are used to calculate the required PAYE deductions. These are constructed with a view to securing so far as possible that the total income tax payable on any income assessable under Schedule E for any tax year is deducted from such income paid during that year. The tables are cumulative so that the income tax deductible or repayable on any payment is such that the total net income tax deducted since the beginning of the tax year is in proportion with that part of the tax year which ends with the date of the payment. This is achieved by a provisional deduction for allowances and reliefs, and subject also, if necessary, to an adjustment for tax overpaid or remaining unpaid on account of income tax under Schedule E for any previous tax year. In estimating the total income tax payable, it is assumed the income paid in the part of the tax year which ends with the making of the payment is pro rata for that part of the tax year.

Interest required to be paid on unpaid tax is paid without any deduction of income tax and is not taken into account in computing any income, profits or losses for any tax purposes.

13.2.2 Meaning of payment for PAYE
(TA 1988, s 203A)

There are rules to be followed in ascertaining when emoluments are treated as paid under the PAYE rules. These are broadly similar to those applying to ascertain the time of receipt of income (TA 1988, s 202B).

13.2.3 Payment by intermediary
(TA 1988, s 203B)

Where any payment of assessable income of an employee is made by an intermediary of the employer, the employer is treated as the payee under the PAYE rules. This treatment is not required if the intermediary deducts income tax from the payment he makes and accounts for it under the PAYE regulations. This procedure is intended to stop the deferment of tax by making payments through an offshore entity.

13.2.4 Employee of non-UK employer
(TA 1988, s 203C)

This applies where:

(1) an employee works for a person in the UK who is not his employer;
(2) any payment of assessable income to the employee for work done in

that period is made by a person who is the employer, or an intermediary (s 203B(4)) of the employer, but who is resident overseas;

(3) the PAYE regulations do not otherwise apply to the person making the payment; and

(4) income tax is not deducted or accounted for by the person making the payment.

The person in the UK for whom the employee works is treated, under the PAYE rules, as making, if the recipient is entitled to a net payment after deduction of any income tax, the gross amount of that payment and the amount of any income tax due; and in any other case, the payment actually made is taken.

13.2.5 Employee non-resident, etc
(TA 1988, s 203D)

A special rule deals with the case where, in a tax year, an employee is not resident or, if resident, not ordinarily resident in the UK; and he works in *and* outside the UK. Here, some of the employee's income is assessable under Schedule E Case II, but an unknown proportion of the income may prove not to be assessable. On an application, the Revenue gives a direction as to the proportion of any payment made which is to be treated, under the PAYE rules, as a payment of the employee's assessable income. If no such direction is made, the entire payment is treated as assessable income and PAYE is operated accordingly.

13.2.6 Mobile UK workforce
(TA 1988, s 203E)

This applies where:

(1) a person has entered into an agreement that employees of a contractor will, in any period, work for, but not as employees of, that person;

(2) payments of the employees' assessable income for work done in that period are likely to be made by or on behalf of the contractor; and

(3) PAYE regulations would apply on the making of such payments but the Revenue considers that it is likely that income tax will not be deducted or accounted for by the contractor in accordance with the regulations.

In such a case, the Revenue may direct that, if:

(1) any employees of the contractor work in any period for, but not as employees of, the person concerned, and

(2) any payment is made by that person for work done by the employees in that period,

income tax must deducted by that person on making that payment.

13.2.7 Tradable assets
(TA 1988, ss 203F, 203FA and 203FB)

Where any assessable income of an employee is provided in the form of a 'readily convertible asset', the employer is treated, for the purposes of the PAYE regulations, as making a payment of that income of an amount equal to that which, on the basis of the best estimate that can reasonably be made, is the amount of income likely to be chargeable to tax under Schedule E in respect of the provision of the asset. 'Readily convertible assets' are assets:

(1) which are capable of being sold or otherwise realised on a recognised investment exchange (within the Financial Services Act 1986) or on the London Bullion Market;
(2) which are capable of being sold or otherwise realised on a market specified in the PAYE regulations;
(3) which are rights which can be passed by assignment, or any other rights, in relation to a money debt that is or may become due to the employer or any other person;
(4) which consist in, or in any right in relation to, any property that is subject to a fiscal warehousing regime (VATA 1994, ss 18–18F);
(5) which are likely (without anything being done by the employee) to give rise to, or to become, a right enabling a person to obtain an amount or total amount of money (other than sterling or euro) which is likely to be similar to the expense incurred in the provision of the asset (eg a reversionary interest in a trust);
(6) for which trading arrangements exist; or
(7) for which trading arrangements are likely to come into existence in accordance with any arrangements of another description existing when the asset is provided or with any understanding existing at that time.

'Trading arrangements' also exist if there are arrangements which enable a person, or a member of his family or household (TA 1988, s 168(4)), to obtain an amount of money that is similar to the expense incurred in the provision of that asset. 'Asset' includes any property and in particular any right or interest falling within the Financial Services Act 1986, Sched 1, Pt I. However, it does not include:

(1) any payment actually made of, or on account of, assessable income;
(2) any non-cash voucher, credit token or cash voucher (see 13.2.9); or
(3) any description of property for the time being excluded from the scope of this rule by PAYE regulations.

There are useful articles in *Tax Bulletins*, February 1997, p 385 (updated article addressing some of the practical considerations of operating PAYE on payments in the form of tradable assets), and August 1998, p 563 (applying PAYE to remuneration in the form of readily convertible assets).

Enhancing the value of an asset
(TA 1988, s 203FA)

It may be that an employee's assessable income includes something which enhances the value of an asset in which the employee or a member of his family or household already has an interest. It may further occur that the asset, with its value enhanced, would be treated as a readily convertible asset (s 203F) if assessable income were provided to the employee in the form of that asset at the time of the enhancement. In such event, the above rule is applied as if the employee had been provided, at that time, with assessable income in the form of the asset (with its value enhanced), instead of with whatever enhanced its value.

Where any assessable income of an employee is provided in the form of a 'readily convertible asset', and its value is enhanced as above, the employer is treated, for the purposes of the PAYE regulations, as making a further payment of that income of an amount equal to that which, on the basis of the best estimate that can reasonably be made, is the amount of income likely to be chargeable to tax under Schedule E in respect of that enhancement.

The PAYE regulations may exclude certain matters from the scope of what constitutes enhancing the value of an asset for these purposes.

13.2.8 PAYE: gains from share options
(TA 1988, 203FB(1)).

These rules are further modified whereby an amount is assessable as a result of an event giving rise to the realisation of a gain from share options etc (TA 1988, s 135, 140A(4) or 140D). Such amount is that which, on the basis of the best estimate that can reasonably be made, is income likely to be chargeable to tax under Schedule E as a result of the event, reduced by the amount of any relief likely to be available under TA 1988, s 187A (relief for NICs in respect of share option gains).

13.2.9 PAYE: non-cash vouchers, credit tokens and cash vouchers

Non-cash vouchers
(TA 1988, s 203G)

Where a non-cash voucher (as described below) is received by an employee, the employer is treated, under the PAYE regulations, as making a payment of assessable income of the employee of an amount equal to the expense incurred by the person at whose cost the voucher and the goods, etc for which it can be exchanged are provided (TA 1988, s 141(1)(a)). This applies if either of the two conditions set out below is fulfilled with respect to the voucher; and the voucher is not of a description for the time being excluded from the scope of this treatment by PAYE regulations:

(1) The first condition is fulfilled if a non-cash voucher is capable of being exchanged for anything which, if provided to the employee at the time when the voucher is received, would be regarded as a readily convertible asset (s 203F).

(2) The second condition is fulfilled with respect to a non-cash voucher if (but for it being excluded by s 203F(4)(b) because it falls within the definition in TA 1988, s 141(1)) it would itself fall to be regarded as a readily convertible asset under s 203F.

On each occasion on which an employee uses a non-cash voucher to obtain money, or anything which, if provided to him at the time when the non-cash voucher is used, would be regarded as a readily convertible asset under s 203F, the employer is treated, under the PAYE regulations, as making a payment of assessable income of the employee of an amount equal to the expense incurred by the person at whose cost the goods, etc are provided (s 142(1)(a)).

Credit tokens
(TA 1988, s 203H)

On each occasion on which an employee uses a credit token (TA 1988, s 142(4)) provided to him by reason of his employment to obtain money, or anything which, if provided to the employee at the time when the credit token is used, would be regarded as a readily convertible asset under s 203F, the employer is treated, under the PAYE regulations, as making a payment of assessable income of the employee of an amount equal to the expense incurred by the person at whose cost the money, goods or services are provided (s 142(1)(a)). This applies where the credit token is not of a description for the time being excluded from the scope of this treatment by PAYE regulations.

Cash vouchers
(TA 1988, s 203I)

Where a cash voucher is received by an employee, the employer is treated, under the PAYE regulations, as making a payment of assessable income of the employee of an amount equal to the sum of money for which the voucher is capable of being exchanged (see TA 1988, s 143(1) and (3)).

13.2.10 Accounting for tax
(TA 1988, s 203J)

Where an employer makes a notional payment of assessable income of an employee, the obligation to deduct income tax requires him to so deduct it from any payment he actually makes to that employee.

437

13.2.11 Agency workers
(TA 1988, s 203L)

Where the remuneration receivable by an individual under any contract is treated by TA 1988, s 134 (agency workers) as the emoluments of an office or employment, the rules described in TA 1988, ss 203B–203K (except section 203E (PAYE: mobile workforce)) apply as if that person held that office or employment under or with the agency.

13.2.12 PAYE repayments
(TA 1988, s 204)

Regulations provide that no repayment of income tax is made to any person if at any time he:

(a) has claimed unemployment benefit for a period including that time; or
(b) has claimed a jobseeker's allowance for a period including that time; or
(c) has claimed a payment of income support under the Social Security Act 1986 or the Social Security (Northern Ireland) Order 1986 for a period including that time and his right to that income support is subject to the condition of availability for employment; or
(d) is disqualified at the time from receiving unemployment benefit because of loss of employment owing to stoppage of work or would be so disqualified if he otherwise satisfied the conditions for entitlement; or
(e) is prevented at the time from being entitled to a jobseeker's allowance because of a trade dispute or would be so prevented if he otherwise satisfied the conditions for entitlement.

13.2.13 Returns of expenses and benefits
(Income Tax (Employments) Regulations 1993 (SI No 744))

By 6 July following the end of each tax year, the employer must provide the Revenue with details on form P11D for employees earning £8,500 or more and directors, and on form P9D (for other employees) showing for each employee:

(1) emoluments received other than in money;
(2) payments made on behalf of the employee and not repaid;
(3) emoluments in the form of non-cash vouchers;
(4) emoluments in the form of credit tokens;
(5) the amount of any tax on a notional payment which is treated as an employee's income because the employer is unable to deduct it from an actual payment;
(6) living accommodation provided for the employee or for members of his family or household;
(7) qualifying removal expenses and benefits to a relocated employee to the extent that they exceed the qualifying limit; and
(8) emoluments relating to business entertainment (TA 1988, s 577(5)) disallowed in computing the employer's taxable business profits.

For employees earning £8,500 or more and directors (TA 1988, s 167), the return must also show particulars of

(9) payments made by the employer to the employee by reason of his employment for expenses (except for qualifying removal expenses as in (7) above);

(10) any sums put at the employee's disposal by the employer by reason of his employment and paid away by him; and

(11) any benefits provided by the employer for the employee (or for any other person) by reason of his employment such as give rise to any charge to tax under special circumstances (see below).

If, or to the extent that, the payments referred to in (1) and (10) above are for qualifying travel expenses, or for amounts expended 'wholly, exclusively and necessarily' in the performance of his duties, the employee may claim relief under TA 1988, s 198.

Items of expenses and benefits for which the inspector has issued a dispensation (TA 1988, s 166(1)) need not be included in the return.

The amount to be entered by an employer on returns of expenses payments on forms P9D and P11D, or by an employee when claiming a deduction for expenses, should include any amount paid by way of VAT, which is reimbursed, whether or not the employer may subsequently recover all or part of that VAT by repayment or set-off (SP A6, A7).

A return P46(Car) is required at the end of any quarter in which a car is first made available or replaced, if a second car is provided, if the employee begins to earn £8,500+ pa or becomes a director, or if a car is withdrawn without replacement.

When a company grants to a director or employee an option to acquire shares or allots or transfers shares under such a right which might give rise to liability under TA 1988, s 135, it must make a return of particulars of such transactions to the Revenue (s 136(6)).

13.2.14 Accounting to the Revenue for PAYE

Regulations impose an obligation on the employer to pay tax deducted under PAYE to the Collector of Taxes or Accounts office within 14 days of the end of the tax month in which the deduction was required. Employers with a monthly liability below £1,500 may choose to account for such deductions on a quarterly basis instead.

The Collector is provided with powers to recover such amounts of PAYE and NICs which are overdue. Further provisions enable such sums to be recovered from the employee rather than employer in certain circumstances.

It is also worth remembering that where an employer has not paid over the PAYE tax to the Collector of Taxes within 14 days of the end of the year of assessment (ie by 19 April), that unpaid tax or NICs automatically carries interest from 19 April until the date of payment.

13.2.15 End of year returns

In addition to paying over the tax and NICs, the employer is required to submit certain documents to the Inspector of Taxes providing details of the employees, their emoluments and tax and NICs due. Individuals' end of year summaries (form P14) and the employer's end of year return or annual return (form P35) are required to be submitted by 19 May following the end of the year to which they relate. Penalties may be charged for late submission. Additional documents may be required where, for example, payments are made to casuals or where students have been employed.

13.3 BENEFITS IN KIND

13.3.1 General rules

The legislation distinguishes between 'P11D employees' (ie directors and employees earning £8,500 or more pa) and other employees. An employer is required to submit form P11D in respect of each P11D employee who may then be assessed on the cost to the employer of benefits in kind received by them. Other employees are normally taxed on benefits only if they are convertible into cash.

Directors are normally within the P11D regime, regardless of whether their remuneration reaches or exceeds the £8,500 limit. An employee falls within the P11D category where remuneration, *together with benefits and reimbursed expenses*, is £8,500 pa or more. Such employees were formerly called 'higher paid' employees. The threshold of £8,500 was set in 1979 and, in accordance with the Government's intentions that all employees should pay income tax on the whole of their earnings, whether received in cash or in kind, this limit has not been increased. By 1989 the term 'higher paid' had become inappropriate and consequently, while there was no change made in the level of the threshold, references to higher paid employees were deleted from the legislation.

Employees are treated as earning £8,500 or more if they are remunerated *at the rate of* £8,500 pa or more. For example, a person whose employment began on 1 January 2000 and who had received a salary of £2,000 and reimbursed expenses of £200 by 6 April 2000 would be within the P11D category as the total amount of £2,200 would give an annual rate greater than £8,500.

Unless a dispensation applies, all reimbursed expenses and other benefits have to be reported on form P11D and count towards the £8,500 limit, even though they may be justified as being for business purposes and no taxable benefit in kind ultimately arises.

Dispensations
(TA 1988, s 166)

The Revenue may grant a dispensation so that certain reimbursed expenses need not be reported on form P11D. This is clearly useful in reducing administration and accounting work and, wherever possible, employers should apply for a dispensation. The expenses covered by it will be set out by the Revenue and any expenses not covered must still be reported. Any changes in the method of reimbursing expenses or scales of allowances must be notified to the Revenue.

13.3.2 Benefits which may result in a tax charge for non-P11D employees

The general rule is that employees who are not within the P11D category are assessable only on benefits capable of being converted into cash or on any benefits provided through an employer meeting an employee's own personal liability. This principle has been modified to some extent so that, for instance, credit vouchers are an assessable benefit even if the employee is not within the P11D category. However, the principle continues to hold good with regard to benefits such as the provision of a company car, free use of assets, beneficial loans etc. Table 13.1 below sets out the position.

Table 13.1 Treatment of benefits received by non-P11D employees

	Taxable	Non-taxable
Benefits capable of being turned to pecuniary account ie convertible to cash	✔	
Luncheon vouchers in excess of 15p per working day	✔	
Credit tokens and vouchers	✔	
Transport vouchers (ie any ticket, pass or other document or token intended to enable a person to obtain passenger transport services)	✔	
Living accommodation	✔	
Payment of employees' personal liabilities	✔	
Relocation expenses (over £8,000)	✔	
Round sum allowances	✔	
Company cars		✔
Free use of assets		✔
Beneficial loans		✔
Medical insurance		✔

13.3.3 Tax treatment of specific benefits where received by non-P11D employee

Benefits capable of being converted into cash

Where the benefit is convertible into cash, the measure of assessable benefit is the amount of cash which could be realised, not the cost to the employer. For example, an employee provided with a new suit by the employer would be taxable only on its second-hand value.

Payment of employee's personal liabilities

A liability arises where the employer pays a personal liability of the employee. This includes such items as home heating and lighting bills and water rates, but special rules apply where the employee is in representative accommodation (see 13.3.4).

Credit tokens and vouchers
(TA 1988, s 142)

The taxable amount on credit tokens and vouchers is the cost to the employer of providing them. Vouchers other than cheque vouchers are deemed to be taxable emoluments as and when they are *allocated* to a particular employee, not when they are *used* by that employee.

Transport vouchers
(TA 1988, s 141)

There is specific legislation to ensure that season tickets provided by employers are taxable. Once again, the measure of the assessable benefit is the cost to the employer of providing the voucher.

Living accommodation
(TA 1988, s 145)

The assessable amount is the greater of the gross rateable value of the property or the rent payable by the employer, less any amount made good by the employee. Following the abolition of domestic rates, estimated values are used for new or substantially altered properties. No assessable benefit arises where the employee occupies representative accommodation (see 13.3.4 below).

Relocation expenses
(TA 1988, s 191A and Sched 11A)

See 13.3.4 below.

13.3.4 Benefits not taxable for any category of employees

There are certain benefits that are not usually taxable even when the employee is within the P11D category. The most common items are described below.

Retirement benefits

Payments by an employer to an *approved* occupational pension scheme to secure retirement benefits for an employee do not give rise to an income tax liability for that employee. Payments into a non-approved scheme are taxable as additional remuneration for the year that the employer makes the relevant contribution. To secure approval, a pension scheme must be established for the sole purpose of providing 'relevant benefits' (ie pensions, death-in-service payments, and widows' and dependants' pensions). In addition, an employee's contributions must not exceed 15% of his remuneration. The pension benefits payable by an approved scheme must not exceed certain limits. Pension schemes are covered in more detail in Chapter 14.

Luncheon vouchers

Non-transferable luncheon vouchers (ie vouchers which are not capable of being exchanged for cash) are exempt from income tax up to a limit of 15p per working day. Vouchers for larger amounts are partly exempt, with the excess over 15p being taxable in full, whether or not the employee is within the P11D category.

Staff canteen and dining facilities

No taxable benefit in kind arises where the canteen etc is used by all staff. Furthermore, the use of a separate room by directors and more senior staff does not prejudice this exemption, unless the meals provided are superior. The Revenue may also accept, in certain cases, that facilities provided by the employer for staff to use a local restaurant may come within the definition of a 'canteen', provided that *all* staff are eligible to use these facilities on the same terms.

There are requirements which need to be strictly observed. For example, there must be no voucher or form of identification which employees need to produce on entering the restaurant. Furthermore, the Inland Revenue may try to withhold exemption from directors and employees earning £8,500 or more who use such a restaurant facility.

Sports facilities
(TA 1988, s 197G)

No taxable benefit arises on the use or availability of sports facilities owned by the employer. Similarly, no taxable benefit generally arises where an employer takes out corporate membership of an outside sports club so that *all* the employees are able to use the club's facilities. An assessment will, however, be made if the employer takes out a subscription for a particular director or employee earning £8,500 or more, or if the subscription covers a small group of such employees and directors.

Works buses and public transport
(TA 1988, ss 197B and 197AA, respectively)

There is no charge for the use of a works bus (more than 17 seats) provided for journeys between home and work or between workplaces. A similar relief is given for support for public transport bus services for such journeys.

Cycles and cycle safety equipment
(TA 1988, s 197AC)

The provision of a cycle and safety equipment is not chargeable if use thereof is restricted to journeys between home and work and between places of work.

Workplace nurseries and crèches
(TA 1988, s 155A)

Employees are exempt from income tax on the benefit derived from the use of a workplace nursery provided by the employer. The exemption applies only to nurseries run by employers alone or jointly with other employers or bodies, either at the workplace or elsewhere. The provision by an employer of cash allowances to employees for childcare, or the direct meeting of an employee's childcare bills by an employer, are taxable benefits.

Relocation expenses
(TA 1988, s 191A & Sched 11A)

Section 191A and Sched 11A provide for a ceiling of £8,000 for the amount which may be paid tax free for any one move. It is not necessary for the individual to dispose of his former residence in order to qualify for the exemption. Payments made to compensate employees for losses on the sale of their old houses are now regarded as taxable. Many practitioners still regard this as debatable and base their arguments on a decision by the House of Lords, *Hochstrasser v Mayes* [1960] AC 376.

From 5 April 1998 relocation expenses are subject to NICs to the extent that they exceed £8,000.

Long service awards
(ESC A22)

Awards to directors and employees to mark long service are exempt provided the period of service is at least 20 years and no similar award has been given to the employee within the previous ten years. The gift must not consist of cash and the cost should not exceed £20 per year of service. An Inland Revenue concession has extended the exemption to gifts of shares in the company which employs the individual or in another group company.

Awards under suggestion schemes
(ESC A57)

Provided the employee concerned is not engaged in research work, he may receive a tax-free payment under a firm's suggestion scheme. The making of suggestions should not, however, be regarded as part of the employee's job. The size of the award should also be within certain limits (ie £25 or less where the suggestion, although not implemented, has intrinsic value). Where the suggestion *is* implemented, the amount should be related to the expected net financial benefit to the employer. The current limits are:

(1) 50% of the expected net financial benefit during the first year of implementation, or
(2) 10% of the expected net financial benefit over a period of up to five years.

There is an overriding maximum of £5,000. Any amount in excess of £5,000 is taxable.

Pool cars
(TA 1988, s 159)

No tax charge arises by reason of the use of a pooled car. A car qualifies as a pooled car only if *all* the following conditions are satisfied:

(1) It is available for, and used by, more than one employee and is not ordinarily used by any one of them to the exclusion of the others.
(2) Any private use of the car by an employee is merely incidental to its business use.
(3) It is not normally kept overnight at or near the residence of any of the employees unless it is kept on premises occupied by the employer.

These requirements are strictly interpreted. Note that a car only qualifies as a pooled car *for a tax year*. There is a danger therefore in a car being taken out of pooled use and allotted to a specific employee towards the end of a tax year. As the car now no longer qualifies as a pooled car, any employee who has had the car available for private use during the same tax year may be assessed. Therefore, if the car is ordinarily parked overnight near the home of one of the users, it will not qualify as a pooled car and will create tax problems for any other employees who use it.

Representative accommodation
(TA 1988, s 145(4))

Living accommodation qualifies as representative accommodation if *any one* of the following conditions is satisfied:

(1) It is necessary for the performance of the employee's duties that he should reside in the accommodation.
(2) The accommodation is provided for the better performance of the employee's duties and it is customary to provide accommodation for such employees.
(3) The employee has to live in the accommodation because of a special threat to his security.

The exemption under the first two conditions is usually only available to directors who (together with their associates) hold 5% or less of the company's ordinary share capital and are full-time working directors. Where the employer pays for heating, lighting, repairs, maintenance etc, the representative occupiers cannot be assessed in respect of such benefits on more than 10% of their emoluments of the employment.

Re-training
(TA 1988, ss 588–589)

Where an employer pays the cost of a course undertaken by an employee (or former employee) for the purpose of providing him with skills for future employment elsewhere (or self-employment), the cost of the course can be a deductible expense of the employer, and may not be a taxable benefit of the employee. Furthermore, TA 1988, ss 200B–200J provide restricted relief to training related to the current employment.

Counselling
(TA 1988, ss 589A and 589B)

Relief in similar form to that available for re-training costs is available for qualifying counselling services for outplacement, coming to terms with redundancy, etc.

Sandwich courses
(SP4/86, re-issued November 1992)

Where an employee is released by his employer to take a full-time educational course at a university, technical college or similar educational institution which is open to the public at large, payments for periods of attendance may be treated as exempt from income tax. There are various conditions which attach to this exemption, ie:

(1) The course must last for at least one academic year with an average of at least 20 weeks of full-time attendance.
(2) The rate of payment must not exceed the greater of £7,000 and the rate of payment that an individual would have received had he been granted a public grant.

Where the rate of payment exceeds the above limits, the full amount is taxable but where the amount of payment is increased during a course, only subsequent payments are taxable.

Computer equipment
(TA 1988, s 156A)

There is a limited exemption for computer equipment and peripheral devices. Relief is limited to the first £500 of the cash equivalent of such equipment made available to an employee.

13.3.5 Free use of assets
(TA 1988, s 156)

A taxable benefit arises where an asset is made available by an employer for use by a director or P11D employee. The annual benefit is 20% of the asset's market value when it was *first* made available for use by the employee. Assets which may be involved include yachts, furniture, television sets, stereo equipment, company vans etc, ie virtually any asset apart from living accommodation and company cars. If the employer rents or hires the item concerned for a sum in excess of 20% of the asset's original market value, the higher rental charge is substituted as the assessable benefit. A deduction is allowed for any contribution or rental payable by the employee.

A further charge may arise if the ownership of assets is eventually transferred to the employee. The amount may be determined either by the market value of the asset at the time of transfer of ownership, or, where a higher figure results, by the original cost of the asset at the time it was first made available as a benefit for *any* person, less any amounts already charged as benefits in connection with the availability of the asset.

The second alternative does not apply to cars.

Example – Transfer of assets

A company provides an employee with the use of a yacht which costs £40,000 with the employee paying a rental of £2,000 pa. After two years the yacht is sold to the employee for its second-hand market value of £20,000. The assessable benefit would be:

	Benefit £
Year one	
£40,000 × 20%	8,000
Less rental paid	2,000
	6,000
Year two	
40,000 × 20%	8,000
Less rental paid	2,000
	6,000
Year three	
Cost of yacht	40,000
Less benefits assessed in years one and two	(12,000)
Amounts paid by employee	(24,000)
	4,000

Where an asset, previously made available to an individual, is transferred at no cost to him (or to another employee), at a time when its market value is still high, it is possible that the overall effect is that the total cost of the benefit for tax purposes exceeds the original cost. In other cases, the rules may operate to impose a high benefit charge upon the transfer of an asset despite the value of the asset having rapidly depreciated during the period of use.

Such rules must therefore be carefully considered when planning the provision of an asset for use by an employee or arranging for its transfer to the employee. It may be that transfer of ownership should be avoided where assets have a relatively short useful life if a tax-efficient remuneration package is desired.

Example – Ownership of assets

A company provides employees with the use of suits which remain the property of the company. The suits cost £200 and have a useful life of two years, after which they are scrapped.

An employee could therefore have an effective benefit of £200 but would be charged tax on only £40 for each of the two tax years.

13.4 TRAVELLING, SUBSISTENCE AND ENTERTAINING

13.4.1 General rules

Travel between home and the ordinary place of work does not rank as business travel. Where an individual is 'on call' and assumes the responsibilities of the employment upon leaving home, it may be possible to argue that home to work travel is business and not private travel, but this usually applies only in exceptional cases.

In order to secure tax relief on reimbursed travelling expenses, the employee must keep adequate records so as to distinguish business from non-business travel. Ideally, expenses claims to the employer should show the actual cost of such travel and, if the employer is to obtain a dispensation, the Revenue needs to be satisfied that such internal controls exist.

Mileage allowances should not be so large as to create a 'profit' element which would of course be taxable. The Revenue has introduced a Fixed Profit Car Scheme setting maximum rates of reimbursement which can be treated as tax free. These are *reduced* when the business mileage exceeds 4,000 miles pa. The rates for 2000–01 are:

	Amount per mile	
Engine size	Up to 4,000 miles	Over 4,000 miles
Up to 1000 cc	28p	17p
1001–1500 cc	35p	20p
1501–2000 cc	45p	25p
Over 2000 cc	63p	36p

Provided these rates are not exceeded and mileage is for business purposes, no benefit in kind will arise. Interest paid on a loan taken out for the purchase of a car used for business purposes may qualify for tax relief. Relief for such interest is not included in Fixed Profit Car Scheme rates and needs to be claimed separately.

13.4.2 Subsistence

The Revenue view is that it is strictly only the extra costs of living away from home which are allowable. If there are continuing financial commitments at home, the whole cost of living away from home is normally allowed. This concession is not available if the employee has no permanent residence, for example an unmarried person who normally lives in a hotel or club and who gives up that accommodation when away on a business trip. There is a specific exemption where an employee performs his duties wholly overseas and needs board and lodging abroad in order to do so.

There is, however, a statutory *de minimis* exclusion for incidental overnight expenses, where an individual is away from home on a 'qualifying 'absence' and the expenses, which would not otherwise be deductible, do not exceed a £5 nightly maximum for absences elsewhere in the UK and £10 if the absence is abroad (TA 1988, s 200A).

13.4.3 Overseas travelling expenses
(TA 1988, ss 192–193)

Where some or all of the duties of an employment are performed abroad, the expenses of travelling to and from the UK to carry out these duties are specifically regarded as having been necessarily incurred in the performance of the overseas employment. It follows, therefore, that if those expenses are reimbursed by the employer, no benefit in kind arises. Recent legislative changes have relaxed the rules further, so that, while the employee is serving abroad, the employer may pay for an unlimited number of journeys made by the employee to and from the UK without any tax charge arising. However, these journeys must be made wholly and exclusively for the purpose of performing the duties of the employment.

Moreover, where an employee travels between places where different jobs are performed, and one or more of these jobs is performed wholly or partly overseas, the expenses incurred in travelling overseas are also deemed to be necessarily incurred in performing the duties carried out overseas, so that once again no benefit in kind arises. In many cases, there is dual purpose in travelling and a taxable benefit in kind arises on the private element. Consequently, where travel expenses relate partly to a foreign holiday taken at the end of the business trip, there would be a taxable benefit in kind.

Similarly, a benefit in kind may be assessed on some or all of the expense where a spouse accompanies a director or employee and where this is not necessary for business purposes.

Maintenance of records

A director or employee who travels overseas should be able to substantiate a claim that expenses were necessarily incurred for business purposes by producing details of the expenses and the time spent away from home. A brief itinerary should be available where travel is undertaken within the overseas country or countries. The Revenue normally expects that an employer will properly control expenditure but in certain cases it may wish to see receipted bills or other vouchers.

13.4.4 Spouse's travelling and subsistence expenses

Where a spouse or other member of the family accompanies the director or employee abroad on a business trip, it is helpful in satisfying the Revenue that no benefit in kind arises if the board of directors minute their decision that the director should be so accompanied. However, this is not generally sufficient in itself and it is necessary to show that the spouse or other relative was able to perform certain tasks which could not be performed by the director.

It may be possible to show this if the spouse has some practical qualification, for example an ability to speak the foreign language concerned. A relative's expenses might also be allowable where the director or employee is in poor health and to travel alone would be impracticable or unreasonable. Where the individual's presence is for the purpose of accompanying his or her spouse at business entertainment functions, the expenses of the trip may be disallowed in calculating the employer's tax liability under the entertainment legislation, even though the expenses may be allowable in determining the employee's tax liability.

13.4.5 Employees working overseas – family visits
(TA 1988, s 194)

Where an employee is abroad for a continuous period of 60 days or more, there is an exemption for amounts borne by the employer for travelling expenses for visits by the employee's spouse and minor children. The exemption is only available for two journeys by the same person in each direction in a tax year. There is no relief if the employee ultimately bears the expense personally.

13.4.6 Entertaining expenses and round-sum allowances

It is not uncommon for directors or employees to have a round-sum allowance to cover such things as travelling, subsistence and entertaining. In the case of travelling and subsistence, the allowance counts as the taxable income of the director or employee, but a tax deduction may be claimed for any part of the allowance which can be shown to have been spent for business purposes. It is very important to have a record-keeping system which enables such claims to be substantiated. It may be better for the employer to dispense with round-sum allowances and reimburse the director or employee for properly substantiated expenditure. In this way, no benefit in kind should arise.

In the case of entertaining expenditure, the situation is rather more complex. If an employer reimburses a director's or employee's entertaining expenditure or pays a round-sum allowance which is specifically intended for entertaining, the expense to the employer is disallowed for tax purposes. The reimbursement or allowance is entered on the director's or employee's P11D but a deduction may be claimed for all the expenditure which is for genuine business purposes. If, on the other hand, the director or employee is given a round-sum allowance not specifically designated as being for entertaining, there is no question of the allowance being disallowed in the employer's tax computation. However, the director or employee would only escape liability on any part of the allowance which could be shown to have been used for business expenditure *other than* entertainment.

13.4.7 Private use of company vans
(TA 1988, ss 159AA–159AC and Sched 6A)

An employee may be assessed on a standard amount of £500 per year for private use of a company van. The amount is reduced to £350 for vans which are four or more years old at the end of the tax year. Any vehicles in excess of 3.5 tons are exempt from tax altogether (unless the vehicle is used wholly or mainly for the employee's private purposes). Where an employee has two or more vans made available for private use at the same time, tax is charged on the scale figure for each van. The standard amount will be reduced *pro rata* where the van is only available part of the year. A reduction is made for any contributions made by the employee towards the private use. Where a van is shared amongst several employees, the standard amount is apportioned among the employees.

13.5 COMPANY CARS

13.5.1 Car benefits
(TA 1988, ss 157, 168A–168G and Sched 6)

The taxable benefit is based on the list price of the car at the time that it was first registered, and not on the cost of the car. The taxable benefit is 35% of the list price which includes delivery charges, standard accessories and optional accessories fitted when the car was first made available to the employee. A separate addition to the list price is also made where accessories are fitted after the car has been made available, but accessories with a list price of less than £100 and accessories installed before 1 August 1993 are left out of account. Where the car is at least four years old at the end of the tax year the benefit is reduced by one-third.

Where the list price of a vehicle exceeds £80,000, the excess is not taken into account.

Where a car is more than 15 years old at the end of the tax year, the car has a market value of at least £15,000 and the market value exceeds the list price, the benefit in kind is calculated by reference to the market value rather than original list price.

The assessable benefit is reduced by one-third where there is at least 2,500 business miles pa. There is a reduction of a further one-third where the business mileage is at least 18,000 miles pa.

Prima facie, if an employee is offered a car in return for a reduction in salary, he may well be taxable under Schedule E on the amount of remuneration foregone (*Heaton v Bell* (1969) 46 TC 211, HL). However this charge is specifically prevented by TA 1988, s 157A.

13.5.2 **Tax treatment of employee contributions**

Contributions made by an employee towards the cost of the car can be deducted from the list price, subject to a maximum deduction of £5,000.

Example – Employee contributions to company cars

Two employees are entitled to company cars. One contributed £4,000 towards a car with a list price of £18,000 while the other contributed £11,000 towards a car with a list price of £25,000. Their assessable benefits in kind for 2000–01 are:

	A	B
	£	£
List price	18,000	25,000
Less capital contribution income of:		
(A) amount contributed	(4,000)	
(B) deduction for capital contribution limited to		(5,000)
	14,000	20,000
35% thereof	4,900	7,000
Assessable benefits	4,900	7,000

Annual payments made by employees for private use of a car may still reduce the assessable benefit on a £1 for £1 basis. In the above example, B would have been better off if he had reduced his initial capital contribution and made annual payments in return for being allowed to use the vehicle for private purposes.

13.5.3 **Returns**

So as to enable coding notices to be amended to reflect changes in an employee's car benefit, employers have to submit returns for directors or employees who either:

(1) have a car provided for the first time;
(2) change vehicles;
(3) have the use of an additional car;
(4) have the use of a car withdrawn;
(5) qualify to be assessed on an existing car either by being appointed a director, or by coming within the 'higher paid' employee category.

Returns, using Inland Revenue form P46 (car), should be returned on a quarterly basis covering the following periods:

Period of return	*Latest date for submission*
6 April to 5 July	2 August
6 July to 5 October	2 November
6 October to 5 January	2 February
6 January to 5 April	3 May

The return provides details as to the make of car, engine size, list price, accessories, capital contributions and anticipated annual business mileage.

The maximum penalty for failing to submit a return by the due date is £300 plus £60 per day until the return is submitted.

The maximum penalty for submitting an incorrect return, either fraudulently or negligently, is £3,000.

13.5.4 Private petrol
(TA 1988, s 158)

An additional scale benefit applies where an employer provides private petrol for use in a car to which a scale benefit charge arises. The scale charge depends entirely on engine size. The scale for 2000–01 is as follows:

Engine size	*Petrol* £	*Engine size*	*Diesel* £
Up to 1400 cc	1,700	Up to 2000 cc	2,170
1401 to 2000 cc	2,070	more than 2000 cc	3,200
More than 2000 cc	3,200		

The scale figures apply regardless of the amount of private fuel provided. If *any* is provided, the fuel scale charge always applies unless the employee reimburses his employer for the full cost. In some cases it may be cost effective for an employee to do this and the position should therefore be reviewed before the start of each new tax year.

13.5.5 Other related costs

The scale benefit does not cover the salary of a chauffeur. If a director is allocated a chauffeur, the full cost to the employer of providing the chauffeur should be included on the director's form P11D and will therefore be potentially assessable as a benefit in kind (subject to a claim for business mileage).

13.5.6 Car parking spaces
(TA 1988, s 197A)

The provision of a car parking space at or near the employee's place of work is not a taxable benefit. Where, however, an employee pays for car parking himself, he cannot claim a deduction for those charges.

13.5.7 Cash alternative
(TA 1988, s 157A)

Where a car is made available to an employee, the mere fact that he is offered a cash alternative to the benefit of the car does not make the benefit chargeable.

13.6 BENEFICIAL LOANS
(TA 1988, s 160)

13.6.1 Type of loans which are caught

A charge generally arises for directors and P11D employees on the annual value of beneficial loan arrangements. The annual value of a loan is taken as interest at the 'official rate' less the amount of interest (if any) paid by the employee. The official rate is revised regularly to keep pace with movements in interest rates generally. An additional taxable benefit arises if the loan is subsequently written off or forgiven.

The beneficial loan provisions can also apply if a loan is made to a member of an employee's family.

Moreover, the Revenue is able to assess benefits even though there may be no formal loan, where credit has been involved. In particular, a director who overdraws his current account with the company is regarded as having obtained a loan and is subject to an assessment.

Almost all loans by employers (and persons connected with them) are caught as the legislation deems such loans to have been given by reason of the employment. Until 6 April 1994, there was only a single exception in that this rule did not apply where the employee was related to the employer and it could be shown that the loan was given for family reasons. There were no other exceptions and there have been cases where bank employees etc have paid a normal commercial rate of interest on money lent to them, but have been assessed on a benefit because the interest they have paid has been less than the official rate.

For 1994–95 and subsequent years, loans made by an employer whose business includes the lending of money to the general public do not give rise to a charge on the employees provided the loans are made on similar terms to the public.

13.6.2 Beneficial loans used for a qualifying purpose

No charge arises on a cheap loan where the money which has been borrowed has been applied for a qualifying purpose, eg for the purchase of shares in a close company in which the individual has a material interest or where he is employed full time in the conduct and management of the company's business.

13.6.3 *De minimis* exemption

There is an exemption for all cheap or interest-free loans made to an individual employee which do not exceed £5,000. This figure excludes loans which qualify for tax relief such as loans of up to £30,000 for house purchase.

13.6.4 Employee loans written off

If the loan is written off, the amount forgiven is treated as assessable income for that year even if the person concerned is no longer employed by that company. The only exception here is if the loan is forgiven on the death of the employee.

Some care needs to be taken if it is decided to clear a loan by making an *ex gratia* or compensation payment to an employee upon the termination of the employment. An income tax liability arises if the loan is formally written off. On the other hand, no liability normally arises if the employee receives a cheque as an *ex gratia* or compensation payment and uses that sum to clear his outstanding loan. It is recommended that professional advice be taken in such circumstances.

13.7 LIVING ACCOMMODATION
(TA 1988, ss 145–146)

13.7.1 Introduction

The income tax charge which generally applies where an employee is provided with accommodation (unless it is representative accommodation—see 13.3.4) depends on whether the property is owned or rented by the employer. In the past, where the employer owned the property, the assessable amount was usually the gross annual value for rating purposes. Despite the abolition of domestic rates, this treatment continues to apply for properties on existing rating lists. For new properties, and those where there have been major improvements, the Revenue makes an estimate of what the gross annual value would have been had rates continued.

Where the property is rented by the employer, the assessable amount is the greater of the rent paid and the annual value as above. In addition a charge may arise on the annual value of any furniture and fixtures, and on any occupier's expenses borne by the company such as water rates, decorations, gardener's wages etc.

An additional charge may arise where the employer paid more than £75,000 to acquire the property. The amount assessable is a percentage of the excess of the cost of the property over £75,000. The percentage to be applied is the official rate of interest used for beneficial loans (see 13.6) as at the *beginning* of the tax year.

Example – Charge on living accommodation in excess of £75,000

A company director occupies a property owned by the company which has a gross annual value of £2,000. The cost of the property was £100,000.
The director is assessed on the following amount for 2000–01:

	£
	£
Gross annual value	2,000
£25,000 × (say) 8% =	2,000
	4,000

13.7.2 Properties owned for more than six years

Where the property is made available to an employee and it has been owned by the company for at least six years, the figure taken into account in computing the additional charge is the market value at the time it was made available rather than the cost. The actual cost (including improvements) to the employer is still used to determine whether the provisions will apply. Consequently, properties whose actual cost was less than £75,000 (including the cost of any improvements) are not within the scope of this additional charge even if their market value exceeds £75,000. Where the actual cost exceeded £75,000, the additional charge is based on the market value.

Example – Charge on living accommodation purchased over six years ago

In the example in 13.7.1, assume that the company has owned the property for more than six years and that in May 1997, when the director first occupies it, the market value is £200,000. As the original cost of the property exceeded £75,000, the director is assessed on the following amount for 2000–01:

	£
Gross annual value	2,000
£125,000 × (say) 8% =	10,000
	12,000

13.7.3 Possible reduction in assessable amount

It may be possible to reduce the assessable amount where the employee is required to occupy a property which is larger than would normally be needed for his or her own purposes. In *Westcott v Bryan* (1969) 45 TC 476 a director was required to live in a large house so that he could entertain customers. He was allowed a reduction in the assessable amount to cover the relevant proportion of the annual value and the running expenses.

Some care is needed if it is intended to claim relief in this way. This claim succeeded because the house was larger than needed for the director and his family. It would not have succeeded had the property merely been more expensive than he would have chosen. It was also helpful that the directors of the company had approved board minutes setting out their requirement and the business reason for it.

Holiday accommodation and foreign properties

Some employers buy holiday flats or cottages etc for use by staff. In practice, the Revenue generally apportions the assessable amount for the year amongst those employees who have occupied the property. The assessment can be reduced by letting the accommodation to third parties when it is not required by directors and employees. A practical problem arises with regard to overseas properties. Because there is no rateable value, the benefit is the annual rent which the property would normally command on the open market.

13.8 MISCELLANEOUS BENEFITS

13.8.1 Council tax

Where an employer pays the council tax on behalf of an employee, this is normally chargeable as part of the employee's remuneration package, resulting in a charge to both income tax and NICs. The one exception to this is where the employee is a representative occupier (see 13.3.4).

13.8.2 Medical insurance
(TA 1988, s 155(6))

The cost of medical insurance is normally assessable on P11D employees. Where the employer has a group scheme, a proportion of the total premiums is related to individual employees. There is an exception in that the premiums are exempt to the extent that they provide cover for an employee working outside the UK.

13.8.3 Telephone rental

The Revenue treats the full amount of the rental paid by the employer as a taxable benefit in kind even though the telephone may be partly (or mainly) used for business calls. The decision in *Lucas v Cattell* (1972) 48 TC 353 was that the expenditure on rental had a dual purpose (ie that a telephone is intended to be used for both business and personal use) and therefore no part of it was allowable.

13.8.4 Club subscriptions

A benefit in kind is deemed to arise where an employer pays or reimburses an employee's subscription to a club, even though the employee may only belong to the club in order to entertain the employer's customers.

13.8.5 In-house tax and financial advice

This is a type of expenditure which the Revenue has ignored in the past, but is now treated as a benefit in kind where the cost can clearly be allocated to particular employees. Similarly the Revenue will seek to assess directors on a benefit in kind where work on their personal taxation affairs has been carried out by the company's auditors, the cost being recovered in whole or in part from the company.

13.8.6 Christmas parties and other annual functions
(Extra-Statutory Concession A70)

The Revenue has said that it will not assess a benefit in respect of 'modest' expenditure on a Christmas party for staff, provided the party is open to all staff. The limit for expenditure to be regarded as modest in this context is currently £75 per head. Although this rule is generally attributed to Christmas parties, it may apply to a function at another time of year.

Where there is more than one annual function and their total costs per head exceed £75, the functions that total £75 or less are not taxed. All other functions are taxed in full.

13.8.7 Legal fees

There may be expenditure which is incurred for the benefit of the company's business but nevertheless is deemed to give rise to a benefit in kind. A leading case in this connection concerned a director of a company who was accused of dangerous driving. It was necessary for the company's business that he should not be imprisoned and the company paid his legal expenses. Although the lawyers engaged by the company were more expensive than the director would have used himself, the expenditure by the company was treated as a benefit in kind.

13.8.8 Outplacement counselling
(TA 1988, s 589B)

The value of outplacement services provided to employees made redundant is exempt from income tax. Such services may include assistance with CVs, job searches, office equipment provisions and advice on interview skills. These types of costs are not treated as part of a termination payment (see 13.18).

13.8.9 Goods and services provided at a discount to the normal price ('in-house benefits')

Where employees are allowed to purchase goods or services from their employer, no tax charge arises provided they pay an amount equal to the employer's cost. The House of Lords has decided that 'cost' meant marginal cost, not average cost (*Pepper v Hart* [1992] STC 898). This normally produces a significantly lower benefit.

Following this, the Revenue published a statement in January 1993 setting out its practice for the future with regard to teachers, employees within the transport industry and other employees who receive goods or services from their employer. The relevant press release stated that Treasury Ministers had the matter under review but, in the event, the decision has not been disturbed.

The Revenue has stated that the decision in *Pepper v Hart* means that:

(1) rail or bus travel by employees on terms which do not displace fare-paying passengers involves no or negligible additional costs;
(2) goods sold at a discount which leave employees paying at least the wholesale price involve no or negligible net benefit;
(3) where teachers pay 15% or more of a school's normal fees, there is no net benefit;
(4) professional services which do not require additional employees or partners (eg legal and financial services) have no or negligible cost to the employer (provided the employee meets the cost of any disbursements).

13.8.10 Director's tax paid by employer
(TA 1988, s 164)

Any tax (as NICs) paid by an employer on behalf of a director must be included as part of his emoluments.

13.8.11 Scholarships
(TA 1988, s 165)

Although scholarships are not taxable upon the recipient (TA 1988, s 331), they are taxed as benefits if the recipient is a member of an employee's family. This does not apply if no more than 25%, in value, of the scholarships is granted to such persons, and the scholarship is not awarded because of the employment.

13.9 END OF YEAR RETURNS

Form P11D can be obtained from the local Revenue office. The form needs to be submitted by 6 June following the end of the tax year. If the forms are submitted late there can be a penalty of up to £300 for each late return, and a continuing daily penalty of up to £60 may be imposed under similar procedures as for forms P35/P14. Penalties up to £3,000 may be charged for each incorrectly completed return.

13.10 PERSONAL SERVICE COMPANIES
(FA 1988, s 60; FA 2000, Sched 12)

13.10.1 Application of the rules
(FA 2000, Sched 12, paras 1–6)

Engagements to which the rules apply

The special rules apply where:

(1) an individual 'worker' personally performs (whether or not by obligation) services for the purposes of a business carried on by the 'client';
(2) the services are provided not under a contract directly between the client and the worker but under arrangements involving a third party (the 'intermediary'); and
(3) the circumstances are such that, if the services were provided under a contract directly between the client and worker, the worker would be regarded for income tax purposes as the client's employee.

Here, 'business' includes any activity carried on by a government or public body or a local authority (in the UK or elsewhere), or a body corporate, unincorporated body or partnership. A third party includes a partnership or unincorporated body of which the worker is a member.

The circumstances referred to in (3) above include the terms on which the services are provided, having regard to the terms of the contracts forming part of the arrangements under which they are so provided. The fact that the worker holds an office with the client does not affect the application of these rules.

Worker treated as receiving Schedule E income

If, in the case of an engagement within these rules, in any tax year:

(1) the conditions specified below are met in relation to the intermediary, and
(2) the worker, or an associate of his:
    (a) receives directly or indirectly from the intermediary a payment or benefit not chargeable to Schedule E tax, or
    (b) has rights entitling him to receive such a payment or benefit from the intermediary,

the intermediary is treated as making a 'deemed Schedule E payment' to the worker in that tax year. The deemed Schedule E payment is treated as made at the end of the tax year unless an earlier date of deemed payment applied in certain cases (Sched 12, para 12; see 13.10.3). A single payment is treated as made in respect of all relevant engagements in relation to which the intermediary is treated as making such payment in the tax year.

Conditions of liability where intermediary is a company

Where the intermediary is a company, the conditions are that the intermediary is not an associated company of the client and either the worker has a material interest in the intermediary, or the payment or benefit not chargeable under Schedule E:

(1) is received by the worker directly from the intermediary, and
(2) can reasonably be taken to represent remuneration for services provided by the worker to the client.

An associated company is one where the client and the intermediary are both under the worker's (whether alone or with associates) control. A material interest means:

(a) beneficial ownership of, or the ability to control, more than 5% of the company's ordinary share capital;
(b) possession of or entitlement to acquire rights entitling the holder to receive more than 5% of any distributions that may be made by the company; or
(c) in the case of a close company, possession of or entitlement to acquire rights that, should the company be wound up or under any other circumstance, entitle the holder to receive more than 5% of the assets that would then be available for distribution among the participators (TA 1988, s 417(1)).

Conditions of liability where intermediary is a partnership

In relation to payments or benefits received by a worker as a member of the partnership, the conditions are that:

(1) the worker (alone or with relatives) is entitled to 60% or more of the partnership profits; or
(2) most of the profits derive from the provision of services under engagements which apply to a single client (whether alone or with associates); or
(3) under the profit-sharing arrangements the income of any partner is based on the amount of income generated by him in providing services to the partnership.

'Relative' means husband or wife, parent of remoter forebear, child or remoter issue, or brother or sister.

With regard to a worker who is not a member of the partnership, the conditions are that the payment or benefit:

(1) is received by the worker directly from the intermediary, and
(2) can reasonably be taken to represent remuneration for services provided by the worker to the client.

Conditions of liability where intermediary is an individual

The conditions under these circumstances are that the payment or benefit:

(1) is received by the worker directly from the intermediary, and
(2) can reasonably be taken to represent remuneration for services provided by the worker to the client.

Exception of certain payments subject to deduction of tax

These rules do not apply to payments subject to deduction of tax under TA 1988, s 555 (payments to non-resident entertainers and sportsmen).

13.10.2 Deemed Schedule E payment
(FA 2000, Sched 12, paras 7–11)

Calculation of deemed payment

There are nine steps to be taken in calculating the deemed Schedule E payment for a tax year.

Step 1 Find the total amount of all payments and other benefits received by the intermediary in that year in respect of the relevant engagements, and reduce it by 5%.

Step 2 Add the amount of any payments and other benefits received by the worker in that year in respect of the relevant engagements, other than from the intermediary, that are not chargeable to Schedule E income tax, and would not be so chargeable if the worker were employed by the client.

Step 3 Deduct the amount of any expenses met in that year by the intermediary that would have been deductible from the emoluments of the employment if the worker had been employed by the client and the expenses had been met by the worker out of those emoluments.

Step 4 Deduct the amount of any capital allowances in respect of expenditure incurred by the intermediary that could have been claimed by the worker under CAA 1990, s 27 (plant and machinery: extension of allowances to employments etc) if the worker had been employed by the client and had incurred the expenditure.

Step 5   Deduct any contributions made in that year by the intermediary for the worker's benefit to a retirement benefits scheme approved under TA 1988, ss 590–612, or to a personal pension scheme approved under ss 630–655, that if made by an employer for an employee's benefit would not be chargeable to income tax as employee's income. This does not apply to excess contributions made and later repaid.

Step 6   Deduct the amount of any employer's NICs paid by the intermediary for that year in respect of the worker.

Step 7   Deduct the amount of any payments or other benefits received in that year by the worker from the intermediary:

(1) in respect of which the worker is chargeable to Schedule E income tax, and
(2) which do not represent items in respect of which a deduction was made under Step 3.

If the result at this point is nil or a negative amount, there is no deemed Schedule E payment.

Step 8   Find the amount that together with the employer's NICs on it is equal to the amount resulting from Step 7.

Step 9   The result is the amount of the deemed Schedule E payment.

Treatment of payments made under construction industry scheme

Where TA 1988, s 559 applies (construction industry subcontractors: payments to be made under deduction), the intermediary is treated for the purposes of Step 1 above as receiving the amount that would have been received had no deduction been made under that section.

Apportionments

In calculating the deemed Schedule E payment, any necessary apportionments are made on a just and reasonable basis of amounts received by the intermediary that are referable to the services of more than one worker, or partly to the services of the worker and partly to other matters.

Application of Schedule E rules

The following provisions apply to calculating the deemed Schedule E payment.

A 'payment or other benefit' includes anything that, if received by an employee for performing his duties of employment within Schedule E, would be an emolument of the employment, or chargeable to tax as such an emolument. The amount of a payment or other benefit is taken to be the amount of payment or cash benefit received, or the cash equivalent of a non-cash benefit. In the case of the latter, the cash equivalent is taken to be the greater of:

(1) the amount that would be chargeable to tax under TA 1988, s 19(1) if the benefit were an emolument chargeable to tax under Schedule E Case I, and

(2) the cash equivalent determined under the rules in TA 1988, s 596B (benefits under non-approved retirement benefit schemes).

A payment or benefit is treated as received when, for a payment or cash benefit, payment is made of or on account of the payment or benefit, or for a non-cash benefit, to be used or enjoyed.

Application of income tax acts: deemed Schedule E payment

The income tax acts (in particular the PAYE provisions) apply in relation to the deemed Schedule E payment as if the worker were employed by the intermediary, and the relevant engagements were undertaken by the worker in the course of performing his duties in that employment. The worker is not chargeable to tax in respect of the deemed payment if or to the extent that any combination of the following factors apply:

(1) the worker is resident, ordinarily resident or domiciled outside the UK,

(2) the client is resident or ordinarily resident outside the UK, or

(3) the services are provided outside the UK.

A deemed Schedule E payment is treated as an emolument of an employment for the purpose of:

(a) determining whether it is employment to which TA 1988, ss 153–168G applies (benefits in kind: provisions applicable to higher paid employment), and

(b) TA 1988, s 198 (deductions for necessary expenses defrayed out of emoluments).

Where the intermediary is a partnership or unincorporated association, the deemed payment is treated as received by the worker in his personal capacity and not as income of the partnership or association.

Where the worker is UK resident, the services are provided in the UK and the client or employer carries on business in the UK, the intermediary is treated as having a place of business in the UK, whether or not it in fact does so.

The deemed payment is treated as the worker's relevant earnings for the purposes of TA 1988, s 644 (relevant earnings for purposes of permissible personal pension contributions).

13.10.3 Supplementary provisions
(FA 2000, Sched 12, paras 12–24)

Earlier date of deemed Schedule E payment in certain cases

If in any tax year:

(1) a deemed Schedule E payment is treated as made, and
(2) before the date on which payment would be treated as made any relevant event occurs in relation to the intermediary,

the deemed payment for that year is treated as having been made immediately before that event or, if there is more than one, immediately before the first of them.

Where the intermediary is a company, the 'relevant events' are where the worker:

(a) is a member of the company, ceases to be a member;
(b) holds an office with the company, ceases to hold such office; or
(c) is employed by the company, ceases to be so employed.

Where the intermediary is a partnership, the relevant events are:

(i) the dissolution of the partnership or its ceasing to trade or a partner ceasing to act as such; or
(ii) where the worker is employed by the partnership, his ceasing to be so employed.

Where the intermediary is an individual and the worker is employed by him, it is a relevant event if the worker ceases to be so employed.

The fact that the deemed payment is treated as made before the end of the tax year does not affect what receipts and other matters are taken into account in calculating its amount.

Relief in cases of distributions by intermediary

A claim for relief may be made where the intermediary:

(1) is a company;
(2) is treated as making a deemed Schedule E payment in any tax year; and
(3) either in that tax year (whether before or after that payment is treated as made), or in a subsequent tax year, makes a distribution.

A claim for relief must be made by the intermediary by notice in writing given to the Revenue.

If on a claim being made the Revenue is satisfied that relief should be given in order to avoid a double charge to tax, it gives such relief by way of amending any assessment, by discharge or repayment of tax, or otherwise, as appears to it appropriate. Relief is given by treating the amount of the distribution as reduced, not the amount of the deemed Schedule E payment.

The Revenue is to exercise this power so as to secure that so far as practicable relief is given by setting the amount of a deemed Schedule E payment against relevant distributions:

(a) of the same tax year before those of other tax years;
(b) received by the worker before those received by another person; and
(c) of earlier years before those of later years.

Where the amount of a distribution is reduced, the amount of any associated tax credit is reduced accordingly.

Provisions applicable to multiple intermediaries

Avoidance of double counting

Where a payment or other benefit has been made or provided, directly or indirectly, from one relevant intermediary to another in respect of the engagement, the amount taken into account in relation to Step 1 or 2 of the calculation in 13.10.2 is reduced to such extent as is necessary to avoid double counting.

Joint and several liability for PAYE deductions

All relevant intermediaries in relation to an engagement are jointly and severally liable to account for any amount required under the PAYE provisions to be deducted from a deemed Schedule E payment treated as made by any of them. An intermediary is not so liable if it has not received any payment or benefit in respect of any engagement.

Calculation of intermediary's profits

In calculating for tax purposes the profits of a business carried on by an intermediary that is treated as making in connection with that business a deemed Schedule E payment, a deduction is allowed for the amount of the payment and of any employer's NICs paid by the intermediary in respect of it. No deduction in respect of these matters may be made except in accordance with this rule. This deduction must be taken into account for the period of account in which the deemed payment is treated as made.

There are special rules for partnerships. Here, the amount of the deduction allowed is limited to the amount that reduces the partnership's profits for the tax year to nil. To the extent that in any tax year the expenses in connection with the relevant engagements exceed the sum of:

(1) the amounts that would be deductible for Schedule E purposes if the worker had been employed by the client and the expenses had been incurred by the worker, and

(2) 5% of the amount taken into account in Step 1 of the calculation as the intermediary's receipts in respect of the relevant engagements,

they shall be left out of account in calculating the partnership's profits.

Meaning of 'associate'

An associate in relation to:

(1) an individual has the meaning given by TA 1988, s 417(3) and (4), subject to the provisions detailed below;
(2) a company means a person connected with the company within the meaning of TA 1988, s 839; and
(3) a partnership means any associate of a partnership member.

Where an individual has an interest in shares or obligations of a company as a beneficiary of an employee benefit trust, the trustees are not regarded as associates of his by reason only of that interest. However, there is an exception where the individual (either alone or with any associate) or any associate of his (with or without any other associate) has at any time on or after 14 March 1989 been the beneficial owner of, or able (directly or through other companies or by other indirect means) to control more than 5% of the company's ordinary share capital. Here 'associate' does not include the trustees of an employee benefit trust by reason only that the individual has an interest in shares or obligations of the trust.

References in these rules to payments or benefits received or receivable for a partnership or unincorporated association include payments or benefits to which a person is or may be entitled in his capacity as a member of the partnership or association.

In these rules, anything done by or in relation to an associate of an intermediary is treated as done by or in relation to the intermediary. Furthermore, a payment or other benefit provided to a member of an individual's family or household is treated as provided to the individual. 'Family or household' refers to an individual's spouse, his sons and daughters and their spouses, his parents, his servants, his dependants and his guests (TA 1988, s 168(4)). A man and a woman living together as husband and wife are treated here as if they were so married.

Transitional provisions

These rules apply for the tax year 2000–01 and subsequent years and applies in relation to services performed, or to be performed, on or after 6 April 2000. Payments or other benefits in respect of such services received before that date are treated as if received in 2000–01.

Deemed discontinuance of business

This applies where an individual or partnership is:

(1) carrying on a business at the beginning of the tax year 2000–01, and
(2) treated as making one or more deemed Schedule E payments for that year in connection with that business.

Where this rule applies, the individual or partnership may elect that:

(a) the business be deemed to have been permanently discontinued at the end of the year 1999–2000, and
(b) a new business is deemed to have been set up and commenced on 6 April 2000.

Notwithstanding the deemed discontinuance, the old business and the new business are treated as the same for the purposes of TA 1988, s 385 (carry-forward of losses against subsequent profits). Any such election must be made by being used in a return made and delivered on or before the due date (TMA 1970, ss 8, 8(1A), and 12AA(2) and (3)).

Agency workers

These rules do not affect the operation of TA 1988, s 134 (workers supplied by agencies).

13.11 GIFTS OF SHARES

A gift of shares to an employee is normally a taxable benefit, with the tax charge being based on the market value of the shares. If the shares are given to the employee by a shareholder, he is normally treated as if he had made a disposal of the shares at their market value, and he may therefore be liable for CGT.

The tax position where an employee is allowed to subscribe for new shares at an undervalue is broadly the same. The employee is taxed on the difference between the amount that he pays to subscribe for the shares and their market value. However, dealing with matters in this way usually avoids any CGT problems for the shareholders (since there is no disposal by the existing shareholders or the company, merely an issue of new shares).

A company normally needs to report the acquisition of shares by an employee within 30 days of the end of the tax year.

13.12 NON-APPROVED SHARE OPTIONS

13.12.1 Introduction

A Schedule E income tax charge may arise on the exercise of a share option or on the growth in value of shares which have been acquired by reason of the individual's office or employment (and, in particular, shares in dependent subsidiaries). The legislation was introduced on a piecemeal basis and it is often difficult to discern any clear or logical structure or principles which underly the legislation.

13.12.2 Non-approved share options
(TA 1988, s 135)

A tax charge may arise on either the grant or the exercise of the option.

Grant of the option

A charge may arise only if the option has a potential life of more than seven years. Even if the option is capable of being exercised more than seven years later, the Revenue is unlikely to assess a value greater than the difference between the value of the shares at the time the option is granted and the aggregate of the amount (if any) paid for the grant of option and the amount payable under the option.

Exercise of the option

A person who is subject to tax under Schedule E Case I may be subject to an income tax charge when he exercises a non-approved share option which has been granted to him by reason of his office or employment. The charge is not dependent upon his selling the shares but arises on any profit or gain that he is deemed to have made by exercising the option. Normally the profit is simply the difference between the market value of the shares at the time that he exercises his option and the price payable under the option.

Example – Exercise of share options

A was granted an option to acquire 1,000 shares in XYZ Ltd at a price of £2 per share. After five years have elapsed, he exercises the option and pays £2,000 to acquire the 1,000 shares. By this time the shares have grown in value to £5 per share.

A will be assessed for the year in which he exercises the option. His profit will be assessed as £3,000, ie:

	£
Market value of 1,000 shares	5,000
Less amount paid	2,000
	3,000

13.12.3 **Residence status of the employee**

No charge arises under these provisions if the employee was not resident and ordinarily resident in the UK at the date that the option was granted. This is because the individual has to be UK-resident and ordinarily resident if he is to be chargeable to tax under Schedule E Case I.

The charge, however, still arises where an individual who was resident and ordinarily resident when the option was *granted* ceases to be UK-resident before the option is *exercised*.

13.12.4 **Other employee share options**
(TA 1988, s 162)

Where an individual exercises an option which was granted to him as an employee, but at a time when he was not chargeable to tax under Schedule E Case I, and he retains the shares, an income tax charge may arise on the eventual disposal of the shares. The legislation on beneficial loans contains deeming provisions which treat the difference between the shares' market value at the time that the option is exercised and the amount payable to exercise the option as if it were a loan. On a subsequent sale or disposal of the shares the loan is deemed to be written off and a Schedule E charge arises if the individual is resident in the UK at that time.

13.12.5 **Returns by employer**

A company which grants an option to an employee must make a return within 30 days of the end of the tax year.

13.13 **PROFIT-SHARING SCHEMES**
(TA 1988, ss 186–187)

These operate by means of a trust, with the trustees receiving payments from the company's profits to enable them to buy shares on behalf of the employees. In computing its profits, the company should get a deduction for the sums paid so long as the trustees apply the money in accordance with the approved scheme rules. The amount which may be appropriated to an employee under the scheme cannot exceed £3,000 or, if greater, 10% of the employee's remuneration for PAYE purposes, with an overall limit of £8,000.

The employee is entitled to dividends paid on the shares during the period of retention by the trustees. The trustees *must* retain the shares for a period of two years; if the shares are then retained by the trustees for a further three years, there is no income tax charge on the employee. If they are sold by the employee within three years of appropriation, an income tax charge arises based on the percentage of the 'locked-in value' ie the lower of the market value of the shares when they were appropriated by the trust fund or the sale proceeds. The percentages are as follows:

Date of disposal	Appropriate %
Before release date	100
After cessation of employment due to injury, disability or redundancy	50
After relevant age*	50
Excess or unauthorised shares	50

*ie the applicable pensionable age

Provided that the shares are held in trust for three years, normally the only liability arising to the employee is to CGT when he disposes of the shares appropriated to him. The capital gains liability arises on the difference between the disposal proceeds of these shares less their open market value on the day on which they were appropriated to him. The growth in value from the date of acquisition by the trust to the date of appropriation is tax free.

Examples – Disposals of shares in a profit sharing scheme

(1)   In March 1996, the trustees of an approved scheme appropriated 500 £1 shares to an employee at a time when the market value was £1.25 each. The locked-in value is therefore 500 at £1.25 = £625.

In June 1998 the shares are sold for £2.35 each. The sale was made between years four and five and consequently an income tax liability arises based on 50% of the locked-in value, ie £312.50.

(2)   The facts are as in example (1) but the sale is delayed until June 1999. The sale is after the end of year five; therefore there is no Schedule E liability. A CGT charge could arise on a disposal of the shares. The gain is the difference between £2.35 per share and £1.25 as adjusted for indexation.

Such schemes are being phased out and replaced with a new approved profit-sharing scheme by FA 2000, Sched 8.

13.14 SHARE OPTION SCHEMES

13.14.1 Introduction

There are two main types of approved share option schemes for employees: save as you earn (SAYE) linked share option schemes and executive share option schemes.

Approved SAYE linked share option schemes were introduced in 1980.

The main features of these schemes are that there is a limit on the value of the shares which may be allocated to an employee and that participation in the scheme must be open to all full-time employees who have completed five years' service.

In 1984 the Government introduced a further category of approved share options intended to cover special arrangements for senior executives. The maximum amounts involved are much more generous and there is no requirement that the option be granted to all employees.

It is possible for an employer to establish both types of scheme and, indeed, to grant non-approved share options as well.

13.14.2 SAYE option schemes

These schemes entail the grant of an option for employees to purchase company shares at a price which must not be 'manifestly less' than 80% of their market value at the time that the options are granted. The employee is required to take out an SAYE linked savings scheme (maximum £250 per month) and may use the proceeds to exercise the share option either five or seven years later, depending on the rules of the particular scheme. No income tax liability arises on the grant of the options or upon their exercise. CGT is charged on an eventual disposal of the shares.

13.15 EXECUTIVE SHARE OPTION SCHEMES

The general principle is that an income tax charge may arise on the exercise of a share option, but certain approved share option schemes may be established which avoid such an income tax liability. CGT may still apply but only on a subsequent disposal of the shares concerned. However, following the Greenbury report, the tax benefits only apply to a restricted extent for options granted after 17 July 1995.

13.15.1 Conditions for approval

In order to receive Revenue approval, the following conditions must be satisfied:

(1) Participation in the scheme must be open only to full-time directors or employees or to part-time employees working at least 20 hours a week. Part-time directors may not participate in this scheme. The Revenue has indicated that it regards a director who works 25 hours per week as full time. The employer may choose which of the employees are to be permitted to participate in the scheme.

(2) Where the employer is a close company, no participant must own (or be entitled to acquire as a result of the grant of the option) more than 10% of the company's shares. Furthermore no individual who has owned

more than 10% of the company's shares within the previous 12 months is able to participate.

(3) The price at which the option is to be exercised must not be 'manifestly less' than the value of the shares at the time that the option is granted. With effect from 1 January 1992, it became possible for options to be granted at a discount of up to 15% of the market value of shares at the time of granting where the company also operates an approved profit-sharing scheme or savings-related share option scheme.

For options granted from 29 April 1996, the discount feature is no longer available, and it is only necessary to compare the aggregate consideration and the market value.

(4) There is a limit on the number of shares over which a particular employee may be granted options. The scheme must limit the employee's options to shares with a market value at the time that the options are granted which does not exceed £30,000. Remuneration for PAYE purposes excludes benefits in kind and reimbursed expenses and is after deducting contributions to an approved pensions scheme.

(5) The shares issued under the scheme must be fully paid ordinary shares of the company or its parent company. They must either be shares quoted on a recognised stock exchange or shares in a non-close company which is controlled by a quoted company or shares in a company not under the control of another company.

(6) Options must not be transferable and must be exercisable only between three and ten years after they are granted. There is an income tax charge on individuals who exercise options under the scheme more than once every three years. This three-year time limit is waived if a director or employee dies, in which case the option must be exercised by the personal representatives within one year of death.

13.16 SPECIAL EMPLOYEE SHARES

There are circumstances where a tax charge may arise on the disposal of shares, or on their being made more valuable by the removal of restrictions. The relevant legislation particularly needs to be borne in mind where the director or employee has acquired shares in a company which is a subsidiary of another company.

Liability to income tax under Schedule E may arise:

(1) when any restrictions affecting the employee's shares are removed; or
(2) when the shareholder receives any special benefit by virtue of ownership; or
(3) where the shares are in a 'dependent subsidiary'.

13.16.1 Shares in a dependent subsidiary

A company which is a subsidiary is deemed to be a dependent subsidiary unless the directors certify each year that it is not a dependent subsidiary and the auditors confirm their agreement to this. A company is regarded as a dependent subsidiary if there is any significant amount of trading with the parent company or another member of the group.

Where an employee holds shares in a dependent subsidiary, a tax charge may arise on the growth in the value which takes place at the earliest of the following times:

(1) the time when he actually disposes of the shares;
(2) the date that the company ceases to be a dependent subsidiary;
(3) the expiry of seven years from the date of acquisition.

A charge may arise even though the company was not a dependent subsidiary when the person acquired his shares if it subsequently becomes a dependent subsidiary.

13.17 NATIONAL INSURANCE CONTRIBUTIONS (NICS)

13.17.1 Introduction

Outline of contributory system
(Social Security Contributions and Benefits Act (SSCBA) 1992, s 1)

NICs are levied under various classes. Employers are concerned with those relating to 'employed earners' (see below):

Class 1   Earnings-related (SSCBA 1992, s 6), being:
             (i)   primary Class 1 contributions from employed earners; and
             (ii)   secondary Class 1 contributions from employers and other persons paying earnings.
Class 1A   Cars (s 10), payable by persons liable to pay secondary Class 1 contributions and certain other persons.
Class 1B   PAYE settlement agreements (s 10A), payable by persons who are accountable to the Revenue for income tax on emoluments under a PAYE settlement agreement.

The amounts and rates of contributions and the other figures which affect the liability of contributors are subject to alteration from year to year. Modified rules apply in the following special cases under SSCBA 1992:

- Women married or widowed before 6 April 1997 (s 19(4))
- Crown employees (s 115)
- HM Forces (s 116)

- Mariners, airmen etc (s 117)
- Married women and widows (s 118)
- Persons outside Great Britain (s 119)
- Employment at sea (continental shelf operations) (s 120).

There are also reductions in state scheme contributions and benefits for members of certified schemes under the Pension Schemes Act 1993.

The rules for computation, collection and recovery of contributions of Classes 1, 1A and 1B otherwise with respect to contributions of those classes are set out in SSCBA 1992, Sched 1.

A person is only liable to pay Class 1, 1A or 1B contributions if he fulfils prescribed conditions as to residence or presence in Great Britain.

Categories of earners
(SSCBA 1992, s 2)

An 'employed earner' is a person who is gainfully employed in Great Britain either under a contract of service or in an office with emoluments chargeable to income tax under Schedule E. By contrast, a 'self-employed earner' is a person who is gainfully employed in Great Britain otherwise than in employed earner's employment (whether or not he is also employed in such employment).

The Social Security (Categorisation of Earners) Regulations 1978 (SI No 1689) provide for certain prescribed descriptions of employment to be categorised as being an 'employed earner' or 'self-employed earner' notwithstanding that such employment would not otherwise fall within that category. The occupations concerned are teachers, lecturers and tutors; office cleaners; ministers of religion; and people employed by their spouses in connection with their spouses' employment.

'Earnings' and 'earner'
(SSCBA 1992, ss 3 and 4)

'Earnings' include any remuneration or profit derived from an employment; 'earner' is construed accordingly (s 3(1)). Regulations set out how the amount of a person's earnings are calculated or estimated.

The regulations make special provision for directors and senior employees for certain categories of income which are not earnings for NICs purposes:

(1) rent paid to a director or an employee who owns the premises and leases them to the company;
(2) payment of a dividend, but the rules for intermediaries may apply;
(3) payment of interest on a current account balance.

The following are treated as remuneration derived from an employed earner's employment:

(1) any sum as:
  (i)   statutory sick pay; or
  (ii) statutory maternity pay; and
(2) any sickness payment made:
  (i)   to the employed earner; and
  (ii) under arrangements by which the secondary contributor makes payments towards the provision of that sickness payment (where the funds for making sickness payments under such arrangements are attributable in part to contributions made by the employed earner, a prescribed part thereof is disregarded).

Additionally, the regulations treat as remuneration derived from an employed earner's employment any payment made by a body corporate to or for the benefit of any of its directors where that payment would, when made, not otherwise be earnings under SSCBA 1992, and also treat any amount on which an employed earner is chargeable to income tax under Schedule E as remuneration derived from the earner's employment.

13.17.2 Personal service companies etc
(SSCBA 1992, s 4A)

The rules by which NICs are applied where a worker performs services for a client through an intermediary in circumstances, whereby if the intermediary were ignored the worker would be classified as an employed earner of the client, are set out in the Social Security Contributions (Intermediaries) Regulations 2000 (SI No 727). These Regulations are virtually identical to the provisions set out in FA 2000, Sched 12 whereby such earnings are chargeable for income tax under Schedule E (see 13.10).

13.17.3 Class 1 Contributions

Earnings limits and thresholds
(SSCBA 1992, s 5)

For each tax year, the limits and thresholds set out below are specified for that year by regulations:

(1) for primary Class 1 contributions:
  (a) a lower earnings limit,
  (b) an upper earnings limit, and
  (c) a primary threshold; and
(2) a secondary threshold for secondary Class 1 contributions.

The amounts for 2000–01 are:

	Weekly (£)	Monthly (£)	Annual (£)
Lower earnings limit	67	291	3,484
Upper earnings limit	535	2,319	27,820
Primary threshold	76	329	3,952
Secondary threshold	84	365	4,385

The amount specified as the lower earnings limit for any tax year is an amount equal to or not more than £0.99 less than the weekly rate of the basic pension in a Category A retirement pension; or that sum as increased by any Act or order passed or made before the beginning of that tax year and taking effect before 6 May in that tax year.

The amount specified as the upper earnings limit for any tax year is an amount which either:

(a) is equal to seven times the sum which is the primary threshold for that year; or

(b) exceeds or falls short of seven times that sum by an amount not exceeding half that sum.

There are equivalent limits or thresholds for earners paid otherwise than weekly.

Primary contributors
(SSCBA 1992, s 6)

Where earnings are paid to or for the benefit of an earner over age 16 for any one employment of his which is employed earner's employment:

(a) a primary (earner's) Class 1 contribution is payable if the earnings exceed the current primary threshold; and

(b) a secondary (employer's) Class 1 contribution is payable if the earnings exceed the current secondary threshold.

No primary or secondary Class 1 contributions are payable on earnings covered by a PAYE Settlement Agreement (PSA).

No primary (earner's) Class 1 contributions are payable on earnings paid to or for the benefit of an employed earner above pensionable age. However, secondary Class 1 contributions are still payable.

There are special rules whereby reduced primary or secondary Class 1 contributions are payable for persons to whom the Employment Rights Act 1996, Pt XI (redundancy payments) does not apply.

Notional payment of primary Class 1 contribution where earnings not less than lower earnings limit
(SSCBA 1992, s 6A)

Where employees are paid an amount which is not less than the current lower earnings limit, but does not exceed the current primary threshold:

(a) the earner is treated as having actually paid a primary Class 1 contribution for that period, and
(b) the earnings are treated as earnings upon which such a contribution has
been paid.

This protects the employee's entitlement to benefits.

Secondary contributors
(SSCBA 1992, s 7).

The 'secondary contributor' in relation to any payment of earnings to or for
the benefit of an employed earner is, under s 7(1), in the case of an earner
employed:

(1) under a contract of service, his employer;
(2) in an office with emoluments, either:
    (a) such person as may be prescribed in relation to that office; or
    (b) if no person is prescribed, the government department, public
    authority or body of persons responsible for paying the emolu-
    ments of the office.

For employed earners who:

(a) are paid earnings in a tax week by more than one person for different
employments; or
(b) work under the general control or management of a person other than
their immediate employer,

regulations provide who is to be treated as the secondary contributor for any
particular employment.

Calculation of primary Class 1 contributions
(SSCBA 1992, s 8)

Where for earnings from employed earner's employment a primary Class 1
contribution exceeds the current primary threshold, but does not exceed the
current upper earnings limit, the amount of that contribution for 2000–01 is
10%. The amounts and rates for 2000–01 are:

	Weekly earnings	Rate of primary contributions
Up to primary threshold	£0.00–£76.00	No contribution
Between primary threshold and upper earnings limit	£76.01–£535.00	10%
Above upper earnings limit	Over £535.00	No further contribution

Alternative rules apply for contracted-out employees (Pensions Act 1993, ss 41 and 42A), airmen, continental shelf workers, mariners, members of HM Forces, married women and widows who have elected for reduced rates, persons resident abroad, and volunteer development workers (Social Security (Contributions) Regulations 1979, regs 81–123F).

Calculation of secondary Class 1 contributions
(SSCBA 1992, s 9)

Where earnings from employed earner's employment exceed the current secondary threshold, the amount of the secondary Class 1 contribution for 2000–01 is 12.2%. The amounts and rates for 2000–01 are:

	Weekly earnings	Rate of primary contributions
Up to secondary earnings threshold	£0.00–£84.00	No contribution
Above secondary earnings threshold	£84.00 and over	12.2%

Alternative rules apply for contracted-out employees under the Pensions Act 1993, ss 41 and 42A and the 1979 Regulations, regs 81–123F (see above).

Calculation of earnings
(1979 Regulations, regs 2–22)

The rules for calculating the amount of Class 1 contributions are set out in detail. Particular attention is drawn to regs 18 (calculation of earnings), 19 (payments to be disregarded) and 19A (certain payments by trustees to be disregarded).

13.17.4 Class 1A contributions

Benefits in kind etc
(SSCBA 1992, ss 10–10ZB)

Class 1A liability is imposed on benefits in kind received by an employed earner employment and who is employed as a director or has annual emoluments, including benefits, of more than £8,500. Such benefits in kind are now subject to Class 1A contributions; prior to 2000–01, the Class 1A liability arose only on the provision of cars and fuel. A deduction is available for business expenses which are allowable for income tax under Schedule E (TA 1988, s 198). Personal expenses paid for an employee by an employer continue, as before, to be included as emoluments subject to Class 1 contributions.

Benefits provided by third parties (including non-cash vouchers) are also subject to Class 1A contributions.

Class 1A contributions are payable at the rate applicable to secondary Class 1 contributors (generally employers) (ie 12.2%).

No Class 1A contributions are payable for any tax year on so much of any emoluments that are taken into account in a PSA (see 13.17.3).

Calculation of earnings
(1979 Regulations, regs 22A–22H)

The rules for calculating the amount of Class 1A contributions with reference to cars are set out in detail in these sections.

13.17.5 Class 1B contributions
(SSCBA 1992, s 10A)

A person who is accountable to the Revenue for income tax on emoluments of his employees under a PSA is also liable to make Class 1B contributions for that tax year. Class 1B contributions are payable on:

(1) the amount of any of the emoluments included in the PSA which are chargeable emoluments; and
(2) the total amount of income tax for which he is accountable for the tax year in question under the PSA.

Class 1B contributions are payable at the rate applicable to secondary Class 1 contributors (generally employers) (ie 12.2%).

Regulations may provide for persons to be excepted in prescribed circumstances from liability to pay Class 1B contributions.

Exception for employees subject to social security system of foreign states
(1979 Regulations, regs 22A–22H)

Certain employees who are subject to the social security system states within the European Economic Area, and under reciprocal agreement arrangements, are not liable to Class 1A contributions.

13.18 ENTERPRISE MANAGEMENT INCENTIVES

13.18.1 Introduction
(FA 2000, Sched 14, paras 1–7)

From 28 July 2000, enterprise management incentives (EMIs) which take the form of non-taxable share options can be granted over shares to key employees of qualifying trading companies. The qualifying rules are similar to those for enterprise investment relief, venture capital trusts and corporate venturing. The option must meet a number of general requirements (set out in Sched 14, paras 8–11), the company must be a qualifying company (paras 12–26), the individual must be an eligible employee (paras 27–36) and the option must comply with certain terms (paras 37–41).

13.18.2 General requirements
(FA 2000, Sched 14, paras 8–11),

An option does not qualify unless it meets the requirements described below:

(1) It must be granted for commercial reasons to recruit or retain a key employee in the company and not as part of an arrangement to avoid tax.
(2) The upper limit on options which can be held by an employee in a company or group is £100,000 worth (by market value) of unexercised options. Once that limit is reached, no further qualifying options can be granted for three years. Account must be taken of options under a non-savings related company share option plan (TA 1988, Sched 9). These are treated as unexercised qualifying options against the £100,000 limit.
(3) The number of employees who can hold EMI options in a relevant company at the same time is limited to 15.

13.18.3 Qualifying companies
(FA 2000, Sched 14, paras 12–26)

The company must be 'independent', and must not be a 51% subsidiary of another company nor under the control (TA 1988, s 840) of another company. Any subsidiaries must be at least 75% owned and must be qualifying subsidiaries. The company or group gross assets must not exceed £15,000,000.

Throughout the qualification period, the company or the group must exist wholly for the purpose of carrying on one or more qualifying trades, or be preparing to do so. In applying this test, there may be disregarded any incidental purposes such as the holding or managing of property used for its qualifying trades. A company intending to carry on a qualifying trade must commence its trade within two years of the share issue.

The company's or group's trade must be carried on wholly or mainly in the UK on a commercial basis with a view to profits. It must not consist substantially of excluded activities. However, research and development carried out for a qualifying trade are not excluded. The following activities are excluded:

- Dealing in land, commodities or futures or in shares, securities or other financial instruments
- Dealing in goods other than in the ordinary course of a wholesale or retail trade
- Banking, insurance, money lending and other financial activities
- Leasing or receiving royalties or licence fees
- Providing legal or accountancy services
- Property development
- Farming or market gardening
- Holding, managing or occupying woodlands, any other forestry activities or timber production
- Operating or managing hotels or comparable establishments or managing property used as a hotel or comparable establishment
- Operating or managing nursing homes or residential care homes or managing property used as a nursing home or residential care home.

13.18.4 Eligible employees
(FA 2000, Sched 14, paras 27–36)

To be an 'eligible employee', an employee must work for the company or for one of its qualifying subsidiaries.

The employee must be committed to work at least 25 hours a week for the company or for one of its qualifying subsidiaries, or, if less, 75% of his working time for the company. However, this does not include non-working by reason of injury, ill health, disability, pregnancy etc.

The employee personally, or together with his associates, must not have a material interest (more than 30%) in the company or its parent or other group company. Options and other rights to acquire shares are included in determining a right to control. However, shares held under approved profit-sharing schemes (TA 1988, Sched 9) or all employee share ownership plans (FA 2000, Sched 8) are disregarded.

13.18.5 Requirements as to terms of option etc
(FA 2000, Sched 14, paras 37–41)

The shares to which the options apply must form part of the ordinary share capital of the company, be fully paid up and not redeemable. The option must be capable of being exercised within ten years from the date of grant and must be non-transferable other than to personal representatives within one year of death.

13.18.6 Income tax treatment
(FA 2000, Sched 14, paras 42–55)

There is no income tax charge on the grant or exercise of the option, provided that the option is exercised within ten years after its grant. However, there is an income tax charge if the shares are acquired at a discount on market value. The charge arises on an amount equal to the lower of the discount, or the excess of the value on exercise over the acquisition cost. If the option is to acquire shares at a nil cost, the charge arises on the lower of the market value at the time of grant or the time of exercise.

An income tax charge also arises if a disqualifying event occurs. These include:

(1) a relevant company coming under the control of another company;
(2) a relevant company ceasing to meet the trading activities requirement;
(3) the employee ceasing to meet the employment or working time requirements;
(4) variations in the terms of the option whereby there is an increase in the shares' market value subject to the option or the requirements of Sched 14, paras 37–41 ceasing to apply;
(5) an alteration to the company's share capital;
(6) a conversion of shares not complying with Sched 14, para 50;
(7) the grant of an option under TA 1988, Sched 9 (FA 2000, Sched 14, para 10);
(8) the company ceasing to prepare to carry on a trade; or
(9) the employee ceasing to work for the requisite period.

13.18.7 Capital gains tax treatment
(FA 2000, Sched 14, paras 56–58)

Qualifying shares also include replacement shares treated as original shares under TCGA 1992, s 127. However, the normal rights issue provisions (TCGA 1992, ss 127–130), which treat the acquisition date of such shares as being the date of purchase of the original shares, do not apply.

The base date for taper relief is the date of the original grant of the original option, not the date of exercise.

13.18.8 Company reorganisations
(FA 2000, Sched 14, paras 59–63)

There are special rules dealing with company reorganisations, takeovers etc.

13.19 TERMINATION PAYMENTS

13.19.1 Redundancy payments
(TA 1988, s 579)

A statutory redundancy payment made under the Employment Rights Act 1996 (ERA) is exempt from tax although it may need to be taken into account in computing the tax payable on a termination payment (see 13.19.3).

Payment to an employee under a non-statutory redundancy scheme is generally treated by the Revenue as exempt under SP1/81 where the following conditions are satisfied:

(1) Payments are made only on account of redundancy as defined in the ERA 1996, s 166.
(2) The individual has at least two years' continuous service.
(3) Payments are made to all relevant employees and not merely to a selected group of employees.
(4) The payments are not excessively large in relation to earnings and length of service.

In *Mairs v Haughey* [1993] STC 569, the Revenue sought to tax a payment made to an employee for giving up contingent redundancy rights. The Revenue argued that the payment constituted an emolument of the employment, but it was held that a redundancy payment is not an emolument and a lump sum paid in lieu of a right to receive such a redundancy payment is equally not an emolument.

This case has also cast doubt on the view generally held within the Revenue that a termination payment is always taxable where the employee is contractually entitled to it. SP1/94 was issued after *Mairs v Haughey*.

13.19.2 *Ex gratia* payments

There has been concern that *ex gratia* payments may be subject to tax under Schedule E as unapproved retirement benefits taxable under TA 1988, s 596A. If this charge arises, the amount received is taxed in full under Schedule E. The Revenue issued SP13/91 in October 1991 and has subsequently clarified the position. An *ex gratia* payment is normally regarded as a retirement benefit taxable under s 596A only where it is paid in connection with an individual's retirement. The Revenue has also given the following guidelines on hypothetical situations:

(1) A person who has worked for a company for 20 years leaves at age 54 to take a senior executive position in another company – 'golden handshake'.
(2) A long-service employee leaves to take a senior executive position in another company at the age of 60 – borderline, probably retirement.
(3) A division of a company is sold and the 55-year-old manager responsible for running it leaves to take a job with the purchaser – 'golden handshake'.
(4) A person in his 50s has a heart attack and is advised by his doctor to leave and seek a less stressful position – 'golden handshake'.
(5) An employee aged 35 is involved in an accident and suffers disabilities that make him unable to continue with his job – 'golden handshake'.
(6) An employee aged 50 leaves to take a job nearer home to be able to nurse her aged parents – borderline, 'golden handshake'. If the employee

did not take a new job, or was nearer normal retirement age, this situation would be treated as retirement.

Ex gratia payments not caught under TA 1988, s 596A are normally treated in the same way as compensation for loss of office (see below).

13.19.3 Compensation for loss of office

Golden handshakes and other termination payments
(TA 1988, s 148)

Where a director's or employee's contract of service is terminated, it may be possible for a compensation payment to be made which is either wholly or partly tax free *provided* the employee is not entitled to the compensation under a contract of service. Where the individual receives compensation, under a term of his contract of employment, the Revenue's view is that it is taxable under Schedule E in the usual way. A payment made to a director as compensation for accepting a reduced salary or any other variation of his service contract is not regarded as a termination payment, and the amount received is normally taxable in full.

13.19.4 Payments for restrictive covenants

A payment made to an employee in return for his giving a restrictive covenant is chargeable to tax under Schedule E (TA 1988, s 313). The employer should operate PAYE.

13.20 HOW THE INLAND REVENUE ENSURES COMPLIANCE

13.20.1 The Collector's audit division

The division exists to monitor the operation of tax deduction and payment under the PAYE and construction industry subcontractors schemes and to monitor NIC compliance.

Method of operation

The Collector of Taxes has a statutory right to inspect documents and records relating to tax deductions. This does not mean Collectors have an automatic right of entry to business or other premises but given their power to inspect documents such a right of entry must to a certain extent follow on. The PAYE Regulations give the Collector the power to specify that the documents should be made available for inspection at a reasonable time at:

- A place agreed by the employer and Collector.
- In default of such agreement, the place in the UK where the documents are normally kept.
- In default of such a normal place, the employer's principal place of business in the UK.

There is no statutory limit to the number of years for which the Collector may ask for documents or records, but the employer is only obliged to keep records for three years after the end of the year to which they relate. It could therefore be said that it is safe for the employer to destroy records after that period has elapsed. The argument against this is that if the Collector finds irregularities in the records for the three most recent years it would be extremely difficult for the employer to refute the suggestions that similar irregularities took place in earlier years. It is therefore advisable that records should be kept for a minimum of six years.

The Inland Revenue's booklet IR71 entitled 'PAYE Inspections' provides brief information on the way in which such inspections are undertaken, whilst IR109 explains how settlements are negotiated at the end of an inspection.

Problem areas

From his previous experience of investigations, and knowledge of the type of business the records of which are being examined, the Collector can identify, in advance, those areas which are likely to be a fruitful source of additional liability. The areas most commonly investigated are:

(1) casuals;
(2) part-timers;
(3) bonuses (eg at Christmas);
(4) round-sum expense allowances including entertaining;
(5) directors emoluments of all types;
(6) payments out of petty cash;
(7) termination payments;
(8) self-employed consultants, out-workers etc.

The Collector will check for failure, or under-deduction, of tax either deliberately or through ignorance, as well as being concerned (and this applies particularly to directors) with the timing of deductions. His responsibility extends to Class 1 and 1A NICs as well as to income tax.

Where employers engage subcontractors in the construction industry the inspection also covers the operation of the Construction Industry Tax Deduction Scheme.

Settlement

Provided the employer agrees with the Collector's conclusions, the unpaid tax and NICs are quantified and the employer is asked to make an offer in settlement of that tax, interest, and possibly penalties.

13.20.2 Role of Schedule E compliance units

While the monitoring of compliance with PAYE and NIC regulations is officially the responsibility of the Collector's PAYE audit teams, visits are increasingly made to employers by Schedule E compliance units.

The units specialise in reviewing the provision of expenses and benefits to directors, and employees earning £8,500 or more pa. Reviews of P11Ds therefore form a large part of their work. Officers also examine employees' own tax returns however, and focus on aspects of the employer's records which indicate or suggest the provision of benefits which have not been declared.

Compliance visits

During the visit, the employer is asked about the possible provision of benefits by third parties to employees or payment of salaries direct to third parties. Questions may also be asked about the provision of inducement and termination payments. The status of individuals treated as casual employees and as self-employed may also be explored.

The principal inquiries however focus upon an examination of the provision of expenses and benefits to directors or employees and members of their family or household with a view to identifying benefits previously undeclared or undervalued.

PAYE Settlement Agreements
(TA 1988, s 206A)

As with PAYE audit inspections, minor errors may result in settlements confined to that year. In other cases settlements, to include in some cases penalties and interest, may cover the previous six years, with earlier years' adjustments estimated on the basis of the errors discovered for the one year reviewed.

The tax liabilities exposed are normally employee liabilities. In the majority of cases both the Revenue and employer are keen to settle matters in such a way that the employer meets the additional liability.

Care should be taken in such cases to ensure that employee's tax rates are taken into account in computing the tax due, although use of a composite rate may sometimes be administratively beneficial and prove acceptable to the Revenue.

While in strictness the liabilities should be grossed up to take into account the additional benefit of the employer meeting the employee's tax liability, the Revenue may be persuaded to forego this for the sake of a quick settlement with the employer as opposed to raising separate Schedule E assessments on all employees involved.

At the close of their inquiries steps are taken to ensure the employer's procedures are now acceptable, and employers should take the opportunity to review existing dispensations, or apply for new dispensations.

14

LIFE ASSURANCE, PENSIONS AND PERMANENT HEALTH INSURANCE

VINCE JERRARD, ALLIED DUNBAR ASSURANCE

14.1 INTRODUCTION

Although the fine print can appear daunting, life assurance, pension and permanent health insurance policies are really just evidence of a contract between the policyholder and the company issuing the policy. In exchange for payment of a contribution or premium, the company promises to make one or more specified payments in certain defined circumstances.

Depending on the type of contract entered into, the payment from the company may be, for example, a lump sum on the death of an individual, an income in retirement for a pensioner, or a replacement income for a person prevented from earning by reason of sickness or disability. Despite the technical appearance of many of these policies (often due to complex tax rules offering relief on payment of premiums or benefits), it is useful to bear in mind the essential simplicity of the idea: payment of premiums (usually regular payments) to the company in exchange for the guarantee or expectation of payments back on the happening of some future event.

With life assurance contracts, there must be an 'insurable interest' before a policy can be effected. Broadly, before a person can effect a life policy he must be able to demonstrate that the death of the person whose life is being insured will cause him financial loss. In addition the amount of the assurance must not exceed the amount of that loss.

Individuals have an automatic and unlimited insurable interest in their own life and the life of their spouse. In other cases an insurable interest must be demonstrated before a person can effect a policy on someone else's life (a 'life of another' policy).

This chapter, in Part I, looks at the contracts themselves and gives an outline of the rules which apply to them. Part II then goes on to consider some basic uses of the contracts with reference to sole traders, partners and small companies.

PART I – THE BASICS

14.2 LIFE ASSURANCE

14.2.1 Types of policy

There are three basic types of life assurance policy.

Whole of life policies are protection-orientated policies which pay the guaranteed sum assured on the death of the life assured, whenever death occurs. As such, they are most appropriate where long-term protection is needed, for example to meet the inheritance tax liability on an individual's death or to protect the family from the consequences of the 'breadwinner's' death. Whole of life policies may, over the years, also acquire significant cash values, although they are not primarily investment vehicles.

Endowment policies pay a guaranteed sum on the death of the life assured during the policy term, or on survival to the end of the term. Such policies provide a valuable mixture of protection and investment and are often used in conjunction with a mortgage to provide for a lump sum which will pay off the loan at the end of the mortgage term, or on the borrower's prior death.

Term assurance policies pay a guaranteed sum assured only if death occurs before the end of the term. They are for protection purposes only and usually provide no return to the policyholder if the life assured survives the policy term. Term assurance policies are usually the cheapest form of life assurance protection. The cover provided by them can be widened by use of renewal or conversion options. A renewal option allows the policyholder to renew the policy at the end of the original term, without further evidence of health being required. A conversion option allows a policyholder to turn his policy into a whole of life assurance or an endowment policy, free of underwriting, should his needs change. A convertible term assurance is particularly useful if the need is for life assurance protection for the whole of the individual's life but it is not possible to afford a whole of life policy at the time. Term assurance policies can also be effected under some pensions legislation (see 14.3.6). These policies have the advantage of tax relief on the premiums paid.

A development in the UK in recent years has been what is commonly called 'dread disease' or 'critical illness' protection. This cover is usually written as an additional benefit to a whole life, endowment or term policy and provides for payment of the sum assured on the life assured suffering one of the several specified diseases or events. Typical dread diseases and events are heart attack, stroke, cancer, major organ transplant, certain types of heart surgery and total permanent disability.

14.2.2 Traditional and unit-linked policies

There are two bases on which policies are offered.

Traditional policy

Under a traditional policy the life assurance company estimates future mortality experience, investment return and company expenses. Using these factors the actuary determines the premium rate for a given sum assured, both of which are then guaranteed by the company. As the assumptions made by the company are, of necessity, conservative, the premiums may often be higher than necessary. To counter this, traditional companies developed 'with profits' policies so that those contracts could share in the extra profits being made by the life company.

Extra profits are allocated to the policy by means of bonuses, either during the policy's term (reversionary bonuses) or on the policy's maturity (terminal bonuses). Once a bonus has been allocated it cannot be taken away, although the level of future bonuses is not guaranteed.

In 1999 the Government introduced the Individual Savings Account (ISA), an investment vehicle to stimulate savings, particularly among the lower paid and those who do not currently have any significant savings. Life assurance is included as an asset capable of being held in an ISA but only to the extent of £1,000 contribution pa (against an annual contribution of up to £7,000 for the tax years 1999–2000 and 2000–01 and £5,000 thereafter).

Unit-linked policies

These are a more recent innovation introduced to the UK in the 1960s. They offer fewer guarantees to the policyholder. Premiums are invested in pooled investment funds maintained by the life company and the policy's performance is linked directly to the fund's actual performance. Freed from having to set up the policy with long-term investment guarantees, the company can adopt an investment policy which is not unduly conservative and so may be able to provide a more realistic level of cover from the outset. The direct linking of the policy and the investment performance of the underlying fund also mean that the policyholder is not subject to the company's discretion in deciding the level of bonuses it should declare.

As unit-linked policies do not usually carry the same investment guarantees as traditional contracts, they usually incorporate the system of reviews by which the company can ensure that the policy stays 'on track'. A review compares the original assumptions about mortality, expenses and investment return with the actual performance achieved. Unfavourable performance usually leads to an increase in premium and favourable performance to an increase in benefits.

14.2.3 Qualifying and non-qualifying policies

The other main method of categorising life assurance contracts is according to whether they are 'qualifying' or 'non-qualifying'. This categorisation arises solely for the purpose of the taxation of the policy proceeds.

The qualifying rules are detailed and complex but, very broadly speaking, a qualifying policy is a regular premium policy with a minimum duration of ten years. The premiums remain fairly level and the sum assured satisfies certain minimum requirements to ensure that it provides a realistic level of life cover protection. Qualifying policies are certified as such by the Revenue, a process known as pre-certification.

The 1994 Budget announced impending changes to the life policy tax regime, with an implementation date of May 1996. After a postponement of the implementation schedule, consultation on the Revenue proposals closed in April 1997. The stated intention was to remove pre-certification and to simplify and modernise the current regime but the proposals set out in the Consultation Document attracted widespread concern among many in the industry for their complexity, the likely high cost of implementation and their failure adequately to protect the legitimate expectations of existing policyholders, particularly in the areas of part surrenders (see 14.2.5) and the taxation of trust-held policies. At the end of 1997 the Revenue confirmed that the proposed radical changes to the policy tax regime would not be implemented. Instead, legislation was introduced in FA 1998 to address the specific issues of the taxation of trusts (specifically, so called 'dead settlor trusts'), personalised portfolio bonds and the fiscal representation in the UK of offshore insurance companies; all areas where the Revenue believed legislation was deficient and abuse could exist.

14.2.4 The advantages of qualifying policies

Premiums paid under qualifying policies issued before 14 March 1984 attracted Life Assurance Premium Relief (LAPR). Qualifying policies issued before that date continue to benefit from LAPR provided that neither the benefits secured are increased nor the term extended after that date.

Subject to meeting the conditions for LAPR, relief was given at approximately half of the basic rate of income tax in force at the time, on up to the greater of ⅙th of the policyholder's income or £1,500 pa. Where LAPR is still available, it applies at the rate of 12½% for the year 2000–01.

The other key advantage of qualifying policies concerns the taxation of policy proceeds. In general, the proceeds from a qualifying policy are entirely free of tax, provided premiums are kept up for at least 10 years (or three-quarters of the term of an endowment policy, if less).

14.2.5 Tax treatment of policies

While a policy is in force all the tax on income and gains attributable to the policy is the responsibility of the life company which pays tax on them according to its own corporate taxation position.

The life company

Life companies are generally taxed on the excess of the investment income and realised capital gains over the management expenses (the 'I–E' basis). For proprietary companies there is a formula to determine the proportion of income and gains to be allocated to policyholders and shareholders, the former's share being taxed at 22% (20% for income from directly held equities) and the latter's share at 30%.

The individual policyholder

The taxation of the individual in connection with income tax and life assurance policies revolves around the concept of the 'chargeable event'. For non-qualifying policies the five chargeable events are:

(1) death of the life assured;
(2) the maturity of the policy;
(3) the total surrender of the policy;
(4) the assignment of the policy for money or money's worth (eg the sale of the policy);
(5) excesses (the system of 'excesses' allows partial surrenders each year of up to 5% of the premiums paid, on a cumulative basis, up to a total of 100% of the premiums paid; only if the cumulative 5% 'allowances' are exceeded does a chargeable event occur).

Chargeable events in the case of qualifying policies are the same as those listed above but with the following amendments:

(1) death or maturity is a chargeable event only if the policy has previously been paid-up within the first 10 years (or three-quarters of the term of an endowment policy, if less);
(2) a surrender or an assignment for money or money's worth or an excess is a chargeable event only if it occurs before the expiry of 10 years (or three-quarters of the term of an endowment policy, if less) or if the policy was made paid-up within that period.

Assignments between spouses or as security for debts are not chargeable events and nor are payments of critical illness claims.

As far as the policyholder is concerned, in most cases life assurance policies (qualifying or not) are free of any personal liability to CGT. Only if the policy is in the hands of someone other than the original owner who gave consideration for it (ie who bought it or gave something of value for it) are proceeds liable to CGT.

Company-owned policies

Special rules apply to post-13 March 1989 policies owned by companies, those assigned to secure a debt owed by a company and those held on trusts created by a company. Broadly speaking, such policies are treated as non-qualifying policies and so may give rise to a tax charge on death, maturity, surrender, part withdrawal or assignment for money or money's worth.

However, policies which would otherwise be qualifying endowments receive more favourable treatment in respect of calculation of the chargeable gain, in certain circumstances where the policy has, throughout its term, been issued to secure a loan to the company which was used to purchase land (or construct, extend or improve buildings) used for the purposes of the company's trade.

14.2.6 Gain on the happening of a chargeable event

Where a chargeable event occurs the gain arising on the event must be computed. The calculation depends on the event's nature but, broadly speaking, it is the investment profit made under the policy, taking into account previous capital benefits enjoyed and the total premiums paid. Any extra amount received by way of death benefit is mortality profit and is not included in the gain for tax purposes.

The rules for calculating the gain as a result of an excess following a withdrawal or partial surrender are somewhat different and take into account the 5% allowable withdrawals. The more favourable treatment for company-owned policies referred to in the previous section is that the amount of the loan (or the lowest amount of the loan during the policy term) is used in place of the sum of total premiums paid when calculating the chargeable gain. Thus, if the loan has remained constant during the policy term and the policy proceeds do not exceed the loan, there is no chargeable gain.

14.2.7 Taxing gains on chargeable events

In outline, tax is payable on a chargeable gain as follows:

(1) Gains made on life policies do not give rise to a tax liability at the basic rate of income tax. Accordingly if the taxpayer's income, including the gain, does not fall into the higher rate tax band there is no income tax charge on the gain.
(2) If the policyholder's income (including any chargeable gain) is taxable at the higher rate, the gain made on the life policy is liable to tax at 18% (the higher rate of 40%, less the basic rate of 22%).

(3) As the gain has accrued over the life of the policy, it would be rather harsh to treat the total gain as the taxpayer's income in the year of receipt. This could push him into the higher rate tax band in that year despite a relatively low income level. Therefore, a measure of relief is afforded by a process known as 'top-slicing'. This involves calculating the rate of tax appropriate to a part of the total gain (a 'slice') and then applying that rate of tax to the whole of the gain.

(4) The taxpayer is usually the policyholder. Exceptions to this are that if the policy is held on trust the charge falls upon the settlor (ie the person who established the trust) if the settlor is alive, otherwise it will fall on the trustees or, if they are not UK-resident, the beneficiaries; if the policy is owned by or held on trusts created, or held as security for a debt owed, by a company, the amount of the gain is treated as part of the company's Schedule D Case VI income (and top-slicing relief does not apply).

Further details of the qualifying rules and taxation of life policies can be found in the *Allied Dunbar Tax Handbook*.

14.3 PENSIONS

14.3.1 Introduction

Pensions are usually regarded as one of the most attractive investments available. Within limits, contributions are deductible at the highest rate of tax paid by the contributor; the underlying pension funds grow, in the main, free of UK taxes on income and gains; and in most cases the pension plan can provide a tax-free cash lump sum to the planholder together with a retirement income in 'old age'.

Over the years UK pensions legislation has undergone substantial reform and development. The Social Security Act 1986 created the framework for the new 'Personal Pensions' and 'Free-Standing Additional Voluntary Contribution Schemes'; reduced the benefits provided by the State Earnings Related Pensions Scheme (SERPS); increased the scope for individuals to contract out of SERPS; and removed the ability of Occupational Pension Schemes to require compulsory membership for employees.

The legislation also allowed, for the first time, banks, building societies and unit trust groups to offer pension plans.

Further changes took place in 1997, this time by virtue of tax changes to the treatment of pension funds. It is now no longer possible for such funds to reclaim the Advance Corporation Tax (ACT) paid by a company when it pays a dividend. This could reduce the overall return from an average pension fund by about 0.8% pa and will have real consequences for pensions funding by companies and individuals in the medium to long term.

From April 2001, a new form of pension will become available. Stakeholder pensions will be available for many individuals as an alternative to personal pensions and, in some cases, in addition to occupational pension schemes.

14.3.2 The state pension scheme

The benefit the state provides to those in retirement falls into two main parts: the basic retirement pension and the supplementary earnings related pension.

Everyone is entitled to the basic retirement pension, subject to payment of the necessary NICs. Currently, for a married man with earnings at the national average level, the aim is to provide a basic pension of approximately 20% of his final earnings level.

SERPS was introduced in April 1978 to provide an additional state pension which is based on earnings (within certain limits) rather than the flat benefit provided by the retirement pension. SERPS also provides a widow's benefit if a husband dies after retirement and also, in certain circumstances, if he dies before retirement. SERPS is funded by the higher rate NICs payable by both employers and employees. The self-employed do not contribute towards, or benefit from, SERPS.

In recent years the state pension scheme has come under pressure from increases in life expectancy and large numbers of retired people in the population. These concerns have led the Government to reduce the benefits under SERPS. Those reaching state retirement age in or after the year 2010 will receive a pension of only 20% of their relevant earnings, instead of the 25% originally intended, and the relevant earnings to be taken into account will be the average of lifetime earnings and not the best 20 years of earnings, as was the original rule for SERPS.

A sliding scale will operate for those retiring between the years 2000 and 2010.

14.3.3 Welfare reform

At the end of 1998, the Government published its proposals for welfare reform. Over the coming years a wide-ranging set of reforms, some of which are already in place, will affect many areas of state pension provision. What follows is a brief summary of the key points.

The basic state pension will be retained and, coupled with the new 'minimum income guarantee', will provide a basic retirement income for all. As now, the state pension will be increased in line with price inflation each year.

SERPS will be replaced by a new 'State second pension', targeted primarily at low earners (ie those earning less than £9,000 pa (at the time of writing)). Those earning less than £9,000 will receive roughly double the amount that SERPS pays to a person on the same earnings.

14.3.4 Contracting-in and contracting-out

Those who are participating in SERPS (ie employees earning more than the lower threshold for standard rate NICs) are said to be 'contracted-in' to SERPS. Since SERPS was introduced it has been possible to opt out of the scheme (referred to as 'contracting-out') in which case NICs are reduced for both the employer and employee but with the loss of SERPS benefits.

The original rules only permitted contracting-out through an occupational pension scheme established by an employer, and only where that scheme provided certain guaranteed pension benefits which were broadly equivalent to the SERPS entitlement the employee was giving up.

Contracting-out is possible through an occupational scheme providing a level of benefits at least broadly equivalent to the SERPS benefits being up or through a contracted-out money purchase occupational scheme (COMPS), or an appropriate personal pension plan (APPP) used by an employee not in an occupational scheme or a member of a contracted-in occupational scheme.

With APPPs the individual and the employer continue to make full NICs and the DSS make payments which are age related direct to the relevant pension plan. Contracting-out through an occupational scheme means lower NICs for employer and employee but the employer is required to make payment of the NICs reduction to the occupational scheme with further age related payments made by the DSS.

If the individual is contracting-out on a money-purchase basis these NICs reductions are known as 'protected rights contributions' and the fund built up from them must be used to purchase protected rights benefits. It is these benefits which, in effect, replace the SERPS being lost through contracting-out and they are treated more restrictively than benefits built up through the employer's or employee's additional contributions. For example, a protected rights pension cannot commence before state retirement age and cannot be commuted for cash.

Whether contracting-out of SERPS is advisable is a decision to be taken by each employee according to his or her personal circumstances. The key factors to be taken into account are the individual's age, sex, earnings and attitude to risk. The decision has to be reviewed each year before the end of the tax year.

It will also be possible to contract out of the State Second Pension when this is introduced.

14.3.5 Occupational pension schemes

These are schemes sponsored by an employer and to which the employer must make a contribution. Schemes are established on one of two bases: either money-purchase (defined contribution) or final salary (defined benefit schemes).

With defined benefit schemes the employee is guaranteed a level of pension benefit based on a fraction (typically $\frac{1}{60}$th or $\frac{1}{80}$th) of his final salary, multiplied by the number of years' pensionable service. A money-purchase scheme does not carry a guarantee of a specific level of pension but invests the contributions and uses the accumulated fund to provide whatever pension can be purchased with the fund at retirement.

To be tax efficient an occupational pension scheme should be approved by the Pension Schemes Office (PSO) which is a branch of the Inland Revenue. 'Approval' prevents contributions paid by the employer being taxed in the employee's hands but the preferable status of 'exempt approval' offers significant further benefits. An exempt approved scheme is able to invest in a fund free of all UK income and capital taxes (although the fund can no longer reclaim ACT paid on company dividends); the employee can claim tax relief on contributions he makes to the scheme; and employers' contributions are deductible business expenses.

Contributions

In general, there are no specific limits on the amount of contributions which can be paid into an occupational scheme but monitoring is necessary to ensure that the scheme does not become 'over-funded'. In other words, contributions may have to be limited if projected funds in the scheme are likely to exceed the amount necessary to meet its obligations. (See below under 'Benefits' for details of the remuneration cap introduced in 1989 for some scheme members.)

Employees may make personal contributions (of up to 15% of 'eligible' remuneration) to the scheme. This may be done on a voluntary basis (by way of additional voluntary contributions to the scheme or by the employee effecting his own Free Standing AVC plan) but the scheme may require some personal contribution from the employee as a condition of membership.

Benefits

To be exempt approved, the scheme must be set up under irrevocable trust for the sole purpose of providing 'relevant benefits'. These are benefits such as an income in retirement, the option to commute part of that income for a lump sum, an income for the employee's widow etc. As a result of the generous tax benefits available to such schemes, there are strict limits on the benefits which may be provided. For example, the maximum pension which can be provided to the scheme member is usually two-thirds of final remuneration and the minimum period of service required to achieve this level of benefits is now 20 years.

A pension for a spouse or dependant can also be provided of up to two-thirds of the deceased member's maximum pension at normal retirement date. A similar pension can be provided on death after retirement.

499

An employee's pension can be commuted for a lump sum, also based on final salary and years of service. The maximum lump sum is $3/80$ths of final salary for each year of service up to 40 years' service or 2.25 times the pension available before commutation, if greater.

FA 1989 introduced new rules for members of schemes established on or after 14 March 1989 and members joining older schemes after 31 May 1989. For such members no benefits can be provided for any remuneration in excess of a specific amount (increased in line with the RPI) which is £91,800 for 2000–01. This remuneration 'cap' restricts funding of such schemes (by the employer and by the employees' personal contributions) as well as payment of the various benefits the scheme can provide.

Schemes may also provide a lump sum of up to four times final remuneration (capped where necessary) on the death, in service, of the employee. This can be paid together with a refund of any personal contributions paid by the employee. It is usually possible to pay the death benefits free of inheritance tax.

The eligibility, contribution and benefit rules changed more than once in the late 1980s and some members of existing schemes will have had their positions protected from some of the subsequent changes. Further details can be found in the *Allied Dunbar Pensions Handbook.*

Top-up occupational schemes

FA 1989 also introduced the concept of unapproved top-up occupational pension schemes. These schemes, for example, allow employers to provide highly paid employees with pension benefits in respect of salary which exceeds the earnings cap, and to provide more than the usual maximum pension benefits.

14.3.6 Personal pensions

Prior to October 1987 the main personal plan was the retirement annuity contract (also called section 226 plans). In October 1987 FSAVC schemes were introduced, enabling an occupational scheme member to effect his own top-up pension as an alternative to making personal voluntary contributions to the employer's scheme. In July 1988 the section 226 plans were replaced by the new personal pension plans.

Retirement annuity contracts

Although it has not been possible to effect a retirement annuity contract since 30 June 1988, plans in force by that date are allowed to continue.

An individual was eligible for one of these plans if he had relevant earnings. These are earnings which do not carry pension rights, eg the earnings of sole traders, the self-employed, partners and employees in non-pensionable employment. Controlling directors of investment companies are excluded from eligibility.

Unlike occupational schemes, these 'section 226' contracts are not controlled by reference to the maximum benefits which can be provided; rather, restrictions are applied to the amount of contributions which can be made. The contribution limit is 17.5% of net relevant earnings, with larger percentages applicable for those over 50 (up to a maximum of 27.5% for those aged over 60). Net relevant earnings (NRE) are, broadly speaking, an individual's earnings after deduction of any business expenses. The earnings cap applicable to other schemes does not apply. Contributions made to these plans up to the limits are fully tax-deductible and the funds in which the plans invest are free of all UK income and capital taxes. Employers are not able to pay contributions to employees' section 226 contracts and they cannot be used to contract out of SERPS.

The plans are issued on a money-purchase basis, the fund accumulated at retirement being used to provide a lifetime annuity for the planholder. The planholder need not actually retire to take the benefits from these plans but the benefits must be paid between the ages of 60 and 75 (earlier for some specified occupations).

The annuity paid can be in various different forms, guaranteed or not, flat rate or increasing etc. If the planholder dies before taking his annuity a lump sum can be paid, not exceeding the contributions made to the plan plus a reasonable amount of interest or bonuses. Alternatively, an annuity can be paid to the individual's widow or dependants. Annuities can also be effected on a 'joint life basis' for the planholder and spouse, so that the annuity payments continue until the surviving spouse's death. The annuity is treated as earned income when it is paid, and the planholder can elect to commute part of his annuity at retirement. This commutation permits a maximum lump sum of three times the remaining annual annuity, but limited to a £150,000 lump sum per contract for contracts entered into on or after 17 March 1987.

In addition to pension benefits, such plans can provide life assurance protection. The maximum contribution which can be used to provide life cover is 5% of NRE (any such contribution is taken into account in determining the overall contribution limit applicable to the individual).

Death benefits payable under such plans can be assigned or put in trust so that payments of benefits on death can be arranged in a way effective for inheritance tax planning.

If, in any year, an individual pays less in contributions to a plan than would be permitted, it is possible to carry forward the shortfall in contributions for up to six years. It is also possible to 'carry back' a contribution to the previous tax year (and sometimes the year before that). Carry-forward ceases from the beginning of the tax year 2001–02.

Personal pension plans

These plans were introduced on 1 July 1988. In many ways they are more flexible than the section 226 contracts which they replaced. For example, employers may make contributions to an employee's PPP; an 'appropriate' PPP can be used by employees to contract out of SERPS; and benefits can be taken between the ages of 50 and 75 (earlier for some specified occupations). Employees' contributions to PPPs are payable net of basic rate income tax under the pension relief at source (PRAS) rules.

PPPs are, like section 226 contracts, money-purchase arrangements with controls on the maximum contributions which can be made. Where an employer contributes to an employee's PPP, the employer's contributions must be taken into account in determining the employee's maximum permissible contributions.

With effect from 1989/90 the maximum contributions allowed (as a percentage of net relevant earnings) are:

Age at beginning of year of assessment	%
below 36	17½
36–45	20
46–50	25
51–55	30
56–60	35
61+	40

However, PPPs are also, with effect from 1989–90, subject to a similar income cap to that referred to in relation to occupational pension schemes (see 14.3.5) and earnings over the appropriate limit must be ignored in calculating entitlement to pay contributions. The benefits provided by a PPP are, again, very similar to those available under a section 226 plan including the use of up to 5% of net relevant earnings to provide life assurance protection, but the tax-free cash which can be taken is a maximum of 25% of the fund.

It is possible to defer taking an annuity but still receive income withdrawals from the fund.

14.3.7 Stakeholder pensions and the new tax regime for defined contribution pensions

From April 2001, a new tax regime will be introduced for stakeholder pensions. The new tax regime will also apply to other types of 'defined contribution' (or money purchase) pension plans, including personal pensions and some occupational pensions.

Contribution limits and benefits will be similar to those for personal pensions. However, for those who contribute less than £3,600 pa there will be no link with earnings for the first time ever. In addition, it will also be possible to have a stakeholder pension, or a personal pension, alongside an occupational pension scheme if earnings are less than £30,000 pa.

All employers with more than four employees who do not offer an occupational scheme will need to provide access to a stakeholder pension scheme and collect contributions by deductions from their employee's salaries.

14.3.8 Moving between different types of pension arrangement

If a self-employed individual effects a PPP but then moves into employment, for example a sole trader incorporating his business, he can continue with his PPP. The same is true with an employee who has a PPP and moves into self-employment. In some cases, however, it is not possible to continue with the same pension plan; for example an employee who is a member of an occupational scheme cannot remain in that scheme if he becomes self-employed. Similarly, if a person with a PPP joins an employer's occupational scheme he cannot continue to pay contributions into the PPP if he has no continuing source of relevant earnings.

In those cases where a change of status affects pension planning it is usually possible for a transfer payment to be made from one scheme to another. Many companies offer such transfers on preferential terms, particularly where the individual is moving between the occupational and personal pension regimes.

The new rules for stakeholder pensions and the changes to the tax rules for personal pensions will make it much easier to continue with the same pension when a change of employment occurs.

Further details of pension plans and planning can be found in the *Allied Dunbar Pensions Handbook.*

14.4 PERMANENT HEALTH INSURANCE

Typically, permanent health insurance (PHI) policies are a means of providing a replacement income if an individual is unable to work through illness or disability. Policies are usually available to those aged between 16 and 60 and cover usually ends no later than the normal retirement date for the individual's occupation.

In the event of sickness or disability the policy usually provides for a deferment period and payment of benefits only commences at the end of this period. Deferment periods may be between one month and one year (usually selected by the policyholder at the outset) and are valuable to the company offering the policy because they reduce the number of short-term claims they have to meet. The longer the deferment period, the cheaper the policy. In some cases, especially those occupations where short-term illnesses affect earnings almost immediately (eg professional sportsmen), the company may decline to offer policies with very short deferred periods.

The benefits payable under the policy are usually limited to approximately 75% of the individual's pre-claim earnings, often taking into account any benefits received from the State and any other policy during the period of claim. Limiting the maximum benefit in this way provides the incentive to the individual to return to work as soon as possible.

Benefits paid by such policies are tax free where the policies are owned by individuals. Where PHI policies are effected by companies to cover their employees, the income is taxable in the employee's hands in the same way as salary would have been.

One of the most important things about PHI policies is the definition of 'disability' which is used in the policy. Under some policies a person is not treated as being disabled if he can do any part of his former job. Others may not treat a person as disabled if he is capable of doing some other job for which he is reasonably suited, even if he is completely unable to do his previous job.

The most flexible PHI policies allow the level of benefit to be increased as salary increases and also give the policyholder the option of paying a higher contribution in exchange for disability income which increases to offer protection against inflation during the period of disability.

PART II – THE USES

14.5 INTRODUCTION

In this second part of the chapter the uses of life assurance, pensions and permanent health insurance are considered with particular emphasis on the business needs of sole traders, partners and small companies. The chapter does not consider more personal uses of life assurance but it is most important that they are not overlooked.

Life assurance is a unique product in the paying of a lump sum on an individual's death at some unknown time in the future. As such it plays a vital role in protection of the family on the breadwinner's death and loss of the family's income. The inclusion of 'critical illness' benefits can also be extremely beneficial as a breadwinner's serious illness can have just as severe an impact as his or her death.

Although most people can see the need for life assurance on the family breadwinner's life, it should not be forgotten that many people are only able to go out and earn an income because their partners are devoting themselves to looking after children and the family home. The non-earning partner's death or serious illness can also cause major financial difficulties such as the need for boarding school fees, a cleaner, a nanny – perhaps even the need for the surviving partner to give up work to look after the family.

Life assurance is also important in inheritance tax planning, being able to provide a fund from which the liability may be met, thus preserving the deceased's estate intact.

Life assurance may be used as a means of investment, even though qualifying endowment policies and single premium savings bonds may have advantages for the individual investor and, in some cases, corporate investment.

14.6 SOLE TRADERS

14.6.1 Life assurance

Keyman assurance – loss of profits

Although the sole trader himself usually is the driving force behind the business's profitability, there may be cases in which an employee is also essential to the undertaking's well-being. Where the death or disability of such a key person would weaken the business's profitability or reduce its capital value as a going concern, the business's owner should consider effecting a life policy (with dread disease benefit) on the keyman's life. The individual's status usually satisfies the requirement for an insurable interest, providing this sum assured is reasonable in view of the keyman's value to the business.

Receipt of the policy proceeds on the life assured's death or disability does not normally constitute a chargeable event, and so does not trigger a tax charge on the policy, if the policy is a qualifying policy. However, it is important to consider whether the policy is an asset owned by the sole trader personally or is a business asset. This determines the ultimate tax treatment of both the premiums paid and the sums received.

If the policy is a business asset contributions paid to it, in general, are tax-deductible provided:

(a) the policy is a short-term assurance; and
(b) the insurance is intended to meet the loss of profit resulting from the employee's death; and
(c) the sole relationship between the policyholder and the life assured is that of employer and employee.

These principles were laid down in a statement in 1944 by the then Chancellor of the Exchequer, Sir John Anderson. In general, the first requirement is an indication that premiums paid on a policy with a term of more than five years will not be tax-deductible.

If premiums are tax-deductible, this usually means that the policy proceeds are, in turn, taxable as a trading receipt of the business. If the premiums do not attract tax relief, usually the proceeds are received as a capital sum, taxable (through Revenue practice) only under the policy tax regime as discussed in 14.2.5. In cases of doubt it may be wise to contact the local tax inspector.

Security for loans

If a sole trader has to borrow money for business purposes, the lender may often require assignment of a life policy on the sole trader as security. The policy should ensure that such loans are repaid on the sole trader's death. Premiums are unlikely to be tax-deductible as a business expense because the plan's purpose is to satisfy a capital liability so that the premiums are not an income expense at all.

Insurance for redundancy payments

If a sole trader's business ceases on his death, his personal representatives are liable for making redundancy payments to eligible employees (see 12.11.8). The amount of any payment depends on various factors, such as salary level and length of service, but for a sole trader employing several staff, such payments could be a significant burden on his estate.

14.6.2 Pensions

For the sole trader

Pension provision for a sole trader must now be through a PPP if no section 226 contract had been effected prior to July 1988. As a sole trader is not an employee, occupational pension schemes are not available and the question of contracting-out of SERPS does not arise.

It should be remembered that the individual can effect life assurance protection through a PPP. This can provide term assurance cover at very competitive rates, because the premiums are tax-deductible, but paying for life cover in this way does lead to a reduction in the contributions which are going towards pension benefits.

For his employees

For a sole trader's employees the choice is wider. The employer could establish an occupational scheme for his staff or, in the absence of an employer's scheme, the employees could effect PPPs for themselves. Most sole traders do not want to assume the responsibility of establishing and running an occupational pension scheme but may well be able to make contributions to their employees' PPPs. Some pension providers offer a group PPP arrangement which is particularly suitable in these circumstances. Members of staff still own individual plans but some aspects of the administration are centralised. If the employer does decide to set up an occupational scheme for his employees, a money-purchase arrangement is likely to be preferable because of the absence of long-term guarantees which have to be met by the employer.

Employees should consider whether contracting-out of SERPS will be beneficial to them. This can be effected in a variety of ways: the employer may offer contracting-out under the main occupational scheme; those in a contracted-in occupational scheme may be able to contract out of SERPS by means of an APPP in the restricted form described at 14.3.4; or the PPPs taken out by those not in the occupational scheme can be used to contract out on an individual basis.

If the sole trader's spouse is employed in the business, he or she is like any other employee as far as pension planning opportunities are concerned, but may be treated more favourably by the employer.

For the sole trader's spouse

If the spouse is not employed in the business, consideration should be given as to whether this could be done, especially if the spouse is not otherwise employed. From April 2001, however, it will be possible for non-earners to take out a stakeholder pension.

The salary paid by the sole trader is deductible at his top rate of tax and, if it is less than the wife's personal allowance and the lower rate for NICs, no income tax or NICs have to be made by either husband or wife in respect of that salary. Of course, it must be possible to justify the employment and the salary being paid by reference to the duties undertaken by the wife.

Once the wife is employed in this way, she could contribute to a PPP, or an occupational scheme could be set up for her by her husband. Although the occupational scheme may be a little more expensive to run and, if it is an insurance company scheme, may have higher minimum contribution levels, it usually offers the chance to provide higher pension benefits for the wife than would a PPP, where the contribution is limited to a percentage of a salary.

To obtain the benefit of tax relief through PPP contributions, the wife should earn more than her tax allowances, but this could lead to payment of NICs. In such cases, it may be better for the husband, as employer, to make the PPP contributions for her.

14.6.3 Permanent health insurance

For the sole trader

It is often the case that if the sole trader is not able to work, the business soon becomes unprofitable. Although state benefits do exist (the sickness and incapacity benefits) they are designed more to avoid poverty than to maintain an individual's standard of living. Accordingly, a PHI policy is one of the first things which the sole trader should consider.

For his employees

A sole trader's employees are will usually be entitled to the same state benefits (with the addition of statutory sick pay) but may be treated more favourably under the terms of their contract of employment.

If the employer has undertaken to maintain the full, or a proportion of, salary during periods of sickness, he should consider effecting a PHI policy on the employee's life, so as to 're-insure' the liability for continuing salary. Benefit received from the policy by the employer is taxable as a trading receipt but normally deductible as a trading expense when paid to the employee.

Even if the employer has not agreed to maintain salary payments beyond that required by statute, he may still consider effecting a PHI policy on key employees to maintain the profitability of the business during their absence from work.

14.7 PARTNERS

14.7.1 Life assurance

The majority of the uses of life assurance applicable to sole traders also apply to partners. Perhaps the main difference with partnerships is that they are more likely to involve key people and that consideration should be given to the partnership's future on the death of one of the partners.

Quite apart from loss of a deceased partner's earning potential, the surviving partners may, subject to the provisions of the Partnership Deed, be faced with having to pay the beneficiaries the value of the deceased's partnership share. For partners who have made no provision, this burden can be acute and might necessitate expensive borrowing or even the sale of vital partnership assets.

Life assurance can help in these circumstances. The partners can set up an arrangement so that each of them has life cover which is paid to the survivors on his death. The survivors then have the funds to pay the deceased partner's share to his heirs, without affecting other aspects of the business's viability.

This partnership assurance arrangement may be achieved by each partner owning a life assurance policy on the life of every other partner, but this can be unwieldy and expensive where there are more than three or four partners. An alternative is for each partner to effect a policy on his own life and write it in trust for the benefit of the other partners.

Both sorts of arrangement should be accompanied by a cross-option agreement by which the surviving partners can compel the deceased's personal representatives to sell the deceased's partnership share to them and vice versa. The cross-option agreement can also contain further provisions to deal with the valuation of the partnership share, time for payment, the destination of surplus policy proceeds and payment of additional capital, should the policy proceeds be insufficient.

A policy incorporating critical illness benefits can also be particularly useful in partnership arrangements where a partner's serious illness can have effects equally severe as his or her death.

14.7.2 Pensions

For the partners

The pension planning routes available to partners are the same as those available to the sole trader, ie a PPP from 1 July 1988 or through a section 226 contract effected before that time. The life cover which can be provided under such pension arrangements can be extremely useful for partnership assurance planning as it provides tax relief on the life cover contributions, at the individual's top rate of income tax. However, these plans are term assurances which must end no later than the individual's 75th birthday, although most life companies will give favourable consideration to a partner applying for a new life policy on the termination of life cover under a pension scheme with that same office.

For their employees

For partnership employees the position is the same as for employees of a sole trader (see 14.6.2); see also that paragraph for the comments made on spouses which also apply to those employed by the partnership.

14.7.3 Permanent health insurance

Partners are in much the same position as sole traders when considering PHI policies (see 14.6.3). A partnership may be better placed to absorb the loss of profits resulting from a partner's long-term absence through injury or illness but a PHI policy can secure the position still further. A policy can be taken out by each partner for his own benefit with the Partnership Deed providing for a corresponding reduction in that partner's share of profits for the period of absence. Alternatively, policies can be owned by all the partners as partnership assets to replace the income at the partnership level. The former method has the advantage of the availability of a tax holiday and of putting this provision into the hands of each individual.

14.8 COMPANIES

14.8.1 Life assurance

Keyman assurance

Keyman assurance is particularly important for small companies where, for example, the managing director, sales director etc may be fundamental to the business's profitability and continuance.

Frequently, small companies effecting keyman policies are not able to obtain tax relief on the premiums but are not taxed on the proceeds other than through the life policy taxation regime (see 14.2.5). This is because the keyman being insured has a material interest in the company so that the relationship between the life assured and the policyholder is not only that of employee and employer.

In the absence of such an interest in the company on the keyman's part, deductibility of premiums might be achieved if the policy is a short-term assurance. A policy of this nature might be appropriate in the early days of the company's existence (eg where it is expected that the company will grow sufficiently over the next five years so as to absorb the loss of the keyman after that time). Although keyman policies are caught by the new rules described in 14.2.5, the high level of life cover being provided usually means that any investment profit under the policy will be small, so that any tax charge on a chargeable event will not cause undue difficulties.

Loan protection and repayment

A form of keyman assurance might also be appropriate where the company is obtaining a loan and the lender requires a life policy on a key executive by way of additional security. Even where the lender has not required a life policy as security for a loan, life assurance has a key role to play in company borrowings. Although the company is usually the borrower, it is common for lenders to require a personal guarantee from one or more directors to ensure repayment of any loan.

By having to give a personal guarantee the director is losing one of the main benefits of trading through a company – that of limited personal liability. Bearing in mind that a key person's death in the company organisation may well precipitate profitability difficulties and so make a calling in of the loan more likely, this is another good reason to effect life assurance on the lives of key individuals. Receipt of the policy proceeds will enable the company to repay its borrowings and so free the guarantor's personal estate from the potential liability.

Repayment of loans should also be considered for any company overdraft which could be called in on a key person's death and in relation to directors' loan accounts where the director's estate may require repayment on the director's death.

Note that the rules described in 14.2.5 mean that policies effected after 13 March 1989 (or older policies which are varied after that date to increase their benefits or extend their term) are treated as if they were non-qualifying and may give rise to a chargeable gain unless they are qualifying endowments and have been used to secure specific types of borrowing.

Key shareholder assurance

Another aspect of small companies which needs to be considered is that of transfer of shares on the death of one of the shareholders. In many cases small companies do not declare dividends on the shares, but those involved in the running of the company draw benefits by way of salary and directors' fees. On a director's death, those inheriting the deceased's shares may find that they have a minority shareholding in the company. The shares may be producing no dividends and may be insufficient to enable the new shareholder to become a director. In such a case the shares may be virtually unsaleable except to the other shareholders who may be able to use their position to depress the value of the shares.

Although in exceptional cases minority shareholders may have some rights against an oppressive majority under company law, the problem can be tackled by life assurance arrangements in at least two specific ways.

The company could effect life policies on the individual shareholders so that, on a shareholder's death, it receives a capital sum to buy the shares from the deceased's heirs. It has been possible for companies to buy their own shares since 1982. An agreement can be entered into between the shareholders and the company itself in which various matters can be addressed; for example, options can be given to both sides to require a sale or purchase of the shares and to determine the method of calculating a fair price for them. The existence of such options usually creates the necessary insurable interest to sustain the life assurance. However, the deceased's personal representatives may have difficulty in enforcing their option to require the company to buy the deceased's shares in some circumstances, eg where the purchase price is to come out of the company's capital. In addition, there are various legal procedures to be gone through before an agreement to buy a company's own shares can be set up and further clearances from the Revenue need to be obtained when the purchase is made to ensure there are no adverse tax consequences.

An alternative and relatively simple method of arranging a share purchase scheme is to establish an arrangement similar to that used for partnership assurance (see 14.7.1). In this way each shareholder effects a policy on the life of each of the others, or each effects a policy on his own life and puts it in trust for the benefit of the other shareholders. The life policies are accompanied by a cross-option agreement which enables both the deceased's personal representatives and the surviving shareholders to enforce the sale and purchase of the deceased's shares and tackles such questions as valuation of the shares etc.

14.8.2 Pensions

For directors and other top executives

The company's directors may plan for their own pension benefits through an occupational scheme or a PPP. In most cases the directors and key executives join a company occupational scheme to enable them to maximise their pension benefits in a tax-efficient way. PPPs with direct contributions from the company are also efficient for the purposes of income tax and NICs, but the limit on the PPP contributions which can be made usually favours the choice of an occupational scheme.

Life assurance protection can be provided under either type of scheme. Usually it is possible to provide a higher sum assured under a PPP (where the maximum life cover contribution is 5% of net relevant earnings) than under an occupational scheme where the maximum sum assured is four times' salary. Despite this, the occupational scheme is often preferable as the provision of life assurance under the PPP reduces the maximum amount which can be paid towards the pension benefits.

For other employees

The choices are very much the same as for the employees of sole traders and partners. If the company does not want to make pension provision for its staff through an occupational scheme, they can plan for themselves by effecting PPPs. The company may choose to make contributions to its employees' PPPs. A group PPP arrangement could be 'sponsored' by the company if it wishes to indicate a greater commitment to the provision of pensions for its employees.

For spouses of the directors

The comments made in 14.6.2 apply equally to employment of, and pensions for, spouses of directors and top executives of small companies.

14.8.3 Permanent health insurance

As with sole traders and partnerships, the smaller the company the more vulnerable it is to the long-term absence of a key individual. The company may effect PHI policies on its directors and top executives either to enable the company to maintain payment of salary or to cushion the company itself from the possible loss of income due to the key person's absence. The question of whether premiums paid on such a policy are tax deductible for the company is not entirely clear.

Despite the policy's long-term nature it seems likely that premiums paid by a company on a PHI policy on an employee, to enable the company to maintain payment of salary to the employee during a period of disability, should be tax-deductible. Certainly it appears that the receipt of payment by the company from the policy would be taxable in the company's hands (although matched by tax relief on the payment of the salary) even though the payment would be made gross by the life company. In cases of doubt, companies should consult their local tax inspector.

15

HEALTH AND SAFETY

JEREMY STRANKS

15.1 INTRODUCTION

The law relating to the health and safety at work of employees and other persons has seen extensive developments over the last decade, and these developments have taken place largely as a result of the implementation in the UK of a range of European Directives.

Indeed, all modern protective legislation, including health and safety at work, food safety and environmental protection, is based on the concept of 'risk assessment'. The requirement on employers and self-employed persons to undertake a 'suitable and sufficient risk assessment' is incorporated in the Management of Health and Safety at Work Regulations 1999 and the Health and Safety Commission (HSC) Approved Code of Practice.

On completion of the risk assessment exercise, employers must appoint 'competent persons' to oversee the preventive and protective measures arising from the risk assessment. The appointed competent person's level of competence will depend on the risks employees are exposed to.

This chapter covers the principal areas of health and safety law. It must be appreciated that employers can incur both criminal and civil liability through failure to comply with legal requirements. In particular, claims for negligence have seen a dramatic increase in the last few years, with extensive damages awarded, particularly in the case of stress-induced injury arising from work. The need, therefore, for well-developed management systems to cover these issues must be seen as an urgent priority by many employers.

15.2 HEALTH AND SAFETY AT WORK ETC ACT 1974 (HSWA)

Under the HSWA, employers, employees, occupiers of premises and people who manufacture and design articles and substances for use at work have both general and particular duties.

15.2.1 General duties of employers to their employees
(HSWA, s 2)

It is every employer's duty, so far as is reasonably practicable, to ensure the health, safety and welfare at work of all his employees. More particularly, this includes:

(1) providing and maintaining plant and systems of work that are, so far as is reasonably practicable, safe and without risks to health;

(2) arrangements for ensuring, so far as is reasonably practicable, safety and absence of risks to health in connection with using, handling, storing and transporting articles and substances;

(3) providing such information, instruction training and supervision as is necessary to ensure, so far as is reasonably practicable, the health and safety at work of employees;

(4) so far as is reasonably practicable as regards any place of work under the employer's control, maintaining it in a condition that is safe and without risks to health, and providing and maintaining means of access to and egress from it that are safe and without such risks;

(5) providing and maintaining a working environment for his employees that is, so far as is reasonably practicable, safe, without risks to health, and adequate as regards facilities and arrangements for their welfare at work.

Every employer must prepare and, as often as is necessary, revise a written Statement of Health and Safety Policy, and bring the Statement and any revision of it to the notice of all his employees.

Every employer must consult appointed safety representatives with a view to making and maintaining arrangements which will enable him and his employees to co-operate effectively in promoting and developing health and safety at work measures and in checking their effectiveness.

15.2.2 General duties other than to employees
(HSWA, ss 3 and 4)

Every employer must conduct his undertaking in such a way as to ensure, so far as is reasonably practicable, that persons not in his employment are not exposed to risks to their health or safety. Similar duties are imposed on self-employed persons. The employer must give such persons information about aspects of his undertaking which might affect their health and safety.

Further, a person who controls premises must ensure, so far as is reasonably practicable, that the premises, access to and egress from them and all plant and substances on them are safe and without risk to non-employees.

15.2.3 **Articles and substances for use at work**
(HSWA, s 6)

Any person who designs, manufactures, imports or supplies any article for use at work must:

(1) ensure, so far as is reasonably practicable, that the article is designed and constructed to be safe and without risks when properly used;

(2) carry out or arrange to carry out such testing and examination as may be necessary to comply with (1) above; and

(3) provide adequate information about the use for which it is designed and test it to ensure that, when put to that use, it will be safe and without risks to health.

In undertaking the design or manufacture of such article, research must be carried out to discover and, so far as is reasonably practicable, eliminate or minimise any risks to health or safety which may arise. An article must be erected or installed to ensure it is safe and risk-free.

Similar provisions as to proper use, testing and the provision of adequate information apply to substances.

15.2.4 **General duties of employees at work**
(HSWA, s 7)

It is the duty of every employee while at work:

(1) to take reasonable care for the health and safety of himself and of other persons who may be affected by his acts or omissions at work; and

(2) as regards any duty or requirement imposed on his employer, to co-operate with him so far as is necessary to enable that duty or requirement to be performed or complied with.

15.2.5 **Duty not to interfere or misuse**
(HSWA, s 8)

No person shall intentionally or recklessly interfere with or misuse anything provided in the interests of health, safety or welfare in pursuance of any of the relevant statutory provisions.

15.2.6 **Duty not to charge employees**

No employer shall levy or permit to be levied on any employee of his any charge in respect of anything done or provided in pursuance of any specific requirement of the relevant statutory provisions.

15.2.7 Enforcement procedures
(HSWA, ss 20 and 21)

The enforcing authorities for the HSWA and other health and safety legislation are:

(1) the Health and Safety Executive (HSE), which is split into a number of specific inspectorates (eg Nuclear Installations, Agricultural, etc) and national industrial groups (NIGs);
(2) local authorities, principally through their environmental health departments; and
(3) fire authorities, for certain fire-related legislation.

Actual enforcement is undertaken by inspectors appointed under the Act and authorised by written warrant from the enforcing authority.

Under HSWA, s 20 an inspector has the power to enter premises at any reasonable time and, where obstruction is anticipated, to enlist the support of a police officer. On entering a premises, he may take with him any person duly authorised by his enforcing authority, and any necessary equipment or materials. He may make such examination and investigation as may be necessary.

The inspector may direct that premises, or any part of them or anything in them, must remain undisturbed while the examination or investigation takes place. He may take any measurements and photographs and make any recordings he considers necessary, and take samples of any articles or substances found in any premises and of the atmosphere in them or in their vicinity.

Where it appears to him that an article or substance has caused or is likely to cause danger to health or safety, he may have it dismantled or subjected to any process or test. He may also take possession of it and to detain it for so long as is necessary to examine it, to ensure it is not tampered with before his examination is completed and to ensure it is available for use as evidence in any proceedings for an offence under the relevant statutory provisions.

The inspector may require any person whom he has reasonable cause to believe to be able to give any information relevant to any examination or investigation to answer such questions as he thinks fit and to sign a declaration of truth. He may require the production of, inspect and take copies of any entry in any books or documents which by virtue of the relevant statutory provisions must be kept, and any other books or documents which it is necessary for him to see for the purposes of any examination or investigation. He may require any person to afford him such facilities and assistance with respect to any matter or things within that person's control or in relation to which that person has responsibilities as are necessary to enable the inspector to exercise any of the powers conferred on him.

After an inspector has completed an investigation or examination, he has a duty to inform safety representatives of the actual matters he has found (s 28(8)) and must give the employer similar information.

Improvement notices

If an inspector is of the opinion that a breach of the relevant statutory provisions has or is likely to occur, he may serve an improvement notice on the employer, occupier or employee. The notice must state which statutory provision he believes has been contravened and the reason for this belief. It should also state a time limit within which the contravention should be remedied.

Prohibition notices

Where an inspector is of the opinion that a work activity involves or will involve a serious risk of personal injury, he may serve a prohibition notice on the owner and/or occupier of the premises or the person having control of that activity. The notice will direct that the specified activities in it shall not be carried on by or under the control of the person on whom the notice is served unless certain specified remedial measures have been complied with. Note that it is not necessary for an inspector to believe that a legal provision is being or has been contravened. A prohibition notice is served where there is an immediate threat to life and in anticipation of danger.

Such notice may have immediate effect after its service. Alternatively, it may be deferred, thereby allowing the person time to remedy the situation, undertake works, etc. The duration of a deferred prohibition notice is stated on the notice.

Prosecution and penalties

Prosecution is frequently the outcome of a failure to comply with an improvement or prohibition notice. Conversely, an inspector may simply institute legal proceedings without service of a notice. Cases are normally heard in a magistrates' court, but there is also provision in the HSWA for hearing on indictment (in the Crown Court). Much depends on the gravity of the offence.

Magistrates may impose fines of up to £20,000 for a breach of ss 2–6 of the Act, and for breach of an improvement or prohibition notice. The maximum fine for other offences is £5,000. Fines in a Crown Court are unlimited.

15.2.8 Hierarchy of duties under health and safety law

Under health and safety law there are three distinct levels of statutory duty.

'Absolute' requirements

Where risk of injury or disease is inevitable if safety requirements are not followed, a statutory duty may well be strict or absolute. An example of an absolute duty is in the Provision and Use of Work Equipment Regulations 1998, reg 5(1), which states:

> 'Every employer shall ensure that work equipment is so constructed or adapted as to be suitable for the purpose for which it is to be used or provided.'

Absolute duties are qualified by the terms 'shall' or 'must' and there is little or no defence available when charged with such an offence. Most of the duties under recent legislation, such as the Management of Health and Safety at Work Regulations 1999, are of an absolute or strict nature.

'Practicable' requirements

A statutory requirement qualified by the term 'so far as is practicable' implies that, if in the light of current knowledge and invention it is feasible to comply with this requirement, then, irrespective of the cost or sacrifice involved, such a requirement must be complied with (*Schwalb v Fass H & Son* (1946) 175 LT 345).

'Reasonably practicable' requirements

A duty qualified by the term 'so far as is reasonably practicable' implies a lower or lesser level of duty than one which is qualified by 'so far as is practicable'. 'Reasonably practicable' is a narrower term than 'physically possible' (ie 'practicable'), and implies that a computation must be made in which the quantum of risk is placed in one scale and the sacrifice involved in the measures necessary for averting that risk is placed in the other. If it can be shown that there is a gross disproportion between these two factors (ie the risk being insignificant in relation to the sacrifice), a defendant discharges the onus upon himself (*Edwards v National Coal Board* [1949] 1 All ER 743).

The mythical reasonable man

A further level of duty is qualified by the term 'reasonable'. For instance, under HSWA, s 7, every employee has a duty while at work to take 'reasonable care' for the safety of himself and other persons who may be affected by his acts or omissions at work. But what is a reasonable person? What is considered 'reasonable' in terms of behaviour changes with time according to society and the norms prevalent at the time.

15.3 CURRENT TRENDS IN HEALTH AND SAFETY LEGISLATION

All modern health and safety legislation is driven by European Directives. For instance, in the UK:

(1) the Directive on the health and safety of workers at work was implemented as the Management of Health and Safety at Work Regulations 1992; and

(2) the Directive on temporary and mobile construction sites was implemented as the Construction (Design and Management) Regulations 1994.

Regulations produced since 1992 do not, in most cases, stand on their own. They must be read in conjunction with the general duties imposed on employers under the Management of Health and Safety at Work Regulations 1999, in particular the duties relating to:

- Risk assessment
- The operation and maintenance of safety management systems
- The appointment of competent persons
- Establishment and implementation of emergency procedures
- Provision of information to employees which is comprehensible and relevant
- Co-operation, communication and co-ordination between employers in shared workplaces (eg construction sites, office blocks)
- Provision of comprehensible health and safety information to employees from an outside undertaking
- Assessment of human capability prior to allocating tasks
- Provision of health and safety information, training and instruction.

Duties imposed on employers tend largely to be of an absolute nature, as opposed to qualified duties, such as 'so far as is reasonably practicable', as with the HSWA. Risk assessment, taking into account the 'requirements and prohibitions imposed on an employer by or under the relevant statutory provisions', is the starting point of all health and safety management systems. Most modern health and safety legislation requires some form of documentation, such as risk assessments and planned preventive maintenance systems, and the maintenance of records.

15.4 MANAGEMENT OF HEALTH AND SAFETY AT WORK REGULATIONS 1999

The 1999 Regulations, which are accompanied by an HSC Approved Code of Practice, require a management-orientated approach to compliance with health and safety legislation generally. Moreover, duties under other regulations must be read in conjunction with the general duties under the 1999 Regulations. Duties on employers are of an absolute or strict nature.

15.4.1 Risk assessment
(1999 Regulations, reg 3)

Every employer shall make a suitable and sufficient assessment of the risks to the health and safety of:

(1) his employees to which they are exposed while at work; and
(2) persons not in his employment arising out of or in connection with the conduct by him of his undertaking,

for the purpose of identifying the measures he needs to take to comply with the requirements and prohibitions imposed upon him by or under the relevant statutory provisions and by Part II of the Fire Precautions (Workplace) Regulations 1997.

Relevant statutory provisions

These are the statutory provisions (ie the HSWA) and those of any regulations made under the statute (eg Noise at Work Regulations 1989).

Principles of prevention to be applied
(1999 Regulations, reg 4)

Where an employer implements preventive and protective measures he shall do so on the basis of the principles specified in Sched 1 to the Regulations.

Health and safety arrangements
(1999 Regulations, reg 5)

Every employer shall make and give effect to such arrangements as are appropriate, having regard to the nature of his activities and the size of his undertaking, for the effective planning, organisation, control, monitoring and review of the preventive and protective measures. These arrangements must be recorded where five or more employees are employed.

Health surveillance
(1999 Regulations, reg 6)

Every employer shall ensure that his employees are provided with such health surveillance as is appropriate having regard to the risks to their health and safety which are identified by the assessment.

Health and safety assistance
(1999 Regulations, reg 7)

An employer must appoint one or more competent persons to assist him in undertaking the measures he needs to take to comply with the requirements and prohibitions imposed upon him by or under the relevant statutory provisions and by Part II of the 1997 Fire Precautions Regulations. This regulation does not apply to self-employed persons and those carrying on a business in partnership where that person or a partner has sufficient training, experience or knowledge as to be considered competent.

Procedures for serious and imminent danger and for danger areas
(1999 Regulations, reg 8)

Employers must:

(1) establish and where necessary give effect to appropriate procedures to be followed in the event of serious or imminent danger to persons at work;
(2) nominate a sufficient number of competent persons to implement these procedures; and
(3) prevent any employee being given access to a danger area unless he has received adequate health and safety instruction.

Contacts with external services
(1999 Regulations, reg 9)

Every employer shall ensure that any necessary contacts with external services are arranged, particularly as regards first aid, emergency medical care and rescue work.

Information for employees
(1999 Regulations, reg 10)

Every employer shall provide his employees with comprehensible and relevant information on:

(1) the risks to their health and safety identified by the assessment;
(2) the preventive and protective measures;
(3) the procedures referred to in reg 8(1)(a) and the measures referred to in reg 4(2)(a) of the 1997 Fire Prevention Regulations;
(4) the identity of the competent persons nominated in accordance with reg 8(1)(b) and the measures referred to in reg 4(2)(b) of the 1997 Regulations; and
(5) the risks notified to him in accordance with reg 11(1)(c) (shared workplaces).

Every employer shall, before employing a child, provide a parent of the child with comprehensible and relevant information on:

(a) the risks to his health and safety identified by the assessment;
(b) the preventive and protective measures; and
(c) the risks notified in accordance with reg 11(1)(c).

Co-operation and co-ordination
(1999 Regulations, reg 11)

Where two or more employers share a workplace (whether on a temporary or permanent basis), each must:

(1) co-operate with other employers to enable them to comply with legal requirements;
(2) take all reasonable steps to co-ordinate the measures he is taking with other employers in order to comply with legal requirements; and
(3) take all reasonable steps to inform other employers of risks to their employees' health and safety arising from his activities.

Persons working in host employers or self-employed persons' undertakings
(1999 Regulations, reg 12)

Every employer and self-employed person shall ensure that the employer of any employees from an outside undertaking who are working in his undertaking is provided with comprehensible information on:

(1) the risks arising in the undertaking; and
(2) the measures taken by the first-mentioned employer to comply with legal requirements and to protect those employees.

These measures include details of emergency and evacuation procedures and the competent persons nominated to implement such procedures.

Capabilities and training
(1999 Regulations, reg 13)

Every employer shall, in entrusting tasks to his employees, take into account their capabilities as regards health and safety. He shall ensure that his employees are provided with adequate health and safety training on their being:

(1) recruited into the employer's undertaking; and
(2) exposed to new or increased risks within the employer's undertaking because of:
    (a) their being transferred or given a change of responsibilities;

(b) the introduction of new work equipment to or a change of work equipment already in use;

(c) the introduction of new technology; or

(d) the introduction of a new system of work or a change of a system of work already in use.

Training shall be repeated periodically where appropriate, be adapted to take account of new or changed risks and take place during working hours.

Employees' duties
(1999 Regulations, reg 14)

Every employee shall use any machinery, equipment, dangerous substance, transport equipment, means of production or safety device provided to him by his employer in accordance both with any training in the use of equipment and the instructions respecting that use provided by the employer in compliance with the requirements and prohibitions imposed upon that employer by or under the relevant statutory provisions. Every employee shall inform his employer or any other employee with specific responsibility for the health and safety of his fellow employees (eg competent person, trade union safety representative) of any:

(1) work situation which he reasonably considers represents a serious and immediate danger to health and safety; and

(2) matter which he reasonably considers represents a shortcoming in the employer's protection arrangements for health and safety.

Temporary workers
(1999 Regulations, reg 15)

This regulation places an absolute duty on employers to provide any person working under a fixed-term contract or employed in an employment business with comprehensible information:

(a) on any special occupational qualifications or skills required to be held by that employee if he is to carry out his work safely; and

(b) of any health surveillance required,

before the employee commences his duties. Further provisions apply in the case of persons carrying an employment business being required to pass on information to employees before working in another employer's undertaking.

Risk assessment in respect of new or expectant mothers
(1999 Regulations, reg 16)

Where employees include women of child-bearing age and the work could involve risk to the health and safety of a new or expectant mother, or to that of her baby, from any processes or working conditions, or physical, biological or chemical agents, the assessment required by reg 3(1) shall also include an assessment of such risk. If in taking other action required by the legislation such an employee would remain at risk, the employer must alter her working conditions or hours of work.

If it is not reasonable to alter working conditions or hours of work, or if it would not avoid such risk, the employer shall, subject to the Employment Rights Act (ERA) 1996, s 67, suspend the employee from work so long as is necessary to avoid such risk.

In relation to risk from any infectious or contagious disease, references to a level of risk is in addition to the level to which a new or expectant mother may be expected to be exposed outside the workplace.

Certificate in respect of new or expectant mothers
(1999 Regulations, reg 17)

Where:

(1) a new or expectant mother works at night, and
(2) a certificate from a registered medical practitioner or a registered midwife shows that it is necessary for her health or safety that she should not be at work for any period identified in the certificate,

the employer shall, subject to ERA 1996, s 67 suspend her from work so long as is necessary for her health or safety.

Notification by new or expectant mothers
(1999 Regulations, reg 18)

Nothing shall require the employer to take any action in relation to an employee until she has notified him in writing that she is pregnant, has given birth within the previous six months, or is breastfeeding.

Protection of young persons
(1999 Regulations, reg 19)

Every employer shall ensure that young persons employed by him are protected at work from any risks to their health or safety which are a consequence of their lack of experience, or absence of awareness of existing or potential risks or the fact they have not yet fully matured. Subject to reg 19(3), no employer shall employ a young person for work:

(1) which is beyond his physical or psychological capacity;
(2) involving harmful exposure to agents which are toxic or carcinogenic, cause heritable genetic damage or harm to the unborn child or which in any other way chronically affect human health;
(3) involving harmful exposure to radiation;

(4) involving the risk of accidents which it may reasonably be assumed cannot be recognised or avoided by young persons owing to their insufficient attention to safety or lack of experience or training; or

(5) in which there is a risk to health from:
- extreme cold or heat;
- noise; or
- vibration,

In determining whether work will involve harm or risks, regard shall be had to the results of the assessment.

Nothing in reg 19(2) shall prevent the employment of a young person who is no longer a child for work where:

(a) it is necessary for his training;
(b) the young person will be supervised by a competent person; and
(c) any risk will be reduced to the lowest, reasonably practicable level.

Provisions as to liability
(1999 Regulations, reg 21)

Nothing in the relevant statutory provisions shall operate so as to afford an employer a defence in criminal proceedings for a contravention of those provisions by reason of any act or default of an employee of his, or a person appointed by him under reg 7 (competent person).

Exclusion of civil liability
(1999 Regulations, reg 22)

Breach of a duty imposed by the 1999 Regulations shall not confer a right of action in any civil proceedings.

General principles of prevention
(1999 Regulations, Sched 1)

Schedule 1 specifies the general principles of prevention set out in Council Directive 89/391/EEC, Art 6(2), ie:

(1) avoiding risks;
(2) evaluating the risks which cannot be avoided;
(3) combating the risks at source;
(4) adapting the work to the individual, especially as regards the design of workplaces and the choice of work equipment and of working and production methods, with a view, in particular, to alleviating monotonous work and work at a predetermined work rate and reducing their effect on health;
(5) adapting to technical progress;
(6) replacing the dangerous by the non-dangerous or the less dangerous;

(7) developing a coherent overall prevention policy which covers technology, organisation of work, working conditions, social relationships and the influence of factors relating to the working environment;
(8) giving collective protective measures priority over individual protective measures; and
(9) giving appropriate instructions to employees.

15.5 CRIMINAL AND CIVIL LIABILITY

15.5.1 Criminal liability

A crime is an offence against the state. Criminal liability refers to the duties and responsibilities under statute, principally the HSWA and regulations, and the penalties that can be imposed by the criminal courts (ie fines, imprisonment and remedial orders). There are two categories of conviction:

(1) *Summary conviction*: for offences regarded as less serious which, in practice, applies to most health and safety offences, and where the case is brought before a magistrates' court (without a jury). The maximum penalty for certain health and safety-related offences is £20,000 and/or six months' imprisonment, and for other health and safety related-offences £5,000.
(2) *Conviction on indictment*: where the case is tried before a judge and jury in the Crown Court. This form of trial is reserved for the more serious offences and offenders can be sentenced to up to two years' imprisonment with unlimited fines.

Thus the criminal courts in question are the magistrates' courts, which handle the bulk of health and safety offences, and the Crown Courts, which deal with the more serious offences. Appeals can be made to the High Court and beyond, to the Court of Appeal and, assuming leave is given, to the House of Lords. Subject to certain criteria, a case may pass to the European Court of Justice.

Criminal law is based on a system of enforcement. Its statutory provisions are enforced by the state's enforcement agencies, such as the police, the HSE, local authorities and fire authorities.

In contrast to civil liability in tort, criminal liability cannot be insured against by employers, directors or employees. However, it is lawful to insure against court costs and the legal expenses of counsel in connection with a prosecution for health and safety offences.

15.5.2 Civil liability

A civil action generally involves negligence and/or breach of a statutory duty. In such actions, a claimant sues a defendant for a remedy (or remedies) that is beneficial to the claimant. In most cases, this takes the form of damages, a form of financial compensation. In a substantial number of cases, the claimant will agree to settle out of court.

Civil liability, therefore, refers to the 'penalty' that can be imposed by a civil court (eg the County Court, High Court, Court of Appeal (Civil Division) or House of Lords), and consists of awards of damages for injury, disease and/or death at work.

15.5.3 Negligence

'Negligence' is defined as 'careless conduct injuring another'. It has been defined at common law as:

(1) the existence of a duty of care owed by a defendant to a claimant;
(2) breach of that duty; and
(3) injury, damage or loss resulting from or caused by that breach.

All the above circumstances must be established by an injured person before a civil claim for damages may be brought.

15.5.4 Breach of statutory duty

In certain cases, a breach of a criminal duty imposed by statute or regulations may give rise to civil liability and a claim for damages. In many cases, a statute or regulations will state that such breach shall not give rise to civil liability (eg the 1999 Regulations). However, where such a statement of exclusion is not made, civil liability is implied.

The standard test adopted by the courts has been to ask the question: Was the duty imposed specifically for the protection of a particular class of people, or was it intended to benefit the public at large? If the answer to the first part of the question is 'Yes', a civil claim may be allowed.

On this basis, the courts have always viewed legislation, such as the safety provisions of the Factories Act 1961, as being directed towards protecting a particular class and have allowed civil claims for damages by persons belonging to these protected classes, namely employees.

15.5.5 Vicarious liability

Vicarious liability is based on the fact that if an employee, while acting in the course of his employment, negligently injures another employee or the employee of another employer, his employer, rather than the negligent employee, will be liable for that injury. Vicarious liability rests on the employer simply as a result of the fact that he is the employer and is deemed to have ultimate control over his employees (ie the master and servant relationship).

This liability must be insured against under the Employers' Liability (Compulsory Insurance) Act 1969. Employers cannot contract out of this liability as this is prohibited by the Law Reform (Personal Injuries) Act 1948 and the Unfair Contract Terms Act 1977.

15.6 WORKPLACE (HEALTH, SAFETY AND WELFARE) REGULATIONS 1992

15.6.1 Introduction

'Workplace' is defined broadly as meaning any premises or part of premises which are not domestic premises and made available to any person as a place of work, and including:

(1) any place within the premises to which such person has access while at work; and
(2) any room, lobby, corridor, staircase, road or other place used as a means of access to or egress from the workplace or where facilities are provided for use in connection with the workplace other than a public road.

15.6.2 Duty to maintain the workplace

Under reg 5 of the 1992 Regulations, there is an absolute duty on employers to maintain the workplace, equipment, devices and systems (including cleaning as appropriate) in an efficient state, in efficient working order and in good repair.

15.6.3 The working environment

Specific provisions apply with regard to environmental factors:

(1) ventilation must be effective and suitable to maintain comfortable conditions;
(2) the temperature must be reasonable during working hours;
(3) lighting must be suitable in terms of the type of lighting and sufficient with regard to the amount of light provided; emergency lighting must be provided where failure of lighting may create danger;
(4) there is a general duty to keep the workplace clean and surfaces (floors, walls, etc) must be cleanable; there must be adequate control over refuse;
(5) sufficient floor area and space must be provided for employees; and
(6) both indoor and outdoor workstations must be suitable for the work carried out; seats provided must be suitable for the person and for the work undertaken.

15.6.4 Structural safety

Specific provisions applying to structural safety include:

(1) floors and traffic routes must be suitable for the purpose, in good repair and free from obstructions;
(2) measures to prevent risks arising from falls and falling objects must be taken, including marking risk areas and covering pits, tanks, etc;

(3) windows and transparent or translucent doors, gates and walls must be of safety material or protected in certain cases, and be suitably marked;

(4) the design of windows, skylights and ventilators must be such that there is no risk when opening, closing or adjusting, and be suitably positioned;

(5) windows etc must be capable of being cleaned safely, including the fitting of suitable devices to buildings;

(6) traffic routes must be organised in such a way as to ensure safe circulation by pedestrians and vehicles;

(7) doors and gates must be suitably designed and constructed, and fitted with certain safety devices; and

(8) escalators and moving walkways must function safely and safety devices and emergency stop controls must be fitted.

15.6.5 Welfare amenity provisions

The provision and maintenance of suitable and sufficient welfare amenities is an important feature of the Regulations. Sanitary conveniences must be suitable and sufficient, adequately ventilated and lit, and kept in a clean and orderly condition with separation of the sexes. Washing facilities must be suitable and sufficient, located in the vicinity of sanitary conveniences (and changing rooms if required), with hot and cold water, and cleaning and drying facilities. They also must be ventilated and well lit, and kept in a clean and orderly condition with separation of the sexes.

Drinking water supply must be wholesome, readily accessible and conspicuously marked, with cups or drinking vessels provided unless from a jet supply.

Accommodation for clothing must be suitable and sufficient, with security for clothing not worn and separate accommodation in some cases. Facilities for drying must be provided which are suitably located. Facilities for changing clothing must be suitable and sufficient, and ensure privacy with separation of the sexes.

Facilities for rest and to eat meals must be suitable and sufficient, including the provision of rest rooms or areas. There must be separation of smokers and non-smokers, and facilities provided for pregnant women and nursing mothers. Facilities must also be provided for taking meals.

15.7 PROVISION AND USE OF WORK EQUIPMENT REGULATIONS 1998

15.7.1 Introduction

'Work equipment' means any machinery, appliance, apparatus or tool or any assembly of components which, in order to achieve a common end, are arranged and controlled so that they function as a whole. 'Use' in relation to work equipment means any activity involving work equipment and includes starting, stopping, programming, setting, transporting, repairing, modifying, maintaining, servicing and cleaning.

15.7.2 Employers' duties

Work equipment must be constructed or adapted to be suitable for the purpose for which it is to be used or provided. It must be maintained in an efficient state, in efficient working order and in good repair. Any maintenance log for machinery must be kept up to date.

Where work equipment incorporates specific risks, its use must be restricted to those persons given the task of using it, and repairs, modifications, maintenance and servicing must be restricted to designated persons. All persons using work equipment must receive appropriate information, instruction and training.

Items of work equipment must conform with any enactment which implements in Great Britain any of the relevant EU Directives applicable to that item of equipment listed in Sched 1 to the 1998 Regulations. Effective measures must be taken to ensure the safety of dangerous parts of machinery, and to provide protection against specified hazards and high or very low temperature.

15.7.3 Specific duties of employers

More specific duties cover:

- Controls and control systems relating to machinery
- Isolation from sources of energy
- Stabilising work equipment
- Lighting where work equipment is used
- Safety of maintenance operations
- Marking work equipment
- The provision of warnings and warning devices.

15.7.4 Mobile work equipment

'Mobile work equipment' is defined as any work equipment which carries out work while it is travelling or which travels between different locations where it is used to carry out work. It may be self-propelled, towed or remote controlled and may incorporate attachments. Employers must ensure that no employee is carried by mobile work equipment unless:

(1) it is suitable for carrying persons; and
(2) it incorporates features for reducing to as low as is reasonably practicable risks to their safety, including wheels or tracks.

Employers must:

(a) minimise the risk of rolling over of mobile work equipment;
(b) fit roll-over protective structures where necessary;
(c) adapt or equip forklift trucks to reduce the risk of overturning;
(d) take specific measures in respect of self-propelled and remote-con-
     trolled self-propelled work equipment; and
(e) either prevent the seizure of drive shafts or, where seizure cannot be
     avoided, take every possible measure to avoid an adverse effect on the
     safety of an employee.

15.8 PERSONAL PROTECTIVE EQUIPMENT AT WORK REGULATIONS 1992

15.8.1 Introduction

These Regulations establish the principles for selecting, providing, maintaining and using personal protective equipment (PPE). They do not replace
recently introduced law dealing with PPE, such as the Control of Substances
Hazardous to Health (COSHH) Regulations 1999 and the Noise at Work
Regulations 1989. Employers need consider only one set of regulations for
all their PPE requirements covering a particular risk.

'Personal protective equipment' is defined as all equipment (including
clothing affording protection against the weather) which is intended to be
worn or held by a person at work and which protects him against one or
more risks to his health or safety, and any addition or accessory designed to
meet that objective.

15.8.2 Employers' duties

There are a number of general duties on employers, namely:

(1) to ensure the provision of suitable PPE to employees, where risks
     cannot be controlled by other means;
(2) where more than one item of PPE is worn or used by an employee, to
     ensure compatibility of those items and that they give effective protec-
     tion against risks;
(3) a duty to assess the PPE's suitability in protecting against risks;
(4) to ensure any PPE is maintained (including replaced or cleaned as appro-
     priate) in an efficient state, in efficient working order and in good repair;
(5) to provide accommodation for PPE not in use;
(6) to provide information, instruction and training for employees to enable
     each employer to know the risks, correct use of the PPE and actions to
     ensure it remains in an efficient state, efficient working order and good
     repair; and
(7) to enforce the use of PPE by employees.

15.8.3 Employees' duties

Employees must:

(1) use PPE in accordance with any training received by them and the instructions respecting that use; and
(2) report any loss or defect.

15.9 MANUAL HANDLING OPERATIONS REGULATIONS 1992

These Regulations apply to all manual handling operations which may cause injury at work. 'Manual handling operations' means any transporting or supporting of a load (including lifting, putting down, pushing, pulling, carrying or moving) by hand or by bodily force.

15.9.1 Employers' duties

Employers have a general duty to avoid, so far as is reasonably practicable, manual handling operations which involve a risk of injury to employees. Where avoidance is not reasonably practicable, the employer must make a suitable and sufficient assessment of all such manual handling operations, having regard to the factors specified in the Schedule (see 15.9.3)

15.9.2 Employees' duty

Employees must make full and proper use of any system of work provided by the employer arising from the assessment.

15.9.3 The assessment

In accordance with the Schedule, this must take into account:

- the task
- the load
- the working environment, and
- individual capability.

15.10 HEALTH AND SAFETY (DISPLAY SCREEN EQUIPMENT) REGULATIONS 1992

The Regulations apply to all identified 'users' and 'operators' of display screen equipment. The following definitions are significant in the interpretation of the Regulations.

'Display screen equipment' means any alphanumeric or graphic display screen regardless of the display process involved. 'User' means an employee who habitually uses display screen equipment as a significant part of his normal work. 'Operator' means a self-employed person who habitually uses display screen equipment as a significant part of his normal work. 'Workstation' means an assembly comprising:

(1) display screen equipment (including software, a keyboard or any other input device);
(2) any optional accessories to the display screen equipment;
(3) any disk drive, telephone, modem, printer, document holder, work chair, work desk, work surface or other item peripheral to the display screen equipment; and
(4) the immediate work environment around the display screen equipment.

The Regulations do not apply to:

(a) drivers' cabs or control cabs for vehicles or machinery;
(b) display screen equipment on board a means of transport;
(c) display screen equipment mainly intended for public operation;
(d) portable systems not in prolonged use;
(e) calculators, cash registers or any equipment having a small data measurement display required for direct use of the equipment; or
(f) window typewriters.

15.10.1 Employers' duties

There are a number of general duties on an employer to:

(1) perform a suitable and sufficient risk analysis of workstations used by users and operators for the purposes of his undertaking;
(2) plan users' activities to ensure regular screen breaks or changes of activity to reduce their workload at that equipment;
(3) provide eye and eyesight tests for existing new users, at regular intervals after the initial tests, and when a user experiences visual difficulties;
(4) provide users with special corrective appliances where normal corrective appliances cannot be used and the eye and eyesight test indicates such need; and
(5) provide information and training in the use of the workstation to users.

15.10.2 Risk analysis

The Schedule covers the requirements to be considered in a workstation risk analysis, namely:

(a) the equipment (display screen, keyboard, work desk or work surface and work chair);
(b) the environment (space requirements, lighting, and reflection and glare, noise, heat, radiation and humidity control); and
(c) the interface between the computer and the operator/user.

15.11 FIRE PRECAUTIONS (WORKPLACE) REGULATIONS 1997

These Regulations came into operation on 1 December 1997, bringing the UK into line with the fire safety aspects of the Framework and Workplace Directives. The Regulations place primary responsibility for workplace fire safety on employers and those in control of workplaces, who must assess and provide the measures needed to prevent or control the risks from fire. The necessary and appropriate measures must be determined by the specific circumstances of individual workplaces.

These Regulations incorporate a new approach to the enforcement of fire safety requirements, allowing most significant breaches of the Regulations to be dealt with by civil sanctions, with the burden of proof on the fire authority sooner than an employer. They amend certain regulations, including the Management of Health and Safety at Work Regulations 1992 and the Safety Representatives and Safety Committees Regulations 1977.

15.11.1 Principal requirements

Every employer and any other person who has control of a workplace, and any person who has an obligation relating to maintenance, repair or safety there, must comply with the Regulations (although see 15.11.5 (excepted workplaces)). In particular, they must:

(1) ensure the workplace is equipped with appropriate firefighting equipment, fire detectors and alarms, and that any non-automatic firefighting equipment is easily accessible, simple to use and indicated by signs;
(2) take measures for firefighting, nominate and train employees to implement those measures, and arrange contacts with external emergency services;
(3) keep emergency routes clear, and comply with specific criteria relating to routes, doors and signs; and
(4) have a suitable system of maintenance for fire precautions in relation to the workplace, equipment and devices, and ensure these are working and in good repair.

15.11.2 Amendment to the Management of Health and Safety at Work Regulations 1992

These Regulations are amended to incorporate the provisions of the 1997 Regulations on:

- Risk assessment
- Health and safety assistance
- Information for employees

535

- Co-operation and co-ordination
- Persons working in host employers' undertakings.

15.11.3 Enforcement

The Regulations are enforced by the local fire authority, either through fire brigade officers or through appointed inspectors. Criminal breaches of the Regulations are liable on conviction in a magistrates' court or Crown Court to a fine, imprisonment or both. Anyone who fails, intentionally or recklessly, to comply with the Regulations and puts employees at serious risk in case of fire (ie death or serious injury) commits a criminal offence.

In situations where non-compliance puts employees at serious risk, the authority can serve an enforcement notice requiring work to be undertaken within a specified period. The recipient has 21 days in which to appeal. Except in situations where the risk is so serious that the service of an enforcement notice cannot be delayed, the authority must give written notice of its intention to serve. Failure to comply with an enforcement notice is a criminal offence.

Where there is a breach of Regulations, whether serious or not, a county court may, on receipt of an application from a fire authority, issue an enforcement order requiring compliance. Before making application for an order, the fire authority must give written notice to the alleged offender of its intention to seek an order, and consider any representations made as a result.

15.11.4 Fire Precautions Act 1971

The scope of this Act, which enables a fire authority to serve a prohibition notice to immediately prohibit the use of premises, including an unsafe workplace in a building, is extended to workplaces in movable structures and in the open air. The Act is not amended and duties under it must be read in conjunction with the Regulations.

15.11.5 Excepted workplaces

The following workplaces are excepted from the requirements of these Regulations:

(1) those having a current fire certificate, or for which an application is pending, under the Fire Precautions Act 1971;

(2) those having a current fire certificate under the Safety of Sports Grounds Act 1975 or the Fire Safety (Safety of Places of Sport) Act 1989;

(3) workplaces covered by the Fire Precautions (Sub-surface Railway Stations) Regulations 1989;

(4) construction sites within the meaning of reg 2(1) of the Construction (Health, Safety and Welfare) Regulations 1996;

(5) ships within the meaning of reg 2(1) of the Docks Regulations 1988;

(6) premises covered by the Fire Certificates (Special Premises) Regulations 1976;

(7) premises covered by the Mines and Quarries Act 1954;

(8) offshore installations within the meaning of reg 3 of the Offshore Installations and Pipelines Works (Management and Administration) Regulations 1995;

(9) aircraft, locomotives and rolling stock, or trailers used as a means of transport, or vehicles having a licence under the Vehicle Excise and Registration Act or which are exempted from duty under this Act;

(10) workplaces which are in fields, woods or other land forming part of an agricultural or forestry undertaking, but which are not inside a building and are situated away from the undertaking's main building.

15.12 LIFTING OPERATIONS AND LIFTING EQUIPMENT REGULATIONS 1998

Under these Regulations, lifting equipment provided for use at work should be:

- Strong and safe enough for its use
- Marked with its safe working load
- Installed and positioned to minimise risks
- Used safely
- Thoroughly examined and, where appropriate, inspected by a competent person on an ongoing basis.

All equipment used at work for lifting and lowering loads, including attachments and accessories, but with the exception of escalators, is covered by the Regulations.

The Regulations apply to all employers or self-employed persons who provide lifting equipment for use at work, as well as those who have control over its use. An ongoing requirement of the legislation is that:

(1) lifting operations must be planned, supervised and carried out in a safe manner by a competent person;

(2) equipment used for lifting people must be marked accordingly, and should be safe for such a purpose;

(3) before being used for the first time the equipment should, where appropriate, be thoroughly examined;

(4) it may also need to be thoroughly examined in use at set intervals (eg six months for accessories and equipment used for lifting people);

(5) all examinations must be carried out by a competent person; and

(6) a report must be submitted by the competent person to the employer following a thorough examination or inspection.

15.13 CONTROL OF SUBSTANCES HAZARDOUS TO HEALTH (COSHH) REGULATIONS 1999

The COSSH Regulations apply to every form of workplace and every type of work activity involving the use of substances which may be hazardous to health to people at work. The Regulations are supported by a number of HSC Approved Codes of Practice, including:

- *Control of substances hazardous to health*
- *Control of carcinogenic substances*
- *Control of biological agents.*

15.13.1 Definitions

'Biological agent' means any micro-organism, cell, culture or human endoparasite, including any which have been genetically modified, which may cause any infection, allergy, toxicity or otherwise create a hazard to human health. 'Substance' means any natural or artificial substance, whether in solid, liquid, gas or vapour form (including any micro-organism). 'Substance hazardous to health' means any substance (including any preparation) which is:

(1) a substance which is listed for supply in Part 1 of the Approved Supply List as dangerous for supply within the meaning of the Chemicals (Hazard Information and Packaging for Supply) Regulations 1994 and for which an indication of danger specified for the substance in Part V of that list is very toxic, toxic, harmful, corrosive or irritant;
(2) a substance for which the HSC has approved a maximum exposure limit or an occupational exposure standard;
(3) a biological agent;
(4) dust of any kind when present at a substantial concentration in air; and
(5) a substance, not being one mentioned in (1)–(4) above, which creates a hazard to any person's health which is comparable with the hazards created by substances mentioned in (1)–(4).

15.13.2 Assessment of health risks
(Reg 6)

This regulation places a duty on employers, where employees may be exposed to substances hazardous to health, to make a suitable and sufficient assessment of the risks (a health risk assessment) created by that work to employees and the steps that need to be taken. The assessment must be reviewed if it is no longer valid or there has been a significant change in the work to which the assessment relates, and any changes, as a result of the review, must be made.

15.13.3 Prevention or control of exposure
(Reg 7)

Exposure to substances hazardous to health must be either prevented or, where this is not reasonably practicable, controlled. Except in the case of a carcinogen or biological agent, prevention or adequate control shall be by means other than the provision of personal protective equipment (PPE).

15.13.4 Use of control measures, etc
(Reg 8)

Every employer shall take all reasonable steps to ensure that any control measure is properly used or applied. Every employee shall make full and proper use of any control measures, return PPE to any accommodation provided, and report defects in control measures to his employer.

15.13.5 Maintenance, examination and test of control measures, etc
(Reg 9)

The employer must ensure that any control measure is maintained in an efficient state, in efficient working order and in good repair and, in the case of PPE, in a clean condition.

15.13.6 Monitoring exposure at the workplace
(Reg 10)

Where appropriate, the employer shall ensure that there is a suitable procedure for monitoring the exposure of employees, including keeping records of such monitoring procedures.

15.13.7 Health surveillance
(Reg 11)

Where appropriate, the employer shall ensure that employees who are liable to be exposed are under suitable health surveillance.

15.13.8 Information, instruction and training etc
(Reg 12)

Where employees are exposed to the risk of exposure, they must be provided with such suitable and sufficient information, instruction and training for them to know those risks and the precautions which should be taken.

15.13.9 Defence in proceedings for contravention of Regulations
(Reg 16)

In any proceedings for an offence consisting of a contravention of these Regulations, it is a defence for any person to prove that he took *all* reasonable precautions and exercised *all* due diligence to avoid the commission of that offence.

15.14 HEALTH AND SAFETY (INFORMATION FOR EMPLOYEES) REGULATIONS 1999

15.14.1 Posters and leaflets

These Regulations require information relating to health, safety and welfare to be furnished to employees by means of posters or leaflets approved and published by the Health and Safety Executive. Copies of posters and leaflets may be obtained from the HSE and HMSO. The Regulations also require the enforcing authority's name and address and the Employment Medical Advisory Service's address to be written in the appropriate space on the poster. Where the leaflet is given to employees, the same information should be specified in a written notice accompanying it.

15.14.2 Certificates of exemption

The Regulations provide for the issue of Certificates of Exemption by the HSE, provide for a defence for a contravention of the Regulations, and repeal, revoke and modify various enactments relating to the provision of information to employees. The Regulations do not apply to the master and crew of a seagoing ship.

15.14.3 Modification to the Regulations

The Health and Safety Information for Employees (Modifications and Repeals) Regulations 1995 amended the 1989 Regulations, allowing the HSE to approve, as an alternative to the basic Health and Safety Law poster, a particular form of poster or leaflet for use in relation to a particular employment or class of employment. When applying for approval to display an alternative poster, applicants must demonstrate:

(1) a clearly defined industry or group of employers;
(2) a clear demand for the alternative poster; and
(3) that the poster would meet the same purposes as the basic poster and that the benefit justifies the development costs.

15.14.4 Abolition of statutory requirements

These Regulations also abolish 53 statutory requirements to display health and safety information, notably the Factories Act 1961, s 139 and a series of regulations made under that Act covering specific industries.

15.15 REPORTING INJURIES, DISEASES AND DANGEROUS OCCURRENCES

The Reporting of Injuries, Diseases and Dangerous Occurrences Regulations 1995 (RIDDOR) cover the requirement to notify and *report* certain categories of injury and disease sustained by people at work, together with specified dangerous occurrences and gas incidents to the relevant enforcing authority (ie the HSE or local authority). The majority of duties on 'responsible persons' (as defined) are of an absolute nature.

15.15.1 Principal requirements of RIDDOR

The responsible person (eg employer) must notify the relevant enforcing authority by the quickest practicable means and subsequently make a report within ten days on the approved form in respect of death, any defined major injury and dangerous occurrence arising out of or in connection with work (reg 3). It is the employer's duty to report the death of an employee where, as a result of an accident at work, the injured employee dies within one year of the accident (reg 4). The employer must also report cases of disease to employees listed in the Schedule (reg 5).

There are duties on certain persons to report gas incidents (reg 6).

A responsible person must keep records of reportable injuries, diseases and dangerous occurrences (reg 7).

15.15.2 Notifiable and reportable major injuries

These are listed in Sched 1 to RIDDOR, as follows:

(1) any fracture, other than to the fingers, thumbs or toes;
(2) any amputation;
(3) dislocation of the shoulder, hip or knee;
(4) loss of sight (whether temporary or permanent);
(5) a chemical or hot metal burn to the eye or any penetrating injury to the eye;
(6) any injury resulting from electric shock or electrical burn (including such burn caused by arcing or arcing products) leading to unconsciousness or requiring resuscitation or admittance to hospital for more than 24 hours;

(7) any other injury:
   (a) leading to hypothermia, heat induced illness or unconsciousness;
   (b) requiring resuscitation; or
   (c) requiring admittance to hospital for more than 24 hours;
(8) loss of consciousness caused by asphyxia or by exposure to a harmful substance or biological agent;
(9) either of the following conditions which result from absorbing any substance by inhalation, ingestion or through the skin:
   (a) acute illness requiring medical treatment; or
   (b) loss of consciousness; and
(10) acute illness which requires medical treatment where there is reason to believe that it resulted from exposure to a biological agent or its toxins or infected material.

15.15.3 Scheduled dangerous occurrences

A dangerous occurrence is a major incident as a rule which has the potential for significant damage and potential loss of life and which is listed in Sched 2 to RIDDOR. Dangerous occurrences are classified under five headings:

(1) General (eg incidents involving lifting machinery, pressure systems, overhead electric lines).
(2) Dangerous occurrences which are reportable in mines (eg fire or ignition of gas, escape of gas, insecure tip).
(3) Dangerous occurrences which are reportable in respect of quarries (eg misfires, movement of slopes or faces).
(4) Dangerous occurrences which are reportable in respect of relevant transport systems (eg accidents involving any kind of train, incidents at level crossings).
(5) Dangerous occurrences which are reportable in respect of an offshore workplace (eg releases of petroleum hydrocarbon, fire or explosion).

15.15.4 Reportable diseases

These are diseases listed in Sched 3 to RIDDOR under three classifications:

(1) conditions due to physical agents and the physical demands of work (eg malignant diseases of bones due to ionising radiation, decompression illness);
(2) infections due to biological agents (eg anthrax, brucellosis, leptospirosis); and
(3) conditions due to substances (eg poisoning by carbon disulphide, ethylene oxide and methyl bromide).

15.16 COMPULSORY INSURANCE

The Employers' Liability (Compulsory Insurance) Act 1969 deals with employers' duties in terms of insuring themselves against claims which may be made by employees.

15.16.1 Employers' duties

Section 1 of the Act requires that every employer carrying on business in Great Britain shall insure and maintain insurance against liability for bodily injury or disease sustained by his employees, and arising out of and in the course of their employment in Great Britain in that business. This insurance must be provided under one or more 'approved policies'. An approved policy is a policy of insurance not subject to any conditions or exceptions prohibited by regulations.

15.16.2 Cover

Cover is required in respect of liability to employees who either:

(1) are ordinarily resident in Great Britain; or
(2) though not ordinarily resident in Great Britain, are present in Great Britain in the course of employment for a continuous period of not less than 14 days.

The amount for which an employer is required to insure and maintain insurance is £2m in respect of claims relating to one or more of his employees, arising out of any one occurrence.

15.16.3 Issue and display of certificate of insurance

The insurer must issue the employer with a certificate of insurance, which has to be issued not later than 30 days after the date on which insurance was commenced or renewed. The certificate must be displayed prominently.

15.16.4 Penalties under the Act

For failure to insure or maintain insurance, the maximum penalty on conviction is a £1,000 fine. For failure to display a certificate of insurance, the maximum penalty on conviction is a £500 fine.

15.17 CONSULTATION WITH EMPLOYEES

Joint consultation between employers and employees is an important feature of the safety management process and may take place specifically with trade union-appointed safety representatives and/or through the operation of a health and safety committee, or as part of a normal employer/employee consultative process.

15.17.1 Safety Representatives and Safety Committees Regulations 1977

The main objective of these Regulations is to provide a basic framework within which each undertaking can develop effective working relationships. These relationships must cover a wide range of work situations (ie different types of workplace and work activity).

Appointment of safety representatives

A recognised trade union may appoint safety representatives from among the employees in all cases where one or more employees are employed by an employer by whom it is recognised. The employer must be notified by the trade union of the names of the safety representatives. Each safety representative has certain prescribed functions, as indicated below.

Functions of safety representatives

Safety representatives have the following functions:

(1) to represent employees in consultation with employers;
(2) to co-operate effectively in promoting and developing health and safety measures;
(3) to make representations to the employer on any general or specific matter affecting the health and safety of
    (a) their members; and/or
    (b) other persons employed at the workplace;
(4) to carry out certain inspections;
(5) to represent members in consultations with the HSE;
(6) to receive information from inspectors; and
(7) to attend meetings of the safety committee if appropriate.

None of these functions, however, imposes a legal duty on safety representatives.

Time off with pay

Employers must give safety representatives time off with pay for performing their functions and for any reasonable training they undergo.

Inspections of the workplace

Safety representatives are entitled to carry out workplace inspections, and employers must give reasonable assistance. Notice to inspect must be given in writing, with a standard inspection every three months. Safety representatives may also inspect the scene of a reportable accident or dangerous occurrence.

Inspection of documents

Safety representatives can inspect any document which the employer has to maintain, other than documents relating to the health records of identifiable individuals.

Approved code of practice

Qualifications and functions of safety representatives

So far as is reasonably practicable, representatives must have two years' experience with the employer or in similar employment. They must keep themselves informed of legal requirements and encourage co-operation between employer and employee. They are entitled to carry out workplace health and safety inspections and must inform the employer of the outcome of these inspections.

Employers' obligations

Employers must provide information to safety representatives on:

- Plans and performance of the undertaking
- Hazards and precautions
- Occurrence of accidents, dangerous occurrences and occupational disease
- Any other information, including the results of any measurements taken (eg from air monitoring).

Safety committees

Basic objectives and functions

The basic objective is to promote co-operation and act as a focus for employee participation. Safety Committees' functions are to consider:

(1) circumstances of individual accidents and cases of reportable diseases; and
(2) accident statistics and trends.

The committee might also:

(a) examine safety audit reports;
(b) consider reports and information from the HSE;
(c) assist in the development of safety rules and systems;
(d) conduct periodic inspections;

(e) monitor the effectiveness of health and safety training, communications and publicity; and

(f) provide a link with the Inspectorate.

Membership

Safety committees should be reasonably compact but allowing for representation of management and all employees. It must be appreciated that safety representatives are not appointed by the safety committee and vice versa. Neither is responsible to or for the other.

Conduct

Meetings should be held as often as necessary; agendas and minutes must be provided.

Arrangements at individual workplaces

Local arrangements should include:

(1) division of conduct of activities;

(2) a clear definition of the committee's objectives, terms of reference, membership and structure; and

(3) publication of matters notified by safety representatives.

15.17.2 Health and Safety (Consultation with Employees) Regulations 1996

These Regulations brought in changes to the law with regard to the health and safety consultation process between employers and employees, largely because many employees are not members of a recognised trade union. Under the Safety Representatives and Safety Committees Regulations 1997, employers must consult safety representatives appointed by any trade unions they recognise.

Under the 1996 Regulations employers must consult any employees who are not covered by the 1997 Regulations. This may be by direct consultation with employees or through representatives elected by the employees they are to represent.

HSE guidance

HSE guidance accompanying the Regulations details:

- which employees must be involved;
- the information they must be provided with;
- procedures for the election of representatives of employee safety;
- the training, time off and facilities they must be provided with; and
- their functions in office.

15.18 CONCLUSION

Most employers are good at assessing the cost of measures to ensure the appropriate levels of protection of employees at work. What they are not good at is assessing the extensive costs arising from death, major injuries and ill-health connected with work activities. Such costs can represent a significant loss as a result of, for instance, fines and damages imposed by the courts, together with increased employers' liability insurance premiums. These are only the direct costs, however. The indirect costs, such as poor levels of morale following a fatal accident, damage to plant and equipment and lost time arising from an accident, are frequently not taken into account.

Indeed, no employer can afford to disregard the current legal requirements for the development and implementation of management systems directed at the prevention of these losses. It should be recognised that loyal, well-trained and safety-conscious employees are the organisation's most valuable asset. Without these people, many employers would not be in business.

16

GENERAL INSURANCE

GILL CLARK, ZURICH FINANCIAL SERVICES (UKISA) LTD

16.1 THE NEED FOR INSURANCE COVER

All businesses, whether large or small, have to take risk. It is essential to recognise the uncertain nature of risk. Can the reader appreciate the financial loss which may be incurred as a result of, for example, an extensive factory fire, or a theft? Adequate insurance cover is a fundamental requirement to ensure the continuation of a business in the event of a loss.

16.2 PROTECTION

It is also important to recognise at this early stage that not all risks can be insured but, in return for a known premium, insurance provides for the uncertainty of most losses in a business environment to be transferred to the insurers who arrange cover for thousands of businesses. A business therefore stands to benefit from insuring the risks to which it is subject since insurance can protect its interests by allowing business plans to continue and by facilitating continued production. There is then no need to make contingency plans or tie up capital in the form of reserves to cater for the possibility of a risk actually occurring and causing a loss which could not otherwise be withstood by the business. Insurance can also free the businessman from many of the worries inherent in the running of the business.

16.3 THE MAIN COMPULSORY INSURANCE REQUIREMENTS

Whilst it is good business practice to arrange insurance to protect the business assets and liabilities, there are several forms of insurance which have been made compulsory for most businesses either by UK statutory law or by EC Regulation. These are explained below.

16.3.1 Legislation relating to employers' liability

Employers' Liability (Compulsory Insurance) Act 1969 and Employers' Liability (Compulsory Insurance) General Regulations 1971

The 1969 Act and 1971 General Regulations introduced compulsory employers' liability insurance with effect from 1 January 1972. Most employers (there are some exceptions) carrying on any business in Great Britain must insure, with an authorised insurer, against liability for bodily injury or disease sustained by their employees arising out of and in the course of their employment in Great Britain in that business. Evidence of this insurance must be provided in the form of an insurance certificate which must be displayed in a prominent position at each place of business at which there are employees. Under 1998 Regulations, employers are required to keep evidence of insurance certificates for 40 years.

16.3.2 Road Traffic Act 1988

This Act consolidated certain legislation relating to road traffic and came into force on 15 May 1989. To comply with an EC Directive on motor insurance, interim regulations gave effect to the Act's requirements from 31 December 1988.

The Act requires that the insurance policy provides unlimited cover for death or bodily injury to a third party (including passengers) and a minimum amount of £250,000 for third party property damage. In practice higher levels of third party property damage are given, usually unlimited for cars and up to £5m for goods vehicles. At present there is no legal requirement for insuring against damage to one's own vehicle.

16.3.3 Statutory examination of engineering plant

By law, many items of plant and machinery (eg pressure systems, power presses, local exhaust ventilation plants, lifts and lifting equipment) must be inspected and certified by a competent person. These examinations are largely in response to the requirements of the Health and Safety at Work Act, and associated legislation.

These services provided by some of the major insurers are sometimes part of a wider policy cover or are on a fee only basis.

16.4 INSURANCE DISTRIBUTION

It is possible to purchase insurance in two ways: direct from the insurance company or through an insurance intermediary. As a commercial buyer of insurance, most businesses currently choose to use an insurance intermediary to assist in identifying the risks which confront the business. The variations in policy wording offered by the different insurers further adds to the complexity of arranging insurance cover.

The insurance intermediaries understand the market and know the various types of cover that can be provided, the most competitive premium rates and the best claims services available. The intermediaries' advice is mainly free since they receive remuneration, in the form of commission, from the insurance company. Therefore the businessman does not pay more for using the service of an intermediary than going to the insurance company itself. However, there has been an increasing move towards intermediaries levying fees to clients for their services. This is based on a perceived benefit to the client, of receiving more favourable premiums from the insurance companies, who would not be then including the intermediaries' commission in their terms, and the potential saving in insurance premium tax (IPT).

Intermediaries act as agents for the insured but sometimes have the authority from the insurance companies to issue cover for certain classes of insurance. Intermediaries can be classified as follows.

16.4.1 Insurance broker

A broker is a full-time intermediary and is expected to have a wide knowledge of the insurance market. The Insurance Brokers (Registration) Act 1977 created the Insurance Brokers Registration Council (IBRC) to govern the registration and regulation of insurance brokers. To be registered as a broker, an individual must have:

(1) an approved qualification; and
(2) been employed by an insurance broker or insurance company for at least three years; or
(3) been employed as in (2) above for five years.

16.4.2 Other intermediaries

There are also insurance agents, consultants, financial advisers, or appointed representatives working on either a full- or part-time basis who may not have had such a wide knowledge of the general insurance market as an insurance broker. The agent, for example, may have been an accountant or solicitor who introduced insurance in the course of his main business activity.

Insurers recognise two main categories of non-registered intermediary:

(1) An 'independent intermediary' who acts primarily for his client and is responsible for the advice and service provided.
(2) A 'company agent' who represents up to a maximum of six insurance companies which accept responsibility for his conduct and advice given.

The Association of British Insurers (ABI), introduced a code of practice in 1981 to compliment the Insurance Brokers (Registration) Act by controlling the non-registered intermediaries with the aim of safeguarding consumers' interests. The code was last reviewed in 1993 and is supported by Government. An independent code monitoring committee, comprising ABI members, consumer groups and DTI representation, reports on the operation of the code annually to interested parties, including Government.

16.4.3 E-commerce

As in many industries, e-commerce is emerging as a powerful force. Internet trading provides opportunities to improve customer service in claims, communications and for all back office activity. The Internet also has strong potential to be a new channel of sale. While currently use of the Internet is limited, there are very clear signs that activity will increase and that for many small businesses it will become their chosen method for placing their insurance.

16.4.4 General Insurance Standards Council (GISC)

The GISC opened for business on 3 July 2000. Its purpose is to regulate the selling of general insurance by insurers, insurance brokers, intermediaries and others acting for them, and Lloyd's. It was set up by the industry in response to the Government's stated wish that sales of general insurance be regulated on a non-statutory basis by a single, independent regulatory body having support across the industry. The Government's intention is that the GISC delivers protection to customers by setting standards for sales, advice and service, to make sure that customers are treated fairly.

Membership will be open to all brokers, intermediaries and direct sellers and initially will be voluntary. In time, however, probably in late 2001 when clearances have been obtained from the Competition Authorities, membership will become mandatory. Insurers will agree only to trade with brokers and intermediaries who are members of GISC unless, in certain circumstances, the insurer accepts responsibility for the actions of its agents. Insurers themselves, through the ABI, have committed to support GISC and will be joining in respect of sales made on a direct basis.

During this interim 'voluntary' period, both the Insurance Brokers Registration Council (IBRC) and the ABI Code of Practice for selling general insurance will continue as present. The Insurance Brokers Registration Act will be repealed when the Financial Services and Markets Act 2000 is brought into force on a date to be announced and with it will go the IBRC. The Code will be withdrawn when the ABI and the Government are satisfied that the GISC has achieved a 'critical mass' (around 60%) of membership. This is not likely to be until the IBRA is repealed with brokers and intermediaries then becoming members of the GISC.

16.5 TYPES OF COVER AVAILABLE

There are many areas of a business which require some form of insurance protection. Various forms of cover are available and these range from insurance against loss or damage to the business assets and the financial loss which would follow, to liability and professional indemnity insurances.

16.5.1 Property insurance – 'material damage'

Material damage insurance provides cover for the actual business assets, for example, the buildings, machinery and stock in trade. Various types of material damage cover are available and the following paragraphs give a brief summary of the forms most commonly requested.

Fire and special perils insurance

A basic 'standard fire' policy gives cover for loss or damage following fire, lightning and a limited form of explosion. However, invariably such limited cover is not enough and wider cover is required. This is provided by a 'fire and special perils' policy which covers a range of additional covers as well as fire. These include full explosion, aircraft, storm, escape of water, riot, malicious damage and impact by road vehicles or animals. The customer may select the extent of cover he requires.

It is also possible to purchase even wider cover by means of an 'all risks' policy which includes all the above perils together with other 'accidental' damage which gives cover for all damage unless caused by an exclusion stated in the policy. These policies are usually sold on an 'all or nothing' basis rather than a selective basis.

The amount chosen to insure the business assets is known as the 'sum insured' and it is essential that this figure is adequate, otherwise any claim will be proportionately reduced. This is known as 'subject to average'. When fixing the sum insured, an allowance should be made for inflation and possible delays in rebuilding time and obtaining alternative equipment or supplies.

It is not sufficient to insure the physical loss or damage to property. It is also essential to insure loss of income following loss or damage and this is provided by means of 'Business Interruption' insurance. Details are explained in 16.5.4.

Theft policy

This provides compensation in the event of the loss of the property insured by theft. It also includes theft damage to buildings. A more detailed description of stock may be necessary, as it is usually this which is attractive to thieves, although it has become more common for computers and computer chips to figure significantly as a target. Commercial theft policies usually require evidence of entry to or exit from premises by forcible and violent means.

Goods in transit insurance

Every business depends upon the movement of goods and documents and as insurance is not provided for business effects under a motor policy, goods in transit insurance is a necessary protection.

An 'all risks' policy is available. If a business owns a small fleet of vehicles, the policy can be arranged to specify the number of vehicles, with individual limits for each vehicle. If a business owns a large fleet of vehicles, it is advised to insure it on 'a declaration basis' whereby the insurance is based on the maximum value in any one vehicle in operation at the inception date of the policy, and a deposit premium charge based on the estimated annual carryings of all vehicles. Any adjustment in the premium is made at each renewal when the actual annual carryings are declared.

A problem arises, however, when goods are sent via a contracted haulier. If the goods are lost or damaged while in the carrier's care, compensation may not automatically be forthcoming as the carrier may be able to prove that he is not liable or, alternatively, can rely on contract conditions to avoid liability.

Various conditions of carriage exist, most notably those resulting from the Road Haulage Association's Standard Conditions of 1991 and the Standard CMR conditions applicable in EC countries. These Conditions should be studied carefully or discussed with an insurance adviser. This being the case, it is advisable that goods are insured under an 'all risks' policy as a carrier's policy ultimately protects the carrier rather than one's business. Such cover can be given on the same policy as for the business's own vehicles, and arranged on a similar basis of maximum any one vehicle and estimated carryings.

If any goods are exported a separate Marine Transit policy may be required.

For goods transported by rail, the liability accepted by the rail authorities is slightly wider than that of the haulage carriers. Even so, additional insurance cover can be arranged at a low premium. This enables any loss or damage to be dealt with by the insurance company and not directly with the rail authorities although it would be expected to first seek whatever compensation is due from such authorities.

The Post Office sets various limits of liability but, as with the above, independent insurance cover can be arranged.

Money insurance

This provides compensation to a business in the event of money being physically stolen or destroyed either at the premises or while being carried to or from a bank. There are various limits which can be arranged. Some companies also provide for compensation if an employee suffers injury from malicious assault while carrying money to or from a bank.

Engineering insurance

An engineering policy provides cover for damage to machinery and can also cover explosion of steam boilers and pressure plant. Cover for electrical and mechanical breakdown is also available for most machinery.

Engineering insurers offer a variety of insurance packages catering for a wide range of machinery and construction risks. Examples include:

(a) machinery breakdown (including loss of profits)
(b) boiler/pressure systems explosion
(c) contract works (eg building and civil engineering, machinery installation)
(d) contractors plant
(e) hired-in machinery and plant
(f) computers and electronic equipment
(g) machinery movement.

Periodic inspection of many types of machinery and plant (eg lifting equipment, pressure systems, local exhaust ventilation, plant power presses) is compulsory by law and most engineering insurers provide such inspection services. Many also offer a range of machinery and health and safety related consultancy services.

It is not sufficient to insure the physical loss or damage to property. It is also essential to insure loss of income following loss or damage and this is provided by means of 'business interruption' insurance (see 16.5.4).

16.5.2 Liability insurances

The day-to-day operation of a business, including the ownership of business premises, business vehicles and the manufacture and sale of goods or other services provided, introduces legal responsibilities to employees, the public and to the consumers of the products or services supplied. It is therefore important that all businesses have adequate insurance protection to protect them against the legal liabilities which may arise. Insurers therefore provide employers, public and product liability insurances and professional indemnity insurances to provide protection against these liabilities. These legal liabilities may be imposed by common law, by statute or increasingly by EC regulation. In addition there may be contractual liabilities, some of which may be uninsurable. Penalty clauses are normally uninsurable.

Employers' liability insurance policy

It is compulsory under the terms of the Employers' Liability (Compulsory Insurance) Act 1969 to effect employers' liability insurance. This Act came into force on 1 January 1972. Most employers (there are exceptions) must take out insurance against liability for bodily injury or disease sustained by employees arising out of and in the course of their employment in the UK. An insurance certificate has to be displayed to provide evidence of the insurance being in force.

An employers' liability policy protects the employer against:

(a) his own personal negligence;
(b) his vicarious liability for the acts of his employees;
(c) failure to provide suitable and safe plant, a safe place of work and competent staff;
(d) the personal negligence of employees and their negligence in carrying out their duties;
(e) breach of statutory duty. There are many statutory enactments relating to the health and safety at work of employees, some of which relate specifically to dangerous substances (eg asbestos). The Health and Safety at Work Act 1974 outlines the main statutory duties imposed on the employer. The Management of Health and Safety at Work Regulations 1992 require employers to:

- assess risks to health and safety
- plan, organise, control, monitor and review measures
- provide health surveillance
- appoint competent people
- set up emergency procedures
- provide information and training.

The Regulations give guidance on personal protective equipment provided, manual handling operations and safety requirements relating to display screen equipment (see generally Chapter 15).

The Employers Liability (Compulsory Insurance) Regulations 1998 require an employer to insure and maintain insurance for £5m for claims relating to employees arising out of any one occurrence. Most insurers now offer a limit of liability of £10m, which sum is inclusive of legal costs. Most insurers provide an option to purchase additional protection up to a limit of £25m, although there are facilities to provide even higher limits.

Employers' liability insurance thus provides cover against an award of damages which a business may have to pay for bodily injury or disease sustained by an employee, and also the costs of defending an action brought under the Health and Safety at Work Act 1974.

Public liability insurance policy

This insurance, unlike employers' liability insurance, is not compulsory by law (other than for the owners of riding establishments), but public liability claims carry the same financial threat to a business.

Public liability insurance provides cover for damages or compensation awarded against a company in respect of accidental bodily injury to third parties and accidental loss of or accidental damage to third party property caused in the conduct of the business (eg the negligence of the employer or employees, or perhaps from defects in the properties owned by the business). There are a number of common exceptions within this cover:

- Liabilities arising from the use of motor vehicles where the RTA applies
- Aviation liabilities
- Marine liabilities
- Claims for damage to property belonging to the policyholder or whilst property is in his custody or control
- Loss of or damage to property which is being worked upon
- Liabilities relating to the sale of products
- Any liabilities relating to professional advice provided by the policyholder for a fee.

The policy has a limit of indemnity which applies to any one claim or a series of claims arising from one original cause. In view of the increasing level of awards made by the courts, a business should ensure that its policy provides an adequate limit of indemnity, probably at least £2m. Additional protection is widely available at reasonable additional cost and limits of £5m, £10m and beyond can be arranged.

The policyholder is normally required to pay the first £100 or £250 of any claim.

Product liability insurance policy

Product liability insurance provides protection in respect of the insured's legal liability to pay damages or compensation for accidental bodily injury to third parties, and accidental loss of or accidental damage to third party property caused by goods sold or supplied or contract work executed by the business. The cover does not extend to apply to the cost of recalling, replacing or repairing the product supplied. This is more properly the subject of product guarantee insurance for which there is a limited market.

Product liability cover is usually available only in conjunction with public liability insurance. A limit of indemnity applies to a product liability policy in the aggregate for any one period of insurance. Again significant limits of indemnity are available.

Consumer Protection Act 1987

The objective of s 1 of the Act was to implement the EC Directive concerning liability for defective products (85/374/EEC). The Directive requires all member states to adopt or adapt national laws so as to impose a strict liability system upon the producers of defective products which cause injury to persons or damage to property. The Act became effective on 1 March 1988.

A person who has suffered damage does not have to prove negligence.

Those liable include the manufacturer of a finished product or component; the producer of raw material; or a person who holds himself out to be a producer (eg by putting an own brand label on the article). Where an article is manufactured outside the EU, the importer is also liable.

In view of the liabilities imposed on the producers of goods, importers etc it is important that they are adequately protected by product liability insurance with an adequate indemnity limit.

Good internal procedures are vital including:

- the adequacy of design and development procedures;
- the effectiveness of quality assurance systems;
- emergency plans for product recall if necessary;
- adequate records identifying suppliers, particularly overseas suppliers, so that any claim can be passed down the chain of supply.

Professional indemnity insurance

This type of insurance provides cover for liability arising from a negligent act, error or omission. The cover is not only required by the established professions (eg doctors, architects and solicitors) but anyone working in an advisory capacity. Cover is therefore required by financial advisers, designers of software or laboratories providing testing facilities.

In recent years the liability of professional advisers has been extended by the courts and they can in some circumstances incur liabilities to others with whom they are not in a contractual relationship.

The professional person must act with reasonable skill and care; if he does not do so he incurs a liability to pay compensation or damages which include compensation for financial losses suffered by the claimant.

The insurance cover is normally written on a 'claims made' basis and again, as with product liability insurance, the indemnity limit is normally capped in the aggregate in any one period of insurance.

16.5.3 Motor insurance policies

Any motorised self-propelled vehicles used or kept on a road or any other public place must be insured for third party liability to meet the requirements of the Road Traffic Act. In addition to this compulsory third party cover a vehicle can also be insured for damage arising from fire and theft; this is known as a 'third party fire and theft' policy. The most common form of cover is the comprehensive policy which includes accidental damage to the employer's own vehicle.

Motor insurance is divided into:

(a) commercial vehicles;
(b) private cars;
(c) motorcycles.

If a business has a number of vehicles, these can be insured as part of a motor fleet policy. This covers all vehicles owned or operated by the business and can also include hired or loaned vehicles, whether they are private cars, goods carrying vehicles or motorcycles.

Comprehensive cover is essential for the small to medium-sized firms which do not have the facilities and resources to repair their own vehicles. If the damage is so severe as to make the vehicle uneconomical to repair, the insurers consider the vehicle to be a 'total loss' and settlement is made on the vehicle's current market value. However, where a car is a total loss and is less than 12 months old at the time of the accident it may be replaced with a new model of the same type.

An excess may be applied in which case the business is liable for the first amount of any claim. This is usually in the region of £100 to £500. An employer can agree to pay a voluntary excess in return for a reduced premium. Other factors such as the vehicle type, the business location and past claims experience are taken into account when assessing the premium.

16.5.4 Business interruption insurance

Formerly known as 'consequential loss', this insurance gives protection against pecuniary loss which is almost certain to follow a fire or other physical damage to property. The business interruption policy is designed to protect the profit or other earnings of the business as well as to meet continuing payments for fixed overheads following a loss by a 'peril' insured under the material damage policy. The range of perils insured under a business interruption policy is usually the same as under the material damage policy.

Insurers invariably insist that a material damage policy exists (usually with the same company) and liability admitted under that policy before a payment can be made under a business interruption policy.

The essential features of business interruption insurance are as follows:

Maximum indemnity period

The businessman needs to assess how long it will take to get the business running normally again and also make sure that the cover will allow enough time for rebuilding or re-equipping the business premises and restoring trade to the level it was at before the loss. This is incorporated into the policy as the 'maximum indemnity period'.

Cover under the policy ceases at the end of the period and thus it is important that the indemnity period selected is more than adequate. Obviously, any estimation of the maximum indemnity period requires in-depth calculations and usually either the insurers or insurance intermediary will help in selecting the correct time period.

Careful consideration should also be given to the business's nature, the machinery used and location of staff. A serious interruption, for example, may force staff to leave, machinery may not be available and stock may not be readily replaced. The maximum indemnity period should take account of all these factors so that the possibility of inadequate cover is minimised.

Loss of gross profit

The most common form of business interruption insurance in the market is loss of gross profit on a 'declaration linked' basis. Under this form of cover, there is no sum insured but the premium is based on an estimate of the gross profit (see below) for the coming year, although this figure has to be pro-portionately increased if the maximum indemnity period is more than 12 months. At the end of the insurance period, this premium is adjusted when the actual gross profit is known, again proportionately increased in line with the maximum indemnity period. This premium adjustment may result in an additional premium to the insurers or a refund due to the insured.

Because the figure chosen is an 'estimate', insurers allow additional cover over that amount, usually 33%, and if in the event of a claim the esti-mate is found to be inadequate, the claim is not proportionately reduced (ie is not subject to average).

It is still possible to insure profit on an actual basis with a sum insured, but the amount has to be accurate, no additional cover is allowed and the policy is subject to average. If, however, at the end of the period the sum insured was in excess of the gross profit (proportionately increased if nec-essary), insurers will allow a refund.

Gross profit for insurance purposes is not the figure shown in trading profit and loss accounts but is calculated in line with the definition stated in the policy. Particular attention should be paid to the future expansion of the business. Thus the figure selected should take into account real growth and inflation as well as being proportionately increased in line with the maxi-mum indemnity period.

Other covers available

Other forms of business interruption insurance often asked for are loss of revenue (suitable for hotel or restaurant owners, churches or dental practices), loss of fees (suitable for professional practices such as solicitors) and loss of rent receivable (suitable for property owners).

Extensions of cover

The business may, of course, be affected by losses outside the premises and therefore most business interruption policies are capable of being extended, the most common being:

(1) Denial of access – neighbouring premises damaged by an insured peril may prevent access to the business premises, thus resulting in a loss of earnings.
(2) Failure of public utilities – access or trade prevented as a result of insured damage at the premises of the gas, water or electricity supply company.
(3) Suppliers of goods or services – premises from which the insured obtains essential supplies or services. If supplies are not available from their usual source, production of the business will be curtailed or even halted until supplies are available again or, as is more likely, an alternative source is found, possibly at an increased cost.

Other extensions exist and vary from insurer to insurer depending on the type of business.

Outstanding debit balances

Any business which allows credit for the payment of goods or services relies on its accounting records for the collection of money due. If these records are destroyed by an insured peril customers cannot be traced and the money they are owed may never be collected.

It is possible to cover these outstanding debit balances by means of a 'book debts' policy. As with the business interruption policy, it is essential for a claim to be agreed in respect of these records under the material policy before a claim can be paid under this one.

The sum insured should represent the maximum amount outstanding at any one time. Each month the insured undertakes to provide the actual amount outstanding and at the end of the year the premium is recalculated on the average of these declarations and a refund is allowed to the insured if this is less than the original amount paid. Furthermore, regular declarations facilitate the calculation of the amount payable in the event of a claim.

16.5.5 Other insurances to consider

Fidelity insurance

This type of insurance is centred around fraud or dishonesty on the part of the employees. Cover is provided for loss of money or goods belonging to or held in trust by the employer, caused directly by an act of fraud or dishonesty committed by an employee. As a condition of the policy, fraud or dishonesty has to be perpetrated and discovered during the period for which the risk is on cover, but commonly a discovery period of one to two years after the expiry date of the time period is provided.

In considering the risk, the insurers will wish to know what systems of check and control the employer has put in place to deter and detect such fraud and dishonesty, the frequency of internal and external audits, and the number of employees. Cover is then provided on an annual basis.

The financial impact of fraud from within can pose a serious threat to a business, particularly if, as is often the case, the fraud has continued and remained undiscovered for a long period of time. Fidelity insurance should thus be considered as a viable insurance option.

Credit insurance

This protects a business against bad trade debts and covers the risk that if goods are sold, the purchaser may not pay for them as a result of insolvency. For foreign transactions, the government has set up the Export Credits Guarantee Department, primarily to assist exporting companies against the risk of not being paid. Premiums are charged on a turnover basis or are adjustable according to the amount of debt outstanding at regular intervals.

Legal expenses insurance

The public in general is becoming more litigation conscious and thus there is an even greater likelihood that at some time or other a business may become involved in legal action. Protection is available in the form of legal expenses insurance. For example, costs may be incurred as a result of legal actions brought about by an aggrieved employee who considers that he has been unfairly dismissed. The insurance cover provides financial support to defend or pursue legal rights. The cover extends to include the solicitor's fees and expenses along with any court costs and opponent's costs if appropriate.

16.6 TYPES OF POLICIES AVAILABLE

The insurance policy issued by the insurance company states what risks are covered by the policy, the premium cost, the insured's name and the period of time over which the cover applies.

16.6.1 Single risk policies

Single policies, such as a fire or a burglary policy, are usually more appropriate to the very large organisation. There is thus one policy for fire, one for consequential loss and for various other single risks. The organisation which is large enough financially may opt to retain several risks through self-insurance.

The disadvantage of a single policy is that the system of one premium and one renewal for each risk insured proves costly from the administrative point of view.

16.6.2 Package/combined policies

Single policies do not appeal to smaller businesses such as shops and offices. For smaller manufacturing or distribution businesses, insurance companies can arrange a combined policy. This incorporates separate sections for fire, consequential loss, liability, theft, money etc. The wordings are the same as if separate policies were issued but the business has the advantage of one policy and one renewal premium. There are, however, usually maximum limits on the premium for this type of policy.

Package policies are also available covering a wider range of business classes including property, loss of earnings, money and legal liability cover. The package policy is capable of covering almost all insurance needs. The combination required is selected from all the options available. Various benefits accrue:

(1) Simplified rating structure;
(2) Only one proposal form to complete;
(3) Only one premium and renewal.

The package policy is therefore flexible in accommodating changing business needs. These package policies are ideally suited to shops, hotels and offices, and can also be available for some of the smaller manufacturing and warehouse businesses, although there may be maximum limits on premiums and values.

16.6.3 Other services

A number of insurers are adding extra services to their Commercial Insurance Contracts and these services are another way of increasing the benefits of arranging insurance (eg the provision of helplines to assist on legal matters or to arrange for emergency repair to buildings). In addition a number of insurers provide booklets which can assist you in improving fire and security precautions at the business premises and risk management for vehicles.

Many insurers provide an advisory service relating to employee safety issues and legislation, product safety assessment and environmental studies.

17

PARTNERSHIP LAW

KEITH HATCHICK, SOLICITOR, PARTNER, MARSHALL HATCHICK

Despite the fact that the principal legislation in this area of law dates back to 1890 (the Partnership Act) this form of business relationship continues to be the most important one after that of the private limited company. It is particularly popular for professional services like solicitors, surveyors, architects and accountants and smaller concerns where the rigours of maintaining a company and complying with the legislation are inappropriate.

17.1 WHAT IS A PARTNERSHIP?

Section 1(1) of the Partnership Act 1890 ('the 1890 Act') defines partnership as being the relationship which subsists between persons carrying on a business in common with a view to profit. All forms of company are expressly excluded under s 1(2).

It should be emphasised that partnership is a 'relationship' and does not have a separate legal status (unlike a company). It is the partners themselves who are and remain responsible for the partnership's activities and it is they personally who will if the circumstances require sue or be sued. In other words, whereas a limited company provides the shareholders with limited liability (up to the amount unpaid on their share capital) a partnership gives no such protection to a third party.

This distinction can sometimes be over emphasised since frequently directors/shareholders of small companies will need to have given personal guarantees before banks will contemplate offering such companies loans etc. The giving of such guarantees in effect counteracts the very point of limited liability since if a company fails it may have the same effect as if the partnership failed.

There are at least three different kinds of partnership envisaged by the 1890 Act (s 32) ie one formed:

(1) for a fixed term which when completed results in its dissolution;
(2) for a particular or defined purpose or undertaking, eg a particular sales promotion – as and when completed the partnership is dissolved;

(3) for an indefinite period eg most forms of professional partnership give each partner an ability to terminate on giving the others a period of notice (see 17.9).

17.2 LIMITED PARTNERSHIP

This vehicle has become increasingly important in the context of offshore planning arrangements. The attractions are various and include:

(1) limited liability to certain of the partners;
(2) it is a registered entity which obtains a Certificate of Registration and a registration number from the Registrar of Companies;
(3) in the UK it is not automatically subject to UK tax (unlike a UK company): if the management and control is situated overseas, the partnership is deemed to be UK non-resident for tax purposes;
(4) there are fewer compliance and disclosure requirements than for a company if one of the general partners is an individual.

A limited company must have at least one 'general partner' who remains liable for all the partnership's debts and obligations. This partner may be a company. The remaining partners can be limited partners who are liable to contribute a fixed sum of capital to the partnership and their liability is limited to this extent. There is no statutory minimum capital contribution.

Where there is a limited partnership the partnership agreement must be signed by all (general and limited) partners and notification must be given to the Registrar of Companies (it is not thought necessary for the agreement to be filed).

The Limited Partnership Act 1907 is the principal governing legislation. This requires notification to Companies House of its existence and failure to notify converts the limited partnership into a normal partnership in which all partners are completely liable for partnership debts. (The notification form which is required to be completed and sent to the Registrar is called an LP5 and when there are changes these must be notified on an LP6.)

A limited partnership must be formed with a view to making a profit – the holding of investments is not in itself sufficient.

17.3 THE LIMITED LIABILITY PARTNERSHIP ACT 2000

Royal assent has been given to this important new Act. No commencement date had been given at the time of writing. The Act creates new status of a limited liability partnership which can be shortened to 'llp' or 'LLP' (or the Welsh equivalent 'pac'/'PAC'). The taxation implications are dealt with elsewhere in this book, but the following is a summary of the principal legal provisions.

There must be a minimum of two member subscribers associated in a business with a view to profit.

An incorporation document containing basic information (eg name of partnership, partners' names and addresses, which partners have limited liability (which may be all of them), address of the registered office (in relation to England, Wales and Scotland only)) needs to be filed with the Registrar of Companies. It is a criminal offence for a person to make a false statement (or one which he believes is not true) in connection with the information. When the formalities have been completed, the Registrar will issue a certificate of incorporation.

A member is any person who has subscribed his name to the incorporation document or who subsequently becomes a member with the agreement of existing members. Being a member does not affect his employment status (s 4(4)); a self-employed partner will remain this after an llp has been formed or he becomes a member of an existing llp unless his existing status is one of being an employee.

Rights between members are governed by any agreement between those members or if these do not exist by the regulations still to be promulgated by the DTI (equivalent to Table A for private registered companies).

Each member is an agent for the llp and binds the llp unless a third party knows that the member has no such authority to do that thing and the member has no such authority (see s 6).

A person's membership continues until such notice of this fact has been delivered to the Registrar. Where notice has not been so delivered, any third party dealing with that person is entitled to assume unless given notice to the contrary that he is dealing with a member (s 6(3)). Where a member is liable to a third party, the llp is to the same extent liable (s 6(4)). It is unclear whether this wording constitutes a joint and several liability and in the author's view this is probably not so.

Membership ceases under s 7 in cases of death, bankruptcy or the grant of a trust deed to creditors or where the whole or any part of a member's share has been assigned. In such circumstances the former member or his representative cannot interfere in management or administration, but can receive amounts that may otherwise be due to that member.

The formalities for the appointment and resignation of designated members is set out in s 8 and new admissions require the agreement of all members. All changes need to be reported to the Registrar within 14 days (where there is a change to the name of the llp the time is 28 days). Notices are required to be in the appropriate form, which will no doubt be issued under statutory instrument made available for this and other purposes prior to commencement.

Some recognition is given to 'overseas llps' with regard to insolvency and winding-up, and the Act refers in particular to the regulations which at the time of writing are still to be released.

17.4 IS THERE AN AGREEMENT?

In almost all partnerships there needs to be a partnership deed, ie a contract between the partners setting out the contractual relationship between them. In the past there have been instances where the courts have taken the view that a contract exists even if there is no formal documentation – so long as it can be shown that there was a contractual intention and some form of relationship based upon that intention.

For the purposes of this chapter it is assumed that the partners wish to enter into a written agreement setting out their relationship. Partners are free to agree upon restrictions between themselves, but this cannot effect the rights of a third party unless they have been made a party to the agreement (under the well-defined contractual rules relating to privity of contract).

The partnership deed is a private document between the partners and does not need to appear on a public register (unlike memorandum and articles of association for a private company which require to be registered at Companies House – there is no such public body to which partnerships need report). A further advantage is that financial information relating to the partnership, eg accounts, partners' drawings and general emoluments etc, remain private and not subject to public inspection. A partner is not an employee since partnership being a relationship between partners, no partner is capable of employing himself. A partnership very commonly employs other people and all the partners have authority to make contracts in the course of a partnership business (eg employing people).

17.5 THE SALARIED PARTNER

The salaried partner is an employee of the partnership who is held out to the outside world as being a partner. He is normally entitled to a fixed remuneration which is not dependent upon profits. A common example of salaried partners is within professional firms where having served apprenticeship it is felt by the equity partners to be appropriate to give an individual the status and prestige of being a partner without the need to consider capital contributions etc. Such a partner's name appears on the notepaper with the other partners and he is able to bind the firm in the same way as any other partner.

It is a question of sometimes great importance whether a person is a partner. The courts have interpreted each case on its own particular circumstances. Irrespective of whether a person is a salaried partner, he is being held out as a partner and as such both he and his fellow partners are jointly and severally liable for his or her actions.

A salaried partner (as a result of his less senior status) is frequently given in the partnership agreement (and if not so given such a partner should insist upon) an indemnity from his fellow partners to compensate him in the event that he suffers liability in his capacity as a partner.

17.6 PARTNERSHIP AND THIRD PARTIES

Since a partnership does not have any separate status under English law it is important to consider in what circumstances a partner is capable of binding his fellow partners and the relationship generally with outsiders.

The basic rule is that a partner is both a principal and an agent for his fellow partners, eg a partner can bind his fellow partners to any contract he signs if acting within his authority. In this way he is binding himself since he is a partner and a principal to that contract, and he is also binding his fellow partners since they are bound under the laws of agency by that contract.

Under s 5 of the 1890 Act it is stated that each partner acts as an agent for the firm. Where a partner does any act in the usual course of business of the kind carried on by the firm he binds the firm and his partners unless that partner has no authority to act for the firm in a particular matter *and the person with whom he is dealing either knows that he has no authority or does not know or believe him to be a partner.*

It is a question of construction and circumstance whether a partnership may be bound under the agency rules. Three factors should be considered:

Nature of the business

An example would be that it is unlikely that a firm of architects could advise upon financial investments whereas a banking partnership may so do. The Court of Appeal considered this question in *United Bank of Kuwait v Hammond* [1983] 3 All ER 418. A solicitor gave false undertakings to the bank concerning money held by the firm on behalf of a client. On the strength of this undertaking the bank advanced money to that client. The court took the view that the solicitor had acted within his ostensible authority in making the allegation since in normal circumstances it would be quite reasonable to expect such funds would fall within the firm's client account as part of normal day-to-day business. The bank was not required to check further since it was reasonable for the partner to be held out by a firm as having such authority.

Carrying on business in the normal way

In one case (*Higgins v Beauchamp* [1914] 3 KB 1192) it was felt that carrying on a cinema business was not in effect a trading business (ie one for purchasing and selling of goods) and therefore a partner could not bind his fellow partner to a debt incurred by him. The carrying on of business in a particular trade or profession can and does over a period of time change and in determining decisions of this nature courts have been flexible.

Knowledge and belief

If a partner has no authority to bind the firm and an outsider dealing with that partner realises it, the partnership cannot be bound by that partner's acts. If a third party does not have knowledge of the partner's lack of authority he can normally rely upon the partner's position as a partner in binding his firm. However, this would not be the case if the outsider did not know or believe that the person he was dealing with was a partner.

17.7 LIABILITY OF PARTNERS

17.7.1 To third parties

Each partner is and remains jointly and severally liable to outsiders for any act or omission committed by any of the partners or their employees in carrying on business. This means that an outsider has a choice of suing all or any of the partners for the full amount of such loss in accordance with normal principles of law. This is irrespective that a person so sued may be a salaried, or indeed a sleeping, partner.

17.7.2 Inter se

Under s 9 of the 1890 Act each partner is liable jointly with other partners for debts and obligations of the firm incurred while he is a partner.

Under s 17 of the 1890 Act a person who becomes a partner does not become liable to creditors of the firm for anything done before he became a partner. Likewise a retiring partner remains liable for debts and obligations incurred before retirement. This rule can be varied if a person either allows himself to be represented as being a partner or represents himself as being one (s 14).

Partnership liability was discussed at length in *Hurst v Bryck* [2000] 2 All ER 193, where Lord Millett delivered the main judgment in the House of Lords. In this case a solicitor argued that he did not need to contribute to the funds required by his fellow partners since they had repudiated the partnership by entering into a separate agreement without his agreement. Lord Millett accepted the argument that there had been a repudiation, but not that the solicitor was discharged, stating that the rights and obligations as at that date did remain. Being a contractual matter it was important to apply the rules of equity which would not accept a discharge of such liability. The court emphasised the need for proper and detailed accounts and a fair accounting procedure.

17.8 PARTNERSHIP AGREEMENT

The relationship between partners in a firm is normally set out in writing in a partnership deed. The 1890 Act also contains a number of implied terms. A partnership agreement typically includes details of the following matters:

17.8.1 Good faith

Like company directors it is clear that partners owe a fiduciary duty to each other. The 1890 Act sets out three such duties in ss 28–30, namely:

Honesty and full disclosure

Partners are bound to 'render true accounts and full information of all things affecting the partnership to any partner or his personal representative'. In one case involving a woollen business, a sleeping partner's share was bought for a gross undervalue since only certain assets had been disclosed. It was held that the other partner had been in breach of his fiduciary duty and should be entitled to a proper value (*Law v Law* [1905] 1 Ch 140). In another case involving property development, unbeknown to one of the partners an offer of purchase was turned down by the other. Eventually the property concerned was sold at a lower value. The court took the view that although the partner conducting the sale had used good faith in rejecting the first offer he should have discussed the matter with the other partner and sought additional advice before rejecting it.

No unauthorised personal profit

A partner shall not make a private gain, even if innocent, and should account to his other partners for any profit made. Section 29 states that 'every partner must account to the firm for the benefit derived by him without the consent of the other partners from any transaction concerning the partnership or from any use by him of a partnership property, name or business connection'. This definition is very wide and has been broadly applied by the courts. For example in one case a discount was offered to a partner which would not have been obtainable by the partnership as a whole. Since the partner made a private profit he should have disclosed this profit and have accounted for it to the practice.

No conflict of duty and interest

This is spelt out in s 30 of the Act 1890 which states that 'if a partner, without the consent of the other partners, carries on any business of the same nature as and competing with that of the firm, he must account for and pay over to the firm all profits made by him in that business'.

17.8.2 Management and control

Under s 24(5) of the 1890 Act each partner may take part in the management of the partnership business. This is a corollary of partners having unlimited liability. Note that the limited partner loses his rights to limited liability if he interferes in the business of a partnership. This question of management is also enshrined in s 24(6) which sets out the basic tenet that partners are self-managers in that 'no partner shall be entitled to remuneration for acting in the partnership business'. In larger partnerships it is normal to find at least one partner spending a substantial amount of time in administration and other non-profit-making work and the partnership agreement frequently includes special provisions for such a partner to ensure that his drawings and participation in any profit are not thereby affected. Section 24(6) does not prevent a partnership from making its own arrangements in this respect.

17.8.3 Meetings, reaching decisions etc

There is no rule on how decisions should be reached. There may be a voting system whereby certain partners qualify for a greater number of votes than others. More usually each partner is given one vote with basic decisions being decided upon by simple majority, but with complicated or controversial matters requiring specified majorities (eg 75% or in the case of taking in/expelling a partner, 100% of the votes (other than the partner being so expelled)). The 1890 Act does not codify this (but see 17.8.6 below – s 24(7)) and it is left up to each partnership to agree this as a matter of contractual negotiation. If a partner feels that he is being unfairly treated by the remaining partners he has very limited remedies. If there has been a breach of contract he may be able to sue. It may also be that he can apply for a receiver to be appointed or possibly for a dissolution on just and equitable grounds. There is however no specific statutory protection. It is for this reason that partnership agreements often contain a settlement of disputes mechanism.

17.8.4 Settlement of disputes

It is common for partnership agreements to require disputes to be referred to arbitration. A popular alternative is for the agreement to contain provision for the appointment of an independent third party to act as an expert whose decision shall be binding on all parties (if the parties cannot agree on the appointment of such an independent expert, he would normally be appointed by a third party, eg President for the time being of the Law Society of England and Wales).

17.8.5 **Financial provisions**

These are probably the most important details from a day-to-day practical view. Under s 24(1) of the 1890 Act it is stated that unless there is contrary agreement all partners are entitled to share equally in the capital and profits of a business and should contribute equally toward the losses (of capital or otherwise) sustained by the firm. Frequently the partnership agreement contains contrary provisions to this to take account of differing roles and participation from each partner. In considering the finances of a partnership it is important to understand the distinction between:

(1) the partnership capital; and
(2) undrawn profits.

Partnership capital means fixed capital which typically is invested in the partnership on its founding or upon new partners being appointed. Upon dissolution or a retirement this is often returned to the partners or the relevant retiring partner with or without the payment of interest. If a partnership is dissolved the amount of surplus over and above the capital is normally deemed to be profit and as such is distributed to the partners in accordance with the profit-sharing rules. In many cases the relevant proportions for a refund of capital are different to those for the division of profits. Each partnership agreement needs to be carefully drawn to ensure that the distinction is clearly provided for. (Section 24 of the Act states other provisions which are frequently incorporated into the partnership agreement, eg under s 24(4) a partner is only entitled to interest on capital when profits have been ascertained. In s 24(3) anything paid over and above capital requirements is entitled to interest at the rate of 5% pa.)

Of greater importance is the requirement that if one partner is sued for a partnership debt under s 24(2), he is entitled to an indemnity from his fellow partners.

17.8.6 **Change of partners**

This normally occurs through death, retirement, expulsion or appointment of a new partner. Under s 24(8) unless stated to the contrary (in the partnership agreement), decisions should be taken by majority vote, but where it is proposed to introduce a new partner, s 24(7) requires the consent of all existing partners. Courts have in the past been called upon to interpret a number of provisions regarding nomination and partnership appointments which do not fall within this ambit. The circumstances of each particular case have been considered and the court's ruling has been based on its merits. In one case where a partner had left his partnership to his widow it was deemed that this constituted an assignment of a partner's share and did not entitle the widow to be a partner. Where a partner was entitled to introduce a qualified person as a new partner, subject to the other partners' consent not to be unreasonably withheld, the court ruled that since consent had not been forthcoming the qualified person did not have the right to become a partner (*Re Franklin and Swathling Arbitration* [1929] 1 Ch 238).

In the context of expulsion s 25 states that 'no majority of partners can expel any partner unless a power to do so has been conferred by express agreement between the partners'. In *Walters v Bingham* [1988] 1 FTLR 260 the court was called upon to consider a dissolution provision in the partnership agreement and ruled that there were three questions that should be considered:

(1) Was the expulsion within the ambit of a dissolution provision?
(2) Had the partners exercising the right of expulsion done so in good faith in accordance with the normal partnership duties?
(3) Had the rules of natural justice been complied with, ie had the partner concerned been given details of the precise cause of complaint against him and been given every opportunity to defend himself?

The implication to be drawn is that if all three conditions have been satisfied a court would uphold any such expulsion. Other cases of expulsion which have come before the courts include a refusal to uphold an expulsion clause where the majority were seeking to obtain the partnership share at a discount (*Blisset v Daniel* (1853) 10 Hare 493); the unlawful expulsion of a partner in circumstances where no details of the particular act complained of were given (living with common law wife) (*Barnes v Youngs* [1898] 1 Ch 414); expulsion held to be lawful where a partner was convicted of travelling on a train without a fare and thereby defrauding the railway company and bringing the partnership into disrepute being a breach of his duties as a partner *(Carmichael v Evans* [1904] 1 Ch 486).

The partnership agreement in many instances includes provisions requiring retirement once a partner reaches a specified age or when certain other conditions occur (eg he becomes bankrupt or subject to the Mental Health Acts).

It is common in a partnership agreement for there to be provisions setting out what is required for the introduction of a new partner (the 1890 Act, as mentioned above, requires the consent of all partners and this applies if the partnership agreement does not make another provision). An assignment of partnership does not create a new partner; it merely assigns an existing partner's rights to partnership assets and/or profits to a third party. It may take the form of, for example, a mortgage or an arrangement made upon the divorce of one partner in favour of his former spouse.

In the case of a voluntary assignment the assignee (the person in whom the assignment is in favour) has no right to interfere in the management or administration of the partnership or the assets or acquire the delivery or inspection of any accounts or books. The only interest an assignee would have relates to a share of profits for which the assigning partner may otherwise have been entitled if there had been no assignment. If however the partnership goes into dissolution the assignee has the right to '(i) receive the assignee partner's share and (ii) to receive accounting details verifying the amount of that share from the date of dissolution'.

17.9 DISSOLUTION AND WINDING-UP OF A PARTNERSHIP

This can occur in two circumstances:

(1) where a partnership splits up – in this case a winding-up of the business would be required;
(2) where surviving or continuing partners take over the whole firm – here there needs to be a valuation of the former partner's share of the business.

Dissolution may or may not arise from insolvency.

Frequently partnership agreements spell out the procedure for dissolution. There are at least three common situations which are usually provided for:

(1) Ability to expel a partner – a number of circumstances are expressly included which enable the partners to expel one of their colleagues from the partnership in certain specified situations, eg if the partner concerned is grossly negligent, brings the practice into disrepute or, in a professional practice, becomes barred from continuing to practice in that position. If a partner is charged with an indictable offence, this also enables the others to expel him.
(2) A partner wishes to retire – the agreement usually incorporates a mechanism whereby a partner can hand in his notice. The notice period is often at least six months or a year and expires on a specified date.
(3) Upon death – since the partner's involvement automatically ceases a procedure is usually inserted for the winding-up of his previous involvement.

Even if nothing is specified in the agreement a partner can apply to court for dissolution under s 35 of the 1890 Act. This gives the court the discretion to dissolve a partnership for the following reasons:

(1) Insanity – if a partner becomes a patient under the Mental Health Act 1983.
(2) Where there is permanent incapacity.
(3) If there is prejudicial conduct – this requires proof with regard to the nature of the business that a partner has conducted himself in a manner 'calculated to prejudicially affect the carrying on of the business'.
(4) Where there have been continual breaches of the agreement – the section refers to 'wilfully or persistently committing a breach . . . or otherwise so conducts himself in matters relating to partnership business that it is not practicable for the other partners to carry on the business in partnership with him'.

(5) If a business is being carried on at a loss – there must be some proof in this circumstance that making a profit is not possible.

(6) If just and equitable – this depends on the particular circumstances presented to court, eg refusal to hold partner meetings, unresolvable dispute (ie where trust and mutual confidence have irretrievably broken down).

17.9.1 Appointment of receiver

In a dissolution it is possible for a receiver to be appointed at the court's discretion. Unlike company law the receiver appointed is responsible for acting in the best interests of all the partners. Courts do not usually authorise the appointment of a receiver where there is only a partial dissolution. (There would therefore need to be a winding-up of the complete partnership as opposed to the buying out of the retiring partner.)

The partnership agreement usually specifies what should occur on dissolution. There is likely to be a valuation of each partner's share (where there is a winding-up) or the respective outgoing partners' shares (where there is a partial dissolution). The valuation needs to take into account such sums which may be owing to creditors etc. It also needs to apply a method for the valuation of goodwill (see 17.9.3 below).

The 1890 Act contains a number of basic provisions for dealing with dissolution:

Section 39

This requires all debts and liabilities of the firm to be paid before the distribution of any surplus (after deducting anything due by the partners to the firm) and gives the right of any partner to apply to court to wind up the business and affairs of the firm.

Section 37

On a dissolution or partial dissolution of a partnership any partner may make a public notice of the dissolution and has a right to require other partners to concur with this action. (It is important to remember that a retiring/former partner is liable for debts incurred after departure unless he complies with a notice provision under s 36 and avoids being represented as a partner (s 14) (see 17.7.2 above)). Normally it is prudent for such a partner to inform the firm's existing clients of his departure and put a notice to that effect in the *London* (or *Edinburgh*) *Gazette*. A further prudent precaution would be for him to ensure that all headed notepaper has been properly altered and any stocks of old paper destroyed.

17.9.2 Assets valuation on dissolution

It is usual for the partnership agreement to contain criteria for the valuation of business assets of the partnership on dissolution, requiring the use of the firm's accountant (or an independent one).

17.9.3 Goodwill

This has been defined as being the difference between the value of a business as a going concern and the value of its assets. Like any other business a partnership over a period of time attracts goodwill which can and often does form part of partnership assets. In certain isolated cases it is illegal to sell goodwill, eg s 54 of the National Health Service Act 1977 which forbids the sale of an NHS practice's goodwill. The sale of goodwill is important in assessing how much a new partner may need to pay on joining a partnership and how much the continuing partners may need to pay on the retirement of a partner. The valuation of goodwill is normally conducted by a firm of accountants and the procedure and criteria to be adopted are time consuming and complicated. It is for this reason that professional partnerships are often disposed to value goodwill at nil. This not only prevents argument as to the valuation, but also reduces the amount of time spent in settling outstanding affairs.

17.9.4 Sharing profits after dissolution

Section 42(1) of the 1890 Act states that on partial dissolution the surviving/ continuing partners should in the absence of any agreement to the contrary share profits made since dissolution which are attributable to the partners' share of partnership assets. Alternatively such partner or his estate has a right to interest at the rate of 5% pa on the amount of his share of partnership assets. A partnership agreement may give continuing partners the right to buy out the former partners in accordance with laid down procedures and valuation provisions, but this would need to be expressly incorporated into the provisions of the agreement.

17.9.5 Insolvency

Assuming the partners are personally solvent, s 44 of the 1890 Act sets out the order of priority for repayment of partnership debts and requires the partners if necessary to contribute in the same proportions that they are entitled to share profits.

The order in which funds should be applied is:

(1) payment of debts and liabilities of the firm to persons, not partners;
(2) payment of each partner rateably of sums due to him from the firm for drawings (not capital);
(3) payment of each partner rateably of amounts due in repayment of capital; and

(4) division of any residue among the partners in the proportion in which the profits are divisible.

Where one or more of the partners are insolvent it is more complicated. It is outside the scope of this chapter to consider this matter in any detail, but there are a number of options open to creditors, eg wind up the partnership, wind up the partnership and bring petitions against insolvent partners (and ultimately bankruptcy), bring an action against the individual partners without winding up the firm or bring proceedings against one or more partners without involving others or the firm itself.

17.10 EEIGS

In order to harmonise the laws of EU member states and each UK Companies Act, the UK has acceded to the Community in seeking to achieve this aim by incorporating various EEC directives into UK legislation. Some areas however have been otherwise treated. For example in 1985, EC Council Regulation 2137/85 was promulgated providing for the European economic interest grouping (more commonly referred to as EEIGs). This was loosely modelled on a French example. Its aim is to enable existing businesses in different member states to form an autonomous body for the provision of common services ancillary to the main activities of its members. All profits made belong to the members of EEIG and they are all jointly and severally liable for any liability.

EEIGs are formed by a written contract between the members. This needs to be registered in the member state in which the official address is situated.

The UK has added to the Regulation in the form of the European Economic Interest Grouping Regulations 1989 under which Companies House is responsible as the registering body. There is provision set out in the Companies Act 1985 and the Insolvency Act 1986 which are applicable.

There are not many examples of EEIGs, but in England there have been a number of firms of solicitors who have used EEIGs as a means of association with lawyers elsewhere in the community.

HOW AN UNINCORPORATED BUSINESS IS TAXED ON ITS PROFITS

DAVID BERTRAM, CLAYFIELD PROFESSIONAL GUIDANCE LTD

This chapter discusses the tax treatment of a 'sole trader' (ie an individual carrying on business on his own account) and partnerships. These are 'unincorporated' businesses, as opposed to companies which are 'incorporated' businesses. The proprietors of unincorporated businesses are self-employed and taxed under Schedule D.

SELF-EMPLOYED INDIVIDUALS

18.1 CURRENT YEAR BASIS

In broad terms, the CY basis of assessment normally means that a trader is assessed on the profits for his accounts year which ends in the tax year concerned (there are special rules for the opening years). Thus, if an individual makes up accounts to 31 August, the CY basis of assessment normally means that his tax assessment for 2000–01 will be determined by his profits for the year ended 31 August 2000.

18.1.1 Opening years

The CY basis has special rules to cope with a business during the first two tax years since there may not be an accounting year which ends in either of those tax years, or the accounting period which ends in the second tax year may be shorter or longer than 12 months. In broad terms, assessments are generally determined as follows:

- first tax year – 'actual' or 'fiscal year' basis;
- second tax year – profits of the first 12 months;
- third tax year – current year basis.

Example of opening years rules

A starts in business on 6 October 1998. His accounts for the year to 5 October 1999 show profits of £48,000. Profits for the year ending 5 October 2000 are £72,000. A will be assessed as follows:

		£
1998–99	'actual' basis ($\frac{6}{12} \times$ £48,000)	24,000
1999–00	First 12 months profits	48,000
2000–01	Current year basis	72,000

18.1.2 No accounts for the first 12 months

The way in which the opening years rules work is more complicated where the trader does not prepare accounts for a period of 12 months ending in the second tax year. It might be that an individual starts business on 1 March 1999 and makes up his first accounts for a 16-month period ending on 30 June 2000. The assessments in such a case will be:

1999–00	$\frac{4}{16}$	$\times$	profits for period
2000–01	$\frac{12}{16}$	$\times$	profits for period
2001–02	$\frac{12}{16}$	$\times$	profits for period

Similarly, if X makes up her first accounts for a six-month period ending on 30 April 2000 and then has accounts for the year to 30 April 2001, the assessments will be:

1999–00	$\frac{5}{6}$	$\times$	profits for six months ended on 30 April 2000
2000–01	$\frac{1}{6}$	$\times$	profits for six months ended on 30 April 2000, plus
	$\frac{11}{12}$	$\times$	profits for year ended 30 April 2001
2001–02			profits of year ended 30 April 2001.

18.1.3 Overlap relief

Because of the way that a new business is assessed during the first two tax years, some profits may be taxed more than once. In the last example, $\frac{11}{12}$ of the profits for the year ended 30 April 2001 are assessed twice, once in arriving at assessable profits for 2000–01, and again in arriving at the assessment for 2001–02. To compensate for this, and to ensure that over the life of the business tax is paid only on the actual amount of profits, overlap relief is given when the business is discontinued or, for partners, when they leave the firm. In some circumstances, overlap relief may also be available if the firm's accounting date is changed (see 18.1.4).

Basis of assessment under opening years rules

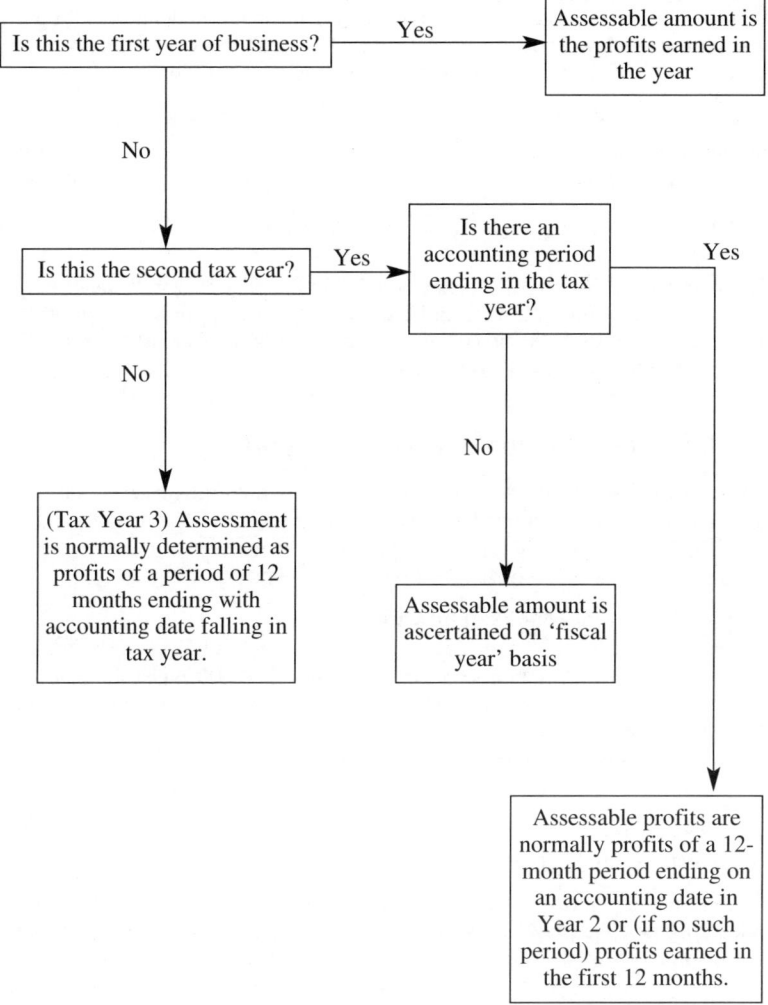

Example of overlap relief

> If the profits for the year ended 30 April 2000 were £36,000, $^{11}\!/_{12}$ would be £33,000. This amount is carried forward and is deducted from A's profits for the final year of trading. Thus, if A retires on 5 October 2002, and his final year's profits are £60,000, the assessment for 2002–03 will be as follows:
>
> | | £ |
> |---|---:|
> | Current year basis | 60,000 |
> | *Less* overlap relief | 33,000 |
> | Taxable profits | 27,000 |
>
> If the overlap relief exceeds the taxable profits for the final year, the balance may be treated as an allowable loss and either set against the individual's other income for that year or the preceding year, or carried back against Schedule D Case I profits of the last three years (see 18.6.7)

18.1.4 Effect of a change in accounting date

Where a firm changes its accounting date to one which falls earlier in the tax year, an adjustment is required to ensure that 12 months' profits are taxed as income of the year in which the change takes place.

Example of how a change is dealt with

> B is in business. She draws up accounts to 30 June until 2000, when she changes to a 30 April accounting date. This means that her accounts which fall in 2000–01 are for a period of only 10 months.
>
> The CY basis requires profits to be ascertained for a 12-month period which ends with the new accounting date. Suppose that the relevant figures were:
>
> | | |
> |---|---|
> | Year ended 30 June 1999 | profits of £120,000 |
> | Period of 10 months ended 30 April 2000 | profits of £140,000 |
>
> B would be assessed for 2000–01 on £160,000 ie $^{2}\!/_{12}$ × profits for the year ended 30 June 1999 plus profits for the 10 months ended 30 April 2000. Once again, some profits will be taxed more than once (the period of two months ending on 30 June 1999) and therefore B would be entitled to increased overlap relief in due course on $^{2}\!/_{12}$ of the profits for the year ended 30 June 1999. The benefit of the overlap relief is enjoyed as and when the firm's accounting date is changed to a date which falls later in the tax year or B ceases business.

18.1.5 Moving accounting date to later in tax year

A different approach is required where a firm extends its accounts to a date which falls later in the tax year. Normally, the assessable profits are those for the entire period which ends in the tax year.

Example of tax treatment of such a charge

C makes up accounts to 31 December. In 2000, he extends his accounting period by three months so that the firm has a 15-month accounting period from 1 January 1999 to 31 March 2000. The whole of the profits for this period is assessed for 1999–00, but C can use some or all of his overlap relief. If C has a potential entitlement to four months' overlap relief of £20,000, and the profits for the 15 months ended 31 March 2000 are £150,000, C would have Schedule D Case I income for 1999–00 of:

	£
Profits for period ended 31 March 2000	150,000
$Less \ \dfrac{3 \ months}{4 \ months} \times$ overlap relief brought forward	15,000
	135,000

18.1.6 Retirement

Where an individual retires and ceases to carry on a business, he is taxed under the CY basis on his profits for a notional period which starts immediately after the basis period for the previous tax year and ends on the date that he ceases.

Example of how taxable income is ascertained for final year of assessment

D makes up accounts to 30 April. Her profits for the year ended 30 April 2000 are £80,000. She ceases business on 30 November 2000 and her profits for the final six months amount to £50,000.

D's assessable income for 2000–01 is her share of profits for the period 1 May 1999 to 30 November 2000, ie £80,000 plus £50,000.

18.1.7 Accounting periods must not exceed 18 months

There is a maximum length of 18 months to an accounting period. Accounts which cover a longer period are rejected as unacceptable for tax purposes under the CY basis.

18.2 CAPITAL ALLOWANCE BASIS PERIODS

18.2.1 Business on CY basis

Capital allowances are computed on exactly the same basis as profits. Normally this means that allowances are computed for the accounts year which ends in the tax year. However, there are special rules which apply for overlapping accounts.

Where there is a gap between accounting periods, the additions and disposals during the intervening period are added to the accounting period which ended before the gap.

Example – Overlapping periods

If a new business is commenced on 1 January 1999 and accounts are drawn up to 31 December 1999, there is an overlap of the period 1 January to 5 April 1999, as this will form part of the profits assessed for 1998–99 and 1999–00 (see 18.1.1).

If the trader spends £10,000 on plant and machinery during the first three-month period, and £40,000 during the period 6 April to 31 December 1999, capital allowances are given as follows:

		£
1998–99	$^3/_{12} \times 25\% \times £10,000$	625
1999–00	Pool brought forward	9,375
	Additions	40,000
		49,375
Allowances ($^9/_{12} \times 25\%$)		9,258

PARTNERSHIPS

18.3 SPECIAL RULES GOVERNING ASSESSMENT OF FIRM'S PROFITS

18.3.1 Assessment under CY basis

Where the CY basis of assessment applies, the Revenue issues separate assessments on each of the individual partners. This is the full extent of their liability; they are not jointly liable for tax payable by their partners (except, possibly, where the partner is not resident in the UK).

Because partners are assessed separately under the CY basis, the continuation election cannot apply. Each partner is dealt with as a 'separate taxable unit' and the opening and closing years rules apply separately to him.

Example – CY opening year rules for new partners

A and *B* have been in partnership since 1 October 1998. They share profits equally and their profits for the first two years are as follows:

	£
Year ended 30 September 1999	90,000
Year ended 30 September 2000	120,000

C joins the firm on 1 October 2000 and thereafter each partner receives one-third of the firm's profits which for the year ended 30 September 2001 amount to £150,000. *B* retires on 5 April 2001 and *A* takes over his share of profits.
   The three partners are assessed as follows:

				£
1998–99	A	⁵⁄₁₂ × 50% of £90,000		22,500
	B	⁵⁄₁₂ × 50% of £90,000		22,500
1999–00	A	First 12 months profits		45,000
	B	First 12 months profits		45,000
2000–01	A	CY basis		60,000
	B	Final year (profits for period 1 October 1999 to		
		5 April 2001)	£85,000	
		Less overlap relief	£22,500	62,500
	C	⁵⁄₁₂ × ⅓ of £150,000		25,000
2001–02	A	CY basis		75,000
	C	First 12 months profits		50,000

18.4 TREATMENT OF OTHER INCOME

Where a partnership receives investment income (eg untaxed interest, miscellaneous income taxed under Schedule D Case VI or dividends), the normal tax treatment was that the income should be assessed on the individual partners. The principle that partners are jointly and severally liable for tax has never applied to investment income received by the firm.

   Under the new CY basis, the way the income assessable on the partners is arrived at has changed. Instead of the income being ascertained by reference to the fiscal year, the income is assessable on the CY basis. Thus, if a firm makes up accounts to 30 April, the partners are assessed for 2000–01 on their share of partnership investment income received during the firm's year ended 30 April 2001. This rule applies even where the income actually arose prior to 5 April 2000.

18.5 QUALIFYING LOANS

Tax relief may be obtained on loan interest where the money is to provide capital into a partnership. Relief is available where the loan is applied:

(1) in purchasing a share in a partnership; or
(2) in contributing capital or advancing money to a partnership where the money advanced is used wholly for the purposes of its trade, profession or vocation; or
(3) in paying off another loan the interest on which would have been eligible for tax relief.

In addition, the borrower must be a member of the partnership throughout the period (and not just as a limited partner). He must not have recovered any capital from the partnership since raising the qualifying loan.

18.5.1 Recovery of capital
(TA 1988, s 363)

If, at any time after the application of the loan's proceeds, the partner recovers any amount of capital from the partnership, he is deemed to have used the withdrawal to repay the qualifying loan on which he is claiming interest relief. This is so whether or not he actually uses the proceeds in this manner. It is therefore advisable to segregate the partners' capital and current accounts in the partnership's books so that any withdrawal can be clearly identified.

18.5.2 Replacement capital

Where a partner has a surplus balance on either his current or capital account with a partnership and he does not already have a qualifying loan, he may withdraw the balance due to him (with the consent of his partners), use the money to pay off non-qualifying borrowings and then borrow further funds to introduce capital into the partnership with tax relief.

Example – Replacement capital

B is a partner in the XYZ partnership. He has a credit balance of £100,000 in his capital account. Outside the partnership, he has bought a yacht for his private use with the help of a £40,000 loan from his bank.

B would withdraw £40,000 from his capital account in the partnership and use the money to repay the yacht bank loan. *B* would borrow £40,000 as a loan (not overdraft) and use the funds to reintroduce capital into the partnership with full tax relief on the interest payable.

Professional advice should be sought in advance on such transactions.

18.5.3 Other partnership loans

Another situation where it may be appropriate to re-structure existing borrowings is where there is a partnership loan outstanding in the business's books. The loan might typically have been used to purchase goodwill or the property from which the practice/business is carried on. In this situation, each partner is required to borrow privately his share of the partnership loan and introduce the moneys raised into the partnership. The partner can then claim tax relief on the interest paid personally as a charge on his income on an actual basis.

The partnership collects the moneys raised by each partner's loan and uses the funds to redeem the partnership loan. As a result, each partner's share of profits becomes correspondingly higher because no interest is now payable by the partnership. However, overall, the situation is the same because the higher profits must be used to finance the private borrowing.

This kind of rearrangement needs considerable attention to detail and timing to be successful and tax effective, and professional advice should always be sought. This is particularly necessary during the transition to the CY basis as there is anti-avoidance legislation to be considered.

18.5.4 Purchase of plant and machinery
(TA 1988, s 359)

Where a partner incurs capital expenditure in the purchase of plant and machinery which is used for the purposes of the partnership's business, and which is eligible for capital allowances, he can claim tax relief on interest paid if the plant or machinery is financed by a loan. The relief is only available in the tax year in which the loan is taken out and the following three tax years. Similar relief is also available for employees who are required to purchase plant or machinery for use in carrying out their duties.

18.5.5 Property occupied rent-free by partnership

Where a partner takes out a loan to purchase property occupied by the partnership for business purposes and the interest is paid by the partnership, no deduction is technically due to the partnership as the interest is not its liability but the partner's. However, SP4/85, issued in February 1985, regards the interest paid as rent so that it then becomes allowable as a deduction. In the partner's hands, the rent is taxable but the interest paid is normally allowed as a deduction in arriving at his Schedule A income.

MISCELLANEOUS

18.6 RELIEF FOR TRADING LOSSES

Relief may be available for a loss incurred by an individual in a trade or profession. The provisions which govern the relief for trading losses are complex and there are several ways in which losses may be utilised.

18.6.1 Carry forward relief against subsequent assessments
(TA 1988, s 385)

A loss incurred by a sole trader or a partner's share of his firm's trading loss may be carried forward and deducted in assessments for later years for the same trade or profession. Where losses are carried forward in this way, they must be used against the assessable profits for the first subsequent year in which profits arise. The loss carried forward in this way may also be relieved against certain income which is connected with the trade even though it is assessed under a different schedule (eg interest earned on temporary investment of trade receipts and dividends from trade investments). There is no limit on the number of years for which a loss may be carried forward provided that the same trade is carried on.

18.6.2 Relief against general income
(TA 1988, s 380)

Where a sole trader or partner incurs a loss and the trade was carried on with a view to profit, the loss may be relieved against his general income for the tax year in which it was incurred (ie his total income for the year). Losses are set against an individual's general income for the preceding year.

18.6.3 Relief by aggregation

Where the profits of different accounting periods are time apportioned (eg on commencement of a business) a loss may be relieved by aggregation with a profit. This situation could arise if a first period of trading is less than 12 months.

Example – Loss relief by aggregation

A started business on 1 January 1999. He made a loss of £9,000 for the period ended 30 September 1999 and a profit of £24,000 for the year ended 30 September 2000. Relief by aggregation would produce the following result:

Profits assessable 1998–99	NIL
Profits assessable 1999–00	NIL
Profits assessable 2000–01	NIL

The reason for this is that the first 12 months' trading is deemed to produce a net loss computed as follows:

	£
Loss for period 1 Jan to 30 Sept 1999	(9,000)
$\frac{3}{12}$ of profit for year ended 30 Sept 2000	6,000
	(3,000)

Relief for the same loss may be obtained more than once when the loss is used by aggregation. This can produce effective relief which exceeds the loss actually incurred.

If a loss is set against other income, it cannot also be relieved by aggregation. Thus, if *A* had claimed relief for the loss that he had incurred in 1998–99, only that part of the loss for the period ended 30 September 1999 which relates to the period 6 April to 30 September 1999 could be taken into account in arriving at the profits of the first 12 months' trading.

Example – Loss set against other income

B commenced trading on 1 August 1998. He has a loss during the nine months ended 30 April 1999 of £36,000. He has profits for the year ended 30 April 2000 of £60,000. If the 1998–99 loss is used by its being set against *B*'s other income, the position is as follows:

1998–99		NIL
1999–00	Profits of first 12 months:	
	nine months ended 30 April 1999	NIL
	$\frac{3}{12}$ × profits for year ended 30 April 2000	15,000
		15,000
2000–01	Profits of first 12 months	15,000

Contrast this with the situation where relief for the loss is obtained by aggregation.

1998–99		NIL
1999–00	Profits of first 12 months	NIL
2000–01	Profits of first 12 months	NIL

18.6.4 Capital allowances and loss claims
(TA 1988, s 383)

The general principle is that where capital allowances cannot be given because there are insufficient profits, the allowances must be carried forward and given in subsequent years. However, it is possible for an individual to claim for capital allowances to be treated as a deduction in

587

arriving at the loss for the year of assessment. Capital allowances which are claimed in this way may either increase a loss or convert a profit into a loss.

The capital allowances to be taken into account are those of the normal basis period which relates to the tax year. This still applies even though the loss itself may be arrived at on the strict basis by apportioning the results of the accounting periods which overlap the relevant tax year.

Example – Capital allowances and loss claims

A commences trading on 6 October. His results are as follows:

	£
Year ended 5 October 1999 – profit	4,000
Year ended 5 October 2000 – profit	12,000
Year ended 5 October 2001 – profit	50,000

Assume that capital allowances are as follows:

1998–99	30,000
1999–00	38,000

If A claims that his capital allowances for 1998–99 should be deducted and the resultant loss relieved under s 380, the position is as follows:

		£
1998–99	$\frac{5}{12}$ × profits for year ended 5 October 1999	2,000
	Capital allowances for 1998–99	(30,000)
	Loss after deducting capital allowances	(28,000)
1999–00	$\frac{7}{12}$ × profits for year ended 5 October 1999	2,000
	$\frac{5}{12}$ × profits for year ended 5 October 2000	6,000
		8,000
	Capital allowances for 1999–00	(38,000)
	Loss after deducting capital allowances	(30,000)

The £28,000 loss for 1998–99 may be set against A's other income for 1998–99 or 1999–00. The £30,000 loss for 1999–00 is available to be set against A's other income for 1999–00 or 2000–01

18.6.5 Losses in early years of a trade
(TA 1988, s 381)

In certain circumstances, relief may be claimed against an individual's general income for the three years of assessment preceding the year in which the loss is incurred. Relief is given against income for the earliest year first. The loss may be computed in the normal way, or it may be augmented by capital allowances as described in 18.6.4. There are certain preconditions for a loss to be claimed:

(1) The loss must arise during the first four tax years in which the business is carried on.
(2) Where a trade is acquired from a spouse, the four years run from the date that the spouse first commenced trading (unless the trade is taken over on the spouse's death).
(3) The trade must be carried on on a commercial basis *and with a reasonable expectation of profits*.

A claim for a loss to be relieved in this way must be made within two years of the end of the tax year in which the loss was incurred. Where a loss is carried back in this way, any repayment normally produces an entitlement to repayment supplement.

18.6.6 Relief for trading losses against capital gains
(FA 1991, s 72)

An individual who has incurred a trading loss may have the loss set against any capital gains which arise in the same year, provided he makes a claim within two years. It is not possible to claim relief for trading losses in this way without first having made a claim for relief under TA 1988, s 380 for the loss to be set against the individual's general income for the year.

It is also possible for a trading loss to be set against an individual's capital gains for the following year provided that a claim is first made under s 380(2) for the trading loss to be set against the individual's general income for that year. A precondition for a loss to be relieved in this way is that the individual has carried on the relevant trade at some time during the following tax year.

18.6.7 Terminal loss relief
(TA 1988, s 388)

Where a trade, profession or vocation is permanently discontinued, a loss incurred during the last 12 months can be deducted from the profits charged to tax in the three tax years before the final year. The relief can include a claim for the loss arising in the tax year in which the cessation takes place, and a proportion of the loss for the previous tax year.

Capital allowances for the final tax year may also be claimed, as can an appropriate proportion of the preceding year's capital allowances, representing the allowances due for the period beginning 12 months prior to the cessation.

The terminal loss may be carried back against profits from the same trade for the three tax years preceding the year of cessation. The relief is given against the latest year's profits first. If interest and dividends would have been included as trading profits (except that they were subject to deduction of tax at source), the terminal loss may be set against such income.

18.6.8 Computation of loss under CY basis

The rules for computing losses under the CY basis are much simplified. They preserve most of the principles explained 18.6.1–18.6.7. The exceptions are as follows:

(1) Losses may only be relieved once. The new rules do not allow duplication of loss claims by aggregation, as was possible under the PY basis.

(2) Relief for losses can be claimed against other income of the year of loss and the preceding year. (Under the PY regime, this was the following year.) Thus a trader who makes a loss in the accounting year to 31 December 2000 will be able to claim relief against other income in 2000–01 and/or 1998–99.

(3) It is not necessary to have separate claims for surplus capital allowances to be converted into losses; under the CY rules, capital allowances are allowed as a deduction just like any other allowable business expense.

(4) The rules for claiming loss relief against future profits from the same trade are slightly modified under the CY basis so that it is not now necessary to make a claim each year when the relief is to be given. All that is required is a claim to establish the amount of the loss. Thereafter the loss is carried forward and offset every year until fully utilised, without the need for any claim.

18.6.9 Anti-avoidance provisions

Farming losses
(TA 1988, s 397)

Restrictions may apply to losses suffered by farmers. The legislation may prevent a farming loss being set against the individual's other income where he has suffered losses for each of the preceding five tax years. The only way of avoiding this restriction is for the individual to show that no reasonably competent farmer would have expected to have made a profit during the period in question.

Losses from limited partnerships
(TA 1988, s 117)

Limited partnerships were widely used in tax avoidance arrangements. The House of Lords decided in *Reed v Young* [1986] STC 285 that a limited partner could be entitled to loss relief for an amount which exceeded his actual liability under the Limited Partnership Act 1907. This led to specific legislation to limit the amount of loss relief to the capital which is 'at risk'. Any losses incurred beyond this amount have to be carried forward to be set against any future share of profits received by the limited partner from the firm.

The provisions of LPA 1907, s 117 of the 1907 Act apply to individuals who are limited partners or members of a joint venture arrangement under which their liability is limited to a contract, agreement, guarantee etc.

18.6.10 Schedule D Case V losses
(TA 1988, s 391)

Profits from a trade managed or controlled abroad are taxed under Schedule D Case V. Loss relief is calculated in the same way as for a loss incurred in a trade, profession or vocation taxed under Schedule D Case I or Case II.

Relief for such losses is given in the same way as for UK trading losses, except that where a loss is to be set against other income, a Case V loss can be deducted only from:

(a) profits from other foreign trades assessable under Schedule D Case V;
(b) foreign pensions and annuities where a 10% deduction is available (see *Allied Dunbar Tax Handbook* 2000–01 at 6.8);
(c) foreign emoluments assessable under Schedule E (see *Allied Dunbar Tax Handbook* 2000–01 at 3.1.1 and 22.2).

18.7 POST-CESSATION RECEIPTS AND EXPENSES
(TA 1988, ss 103–104)

18.7.1 Post-cessation receipts

Where a person has been assessed on the cash basis (see eg 4.5.16) special rules apply if the trade or profession is discontinued. Subsequent receipts are normally taxed under Schedule D Case VI as income for the year in which they come in, although an election may be made for the post-cessation receipts to be treated as arising in the year of discontinuance.

Expenses may be deducted in so far as they were incurred wholly and exclusively for business and are not otherwise allowable. For example, a solicitor who had post-cessation receipts would be able to deduct premiums paid on a professional indemnity policy where the cover related to the period after the solicitor had ceased to carry on his profession.

A similar charge may arise where a change occurs in the treatment of a trader's profits so that the cash basis ceases to apply and his profits are assessed on the earnings basis. Amounts received from customers after the change which relate to invoices issued when the business was dealt with on the cash basis are treated as post-cessation receipts.

18.7.2 Post-cessation expenses
(TA 1988, s 109A)

Relief can be due for expenses incurred by a person after he has ceased carrying on a trade or profession. This relief can be due on any such expenditure incurred within seven years of the date of cessation. The following types of expenditure may qualify for relief:

(a) the costs of remedying defective work done, goods supplied, or services rendered while the trade or profession was continuing and damages paid by the taxpayer in respect of such defective work, goods or services whether awarded by a court or agreed during negotiations on a claim;
(b) insurance premiums paid to insure against the above costs;
(c) legal and other professional expenses incurred in connection with the above costs;
(d) debts owed to the business which have been taken into account in computing the profits or gains of the trade or profession before discontinuance but which have subsequently become bad;
(e) the costs of collecting debts which have been taken into account in computing the trade's profits before discontinuance.

The amount of this relief is reduced by any expense allowed as a deduction in the final accounting period which remains unpaid at the end of the year of assessment in which the relief is given. Expenditure which qualifies for the relief is set against income and capital gains of the year of assessment in which the expense is paid. Where there is insufficient income or capital gains to cover the expenditure, the unrelieved expenditure of that year cannot be carried forward under the new relief arrangements against future income or capital gains. However, the unrelieved expenditure is still available to be carried forward under the existing rules and set against subsequent post-cessation receipts from the trade or profession.

PRACTICAL ASPECTS AND INTRODUCTION OF SELF-ASSESSMENT AND HOW IT AFFECTS SELF-EMPLOYED INDIVIDUALS

18.8 OUTLINE OF NEW REGIME

18.8.1 Background

The 1997 changes amount to a fundamental change to the tax system. The Revenue no longer needs to initiate proceedings by issuing an assessment; liability for tax arises automatically.

Under the new regime, taxpayers are required to submit tax returns which incorporate a calculation of the tax to be paid (or in some cases, tax to be repaid) and payment of the amount due. In effect, instead of being required to deliver a return, the legislation requires taxpayers to make a self-assessment. This replaces the former system where a taxpayer was sent several different assessments on different sources of income and capital gains. Because of this, and because the Revenue no longer has to issue estimated assessments and amended assessments, there should be a significant reduction in paperwork.

The self-assessment form is capable of being processed by computerised scanning equipment, which further reduces the clerical work required at the Revenue's offices.

18.8.2 Liability to make self-assessments

Any person served with a notice by an Officer of the Board of Inland Revenue must file a return. Normally, the filing date is 31 January following the end of the tax year. However, if the officer is late in serving notice on an individual for him to make a self-assessment, the filing date may be extended. Basically, the officer must give the individual at least three months to make the self-assessment. Thus, if the notice requiring the delivery of a self-assessment is served after 31 October, it does not need to be delivered to the Revenue until three months later.

18.8.3 Alternative to self-assessment

Provided a return of income and chargeable gains is delivered to the Revenue not later than 30 September following the end of the tax year, the Revenue calculates the amount of tax payable and issues an assessment.

If the officer is late in issuing the notice to make a self-assessment, the 30 September deadline may be extended. The taxpayer is given at least two months in which to complete and deliver the return and so if the officer serves the notice after 31 July the deadline for filing the return is later than the normal 30 September deadline.

The Revenue has confirmed that if it receives a return by 30 September, but does not issue a notice of the tax payable by 31 December, the trigger date for interest and surcharge is 30 days after the issue of the statement of tax which is payable.

18.8.4 Inclusion of estimates

The Revenue has stated its intention that if a taxpayer includes an estimate in his return, the rest of the return becomes final within the normal timescale provided it is completed to the best of his knowledge and belief. The Revenue stated that the estimate should be corrected as soon as the missing information is reasonably available, in accordance with TMA 1970, s 97.

The need for estimates often arises in relation to CGT (eg valuations at 31 March 1982). It should be borne in mind that a valuation is not treated as an estimate, unless designated as such by the taxpayer. On the other hand, not all valuations are estimates, although they may be subject to dispute. The Revenue has agreed that it will not be able to reopen the position where no enquiry into a valuation is made within 12 months and the valuation falls within the range of bona fide valuations which could arise between valuers who were fully instructed on the facts.

18.8.5 Submission of supporting documents with self-assessment

The notice which the officer sends asking for the self-assessment may specify that certain accounts, statements and documents relating to information in the return should be filed at the same time. The Revenue will certainly continue to require business accounts for a sole trader or a partnership. Other documents which may be required include books, contracts, deeds, receipts etc.

The legislation specifies that records must be retained for a minimum period after the submission of the self-assessment, in case they are required by the officer. Personal records must be retained for 12 months after the filing date. Business records must normally be retained for a minimum period of five years after the filing date.

FA 1994 also sets out the business records which should be retained for examination. The following need to be retained:

(a) records of all amounts received and expended in the course of the trade or profession, and the matters in respect of which the receipts and expenditure took place; and

(b) all supporting documents relating to such items.

This requirement is extremely wide and general in nature. However, the taxpayer is protected if he has preserved information in such a way that original documents can be reproduced. This means that a microfilming system is as acceptable as the retention of the original documents. Moreover, the Revenue has published guidance notes on what records should be retained. A penalty of up to £3,000 can be imposed for failure to keep records.

18.8.6 Amendments to self-assessment after it has been filed

A notice may be given to the Revenue amending the self-assessment. This notice may be given within 12 months of the filing date (ie 31 January or three months after the officer gives notice asking for the self-assessment, whichever is the later). The Revenue may also amend the self-assessment within nine months of receiving it to correct obvious errors of principle, arithmetical errors and the like (this is called 'repairing' a self-assessment).

18.8.7 Revenue enquiries and right to audit

The Revenue may start an enquiry into a self-assessment (or, where the taxpayer has filed an amendment, into the amended self-assessment). However, the officer must give written notice of his intention to make an enquiry. Furthermore, that notice must be served within a strict time limit of:

(a) 12 months after the date that the self-assessment was delivered; or

(b) where the self-assessment is delivered after the filing date, the quarter date following 12 months after delivery. For this purpose, the quarter dates are 31 January, 30 April, 31 July and 31 October. Thus, if a self-assessment which is due on 31 January is not in fact delivered until 31 March, the time limit for the Revenue starting an enquiry expires on 30 April of the following year.

Note also that the Revenue is not be allowed to institute more than one enquiry during the time limit. Once a return or an amendment has been subject to enquiry, no further notice may be given.

Where a notice of intention to enquire has been issued, the officer may issue a notice requiring the production of documents which are in the power or possession of the person on whom the notice has been served. These must be documents, etc which are reasonably required by the officer to determine to what extent, if at all, the self-assessment or amendment is incorrect. The notice may also require accounts or other particulars which he may reasonably require. The notice must give a time limit for the production of the documents, etc and the taxpayer must be allowed at least 30 days to produce the documents.

An appeal may be made to the Commissioners against such a notice. They can set the notice aside if they think that it is invalid. If they decide it is valid, the documents must be produced within 30 days of their decision. Continued failure to comply may then result in a penalty of up to £150 per day.

There is no specified time limit in which the officer must complete an enquiry but the Government has stated that a code of practice will be issued on the conduct of enquiries. One aspect to be covered in the code will be a general requirement for the Revenue to proceed with reasonable speed once it has launched an enquiry and not to drag the process out unnecessarily. The code of practice will also set other ground rules which will apply to Revenue offices when they conduct an enquiry.

Once the officer who is conducting the enquiry has completed his investigation, he must say so and state his conclusions as to the correct amount of tax which should be in the self-assessment.

18.8.8 Correction of self-assessments

There are provisions for the self-assessment to be amended by the taxpayer in accordance with the conclusions notified by the officer who has conducted the enquiry. However, if the taxpayer does not correct the self-assessment in accordance with the officer's conclusions, the officer issues a notice of amendment (in effect an assessment) against which an appeal may be made within 30 days. If the dispute cannot be settled by agreement, the Commissioners adjudicate.

18.8.9 Requirement to notify chargeability

An individual who is liable for unpaid tax but who has not been served with a notice requiring him to make a self-assessment must notify the Revenue within six months of the end of the tax year.

18.8.10 Payment of tax

An individual is required to pay two equal amounts on account of income tax on 31 January during the year of assessment and on 31 July following the end of the tax year. The amount of the tax payable in this way is normally equal to the total income tax assessed for the previous year. However, it is open to a taxpayer (or his advisor) to make a claim before 31 January (ie the normal filing date) for the payments on account to be reduced to 50% of the tax believed to be payable for the year. The Revenue generally requires an explanation for why it is believed that the tax payable will be less than that for the previous year.

When the self-assessment is delivered on the following 31 January, any difference between the payments on account already made and the amount shown as payable for the year needs to be settled. At the same time, it is necessary to make a payment equal to the CGT liability for the year concerned.

18.8.11 Amended self-assessments

Tax is payable or repayable on the later of:

(a) 31 January following the end of the tax year; and
(b) 30 days from the date on which the amendment to the self-assessment was given.

In cases where the Revenue discovers that a source of income has not been assessed or has been inadequately assessed, the officer normally makes an assessment and the tax is payable 30 days after the assessment has been issued.

18.9 PENALTIES AND INTEREST CHARGES

18.9.1 Surcharges

Where tax is paid more than 28 days after it fell due, there may be a 5% surcharge levied by the Revenue. This 28-day period applies both to the payments required on 31 January and 31 July and also to tax which is due 30 days after an assessment has been made. If the tax remains unpaid more than six months after the due date, there is a further 5% surcharge.

18.9.2 Appeals against the surcharge

The Revenue may mitigate the whole or part of a surcharge where there is a reasonable excuse for the delay. In cases where there is a dispute with the Revenue over whether there is a reasonable excuse, the Commissioners can be asked to adjudicate. However, FA 1994 specifically states that inability to pay is not to be regarded as a reasonable excuse.

18.9.3 Interest

Interest is payable for periods up to the date on which payment is made and is in addition to the surcharges referred to above. This interest does not attract any tax relief.

18.9.4 Penalties

A penalty of £100 is due if the self-assessment is not delivered by the filing date. The Revenue may then appeal to the Commissioners for a continuing penalty of up to £60 per day. The starting date for this continuing penalty is the day on which the Commissioners direct that it should be imposed. It is avoided if the self-assessment is delivered before the Commissioners make their decision. However, even if no continuing daily penalty is imposed, there is a further £100 penalty if the self-assessment is delivered more than six months after the filing date.

Where the failure continues beyond 12 months the penalty, in addition to anything mentioned above, is a maximum of the tax due as shown in the return.

Penalty determinations may attract an interest charge, where the penalties are not paid promptly, as the determination is treated as if it were an assessment for the purposes of interest charged on late payment of tax.

18.9.5 Appeals

It is possible to appeal against the determination of a penalty by the inspector. However, the Commissioners may only set aside the £100 fixed penalties if there is a reasonable excuse for the taxpayer not having delivered the return throughout the period it was overdue. Where this condition is not satisfied, the Commissioners are required to confirm the penalties in full.

18.9.6 Partnerships

The basic rules are modified to take account of partnerships.

Partners' obligations to make returns

Individual partners are required to deliver self-assessments. However, the partnership is also required to make a return (not strictly speaking a self-assessment) if the Revenue serves a notice. The Revenue may serve the notice on any partner (the 'representative partner').

The notice asks for delivery of the return together with accounts and such other statements as the Revenue requires. The representative partner is required to make a return and all items relevant to the agreement of profits assessable under Schedule D Case II must be included in that return. It is not possible for individual partners to claim a deduction for expenses incurred by them unless they are shown in the partnership return. The notice requires the partnership return to include:

(a) the names, addresses and tax references of all persons who have been partners at any time during the period covered by the return; where partners have been in the firm for only part of the year, the precise period must be specified;
(b) full details of each partner's entitlement to profits (and losses) from each source of partnership income;
(c) particulars of the disposals of partnership assets as if the partnership itself (not the individual partners) were liable to tax on any chargeable gains and details of each partner's share of such capital gains;
(d) details of acquisitions of property by the partnership;
(e) the amount of annual charges borne by each partner (eg annuities paid to former partners or their dependants).

It is possible for the partnership to amend its return and for the Revenue to amend it after an enquiry.

Revenue investigations into partnership returns

The Revenue has the power to enquire into partnership returns on the same basis as they may enquire into returns made by individuals. That is to say, a notice must be issued within 12 months of the filing date or, if the return is delivered after the filing date, at the quarter date following 12 months after the delivery date.

A notice served on the partnership is deemed to include similar notices issued to the individual partners to the extent that they have actually delivered self-assessments.

Partnership returns

Each partner is liable to a £100 penalty if the partnership return is submitted late. This applies to any person who was a partner at any time during the return period. The continuing daily penalties and the six-month £100 penalty also apply to each partner.

Appeals against penalty notices imposed on partners

Where penalty determinations have been made so as to impose either the £100 penalty or the continuing daily penalty on two or more partners, appeals may be brought only by the representative partner. He then makes a composite appeal. Once again, the £100 penalty must stand unless the Commissioners are satisfied that there was a reasonable excuse which applied throughout the period of default.

18.9.7 Incorrect returns

If an incorrect self-assessment is delivered and it is wrong because of negligent or fraudulent conduct, the maximum penalty remains 100% of the tax understated in the self-assessment.

A partnership return, which includes accounts and statements, and which is incorrect due to negligent or fraudulent conduct, can give rise to a penalty on each partner, with the maximum amount of the penalty being the tax under assessed on him. It is possible for this penalty to apply even though the individual partner has not completed the partnership return and has not himself been guilty of negligent or fraudulent conduct. Basically, the conduct of the representative partner who made the partnership return is all that matters.

18.10 ACHIEVING FINALITY

It has generally been accepted that any new regime should afford taxpayers the same degree of certainty that liabilities have been finalised as exists at present where an assessment is appealed against and there is a determination under TMA 1970, s 54.

The legislation specifically provides that the Revenue may make assessments to correct a loss of tax which has been discovered. However, the Act makes it plain that this may not be done where there has been an error or mistake in a return as to the basis of computing a liability but the basis which was adopted accorded with the practice generally applying at the time.

The Act makes it clear that no discovery assessment may be made where all the facts were clearly made known to the Revenue and the matter was concluded without an enquiry, or with the officer being satisfied after carrying out an enquiry. The distinction that the Revenue presently draws between points which are fundamental to the determination of the liability does not feature in the legislation for the new regime and, therefore, to that extent a taxpayer may have greater certainty once an enquiry has been concluded or the time limit for the officer to initiate an enquiry has passed.

ANNUAL PAYMENTS, NICS ETC

18.11 MISCELLANEOUS PRACTICAL ASPECTS

18.11.1 Class 4 NICs

A deduction is available for half of the trader's liability for national insurance Class 4 contributions in arriving at the trader's income tax liability. Contributions are payable by self-employed individuals according to the level of their profits as determined for income tax purposes. For 2000–01 Class 4 NICs are levied at the rate of 7% of Schedule D profits between £7,530 and £23,435.

Where an individual pays interest on a business loan or has suffered trading losses, such amounts may be set against his earnings for the purposes of assessing liability for Class 4 NICs. This situation applies even where the losses have been relieved for income tax purposes by way of offset against his other income.

18.11.2 Annual payments
(TA 1988, ss 349 and 387)

These include any annuity or other annual payment (other than interest) and any royalty or other sum paid in respect of the use of a patent. These payments are normally made out of profits or gains chargeable to income tax.

Example of treatment of annual payments

In 2000–01 *A* has taxable profits of £20,000. He pays an annuity to a former partner of £10,000 (gross).

A cannot deduct the annuity, but he can take basic rate relief at source. This means that he pays only £7,800 to the person entitled to the annuity, ie £10,000 less 22% tax. The tax withheld of £2,200 comes out of the tax that he would have paid in any event on his profits of £20,000. Furthermore, *A* may be able to secure higher rate relief on the £10,000 annuity. If, for example, his total income were £60,000 his liability for higher rate tax would be computed as follows:

	£
10% and basic rate band	28,400
Gross amount of annuity	10,000
	38,400
Income subject to 40% rate is:	
Taxable income	60,000
Less	38,400
	21,600

On the other hand where a person making an annual payment has an insufficient tax liability to cover the tax withheld, he must account for this separately to the Revenue. Thus if A had taxable income of only £8,000 (after allowances but before the annuity) his 2000–01 normal tax liability would be:

	£
Tax at 10% on £1,520	152.00
Tax at 22% on £6,480	1,425.60
	1,577.60

However, because he has deducted tax from an annuity of £10,000 he will instead be required to pay £2,200 to the Revenue, to cover the tax relief taken by him at source.

19

COMPANY LAW

KEITH HATCHICK, SOLICITOR, PARTNER, MARSHALL HATCHICK

This chapter gives an overview of a vast body of corporate law which affects business life.

19.1 WHAT IS A COMPANY?

The fundamental principle of a company is that it is a separate legal entity distinct from its members. Two important points should be noted:

(1) Property belongs to a company and not its members. Directors and shareholders can be prosecuted for theft in appropriate circumstances.
(2) A company's debts and liabilities in themselves cannot in general be enforced against that company's members.

19.1.1 Limited liability

Most companies are formed with limited liability. This means that share-holders are only obliged to pay the company such amounts that remain unpaid on any shares they hold. In the case of companies limited by guarantee (ie without a share capital – see 19.1.2 below) shareholders are only obliged to contribute the amount they have guaranteed to contribute to the company should it be wound up. Other typical characteristics of a company are:

(a) a company can be sued in its own name;
(b) a death or change in the membership does not affect its continued existence; a company continues indefinitely until wound up or dissolved;
(c) members hold shares which constitute property and can be transferred to others without affecting the company's existence;
(d) the company has power to give security for its borrowing through the creation of a floating charge over all or any part of its assets.

19.1.2 Types of company

The Companies Act (CA) 1985 provides for three types of companies:

(i) companies limited by guarantee;

(ii)   unlimited companies; and

(iii) companies (either private or public) limited by shares.

Companies limited by guarantee

These are generally formed for non-trading purposes (eg charities, clubs, trade associations). Prior to the CA 1980 they could be formed with a share capital. This option was rarely used since it exposed members to liability with respect both to their guarantee in a winding-up and anything unpaid on their shares. Since the 1980 Act it has not been possible to form a company limited by guarantee with a share capital.

The memorandum of association must contain a provision stating that each member undertakes to contribute to the company's assets if it should be wound up either while he is a member or within one year thereafter. The liability is limited to a specified maximum (usually £1).

Companies limited by guarantee frequently dispense with the requirement that they should use the word 'limited' in their name. To obtain such an exemption permission must be sought from the Registrar of Companies. This is usually provided so long as

(a) the company's objects are for the promotion of commerce, art, science, education, religion and charity or any profession, and

(b) the articles or memorandum of association prohibit the payment of dividends to members, and

(c) profits, if any, are applied in promoting its objects, and

(d) on a winding-up any assets must be transferred to another similar body (ie not to its members).

Unlimited companies

These are not widely used since members, as the name implies, have no limitation on potential liability in the event that the company is wound up with debts that it is unable to pay. While the company is a going concern members can only be called upon to pay any sums that remain unpaid on their shares. Creditors of the company can, if debts owed to them remain unpaid, obtain a petition for winding up the company, but they cannot sue the members directly.

Private limited companies

The CA 1985 contains an unhelpful definition of a private company being 'one which is not a public company'. Effectively this means that a private company is one that is not allowed to offer shares to the public, eg by seeking admission on the Stock Exchange or by issuing an advertisement offering security to be issued by it. A private company is the most popular form for profit-making business entities.

Public companies

The CA 1985 contains a technical definition of a public company. The real differences between a public and a private company are:

(1) Its name must finish with the words 'public limited company' or 'plc' (for a Welsh company 'cwmni cyfyngedig cyhoeddus' or 'ccc'). A memorandum of association also needs to highlight the fact that it is a public company.

(2) There must be an authorised share capital of not less than £50,000 (this figure can be varied by the Secretary of State by statutory instrument) of which at least one-quarter and the whole of any premium has been paid up.

The advantage of a public company over a private one is that, subject to certain exceptions, a public company is entitled to issue advertisements offering securities to be issued to members of the public. The disadvantages are that public companies are subject to far more stringent controls than private ones. Public companies do not need to be and frequently are not listed on the Stock Exchange.

19.2 MEMORANDUM OF ASSOCIATION

Every company needs a memorandum of association; it acts as a company's charter and regulates the company's external affairs. Its purpose is to enable persons who invest in or deal with it to establish such facts as:

(a) its name;
(b) whether it is a private or public company;
(c) what its objects are;
(d) whether liability of its members is limited or unlimited;
(e) the location of its registered office (England, Wales or Scotland);
(f) if there is a share capital, and if so the amount and how it is divided (eg £1,000 divided into 1,000 ordinary shares of £1 each).

For a company limited by guarantee the memorandum must also state the maximum guaranteed liability of such members (see 19.1.2 above).

19.2.1 The name

The name chosen must end with the word Limited (or Ltd) or public limited company (or plc) unless a dispensation has been granted (see 19.1.2 above) or the Welsh equivalent (see 19.1.2) in the case of Welsh companies. It should not be the same as any other registered company or be offensive or commit a criminal offence. It should not be of a 'sensitive nature'. The Registrar keeps a list of such sensitive names and under what circumstances those names are granted. For example use of the words 'Group' or

'Holding' requires the company using the name to have at least two subsidiary companies. Use of words like 'Royal' are also restricted, normally to companies holding a royal charter.

Passing off

In forming a new company or changing the name of an existing company, attention should always be given to the name chosen since use of a similar name to an existing company may potentially give rise to a passing off action. This is where the use of a name is sufficiently similar to another as it may mislead members of the public. For example, if a company is called 'AG Honey Ltd' and a new company is formed called 'G A Huney Ltd' and both are in the same line of business (eg the extraction of honey), it may be that the first company would have an action for passing off due to its loss of goodwill. The normal action brought is one of damages, but more frequently the earlier company seeks to obtain an injunction to stop the newer company from continuing under that name. Guidelines were set down in *Warnink BV v Townend & Sons Ltd* [1979] AC 731. To establish a case there needs to be:

(a) a misrepresentation by a trader in the course of his business to a prospective customer or consumer;

(b) damage to goodwill of the existing business – it is sufficient if such damage is reasonably foreseeable as a consequence of any such misrepresentation;

(c) 'a common field of activity' – in one case a radio broadcaster failed to prevent a cereal producer from using the same name for his product (*McCulloch v May* [1947] 2 All ER 845).

19.2.2 Articles of association

The articles of association regulate a company's internal affairs, dealing with such matters as:

(a) issue and transfer of shares;
(b) alteration of share capital;
(c) holding of meetings and voting rights;
(d) directors' appointments and retirements;
(e) appointment of a secretary;
(f) declaration of dividend;
(g) accounts, auditing etc; and
(h) winding-up etc.

Both the memorandum and articles of association form a contract between the company and each member and between the members.

19.2.3 Formation requirements

The following documents should be sent to Companies House together with the relevant statutory fee (currently £20).

(1) A copy of the memorandum and articles of association. For a private company if no articles are filed Table A of the Companies (Tables A to F) Regulations 1985 automatically applies. For companies limited by guarantee the forms of memorandum and articles of association set out in Tables C and D of the same regulations must be used. These need to be signed by all members and witnessed.

(2) Form G10 – This needs to be completed by each director and the secretary. It also gives the address of the company's registered office.

(3) Form G12 – This must be completed by the solicitors engaged in the company formation (but can also be signed by a person named or a director or secretary in the Form G10). It confirms compliance with the companies legislation.

19.3 RE-REGISTRATION

At some stage during the currency of a company it may wish to convert into a company of a different form. Part II of CA 1985 anticipates that by considering four particular forms:

(a) a private company becoming a plc;
(b) a plc becoming a private company;
(c) a limited company becoming unlimited; and
(d) an unlimited company becoming limited.

19.3.1 Private company to plc

There must be the passing of a special resolution (or written resolution) that the company should be registered. The company must be able to show that it has an authorised share capital of at least £50,000 with not less than 25% paid up. There are various other considerations set out in CA 1985, s 45 which may need to be considered.

A copy of the special or written resolution needs to be sent to the Registrar within 15 days of the date of the meeting (or in the case of a written resolution the date it was signed by the last member). A Form 43(3) should also be completed. This needs to be accompanied by:

(a) a printed copy of the up-to-date articles and memorandum;
(b) a statement signed by auditors that in their opinion the balance sheet shows net assets not less than the aggregate of called up share capital and undistributable reserve;
(c) a copy of the balance sheet with an unqualified auditors report. The

report needs to state that if there is a qualification it is not material for purposes of determining whether (at the balance sheet date) the net assets exceeded the aggregate of its called-up share capital and distributable reserves.

A Form 53(3) should be completed and sent to the Registrar as outlined above. It contains a statutory declaration confirming that all required procedures have been complied with and the share capital requirements have been satisfied.

19.3.2 A plc to a private company
(CA 1985, ss 53–55)

A company must pass a special resolution changing the name from plc to Ltd and amend all references in the memorandum and articles accordingly.

A Form 53 needs to be completed and sent with the special resolution to the Registrar within 15 days. A shareholder is entitled to apply to court for an order of cancellation and the court will either cancel or confirm the resolution. In order for a shareholder to apply to court he or it must either

(a) hold not less than 5% of the issued share capital (of any class of share);
(b) consist of not less than 5% of members of a company; or
(c) consist of not less than 50 members.

Where there is a reduction of the plc's share capital which has the effect of bringing the nominal value of the company's allotted shares below the authorised minimum, the company must cease to be a plc under CA 1985, s 138. A court may further order that a company shall be re-registered as a limited company and in this case it dispenses with the necessity for the company to pass a special resolution so re-registering. If a company cancels shares under CA 1985, s 146 and it results in its share capital being below the authorised minimum, the company is obliged to apply for re-registration as a limited company.

19.3.3 Unlimited companies

Under CA 1985, s 49 if a private limited company wishes to re-register as an unlimited company all members must approve that re-registration and its memorandum and articles must be altered to comply with the Act. A Form 49 must be completed and filed with the Registrar of Companies, attached to which must be a confirmation signed by each member and a statutory declaration by the director confirming that all members have agreed. On receipt of this documentation Companies House issues a revised certificate of incorporation.

If an unlimited company wishes to re-register as a private company it must pass a special resolution and complete a Form 51. If a limited company has already registered as an unlimited company it cannot again re-register as a limited company.

There are provisions in the Act enabling an unlimited company to register as a plc and a plc to register as a private unlimited company. These are very rarely used in practice, but the procedure is set out in ss 48–53.

19.3.4 Stamp duty

This is charged on any document transferring ownership of shares, debentures and other security. It is an *ad valorem* tax levied at the rate of 0.5%. The minimum payable is £5 (increased from 50p in October 1999), but if for example shares are transferred for £120, stamp duty is £1 (ie it is rounded up to the nearest £5).

Stamp duty is chargeable to the purchaser of shares. In certain cases there may be exemption from stamp duty (eg transactions involving shares in the same group of companies on a re-organisation), but this area of law is complicated and professional assistance should be sought.

Stamp duty reserved tax (SDRT) arises when there is no stampable document used (eg when a block of shares is sold on the Stock Exchange). In this case the SDRT amount paid would equal that which would arise from stamp duty.

A number of pronouncements concerning the future of stamp duty have been made. It is likely that stamp duty for these transfers and other non-property documents will be limited, but nothing has yet been settled.

19.4 AFTER INCORPORATION

When the formalities referred to above have been completed and a certificate of incorporation has been received (and also in the case of a public company a certificate confirming that the share capital requirements have been complied with) the company should hold its first board meeting. The normal business of this meeting includes the following:

(1) adoption of the company seal (an impression is normally made in the margin of the minutes);
(2) appointment of a chairman (if appropriate) and any additional directors and the approval of any service contracts;
(3) appointment of auditors;
(4) stock transfer forms transferring subscriber shares to intended members of the company;
(5) completion of the company's bank mandate form setting up banking arrangements;
(6) adoption of an accounting reference date (ARD) to which the company's accounts will be prepared (in the event that the Registrar is not notified of the ARD within six months of the incorporation the statutory ARD will apply as of 31 March).

The following company forms typically need to be filed with the Registrar following the first board meeting (and subsequently when appropriate changes are made):

(a) Form 88(2) setting out details of shares which have been allotted for cash (if there is a non-cash consideration a Form 88(3) will need to be completed);

(b) Form 288 (Appointment of any new director or secretary), which needs to be signed by each new director and the secretary: resignations should also be recorded on the same form;

(c) Form 224 which is notification of the accounting reference date chosen by the company.

Any completed stock transfer form also needs to be sent to the Revenue for stamping (this is an ad valorem tax and is assessed at the rate of 50p per £100 or part thereof (see further below)). If there are any declarations of trust regarding the holding of such shares, such a declaration of trust form also needs to be stamped £5.

19.4.1 Continuing requirements

In addition to notifying the Registrar about day-to-day changes (eg:

(a) the appointment or resignation of a director or secretary (Form 288);

(b) a change of accounting reference date (Forms G225(1) and (2));

(c) a change of registered office (Form 287);

(d) a change of auditor, etc),

the company also has an obligation to prepare accounts. For the first accounting reference date, the accounts must be for a period of more than six months but not more than 18 months beginning with the date of incorporation. There is no minimum duration for subsequent periods but no period may exceed 18 months.

In each financial year the company's directors must lay before the company in general meeting copies of its annual accounts and the directors and auditors report. A copy of this material needs to be delivered to the Registrar within ten months of the end of the appropriate accounting reference period for a private company, or within seven months for a public company. In the case of a first accounting period of a company which is more than 12 months, the period allowed is ten and seven months respectively from the first anniversary of the company's incorporation (or three months from the end of the accounting reference period whichever last expires). If a company fails to deliver accounts to the Registrar within those periods civil penalties are charged of up to £5,000 for a public company, and up to £1,000 for a private company.

A private company may pass an elective resolution (see 19.6.6 below) to dispense with laying the accounts or reports before the company in general meeting (see 19.6.1 below). Any such election does not relieve the company from the obligation to send copies of the accounts to all members and other people entitled to receive them (including the Registrar).

There are special provisions for dormant companies which may, by special resolution, resolve not to appoint auditors. A dormant company for this purpose means one which has not had transactions requiring entries in the company's accounting records since the end of the previous financial year (or the date of incorporation as the case may be).

19.4.2 Annual return

Each company must deliver to the Registrar on a Form 363a details made up to a date not later than the anniversary of the company's incorporation for a new company, or the anniversary of the date of the last return for other companies. The return must be delivered to the Registrar within 28 days of the relevant date.

The annual return needs to specify the following:

(1) The relevant date as it is made up.
(2) The registered office address.
(3) Details of the company's main business activities.
(4) Names and addresses of the company secretary and each director of the company. For directors, additional information is required (including nationality, date of birth, business occupation and other directorships).
(5) Where the register of members is kept (if not at the registered office).
(6) The share capital of the company and its members.

19.4.3 Borrowing

Trading and commercial companies have employed powers to borrow money for all purposes of its business and this power is invariably enshrined in a company's memorandum of association. A borrowing or loan is an agreement under which one party advances or otherwise makes available to another a sum of money in consideration of a promise, whether expressed or implied, to repay the amount advanced, whether or not at a premium and whether or not with interest. An agreement relating to borrowing must be validly entered into by the company and borrowing must not be unlawful or for some unlawful pursuit.

Borrowing takes two forms:

(a) secured debt (borrowings secured subject to a charge that has been granted on some or all of the company's property); and
(b) unsecured debt, eg bills of exchange, promissory notes and bonds etc issued by the company.

Restrictions on borrowing

Frequently articles of association limit the amount of debt in the form of borrowings which can be outstanding at any time without the shareholders' prior consent. In the case of a listed company the Stock Exchange no longer requires the articles to restrict borrowings and it is left to the company and its advisors to determine limitations; obviously they need to take a view to ensure marketability of its securities. Section 6 of Chapter 1 of *The Admissions of Securities Listing* (the 'yellow book') makes it a requirement of the Stock Exchange that in most cases a listed company needs to obtain the shareholders' approval to a transaction, a principle purpose or effect of which is the granting of credit (including lending money or guaranteeing the loan) by the company or any one of its subsidiaries to, or to an associate of, a director or substantial shareholder ('a class IV transaction'). 'Director' and 'substantial shareholder' includes a person who occupied that position within the preceding 12 months.

Agreements usually require the company to undertake to keep its borrowings and those of any subsidiary within a specified limit. In the event that the company fails to comply with this provision a lender would have remedies against the company for breach of contract and may also seek to bring an injunction. It may also be possible that those who authorised such offending loan may be personally liable.

19.4.4 Debentures

There is no precise meaning of 'debenture'. The broad legal meaning is that it is a document which either creates or acknowledges indebtedness. For the purposes of this section debenture is used in its banking context, ie a document signed by the company covenanting to repay all monies that may be due to the lender and creating a fixed charge over the company premises etc and a floating charge over the concern's business and undertaking.

If there is a default in the repayment of the debenture which is unsecured, the main remedy is for the holder to sue for the debts if it remains unpaid. He needs to obtain a judgment and seek distress against the company's property and possibly present a petition for the company's winding-up. In the case of a secured debenture the holder is in a far stronger position since in addition to the powers already referred to he can also appoint a receiver or administrative receiver.

19.4.5 Mezzanine finance

This is a type of debt which has in recent years become quite popular with highly geared companies. It is a form of subordinated debt which ranks behind all or certain other specified debts of the company. This type of debt may be secured by charges, but these invariably rank behind other creditors.

The principal advantage to the creditor in offering this form of finance is that since the risk is high, so is the interest chargeable.

19.4.6 Charges and secured debentures

There is a temptation to use the words 'charge' and 'mortgage' interchangeably. There is an important difference between them since a mortgage arises when a property is transferred subject to a right of redemption. Conversely a charge does not transfer or convey anything but just gives the person holding the charge (the chargee) certain defined rights over the property as security or a loan.

A fixed or specific charge is one linked to either existing or future property and which attaches to that property. (For future property it attaches when that property has been ascertained.) When a fixed charge has been given relating to specific property the owner or company giving the charge is prohibited from dealing with the property without the consent of the company or individual to whom the charge was given.

A floating charge, as its name implies, floats over the relevant property until a specified event happens which would then cause it to fasten on to the subject matter of the charge. Until this occurs the relevant company can carry on its day to day activities and sell or deal with its assets without first requiring the holder's consent. If an event occurs which causes the charge to 'crystallize' (fasten), the holder of the floating charge becomes entitled to a specific or fixed charge over the property and any further dealing by the company of that property requires his or its consent. A floating charge crystallizes in circumstances including the following:

(a) upon the winding-up of the company;
(b) if an administrative receiver is appointed;
(c) if a company has sold substantially all its property and assets so that it can no longer carry on business;
(d) if possession of any assets is taken by the holder of a charge; and
(e) any other floating charge that may have been granted crystallizes or if the company granting the floating charge failed to repay money on demand.

19.4.7 Registration of charges

Section 395(1) of CA 1985 requires that if any security of a company's property or undertaking has been granted, such security shall cease to prevail unless details of the charge together with a document creating the charge has been delivered to the Registrar within 21 days. Section 396(1) lists nine types of charges to which the obligation of registration applies. The categories listed are broad, but exclude such items as fixed charges over shares which the relevant company may hold in another company and also interest under insurance policies.

To register a charge, a Form 395 must be completed as accurately as possible. To ensure that the charge is valid, full details of the nature of the charge should be set out in the form. A mistake or omission in the completion of the form can prejudice the effectiveness of that security against competing claims in the event of a winding-up. It is most important that professional assistance is sought in the drafting and registration of charges to avoid potential pitfalls. Information required to be inserted on Form 395 includes the following:

(1) Company name and number.
(2) Date of creation of charge.
(3) Description of the instrument.
(4) Names and addresses of persons entitled to charge.
(5) Particulars of property charged.

19.4.8 Failure to register a charge

If a charge is not registered within the required 21-day period:

(a) it becomes void as against the liquidator and administrator, any creditor of the company and any person who has acquired proprietary rights to an interest in assets which are subject to a charge;
(b) the money which it secures becomes immediately repayable when the time for registration expires;
(c) the company and every officer in default becomes liable to a fine under CA 1985, s 399(3).

If registration is late it is normal to execute a fresh charge, etc and duly register that within 21 days (but this may be subject to any others that may have been created in any intervening period). This second charge might also be subject to being set aside by a liquidator or administrative receiver as being a preference or possibly a transaction at an undervalue (see Insolvency Act 1986, ss 244 *et seq*).

19.4.9 Foreign companies

If a company incorporated outside Great Britain has an established place of business in England and Wales, it is required to submit particulars of any charge on property in England and Wales. Charges etc created prior to an establishment of a place of business remain valid even if the charge subsequently establishes the place of business.

Where a lender takes a charge from a foreign company relating to present or future property in England and Wales he should submit particulars of the charge and relevant documentary evidence to the Registrar. Even if the particulars are subsequently returned to the sender Companies House now maintains an alphabetical index of the names of overseas companies for which charges for registration have been delivered (this is known as the Slavenburg Index after an important case involving this foreign bank).

19.5 DIRECTORS

Regulation 70 of Table A of the Companies (Tables A to F) Regulations 1985 states the general precept of company law, namely 'subject to provisions of the [companies legislation] and the articles and to any directions given by special resolution, the business of the company shall be managed by the directors who may exercise all the powers of the company'. There is broad statutory definition of 'director' since CA 1985, s 741(1) refers only to a person occupying the position of a director by whatever name called. Directors are those people who have agreed to become directors, for example by completing a company Form 288, but may also include individuals who take that role upon themselves (eg a major shareholder in a small company who meddles in day-to-day business). It could also be deemed to include a senior manager of a larger company who makes significant decisions regarding that company's day-to-day business. It is clear that just because a person is not called a 'director' may be of little importance in establishing what is the position *de facto*. Such quasi directors are normally referred to as 'shadow directors'. In *Re Tasbian Ltd No 3* [1992] BCC 358 the Court of Appeal supported the claim that in the circumstances presented to the court the company doctor, who had been required to assist in a corporate recovery case, could have been treated as a director or a shadow director in the context under the Company Directors Disqualification Act 1986.

There is no maximum number of directors that can be appointed to a company and a private company may have one director. In the case of a public company it must have at least two directors. If a private company only has one director there must be at least two people involved in the running of the company since CA 1985, s 283(2) requires that a sole director cannot also be a secretary. There is nothing to stop a director – and indeed a secretary – being another company, but this should not lead to a circumvention in the requirement that there are only two individuals involved.

19.5.1 Appointment of directors

Founding directors complete company Form G10, which must be presented to Companies House before a certificate of incorporation is granted (see 19.2.3 above). Appointment of subsequent directors is determined in accordance with the company's articles. A typical such provision appears in reg 79 of Table A of the 1985 Regulations which states that the existing directors may appoint such person who is willing to act to be a director; this could either be to fill a vacancy or due to a requirement to have additional directors. Occasionally the articles will provide special provisions relating to a director appointment and it is not unusual for the articles to require a rotating system (ie a proportion of all the main members retire and offer themselves for re-selection at each annual general meeting). Sometimes the articles also require a director to hold a number of shares in the company concerned. Such shares are frequently held on the basis that on resignation they are resold to the company's other members.

Neither the managing director nor the chairman has specific powers accorded to him by law, but regulation 84 of Table A does allow the appointment of a managing director. Each meeting requires a chairman to preside. Normally one of the directors takes this role, but larger companies appoint a specific person to fill this slot. Table A requires that the chairman ought to be a member of the board. The position of chairman is a difficult one for he is in charge of the meeting and needs to check the meeting is properly conducted. Regulation 50 of Table A gives the chairman a casting vote at meetings in addition to any other vote he may have (whether on a show of hands or a poll).

19.5.2 Non-executive directors

This has been a characteristic of larger companies for many years. It refers to a director who is not employed by a company under a service contract. Frequently he is seen as being a useful nexus between the board and the shareholders' interests and is able to offer an independent stand which may not otherwise be available at board level. Company law does not recognise any division between a director and a director's responsibilities and duties. In recent years the importance of non-executives has been underlined by various guidelines on corporate governance, such as the Cadbury, Greenbury and Hampel Reports.

An executive director should have a service contract with the company. Regulation 82 of Table A provides that the director should be entitled to such remuneration as the company may by ordinary resolution determine. For a director who works without having a service contract there is a presumption that he should be paid for the work done for the company on a merit basis (*Craven-Ellis v Cannons Ltd* [1936] 2 KB 403).

19.5.3 Director meetings

The day-to-day management of a company is centred upon the decisions of the Board of Directors. Directors, unless otherwise required by the articles (or a shareholders' agreement etc), meet at such times and intervals as they feel fit. Frequently meetings, if permitted by the company's articles, are held with little formality. Notice is similarly dealt with on an informal basis, but must be given to each director. Article 88 provides that no notice need be given to a director who is absent from the UK. Table A also permits a director to appoint an alternate to represent him.

The company's articles will specify what constitutes a quorum. A sole director who can only act in limited circumstances without a meeting will usually need acts by written resolution to be effective. Each director will have a vote and in addition Table A gives the chairman a second or casting vote if votes are equal. There is little law to determine how such a casting vote should be exercised but it is recognised that it should not be exercised arbitarily or capriciously (it does not though need to be exercised in the same way as the chairman's first vote).

Meetings are increasingly being held by telephone: this is tolerated by law, but is not preferable to an actual meeting. The validity of such a meeting depends on ensuring the normal procedures are adopted. Due to the normal requirements of a meeting it is unlikely that meetings can effectively be held by e-mail.

19.5.4 Resignation or retirement

A director can at any time resign his directorship, but if in so doing he has breached a contract of service this could result in liability for damages. In the case of public companies and private companies which are subsidiaries of private companies, CA 1985, s 293 states that a director must retire from office at the AGM following his 70th birthday. This does not apply if a director's appointment has been approved by a resolution of the general meeting at which special notice giving details of the director's age has been circulated to members (at least 28 days prior to the meeting). If such notice is not practical it can take the form of a newspaper advertisement or any other method allowed by the articles, but this needs to be done at least 21 days before the meeting.

19.5.5 Disqualification

This can take two forms:

(1) The articles normally set out regulations under which a director is required to vacate office in certain circumstances (eg ceasing to hold qualifying shares (if required), becoming of unsound mind, bankruptcy etc).
(2) The Company Directors Disqualification Act 1986 sets out three circumstances:
    (a) disqualification for misconduct in relation to the company (eg if a director has been convicted of an indictable offence in connection with the company);
    (b) disqualification for unfitness (eg persistent breaches of company's legislation like failing to deliver documents or returns to Companies House on a regular basis); and
    (c) other cases of disqualification (eg if a director has participated in fraud or a breach of duty or has participated in fraudulent trading which comes to light during a winding-up).

An application may be sought for disqualification by the Secretary of State, the official receiver or the liquidator, past or present members of a company, or a creditor of a relevant company. It is within the court's discretion whether to make an order. For cases of fraud and misconduct such disqualification can be up to a maximum of 15 years, in other circumstances up to five years. Under s 6 of the 1986 Act a court must disqualify a director for not less than two years and not more than 15 years in the case where a company becomes insolvent (whether while he was a director or subsequently) and his conduct was such as to make him unfit or concerned in the management of the company. Under s 8 the Secretary of State can apply to court for a disqualification order for up to 15 years.

See *Re Sevenoaks Stationers (Retail) Ltd* [1991] Ch 164 in which the Court of Appeal set out guidelines on how the Act should be interpreted.

19.5.6 Removal of director

Section 3 of CA 1985 allows a director to be removed by ordinary resolution of the company so long as special notice of at least 28 days has been given. Such notice must be served on the company. The director affected has the right to receive a copy of the notice and be heard at the meeting whether or not he is a member of the company. He can, if he requires, oblige the company to circulate written representation to the members before the meeting (there is though a right to apply to the court to have this curtailed).

The removal of the person as a director does not deprive that person from obtaining compensation damages with respect to determination of his appointment. It may also be open to him to petition for the company's winding-up under s 122(1)(g) of the Insolvency Act 1986 on the 'just and equitable' ground. In one case the petition was held to be successful since the director had such a substantial stake in a small family company that it was felt to be based upon a personal relationship involving mutual confidence (this area of law was carefully considered by the House of Lords in *Ebrahimi v Westbourne Galleries* [1973] AC 360).

19.5.7 Directors' duties

The duties can be summarised under two heads:

(a) the duty of good faith and loyalty (more usually referred to as fiduciary duties), and
(b) the requirement to use skill and care in carrying out their duties.

Fiduciary duties

This is an individual duty imposed upon each director of a company and it is owed to the company. From this fundamental principle certain strands have developed:

(1) In exercising good faith, directors must act in what they believe to be the company's best interests.

(2) They should not prejudice their ability to make decisions or restrict how they should act.
(3) They should not place themselves in the position where their personal interests or relationships to other persons may conflict with their duties to the company.
(4) They should not use the powers placed upon them for different purposes from those with which they were conferred.

Illustrations

In *Re W & M Roith Ltd* [1967] 1 WLR 432 a controlling shareholder and director made provision for his widow under his service agreement that she should be entitled upon his demise to a pension for life. The court held that this was not binding upon the company since no thought had been given to the question of whether this provision was for the company's benefit. Here the sole object was to make a provision for the shareholder/director's widow.

In *Re Kuwait Bank v National Nominees* [1991] AC 187 the bank, which held 40% of the shares in the company, had appointed two of its employees as directors, but continued to pay them for time spent in carrying out their duties. The court held that although they continued to owe a duty to the bank (ie their employers), their primary duty when acting as directors was to the company and that they should when circumstances dictated have ignored the bank's interests and wishes.

In *Re Aberdeen Railway v Blaikie Bros* (1854) 1 Macq 461 a contract was revoked between the company and the partnership since one of the directors was a partner. Lord Cranworth in discussing fiduciary duties said 'it is a rule of universal application that no one, having such duties to discharge, shall be allowed to enter into engagements in which he has, or can have, a personal interest conflicting, or which possibly may conflict, with the interests of those whom he is bound to protect . . . no question is allowed to be raised as to the fairness or unfairness of a contract so entered into . . .'.

Section 317 of CA 1985 requires a director of a company who is in any way 'whether directly or indirectly' interested in a contract or a proposed contract to declare his interest at a meeting of directors. If a director fails to declare his interest he is liable to a fine. Recent cases before the House of Lords and the Court of Appeal have been particularly interesting since in *Hely-Hutchinson v Brayhead Ltd* [1968] 1 QB 549 and *Guinness v Saunders* [1988] 1 WLR 863 both companies had in their articles of association provision that so long as the director disclosed his interest in accordance with s 317, he would be exonerated from the normal duty to account to the company for benefit resulting from such transaction. In each case the director failed to declare his interest. The courts' judgments were clear that, if the company wished, it could avoid the transactions and any such benefits received by directors would be recovered. In each case the court appeared to accept that had the interest been declared the transaction would be upheld even if it had not specifically consented to the director placing himself in a position where his duty to the company and his interests could conflict.

There are a number of examples of the use of corporate property where directors have been required to return funds which had been misappropriated. In *Guinness v Saunders*, although Mr Ward thought he was entitled to £5.2m from the company, he was required to return it.

In *Re Regal (Hastings) Ltd v Gulliver* [1942] 1 All ER 378 the directors decided to purchase two additional cinemas with the view that the company would then be sold. The directors were unable to obtain the required funds. The directors and their friends subscribed for shares in a second company, making a profit. The first company fell into different hands and brought an action against its former directors to recover profits they had made. Despite the fact that the original company would not have been in a position to make these profits it was held by the House of Lords that the directors were liable to account since they acquired their knowledge as directors while managing the original company and their actions resulted in profit.

There has been a line of cases concerned with directors who had retired to obtain remunerative work that their original companies had been denied. In each case the relevant directors have been required to account to the company for profits they made. (See further *Industrial Development Consultants v Cooley* [1972] 1 WLR 443; *Canadian Aero Service v O'Malley* [1971] 23 DLR (3d) 632.)

Section 309 of CA 1985 requires directors of a company to have regard in the performance of their functions to the interests of the company's employees in general in addition to those of its members. Section 310 states that 'any provision whether contained in the Company's articles or in any contract with the Company or otherwise which attempts to exonerate an officer (or auditor of the company) from, or indemnify them against liability for negligence, default, breach of contract, breach of trust which he may be guilty in relation to the company is unenforceable'. There is a difficulty reconciling this statutory provision with the wording in Table A, regs 85 and 86.

19.5.8 Directors' remuneration

Section 318 of CA 1985 obliges a company to keep copies of a service agreement for each director of the company or its subsidiaries. These should be kept at the registered office or at its principal place of business and must be open for inspection by any member of the company without charge.

Section 319 makes it unlawful for any provision in a director's contract which may make it last for more than five years without being terminated (ie other than through causing a breach of contract) unless the relevant term is first approved by the company in general meeting. There are special provisions relating to inspection being available without charge to members for a period prior to the meeting and at the meeting itself.

19.5.9 Substantial property transactions

Section 322 of CA 1985 requires that the company approve in advance any arrangement under which a director or person connected with such director will acquire from the company or the company will acquire from such person non-cash items of requisite value (being £100,000 or 10% of the company's net assets if more than £2,000). The need for approval does not apply to intergroup transfers when the property is to be acquired by a holding company from one of its wholly owned subsidiaries or vice versa or from one wholly owned subsidiary to another of that same holding company. If a director authorises an arrangement or transaction in violation he is liable to account to the company for any gain he makes.

19.5.10 Loans to directors

Section 330(2) and (3) of CA 1985 prevents the company making a loan to a director of it or its holding company or from entering into any guarantee or providing security in connection with a loan made by any person to such director. This also covers a prohibition on 'quasi-loans' (these are when a director makes some financial benefit as a result of the company being party to a transaction), eg a gift of a holiday or some other benefit in kind. The grant of credit is also prohibited and the assignment of any rights, obligations and liability could also fall within this scope (s 330(4) and (6)).

There are certain exceptions to these rules and these should be carefully considered prior to any such potential 'loan'.

19.5.11 Directors' duties of care

Re City Equitable Fire Insurance Co [1925] Ch 407 laid down the standard of care required under three heads:

(1) In the performance of his duties a director does not need to show any greater skill than would reasonably be expected from a person of his knowledge and experience.
(2) A director's duties are of an intermittent nature and should be formed at periodic board meetings or any committee of that board on which he serves. He is not required to give continuous attention to the company's affairs.
(3) A director may rely upon agents or employees of the company not being directors to carry on day-to-day duties of the company. In particular a director can only be liable on the basis of his own personal negligence.

There are two important statutory provisions which should be noted which affect the director's duty of care:

(1) Section 214 of the Insolvency Act 1986; this provision can potentially make a director personally liable if there is 'wrongful trading' (see further 19.5.13 below)
(2) The Company Directors Disqualification Act 1986 (see 19.5.5 above).

19.5.12 Personal liability of directors

There are a number of circumstances referred to above and also with respect to the insolvency legislation in which directors can potentially be personally liable. The articles cannot relieve directors from their duty to act bona fide in the interests of a company nor can a resolution of a company in general meeting make good default, but the courts have indicated that a transaction may sometimes be validated (and the directors thereby excused from liability) if:

(a) all relevant facts are disclosed in a notice convening a general meeting or in a circular accompanying that notice;
(b) it can be shown that the resolution was 'bona fide in the interests of the company'.

In *Williams v Natural Law* (1996) inaccurate financial projections were provided to an applicant to a franchise which persuaded him to enter into a franchise. The result was a substantial loss of money. The plaintiff had no difficulty in showing that there was gross negligence (there was clearly a duty of care to ensure projections were correct and reasonably and properly prepared). It was held that in the particular circumstances of the case the director had, since the plans were presented relying upon the personal expertise and experience of the director, effectively assumed a personal duty to the plaintiff (and was therefore personally liable). The court did however emphasise that a director who merely had control or ownership of the company in itself was not sufficient to create such a liability.

It is clear that English courts have been extending liability for directors and that a more objective test (common in Australian case-law) is beginning to be recognised (ie directors are expected to use skill and diligence and not just be enthusiastic amateurs).

19.5.13 Insurance

It has been customary for the personal liability of directors and other officers to be covered by insurance. Before CA 1989 it was unclear whether under CA 1985, s 310 such insurance was enforceable. A new provision was inserted by s 137 of the 1989 Act under which a new subs 310(3) was incorporated in the 1985 Act. This makes it clear that a company can purchase and maintain insurance for its officers if its memorandum and articles of association so allow. The normal form of cover protects past, present and future officers of a specific company (including shadow directors), but does not protect outsiders (eg an auditor or liquidator).

Indemnity insurance normally takes two forms:

(i) protecting officers of a company where an indemnity from the company is not available, and

(ii) where the company reimburses its officers for liability it would in turn make this good to the company.

It is normal for a company to protect against:

(a) paying damages and costs of any action for a 'wrongful act' (broadly defined and includes actions for wrongful trading under s 214 of the Insolvency Act 1986);

(b) legal expense incurred (except the exclusions from policy are normally limited to public policy items such as dishonesty, fraud, malicious conduct, indemnity for fines and penalties);

(c) specific risks which should be insured elsewhere (eg negligence or a breach of professional duty by an auditor or solicitor).

19.6 MEETINGS

19.6.1 General meetings

There are two types:

(a) annual general meetings (AGMs), and

(b) extraordinary general meetings (EGMs).

Every company must hold an AGM each calendar year with not more than 15 months between one AGM and the next. A newly formed company need not hold its first AGM for up to 18 months from the date of incorporation (see generally CA 1985, s 366).

An EGM is any general meeting that is held other than an AGM, and is usually convened by the company's directors when they so require. Under CA 1985, s 368 the directors are bound to convene an EGM if the holder of not less than one-tenth of the company's voting shares (or for companies without a share capital, of not less than one-tenth of voting rights) so requires. The people calling the meeting must give written notice setting out the meeting's objects and sign that notice. If the directors are requested to hold an EGM by the shareholders or those with voting rights they must fix the actual date within 28 days (ie allowing a maximum of 49 days before a meeting is actually held).

The directors of a plc are required to convene an EGM under CA 1985, s 142 if there is a serious loss of capital (where the net assets are half or less of its called-up share capital). In this instance the meeting must be convened in 28 days for a date not later than 20 days after such notice.

Before the company can hold an AGM or EGM written notice must be given to the members:

(a) for an AGM, at least 21 days' notice;

(b) for an EGM, not less than 14 days unless a special resolution is proposed, in which case it must be 21 days. In sending out the notice a company should carefully ensure that extra days are given since frequently the article requires 'clear' days' notice (eg reg 38 of Table A).

Shorter notice can be given if this is agreed by all members entitled to attend in the case of an AGM or for an EGM those holding not less than 95 per cent of the voting shares (or having such voting rights).

Notice needs to be sent to every member of a company, but frequently the articles state that accidental omission to give such notice (or non-receipt of such notice) does not invalidate proceedings of a meeting (eg reg 39 of Table A). Table A also (in reg 38) requires that the notice should state the:

(a) time and place of the meeting;

(b) general business to be transacted (eg retirement, re-election of directors); and

(c) appointment of auditors.

Where a special resolution is to be proposed the notice must set this down.

For a company with share capital, the notice must also contain the statement in reasonable prominence that a member is entitled to attend and vote and may also appoint a proxy to attend and vote in his place and that this proxy need not be a member of the company (s 372). If a company's members wish to include a resolution at an AGM and such member or members hold not less than ¹⁄₂₀th of the voting rights (or 100 members entitled to vote with an average paid-up share capital of not less than £100 per member), the company must circulate:

(a) notice thereof to each member of the company that a resolution will be proposed at the AGM; and

(b) a statement of not more than one thousand words relating to the proposed resolution (s 376). The company and 'any aggrieved person' has the right to petition the court to prevent any such statement being circulated.

The court has power to call a meeting (s 371). This power is normally used if no quorum can be achieved (eg a shareholder argument) or a meeting may end in violence. An example of such use was a meeting held by the British Union for the Abolition of Vivisection: the court held that only the executive committee should meet, with all other members having a postal vote.

19.6.2 Special notice

This is required for the:

(a) appointment of a director who has attained the age of 70;

(b) removal of directors;

(c) appointment and removal of auditors.

Notice in this respect must be given to the company not less than 28 days before the meeting and the company must give notice to each of the members when it circulates a notice for the meeting (or if this is not practical through newspaper advertisement or any other form allowed by the articles not being less than 21 days before the meeting).

19.6.3 Quorum

The articles of association normally provide that a specified number of people must be present before a meeting can be held. Under CA 1985, s 370 unless the articles otherwise state, two members must be present in person for a meeting to be held. Table A, in reg 41, states that where a meeting cannot be held it should be adjourned to the same day in the following week at the same time and place (or such time and place as the directors may determine) and if after half an hour at that adjourned meeting there is no quorum the members present shall form that quorum (even if it is a single person).

A meeting can be held in more than one room at the same time provided there are audio visual links (*Byng v London Life Association* [1990] Ch 170).

19.6.4 Voting

This is normally done by show of hand with each person present having one vote, unless a poll is demanded in which case a member has a vote for each share he holds. Section 372 of CA 1985 gives the right of voting by proxy (ie appointing another person to attend and vote in his place). There are two forms of proxy:

(1) a general proxy appointing a person to vote as he thinks fit having regard to what is said at the meeting; and

(2) a special proxy where a person is required to vote for or against a particular resolution (frequently called 'a two-way proxy').

19.6.5 Minutes

Minutes should be taken of proceedings of general meetings. These are signed by the chairman of that meeting either at the end of the meeting or at the next meeting. Frequently articles state that when signed they are conclusive evidence of what took place at the meeting, but if the articles do not so provide it does not form conclusive evidence. Members are entitled to inspect the minute book at the registered office without charge; if this is refused or not made available the court can compel inspection.

19.6.6 Resolutions

There are four types of resolutions.

Ordinary resolution

Unless the company's articles or memorandum state otherwise a motion can be passed by ordinary resolution – by simple majority of votes of members entitled to vote and voting in person.

Extraordinary and special resolutions

These require to be passed by at least a three-quarter majority of the voting members entitled to vote in person at a general meeting.

Elective resolution

This was introduced by CA 1989 for use in a private company. It can be used for the following:

(a) with respect to authority of directors to allot shares;
(b) to dispense with the laying of accounts and reports for a general meeting;
(c) to dispense with the appointment of auditors;
(d) to reduce a percentage required before sanctioning short notices of meetings or special resolution; and
(e) to dispense with the holding of an AGM.

To pass an elective resolution needs at least 21 days' notice in writing. The notice needs to set out the terms of the resolution which needs to have unanimous consent of those entitled to attend and vote at the meeting (ie one shareholder can veto it). Any election can be revoked by ordinary resolution and is automatically revoked if, for example, the company becomes a plc. An elective resolution, or one revoking an elective resolution, must be registered at Companies House in the same manner as a special resolution.

19.6.7 Filing of resolution

Companies House must be sent copies of the following:

(a) special resolutions;
(b) extraordinary resolutions;
(c) elective resolutions;
(d) written resolutions;
(e) other resolutions agreed by all members (which would otherwise not be effective unless passed as a special or extraordinary resolution);
(f) a resolution passed by all members of a class of shareholders;

(g) an ordinary resolution increasing share capital.

Copies of all such resolutions must be sent to the Registrar within 15 days after they are passed or made.

The following are examples of ordinary resolutions:

(a) removal of a director (CA 1985, s 303);
(b) appointment or removal of an auditor (ss 384 and 386);
(c) increase in share capital.

Extraordinary resolution examples are few but do occur in insolvency:

(a) in sanctioning the exercise of certain powers of liquidation and a member's voluntary winding-up under the Insolvency Act 1986, s 165;
(b) for the initiation of a creditor's voluntary winding-up when the company is insolvent under s 84 of that Act.

A special resolution is required for more important situations:

(a) alterations of the objects clause in the memorandum of association (CA 1985, s 4);
(b) alterations of articles (s 9);
(c) reduction of capital (s 135).

19.6.8 Written resolutions

For some years the courts have accepted that it is not necessary that the company should always hold a meeting, and that all shareholders having a right to attend and vote at general meetings and give notice in written form constitute a binding resolution on the company. The CA 1989 now formally allows private companies to pass resolutions without holding any meeting provided all those who could have attended the meeting and voted sign such a resolution. This can only take effect when the last relevant member signs. A written resolution cannot be used to dismiss a director under CA 1985, s 303 or an auditor under s 391. The CA 1985 requires that the written resolution should be sent to the auditor who can, within seven days, notify the company that it should be considered by a formal meeting. In this case a meeting needs to be held to consider the resolution. If the written resolution in effect transacted business which would otherwise be done by special, extraordinary or elective resolutions, it must be sent to the Registrar for filing.

19.6.9 The shareholder

There is no clear definition of what a share is in law, but it is clearly recognised as being an item of property which can be bought, sold, mortgaged and approved. Normally a shareholder's rights consist of three items:

(a) dividends;

(b) in the event of a winding-up, a return of capital (also in the event of an authorised reduction of capital); and

(c) voting and attendance at a meeting.

Unless the articles state to the contrary all shares confer rights with respect to each of these characteristics.

Either a general meeting resolution or alternatively the company's articles must empower the directors to allot shares in the company (right to subscribe, convert, etc) (CA 1985, s 80). Such authority also needs to state the maximum number of shares, etc which can be issued under that power and the power can only be that for up to five years. Thereafter further authorisation must be given by the general meeting.

Sections 89–96 of CA 1985 grant pre-emptive rights to the existing shareholders, ie giving them the ability to protect the proportion of total equity that they may hold at any one stage (the provisions require that the company should not allot shares to any person unless it is first offered, on the same or more favourable terms, to each person who holds relevant shares a proportion of shares which as nearly as practicable equals his existing proportion in nominal value of his aggregate holdings of relevant shares). The difficulty with these pre-emption provisions is that they can be modified or extinguished since under CA 1985, s 31 the need to offer pre-emptive rights can be excluded in the memorandum and articles of a private company (in each case or in respect of a particular allotment).

With reference to public companies, CA 1985, s 95 empowers directors who have general authority by the articles or through a resolution at general meeting to allot shares as if the pre-emption provisions do not apply.

19.6.10 Types of shares

In a company with more than one type of share (frequently referred to as a 'class') there must be equal treatment for all holders of those shares. Frequently a company has more than one class of share with different rights with respect to

(a) dividends,
(b) return of capital,
(c) voting rights, and
(d) nominal values.

Each class of share has its own rights; this is referred to more generally at 19.6.14 below.

Preference shares

These, as the name implies, have a preferential right in comparison with ordinary shares. The preference is normally dividend or return of capital. The rights of the holder of such shares are normally set out in the articles of

627

association. Where this share has priority with respect to dividend it normally takes two forms, either cumulative or non-cumulative. The former safeguards the shareholder in the event that a dividend is not declared since in effect it is added to the next time a dividend is paid. In the latter case, if a dividend is not paid the right is lost forever.

Ordinary shares

If there are special rights given to another class of share (eg preference shares) until these preferential rights have been satisfied claims by the ordinary shareholder are delayed. It is for this reason that ordinary shares are sometimes referred to as 'risk capital'. Sometimes such shares are themselves divided into different classes.

Employee shares

These are shares normally allotted to full-time employees under an established scheme (frequently taking advantage of tax benefits under approved option schemes. This may include present and past employees within the group and spouses etc. Sometimes a special class of share is created to cater for the rights of these holders, but more usually they form part of an established class with special rules regarding allotment, finance and repurchase. There is frequently also a trust document setting out various rights.

19.6.11 Debenture holder

This has sometimes been classified as a type of share, but does not really conform to the characteristics of shares discussed above. The relationship is really one of debtor creditor (frequently coupled with some form of security against some or all of the company's assets). The distinction sometimes becomes blurred, eg where a debenture holder may be able to appoint a director, obtain a share of profit (this may be irrespective of whether a dividend is declared), to attend and vote at meetings and sometimes to have the right to convert his debentures into equity shares.

19.6.12 Bonus issue

This is frequently also called a 'capitalisation' issue (and sometimes a 'scrip' issue). If a cash rich company wants to increase the network of its share capital to its shareholders it may issue them with bonus shares. It is a method of capitalising reserves by issuing new-paid-up shares to its existing shareholders (eg if a book value of a company was, say, £10m and the company had an issued share capital of 5m shares of £1 each the shares are effectively worth £2). If a company then decides to make a one-for-one paid-up bonus issue (which is paid out of the share premium account or any free reserves) the shareholder effectively receives for each of his shares (worth £2) two £1 shares each worth £1. The sole effect is that the company can reduce the amount held in its share premium account and replace it with issued shares. Sometimes a listed company achieves the same effect by allowing shareholders to exercise an option and take shares in place of dividends.

19.6.13 CREST

After nearly ten years of work, settlement of dealing in shares can now be dealt with on a computerised basis, rather than a lengthy paper system. The CREST system was inaugurated on 15 July 1996; it is run by CRESTCo, owned by 69 institutions from various parts of the securities industry.

The computer system in its simplest form works from a computer which receives instructions for the transfer of shares and acts upon those instructions. Companies and shareholders are therefore disassociates and communicate only by electronic media through the centralised computer. Companies will continue to keep registers of members and dividends and voting remains unchanged.

CREST is a voluntary system and an issuer can choose whether to use it – even when a security is dealt with by CREST a shareholder can choose whether to hold it in a certificated or uncertificated format.

19.6.14 Class rights

Three particular types of rights are identified:

(1) Those rights which clearly attach to a class of share (eg dividend and rights to participate in surplus assets on a winding-up).
(2) Where the articles purport to confer rights on individuals not as shareholders (eg a solicitor who becomes a member of a company cannot enforce a provision that he should be the company's solicitor). Rights of this sort are clearly not a class right since it could not be said to attach to a class of share.
(3) Rights that although not attached to any particular share are nonetheless conferred upon the beneficiary in the capacity of member or shareholder of the company (eg the right of the holder of 10% of the issued shares to nominate a director) (*Cumbria Newspapers Group v Cumberland & Westmorland Herald Newspaper & Printing Co Ltd* [1987] Ch 1). It was felt that this constituted class rights.

Where class rights exist they can only be varied:

(a) if the holders of three-quarters of the nominal value of the issued share of that particular class consent in writing; or
(b) a separate general meeting of holders of that class is held and an extraordinary resolution passed; or

(c) in either instant all relevant provision of a memorandum and articles of association or any agreement binding upon the shareholder is satisfied.

If variation provisions of class rights are incorporated in the memorandum and articles of association it is sufficient that variations are carried out in compliance with such provisions. If there is no such variation provision included and the rights are set out in the memorandum it can only be varied if all members of a company agree to the variation (CA 1985, s 125(5)).

Strict compliance is necessary to the length of notice to be given for any such class meeting and CA 1985, s 369 and for the holding of that meeting and voting (s 370) and the circulation of resolutions (ss 376 and 377).

Under CA 1985, s 127 a dissenting minority of not less than 15% of the issued shares of a class whose rights have been varied in the manner permitted may apply to the court to have any variation cancelled. Such application needs to be made within 21 days after consent was given or the resolution passed. When such an application has been made the variation has no effect until it is confirmed by the court. If the court is satisfied the variation would unfairly prejudice the shareholder of the class represented by the applicant it will cancel the variation, but if it does not disallow the variation the court must confirm it.

19.6.15 Members' rights and duties

The company in general meeting has the power to act in place of a board if for any reason the board cannot function. For example if no quorum can be obtained for a meeting of directors or there is deadlock on the board it is well established that the company in general meeting may act instead. Similarly if the directors are in breach of duty in some circumstances this can be authorised or ratified by the company in general meeting.

There is an obligation upon directors in carrying out their duties to act for the benefit of a company as a whole, but if they are members themselves can they vote in support of their own personal interests? This has led the courts to develop the concept of 'fraud on the minority'. Fraud in this context does not mean deceit, but refers to an abuse of power; the victim of such an abuse does not need to be a 'minority of members' – it is enough if the injured party is a company. There is a large body of cases giving examples of circumstances which have amounted to 'fraud on the minority'. In practice it is likely that a new statutory provision incorporated in CA 1985, s 459 can now be used more frequently (see 19.6.16 below).

Fraud has taken three particular forms, as follows.

Resolution permitting expropriation of property belonging to company

In *Cook v Deeks* [1916] 1 AC 554 directors diverted to themselves contracts which should have been taken up by the company and passed a resolution ratifying and approving this. The court held that the directors should hold the benefit of such contracts on trust for the company and could not be permitted to make a present of it to themselves. In *Menier v Hooper's Telegraph Works* (1874) 9 Ch App 350, those holding a controlling interest in a company compromised a pending action to their advantage (in a rival concern) which had the effect of gaining the company's assets to the exclusion of a minority. Again the court supported the minority's case.

Resolutions which relieve directors of liability

It is likely that if a director makes a full and frank disclosure to the company's members and the resolution can be shown to be bona fide in the company's interests it is unlikely that a minority is now able to successfully bring an action for fraud. Further, under CA 1985, s 35, if directors have failed to observe limitations on their power in the memorandum of association they can now be released from any liability by a special resolution.

Resolution that exappropriates members' shares

In *Brown v British Abrasive Wheel Company* [1919] 1 Ch 290 a public company was unable to buy out a 2% minority so proposed by special resolution to acquire the shares. Here it was felt that the resolution could not be said to benefit the company as a whole, but only benefit the majority. An injunction was granted.

Other similar cases, though, have not followed this particular case and it is clear the courts will look carefully at the circumstances of each particular action. Further discussion on this general principle is outside the scope of this book, but a full discussion of the principles involved is discussed at length by the Court of Appeal in the influential case of *Greenhalgh v Arderne Cinemas* [1946] 1 All ER 512 (especially the judgment of Evershed MR).

19.6.16 Other remedies available to shareholders

Section 210 of the Companies Act 1948 gave protection to minorities where there had been conduct of an 'oppressive nature'. The remedy granted in the circumstances was to petition for a winding-up order on the grounds that such a remedy was just and equitable. The new law is incorporated in CA 1985, s 459 which allows a member of a company to petition a court on the ground that the affairs are being carried out or conducted in a manner which is 'unfairly prejudicial to the interests of its members generally or some part of the members (including at least himself) or that any actual or proposed act or omission of the company (including any act or omission on its behalf) is or would be so prejudicial'.

Once the court is satisfied that the petition is well founded, it makes 'such order as it thinks fit for giving relief in respect of the matter complained of'. The section goes on to give some examples:

(a) give instructions regulating the conduct of a company's affairs in future;
(b) give instructions prohibiting the company from doing an act complained of or requiring it to make an omission;
(c) authorise a company to bring in its name civil proceedings;
(d) require the purchase of shares of any member of a company either by the company itself or other members (if the company was to purchase its own shares under this head it would not need to comply with the special requirements for purchase of company's own shares) (see 19.7.5 below).

Recent cases concerned with ascertaining whether there was unfairly prejudicial conduct have indicated that there is no need to show either bad faith or a conscious intent to be unfair. It was also not essential to show a reduction in share value although that could be helpful.

In *Re Noble* [1983] BCLC 273 the judge felt that the shareholder had contributed to his own exclusion from the management of the company by showing no interest in its affairs. In *McGuinness & Anor v Bremmer plc and others* [1988] BCLC 673 it was held that a delay in holding a meeting was unfairly prejudicial even though it was within the terms of the 1985 Act.

Where a letter from the directors had deprived shareholders the chance of selling shares to the highest bidder or had reduced their chance of doing so this would also justify an action under CA 1985, s 459 (*Re a Company (No 008699 of 1985)* [1986] PCC 296).

Where a member had risked his capital in the business (a small limited company) it was justifiable that he would expect to be retained as a director. When he was dismissed it was held to be an unfairly prejudicial treatment of his interests as a member (*Re a Company (No 00477 of 1986)* [1986] PCC 372), but where a director was causing friction and difficulties his dismissal was not deemed to be unfairly prejudicial (*Re a Company (No 002470 of 1988), ex p Nicholas* [1991] BCLC 480).

In addition to a remedy from the court there remains a broad power of the Department of Trade and Industry to investigate where there is some cause of disquiet. This has led to a significant increase in publicity and the number of legal actions which have followed.

19.7 SHARE CAPITAL

The memorandum of association for a company with a share capital must declare the amount of share capital it proposes to be registered and the division of that share capital into shares of fixed amounts. For example this provision in the memorandum may state that a company's share capital shall be £1,000 divided into 1,000 ordinary shares of £1 each. The level of authorised share capital tends to be a formality and its purpose really is to prescribe the maximum number of shares which a company is able to issue without first increasing its authorised share capital. It also indicates the nominal value which it has chosen to place on shares into which the share capital is divided. In order to increase authorised share capital the company merely has to pass an ordinary resolution in general meeting. This, together with a Form 123, is then filed with the Registrar within 15 days of the passing of such resolution.

19.7.1 Issued share capital

The general rule is that shares must not be issued at a discount of a nominal par value (eg £1 shares must be issued at not less than £1). Payment does not necessarily need to be in cash; it can be made in kind and the party's valuation of non-cash consideration is usually accepted as conclusive unless the inadequacy appears on the face of a transaction or there is bad faith. Private companies are, however, required under CA 1985, s 88 to complete a return of allotment form (Form 88) reporting upon how many shares are issued and for what consideration.

There are stricter rules regarding non-cash consideration for public companies. A plc may not accept an undertaking by a person that he will work or perform services for a company in payment for shares; there are other similar rules set out in CA 1985, s 99. Further, under s 103, a plc may not allot shares as fully or partly paid up unless certain circumstances exist:

(a) the consideration needs to be valued;
(b) a report needs to be prepared for the company during the six months preceding such allotment; and
(c) a copy should be sent of this report to the proposed 'purchaser'.

19.7.2 Reductions of capital

The general rule is that a company's capital cannot be reduced without a court order being sought. Under CA 1985, s 135 a company may, if authorised by its articles, reduce its share capital so long as it has obtained court confirmation under ss 136–138. The procedure is as follows:

(1) It must pass a special resolution to reduce its share capital either by reducing or extinguishing an amount of uncalled liability on shares or cancelling any paid-up share capital which it 'lost or unrepresented by available assets', or by paying off any paid-up share capital which is in excess of the company's wants. It needs to alter reference in its memorandum of association to its share capital etc.
(2) After passing such resolution the company needs to apply to court to confirm the resolution. The court will be concerned to ensure that all creditors have been notified and given an opportunity to object. Once a court is satisfied that every existing creditor has consented or that his debt or claim has been discharged or secured, it will then make an order confirming the reduction on such terms as it sees fit.

(3) If any creditor has been overlooked or is ignorant of a reduction pro-
ceeding and the company goes into insolvent liquidation the court on
the application of that creditor may order members whose uncalled liability has been reduced to contribute as if it had not been to the extent
necessary to pay off the creditor.

In practice this procedure is rarely used since most companies use
Companies Act procedures for the purchase of its own shares.

Just because the net asset may fall below a company's capital it does not
necessarily indicate that it must cease trading. The usual effect is that the
company is not able to pay dividends. In the case of a plc CA 1985, s 142
states that if net assets become half or less of its called-up share capital it
must within 28 days of such becoming known to a director convene an
EGM for not later than 56 days thereafter (of it becoming known) to consider what steps should be taken to deal with this problem.

19.7.3 Acquisition of own shares

Traditionally even if there was an express provision in the memorandum it
has been held that a company cannot purchase its own shares since this
results in a reduction of share capital. This general rule has been eroded by
practical necessity over a number of years and in CAs 1980 and 1981 it was
formally codified. This is now incorporated in ss 143–181 of the 1985 Act.

The general rule states that a company 'shall not acquire its own shares
whether by purchase, subscription or otherwise'. Violation of it renders
every officer and company liable to a fine and any purchase carried out is
void. There are five exceptions:

(a) where fully paid shares are acquired otherwise than for valuable consideration, eg where the shares were given to the company and held by
a nominee for it (as was the case in *Re Castiglione's Will Trusts, Hunter
v MacKenzie* [1958] Ch 549);
(b) the redemption or purchase of shares in accordance with CA 1985, ss
159–181 (see below);
(c) the acquisition of shares on a formal reduction of capital that has been
confirmed by the court (see 19.7.2 above);
(d) the purchase of shares as a result of an order of court;
(e) where shares have been forfeited due to non-payment.

19.7.4 Redeemable shares

Companies have been allowed to issue redeemable shares since CA 1929.
Prior to CA 1981 only preference shares could be issued as redeemable but
under CA 1985, s 159 a company (if authorised by its articles) can issue
shares of any class which can be redeemable or liable to be redeemed
whether at the option of the company or of the shareholders. A company

cannot just issue redeemable shares, but must also issue shares which are not redeemable. It also may not redeem shares until they are have been fully paid by the holders of the redeemable shares.

Normally redeemable shares can only be redeemed out of distributable profits or out of the proceeds of a fresh issue of shares made for that particular purpose. If any premium is payable this should also be made out of distributable profits.

Where shares are redeemed out of profits the amount by which the issued share capital is diminished should be transferred to a reserve called the 'capital redemption reserve' (or the proportion if partly paid out of proceeds).

19.7.5 Purchase of own shares

Up to CA 1981 a company had to issue preference shares to enable it to purchase its own shares (or required a court order).

A listed company cannot make a purchase of its own shares unless under CA 1985, s 166 it has first been authorised by the passing of an ordinary resolution. The resolution when passed needs to be filed at Companies House within 15 days. The authorisation may be a general one or limited to a class of shares and may if the company wishes be conditional. It must however state the maximum number of shares to be acquired and the maximum and minimum prices and give a date on which it expires (not later than 18 months after passing the resolution). There are various other safeguards set out in CA 1985, ss 164–169.

The situation with private companies is more straightforward and is now contained in CA 1985, ss 171–177. If the company is authorised by articles it can make a payment for the redemption or purchase of shares otherwise than out of distributable profits or the proceeds of a fresh issue of shares. It must not though exceed 'the permissible capital payment' – the amount by which available profits exceed the proceeds of any fresh issue made for the purposes of redemption. If the principal capital payment is less than the nominal value of shares redeemed or purchased the amount of the difference must be transferred to a capital redemption reserve, but if more the amount of issued share capital and undistributable reserves can be reduced by a sum not exceeding the extent of such excess.

'Available profits' is defined in CA 1985 as being those that are available for distribution under the dividend rules (see 19.8 below) and must be calculated in accordance with the usual accounting procedures used by the company's auditors. The following steps must be carried out:

(1) The directors need to make a statutory declaration in the prescribed form (Company Form 173). This needs to contain the following information:
    (a) amount of permissible capital payment;
    (b) confirmation that the directors have enquired into the affairs and prospects of the company;

    (c) it is their opinion that 'immediately following payment there will be no grounds on which the company could be found unable to pay its debt and . . . for the year following the company will be able to continue to carry on business as a going concern and to pay its debts as they fall due throughout that year'.

(2) The declaration needs to have attached to it a report by the company's auditors confirming they have enquired into the company's business and the amount stated as permissible capital payment has been properly ascertained and they are not aware of anything in the directors' statement which is 'unreasonable'.

(3) The capital payment needs to be authorised by special resolution (or one in writing) and should be passed on all within the week immediately following the making of a statutory declaration and the payment of capital must be made no earlier than five nor more than seven weeks after the date of such resolution.

There are also similar statutory protections required for public companies, eg:

(a) a member of the company whose shares are to be redeemed or bought cannot vote (if he does the resolution will be ineffective if it would not have passed without his vote);

(b) the statutory declaration and auditor's report must be available for inspection by members at the meeting;

(c) within a week of a resolution a notice must be published in the *Gazette* and also an 'appropriate national newspaper' (unless it has notified all creditors in writing); the notice must give full details of a resolution and state the creditors may within five weeks of the resolution apply to court under CA 1985, s 176 for an order prohibiting payment;

(d) on or prior to the notice's publication, the company needs to send to the Registrar the completed Form 173 and also the auditor's report (copies must also be available at the company's registered office for inspection by any member or creditor).

A member (who has not consented or voted for the resolution) and creditor may not later than five weeks after the passing of the resolution apply under s 176 to the court for cancellation. The court has wide powers under s 177 to cancel, confirm or make such an order as it thinks fit for the purchase of dissenting members' shares.

19.7.6 Financial assistance by company for purchase of own shares

Section 54 of CA 1948 became notoriously difficult to operate and the 1981 Act sought to clarify the position. The new provisions are found in CA 1985, ss 151–158. The general rule is that where a person is acquiring or proposing to acquire shares in a company it is unlawful for a company or any of its subsidiaries to give 'financial assistance directly or indirectly for the purpose of that acquisition before or at the same time as the acquisition takes place'. Financial assistance can also take the form of acquiring a liability which directly or indirectly gives financial assistance (eg gifts, loans, guarantees, waivers, indemnities etc). The definition of 'financial assistance' is very broadly worded and even if a form of financial assistance does not expressly fall within the provision it may nevertheless be unlawful if a company has no net assets or the consequence of assistance is to reduce its net assets. This section gives a particularly wide definition to the word 'liability' and seems to suggest that before a company can give any financial assistance to any person (whether or not a potential 'purchaser') it must assess that person's overall financial position before and after the acquisition and if afterwards it has deteriorated the company must refrain from any form of financial assistance which is not covered by one of the exceptions.

19.7.7 Exceptions

Section 153 sets out a number of exceptions and these include:

(a) bonus shares;
(b) lending money in the ordinary course of business;
(c) contributions to employee share schemes (public companies have an additional net asset test in this case); and
(d) lawful declaration of a dividend.

A complication exists under s 153 since it does not prohibit a company from giving financial assistance if:

(a) the company's principal purpose in giving that assistance is not for the purpose of acquisition of shares of a company or its holding company but is an incidental part of some larger purpose of a company; and
(b) the assistance is given in good faith in the company's interests.

The House of Lords has considered this wording in the important case of *Brady v Brady* [1989] AC 755 which has narrowly interpreted this wording. Advice should always be sought if seeking to fall within this exception.

Special relaxation provisions apply to private companies under CA 1985, ss 155–158. The underlying principle is that financial assistance can only be given if a company has net assets which are not thereby reduced or to the extent they are reduced assistance is provided out of distributable profits (s 155). The relaxation can only be used by genuine independent private companies (ie those not members of a group where there is a plc). The procedure is as follows.

The relevant company giving financial assistance needs to make a statutory declaration similar in terms to the one referred to at 19.7.5 above for the purchase of shares. This declaration must identify to whom the assistance is to be given and must confirm in their opinion that immediately following such assistance there are no grounds on which a company can be found unable to pay its debt and that this will apply during the preceding 12-month period or if wound up in this period it could pay its debts in full.

The declaration must have attached to it an auditors' report stating in effect that they are not aware of anything unreasonable in the circumstances in the directors' opinion.

A special (or written) resolution needs to be passed by the company giving assistance (and in the case of a subsidiary giving financial assistance to a holding company the holding company also needs to pass a special resolution). The special resolutions must be passed on or within a week of the day on which the directors make the statutory declarations and are not effective unless the declaration and auditors' reports are available for inspection by the members at the meeting.

A copy of a statutory declaration (on Company Form G155(6)(a)) and the auditors' report needs to be delivered to the Registrar within 15 days of the declaration and must be accompanied by copies of a special resolution.

Financial assistance must not be given before the expiration of four weeks beginning the date upon which the resolution was passed (or if more than one on the date of the last such resolution). This enables any member not consenting or voting in favour of the resolution to apply to court to cancel the resolution under s 157. If an application is made financial assistance must not be given until the court has given a ruling.

The financial assistance provided for must be given not later than eight weeks from the date of statutory declaration. If all members voted in favour of the resolution the assistance may be given immediately after the delivery to the Registrar of the statutory declaration and report, but must not be given after eight weeks from that date.

Application to court under s 157 needs to be made by holders of not less than 10% of the company's issued share capital or if a company has no share capital by 10% of the members. The court has similar rights as set out above in connection with purchase of such shares for determining the position.

19.8 DIVIDENDS

An underlying principle of company law is that the company subscribed money capital (ie issued share capital plus share premium) must be maintained. Dividends should not be paid out except from accumulated realised profits. Sections 263–281 of CA 1985 set out the position. A distribution covers any payment of the company's assets to members which is not a bonus share, a redemption or purchase of the company's own shares, an authorised reduction of share capital, or a distribution and winding-up. Distributions can only be made out of profits made available for that purpose.

The company's profits available for distribution can be summarised as being the accumulated realised profits (not already distributed or capitalised) less its accumulated realised losses not written off under the capital reduction provisions. This realised profits test applies to all companies. In addition a plc is subject to a net assets test. Thus even if it has realised profit it can only make a distribution if its net assets are less than the aggregate of its called-up share capital and its undistributable reserves and also the proposed distribution will not reduce the amount of the assets to less than that aggregate.

Net assets for this purpose is defined as being the aggregate of its assets less the aggregate of its liabilities (uncalled share capital cannot be used as an asset for determination). Special rules regarding distribution apply to companies in various particular industries (eg investment companies and insurance companies).

A shareholder who receives a distribution he knows or has reasonable grounds to believe was paid in breach of the rules must repay any amount received by the company in addition to any other liability he may have. Further a director who is knowingly a party to such payments is jointly and severally liable to the company to replace the amounts of dividends so paid with interest (ratification to bind the company is not possible). The director would however be entitled to be indemnified by each shareholder who received dividends knowing they have been paid out of capital to the extent such dividends have been received.

The procedure for declaring dividends is relatively straightforward. The articles normally provide for it. Regulation 102 of Table A states that a company is made by ordinary resolution to declare dividends, but no dividends should exceed the amount recommended by directors. It is at the AGM that a final dividend is normally declared, but an interim dividend can be paid at any date between AGMs. Article 103 of Table A states that directors may pay interim dividends if it appears to them to be justified by the profits of the company available for distribution, but must act in good faith and not incur any liability to the holders of shares conferring preferred rights etc.

The director of a company needs to carefully consider a company's assets before recommending a dividend. A declaration of dividend creates a contract to pay a debt which would have become statute barred after six years from the date of declaration. Whether a company is able to forfeit the amount held after this period depends on its articles; for example, reg 108 of Table A states that it must be unclaimed for 12 years before a dividend can be forfeited.

The articles usually also provide that dividends payable in cash can be sent by cheque through the post to a shareholder's registered address (or such other address as the shareholder may notify the company).

19.9 ULTRA VIRES

This used to be an area of some complication, but since the passing of CA 1989 the position has been simplified. The words 'ultra vires' in relation to company law are largely used to explain a situation which arises when a company's officers or employees act beyond their legal power. There are two principal elements of this rule:

(a) where the directors, officers or employees act outside their power, eg purport to bind the company when they have no authority so to do; and
(b) when the company acts beyond its objects, ie does an act to which the objects clause of its memorandum of association does not extend.

The effect of the new provisions in CA 1985 (ss 35A and 35B, as inserted by CA 1989, s 108(1)) is that an innocent third party is entitled to rely upon the board of directors or a person authorised by the board and that the transaction agreed and enforceable in the normal way binds the company.

The difficulty that remains is that where a company, for example, is very small or a transaction is large a third party may have no dealings with the board and may instead be dealing with an executive of the company or a junior employee. In these circumstances the third party is unlikely to know whether the transaction has actually been authorised by the board. In this circumstance it is necessary to look at the laws of agency as interpreted by the celebrated legal case of *Royal British Bank v Turquand* (1856) 6 E&B 327. This case enunciated the rule that when a person conducts a company's affairs, in a manner which seems perfectly normal, the third parties dealing with them are not to be affected by any irregularities which may take place in the internal management of the company.

Section 285 of CA 1985 also states that the acts of a director or manager are valid irrespective of any defect which may be discovered afterwards in that director or manager's appointment or qualification.

It is unlikely that a person dealing with a company is deemed to have notice of who the true directors are, but if that third party is actually aware of the potential ultra vires problem he would no longer be said to be acting in good faith and therefore probably not be able to rely on either s 35A or 35B or the common law position. The new legislation does not though protect a third party dealing with the company through an unauthorised officer. In this circumstance the company is only bound if an unauthorised officer acts within his actual or apparent authority or the company ratifies what he has done.

Case law has recognised that where managerial powers have been delegated by the board to other officers their acts can be regarded as binding the company.

19.10 AUDITORS

Every company other than a dormant one needs to appoint an auditor. The appointment is done at each general meeting at which the accounts and reports are laid and the appointment must be from the conclusion of that meeting until conclusion of the next such meeting (this would not be the case where a private company has elected to dispense with the laying of accounts). It is to the members of the company that the auditors' report is addressed. Normally an auditor continues to be reappointed until he wishes to retire or the directors wish to appoint someone different.

For private companies which have elected to dispense with the laying of accounts, the appointment of auditors needs to be dealt with within 28 days after the date copies of the accounts are sent to members. If a private company has, by elective resolution, dispensed with the obligation to appoint auditors annually, the auditors are deemed to have been appointed for each succeeding financial year until a resolution is passed ending this appointment. Many small companies have been exempted from the requirement for an audit report. This though does not affect the statutory requirements to prepare file accounts.

A company is totally exempt from the need to have an audit if it is a small company with a turnover of £350,000 or less (£90,000 or less if it is a charity) and its balance sheet total is not more than £1.4m. Exemptions to audit are *not* available to public companies, banks or insurance companies or those which constitute authorised pension funds under the Financial Services Act 1986 (to be replaced from a date to be announced by the Financial Services and Markets Act 2000). Companies also qualify as an exception from audit.

An auditor has a statutory right of access at all times to the company's books, accounts and vouchers and can require from the company's officers such explanation as he thinks necessary for the performance of his duties as auditor. In addition he is entitled to receive all notices and other communications concerning general meetings and to be heard with respect to business which concerns him.

A company can by ordinary resolution remove an auditor from office irrespective of any agreement it may have with him but such a resolution requires special notice to be given to the company of a resolution and copies have to be given to the auditor and to the person to be appointed in his place. The auditor is also entitled to make written representation and may have rights to compensation.

Under CA 1985, s 392 an auditor may resign at any stage by depositing a notice in writing to the effect at the company's registered office. This must be accompanied by a statement providing the reasons why he wishes to resign and should contain any details he feels should be brought before the members or creditors. The company must then within 14 days send copies of it to any person who is entitled to be sent copies of the accounts. The company has the right if it wishes to apply to court, but must in these circumstances notify the auditor. Where no court application is made the auditor must send a copy of the statement to the Registrar within 21 days.

19.10.1 Auditor's negligence

It is primarily the directors who are responsible for the published accounts but an auditor can be shown to be negligent in certifying the accuracy. Auditors are required to display care and skill expected from such professionals and this has led in recent years to numerous well publicised cases. The House of Lords in *Caparo Industries plc v Dickman* [1990] 2 AC 605 established:

(a) the general responsibility for preparation of accounts which should give a true and fair view of the company's position rests on the directors' shoulders;

(b) the auditors provide independent reports to members on the proper preparation of the balance sheet and profit and loss account and as to whether these documents give a true and fair view (ie their role is investigative rather than creative);

(c) auditors have a duty to obtain information from directors and officers and failure to so obtain could amount to negligence.

This chapter largely concerns private companies, but a large number of provisions apply to public companies. In the case of a public company which is also listed on the London Stock Market (whether fully listed or admitted to the AIM), such companies need to comply with the rule books and codes of the relevant market and also the guidelines which have been produced by recommendations made by the Cadbury, Greenbury and Hampel reports. Plcs are also expected to respect guidelines produced from time to time by the Association of British Insurers (ABI) and the National Association of Pension Funds (NAPF).

The rules produced by The Stock Market or under the auspices of one of the regulating authorities have quasi statutory force by most plcs and also by the largest private companies, since they are seen as being recommendations of good husbandry and reassure investors, shareholders and creditors. The various bodies concerned can provide full details of their recommendations and it is really outside the scope of this book to make any consideration of their requirements. The author, though, refers readers to his *Alternative Investment Market Handbook*, the second edition of which is to be published by Jordans in 2000, which has a more detailed commentary.

19.11 SELECTION OF ADMINISTRATIVE DOCUMENTS TO BE FILED AT COMPANIES HOUSE

19.11.1 Formation

(1) Copy of memorandum and articles of association
(2) Form 10 – Statement of first directors and secretary and intended situation of registered office.
(3) Form 12 – Statutory declaration of compliance with requirements on application for registration of a company (to be completed by the solicitors engaged in the company formation).

19.11.2 Capital

(1) Form 88(2) – Return of allotment of shares for cash. To be filed within one month of making the allotment.
(2) Form 88(3) – Return of allotment of shares for non-cash consideration. To be filed within one month of making the allotment.
(3) Form G122 – notice of consolidation, division, subdivision, redemption, etc of share capital.
(4) Form 123 – Increase of share capital. Filed within 15 days after passing resolution. Resolution should also be filed.
(5) Reduction of share capital forms:
    (a) Form 155(6)A and B – Declaration in cases of financial assistance.
    (b) Form 157 – Application to court for cancellation.
    (c) Form 169 – Return to be made by a company purchasing its own shares.

19.11.3 Directors or secretary

(1) Form 288 – Change of directors or secretary. Notification to be given within 14 days. (Notification of interests and changes of interest in shares or debentures is to be made by the director to the company within five working days of the event.)
(2) Form 288a – Appointment of a director or secretary.
(3) Form 288b – Resignation of a director or secretary.
(4) Form 288c – Change in particulars of a director or secretary.

19.11.4 Notice of accounting reference date

(1) Form G224 – Names an accounting reference date to which statutory accounts are to be prepared. A company has nine months from the date of incorporation to file such a form.
(2) Form G225(2) – New account reference date given after the end of an accounting reference period by a parent or subsidiary undertaking or by a company subject to an administration order.

19.11.5 **Annual return**

Every company is required to deliver to the Registrar of Companies successive annual returns, each of which is made up to a date which is not later than the company's 'return date', that is:

(a) the anniversary of the company's incorporation; *or*
(b) if the last return lodged by the company was made up to a different date, the anniversary of that date.

The annual return must be lodged within 28 days after the date to which it is made up.

19.11.6 **Registered office**

Form 287 – a company can change its registered office by filing this form.

19.11.7 **Charges, mortgages and debentures**

(1) Form 395 – notification of particulars or charges created by a company. Filed within 21 days after the date of their creation and the relative instrument creating the charge must also be produced.
(2) Form 397 – particulars for the registration of a charge to secure a series of debentures.
(3) Form 400 – particulars of a mortgage or charge subject to which property has been acquired.
(4) Form 403a – declaration of satisfaction when a charge has been wholly or partially redeemed.
(5) Form 403b – declaration of satisfaction where the declaration relates to release of part of property or undertaking from the charge; or where the part of the property or undertaking charged no longer forms part of the company's property or undertaking.

19.11.8 **Resolutions**

Copies of the following types of resolution must be filed within 15 days of their being passed:

(1) Special/Extraordinary.
(2) Elective.
(3) Ordinary:
 (a) authorising increase of capital;
 (b) giving, varying, revoking or renewing an authority to allot;
 (c) shares under s 80;
 (d) revoking an elective resolution.
(4) Resolution for winding up voluntarily under the Insolvency Act 1986, s 84(3).

20

HOW COMPANIES ARE TAXED

DAVID BERTRAM, CLAYFIELD PROFESSIONAL GUIDANCE LTD

20.1 LIABILITY FOR CORPORATION TAX AND HOW 'PROFITS' ARE DEFINED

20.1.1 Liability for corporation tax
(TA 1988, ss 11 and 12 ; FA 1988, s 66)

Corporation tax is levied on the chargeable profits (see 20.1.2 below) of companies which are resident in the UK for tax purposes. A company is generally defined as meaning any body corporate or unincorporated association, but does not include a partnership, a local authority or a local authority association.

Corporation tax also extends to non-resident companies carrying on a trade in the UK through a branch or agency. Such companies are chargeable to tax on any income attributable to the branch or agency and on any capital gains arising on the disposal of assets used in the UK for the purposes of the branch or agency.

A company which was incorporated in the UK is regarded as resident there regardless of where the directors exercise their management and control. However, some of the double taxation conventions negotiated with other countries override this in practice and treat a dual resident company as if it were not resident in the UK. A company which was incorporated overseas may still be regarded as UK-resident on the basis that its central management and control is exercised in this country. Questions relating to the residence status of a foreign incorporated company are usually determined by reference to the guidelines set out in SP1/90.

20.1.2 Computation of profits
(TA 1988, s 6)

A company's profits are made up of its income and chargeable gains. The computation of chargeable profits can be a very complex process because of the lengthy and detailed tax legislation and the extensive case-law. There are also a multitude of Revenue statements of practice, press releases and extra-statutory concessions which may need to be borne in mind when calculating profits upon which corporation tax is payable.

The general principles for computing taxable profits closely follow the rules for income tax and each different type of income is charged under the relevant schedule.

20.1.3 Capital allowances
(CAA 1990, s 144)

Although depreciation is not regarded as an allowable expense for tax purposes, tax relief is given for expenditure on qualifying capital assets by means of capital allowances. Capital allowances in respect of a trade carried on by a company are regarded as trading expenses for the accounting period in which they arise. They are therefore taken into account in arriving at the chargeable profits or allowable loss for the accounting period.

Capital allowances on certain leasing activities are primarily deductible from the income arising from that source.

20.1.4 Interest and other annual payments
(TA 1988, s 338)

A company is liable to account to the Revenue for income tax on certain annual payments which it makes. Such annual payments (termed 'charges on income') are deductible from a company's profits in arriving at the amount assessable to corporation tax. The basic principle is that these charges on income are offset against the payer's total profits, not merely against a particular source of income with which the payment is connected. A payment counts as a charge on income only if the following conditions are met:

(1) It has been made out of the company's profits brought into charge to corporation tax.
(2) It is made under a liability incurred for a 'valuable and sufficient consideration' (or the payment is a covenanted donation to charity).
(3) The payment must not be one charged to capital or one not ultimately borne by the company.
(4) It must not be in the nature of a dividend or distribution made by the company.

Payments of interest are not treated as charges on income, but are dealt with under the FA 1996 loan relationship regime. Payment must actually be made in the accounting period for it to count as a charge for that period. Where there is a requirement to deduct and account for income tax on the payment, no deduction is allowed until this requirement is satisfied.

Where the total profits for an accounting period are insufficient to absorb charges on income, excess charges in respect of payments made wholly and exclusively for the purposes of the company's trade may be carried forward and utilised against the company's future trading income. Non-trade charges may not be carried forward in this manner and no further relief is available.

20.2 ACCOUNTING PERIODS, RATES AND PAYMENT OF TAX

20.2.1 Accounting periods for tax purposes
(TA 1988, s 12)

Companies pay corporation tax by reference to their accounting periods and the income included is assessed on an actual or accruals basis. Accounting periods may straddle two financial years (which for corporation tax purposes run from 1 April to 31 March). If this is the case, the chargeable profits are apportioned on a time basis for the purposes of determining the rate of tax to apply to the overall profit. An accounting period begins for corporation tax purposes:

(1) when the company comes within the charge to corporation tax either by becoming resident in the UK or acquiring its first source of income; or
(2) when the company's previous accounting period ends without the company ceasing to be within the charge to corporation tax.

An accounting period normally runs on for a maximum of 12 months from its commencement. In some instances, the accounts year end may vary slightly for commercial reasons (for example where accounts are made up to the last Friday of a specified month). Provided the variation is not more than four days from the 'mean' date it is normally acceptable to treat each period of account as if it were a 12-month accounting period ending on the mean date.

An accounting period runs for a period of less than 12 months if the company's own accounting date falls within the 12 months; it also ends if the company:

(a) ceases to trade;
(b) begins or ceases to be resident in the UK; or
(c) ceases to be within the charge to corporation tax altogether.

Example of how accounting period is ascertained

A Ltd is formed on 1 January 2000. It remains completely dormant until 1 February 2000 when it starts to trade. The first set of accounts are made up for a period of 15 months ending on 31 March 2001.

In strictness, there is a first accounting period of one month from 1 January to 31 January 2000. There is then a 12-month accounting period for the year ending on 31 January 2001. There is then a two-month period from 1 February to 31 March 2001 when the company makes up its accounts.

20.2.2 How profits are apportioned

Where accounts are made up for a period of more than 12 months, the income is usually apportioned on a time basis to the relevant accounting period. Thus, in the above example, if A Ltd had profits of £140,000 in its accounts for the 15 months ending on 31 March 2001, these would normally be apportioned as follows:

Accounting period ended 31 January 2000	Nil
12 months ended 31 January 2001	£120,000
Period 1 February–31 March 2001	£20,000

However, where a more appropriate basis of apportionment is available, the inspector may apply that basis instead (*Marshall Hus & Partners Ltd v Bolton* [1981] STC 18).

20.2.3 The corporation tax rates
(TA 1988, s 6)

The rate of corporation tax is fixed for each financial year which, for these purposes, starts on 1 April. The rate of tax for the financial year 2000 (ie, 1 April 2000 to 31 March 2001) is 30% and the following table shows the full corporation tax rate applicable for previous financial years.

Financial year	Rate (%)	Financial year	Rate (%)
1995	33	1998	31
1996	33	1999	30
1997	31	2000	30

20.2.4 Starting rate

From April 2000, a new starting rate of corporation tax of 10% applies for profits of up to £10,000. There is marginal rate relief at ¼₀th for profits from £10,001 to £50,000, giving an effective marginal rate of 22.5%.

20.2.5 Small companies rates and associated companies
(TA 1988, s 13)

A reduced rate of corporation tax (known as the 'small companies rate') applies to a company's profits where those profits do not exceed a maximum level. The current rate of tax is 20% and the current profit level below which the small companies rate applies is £300,000. The following table shows the small companies rate and maximum profit level for earlier financial years:

Financial year	Rate (%)	Max profit level (£)
1995	25	300,000
1996	24	300,000
1997	21	300,000
1998	21	300,000
1999	20	300,000
2000	20	300,000

Where profits exceed the maximum profit limit for small companies rate purposes, an element of marginal relief is given for profits between £300,000 and £1,500,000. This relief operates on a tapered basis at $\frac{1}{40}$th by charging the profits to the full corporation tax rate but gives an element of credit for the reduced corporation tax rate which would have been applicable to the initial tranche of profit.

Example of marginal small companies rate

B Ltd has profits for its year ended 31 March 2001 of £350,000. Its corporation tax liability is arrived at as follows:

	£
Corporation tax at 30% on £350,000	105,000
Less $\frac{1}{40}$ × upper limit (£1,500,000 – 350,000)	28,750
	76,250

If B Ltd's profits were £450,000, the computation would be:

Corporation tax at 30% on £450,000	135,000
Less $\frac{1}{40}$ of (£1,500,000 – 450,000)	26,250
	108,750

Thus the additional tax due to B Ltd having an extra £100,000 profits is £32,500 (32.5%).

20.2.6 Restriction where there is associated company

The profit limits applicable to small companies relief are restricted, based upon the existence of any 'associated' companies which the company has during the accounting period concerned. A company is an associated company of another if they are under common control or one has control of the other. 'Control' for this purpose is defined as the ability to exercise direct or indirect control over the company's affairs and in particular:

(a) the possession or entitlement to acquire more than 50% of the share capital or voting rights in the company;

(b) entitlement to receive the greater part of income distributed among the shareholders;
(c) entitlement to receive the greater part of the company's assets in the event of a winding-up.

For example, if a company has one associated company, the small companies profit limits are divided by two, ie one plus the number of associated companies. However, an associated company which has not carried on any trade or business at any time during the accounting period concerned is disregarded. Where a company's accounting period straddles more than one financial year and the marginal relief limits for each financial year differ, the 12-month period is treated as separate accounting periods for the purpose of calculating marginal relief.

20.2.7 Payment of tax
(TA 1988, s 10)

The basic rule is that corporation tax is automatically due and payable nine months and one day after the end of an accounting period. However, 'large companies' must pay corporation tax by instalments. A large company is one the taxable profits of which are in excess of £1.5m pa, divided by one plus the number of active associated companies (if any) that it has. A company that would otherwise be classified (by reference to taxable profits) as a large company is not so treated if its tax liability for the accounting period concerned does not exceed £10,000 (or £5,000 for accounting periods ending prior to 1 July 2000). Furthermore, a company is not classified as a large company if it was not a large company in the 12 months preceding the accounting period in question, and its profits for that accounting period do not exceed £10m, divided by one plus the number of active associated companies (if any) that it had at the end of the preceding accounting period. These limits are reduced pro rata for accounting periods of less than 12 months.

Payment is required in four instalments. The first payment must be made 14 days after the first six months of the accounting period in question and are due in four quarterly instalments. Quarterly instalments for a company with an accounting period ended on 31 March 2001 would fall due on 14 October 2000, 14 January 2001, 14 April 2001 and 14 July 2001.

There are transitional rules whereby a company pays 60% of its liability due by instalments in year one, with the balance due nine months after the end of the accounting period. This increases to 72% in year two, 88% in year three and 100% in year four. Interest is charged on any unpaid tax and is an allowable deduction. Interest is paid to the company on overpayments. This interest is taxable.

20.3 COMPANIES' CAPITAL GAINS

20.3.1 Computation of gains

Capital gains made by companies are included in their chargeable profits and are subject to corporation tax. Capital gains tax (CGT) therefore does not apply to companies, although chargeable gains and losses are computed in accordance with the detailed provisions of CGT (see Chapter 5). The main differences between CGT and corporation tax on chargeable gains for companies are, first, that provisions which clearly apply only to individuals (eg annual exemption) have no application as far as companies are concerned, and secondly, that computations of chargeable gains are prepared on an accounting period basis rather than by income tax years of assessment. The total chargeable gains for an accounting period less a deduction for allowable losses are brought into charge to corporation tax in the same way as income.

Capital losses can only be offset against chargeable gains; they cannot be offset against trading or other income.

20.3.2 Roll-over relief
(TCGA 1992, ss 152–158 and 175)

Roll-over relief is available where the proceeds on the disposal of a qualifying asset used in the company's trade are reinvested in further qualifying assets (see 6.3). It provides a deferral of the corporation tax which would otherwise be payable on the chargeable gain. Relief is normally dependent upon the proceeds being fully reinvested in qualifying assets within a period of 12 months before and three years after the date of disposal.

Where the proceeds are only partly reinvested, a proportion of the gain is deferred or 'rolled over' and the balance (equivalent to the amount of proceeds not reinvested) is left in charge. The part of the gain which is deferred or 'rolled over' is deducted from the base cost of the new asset for capital gains purposes. This operates to increase the potential gain on the eventual sale of the new asset acquired, hence the term 'roll-over relief'.

Qualifying assets for this purpose are freehold and leasehold land and buildings, goodwill, ships, aircraft and hovercraft, fixed plant and machinery, satellite space stations and spacecraft, and certain agricultural quotas. Expenditure on an asset acquired from a group company (see 20.7) does not rank as qualifying expenditure for roll-over relief.

20.4 INTEREST AND OTHER CHARGES

20.4.1 Loan relationships
(FA 1996, ss 80–84)

The 'loan relationships' regime covers all loans made to a company (eg bank overdrafts, long-term finance etc) and all loans made by a company (eg holdings of gilt-edged securities and corporate bonds). Thus all interest paid or received by a company is brought into account on an accruals basis (so that account is taken of amounts paid in arrears and in advance – this is the normal basis of accounting for these items). Any profits or losses made on loan relationships are treated as income or expenditure on an accruals basis. Certain companies who deal in gilt-edged securities and bonds prepare their accounts on a 'mark to market' basis, and their profit or loss takes account of the market value of securities and bonds held at the beginning and at the end of the accounting period.

Profits or gains made by a company from loan relationships are taxable as trading income, to the extent that the company is a party to the loan relationships in the course of activities which are an integral part of its trade. Losses or deficits are treated as allowable deductions in arriving at the overall profit or loss of the trade.

In other cases where the loan relationship is for non-trade purposes a surplus is brought into tax under Schedule D Case III. If a deficit is suffered on loan relationships, loss relief can be claimed by:

(1) set-off against profits of the same period;
(2) group relief;
(3) carry-back against loan relationship profits of the preceding accounting period;
(4) carry-forward against all profits, other than trading profits of the next period;
(5) carry-forward against future profits from non-trading relationships.

20.4.2 Annual charges
(TA 1988, ss 338–339)

A company may make annual payments in respect of annuities, royalties, covenanted payments etc, which are available for offset as charges on income against the company's chargeable profits on a paid basis.

20.4.3 Income tax deduction at source

Companies must deduct and account to the Revenue for income tax on payments of charges on income. A return Form CT61 is required to be submitted on a quarterly basis detailing payments made and computing the income tax payable to the Revenue. In arriving at the income tax liability due, any income tax suffered on income received under deduction of tax may be offset. Where the income tax suffered on income received exceeds the income tax payable on annual charges, the surplus may be carried forward to the next quarterly return. If at the end of the accounting period it has not proved possible to obtain credit against income tax payable, credit may be obtained against the corporation tax liability for the accounting period (and if there is no or insufficient corporation tax liability to offset any income tax credit, a repayment may be obtained from the Revenue).

20.4.4 Connected parties
(FA 1996, s 87)

Special rules apply where the other party to a loan relationship is a connected company. For this purpose, companies are connected if they are under the same control, or one controls the other, either in the accounting period concerned or in the two preceding years. A person controls a company by owning the greater part of the shares, voting rights or other capital giving entitlement to more than one-half of the assets in a winding-up.

These rules also apply if the other party, or its 'associate', is or was at any time in the two preceding years a 'participator' in the accounting period. In general, participators are shareholders, and associates are relatives, partners or trustees of settlements where a relative or the participator is or was the settlor.

If two parties are connected, then interest is only allowable on an accruals basis when paid to a connected party where the recipient is liable to UK corporation tax on the full amount of interest received, or the interest is paid within 12 months after the end of the accounting period concerned. Therefore, if the recipient is an individual, trustee, non-resident company or exempt body such as a charity, the interest must be paid by the anniversary of the accounting period if a deduction is to be obtained.

No tax relief is available for any bad debts on connected party loan relationships, and conversely no liability to tax arises when a debt is waived.

20.5 TAXATION OF COMPANY DISTRIBUTIONS
(TA 1988, ss 238–241)

Company distributions are defined as any dividends, and any other distribution out of the company's assets, paid by a company in respect of shares in the company. The main exception to this is that any repayment of share capital is not normally regarded as a distribution of assets.

The amount of the tax credit accompanying any dividend or other distribution from a UK company made after 5 April 1999 is 10% of the aggregate of the distribution and the tax credit.

For tax years 1999–2000 onwards there is no further tax to pay for share-holders liable at the lower or basic rate, and no increase in charge for individuals liable at the higher rate. The overall effect of this is that the double taxation effect, by charging corporation tax, as well as income tax, is mitigated to the same extent as it was prior to 6 April 1999.

The system prior to 6 April 1999 went further than simply mitigating any double charge to tax. If a person was exempt from tax, or if the tax credits exceeded their tax liability, the tax credit was paid over to them. The payment of tax credits to certain shareholders meant that profits paid out by a company could actually face a substantially lower effective tax charge than profits which were retained by the company and reinvested.

The first stage in the correction of this distortion removed the entitlement to payment for pension providers and other UK companies with effect from 2 July 1997. The second stage of the change extended the restrictions on payment and set-off of tax credits to nearly all shareholders with effect from 6 April 1999.

There is one class of shareholders who still obtain payment of tax cred-its. Under the terms of some of the UK's double taxation agreements with other countries, specific provision is made, within the agreements, that tax credits can be paid to shareholders resident in that other country. These agreements have effect as long as there is any tax credit made available to UK-resident shareholders, whether that credit is payable or not. The double taxation agreements normally only pay a proportion of the tax credit, so that the effect of the reduction of the rate of tax credit is that the amount of tax credit paid will be very small.

The rates of income tax charged on dividends and similar income are, from 1999–2000, 10%, while the rate charged on those who are liable at the higher rate is 32.5%.

'Schedule F ordinary rate' applies to certain income of dividends and other distributions of UK companies, and equivalent foreign income. Hitherto savings income has been the top slice of income for the purposes of computing the charge to tax. Under the new rules Schedule F and equiv-alent foreign income is treated as the top slice above other savings income. There is also a 'Schedule F upper rate' that would otherwise be chargeable at the income tax higher rate. The Schedule F upper rate is set at 32.5%.

Under the new rules, in 1999–2000 on a dividend of £80 there is a tax credit of £8.89. Taxpayers who are not liable at the higher rate are charged to tax at the new rate of 10%. So the tax due is £8.89 (ie the total of the div-idend and associated tax credit of £88.89 at 10%). The liability is matched exactly by the tax credit, leaving no tax to pay. For a higher rate taxpayer receiving a dividend of £80 in 1999–2000 the tax due is £28.89 (ie the total of the dividend and tax credit of £88.89 at the new upper rate of 32.5%). The tax credit of £8.89 can be set against the tax liability, leaving the higher rate taxpayer with £20 to pay.

Prior to 6 April 1999, UK recipients of distributions were entitled to a tax credit. This aggregate amount was described as a 'franked payment' and, as far as individuals were concerned, represented the gross equivalent of the dividend received. This amount was taxable income, but the shareholder could set the tax credit against his tax liability on the 'grossed-up' amount.

Dividends received by a company from another UK company were termed 'franked investment income'. This income was regarded as having already borne tax and therefore did not form part of the chargeable profits of a company, and was not taxable.

Until 5 April 1999, there was a liability to account for advance corporation tax (ACT) where a company made a qualifying distribution to the shareholders. The ACT rate of was $^{20}/_{80}$ths of the dividend (ie 20% of the 'grossed-up amount). As its name suggests, ACT was treated as an advance payment of corporation tax and relief was obtained by deduction from the mainstream corporation tax liability payable on the profits of the accounting period in which the distribution was made.

The maximum relief against mainstream corporation tax for ACT paid on distributions made in an accounting period was equivalent to the ACT that would have been due on a franked payment equal to the profits chargeable to corporation tax for that accounting period. Where ACT exceeded this maximum amount, relief could be obtained in the following ways:

(1) carry-back to accounting periods beginning in the preceding six years;
(2) carry-forward and treated as ACT payable for the next accounting period, and so on, until utilised;
(3) surrender to a 51% subsidiary resident in the UK, and treated as ACT paid by that subsidiary.

Even after the abolition of ACT on 6 April 1999, surplus ACT remains available for relief. The company must calculate the 'shadow ACT' due on distributions after 6 April 1999.

Shadow ACT is not actually paid to the Revenue, but merely serves as a method to calculate the extent to which surplus ACT can be set against further corporation tax liabilities. The shadow ACT position has to be calculated for each accounting period ending after 5 April 1999 as if ACT were payable on the dividends, and the shadow ACT were then set against mainstream corporation tax as described above.

Shadow ACT is relieved in priority to actual surplus ACT brought forward from before 6 April 1999. If there is spare capacity (ie where the 'shadow ACT' is less than the maximum which can be offset against mainstream corporation tax), surplus ACT from prior to 6 April 1999 can be utilised against the available balance of profits. Any unrelieved 'shadow ACT' is carried forward and again must be utilised before any actual unrelieved ACT.

If a company is of the opinion that it will never be able to access actual unrelieved surplus ACT, it is not required to carry out 'shadow ACT' calculations.

20.6 LOSSES

20.6.1 Losses arising in the accounting period
(TA 1988, s 393)

When a company makes a trading loss for an accounting period, it may claim that the loss arising may be set off against other profits including chargeable gains arising in that accounting period. A tax loss is computed in the same manner as taxable profits, but is restricted to losses arising from trading activities carried out on a commercial basis and with a view to the realisation of profit.

20.6.2 Different ways of claiming relief for losses

There are a number of ways in which a trading loss may be relieved for tax purposes apart from being offset against other profits arising in the accounting period. The loss can be carried forward and offset against trading profits arising in succeeding accounting periods. Losses can be carried forward indefinitely in this manner for as long as the company carries on the trading activity which generated the loss. A loss may also be carried back and offset against total profits for the period of three years which ended immediately before the period in which the losses were incurred (provided the company was carrying on the relevant trade in the earlier periods). Partial relief claims are not allowed, and relief is obtained for later years before earlier years. Relief must be obtained for the loss against other profits of the accounting period before computing the balance of the loss available for carry-back.

Section 39 of F(No 2)A 1997 restricts the period against which a company may claim to carry back trading losses to set against the profits of an earlier period. The amended rules, which apply to trading losses incurred in accounting periods ending after 1 July 1997, allow a loss to be carried back only to an accounting period falling wholly or partly within 12 months of the start of the period in which the loss was incurred. For accounting periods ending before 2 July 1997 the carry-back period is three years. Losses made in periods which straddle that date are apportioned, with the new and previous rules being applied appropriately.

However, the 12-month period remains at three years in two circumstances: first, where the trading loss arose in the 12 months immediately before the company ceased to trade (a terminal loss); secondly, where the losses result from the special allowances given for the costs of decommissioning North Sea oil and gas installations.

Example

> A Ltd makes a trading loss of £1m in its accounting period ending on 31 August 2000. If A Ltd has other income of £150,000, it can choose between the following:
>
> (1) Carry forward the £1m loss to be set against future profits from the same trade – in this case A Ltd will have taxable profits of £150,000 for 2001.
> (2) Set part of the loss against profits of 2000 and carry forward the balance of £850,000 for eventual off-set against future profits from the same trade.
> (3) Set off part of the loss against 2000 profits and carry back the £850,000 against profits of the year 1999. Any balance can then be carried forward for off-set against future trading profits.

20.6.3 Capital losses

Capital losses, like capital gains, are computed in accordance with CGT rules, although the net capital gains are subject to corporation tax as part of the overall chargeable profits for the accounting period. Capital losses may be offset against capital gains in computing net chargeable gains, and capital losses which cannot be relieved in this way may be carried forward and offset against gains arising in subsequent accounting periods without limit. The carry forward of capital losses is not dependent upon whether the company continues to carry on its trading activity, and may be offset against gains arising on trade and non-trade assets. There are, however, restrictions on pre-entry losses where a company joins a group of companies.

Certain capital losses realised by an investment company (see 20.8.5) may be set against the company's profits (see 6.2.4 on this).

20.6.4 Surplus charges on income
(TA 1988, s 393(9))

Relief for charges on income is generally given as the last of all reliefs other than group relief (see 20.7). It is given against the total profits of the period in which the charges are paid. If profits are insufficient to absorb the charges, the amount of charges paid wholly and exclusively for the purposes of the company's trading activities may be carried forward to the next accounting period and treated as a trading loss to be offset against future trading income of the company. Non-trade charges on income may not be so carried forward and therefore relief is lost.

20.6.5 Charges paid in company's final accounting period
(TA 1988, s 388)

A trading loss may be carried back and offset against profits of the previous year. A company's charges are normally ignored for this. However, charges paid wholly and exclusively for the purposes of the trade are treated as trading expenses for the purpose of computing a loss for the accounting period in which the company's trade comes to an end, and these can be carried back.

20.6.6 Changes in company ownership
(TA 1988, s 768)

There are anti-avoidance provisions designed to ensure that trading losses carried forward can only be utilised against future trading income from the trading activity which generated the losses. Losses may not be carried forward if:

(a) within any period of three years there is a change in the company's ownership preceded or followed by a major change in the nature or conduct of the trade carried on by the company; or

(b) there is a change in the company's ownership at any time after the scale of activities in a trade carried on by the company has become small or negligible, and before any considerable revival in the trade.

A 'change in ownership' means a change in more than 50% of the ownership of the ordinary share capital in the company. A 'major change in the nature or conduct of a trade' includes a major change in the type of property dealt in, or the services or facilities provided in the trade, or in customers, outlets or markets. The Revenue has issued guidelines on some of the factors which will be relevant in determining whether there has been a major change in the nature or conduct of a trade or business (see SP10/91).

20.7 GROUPS OF COMPANIES

20.7.1 Group relationships
(TA 1988, s 402)

There are special rules which apply to groups of UK-resident companies. For corporation tax purposes, a group relationship exists between two companies if one company holds not less than 75% of the ordinary share capital of the other, or if both companies are 75% subsidiaries of a third company. Note that these rules are quite different from those used for VAT and stamp duty purposes (see 7.4.1 and 8.3.8).

20.7.2 Use of losses
(TA 1988, ss 402–413)

Where one company in a group makes a loss for tax purposes, it may 'surrender' that loss as group relief to another member of the group for offset against that company's taxable profits for its 'corresponding accounting period'. For this purpose, losses available for surrender include charges on income to the extent that they exceed profits chargeable to corporation tax. For group relief purposes, the requirement for a 75% shareholding relationship is extended so that the company owning the shares must also be beneficially entitled to 75% or more of the profits available for distribution to equity shareholders, and of assets available for distribution in a winding-up.

Where the accounting periods of the surrendering and claimant companies do not coincide (ie 'correspond'), the amount of loss to be surrendered is restricted on a time basis reflecting the length of the accounting periods common to both companies.

20.7.3 Transfers of assets between group companies
(TCGA 1992, ss 171–174)

Where a trading activity is transferred from one group company to another, relief is available under TA 1988, s 343 to ensure that the company transferring the trade does not suffer balancing charges on assets which have qualified for capital allowances. The successor company takes over the assets at their written-down value for capital allowances purposes relating to those assets. It is also possible to elect under CAA 1990, s 158 that properties may be transferred between group companies at tax written-down value for the purpose of industrial buildings allowances. Where s 343 applies, any unrelieved trading losses pass across to the successor company.

Section 343 can also apply where a trade is transferred to another company which is under common control, even though it is not a member of a group.

20.7.4 Payment and interest
(TA 1988, s 247)

The payment of interest by one company to another normally requires the payer to account for income tax deducted from the interest payment. Where the two companies concerned are members of the same group for tax purposes, relief is available from these procedures by lodging, with the Revenue, an election under TA 1988, s 247. This is effective for as long as both companies remain UK-resident and one company beneficially owns more than 50% of the ordinary share capital of the other.

20.7.5 Capital gains and transfers within a group
(TCGA 1992, s 171)

For the purposes of capital gains, chargeable assets may be transferred from one group company to another without tax consequences. Such transfers are treated as if made at a 'no gain/no loss' price and the recipient company takes over the capital gains base cost of the asset concerned from the transferor company.

Example of intra-group transfers

X Ltd has two wholly owned subsidiaries Y Ltd and Z Ltd. X Ltd transfers a property to Y Ltd for its current market value. No chargeable gain arises to X Ltd on this transfer. This is ignored when working out any capital gain or loss when Y Ltd eventually disposes of the property. Y Ltd is treated as if it had acquired the property for A's original cost plus indexation to date.

The same treatment would apply if Y Ltd transferred an asset to Z Ltd, its 'sister company'.

20.7.6 Company leaving a group after an intra-group transfer

If a company leaves a group, and it owns an asset transferred to it from another member of the group within the previous six years, a tax charge may arise under TA 1988, s 179 as if the asset had been sold for its market value at the time of the intra-group transfer.

Example of tax charge on company leaving a group

If X Ltd had transferred a property in 1996 to Y Ltd which was then worth £10m, and a gain of £2.5m would have arisen to X Ltd were it not for the relief under TCGA 1992, s 171 there would be a notional disposal for Y Ltd if it leaves the X Ltd group in 2001. Basically, Y Ltd would be regarded as having made a chargeable gain of £2.5m at the time that it leaves the group.

Note that the charge is based on the value at the time of the intra-group transfer and the £2.5m gain would still arise even if the property were worth £25m (or £7m) in 2001 when Y Ltd leaves the group.

20.7.7 Roll-over relief and groups of companies

For the purposes of roll-over relief (see 20.3.2), all the trades carried on by group companies are treated as a single trade and therefore it is possible to roll over a gain made on qualifying assets by one member of a group against qualifying expenditure incurred by another within the appropriate timescale. Roll-over relief is generally available only for trading companies within a group although, concessionally, relief is also available for a property holding company where the properties concerned are used for trading purposes by the other members of the group.

20.8 CLOSE AND INVESTMENT COMPANIES
(TA 1988, s 13A)

20.8.1 Close companies
(TA 1988, ss 414–415)

Companies which are under the control of five or fewer persons, or under the control of their directors, are known as 'close companies'. There are special provisions which are designed to ensure that such individuals cannot take undue advantage of corporation tax legislation by virtue of their positions of influence over a company's affairs.

A person controls a company if, in fact, he is able to exercise control directly or indirectly over its affairs by owning the greater part of its share capital, voting capital, or other capital giving entitlement to more than half the assets on a winding-up. Shareholders and certain loan creditors in a close company are known as participators. Rights held by certain 'associates' are attributed to participators in order to determine whether they have control.

An associate is defined for these purposes as any relative or partner of the individual concerned, or a trustee of a settlement where the individual (or a relative) was the settlor. A relative is defined as meaning spouse, parent, grandparent, child, grandchild, brother or sister. Where the individual is a beneficiary of a trust, the trustees may also be regarded as his associate.

20.8.2 Loans to participators
(TA 1988, s 419)

Where a close company makes a loan or advances any money to a participator, or to his associate, there is a liability to account for an amount of tax equal to the ACT liability which would arise if the loan or advance were treated as a dividend payment. The tax payable under s 419 is due within 14 days after the end of period for the purposes of interest on overdue tax. The company does not receive any relief even though the tax payable is calculated in the same way as ACT.

If the loan is repaid, the tax is repaid accordingly, but if the loan is wholly or partly written off or released, the borrower is treated as receiving, as part of his total income, an amount equal to the amount so written off, grossed up at the lower rate of income tax. While no basic or lower rate tax liability arises, there may be a further liability to higher rate tax.

20.8.3 Benefits to participators
(TA 1988, s 418)

Where benefits in kind are received by participators in a close company (or their associates) and the individual is not taxed under Schedule E, the cost to the company of providing the benefit can be treated as a distribution (see 20.5).

20.8.4 Directors' defalcations

Cash diverted by a director and misappropriated by him may have to be written off as irrecoverable. However, such losses are not allowable in computing the company's profits for tax purposes.

20.8.5 Investment companies
(TA 1988, ss 75 and 130)

An investment company is any company the business of which consists wholly or mainly of the making of investments and the principal part of its income arises as a result of that activity. The expenses of managing a UK-resident investment company are deductible in computing its total profits for corporation tax purposes. Where management expenses exceed the company's chargeable income and gains for an accounting period, the surplus may be carried forward and treated as management expenses incurred in the next succeeding accounting period, and may continue to be carried forward until relieved. Surplus management expenses may also be surrendered as group relief from one group company to another. Expenses brought forward from previous periods are not available for surrender as group relief. Unrelieved management expenses of an accounting period may also be set off against surplus franked investment income by a claim under TA 1988, s 242(2), for the purposes of claiming repayment of the tax credit attaching to it.

Relief for excess management expenses and charges brought forward is not available where there is a change in the ownership of the investment company and:

(a) after the change there is a significant increase in the amount of the capital of the investment company; or
(b) within the period of six years beginning three years before the change there is a major change in the nature of conduct of the business carried on by the company; or
(c) the change in the ownership occurs at any time after the scale of activities in the business carried on by an investment company has become small or negligible and before any considerable revival of the business.

20.8.6 Close investment-holding companies
(TA 1988, s 13A)

A close investment-holding company means a close company carrying on specific investment-holding activities. For this purpose, investment-holding activities do not include the carrying on of a trade on a commercial basis, property holding, or holding shares in companies carrying on either of these activities.

A close investment-holding company does not qualify for the small companies rate of corporation tax. In addition, the Revenue has power to restrict repayment of tax credit to shareholders receiving dividends from a close investment-holding company where it appears that arrangements have been made in relation to the distribution of profits, the main purpose of which is to enable the individual shareholder to obtain the tax repayment.

20.9 DOUBLE TAXATION RELIEF ON FOREIGN INCOME
(TA 1988, ss 788–806)

20.9.1 The main reliefs

A UK-resident company may claim a credit for foreign tax paid on income or capital gains arising from any overseas source. Credit is available against the corporation tax liability payable on the same income or gains. Relief may be due either under the provisions of a double taxation agreement between the UK and the overseas country concerned, or under the general rules for 'unilateral relief' as provided in TA 1988, s 790. Where credit is due under a double taxation agreement, the relevant agreement takes precedence over UK domestic legislation.

For most types of income and gains, the full amount is brought into charge for the purpose of computing the corporation tax liability on chargeable profits for the accounting period. Any overseas tax suffered is then offset by way of credit against the corporation tax liability. The amount of credit which is available is limited to the corporation tax liability on the source of income or gain which has suffered overseas tax. No relief is due for the excess foreign tax paid.

Where double tax relief would be lost (eg where no corporation tax liability arises for the accounting period), it is possible to obtain relief by treating the foreign tax as an expense in computing profits for the purposes of Schedule D Case I.

20.9.2 Double tax relief on dividends from foreign companies

In addition to relief for withholding or other foreign taxes suffered on payment of the dividend, relief may also be available for the foreign tax suffered on the profits out of which the dividend has been paid. This is known as 'underlying tax', for which relief is given automatically if the UK-recipient company controls, directly or indirectly, 10% or more of the voting share capital in the overseas company paying the dividend. The dividend taxable in the UK is grossed up at the rate of underlying tax applicable to the profits out of which the dividend has been paid. This, together with any withholding and other taxes suffered on payment of the dividend, can then be offset against the corporation tax liability arising on the grossed-up equivalent of the dividend received (subject to the restriction that underlying tax relief cannot exceed the corporation tax liability on the same income).

20.9.3 Unremittable income

Where an overseas source of income is taxable on an arising basis but it is not possible to remit the income due to government policy in the foreign country concerned, it is possible to make a claim to defer the corporation tax liability until such time as sufficient funds can be remitted to the UK to satisfy the liability. A claim under these circumstances may be made to the Revenue at any time within six years of the end of the accounting period in which the income arises.

20.10 CONTROLLED FOREIGN COMPANIES AND ANTI-AVOIDANCE LEGISLATION

20.10.1 Reason for legislation on controlled foreign companies

Legislation was introduced in 1984 with a view to countering the use of tax haven companies. The Government made it clear that the legislation was aimed at the following types of companies:

- 'Money box companies' (ie companies which simply accumulate investment income outside the UK);
- 'Dividend trap companies' (ie companies which are interposed between overseas subsidiaries and a UK parent company and which catch dividends before they reach the UK company and so prevent a UK tax liability);
- Offshore 'captive insurance companies';
- Sales, distribution or services companies which are used to enable profits to be put in a company which is subject to a low tax regime;
- Patent holding companies which enable royalty income to be sheltered from UK tax.

20.10.2 Definition of a CFC

A controlled foreign company (or 'CFC') is a foreign company which is controlled by UK resident persons. Basically, where a UK company has a material interest (ie normally a 10% or greater entitlement to share in the profits of a non-resident company) it may be taxed on a proportion of the overseas company's income. Note that the CFC's income is computed according to normal UK tax principles. It is also worth noting that capital gains realised by such a company are not subject to tax under the CFC legislation (but see 20.10.7).

There are various escape routes which enable a UK company to avoid any tax on its share of a CFC's profits. The escape routes involve the CFC meeting one of the following:

(a) the motive test;
(b) the exempt activity test;
(c) the acceptable distribution test; or
(d) the public quotation test.

20.10.3 Motive test

The legislation provides that no tax charge arises if the Board of Inland Revenue is satisfied that the motive for forming the CFC was not to avoid UK tax. In practice, the Revenue accepts that the test is satisfied if the CFC is resident in certain countries which impose tax at a rate comparable to UK tax. Companies which are resident in the following countries are therefore outside the legislation altogether.

Australia	Germany	Poland
Austria	Ghana	Romania
Bangladesh	Honduras	Senegal
Bolivia	Hungary	Sierra Leone
Botswana	Iceland	Slovak Republic
Brazil	India	Solomon Islands
Canada	Indonesia	South Africa
China	Ivory Coast	(excluding the
Colombia	Japan	Homelands)
Czech Republic	Korea, Republic of	Spain
Denmark	Lesotho	Swaziland
Dominican Republic	Malawi	Sweden
Falkland Islands	Mexico	Tobago
Fiji	New Zealand	Trinidad
Finland	Nigeria	Zambia
France	Norway	Zimbabwe
Gambia	Papua New Guinea	

A limited exclusion is available for certain other countries (eg Eire and The Netherlands).

Quite separately from the above, a company is not treated as a CFC if its tax liability in the country in which it is resident amounts to at least 75% of the tax which would be payable if it were a UK-resident company.

20.10.4 Exempt activity test

This test requires that the CFC should have premises in the country in which it is resident and use these premises for carrying on a business. Furthermore, the exempt activity test is satisfied only if it can be shown that the CFC's business is effectively managed in the country in which it is resident and that there are a number of employees based there who are adequate to deal with the volume of the company's business.

This test cannot be satisfied where the CFC's main business consists of any of the following:

(a) the holding of securities, patents or copyrights;
(b) dealing in securities;
(c) leasing;
(d) dealing in goods for delivery to or from the UK;
(e) dealing in goods for delivery to or from a connected or associated person.

20.10.5 Acceptable distribution test

This test applies in the following way. Provided the CFC distributes an acceptable proportion of its profits within 18 months of the end of its accounting period, no tax charge can arise for the UK companies who have a material interest.

Where the CFC is a trading company, the requirement is that the CFC should distribute at least 50% of its profits. Where the CFC is an investment company, the requirement is that it should distribute at least 90% of its income.

20.10.6 Public quotation test

There is also an exemption from the CFC legislation where the subsidiary is quoted on a recognised overseas Stock Exchange.

20.10.7 CGT legislation on non-resident companies

Shareholders in a non-resident company may be subjected to tax on its capital gains. The legislation is contained in TCGA 1992, s 13 and applies if the company would be a close company (see 20.8) if it were a UK-resident company. Basically, any shareholder who has at least 5% of the shares in the non-resident company may be charged tax as if a proportion of the non-resident company's capital gains belonged to him. The proportion is determined by the shareholder's entitlement in a winding-up.

Capital gains may not be apportioned in this way where any of the following conditions are satisfied:

(1) The non-resident company distributes the capital gain within two years, whether the distribution takes the form of a dividend, capital distribution or a payment by the liquidator etc on the winding-up of the company.

(2) The capital gain arises on the disposal of tangible property which is used (and used only) for the purposes of a trade carried on by the non-resident company wholly outside the UK.

(3) The capital gain accrues on the disposal of foreign currency where that currency represents money in use for the purposes of a trade carried on by the non-resident company wholly outside the UK.

(4) A non-resident company is charged tax on the capital gain because the gain arises on the disposal of an asset used by that non-resident company in connection with a UK branch or agency (see 20.1.1).

20.11 FOREX TRANSACTIONS

20.11.1 Outline of the basic rules

The main rules are set out in the flow-chart overleaf. These rules apply to:

(1) Qualifying assets such as currency, cash or bank accounts, and debts.

(2) Qualifying liabilities, including money debts, and provisions for trading liabilities.

(3) Currency contracts involving simultaneous exchange of two currencies such as currency swaps and forward and future contracts. It includes transactions where settlement is made by a single payment instead of actual exchange of currencies.

Forex gains and losses on the above items are taxed as income on an accruals basis. Generally the accounts figures are recognised for tax purposes so long as accounts are prepared using normal accountancy practice. Transactions entered into for trading purposes are taxed as trading profits or losses under Schedule D Case I. Where this is not the case (eg where the company is an investment company) they are taxed as Schedule D Case VI income. Special rules provide for Forex losses arising under Schedule D Case VI to be relieved first against other Case VI profits and then:

(a) offset against other current period profits;

(b) group relieved;

(c) carried back against other Forex or Financial Instruments (FI) profits of the three preceding years;

(d) carried forward against other Forex or FI profits;

The new rules apply from a company's 'commencement date' ie the first day of its accounting period which starts on or after the 'appointed day'

New Forex regime for companies

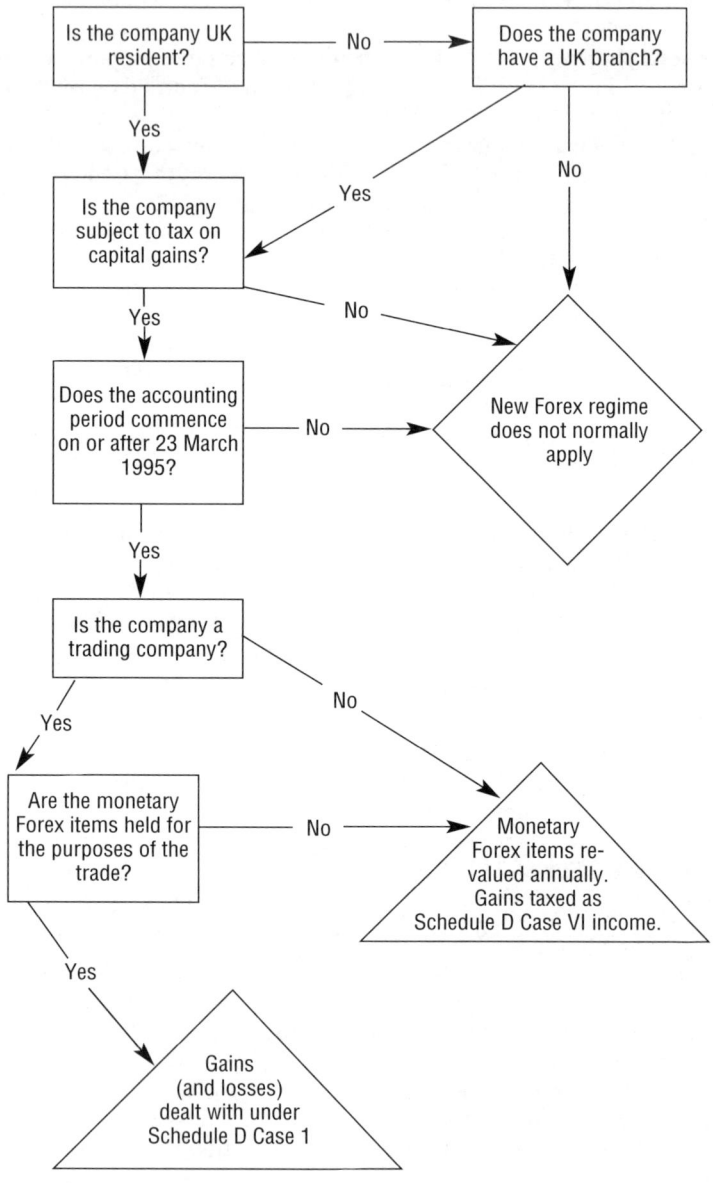

which was 23 March 1995. Thus the commencement date of a company will be 1 January 1996.

There are important reliefs available in respect of the above rules.

20.11.2 Matching

An election is available to match Forex gains and losses on certain borrowings and currency contracts with Forex gains and losses on certain categories of non-qualifying assets such as holdings in shares or convertible securities in non-UK resident companies, and net investments in overseas branches where a local currency election has been made (see below). The election can also be made in respect of ships and aircrafts. The effect of the election is that Forex gains and losses on the matched borrowings or currency contracts are taxed on realisation of the asset as capital gains or losses, or in the case of net investments in overseas branches are left out of account altogether. The election is irrevocable and only applies to assets and liabilities matched within the same company. This may be of concern to groups of companies where assets and liabilities are not economically matched within the same company.

20.11.3 Local currency election

Generally Forex gains and losses are calculated by reference to sterling but, in certain circumstances an election can be made to calculate *trading* profits by reference to other currencies. For example, a company which carries on an overseas trade may elect to calculate Forex gains and losses by reference to the relevant overseas currency. An overseas company with a UK trade may elect to use its 'home currency'. The effect of the election is that the trading profits or losses, including Forex gains and losses, are first computed in the local currency, then translated to sterling and adjusted for capital allowances.

20.11.4 Deferral relief

Relief is available to enable unrealised Forex gains on long-term capital assets and liabilities to be deferred for tax purposes. The amount available for deferral is the excess of the lower of either the *unrealised* Forex gains (net of losses) or *total* Forex gains (net of losses) in so far as they exceed 10% of taxable profits for the period.

A claim must be made for the relief and the excess is then carried forward and included in taxable profits of the next accounting period (when a further claim may be appropriate). Where the claimant is a member of a UK group, the amount available for deferral is calculated after taking into account gains and losses of other group companies.

20.11.5 Transitional rules

There are detailed rules dealing with the transition to the new regime. These cover the following aspects:

(1) Generally speaking qualifying assets and liabilities and currency contracts in existence at commencement date are revalued as if there had been a disposal at that date.
(2) No adjustment should be required for items previously included in trading profits unless the gains and losses were previously recognised on a realisation rather than an accruals basis.
(3) Pre-commencement gains and losses on qualifying assets previously dealt with under the capital gains regime are carried forward and offset against post commencement gains and losses. Similar rules apply to pre-commencement gains and losses on trading items previously dealt with on a realisation basis.
(4) There are special rules to deal with qualifying assets and liabilities previously outside the scope of tax, such as capital borrowings. Pre-commencement Forex gains and losses arising on fixed debts are not recognised, but there is a 'kink' test to ensure that the post-commencement gain or loss does not exceed the overall gain or loss over the entire life of the debt. Fluctuating debts are 'grandfathered' for six years with the result that gains and losses are not recognised during that period. If the latter treatment is not favourable a claim can be made to include the fluctuating debts within the new regime.
(5) Currency contracts entered into prior to commencement date are dealt with by a combination of the Forex and the Financial Instrument rules (see 20.11.6). These are intended to ensure that gains and losses are not taxed twice under both the new rules and under pre-commencement capital gains rules.

As might be expected, there are anti avoidance rules which may deny or restrict relief for Forex losses, where the loss is the main benefit expected to accrue from the transaction, or the transactions involved are not on arm's length terms. There are also rules dealing with benefits obtained from changing the company's accounting reference date.

20.11.6 Financial Instruments

The new rules which were included in FA 1994, but came into operation on the same date as the Forex rules, apply to currency contracts (eg swaps), currency options, interest rate contracts and interest rate options. The payments and receipts covered include periodic payments, premiums, fees, costs and payments for variation, termination and compensation.

The overall objective, as with Forex, is to tax the instruments as income, using the accruals or 'market to market' basis. The treatment of trading and non-trading transactions is exactly the same as for Forex transactions and the same rules apply for relief of Schedule D Case VI losses (see above).

Once again there are special transitional rules for contracts in existence at commencement date. The new rules apply to currency contracts but there are provisions to ensure that gains and losses are not taxed twice, under both the new and the old regime. Interest rate contracts and options in existence at commencement date are not dealt with under the new regime until six years after commencement date, unless the company elects to include them within the new rules.

There are anti-avoidance rules which may deny or restrict relief where a transaction is not on arm's length terms or a benefit is given by a transfer of value to an associated person.

20.11.7 Tax planning for Forex and Financial Instrument transactions

It is vital to review the existing position of a company before the commencement date to establish what, if any, measures need to be taken before commencement date and to assess the impact of the new legislation after commencement date. In particular, the following need to be considered:

(1) Whether existing borrowing arrangements need to be restructured to take best advantage of reliefs available and the impact of the transitional rules.
(2) Whether it is beneficial to terminate existing contracts or arrangements before commencement date.
(3) Whether matching relief is beneficial and whether relevant assets and liabilities are located and structured in the best way.
(4) Whether intra-group arrangements are affected by the new rules.
(5) Whether there is potential exposure to anti-avoidance provisions.
(6) The time limits for making the various claims and elections available, which in some cases are within 92 or 183 days of the commencement date.

20.12 CLAIMS AND ELECTIONS

20.12.1 General

Throughout the Taxes Acts, there are various claims for relief from corporation tax which must be lodged with the Revenue and, in practice, are made to the Inspector of Taxes dealing with the company's affairs. Unless otherwise specified by legislation, claims must be made within six years of the end of the accounting period to which they relate. The most common claims and elections are set out below together with the time limit by which the claim or election must be made. The Inspector does not generally have discretion to accept claims made after the time limit has expired for a particular claim unless the legislation (or Revenue practice) allows otherwise.

Relief may be claimed within the normal six-year time limit against any over-assessment to corporation tax due to an error or mistake in, or an omission from, any return or statement. No relief is due where the information was not used to form the basis of an assessment, or where the assessment was made in accordance with practice generally prevailing at the time of issue. An error or mistake claim under TMA 1970, s 33 should be made to the Revenue.

For accounting periods ended after 30 September 1993, group relief and capital allowances claims are no longer made by submitting formal claims to the Inspector. Such claims are made in the pay and file return Form CT200, as are claims for repayment of tax deducted at source.

Table 20.1   Time limit for claim submission reference

Claim	Period (years)	Legislation	Paragraph reference
Trading losses carried forward	6	TA 1988, s 393	20.6.2
Trading losses offset against other income of accounting period	2	TA 1988, s 393A	20.6.2
Trading losses carried back	2	TA 1988, s 393A	20.6.2
Terminal loss relief	2	TA 1988, s 393A	20.6.2
Disclaimer of capital allowances	2	CAA 1990, s 24	20.1.3
Group relief	2	TA 1988, s 412	20.7
Surrender of ACT	6	TA 1988, s 240	20.5
Carry back of ACT	2	TA 1988, s 239	20.5
Surplus franked investment income	2 (6 for charges on income and management expenses)	TA 1988, s 242	20.5
Roll-over relief	6	TCGA 1992, s 152	6.3 and 20.3.2
CGT rebasing at 31 March 1982	2 after the end of the accounting period in which the first relevant disposal is made after 31 March 1988	TCGA 1992, s 35	5.5 and 20.7.7

21

TAX PLANNING FOR SOLE TRADERS AND PARTNERS

DAVID BERTRAM, CLAYFIELD PROFESSIONAL GUIDANCE LTD

This chapter covers some wider issues for proprietors of unincorporated businesses such as sole traders and partners. We address issues such as bringing in a partner or merging with another firm. We also describe some of the advantages (and disadvantages) which might apply if an unincorporated business were transferred to a company. Assuming that an unincorporated business has grown to the point where it should be incorporated, we set out some of the tax aspects concerning the best way in which this should be achieved. Finally, we look at some tax considerations to be borne in mind where the proprietors of an unincorporated business sell out or cease trading.

OPERATING AS AN UNINCORPORATED BUSINESS

21.1 BRINGING IN A PARTNER (AND BECOMING A PARTNER)

21.1.1 Relief for loans where new partner borrows to finance his capital

Income tax relief is available under TA 1988, s 362 for interest on personal loans taken out by partners in order to contribute partnership capital, or to make a loan to the firm (see 18.5).

21.1.2 Interest on capital

It is generally appropriate for interest to be paid on partners' capital accounts, especially where there is some disparity between the amounts of capital provided by each partner.

'Interest' paid in these circumstances is treated as an allocation of Schedule D Case I profits rather than as interest taxable under Schedule D

Case III. This has the effect that the partner's relevant earnings for personal pension purposes (see 14.3.6) are likely to be higher than if the firm borrows from a bank to meet its working capital requirements.

Example – Treatment of partnership interest

A is a sole trader. His profits are running at the rate of £50,000. He brings in a partner and finances the practice by a loan which he raises in his personal capacity. At the end of the year, his position may be:

	£
Interest on capital	12,000
Share of profits	50,000
Interest paid on personal borrowings	(10,000)
	52,000

However, for personal pension purposes (see 14.3.6), his relevant earnings are £62,000 – ie there is no deduction for interest relieved under TA 1988, s 362.

21.1.3 Capital gains tax considerations

There is normally no CGT charge if a sole trader and his new partner each puts in capital on an equal basis – or in proportion to their profit-sharing ratios. However, it is possible that a sole practitioner may require the incoming partner to put in capital to match the value of his interest in the firm. The normal way to account for this is to re-value goodwill, and this could give rise to a capital gain.

Example – Valuation of goodwill

A brings *B* into partnership, sharing profits equally. *B* is required to pay £50,000 capital into the firm, but *A* does not need to pay any money into the firm, and, indeed, is free to withdraw all his undrawn profits. On the other hand, it is agreed that half of the goodwill now belongs to *B*.

A situation like this really amounts to an agreement that *A*'s goodwill is worth £50,000. After admitting *B* as a partner, he is entitled to only half of this, but he is also entitled to half of the £50,000 cash that *B* has put into the firm. So, in effect *A* has received a capital payment for a disposal of half of the goodwill and there may be a CGT charge on this.

21.1.4 Keeping certain property assets outside the firm

A sole trader may wish to retain personal ownership of the office premises etc, rather than share them with the incoming partners. This problem may be more apparent than real since there is no requirement that partners should share capital profits in the same way as they share ordinary profits. Nevertheless, many people prefer to keep the premises outside the firm altogether.

In such a situation the former sole trader can rent the premises to the firm, preferably under a formal agreement which gives the firm a tenancy or a licence. He can also charge rent, but if he does so the consequences for CGT retirement relief should be borne in mind (see 6.7–6.8).

It is also possible for the partner to forgo rent, but to receive the benefit of an appropriate adjustment in the partnership accounts, as a prior charge on profits in the same way as interest on capital is charged. If the partnership agreement is drafted correctly, this effectively converts Schedule A rental income for the partner into profits falling under Schedule D Case I. It also avoids any restriction on CGT retirement relief.

21.1.5 Admitting a partner under CY basis rules

Where the firm is already on the CY basis, either because the business was started after 5 April 1994 or because a partner retired from the firm after that date and no continuation election was made, matters are much more straightforward.

Basically, the partnership's profits are assessed on the CY basis (bear in mind the opening rules (see 18.1.1)). Each partner is separately responsible for settling his own tax; there is no principle of joint and several liability for the firm's income tax.

Where a firm is assessed on the CY basis, any changes in the partners do not give rise to a cessation as there is an automatic 'continuation' for the ongoing partners. Thus, on a partnership change under the new rules, the tax liabilities of past years are not affected because the change does not trigger a Revenue review of tax assessments for the penultimate and ante-penultimate years.

21.2 BUYING OUT A PARTNER

21.2.1 Change in status to salaried partner

Where circumstances permit, there could be some advantage for the outgoing partner to revert to salaried partner status and be taxed under Schedule E.

There can be other benefits in switching from Schedule D status to Schedule E. The continuing partners could undertake to fund an approved pension scheme (see 14.3.5), which in turn may enable a tax-free lump sum to be provided where the outgoing partner had previously been an employee (or a salaried partner). Benefits under an approved scheme must relate to periods of service as an employee, but there is no statutory requirement that the periods be continuous as opposed to two periods separated by a period as a Schedule D partner.

21.2.2 Consultancy arrangement

It could be that the individual agrees to retire from the firm only if he receives a 'retainer' under which the firm is committed to consult him (and pay him) for a minimum number of days over a specified period. Unless the retainer is substantial, it is unusual for the Revenue to seek to classify an ex-partner consultant as an employee, even though he may not undertake work for many other clients (if any). However, this possibility should be borne in mind and the consultancy agreement carefully drafted to avoid any suggestion of a 'master/servant' relationship (see 12.3). If there is any doubt, the partnership needs to withhold PAYE from the consultancy fees.

While it may suit the individual to be taxed as a consultant under Schedule D Case I, particularly if there are expenses that he can claim against his consultancy income (such as the cost of maintaining an office in his home, payment to a spouse for secretarial services and business use of a car), the firm must protect its position. In particular, where the consultancy fee exceeds the VAT threshold, the firm must obtain a valid VAT invoice.

During the transitional period, it may be better for the continuing partners if the retiring partner is paid an annuity rather than consultancy fees, as this may mean that greater relief is available (see below).

21.2.3 Annuity arrangements

An annuity may effectively be paid out of pre-tax income since the payer is normally entitled to relief at his marginal rate of tax. An annuity of £10,000 is satisfied if the partners pay £7,800 (ie £10,000 less basic rate tax), and they can then claim the full amount as a deduction in arriving at their total income for higher rate tax purposes.

As already mentioned, payment as an annuity may be more tax-efficient than consultancy payments during the transitional basis period. The main drawback with annuity payments is that the continuing partners cannot raise qualifying loans in order to meet these obligations.

So far as the outgoing partner is concerned, a capital sum may be preferable, especially where retirement relief (see 6.7) or roll-over relief (see 6.3) may be relevant. On the other hand, the annuity should not attract a CGT liability unless it exceeds two-thirds of his average share of profits over a period of three years which falls within the last seven years in which he is a partner.

21.2.4 Payment of a capital sum

A capital sum may be paid direct to an outgoing partner, or an adverse balance on his capital account may be written off – this is in effect a capital payment by means of a transfer from the continuing partners' capital accounts.

21.2.5 Borrowing by partners to fund the buyout

Where one or more partners raise personal loans to make a capital payment to buy out a colleague, interest normally qualifies for relief under ICTA 1988, s 362. If, exceptionally, the interest on such a loan exceeds the partnership profits, the excess may be carried forward as if it were a Schedule D Case I loss. However, it is important to bear in mind that if the buyout does not take place, and the borrower ceases to be a partner, his loan ceases to qualify for tax purposes. This has been a real problem for the proprietors of firms which have subsequently found themselves in financial difficulties.

21.2.6 Capital gains tax implications

A partner who is being bought out may have a CGT liability unless he can make use of roll-over relief or his gain is covered by retirement relief (see 6.7).

21.2.7 Splitting the practice

In some situations, the outgoing partner effectively takes over one particular office and continues to practice on his own account. This is a 'demerger' situation and the tax treatment depends on whether continuation elections are made.

21.2.8 Demergers

Where some partners buy out part of a firm's business they are usually treated as starting a new business. The partners who continue in the original firm can avoid a cessation by making a continuation election. Alternatively, it may be possible to satisfy the Revenue that a demerger consists of separating two businesses which were different businesses all along. Thus, if a firm of estate agents consists of five offices in different towns, it could be argued that one particular office was always a distinct business and its separation from the rest of the partnership does not amount to commencing a new business. This enables both the continuing partners in the main firm, and the partner(s) who have taken on the office which has demerged, to make continuation elections. Indeed it also allows the partners in the original firm to have a cessation, even though the partners who have demerged chose to make a continuation election.

Capital gains tax

The partners who have demerged will normally have disposed of their interests in the assets of the main firm and acquired enlarged interests in the assets of the demerged firm. Depending on the relative values, any capital gains may well be covered by roll-over relief (see 6.3).

VAT

As partners are jointly and severally liable for VAT, it is important to notify Customs of the departure of partners immediately the demerger takes effect. Joint and several liability continues up to the date the change is notified.

OPERATING AS A LIMITED COMPANY

21.3 GENERAL TAX CONSIDERATIONS

There is no simple answer to the question 'is it better to operate via a company?' There can be both advantages and disadvantages in carrying on business through a limited company rather than as an unincorporated business, and it is generally appropriate to take professional advice. There are commercial considerations as well as tax aspects, eg limited liability may be an important consideration, either for the current proprietors of the business or to attract finance from an outside investor. However, the apparent protection given by limited liability is often illusory, since banks or other lending institutions normally require personal guarantees from directors for any loans made to the company.

21.3.1 Lower rate of tax on profits

Having a company often means that a lower rate of tax applies to retained profits, ie profits which are not taken out as remuneration or dividends.

The starting rate of 10% (see 20.2.4) applies to profits up to £10,000, with marginal relief of up to £50,000 provided there are no associated companies.

The small companies rate of 20% (see 20.2.5) applies to profits up to £300,000 provided there are no associated companies. If there are associated companies, the threshold at which profits attract tax at either the full 30%, or the marginal small companies rate, is reduced. If there are no associated companies, the small companies rate can produce a substantial saving.

21.3.2 Possible ways of deferring tax

There is a useful timing difference where a business is carried on through a company in that remuneration can be deducted from the profits of the company even though it is not paid (and is not taxable income of the individuals until it is paid). Provided that the remuneration is actually paid within nine months of the company's year end, the company is normally entitled to a deduction in arriving at its profits.

Example – Timing of tax payments

If a company draws up accounts to 31 March 2001, it may secure a deduction for directors' remuneration of £150,000 even though the remuneration is not paid until 31 December 2001, in which case PAYE tax does not have to be paid over until 14 January 2002 in accordance with the timetable for self-assessment payments.

21.3.3 Other tax considerations

Pension contributions

Another aspect which favours having a company is that it is possible for a company to fund pensions for directors more generously than is permitted for personal pensions. For example, if an individual is aged 44, the maximum personal pension contribution the individual may make for the year is 20% of relevant earnings up to the amount of the earnings cap (currently £91,800 for 2000–01) (see 14.3.5). In contrast, a company would normally be permitted by the Pension Schemes Office to fund a pension scheme for the benefit of the individual at the rate of 100% of remuneration up to the amount of the earnings cap.

Payment of remuneration may prevent personal allowances going to waste

Where an unincorporated business operates at a loss, and the individuals have no other income, the benefit of their personal allowances is lost forever. By trading through a company, it is possible to vote remuneration equal to the individuals' personal allowances, and the remuneration voted in this way increases the amount of the company's loss which can be carried forward and set against subsequent profits.

Greater scope for raising new finance

An outside investor normally prefers to be a shareholder rather than a partner. While he could in theory limit his exposure by being a limited partner, this is not familiar territory. Furthermore, a limited partner loses the protection of limited liability under the Limited Partnership Act 1907 if he takes part in the management of the firm's business. Most outside investors are therefore prepared to invest only if they can acquire shares and act as directors of a company.

Having a company also opens the way to attracting outside investment under the Enterprise Investment Scheme (see 22.10.1) or from investors who wish to secure CGT reinvestment relief (see 6.4).

21.4 POSSIBLE DISADVANTAGES

Possible disadvantages of operating through a company include the following.

21.4.1 Extra administration

Companies are subject to more statutory requirements concerning the keeping of books, filing of annual accounts, disclosure etc than unincorporated businesses. An unincorporated business does not normally need to file annual accounts at all, whereas a company needs to file accounts with Companies House, and to make an annual return.

21.4.2 Loss of privacy

A limited company must file its accounts annually, and they are available for public inspection. In contrast, an unincorporated business's accounts are a private document which need not be made available to anyone other than the proprietors and the Revenue (and, possibly, the business's bankers).

21.4.3 Relief for losses

A proprietor of an unincorporated business may secure tax relief for any losses by setting them against other income. Losses suffered during the first four tax years in which a business is carried on may be carried back and set against income of the previous three years.

In contrast, losses made by a company can only be set against the company's other profits for the year (or the previous year). Any unrelieved losses may then be carried forward and can be off-set against future trading profits only.

21.4.4 Admitting future partners

If profits are retained, this may make it increasingly difficult for individuals who come up through the business to become shareholder directors. For example, if a company has 100 £1 shares in issue, and retains profits after tax of £15,000 pa for ten years, each share is worth £1,500 more at the end of the ten years than at the start of the period. An individual seeking to acquire a 10% shareholding would normally have to raise sufficient finance to pay for the shares at this increased value. The problem does not, though, arise in the case of a partnership, since the normal procedure is to allocate past profits to partners' capital accounts and then admit a new partner on the basis that he shares in future profits at a specified percentage. Having said this, the disadvantage in having a company can be over-stated. For example, if the shareholders so wished, they could arrange for the company to make a bonus issue of preference shares before allowing an incoming director to subscribe for ordinary shares. This is not always appropriate, but where it can be done, the shareholder/directors are not disadvantaged through having a company rather than a partnership and the new shareholder/ director need not put in very large amounts of new share capital.

21.4.5 Tax savings may only be a deferment

The traditional analysis has been that tax generally becomes payable by shareholders on their share of retained profits, either when the shareholders sell their shares and realise a capital gain, or as and when they extract retained profits by taking a dividend. On this analysis, the saving of tax on retained profits is often little more than a deferment of tax. The validity of this view has been brought into question by the substantial increases in CGT retirement relief during recent years (see 6.7). The fact that gains may be exempt up to £500,000 if a husband and wife both qualify for the maximum retirement relief means that the traditional analysis is often no longer valid since shareholder/directors are generally able to enjoy the full value of their shares on a sale or liquidation of the company.

21.4.6 Increased liability for NICs

A company is required to pay Class 1 NICs on all amounts paid as remuneration. There is no ceiling akin to that which applies to employees' own contributions. This can give rise to a substantially increased burden for a company as compared with an unincorporated business. Comparing an unincorporated business owned by four equal partners with a company which has four 25% shareholders (and it is assumed that in both cases the individuals will have income of £75,000 each), the national insurance bill for 1997–98 is as follows:

		Partnership £		*Company* £
Class 2		104.00	Employees' Class 1	2,388.00
Class 4		1,640.45	Employer's Class 1	8,615.03
		1,744.45		11,003.03
× 4 =		6,977.80	× 4 =	44,012.12

While the benefits payable to employees are better than those received by the self-employed the higher NIC costs can be a very expensive way of financing such benefits.

21.5 OTHER TAX ASPECTS

21.5.1 Work in progress

In principle, a professional firm should not include partner time in arriving at the cost of work in progress. This means that the figure brought into account should be lower because of this. However, if a business is carried on by a company, time put in by a director should be included when valuing work in progress.

21.5.2 Potential double charge for capital gains

Where a valuable asset is held within a company, a tax liability may arise at two stages before the shareholders can enjoy the sale proceeds. For example, if a company acquires a property at a cost of £150,000, and five years later it is worth £550,000, there might be a gain for the company (after indexation) of £400,000. The company then pays tax on this capital gain either at the marginal small companies rate or at 30%. If a tax charge at 30% is assumed, the company has net funds available after paying tax of £318,000, ie:

	£	
Profit for accounting purposes	450,000	
Less tax on gain	120,000	(£400,000 at 30%)
	330,000	

If the company is then wound up, and the cash distributed to the shareholders, they are likely to have a personal CGT liability on the £330,000. If retirement relief is not available, the CGT payable by them could be £132,000 (ie £330,000 at 40%). This figure assumes that other assets and retained profits within the company are such that there would have been capital gains for the shareholders in any event, even if the company had not held the property concerned.

However, once again, the traditional analysis is open to question. If the company had paid a dividend in order to transmit the £330,000 cash to shareholders, their personal liability could not exceed £82,250. Consequently, while it is not generally good policy to have appreciating assets within a company, the extent of the extra tax payable is not as great as it was in the past. Furthermore, while some additional tax is likely to be payable if an appreciating asset is held within a company, this is not in itself an argument against a business operating through a company but rather an argument in favour of shareholder/directors holding such assets in their personal capacities outside the company. It should be borne in mind here that retirement relief is available to a full-time working director who disposes of a property which is used by his family company provided that a disposal is associated with a disposal of shares in the company.

21.6 TRANSFERRING A BUSINESS TO A COMPANY

Where a person transfers a business to a company (ie he 'incorporates the business'), there is a disposal of the assets which are transferred to the company. Not all the assets are necessarily chargeable assets for CGT purposes, but a gain may arise on the transfer of assets such as land, buildings and goodwill to the company. Fortunately, there is a relief which may cover such situations (TCGA 1992, s 162).

21.6.1 Nature of relief

The main relief applies only where a business is transferred to a company in return for an issue of shares to the former proprietors of the business. Where the necessary conditions are satisfied so that s 162 relief is available, the gains which would otherwise arise on the transfer of chargeable assets are 'rolled-over' into the cost of the shares issued.

Example – Transfer of a business to a company

A transfers a business to X Ltd in return for shares which are worth £75,000. There are capital gains of £48,000 on the assets transferred to the company. If TCGA 1992, s 162 relief applies, A will not have any assessable capital gain, but A's shares in X Ltd will be deemed to have an acquisition cost of £27,000 computed as follows:

	£
Market value	75,000
Less rolled-over gain	48,000
	27,000

21.6.2 Conditions which must be satisfied

For s 162 relief to be available, *all* the assets of the business other than cash must be transferred to the company. It is not acceptable to the Inland Revenue for certain assets of the unincorporated business, such as trade debts, to be excluded, even though this might otherwise be desirable to save stamp duty.

Relief is available only in so far as the company issues shares rather than other consideration such as loan stock. However, some relief is still available if the business is transferred to the company in return for a mixture of shares and loan stock, or shares and cash. The formula to be used is:

$$\text{Chargeable gain} \times \frac{\text{value of shares received}}{\text{value of whole consideration received}}$$

Thus if B transfers a business to Y Ltd, and receives shares worth £10,000 and loan stock worth £200,000, only one-third of any capital gains arising on the transfer of the business assets can be rolled-over under TCGA 1992, s 162.

21.6.3 Limitations of s 162 relief

The market value of the shares issued in return for the transfer of the business must be at least equal to the capital gains arising on the transfer of assets, or there will still be a CGT charge on the transfer of the business to the company. Thus if C transfers a business with a net value of £400,000 to Y Ltd, a new company specially formed for the purpose, the shares in Z Ltd will have a value of £400,000. However, it may be that closer examination reveals that the business's value is depressed by heavy bank borrowings. If so, it may be that capital gains totalling (say) £490,000 arise on the chargeable assets transferred as part of the business. Section 162 relief is then limited to £400,000. The balance of £90,000 is taxable in the normal way.

21.6.4 Conditions which do not apply

(1) Relief is not confined to a transfer of a business to a company by a sole trader; the same relief is available where a partnership transfers its business to a company.
(2) The shares which are issued need not be ordinary shares.
(3) Relief is not confined to a business which is classified as a trade which falls under Schedule D Case I or II. It is arguable that the relevant business might, for example, consist of letting group of properties.
(4) There is no requirement that the company should be incorporated or resident in the UK. It can be both of these, but relief is not prejudiced just because a foreign company is involved.

21.6.5 Alternative way of incorporating a business

It may sometimes be possible to transfer a business to a company and avoid any CGT liability by relying on the hold-over provisions for gifts (see 6.4). Thus if A establishes a new company, X Ltd, and he owns all the shares, he could give his business to X Ltd and 'hold over' any capital gain. If A's acquisition cost was £15,000 and indexation relief (see 5.5.5) amounts to £7,000, he is deemed to transfer the business assets for £22,000 and the company takes over the assets for a notional acquisition value of £22,000. This could be a suitable way of transferring a business to a company where the proprietors do not wish to transfer all the assets to the company, as required by TCGA 1992, s 162 (eg where the proprietors wish to retain properties used in the business).

Professional advice is essential to such arrangements. Problems are particularly likely to arise if there is some consideration involved, even if it does not correspond to the market value of the business at the time of transfer.

21.6.6 Income tax consequences

Although there are specific CGT reliefs, there are no similar provisions for income tax purposes. Where individuals transfer a business to a company, they cease to carry on the business and the Schedule D closing year rules may apply.

Furthermore, the transfer of stock to the company may give rise to a taxable profit. Normally, stock is deemed to be transferred at market value in these circumstances. However, it is possible for the proprietors of the unincorporated business and the company to jointly elect for the stock to be transferred at the lower of its cost or carrying value in the unincorporated business's accounts.

The transfer of plant and machinery, and other assets which qualify for capital allowances, might give rise to a balancing charge. However, it is possible for the proprietors and the company to make a joint election so that the plant and machinery etc are deemed to be transferred at their tax written-down value.

21.6.7 VAT consequences of the transfer

The VAT legislation provides that a transfer of a business is not a taxable supply if the following conditions are satisfied:

(1) the assets transferred are to be used by the transferee to carry on the same kind of business as that carried on by the transferor; and
(2) where the transferor is a taxable person the transferee is already, or as a result of the transfer becomes, a taxable person;
(3) where part of a business is transferred, that part is capable of separate operation, ie it must have the substance of a business activity.

The above conditions are normally satisfied where a business is transferred to a limited company as a going concern. Where this happens, it is possible for the unincorporated business's VAT registration number to be taken over by the company if the following conditions are satisfied:

(1) an application on form VAT 68 must be made both by the individuals previously in business and the company; and
(2) the unincorporated business's registration must be cancelled from the date of the transfer; and

(3) the company must not already be registered, although it will of course be liable to be registered as a result of the transfer of the business to it.

The effect of such an application is that the company stands in the shoes of the proprietors of the unincorporated business and takes over all the rights and obligations of those proprietors. Thus, the company becomes liable to furnish any outstanding returns and to pay any VAT due to Customs and Excise at the date of the transfer. This includes any undetected errors in VAT returns which emerge at any subsequent VAT control visit.

21.6.8 Stamp duty on the transfer

The general principles of stamp duty in relation to the transfer of a business to a company are set out at 8.3.7. It is appropriate to go into a little more detail here, and in particular to look at possible ways of avoiding stamp duty on the transfer of land and buildings.

Land and buildings can be transferred for a consideration below market value, eg an issue of preference shares. Where this happens, stamp duty is payable only on the actual consideration which passes.

It is also possible that ad valorem duty could be deferred or even avoided altogether if the proprietors of the unincorporated business contract to sell the land and buildings to the company but do not complete that contract.

An agreement for the sale of an interest in land is specifically excluded from the charge to stamp duty under Stamp Act 1891, s 59 and therefore there is no stamp duty on the contract. Beneficial ownership of the property passes to the company as soon as the contract is executed and the company issues its shares as consideration. If the contract were ever completed, stamp duty is then payable. However, it may well be that the directors of the company would be safe to rely on the existence of the contract and allow the legal estate to remain in the names of the proprietors of the unincorporated business. As and when the company wishes to sell the property to a third party, the legal estate can be transferred directly from the former proprietors with only one charge to stamp duty arising, this being the duty payable by the new owner on his purchase consideration. It is essential that professional advice be taken on this.

21.6.9 Carry forward of past trading losses
(TA 1988, s 386)

Where a business has been carried on by an individual (either as a sole trader or in partnership) and the business is transferred to a company, it is possible for any unused trading losses to be relieved against the individual's income from the company in subsequent years. This relief is available only if the business is transferred to a company in return for an issue of shares and the individual has retained ownership of those shares throughout the tax year concerned. In practice, the Revenue does not withhold relief provided the individual has retained at least 80% of the shares.

21.6.10 Other tax aspects

Where CGT incorporation relief is sought under TCGA 1992, s 162 (see 21.6.1 above) it is important to bear in mind that if the limited company takes over the liability of the incorporated business to pay the partners the balance on their current accounts, this counts as a form of consideration and CGT may be payable. It is generally thought advisable for the partners to withdraw the balances on their current accounts shortly before the business is transferred to the limited company. If necessary, short-term bank borrowings may be taken on to bridge the situation, with the individuals then lending money to the company after it has acquired the business. This is clearly another aspect on which professional advice should be taken.

Partners in a firm should plan ahead. Retirement relief is an important long-term consideration and there can be some pitfalls. For example, an individual who personally owned an asset used by the partnership can qualify for retirement relief on an associated disposal of the property (see 6.7.2). Directors who personally own an asset used by their personal trading company (see 6.8.1) can also claim relief on an associated disposal, but only if they work full-time for the company.

Inheritance tax should be borne in mind as well. While they were partners, the individuals would have been entitled to 100% business property relief. As shareholders in a company which has taken over their business, the relief is limited to 50% unless the individual concerned has more than 25% of the voting shares. Thus, if five individuals who share profits equally transfer their business to a company, each of them has only a 20% shareholding, and his or her entitlement to business property relief is only 50%.

SALE OF THE BUSINESS AND CESSATION

21.7 SALE

21.7.1 Apportionment of sale consideration

When the proprietors of an unincorporated business dispose of it, they actually make separate disposals of different assets. The contract under which the business is sold normally allocates a specific part of the consideration to each separate asset, eg stock, plant and machinery, land and buildings and goodwill. The Inland Revenue may challenge the way in which the sale consideration is apportioned if it seems unrealistic and, if no apportionment is contained in the contract, a just and reasonable apportionment may be made. This may have income tax implications as well as CGT consequences.

Example – Apportionment

A sole trader, *A*, sells his business for £180,000. It is decided that this sum breaks down into the following components:

	£
Stock	40,000
Plant and machinery	35,000
Leasehold property	25,000
Goodwill	80,000
	180,000

The £40,000 for stock is brought into account as a trading receipt. The £35,000 for plant and machinery needs to be set against the 'pool' balance (see 4.6.12) and there may be a balancing charge if it exceeds the pool figure. The £25,000 for the sale of the leasehold property and the goodwill may produce capital gains.

21.7.2 Transfer of business to company immediately before sale

Where a business is to be sold and the gain is likely to exceed any amount covered by retirement relief, there can be some advantage in first transferring the business to a limited company under TCGA 1992, s 162 (see 21.6), the company later selling on the business.

Example – Transfer to a company

Using the figures in the example in 21.7.1, let us suppose that a disposal of the goodwill for £80,000 would produce a capital gain of £70,000. If *A* had no entitlement to retirement relief, tax of up to £28,000 might be payable.

However, if *A* transferred the entire business to A Ltd in return for an issue of shares, A Ltd's acquisition value of the business is its market value at the time of the transfer (ie £180,000). The company would have a capital gain on a sale of the goodwill etc only if the assets appreciated after being transferred to A Ltd.

A would have a capital gain if he disposed of his shares in A Ltd, but in practice he may not need to do so and could use the company for some other purpose (eg as an investment company).

21.8 CESSATION

The proprietors of an unincorporated business may not be able to sell it to anyone else and may simply have to terminate the business themselves. A number of tax points arise in this connection.

21.8.1 **VAT**

Where assets such as stock or plant and machinery are still held by the business at the date that it ceases to make taxable supplies, there is a deemed supply and the assets are treated as if they have been sold. VAT is then due to Customs based on the open market value (except in the situation where the value is less than £250).

There are minor exceptions to this rule, ie there is no deemed supply where the goods retained by the proprietors are motor cars or goods obtained under a second-hand scheme.

21.8.2 **Redundancy costs**

Payments made to former employees on the cessation of a business do not qualify for relief under TA 1988, s 74 as the payments are not made for the benefit of the trade but are expenditure incurred in bringing that trade to an end. However, TA 1988, s 90 allows a deduction for payments of up to three times the statutory redundancy payments which are due.

21.8.3 **Post-cessation expenses**
(TA 1988, s 109A)

Relief is available for expenses incurred by a person after ceasing to carry on a trade or profession provided it is incurred within seven years of the date of cessation. The following types of expenditure may qualify for relief:

- the costs of remedying defective work done, goods supplied, or services rendered while the trade or profession was continuing, and damages paid by the taxpayer in respect of such defective work, goods or services, whether awarded by a court or agreed during negotiations on a claim;
- insurance premiums paid to insure against the above costs;
- legal and other professional expenses incurred in connection with the above costs;
- debts owed to the business which have been taken into account in computing the profits or gains of the trade or profession before discontinuance but which have subsequently become bad;
- the costs of collecting debts which have been taken into account in computing the profits of the trade before discontinuance.

The relief is reduced by any expense allowed as a deduction in the final accounting period which remains unpaid at the end of the year of assessment in which the new relief is given.

Expenditure which qualifies for this relief is set against income and capital gains of the year of assessment in which the expense is paid. Where there is insufficient income or capital gains to cover the expenditure, the unrelieved expenditure of that year is not eligible to be carried forward under the new relief arrangements against future income or capital gains. Any unrelieved expenditure is then available to be carried forward under the existing rules and set against subsequent post-cessation receipts from the trade or profession.

22

TAX AND THE COMPANY PROPRIETOR

DAVID BERTRAM, CLAYFIELD PROFESSIONAL GUIDANCE LTD

In this chapter, we look more closely at tax planning for proprietors; points to bear in mind when buying a company; the treatment of shareholder directors, and the way in which they are assessed on benefits received by them (and by members of their family); how cash may be extracted from the company in the most tax-efficient manner; and the tax implications of various transactions with the company.

22.1 BUYING A COMPANY

There are several points to bear in mind where an individual or group of individuals are purchasing an existing company.

22.1.1 Relief for financing costs

Where an individual finances such a purchase through a qualifying loan, the interest payable on the loan may qualify for income tax relief under TA 1988, s 360. The conditions which need to be satisfied for a loan to be a qualifying loan are:

(1) The loan must be a formal loan and not merely an overdraft.
(2) The loan must be used to acquire ordinary share capital of a close trading company or ordinary share capital of a company which is the holding company of a trading group or to make a loan to such a company.
(3) The borrower must have a material interest in the close company or be employed full-time by the company at the time the interest is paid.

As can be seen from the above, it is a requirement that the company is a close company and that the individual has a material interest. Close companies are defined at 20.8.1 above. An individual is regarded as having a material interest if he owns more than 5% of the ordinary share capital of the company. In fact, the 5% test applies to the individual taken together with his associates, so that if an individual held 4% personally and his wife owned 2%, he is deemed to have a material interest.

The requirement that the individual should have a material interest does not apply if he works full time for the company. Working full-time means that the individual works for the greater part of his time in the management of the company, and he must therefore be a director or a person who has a wider management role that affects the company as a whole and not merely a particular department within the company.

22.1.2 Income tax relief for capital losses

As explained at 6.2, a UK-resident individual who has subscribed for ordinary shares in an unquoted company may be able to claim income tax relief for any loss realised on a disposal of those shares. This contrasts with the normal position where capital losses may be set only against an individual's capital gains and not against income.

In practice, where an individual or group of individuals are considering purchasing an existing company, they may be better advised to form a new company, subscribe for shares in that company, and have that company ('Newco') purchase the target company. If Newco has no assets or activities apart from holding shares in the target company, there would be a very close relationship between the value of the shares in Newco and the shares in the target company. If the target company fails, the shares in Newco are likely to become worthless and this produces a capital loss. Because the individuals will have subscribed for shares in Newco, and the other requirements of TA 1988, s 574 are satisfied, it should be possible for them to secure income tax relief (see 6.2).

22.1.3 Checklist of tax points when buying a company

(1) Establish whether the target company has any assets which have been the subject of a roll-over relief claim (see 6.3).

(2) Ensure that none of the company's assets have been transferred to it from another group company within the past six years as this could give rise to a tax charge on the company under TCGA 1992, s 179 (see 20.7.6).

(3) Obtain appropriate indemnities against any tax payable for back years because of failure to make PAYE and NIC deductions, failure to make correct end of year returns, problems in operating the sub-contractors scheme, or interest or penalties payable under the VAT legislation following an investigation.

(4) Take professional advice if the vendors are to receive compensation for loss of office or *ex-gratia* payments, as these payments are not always an allowable deduction for corporation tax purposes.

(5) Take professional advice on possible ways to minimise stamp duty (see 8.3).

22.2 CORPORATION TAX PLANNING

22.2.1 Maximising benefit of small companies rate

There can be a tax penalty where there is more than one associated company (see 20.2.6) and the profits of the two companies are not equally distributed. Even though the combined amount may fall within the limits which would apply for small companies rate if there were only one company, the way in which the rules work can produce a situation where one company's profits suffer tax at the full 30% rate.

Example – Adverse tax position

A Ltd and its wholly owned subsidiary B Ltd may have total profits of £300,000 which would attract corporation tax at only 20% if they arose within A Ltd and A Ltd had no associated companies. If, however, A Ltd has profits of £250,000 and B Ltd has profits of £50,000, the total corporation tax payable is as set out below.

	£
A Ltd	
£250,000 at 30%	75,000
Less: Marginal relief $\frac{1}{40}$ × (£750,000 – £250,000)	12,500
	62,500
B Ltd	
£50,000 at 20%	10,000
Total corporation tax payable	72,500

The effect in this particular case of having two companies rather than a single company is that the overall rate of tax is increased from 20% to 24.17%.

22.2.2 Commercial considerations

Tax is not, however, the only consideration. There may be good commercial reasons why the directors prefer to keep certain trading operations in a separate company. For example, this may be a way of ensuring that valuable properties within a holding company are not put at risk if those trading operations result in insolvency.

It is sometimes possible to have the small companies rate computed on the basis that a company is left out of account. In particular, if the company is a pure holding company which has no business operations apart from holding shares in one or more subsidiary companies, or holding property used by such subsidiary companies, and the holding company has no profits for corporation tax purposes, it may be left out of account.

22.2.3 Companies controlled by associates

The Revenue also operates a concession where there is no trading interdependence or connection between two companies and they are technically associated companies only because the individuals who control each of the companies are associated with one another (eg an individual controls company A and his brother controls company B). This is an area where professional advice should be taken in the light of the precise wording of ESC C9.

22.2.4 Avoiding disallowable expenditure

If it is decided to have a group of two (or more) companies or associated companies (ie companies which are under common control but are not parent/subsidiary), each company should avoid incurring expenditure which is partly or wholly for the benefit of the other company's trade. Such expenditure is not allowable in computing profits for corporation tax purposes.

22.2.5 Managing a group's tax affairs

It is most important that the necessary elections are in place to enable interest and other annual payments to be paid from one member of a group of companies to another, and for any dividends to be paid within the group, without the company which declares the dividend having to account for ACT. Bear in mind that such elections do not take effect automatically. The proper procedure is to submit the elections to the Inspector of Taxes. They then take effect after three months, or at some earlier date if the Inspector gives notice that he agrees that the elections are valid.

Care is needed if any shares in a subsidiary company are held by outside shareholders. Certain reliefs, and specifically group relief, are dependent on the holding company being entitled to at least 75% of the ordinary share capital of subsidiaries. Other tests also have to be satisfied and group relief might not be available if an outside investor holds preference shares or convertible loan stock, which might mean that less than 75% of the subsidiary's profits, or assets available for distribution on a winding-up, would belong to the holding company (see 20.7.2).

Group relief is available only to cover profits of a corresponding accounting period. It cannot be carried back and set against a subsidiary's profits for an earlier accounting period. There may also be problems where a subsidiary has a different accounting date from that of its parent company.

Some of the above points would be dealt with by the company's tax advisors, but a prudent director will wish to understand the statutory requirements and to ensure that the advisors are on top of the matter. The following checklist may be of assistance in this connection.

22.2.6 Checklist of tax considerations for group of companies

(1) The position should be monitored to identify cases where a subsidiary may have a loss for tax purposes. It may be possible to maximise tax relief if certain action is taken before the end of the accounting period in which the loss will arise. Professional advice is appropriate.

(2) The company's accountant should be consulted before a subsidiary company pays a dividend.

(3) A valid group dividend election should be in place. It is also worth checking with the group's accountant that it will not be more beneficial for the dividend to be paid outside the group election.

(4) Annual charges such as interest should actually be paid by the company's year end as no tax relief is otherwise available.

(5) Advice on the tax implications of any transfers of assets between group companies should be taken. Tax on a gain which is covered by TCGA 1992, s 171 may become payable if a subsidiary leaves the group within six years (see 20.7.6).

(6) The deadlines for submitting formal claims to the Inspector of Taxes, explained below, should be kept in mind.

22.3 TREATMENT OF REMUNERATION FOR PAYE AND NICS PURPOSES

In essence, shareholder directors are treated in the same way as all other directors and P11D employees (see 13.3.1) in that their remuneration is taxed under Schedule E, and the same rules govern the tax treatment of benefits in kind. However, directors who are also significant shareholders in the company are likely to be affected more by certain aspects of the legislation.

22.3.1 How receipts basis applies to shareholder/directors

Where remuneration is deemed to have been received, PAYE must be accounted for and it is assessable as income in the year of receipt.

Special provisions define the date on which an individual is deemed to receive remuneration, as the earlier of:

(1) the date when payment is actually made; and
(2) the time when the employee becomes entitled to payment.

In the case of directors, the date can be earlier than above, in that payment is deemed to take place on the earliest of (1) and (2) and

(3) the date that income is credited to the director in the company's accounts or records; and
(4) the date when the accounts of income for a period is determined.

22.3.2 **NIC problem areas**

One major problem concerns directors' drawings. The DSS takes the view that where a director arranges for a personal liability to be settled by his company and charged to his drawings account, the payment constitutes earnings for national insurance purposes unless the drawings account is in credit. Thus, payments are treated as earnings for PAYE purposes if:

- payment has actually been made;
- the individual has become entitled to payment;
- the individual is a director;
- the money has been credited to the director's account with the company; and
- the amount of income for a period has been determined.

Example – Directors' drawings

> *A* has a drawings account with his company which is £60 in credit. The company pays a personal bill for *A* of £100 and debits his drawings account with £100, thus turning the credit balance into an overdrawn balance of £40.
>
> The Contributions Agency takes the view that £60 of the payment of the £100 bill is a repayment of a loan and attracts no national insurance liability, but the balance of £40 is a payment of earnings and the grossed up amount is subject to NICs.

22.3.3 **Loans by the employer**

Curiously, the Contributions Agency takes the view that if an individual arranges for a loan from his employer and the loan is used to settle a personal liability, there is no liability for NICs unless (and until) the loan is written off by the employer.

There is clearly a need for considerable care in dealing with any documentation and structuring the arrangements to minimise liability for NICs on payments of this nature. It should, though, be borne in mind that in general it is unlawful under the Companies Acts for an individual to be given a loan from a company of which he is a director.

22.4 BENEFITS IN KIND

22.4.1 **Benefits for a director's family**
(TA 1988, s 154(1))

A tax liability may arise even though the director or employee has not personally received a benefit in kind, as where a benefit is made available to a member of the director's or employee's household by reason of his employment. The Revenue may say that substantial benefits in kind enjoyed by a director's family are provided by reason of that person's employment even though the recipient may also be a company employee. The Revenue is especially likely to argue this where a director's spouse is employed by the company and receives abnormally large benefits in kind for employees of that category.

22.4.2 Benefits for 'participators'
(TA 1988, s 418)

The legislation also covers a slightly different situation where shareholders receive benefits because they are shareholders, or associates of shareholders, rather than by reason of their own or anyone else's employment. The legislation applies only to *close* companies (see 20.8) and effectively treats the individual as if he or she had received a dividend equal to the value of the benefits as measured for Schedule E purposes (see 13.1). This is a complex subject on which professional advice should be taken.

22.5 DIVIDENDS

The usual reason why directors take cash from their company in the form of dividends rather than remuneration is because of the national insurance savings. Where the company is subject only to the small companies rate (see 22.2.1) there can be a considerable saving by taking dividends.

22.5.1 Possible drawbacks

There are other aspects to bear in mind, in particular the potential effect on the director's pension entitlement. Where the director is within ten years of normal retirement date, his final remuneration may have to be determined as the average of the three best consecutive years' remuneration. Taking dividends rather than remuneration may have the effect of reducing the individual's potential pension benefits.

22.6 LOANS TO THE COMPANY

22.6.1 Qualifying loans to the company

Where an individual borrows from a bank (other than under an overdraft) and then lends the money on to a company, he is entitled to income tax relief on the interest paid on the borrowings, provided:

- the company concerned is a close company (see 20.8) and the individual is a full-time director or employee involved in the management of the company's business; or

- the company concerned is a close company and the individual has a material interest in it (normally this means having more than 5% of the ordinary share capital); or
- the company is 'employee controlled' and the individual is a full-time employee.

However, the interest ceases to qualify for tax relief to the extent that the individual recovers capital from the company.

Example – Effect on a qualifying loan recovering capital

A has a 'material interest' in a close trading company. He borrows £150,000 from the bank and lends this money to the company for use in its business.

In year one, all the interest that A pays to the bank is an allowable deduction in arriving at taxable income. In year two, A withdraws £70,000 as part repayment of the loan to the company, but uses this for personal expenditure and does not clear his bank borrowings. From this point, only part of the interest payable on the bank loan qualifies for income tax relief.

22.6.2 Consequences if the company fails

Where an individual has raised a qualifying loan, his entitlement to income tax relief ceases when the company ceases to qualify. Thus, if an individual has borrowed £100,000 to finance his investment in a close trading company, and the company is wound up, the individual is not entitled to relief for any interest paid after the company ceased trading. If he is unable to repay the borrowings, he is left with having to pay interest which does not qualify for any tax relief whatsoever.

22.7 LOANS BY THE COMPANY

In the past, many companies operated on the basis that a director drew sums from the company in anticipation of bonuses or other remuneration which would be voted after the end of the company's year, perhaps when draft accounts were available. In many cases, the directors' account was effectively overdrawn at the year-end, and was restored to credit only because of the bonus approved after the year-end at the company's annual general meeting.

The Revenue normally maintains that bonuses should be treated as having been credited to a director only when the accounts were approved at the annual general meeting, and not at the company's year-end. It is generally difficult to resist such an argument since a director normally becomes entitled to a bonus only when the accounts are approved, and credit for such a bonus should not be applied retrospectively.

Where a director's loan account is effectively rewritten and is found to be overdrawn at the year-end, the Revenue is likely to seek to assess a benefit in kind as if the director had received a beneficial loan (see 13.6). Furthermore, there may be a liability on the company under the provisions of s 419 (see 20.8.2).

22.8 SALE AND PURCHASE OF ASSETS BY THE COMPANY

Where a director, or some other person connected with the company (eg a shareholder or an associate of a shareholder) purchases an asset from a company, there may be an income tax charge on any benefit enjoyed by the purchaser. Furthermore, the CGT legislation often requires the company's capital gain to be calculated if the company had disposed of the asset for its market value.

The company law aspects also need to be borne in mind. The purchase of an asset by a director normally needs to be disclosed in the company's annual accounts. It may be necessary, or at the very least advisable, for the transaction to be approved by the members of the company in a general meeting.

22.8.1 Purchase of assets by a director

Where a director (or other employee) acquires an asset from the company, the Revenue needs to be satisfied that the price paid is market value. If, in fact, the asset has been purchased at less than market value, the undervalue is treated as a benefit subject to income tax under Schedule E (see 13.1). Thus, if A acquires a property from A Ltd for £150,000, but its market value is £250,000, he is charged income tax on a benefit of £100,000. The fact that the buyer has purchased the property at an undervalue needs to be disclosed on form P11D (see 13.3).

In addition to the above, TCGA 1992, s 18 means that the company is deemed to have disposed of the property at its market value (ie £250,000). Thus, the company may have a tax charge based on value which it has not in fact received.

In the past, the Revenue made matters worse in such cases by resisting a claim by the company for a tax deduction in arriving at its profits. It is thought that this is not correct, and in the above example A Ltd ought to be entitled to a deduction of £100,000 (ie matching the amount assessed on A under Schedule E). However, the position remains uncertain and problems of this type are best avoided if at all possible.

22.8.2 Purchase of assets by associate of a director

Much the same treatment applies if, in the above example, the property had been purchased by A's wife rather than by A himself. In general, the Revenue normally argues that a benefit obtained by a close relative or other associate of a director should be treated for tax purposes as if the director had enjoyed the benefit himself.

22.8.3 Capital gains tax treatment of the director

Where a director etc has acquired property from his company, and has been assessed under Schedule E on any undervalue, he should be able to deduct the property's market value at the time of acquisition in arriving at any capital gain when he eventually disposes of the property.

Example – Value of capital gain

> If *B* acquires a property worth £300,000 from his employer but pays only £180,000, he is assessed to income tax under Schedule E on £120,000.
>
> If he later sells the property for £350,000, his capital gain is £50,000 (before indexation), and not £170,000.

22.8.4 Acquisition of property by shareholder

An individual who is a shareholder in a company, but not a director or employee, may likewise purchase an asset at an undervalue. In this situation, the amount of the undervalue is treated as if it were a distribution (ie dividend). The company needs to account for ACT on the amount of the undervalue. Moreover, the company's capital gain is once again calculated as if it had in fact received market value.

Thus, if *B* in the above example had been not a director or employee, but a shareholder, the company may need to account for ACT on £120,000, and *B* would be treated as receiving £150,000 income, less tax at the basic rate.

22.8.5 Sales of assets to the company

Much the same considerations arise where a director or shareholder sells an asset to the company. If the company is deemed to pay too much, the amount of the overvalue is treated as subject to income tax.

22.8.6 Capital gains aspects

Where an individual gives an asset to a company or sells it at an undervalue, he is often treated as if he were making a disposal to a connected person. This is particularly likely where the individual controls the company, or he and his associates, when taken together, have control. In such a case, TCGA 1992, s 18 normally requires the individual's capital gain to be calculated as if he had in fact received market value.

Where the asset concerned is a business asset, however, used either by the individual in a trade carried on by him personally, or by the company in the course of its own trade, it is possible for any gain to be avoided by the two parties making a joint election under TCGA 1992, s 165 (see 6.4 on holdover relief).

Example – Transfer for no consideration

C is the main shareholder in C Ltd. He owns a warehouse used by C Ltd which is currently worth £1m. His original cost was £100,000, the 31 March 1982 value is £300,000, and indexation relief amounts to £200,000. If C transferred the warehouse to C Ltd for no consideration, and an election were made under TCGA 1992, s 165, C would not have a capital gain and C Ltd would be deemed to acquire the property for £500,000.

22.8.7 Sale at an undervalue

The treatment is slightly different in the case of a sale at an undervalue. The excess of the amount paid to the transferor over the unindexed cost must be deducted in arriving at the amount of the gain which is eligible for hold-over relief. Thus if, in the example above, C had sold the warehouse to C Ltd for £700,000, the hold-over relief would be limited to £300,000 and C would have a chargeable gain of £200,000.

22.8.8 Interaction with retirement relief

Retirement relief (see 6.6) is mandatory, ie it does not have to be claimed. Thus, if C met all the conditions in relation to the disposal described in the example in 22.8.6, his held-over gain would be reduced by £375,000 retirement relief and this relief is not then available to cover gains on any other disposal.

22.8.9 Company law aspects

The Companies Acts contain many provisions intended to ensure that directors do not obtain personal benefits at the expense of their companies. The main safeguards which apply where a director buys or sells an asset are contained in CA 1985, s 320. This provides that the company may not enter into an arrangement for the purchase/sale of a non-cash asset of the 'requisite value' unless the arrangement is approved in advance by the company's shareholders. The requisite value is 10% of the company's net asset value, subject to a minimum of £1,000 and a maximum of £50,000. The CA 1985 also requires such transactions to be disclosed in the company's accounts.

There are specific rules which preclude a public company from entering into a 'credit transaction' with a director or connected person. A credit transaction is defined as including the sale of an asset on terms such that payment may be deferred. Thus, where a public company sells an asset to a director or connected person, it is normally necessary for full payment to be made at the time the purchase contract is entered into.

22.9 SELF-ADMINISTERED PENSION SCHEMES

In the past, one way in which directors arranged their affairs to best advantage was by having the company form a small self-administered pension scheme, with the trustees making loan-backs to, or other investments in, the company. In effect, a company could secure tax relief while still having the use of the money paid into the pension scheme. There are now, however, special rules which apply to small self-administered schemes (ie schemes which have fewer than 12 members). The Revenue is particularly anxious to monitor such schemes to ensure that they operate as pension schemes and not for the benefit of the directors or as a way of financing the company.

The Revenue requires one of the trustees to be a pensioneer trustee, ie an individual or body widely involved in pension scheme work and having regular dealings with the Pension Schemes Office (PSO). A pensioneer trustee is required to give an undertaking to the PSO not to acquiesce in any arrangements which are considered by the PSO to be inconsistent with a scheme operating as a *bona fide* pension scheme.

22.9.1 Prohibition on loans to members

Loans to scheme members, or anyone connected with a scheme member, are specifically prohibited. Moreover, there are restrictions on the purchase of assets from scheme members.

22.9.2 Loans to the company (and associated companies)

There is a general rule that not more than 25% of the self-administered pension fund's assets may be lent to the company within the first two years. Moreover, the 25% rule applies to the value of the fund contributed by the company (and the members), and does not include any value arising from a transfer to the fund from another approved scheme. After the first two years, the proportion of the fund which may be invested in this way increases to 50%.

Even where a loan is not barred by the above rules, there are other conditions which need to be satisfied. The money must be lent to the company for business purposes and not for a purely speculative purpose such as the purchase of shares or other investments. Any such loan must be for a fixed period and on arm's length terms. The Revenue has indicated that in general such loans must carry a commercial rate of interest, equivalent to clearing bank base rate plus 3%.

22.9.3 Investment in shares in the company

This is another area where the Revenue has tightened the rules. The 50% ceiling referred to in 22.9.2 applies to both loans to the company and investment in its shares. Moreover, there is a separate limit in that a self-administered pension scheme's investment in any unlisted company must not exceed 30% of the shares in that company. Furthermore, where a self-administered scheme purchases shares from a director, it is normally advisable to seek prior clearance, and, indeed, for the directors to seek clearance under TA 1988, s 707 (see 22.14.1). This is very much an area where specialist advice is required.

22.9.4 Investment in property used by the company

The PSO is less difficult where a small self-administered pension scheme acquires a property to be used by the company. The relevant memorandum issued by the PSO states:

> it is not for the Inland Revenue to interfere in the way the trustees invest trust monies, except where tax avoidance is in point, or where the investment appears to be irreconcilable with the *bona fides* of the scheme having regard to its cash needs for purchasing annuities. Investment in land or buildings may be a good long term investment for a scheme where the members are many years from retirement, but even so, questions would need to be asked if the property purchased appeared to be an important part of the employers own commercial premises, and thus potentially difficult to realise.

One particular point is that the PSO does not normally sanction a situation where the trustees take on borrowings which exceed three times their equity in the property.

There is a specific prohibition for residential property. The PSO Memorandum states that investment in residential property is prohibited except where it is for occupation by:

- an unconnected employee as a condition of employment (eg a caretaker), or
- someone unrelated to the members of the scheme (or to a person connected with a scheme member) in connection with his or her occupation of business premises (eg the occupier of a shop with an integral flat above) where the business premises are held by the trustees as a scheme asset.

22.9.5 Overall limit on borrowings by trustees

The Revenue has a well established rule that any borrowings by the trustees should not exceed 45% of the market value of the investments held by the trustees plus three times the ordinary annual contributions payable by the employer.

703

22.10 RAISING BUSINESS FINANCE

A successful private business often finds itself prevented from fully developing and expanding its business because of lack of finance. There may be a limit on the finance available from a bank in the form of medium-term loans, and in practice many companies survive on overdraft. The proprietors may come to see that they can develop the company to its full potential only if they can attract new equity finance.

There are various commercial aspects to raising new business finance and directors should take professional advice from an accountant and a solicitor who are experienced in venture capital work. From a tax point of view there are three major aspects to bear in mind.

22.10.1 Enterprise Investment Scheme

It may be possible to raise new equity finance from business 'angels' by issuing shares which qualify under the Enterprise Investment Scheme (EIS). An individual who invests at least £500 under the EIS may secure 20% income tax relief, and may also be able to secure CGT deferral relief which may be worth another 40%.

The provisions governing EIS relief which apply to an investor are set out in the *Allied Dunbar Tax Handbook 2000–01* at 11.8. From the company's point of view, the following provisions are relevant in determining whether the company can issue shares which qualify under the EIS.

22.10.2 Qualifying companies

A qualifying company is defined as an unquoted company which either:

(1) exists wholly for the purpose of carrying on one or more qualifying trades 'or which so exists apart from purposes capable of having no significant effect (other than in relation to incidental matters) on the extent of the company's activities'; or
(2) has a business which consists wholly of:
   (a) the holding of shares or securities of, or the making of loans to, one or more qualifying subsidiaries of the company; or
   (b) both the holding of such shares or securities, or the making of such loans, and the carrying on of one or more qualifying trades.

There are also certain other conditions which need to be satisfied if it is to be a qualifying company:

(1) The company's share capital must not include any issued shares that are not fully paid up or would not be fully paid up if any undertaking to pay cash to the company at a future date were disregarded.
(2) The company must not control another company apart from a qualifying subsidiary, either on its own or together with a connected person,

and there must not be any arrangements in place under which the issuing company can acquire such control.

(3) The company must not be under the control of another company or under the control of another company and persons connected with it, and once again there must be no arrangements in place whereby such a company may acquire control of the issuing company.

22.10.3 Qualifying trades

There are certain trades which are excluded under TA 1988, s 297, ie the company's business must not consist to any substantial extent of any of the following:

(1) dealing in land, in commodities or futures or in shares, securities or other financial instruments;

(2) dealing in goods otherwise than in the course of any ordinary trade of wholesale or retail distribution;

(3) banking, insurance (but not insurance broking), money-lending, debt-factoring, hire-purchase financing, or other financial activities;

(4) oil extraction activities;

(5) leasing (except for certain short-term charters of ships) or receiving royalties or licence fees;

(6) providing legal or accountancy services;

(7) providing services or facilities for any trade carried on by another person (other than a parent company) which consists to any substantial extent of activities within any of paragraphs (1)–(6) above and in which a controlling interest is held by a person who also has a controlling interest in the trade carried on by the company.

22.10.4 Wholesale and retail distribution trades

Wholesale and retail distribution trades qualify only if they are 'ordinary' trades. Section 297(3) states that a trade does not qualify as an ordinary trade of wholesale or retail distribution if:

(1) it consists to a substantial extent of dealing in goods of a kind which are collected or held as an investment; and

(2) a substantial proportion of those goods are held by the company for a period which is significantly longer than the period for which a vendor would reasonably be expected to hold them while endeavouring to dispose of them at their market value.

The following are taken as indications that a company's trade is a qualifying trade:

(1) The goods are bought by the trader in quantitites larger than those in which he sells them.

(2) The goods are bought and sold by the trader in different markets.

(3) The company incurs expenses in the trade in addition to the costs of the goods, and employs staff who are not connected with it.

The following are 'indications' that the trade is not a qualifying trade:

(1) There are purchases or sales from or to persons who are connected with the trader.

(2) Purchases are matched with forward sales or vice versa.

(3) The goods are held by the trader for longer than is normal for goods of the kind in question.

(4) The trade is carried on otherwise than at a place or places commonly used for the type of trade.

(5) The trader does not take physical possession of the goods.

The above are only indications and are not conclusive that a company's trade is or is not a qualifying trade, but it will be difficult to persuade the Revenue that a trade qualifies if there are a number of indications to the contrary.

22.10.5 Qualifying subsidiaries

A qualifying subsidiary is one in which the issuing company or one of its subsidiaries holds at least 90% of the share capital (TA 1988, s 308(2)). In addition, the company must meet one of the following tests:

- it must be carrying on a qualifying trade; or
- it must exist to hold and manage a property used by the parent company, or by a fellow 90% subsidiary, for the purposes of a qualifying trade; or
- it must be dormant.

22.10.6 Three-year period

EIS relief is withdrawn if a company, having initially satisfied the requirements set out in 22.10.2–22.10.5, ceases to satisfy them within three years.

22.10.7 Individuals excluded from EIS relief

A qualifying investor is defined as an individual who is not 'connected with the company'. This means that he must not own more than 30% of:

- the issued ordinary share capital of the company, or any of its subsidiaries;
- the loan capital and issued share capital of the company or any subsidiary; or
- the voting power in the company or any subsidiary; or
- any loan capital in a subsidiary of the company.

An individual is also connected with the issuing company if he directly or indirectly possesses, or is entitled to acquire such rights as would, in the event of the winding-up of the company (or any of its subsidiaries), mean that he is entitled to receive more than 30% of the assets available for distribution to equity holders of the company.

Rights of 'associates' need to be taken into account. For these purposes, an 'associate' means partner, spouse, parent, grandparent, great grandparent, child, grandchild, great grandchild and certain family trusts.

22.10.8 Individual must not be previously 'connected with the company'

An individual is also deemed to be connected with the company if he is:

- a paid director of the issuing company or any of its subsidiaries;
- an employee of the issuing company or any of its subsidiaries;
- a partner of the issuing company or any subsidiary; or
- an associate of someone who is a director or an employee or a partner of the issuing company, or any of its subsidiaries.

An individual is disqualified if he falls into any of the above categories during the two years prior to the date that the EIS shares are issued. Furthermore, an individual does not qualify for EIS relief if he is connected with the issuing company at the time the shares are issued, unless he is a business angel who qualified for EIS relief on his original investment and is now acquiring additional shares and he is connected only because he is a paid director.

22.10.9 Five-year period

EIS relief is withdrawn if the individual breaches the 30% limit within a period of five years.

22.10.10 Purchase of own shares/redemption of shares

There may be a partial withdrawal of EIS relief if the company (or a subsidiary) purchases its own shares or redeems shares within the five-year period. See further, *Allied Dunbar Tax Handbook 2000–01* at 11.6.12.

22.10.11 Approved investment funds

As well as seeking investment from business angels and other private individuals, it is possible for a company to issue shares to an approved EIS fund which operates in a similar way to a unit trust. From the point of view of the directors of the company which issues the shares, the same requirements apply as for shares issued to individuals direct.

22.10.12 Venture capital trusts

It may also be possible for an unquoted company to attract new equity finance from a venture capital trust (see *Allied Dunbar Tax Handbook 2000–01* at 11.7). The following parameters apply in determining whether a venture capital trust may invest in a company.

(1) The company must exist wholly for the purpose of carrying on wholly or mainly in the UK one or more qualifying trades (defined as for the EIS).
(2) Venture capital trusts may count annual investments of up to £1m in total in any one qualifying unquoted company as a qualifying holding.
(3) The gross asset of the unquoted company must not exceed £10m, immediately prior to the investment by the venture capital trust.

22.10.13 The Alternative Investment Market

The Alternative Investment Market (AIM), provides smaller companies, including companies which have only recently been set up, with a way of raising new equity finance. AIM shares qualify for the following reliefs:

- income tax relief under the EIS;
- CGT reinvestment relief;
- income tax relief for capital losses realised by an individual who sub-scribed for shares in an AIM company;
- CGT hold-over relief for gifts of shares;
- IHT business relief, provided the shares have been held for at least two years.

In addition, the Revenue has announced that venture capital trusts are per-mitted to invest in AIM securities.

In practice the availability of CGT reinvestment relief and IHT business relief are the most important tax incentives for investors. EIS relief is not available for investment in *all* AIM companies, only those carrying on qualifying trades and having no quoted securities. Thus, shares dealt in on AIM do not qualify for EIS relief if the company has preference shares or loan stock which are quoted on the main market. Where the necessary con-ditions are satisfied, however, investment in an AIM investment could qualify for 60% tax relief.

22.11 PURCHASE OF OWN SHARES

Since 1980, it has been possible for a company to purchase its own shares. The tax legislation contains specific provisions covering such transactions.

The general rule is that any amount paid by the company in excess of the amounts originally paid for the issue of the shares may be treated as a distribution (TA 1988, s 209). Where certain strict conditions are satisfied, however, it is possible for an unquoted trading company to buy in its own shares without the payment being treated as a distribution.

22.11.1 Conditions for capital treatment to apply

The following conditions need to be satisfied if a purchase by a company of its own shares is not to be treated as giving rise to a distribution:

(1) The company must be an unquoted company.
(2) It must be a trading company or the holding company of a trading group.
(3) The vendor shareholder must be resident and ordinarily resident in the UK.
(4) The vendor must have owned his shares for at least five years.
(5) The vendor's interest in the company must be substantially reduced.
(6) The company must purchase its own shares to benefit its trade.

22.11.2 Definition of unquoted company

For these purposes, a company is regarded as a quoted company if any of its securities are quoted on the Stock Exchange. On the other hand, the fact that shares are dealt in on the USM or the AIM does not make the company a quoted company.

22.11.3 Ownership of shares for five years

The legislation provides that the vendor shareholder must have owned his shares throughout a period of five years ending with the purchase. There are exceptions to cover situations where an individual acquired the shares by a gift from his or her spouse, or inherited them.

Section 220(6) of TA 1988 provides that an individual may count any period of ownership by his spouse towards the five-year period, provided they are not separated or divorced at the time the company purchases its own shares.

Section 220(7) of TA 1988 reduces the five-year period to three years in cases where the shareholder inherited his shares. Moreover, it is also possible to include the period during which the shares were owned by the person from whom he inherited them.

22.11.4 Substantial reduction

The legislation states that a shareholder shall be regarded as substantially reducing his interest in the company only if his interest is reduced by at least 25%. Furthermore, in looking at an individual's interest in the company, it is necessary to take account of his interest as a loan creditor (ie someone who has lent money to the company) as well as a shareholder. Although the legislation refers to a minimum reduction of 25%, the Revenue normally expects a much greater reduction.

22.11.5 Benefit to the company's trade

The legislation states that a purchase of own shares by a company is regarded as a distribution unless the purchase is made wholly or mainly for the purpose of benefiting a trade carried on by the company or by any of its 75% subsidiaries. The legislation also requires that the purchase must not be part of a 'scheme or arrangement' the main purpose of which is to enable the individual to avoid tax or to participate in the profits of the company without receiving a dividend.

22.11.6 Advance clearance procedure

It is possible to submit details of the commercial reasons for a proposed purchase of own shares with a view to securing confirmation from the Revenue that the purchase will be treated as a capital transaction and not as a distribution. The basic information required by the Revenue is set out in SP2/82.

22.12 DEMERGERS

It often happens with family companies that different members of the family wish to develop the business in different directions. If the founding generation has passed control to their children, a company may be run by two cousins or more distant relatives who have markedly different ideas and ambitions. There is a way in which the businesses can be separated in a tax-efficient way so that each of the different sides of the family can have a separate company with a distinct business.

Demergers are not confined to family companies and may also be appropriate where individuals who have been business partners wish to go their separate ways.

22.12.1 Form of the demerger

Demergers may take one of three forms, but they all involve the distribution of assets to shareholders out of distributable profits. The three types of transaction are as follows:

- distribution of shares in a subsidiary company to shareholders (ie the holding company declares a dividend);
- transfer of shares in a subsidiary to another company ('Newco') in return for its issuing shares to the shareholders of the holding company;

- transfer of a business to another company (again Newco) in return for that company's issuing shares to the shareholders in the holding company.

Where the Revenue gives approval to a demerger, the value transferred to the shareholders in one of the above three ways is not subject to income tax or CGT.

22.12.2 Conditions which must be satisfied

Demerger relief is available only where the purpose of the demerger is to separate two distinct trading activities. Relief is not intended to be available where the purpose is to separate trades from investments or other assets. It is also necessary to show that the purpose of the demerger is to benefit the trade being demerged. This condition is normally satisfied if it can be shown that the directors have irreconcilable differences as to business policy and the trade of the company to be demerged is being inhibited or held back because of these policy differences.

The demerger reliefs are not available where the demerger forms part of a scheme or arrangement where the main purpose is either:

- the avoidance of tax, or
- the acquisition by any person other than a shareholder of the distributing company of control of that company or any other company involved in the demerger.

22.12.3 Advance clearance

It is possible to secure advance clearance from the Revenue that a proposed demerger qualifies for the tax reliefs. In practice, it is necessary to make out a case to the Revenue that there are good commercial reasons for the demerger and there is no immediate likelihood of one of the demerged companies being sold.

22.12.4 Informal demergers

It may sometimes be possible to achieve a demerger which separates assets from trading activities, but this is not possible under the above rules for statutory demergers.

Informal demergers are a type of reconstruction which relies on SP5/85. Specifically, the transactions involved are normally as follows:

(1) the company's ordinary share capital is re-classified so that A shares carry the right to participate only in the profits of one trade or business and B shares carry similar rights over another business;
(2) the company is put into liquidation;
(3) the liquidator transfers the assets and undertakings which relate to the A shares to a company ('Newco') which issues its share to the A shareholders. The process is repeated in relation to the B shareholders.

In some circumstances it is shares in a subsidiary which are transferred to the new company, which issues shares to the A and B shareholders.

The transfer of the business or undertaking to Newco A and Newco B does not normally give rise to a tax charge for the transferor company because this is specifically covered by TCGA 1992, s 139. Similarly, the issue to the A and B shareholders of shares in Newco A and Newco B does not normally give rise to a CGT charge because of reliefs available under TCGA 1992, s 136. However, both these sections apply only where the transactions are carried out for *bona fide* commercial reasons and not for the avoidance of tax.

Once again there is a clearance procedure, which clearly should be contemplated only after taking appropriate professional advice.

22.13 LONGER TERM CAPITAL GAINS TAX PLANNING

Inevitably, medium- to long-term CGT planning depends upon a person's particular circumstances, and the following are merely suggestions to be borne in mind.

22.13.1 Should investments be held by trustees?

There is a major distinction between capital gains realised by an individual and gains made by trustees of an interest in possession trust. An individual's capital gains are effectively added to his taxable income and, if the aggregate amount exceeds £28,400, the gains are subject to 40% tax (see 5.1.4). In contrast, where gains are realised by trustees, the rate of CGT is 34%, regardless of the amount of the gain. It follows that if an individual is a beneficiary of an interest in possession trust, whether this be a trust created by another person's Will, or a settlement created by a relative etc, then it may well be more appropriate from a tax point of view if the trustees, rather than the individual himself, hold shares in a private company.

Example – Shares held by trustees

> *A* has 500 shares in X Ltd. His brother does not have any shares but is the life tenant of a trust created by his father which owns the remaining 500 shares.
>
> If X Ltd is taken over and *A* and the trustees both have a capital gain of £400,000, *A* pays tax of £160,000, but the trustees are liable for CGT of only £100,000.

22.13.2 Special rules where settlor or spouse a beneficiary

The treatment described in 22.13.1 does not apply if the settlor or his spouse can benefit. If so, the trustees' gain is taxed as if the settlor had realised it himself.

22.13.3 Forward planning for retirement relief

Both spouses may qualify for the full measure of retirement relief (see 6.6–6.8) provided they meet the conditions for that relief. In practice, this means that both husband and wife should hold at least 5% of the voting shares for a period of ten years up to the time of a disposal, and they should both be full-time officers or employees of the company.

Example – Maximising retirement relief

A and his wife both work full-time for their private company, X Ltd. *A* holds 99% of the shares and his wife holds only 1%.

In due course, a capital gain of £1m arises on the sale of the company. *A*'s share is £990,000 and his tax is as follows:

	£
Capital gain	990,000
Less exemption	250,000
	740,000
Less 50% exemption	370,000
	370,000

If he has used his annual exemption elsewhere, the tax normally amounts to £148,000.

If *A* and his wife had each held 50% of the shares, the tax would instead have been calculated as follows:

	£
Capital gain for both husband and wife	500,000
Less exemption	250,000
	250,000
Less 50% exemption	125,000
	125,000

The maximum tax payable would then be £100,000 (ie £50,000 each).

22.13.4 Assets owned privately but used by personal company

In many situations, the company concerned is not particularly valuable and the proceeds which are likely to arise on a disposal are insufficient to allow retirement relief to be taken up in full. On the other hand, the individual may have charged rent for making a valuable asset (eg a property owned by the director concerned) available to the company for use in its business. A gain on the disposal of the property does not qualify for retirement relief at all if a market rent has been charged (see 6.8.3), so retirement relief may go to waste.

One solution may be for the individual to transfer the property to the company by way of a gift, or a sale at an amount equal to his acquisition value. There should be no problem from the point of view of IHT provided all the shares in the company are held by the individual and spouse. The overall effect is that the individual realises a larger gain on the eventual disposal of his shares and this should qualify for retirement relief in full.

In some situations, it may also be possible for the individual to sell the property to the company for full consideration and to cover any capital gain which arises by using the sale proceeds to subscribe for new shares in the company concerned. Such an investment should qualify for reinvestment relief (see 6.4) and this should mean that no CGT is payable on the disposal of the property. In due course, when the shares and the company are sold, retirement relief should be available to cover any capital gain (subject to the normal limits).

22.14 ANTI-AVOIDANCE LEGISLATION

22.14.1 Transactions in securities

Section 703 of TA 1988 enables the Revenue to treat certain capital sums as if they were income. This section has particular application to a sale of shares in a private company.

For the Revenue to invoke s 703, one of the five prescribed circumstances set out in TA 1988, s 704 must apply. Several of these prescribed circumstances refer to an abnormal dividend and it is therefore particularly dangerous for a person to sell shares as part of a series of transactions under which another person (eg the purchaser) receives an abnormal dividend. However, s 704D can also apply to a series of transactions which does not involve an abnormal dividend but has the effect of extracting cash which could have been distributed as dividend.

There is an exemption for transactions which are carried out for *bona fide* commercial reasons or in the ordinary course of making or managing investments. However, it needs to be shown that none of the transactions was entered into with the main object, or one of the main objects, of obtaining a tax advantage.

Fortunately, TA 1988, s 707 provides an advance clearance procedure whereby a taxpayer may require the Revenue to state whether s 703 would apply to a proposed transaction. The taxpayer must set out all the material facts in his application. If the Revenue is not satisfied that clearance can be granted, or if it requires further information, notice must be given within 30 days. Once the Revenue has given clearance, an assessment cannot be made under s 703 unless it can be shown that the application did not fully and accurately disclose all the proposed transactions.

22.14.2 CGT anti-avoidance provisions

There are two anti-avoidance provisions in respect of CGT, both relating to value shifting.

22.14.3 Controlling shareholders

Section 29 of TCGA 1992 can apply where a controlling shareholder takes actions (or refrains from action) so as to cause value to pass out of his shares and into shares held by some other person with whom he is connected. Section 29 allows the Revenue to treat such a controlling shareholder as if he had disposed of his shares for their value at the time when he exercised his control to shift value into the other shares.

Example – Value shifting

A holds 51% of the ordinary shares in X Ltd and his son holds the remaining 49%. A arranges for the company to offer ordinary shareholders the option of converting their shares into preference shares. A accepts this offer but his son does not. This means that control of the company shifts from A to his son since, after the conversion of ordinary shares into preference shares, all the ordinary shares are held by his son. If the Revenue invokes s 29, it will assess A as if he had disposed of his 51% shareholding at its market value before the shares were converted into preference shares.

22.14.4 Section 30 of TCGA 1992

This legislation can apply to a scheme or arrangement under which the value of an asset which has been transferred has been materially reduced and a tax-free benefit has been obtained. Fortunately, there are specific exemptions for the following transactions:

- disposals between husband and wife;
- disposals by personal representatives to legatees;
- disposals within a 75% group of companies.

Nevertheless, this anti-avoidance section is important in connection with any transactions which may affect the balance of control within a family over a private company. Proprietors of companies should therefore take appropriate professional advice.

22.14.5 Share exchanges and take-overs

The exchange of shares or securities in Company A for shares in Company B which is making a take-over bid or acquiring a 25% shareholding in Company A can give rise to a CGT liability for shareholders in Company A unless they had no more than 5% of Company A or advance clearance had been obtained (see 5.4.4). This legislation therefore needs to be borne in mind where shareholders in an unquoted company take shares or loan stock issued by an acquiring company.

22.15 SALE OF THE COMPANY

Once again, the purpose of this section is to outline some of the more common ways in which CGT may be mitigated.

22.15.1 Pre-sale dividends

Vendors of a private company may have a choice. They can sell their shares for a capital sum or they can take a pre-sale dividend and a reduced amount on the sale of their shares. There may be a significant benefit if the shareholders organise a pre-sale dividend.

22.15.2 Using CGT hold-over relief

Where an individual makes a gift of shares in an unquoted trading company, it may be possible to secure hold-over relief. The conditions which must be satisfied are basically that:

- the company is an unquoted company;
- it is a trading company or the holding company of a trading group;
- the recipient of the gift is UK resident;
- the recipient joins in a hold-over election.

A restriction on hold-over relief may apply where the company has chargeable assets which are investment assets. (See 6.4.)

Where hold-over relief is obtained, the person transferring his shares does not normally have a capital gain but the recipient of the gift takes over his acquisition cost for the purposes of CGT.

Where substantial amounts are involved, it may be worthwhile for an individual to use this relief to make gifts to his children, or to a settlement for the benefit of his children.

Example – Hold-over relief

A receives an offer for his shares in X Ltd and stands to realise a capital gain of £2m. If he transfers a quarter of his shares to an interest in possession trust for his children, and makes a hold-over election, the trustees take over his CGT acquisition value. The position on the sale to the third party is that A now realises a gain of £1.5m and the trustees realise a gain of £500,000. Their rate of tax is 25% rather than 40% so A's family saves £75,000 at the Revenue's expense.

22.15.3 Taking loan notes or other paper from the acquirer

Where a public company is acquiring an unquoted company, it may be attractive for the vendors to take loan stock (or other securities) issued by the quoted company. Provided that clearance has been obtained under TCGA 1992, s 138 (see 22.14.5) no capital gain arises to the extent that the vendors take such consideration. They do, however, realise a capital gain as and when they dispose of the loan stock or other securities.

Taking loan stock can be attractive where the vendors anticipate that they may subsequently cease to be resident or where they can cash in the loan stock in stages, so as to realise modest gains in different tax years to take advantage of the CGT annual exemption for those years.

22.15.4 Consideration payable by instalments

One potential problem area is where a person sells shares (or any other asset) with the sale consideration being receivable in instalments. The CGT legislation requires the full amount to be brought into account for the year in which the disposal takes place. In some cases this might cause hardship in that a vendor is assessed for CGT but does not yet have sufficient cash to cover this liability. The legislation caters for this by allowing payment of CGT to be made by instalments over a period of up to seven years. However, this is not automatic and the basis on which payment may be made by instalments needs to be negotiated with the Inspector of Taxes.

Where it subsequently transpires that not all the consideration is actually received, the CGT assessment may be reduced.

22.15.5 Contingent liabilities

If a person sells shares (or any other assets) but is under an obligation to return part of the money in certain circumstances, the legislation requires that his capital gain should be computed without reference to the contingent liability. However, if and when the contingent liability becomes an actual liability, the CGT assessment is then adjusted to reflect this (see 5.5.1).

22.15.6 Earn-outs

It is also possible for a person to sell his shares for an amount in cash, plus a further amount based on the future result of the company's business. The House of Lords decision in *Marren v Ingles* [1980] STC 500 has established that such a vendor must be deemed to have received two types of consideration at the time of his disposal: the cash amount, plus the contingent right to receive further sums in the future. The technical term for the right to receive sums in the future is a *chose in action*. The House of Lords decided that CGT must be charged on the cash received plus the market value of the *chose in action*.

Example – Tax treatment of earn-out transaction

A sells out for £1.5m plus a contingent right to receive up to another £1m if his company achieves profit targets.

The present value of this contingent right or chose in action is £450,000 and so *A* is assessed as if he had received £1.95m. If the full amount of £1m is eventually received, he then has a further gain in the year that this is paid out. His gain in that year is:

	£
Proceeds	1,000,000
Less market value of chose in action when acquired	450,000
Capital gain before indexation	550,000

TCGA 1992, s 138A deals with the above problem and states that where the earn-out consideration consists only of shares or other securities to be issued by the acquiring company, those securities may be treated as if they were securities issued by the acquiring company on the take-over.

Example

If the sale contract in the example immediately above provides that *A*'s further £1m consideration must be satisfied by an issue of shares by the acquiring company, he would then be taxed only on the £1.5m cash, and tax would not be payable on the *chose in action* or on the issue of the shares, but only as and when he disposes of those shares.

22.15.7 Qualifying corporate bonds

Some caution is required where a private company is being disposed of and the vendors are offered a share exchange involving the issue of qualifying corporate bonds (QCBs). A QCB is a special type of loan stock (see 5.3.2). It is called a *qualifying* corporate bond because no capital gain may normally arise on its disposal (similarly, no allowable loss normally arises on its disposal).

However, where a company has been taken over, and the acquiring company issues a security which is a QCB, the legislation provides that the vendors' capital gain may be deferred only until such time as the QCB is disposed of.

This can cause real problems if the acquiring company gets into financial difficulty and cannot redeem the QCB. The deferred gain may become chargeable, as a disposal is deemed to take place when the acquiring company is wound up, and there is no relief for the loss due to the QCBs becoming worthless. This is an area where a potential vendor should obtain professional advice.

INHERITANCE TAX AND BUSINESS PROPERTY

DAVID BERTRAM, CLAYFIELD PROFESSIONAL GUIDANCE LTD

Inheritance tax (IHT) is a combined gift tax and death duty. It applies to certain gifts and deemed gifts made during a person's lifetime and to the estate on death. The first £234,000 of chargeable transfers (the nil rate band) is free of IHT. Cumulative transfers in excess of this, which take place either at death or within seven years before death, are taxed at 40% (though the overall impact may be reduced on transfers that take place more than three years before death).

23.1 PERSONS SUBJECT TO IHT

A UK-domiciled individual is subject to IHT on all property owned by him, whether it is located in the UK or overseas. In contrast, a person who has a foreign domicile is in general subject to IHT only on property situated in the UK. Foreign nationals and individuals with family connections overseas should refer to the *Allied Dunbar Tax Handbook 2000–01* at 22.1 and 22.15 for further details. This chapter concentrates on the position of individuals domiciled in the UK.

23.2 WHEN A CHARGE ARISES

Inheritance tax can apply in the following circumstances:

- .on a gift made by an individual during his lifetime;
- on a lifetime transfer of value which is regarded as a 'chargeable transfer';
- on death.

A person who has an interest in possession under a trust or settlement is normally regarded as entitled to the capital. When the beneficiary dies, the full value of the trust property is treated as part of his estate for IHT purposes (see 23.11.1).

Figure 23.1 opposite indicates the circumstances under which a gift may be a chargeable transfer for IHT purposes.

Figure 23.1 – Chargeable or exempt transfer

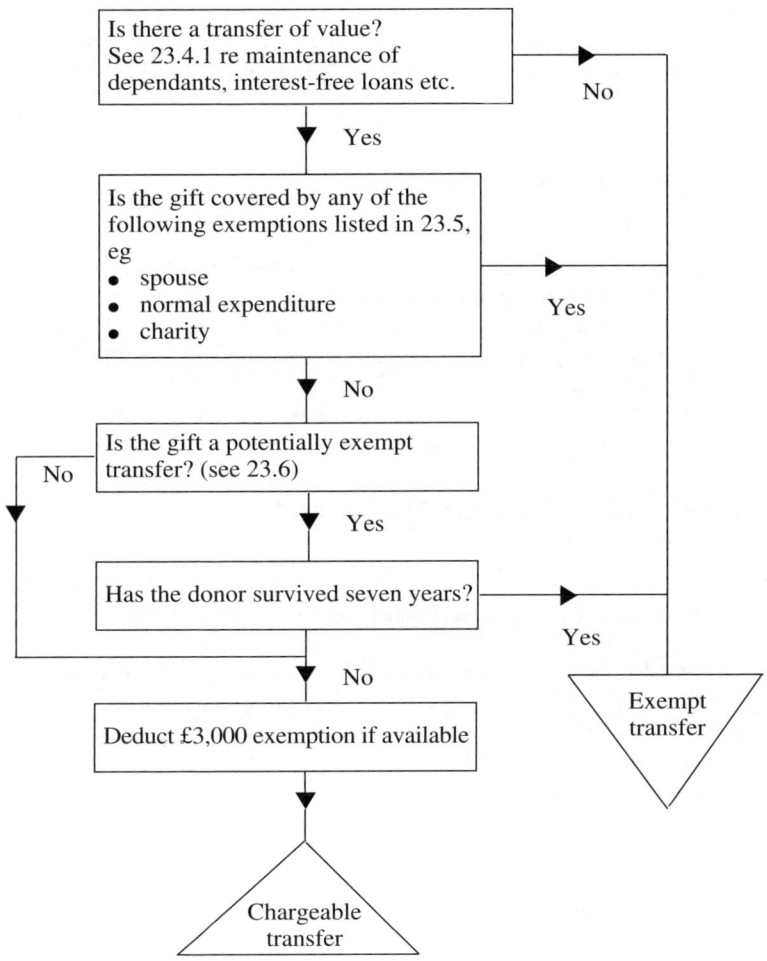

23.3 TRANSFERS OF VALUE

23.3.1 Transfers which do not amount to gifts
(IHTA 1984, s 3)

The legislation refers mainly to *transfers* rather than gifts. The reason is that all gifts are transfers of value but not all transfers of value are gifts. For example, where a person deliberately sells an asset at less than market value, he may not be making a gift but he is certainly making a transfer of value. Similarly, deliberately omitting to exercise a right can also be a transfer of value, but this is not a gift in the normal sense of the word. To give a third example, a transfer can feature property which is not even owned by the person making it since the IHT legislation deems that a person has made a gift if his interest in possession under a trust comes to an end (see *Allied Dunbar Tax Handbook 2000–01* at 18.4.15).

23.3.2 Gratuitous intent
(IHTA 1984, s 10)

IHT does not normally apply to a transaction unless there is an element of 'bounty' (ie a deliberate intention to make a gift). An unintentional loss of value (eg a loss made on a bad business deal) is not subject to IHT because there was no intention to pass value to another person. On the other hand, it may be difficult to satisfy the Capital Taxes Office (CTO) that there was no gratuitous intent to benefit a relative or connected person if the terms of the transaction seem unusually favourable.

23.3.3 Calculating the value of a transfer
(IHTA 1984, s 3)

The amount of any transfer of value is determined by the reduction in the donor's wealth. This is not necessarily the same as the increase in the recipient's wealth.

This can be illustrated by considering the situation where a person owns 51 out of 100 shares in a company. He has control because he has the majority of the shares. If he were to give two shares to his son, he would relinquish control of the company and his remaining 49 shares might be worth disproportionately less because of this. The two shares given to his son might not be worth particularly much in isolation, and the son may not have acquired a particularly valuable asset, but the father's estate would have gone down in value by the difference between the value of a 51% shareholding and the value of a 49% shareholding. Contrast the way that market value is ascertained for CGT purposes (see 5.5).

23.4 GIFTS WHICH ARE NOT TRANSFERS OF VALUE

Certain gifts and other transactions are not regarded as transfers of value so the issue of whether they are chargeable transfers simply does not arise. These include:

- maintenance of family, dependants etc
- waivers of dividends
- waivers of remuneration

- interest-free loans
- disclaimers of legacies
- deeds of variation.

23.4.1 Maintenance of family, dependants etc
(IHTA 1984, s 11)

The legislation specifically provides that the following lifetime payments are not transfers of value:

(1) Payments for the maintenance of a spouse or former spouse.
(2) Payments for the maintenance, education or training of a child or stepchild under the age of 18.
(3) Payments made to maintain a child over 18 who is in full-time education or training.
(4) Reasonable provision for the care or maintenance of a dependent relative, ie someone who is incapacitated by old age or infirmity from maintaining himself, or a widowed, separated or divorced mother or mother-in-law.

23.4.2 Waivers of dividends
(IHTA 1984, s 15)

A waiver of a dividend is not regarded as a transfer of value provided certain conditions are satisfied:

(1) The dividend must be waived by deed.
(2) The deed must not be executed more than 12 months before the right to the dividend has accrued.
(3) The deed waiving the dividend must be executed before any legal entitlement to the dividend arises.

There is a difference in the treatment of interim and final dividends, as the time at which entitlement may arise can be different.

Interim dividends

A shareholder has no enforceable right to payment before the date on which the board declares that a dividend shall be payable. Therefore, a deed waiving a dividend should be executed before any board resolution is passed.

Final dividends

A company might declare a dividend without stipulating any date for payment. In such circumstances, the declaration creates an immediate debt and it is therefore too late to execute a waiver.

In other cases where a final dividend is declared as being payable at a later date, a shareholder *may* waive his entitlement but must do so before the due date for payment.

In practice, a final dividend requires the shareholders' approval; an individual shareholder may therefore waive a dividend provided that the deed is executed before the company's annual general meeting.

23.4.3 Waivers of remuneration
(IHTA 1984, s 14)

There is a specific provision that a waiver of remuneration does not constitute a transfer of value. The terms of this exemption are based on income tax treatment. In practice, the Revenue normally accepts that remuneration is not subject to income tax under Schedule E if it is waived, and the Schedule E assessment has not become final and conclusive, provided:

(1) the remuneration is formally waived (usually by deed), or, if it has already been paid, it is repaid to the employer; and
(2) the employer's assessable profits are adjusted accordingly.

23.4.4 Interest-free loans
(IHTA 1984, s 29)

The IHT legislation specifically provides that an interest-free loan is not to be treated as a transfer of value provided that the loan is repayable on demand.

This exemption would not cover a situation where a loan was made for a specific period, with the lender having no legal right to call for repayment before that time has expired. The grant of such a loan could be a transfer of value. The Revenue would assess the value of the transfer as the difference between the amount of the loan and the present market value of the loan if it were to be assigned.

23.4.5 Disclaimer of legacies
(IHTA 1984, s 142)

If a person becomes entitled to property under a Will or on an intestacy, or under a trust (for example, a life tenant's death), he may disclaim his entitlement. Where such a disclaimer is made, the legacy or other entitlement is not treated as a transfer of value provided that:

(1) no payment or other consideration is given for the disclaimer, and
(2) the person has not already accepted his entitlement, either expressly or by implication.

23.4.6 Deeds of variation
(IHTA 1984, s 142)

A deed of variation may be entered into where a person has died leaving property to a beneficiary, the effect being to redirect the property. Where the necessary conditions are fulfilled, the revised disposition is treated as having taken place on the deceased person's death. Once again, a person who gives up an entitlement is not treated as making a transfer of value.

The following conditions need to be satisfied:

(1) The deed of variation must be executed within two years of the death.
(2) The deed must be in writing and must specifically refer to the provisions of the Will etc which are to be varied.
(3) It must be signed by the person who would otherwise have benefited, and anyone else who might have benefited.
(4) Only one deed of variation in respect of a particular piece of property can be effective for IHT purposes.
(5) No payment or other consideration may pass between beneficiaries to induce them to enter into the deed of variation (except that a variation which consists of an exchange of inheritances and a cash adjustment is permitted).
(6) The deed must be submitted to the CTO within six months of its being executed.

23.5 EXEMPT TRANSFERS

Even if a transfer takes place, it does not attract IHT if it is an exempt transfer. The following are exempt transfers.

23.5.1 Gifts to spouse
(IHTA 1984, s 18)

There is normally an unlimited exemption for transfers between husband and wife. For this purpose, a couple is regarded as husband and wife until a decree absolute has been made. The exemption covers outright gifts, legacies and transfers of property to a trust under which the spouse has an interest in possession. (The transfer may be either a lifetime transfer or a transfer which takes place on death.)

The exemption is restricted where a UK-domiciled individual makes transfers to a foreign domiciled spouse. In this situation, the exemption is limited to £55,000 (see *Allied Dunbar Tax Handbook 2000–01* at 17.5.1).

23.5.2 Normal expenditure out of income
(IHTA 1984, s 21)

A lifetime gift is exempt if it is shown that it was made as part of the donor's normal expenditure and comes out of income. The legislation requires that the gift should be 'normal', ie that the donor had a habit of making such gifts or must have intended to make a series of such gifts. The legislation also requires that by taking one year with another, the pattern of such gifts must have left the donor with sufficient income to maintain his normal standard of living.

Gifts which take the form of payments under deed of covenant or the payment of premiums under life assurance policies written in trust frequently qualify as exempt because of this rule.

23.5.3 Small gifts
(IHTA 1984, s 20)

Any number of individual gifts of up to £250 in any one tax year are exempt. But where gifts to any one individual exceed £250, the exemption is lost completely.

23.5.4 Annual exemption
(IHTA 1984, s 19)

This exemption is available to cover part of a larger gift. The exemption is £3,000 for each tax year. Furthermore, both husband and wife have separate annual exemptions.

If the full £3,000 is not used in a given year, the balance can be carried forward for one year only, and is then allowable only if the exemption for the second year is fully utilised.

23.5.5 Gifts in consideration of marriage
(IHTA 1984, s 22)

Gifts made to a bride or groom in consideration of their marriage are exempt up to the following amounts:

Gifts made by	Maximum exemption
Each parent	£5,000
Grandparents	£2,500
Bride or groom	£2,500
Any other person	£1,000

23.5.6 Gifts to charities
(IHTA 1984, s 23)

Gifts to charities which are established in the UK are exempt regardless of the amount. A charity may be established or registered here even though it carries out its work overseas and the exemption covers gifts to such charities. However, donations made to a foreign charity which is established abroad do not normally qualify.

23.5.7 Gifts for national purposes
(IHTA 1984, s 25)

Gifts to certain national bodies are totally exempt. These bodies include colleges and universities, the National Trust, the National Gallery, the British Museum and other galleries and museums run by local authorities or universities.

23.5.8 Gifts for public benefit
(IHTA 1984, s 26)

This exemption covers gifts of eligible property such as historic buildings, land of outstanding scenic, historic or scientific interest, works of art and collections of national, scientific, historic or artistic interest. It is necessary to clear the position in advance with HM Treasury if the exemption is to be available.

23.5.9 Gifts to political parties
(IHTA 1984, s 24)

Gifts to 'qualifying political parties' are exempt only if certain conditions are satisfied. A political party qualifies if it had at least two MPs returned at the last general election, or if it had at least one member and more than 150,000 votes were cast for its candidates.

23.5.10 Certain transfers to employee trusts
(IHTA 1984, s 28)

Transfers by an individual to an employee trust of shares in a company can be exempt provided all the following conditions are satisfied:

(1) The beneficiaries of the trust must include all or most of the persons employed by or holding office with the company.
(2) Within one year of the transfer:
  (a) the trustees must hold more than 50% of the company's ordinary share capital and have voting control on all questions which affect it as a whole; and
  (b) the trustees' control must not be fettered by some other provision or agreement between the shareholders.
(3) The trust deed must not permit any of the trust property to be applied at any time for the benefit of:
  (a) a participator in the company (ie a person who holds a 5% or greater interest);

(b) any person who has been a participator at any time during the ten years prior to the transfer; or

(c) any person connected with a participator or former participator.

A further restriction may apply where a company makes a transfer to an employee trust.

23.6 POTENTIALLY EXEMPT TRANSFERS
(IHTA 1984, s 3A)

23.6.1 Definition

Irrevocable gifts made during an individual's lifetime may, provided certain conditions are satisfied, be 'potentially exempt transfers' (PETs). These gifts become actually exempt only if the donor survives for seven years. If the donor dies during that period, the PET becomes a chargeable transfer. The tax payable depends on the rates of IHT in force at the date of death. The donee is liable to pay the tax.

The main conditions to be satisfied for a gift to be a PET are that:

(1) the gift is made to an individual; or

(2) the gift is made to a trust for a disabled person (see *Allied Dunbar Tax Handbook 2000–01* at 18.7);

(3) the gift is made to an accumulation and maintenance trust (see *Allied Dunbar Tax Handbook 2000–01* at 18.6).

A gift which is subject to a reservation of benefit (see 23.7) cannot be a PET. Furthermore, a gift to a discretionary trust is a chargeable transfer (see 23.10).

23.6.2 Taper relief
(IHTA 1984, s 7)

Where an individual makes a PET and dies within the seven-year period, taper relief may reduce the amount of tax payable. The tax payable on the transfer which has become a chargeable transfer is subject to the following reduction:

Years between gift and death	Percentage of the full charge
Three to four	80
Four to five	60
Five to six	40
Six to seven	20

23.7 RESERVATION OF BENEFIT
(FA 1986, s 102 & Sched 20)

23.7.1 Introduction

Property which has been gifted may still be deemed to form part of a deceased person's estate unless:

(1) possession and enjoyment of the property was *bona fide* assumed by the donee; and
(2) the property was enjoyed virtually to the entire exclusion of the donor and of any benefit to him by contract or otherwise.

The reference under (2) above means that for all practical purposes this is an 'all or nothing' test. The Revenue view is that the exception is intended to cover only trivial benefits, for example, where the donor of a picture enjoyed the chance to view it when making occasional visits to the donee's home.

The term 'by contract or otherwise' is meant to embrace arrangements which are not legally binding but which amount to an honourable understanding. This might arise where a person gives away a house but remains in occupation. A reservation of benefit would arise even if there is no legal tenancy and the donee could, in law, require the donor to vacate the property at any time.

23.7.2 Two specific exemptions

The legislation specifically states that occupation of property or use of chattels does not count as a benefit provided a market rent is paid by the donor. The legislation also provides for the benefit enjoyed by a donor who occupies property he has given to another where the donor's financial circumstances changed drastically for the worse after the gift was made.

23.7.3 Ending of reservation of benefit

Where a person makes a gift and initially reserves a benefit, but then relinquishes that reservation, the donor is treated as making a PET at the time that he gives up the reserved benefit. The amount of the PET is governed by the market value of the property at that time.

Example – Giving up reservation of benefit

A gives property worth £150,000 in July 1996 but reserves a benefit. The benefit is relinquished in July 2001 when the property is worth £220,000. *A* dies in October 2002.

If no benefit had been reserved, the gift would have been completely exempt by August 2003 (ie seven years after the gift), but because a benefit was retained until July 2001, the seven-year period starts only from that date.

The full £220,000 (ie the value at July 2001 when the reservation of benefit came to an end) would form part of *A*'s estate for IHT purposes.

23.7.4 Settlements and trusts

The Revenue has confirmed that a settlor may be a trustee of a settlement created by the settlor without this constituting a reservation of benefit. Also, where the settled property includes shares in a family company, the settlor/trustee may also be a director of the company and may be permitted under the trust deed to retain his remuneration provided it is reasonable in relation to the services rendered.

The position is less clear where a person has sought to reserve the *possibility* of a benefit, eg where an individual has created a settlement and is a potential beneficiary. It is the Revenue's view that a benefit is reserved where the settlor creates a discretionary trust and is a member of a class of potential beneficiaries. This would also apply where the settlor may be added to a class of potential beneficiaries. However, the Revenue has confirmed that no reservation of benefit arises where a person creates a settlement and is a contingent or default beneficiary. This might apply, for example, where property is put into trust for the settlor's children but would revert to the settlor if the children die or become bankrupt.

The legislation does not require that the donor's spouse should be excluded from benefit, and where a discretionary settlement is created it would be possible to include as a potential beneficiary the donor's spouse, any future spouse or widow/widower. However, if property were to be distributed to the donor's spouse from the trust and that property were then to be applied for the benefit of the *settlor,* the Revenue might well take the view that, looked at as a whole, there had been a reservation of benefit.

It is often difficult to distinguish between making a gift with reservation and giving away a part only of what one possesses. In *Munro v Stamp Duty Commrs of NSW* [1934] AC 61 it was held that arrangements made between a donee and a third party to give the donor a benefit were caught, whereas the retention of rights under a contract which was separate from the gift and made before it were not. This gave rise to the 'shearing' or 'carve-out' of the scheme, whereby a gift of land which was already subject to a lease was not a gift with reservation because the lease was not part of the gift. However, a gift of land which was subject to an agreement for a lease back, whether created at the same time or later, was a gift with reservation, the reason being that the gift comprised the grant of the whole, subject to something reserved out of it, as contrasted with a gift of a partial interest leaving something retained in the hands of the grantor (*Nichols v CIR* [1975] STC 278, CA).

The most recent case is *Ingram and Palmer-Tomkinson (Lady Ingram's Executors) v CIR* [1999] STC 37. Lady Ingram transferred a property to the solicitor, who held the property as her nominee. He then executed a lease in favour of Lady Ingram giving her a rent-free lease for 20 years. The land subject to the lease was transferred to a family trust. The executors' appeal was allowed. It was stated: 'Although [FA 1986, s 102] does not allow a donor to have his cake and eat it, there is nothing to stop him from carefully dividing the cake, eating part and having the rest.' It is thus important to define precisely what interests are being given away and those that are being retained. In this case the gift was the capital value of land after deduction of a leasehold interest. Although an owner of property cannot grant a lease to himself (*Rye v Rye* [1962] AC 496), in English law a trustee is not an agent for his beneficiary. The position is different in Scotland where a nominee cannot create an effective lease in favour of his principal, and a person cannot create a lease in favour of himself (*Kidrummy (Jersey) Ltd v CIR* [1990] STC 657).

As they apply to gifts of land, the gift with reservation rules are extended where:

(1) the donor retains a right to continue to occupy the land or enjoy a right in relation thereto for less than full consideration; and
(2) the gift is made within seven years after the interest which gives the continued right of occupation, etc is created.

The extended gift with reservation rules do not apply where:

(a) the gift is covered by an exemption from IHT;
(b) the benefit to the donor is negligible from the donee's point of view;
(c) the donor pays full consideration for the benefit; and
(d) the donor's occupation is forced upon him because of an unexpected hardship arising after the gift.

23.8 BUSINESS PROPERTY
(IHTA 1984, ss 103–114)

23.8.1 Basic requirements

A special deduction from liability to IHT is given in respect of value of business property where the following conditions are satisfied:

(1) The property must have been owned during the previous two years; or it must have been inherited from a spouse and, when the spouse's period of ownership is taken into account, the combined period of ownership exceeds two years.
(2) The property must not be subject to a binding contract for sale.

There is no requirement that the business should be carried on in the UK.

23.8.2 Rates of business property relief

Unincorporated businesses

A sole proprietor's interest in his business qualifies for a 100% deduction. A partner's interest in his firm also qualifies for 100% relief. A 50% deduction is available in respect of an asset owned by a partner but used by his firm.

Shares and debentures

Business relief on shares is available only where the company concerned is a trading company or the holding company of a trading group.

The 100% relief is available on shares and debentures in an unquoted company where the transferor had voting control before the transfer. Relief of 100% is also available for a controlling interest in a quoted trading company.

The 100% relief is also available for a transfer of shares in an unquoted trading company provided that the transferor had control of more than 25% of the voting rights before the transfer. Specific legislation on 'related property' means that where a husband and wife's combined shareholding exceeds 25%, the 100% relief is available even though neither spouse has more than 25% when looked at in isolation. A 100% deduction is given for other shareholdings in unquoted trading companies. Shares dealt in on the USM or the AIM are regarded as unquoted shares.

Relief of 50% is available where a controlling shareholder transfers an asset which is used by his company, or where such an asset passes on his death.

23.8.3 Businesses which do not qualify

Business relief is not normally available where the business carried on consists wholly or mainly of dealing in securities, stocks or shares, or land or buildings, or in making investments.

Where the transfer is of shares, business relief may be restricted if the company owns investments. The legislation refers to such investments as 'excepted assets', which are defined as assets which are neither:

(1) used wholly or mainly for the purposes of the business, nor
(2) required for the future use of the business.

Example – Restriction on business property relief

A dies holding shares in X Ltd, and X Ltd's balance sheet shows the following assets:

	£
Investments	750,000
Factory	1,000,000
Stock	300,000
Debtors	200,000
Cash	1,250,000

Only part of the value of the shares qualify for business relief. The part which would not qualify is normally:

Investment	750,000
Total assets	3,500,000

If the cash were excessive in relation to the likely needs and requirements of the business, there could also be a restriction on this count.

23.8.4 Test normally applied on a 'consolidated basis'

Where a company has subsidiaries, it is necessary to look at the group situation (ie shares in subsidiaries may have to be treated as excepted assets if the subsidiaries are investment companies). The CTO has confirmed that business assets held by subsidiaries of subsidiary companies should qualify for business relief.

23.9 AGRICULTURAL PROPERTY
(IHTA 1984, ss 115–124B)

Relief is available on the agricultural value of farmland in the UK, Channel Islands or Isle of Man.

23.9.1 Land occupied by the transferor

Relief is available where the individual had occupied the farmland for the two years prior to the date of the transfer. Where a farm has been sold and another farm acquired, the replacement farm normally qualifies for agricultural property relief provided that the owner occupied the two farms for a combined period of at least two years in the last five years. Agricultural property relief is also available for land owned by an individual but occupied by a firm of which he is a partner, or by a company of which he is the controlling shareholder for the two years preceding the date of the transfer.

23.9.2 Tenanted land

To qualify under this head, the individual must normally have owned the land for at least seven years.

A 100% deduction is available on land which is not occupied by the owner provided he has (or had at the date of his death) the legal right to regain vacant possession within a period not exceeding 12 months.

A 100% deduction is available for tenanted farmland where the owner cannot obtain vacant possession within 12 months. This is generally the case where the land is let under an agricultural tenancy.

23.10 COMPUTATION OF TAX ON LIFETIME TRANSFERS

In practice, IHT is likely to be paid during a person's lifetime only for chargeable transfers made by him to a discretionary trust or on transfers effected through a gift of assets to a company. The IHT is computed as follows:

Table 23.1 IHT payable on lifetime transfers

Initial calculation		
Chargeable transfers made during the preceding seven years		$\boxed{A}$
Add	Amount of chargeable transfer	$\boxed{B}$
		$\boxed{C}$
Deduct	Nil rate band	$\boxed{D}$
		$\boxed{E}$
	IHT thereon at 20%	$\boxed{X}$
Deduct	IHT on a notional transfer of $\boxed{A}$ minus $\boxed{D}$ as if	
	it took place at the same time	$\boxed{Y}$
	IHT payable in respect of the chargeable transfer	$\boxed{Z}$
Position if the donor dies within three years		
Chargeable transfers made during the previous seven years		$\boxed{A}$
Add	Potentially exempt transfers caught by the seven-year rule	$\boxed{B}$
		$\boxed{C}$
Add	amount of chargeable transfer	$\boxed{D}$
		$\boxed{E}$

Table 23.1 *Cont.*

Deduct   Nil rate band $\boxed{F}$

$\boxed{G}$

IHT thereon at 40% $\boxed{H}$
Deduct IHT at 40% on a notional transfer
of $\boxed{A}$ minus $\boxed{F}$ $\boxed{I}$

$\boxed{J}$

The donee is liable to pay additional IHT of $\boxed{J}$ minus the amount already paid under $\boxed{Z}$ above.

23.11 COMPUTATION OF TAX PAYABLE ON DEATH

23.11.1 Normal basis

The charge on death is normally computed as shown in Figure 23.2. The IHT is the tax on the figure in box 6, minus the tax payable on a normal transfer equal to the amount in box 4 as if the notional transfer took place immediately prior to the death. Some taper relief may be due on the PETs caught by the seven-year rule, see 23.6.2.

A number of special reliefs may be available.

23.11.2 Sales of land at a loss
(IHTA 1984, ss 190–198 as amended by FA 1993, s 199)

Relief is due where land and buildings are sold at a loss within four years of death, provided the loss is at least £1,000 or 5% of probate value (whichever is less). The net proceeds are substituted for the value at the date of death and the IHT is re-computed. However, this relief applies only where the property is sold to an arm's length purchaser rather than to a connected person.

23.11.3 Debts which may be disallowed
(FA 1986, s 103)

As a general rule debts are not deductible where the deceased made a capital transfer to a person who subsequently made a loan-back to the deceased. This rule applies only to loans made after 18 March 1986 but there is no such time limit on the capital transfers. A debt may be disallowed because the deceased had made a capital transfer to the lender even though that

Figure 23.2   IHT payable on death

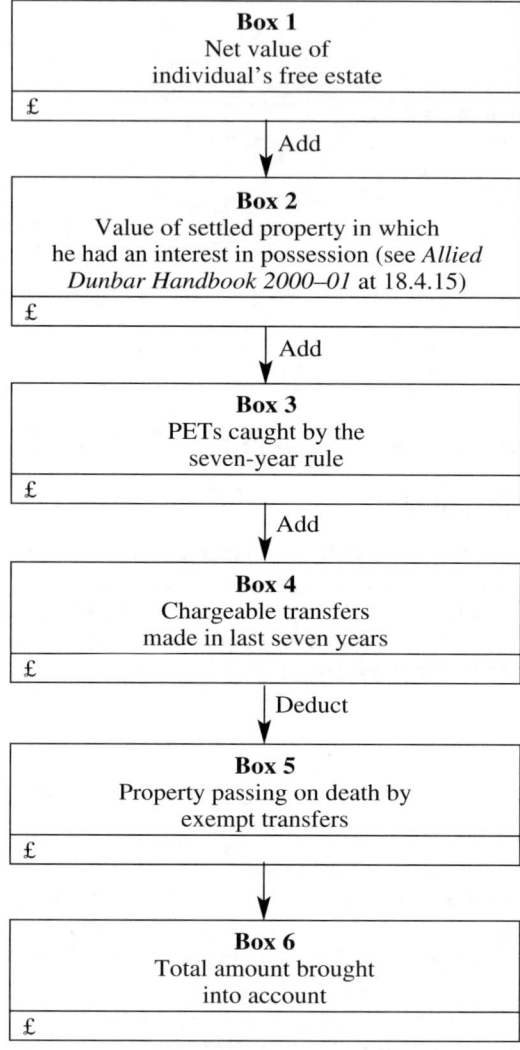

| **Box 1** |
| Net value of |
| individual's free estate |
| £ |

↓ Add

| **Box 2** |
| Value of settled property in which |
| he had an interest in possession (see *Allied* |
| *Dunbar Handbook 2000–01* at 18.4.15) |
| £ |

↓ Add

| **Box 3** |
| PETs caught by the |
| seven-year rule |
| £ |

↓ Add

| **Box 4** |
| Chargeable transfers |
| made in last seven years |
| £ |

↓ Deduct

| **Box 5** |
| Property passing on death by |
| exempt transfers |
| £ |

↓

| **Box 6** |
| Total amount brought |
| into account |
| £ |

capital transfer took place before 18 March 1986. Nor is it of any help that the loan was made on normal commercial terms and a market rate of interest was payable.

23.11.4 Treatment of gifts caught by seven-year rule
(IHTA 1984, s 113A)

Tax on a PET which becomes a chargeable transfer because of the transferor's death is payable by the recipient of the gift.

Business relief is available on a PET that becomes a chargeable transfer only if the conditions in 23.8 are satisfied both at the time of the gift and at the time of death.

Examples – Business relief on PETs

(1) *A* owns all the shares in a family company. He gives his son a 24% shareholding. Three years later, the company is sold and the son receives cash for his shares. One year after that *A* dies.

Business relief is not normally available as the necessary conditions are not satisfied by the donee at the time of *A*'s death. If the son had reinvested the proceeds in another private company, business relief might have been available after all.

(2) In this case the basic position is as in (1), ie *A* has made a gift to his son of a 24% shareholding. However, this time, the son retains his shares, but by the time *A* dies, the shares are quoted. No relief is due as the son does not control the company and his shares are quoted shares.

(3) The basic position is as in (1) but, in this case, the son retains the shares and they are still unquoted at the time of *A*'s death. The shares attract the 100% relief and this is not lost even if the son disposes of the shares shortly after *A*'s death.

23.11.5 Replacement property

Where a donee has disposed of business property but acquires replacement property, the PET may yet attract business relief. The replacement property must be acquired within three years.

23.12 HANDING ON THE FAMILY BUSINESS/COMPANY WITHOUT ATTRACTING IHT

23.12.1 General strategy

Many proprietors are reluctant to transfer ownership of their businesses or family companies to the next generation. There may be good reasons for this: perhaps the proprietor's children are too young to take on the responsibility or they may not appear to have much aptitude for business. Experience is that most proprietors wish to retain control during their lifetime, but are equally anxious that their work should not go to waste, and often wish to take appropriate steps to avoid heavy death duties on the business.

The best way for a proprietor to plan varies according to the particular circumstances, although the following general strategy suits most situations:

(1) A proprietor should endeavour to provide himself with a guaranteed 'income stream' which is not dependent on the family business/company. Once he has secured this (eg by funding a personal pension plan) he is in a position to contemplate gifts.

(2) Effective use of insurance and pension arrangements can help to cover the position in the short and medium term.

(3) The benefits of business property relief or agricultural relief should be maximised. It is particularly important to make sure that no action is taken which jeopardises these very valuable reliefs.

(4) The proprietor should draw up a Will in the most tax-efficient way.

(5) It usually makes sense for gifts to be made sooner rather than later, especially if the business is growing in value. Ideally, such gifts should be PETs.

(6) Transferring property to a trust may enable the individual to mitigate IHT without relinquishing control of the capital during his lifetime.

23.12.2 Pension arrangements

The tax advantages of funding a pension scheme cannot be overstated. An individual who funds a personal pension plan will secure income tax relief at his marginal rate. Where a company funds a pension scheme for a director, the company normally secures relief against its corporation tax liability.

The pension which results from such contributions confers a degree of financial independence so that the individual relies less on income from his business or family company and is therefore more able to consider giving away part or all of his interest in that business.

Furthermore, most pension arrangements provide death-in-service cover which means that a lump sum may be paid out, free of IHT, if the individual dies before drawing his pension. The existence of such cover (which in the case of company directors may be up to 400% of the individual's salary and other remuneration) means that funds should be available to cover any IHT liability which may arise if the proprietor should die in the short term.

23.12.3 Maximising business relief

It is crucially important that any loans are secured on non-business assets. The reason for this is that business (and agricultural) relief is due only on the net value after deducting any loan secured against the property.

Example – Securing loans

> A owns a business worth £500,000. The business assets include a factory which is subject to a £300,000 mortgage. If A should die, business relief is due only on £200,000. In contrast, if A had borrowed against other assets, business relief might have been due on the full £500,000.

It may be possible to secure the best of both worlds. Income tax relief on interest is available where a loan has been raised for a particular purpose, regardless of how the loan is secured. Thus, it seems possible in principle for a person to borrow for a qualifying purpose but secure the loan against another asset (eg his main residence) so that business relief is not restricted on death.

23.12.4 Avoiding buy/sell clauses

In the past, many partnership agreements included a clause intended to protect the widow and family of a deceased partner. Typically, such agreements contained a clause (often called a buy/sell clause) requiring that on the death of a partner the surviving partners purchase the deceased's interest in the firm. Similar arrangements were often contained in shareholder agreements entered into by working shareholder/ directors in private companies. While such arrangements are commercially sensible, there is a problem in that the Revenue regards them as amounting to a binding contract for sale and so not eligible for business property relief at all (see 23.8.1).

This problem can be avoided. It is possible to have a legally enforceable agreement which has almost exactly the same consequences as a buy/sell agreement but which does not jeopardise business relief. The recommended arrangement involves options. Each partner or shareholder/ director grants his colleagues an option and his colleagues grant him an option. The options are exercisable on death and enable the deceased's executors to require the surviving partners/shareholder/directors to buy them out at a fair price.

The Revenue has specifically confirmed that the existence of such options does not preclude availability of business relief or agricultural relief; see SP12/80.

23.12.5 Assets owned by a partner but used by the firm

Where a partner owns an asset (eg a building) which is used by the partnership for its business, business relief is available at the rate of 50%. In some family situations, it may be appropriate for the asset to be brought into the partnership so that on the death of the owner 100% business property relief, rather than 50%, is available.

23.12.6 **Assets owned by shareholders**

Similarly, a shareholder may own an asset which is used by a private company in which he is a shareholder. Unfortunately, no business property relief is available unless he is a controlling shareholder. It follows that a minority shareholder should carefully consider giving away such an asset (see 23.6 on PETs). Alternatively, it could make sense from this particular point of view to add to his shareholding so that he becomes a controlling shareholder.

23.12.7 **Tax-efficient Wills**

It is usually desirable for a proprietor to fully utilise the nil rate band rather than leave his entire estate to his spouse. However, this is general advice and the best way of drawing a Will depends upon the individual's particular circumstances.

In some cases, it is likely that property which qualifies for business property relief may be sold after the individual has died. If this property passes in the first instance to the individual's widow, it means that IHT is payable in the long term, when she dies. In a case such as this, it may be appropriate for the individual to draw his Will so that business property passes into a discretionary Will trust. No IHT should be payable if 100% business property relief is available, and the burden of IHT is much reduced in a situation where 50% relief is available. Property held in a discretionary trust will not form part of the widow's estate on her death, even if she is one of the beneficiaries of the Will trust, and in fact receives most of the income. There may be a charge on property held by the trustees once every ten years, but the rate is relatively modest compared with the normal 40% rate which applies where an individual owns non-business property or has an interest in possession.

Example – Planning a Will

A is the managing director and a substantial shareholder in X Ltd. His shares qualify for 100% business property relief on his death. However, his children are not involved in the business and the executors sell the shares for £1m.

If A had left the shares to his children, the IHT position would be satisfactory in that no charge would arise on A's death or on Mrs A's death.

If A left the whole of his estate to his widow, an IHT charge would eventually arise on capital of £1m, and additional IHT of £400,000 might be payable on Mrs A's death.

If A left the shares to a discretionary will trust, Mrs A could benefit during her lifetime but there would be no IHT charge on her death. The trustees may be liable for the periodic charge every ten years but the maximum rate at present is 6% (see *Allied Dunbar Tax Handbook 2000–01* at 18.5.12).

23.12.8 Property which cannot attract business property relief on widow's death

An individual may be a partner in a business which the widow cannot take over, eg the individual may be a doctor, dentist or solicitor. If he owns an asset used by the firm (eg the business premises) there is 50% business property relief if the property passes on his death to someone other than his widow. However, there is no business property relief if the property is left to the widow and then forms part of her estate on her death.

23.12.9 Double business property relief

It is sometimes possible to obtain business relief twice. For example, B dies owning non-business assets worth £2m and a 26% shareholding in an unquoted trading company worth £1m; his Will leaves all the non-business assets to his widow and the 26% shareholding to a discretionary Will trust. The position is:

	£
Will trust	1m
Less business relief	1m
Chargeable transfer for IHT purposes .	NIL

If the Will trustees then buy £1m of the non-business assets from the widow and sell the 26% shareholding to her, it may qualify for business property relief on her death (provided she survives two years). The position is then:

	£
Will trust	1m
(no charge on widow's death as it does not form part of her estate)	
Widow's free estate	2m
Less business property relief	1m
IHT payable on	NIL

23.12.10 Deeds of variation

Even if an individual's Will is not drawn up in the most tax-efficient way, it may be possible for the family to reorganise matters during the two years after his death by taking advantage of the provisions on deeds of variation (see 23.4.6).

23.12.11 Family trusts

One advantage for an individual who makes a gift into a settlement is that he may be a trustee and can therefore continue to control the way in which the capital is used.

The Revenue has specifically confirmed that the fact that a settlor is the first named trustee and can therefore exercise voting rights attaching to shares which he has put into trust does not mean that he has reserved a benefit. The Revenue has also confirmed that an individual may include his or her spouse as a potential beneficiary without the trust being caught by the gift with reservation rules. However, this may have adverse income tax consequences in that any income arising to the trustees is taxed as if it were the settlor's income. Accordingly, settlements are usually drawn up so that the spouse cannot benefit during the settlor's lifetime, but can benefit as the settlor's widow. Where the trust deed is worded in this way, the adverse income tax consequences do not arise.

GLOSSARY

Actual basis of assessment   This describes the situation where a person carrying on a trade or profession is assessed according to the profits which he has actually earned during the tax year concerned.

Accounting reference date   The date to which accounts are made up for a company. In practice, when a company is formed, the accounting reference date is normally the last day of the month in which the anniversary of its incorporation falls.

Ad valorem duties   Duties which are charged as a percentage of the value of the asset concerned, particularly stamp duty.

Administrator   An officer appointed by the court who takes charge of the company's affairs on insolvency and one of whose aims is to secure the company's survival.

Agricultural buildings allowances   A form of capital allowance given for expenditure on buildings used for agricultural purposes.

Agricultural property relief   A relief given for inheritance tax purposes. The relief is either 50 or 100% of the value of agricultural land. To qualify, the land must be situated in the UK, Channel Islands or Isle of Man.

Alternative Investment Market   The Stock Exchange launched the AIM in June 1995 to enable investors to deal in shares in unquoted companies. The AIM replaces the Unlisted Securities Market, a market for dealing in unquoted shares which is now closed to new entrants.

Annual charges   Certain payments made by a company are allowable in computing its corporation tax liability. Such payments include interest and payments under deed of covenant. In general, when the company makes an annual payment it must deduct tax at the basic rate and account for this at the end of the quarter on form CT61.

Annual exemption   An individual is entitled to an annual exemption for CGT purposes of £7,200. There are two types of annual exemption for IHT. An individual may give away up to £250 to any number of people in a tax year. This is generally called the 'small gifts exemption'. Separately from this, an individual is allowed to make chargeable transfers of up to £3,000 pa which are treated as exempt.

Arrival   A VAT term used for imports from other EU member states, particularly in connection with reporting trade statistics.

Articles of association   A company's regulations which govern its procedures, day-to-day operations and the members' relationship between themselves.

Associated companies   Companies controlled by the same person or groups of persons.

Business property relief   This is a deduction of either 50 or 100% which is made from the value of business property when it is assessed for IHT purposes.

Buy/sell clause A legally binding agreement under which two shareholders agree that in the event of certain things occurring in the future, one shareholder will offer the other his shares and the other will be required to buy them.

Capital *Authorised or nominal* – The limit of capital to which the company can go to in issuing new shares without passing a resolution to increase its capital.

Issued or allotted – The amount of shares actually issued by the company to its members.

Paid up – The amount of issued or allotted share capital paid up by the members.

Capital allowances These are allowances given for plant and machinery, industrial buildings and commercial property in enterprise zones. In general terms, capital allowances represent a form of relief which corresponds to depreciation.

Capital expenditure This is expenditure of a once and for all nature to achieve an enduring benefit for a trade. It is not a cost which may be deducted in arriving at profits for tax purposes, although capital allowances may be available. Contrast revenue expenditure.

CFC legislation There is special legislation on controlled foreign companies (CFCs). A UK-resident company which has an interest in a CFC may be taxed on a proportion of the CFC's profits.

Charge Security for the payment of a debt or performance of an obligation. In property law the most common charge is by way of legal mortgage. In company law a charge can be fixed on a particular asset or a floating charge.

Chargeable transfer A gift or other transfer of value made by an individual which is not covered by any of the various exemptions and which is therefore a transfer for IHT purposes.

Class rights Rights attaching to different classes of shares in the articles.

Closing years' rules Under the Schedule D preceding year rules basis, a firm is assessed on the actual basis for the tax year in which it ceases to carry on business. Furthermore, the Revenue has the right to adjust the assessments for the two preceding years so that those years may also be assessed on the actual basis if this produces higher assessments than under the preceding year basis.

Condition Under English contract law, a condition is a term of a contract of such importance that if a party to the contract breaches it the other party may repudiate the contract.

Conditional sale A type of contract for sale which does not become legally binding until some condition is satisfied.

Consideration In general, a contract becomes legally binding under English law only if it is entered into for consideration, ie for money or monies worth.

Constructive dismissal Under employment law, an employee who has resigned because of unfair action taken by an employer may argue that the employer has broken the contract of employment and thus constructively dismissed the employee.

Contingent liabilities A contingent liability to make a payment, or return part of sale proceeds, if certain events occur (ie if contingencies occur).

Copyright The exclusive right of printing and copying a published literary work or other original material and the right to prevent all others from doing so.

Corporation tax This is a tax levied on companies' profits. The full rate is 30% but many companies qualify for the small companies rate (see below).

Covenant An obligation which is contained is a deed and can be negative or restrictive on the one hand and positive (ie requiring some act or payment) on the other.

Current year basis   This is the Schedule D basis of assessment whereby an individual is assessed on his profits for the firm's year which ends in the tax year.

Debenture   A document evidencing a loan to a company. Such a document often enables the lender to have a charge over the company's property.

Deeds of variation   A lease can be varied by agreement. In addition it is a special term for IHT purposes. Where the provisions of a person's Will are varied by the beneficiaries' mutual consent, and the necessary deed of variation is executed within two years of the relevant death, IHT may be computed as if the deceased's Will had contained the revised provisions from the outset. A similar treatment may apply where a person has died without making a valid Will, and the individuals who would benefit under the intestacy rules mutually agree to vary the position.

De-registration   De-registration occurs when a trader who has been registered for VAT purposes is permitted to deregister. Once the trader has deregistered, he must not charge VAT on any supplies subsequently made by him in the course of his business.

Despatches   A VAT term used for exports in EU trade.

Directive   EU legislation which must be implemented in the national legislation or administrative provisions of each of the member states.

Dispensations   An employer is required to make annual returns of payments and benefits provided to employees (form P11D). A dispensation may be negotiated with the Revenue whereby certain expenses and other payments need not be reported on form P11D.

Distribution   A distribution of a company's assets to its members (ie shareholders), for example a payment of a dividend. Distributions may also be made by a liquidator. Where assets are distributed to members of the company during the course of a liquidation, there is said to be a distribution *in specie*.

Dividends   A dividend is a cash amount paid to a member of a company according to the number of shares held by him. Dividends may only be declared out of distributable profits.

Earnings basis   Accounts should be prepared so as to reflect a trader's earnings for a year rather than just cash received. Thus, accounts should include debtors, ie bills which have been issued but which have not been paid by the year end.

Election to waive exemption   A VAT term used in commercial land and property transactions. Otherwise known as the option to tax. A landowner has the option to make what would otherwise be an exempt supply into a taxable supply. Formal notification to Customs is required.

Enhancement expenditure   This is a term used in the context of CGT. In computing a person's capital gain, it is possible to deduct the costs incurred in acquiring the asset and any enhancement expenditure on improvements etc which is reflected in the state of the asset at the date of disposal.

Enterprise Investment Scheme   This is a scheme under which individuals may receive income tax and CGT relief when investing in qualifying unquoted trading companies.

Enterprise zones   The Government has designated certain areas as enterprise zones. Designation normally lasts for a period of ten years. During that period, a person carrying on a business within the enterprise zone is exempt from business rates. There is also considerable freedom from planning controls.

Expenditure on commercial buildings situated in an enterprise zone qualifies for capital allowances. The acquisition of an unused commercial building, or a building which has been let only during the preceding two years, attracts a 100% allowance.

EU   The European Union comprises Austria, Belgium, Denmark, Finland, France, Germany, Greece, Ireland, Italy, Luxembourg, the Netherlands, Portugal, Spain, Sweden and the UK.

Exempt supplies   Supplies which are not liable to VAT. A person who makes only exempt supplies cannot recover input VAT suffered by him.

Exempt transfers   The following transfers are exempt from inheritance tax: gifts to spouse; normal expenditure out of income; £250 small gifts exemption; annual £3,000 exemption; exemption for marriage gifts; gifts to charities; gifts for national purposes; gifts for public benefit; gifts to political parties; certain transfers of employee trusts.

Ex-gratia   A person makes an ex-gratia payment when he does so without admitting liability.

Fiduciary duties   A director is under a duty not to let his own interests conflict with those of the company.

Floating charge   This is a type of charge or security that may be granted to lenders. A floating charge differs from a fixed charge in that it does not apply only to a specific asset or assets but rather applies to a class of assets.

Forex   Extensive tax legislation which deals with foreign exchange gains and losses as recognised for tax purposes. The Forex regime may result in a tax liability on certain profits which are recognised for accounting purposes but are unrealised profits in that no disposal has occurred during the accounting period concerned.

Form CT61   A quarterly return required for a company in respect of annual payments made under deduction of tax.

Form P11D   An annual return made by employers of expenses payments and benefits in kind provided for an employee.

Full-time working directors and managers   This is a concept which applies for the purposes of CGT retirement relief. A person selling shares in a company qualifies for retirement relief only if he is a full-time worker or manager, ie someone who is required to spend the greater part of his time working for the company in a managerial capacity.

Groups of companies   There are various different rules under which companies may be regarded as part of a group.

A parent company may have subsidiaries, ie other companies in which the parent company has a majority shareholding. The companies constitute a group for company law purposes.

The conditions which need to be satisfied for companies to form a group for tax purposes vary, but in general the parent company needs to have a 75% interest in its subsidiaries.

Group registration for VAT purposes   Companies which are under common control may register for VAT purposes as a single unit or VAT group. Where this happens, all supplies between the companies concerned are disregarded for VAT purposes. VAT is charged only on supplies outside the group.

Hold-over relief   This is the relief given to a donor or other transferor of business assets. Where an individual etc is entitled to hold-over relief, his gain is not charged but is deducted from the asset's market value in determining the transferee's acquisition value for CGT purposes.

Indemnity   A collateral contract or security which prevents one person from suffering loss from the act or a default of the other.

Indexation   This is an adjustment made for CGT purposes to allow for inflation. The adjustment is computed by reference to the increase in the retail price index between the month of acquisition (or March 1982 if later) and the month of disposal.

Industrial buildings   Buildings which are occupied for the purposes of a qualifying trade may qualify as industrial buildings. The significance of this is that a person who incurs expenditure on an industrial building may claim industrial buildings allowances. Normally, allowances are given at the rate of 4% pa over a 25-year period.

Industrial tribunal   This is a body set up to hear complaints concerning statutory employment rights such as unfair dismissal, redundancy etc.

Inheritance tax   Inheritance tax is a combination of a gift tax and death duties. Tax is payable on chargeable transfers made by an individual during his lifetime and on his estate at the time of his death.

Input VAT   The VAT paid to suppliers of goods and services. Where a person has paid for such goods and services and he is himself VAT registered, he may recover input VAT by offsetting the tax paid by him against tax charged on his own supplies.

Insolvency   This is the situation where a person or business is unable to pay his or its debts in full.

Intrastats   Statistical returns which record EU arrivals and dispatches. Commonly known as SSDs.

Investment companies   An investment company is a company which exists wholly or mainly for the purpose of carrying on a business of managing investments.

Joint and several liability   Applies where two or more persons enter into an obligation jointly and severally so that each is liable separately and all are liable jointly. A creditor may choose to sue one or more severally or all jointly.

Know-how   Certain expenditure by a person carrying on a trade to acquire information required to carry out certain industrial or manufacturing processes may qualify for a form of capital allowances.

Lien   The right to hold the goods or property of another as security for the performance of a particular obligation such as an unpaid invoice.

Liquidator   A person who presides over and administers the winding-up or dissolution of a company.

Market value rule   Where an asset is transferred to a person by way of a gift or some other disposal which is not an arm's length transaction, CGT may be charged as if the person making the disposal had in fact received market value.

Members of a company   Shareholders.

Memorandum of association   This is a document setting out a company's constitution and in particular giving its name, the objects for which the company was formed, terms under which shares are issued etc.

Misrepresentation   A statement or act which conveys a false or wrong impression.

National insurance contributions   These are Social Security Contributions. Class 1 NICs are payable by an employer and employees. Class 2 and Class 4 NICs are payable by self-employed individuals. The collection of NICs is undertaken by the Revenue.

Opening years rules   Under the Schedule D current year basis, there are special rules for computing the assessable profits for the year in which the business commences, and the subsequent tax year.

Options   Legally binding contracts under which one party to a contract is bound to buy or sell an asset to the other party. A call option is an option under which the person granting the option agrees to sell an asset to the other party if he exercises his option. A put option is where a person has the right to require the other party to buy an asset from him.

Output tax   The VAT chargeable on goods or services supplied in the UK. The trader must account for VAT charged on such supplies by completing a VAT return, normally on a quarterly basis.

Outworkers   Some industries have outworkers who work on their own premises. However, depending on the circumstances, outworkers may be regarded as employees and not as self-employed individuals. This means that payments made by the person using the outworkers' services may be subject to PAYE and employers' national insurance contributions.

Overlap relief   Under the Schedule D current year basis of assessment, there are special provisions to cover the way in which profits are assessed for the opening years. The general principle is that the total amount of profits which are assessed over the life of the business should precisely equal the actual profits earned by the business. Overlap relief covers situations where a particular year's profits are assessed more than once (usually under the opening years' rules) and is effectively an adjustment to ensure that this does not result in excessive amounts being assessed overall.

Overlap relief is given by way of a deduction from an individual's profits when he ceases to carry on his business or profession, or when the firm's accounting date is changed to a date which falls later in the tax year.

Partially exempt traders   This is a VAT concept. A partially exempt trader is a person who makes a mixture of standard-rated or zero-rated supplies and supplies which are exempt for VAT purposes.

A partially exempt trader may not be able to claim full credit for his input tax.

Partnership   The relationship which subsists between persons carrying on business with a view to profit.

Patent   The exclusive use and benefit of a new invention.

Pay as you earn (PAYE)   This is a compulsory system for deduction of tax at source from cash payments to employees. There are different rules for PAYE and national insurance contributions and an individual's earnings may be different for the purposes of these two systems.

Personal pension scheme   An approved pension scheme run by an insurance company, bank, building society or unit trust group. An individual who is self-employed or who is in non-pensionable employment may make contributions to a personal pension scheme.

Plant and machinery   Plant and machinery attract capital allowances if used by a person in the course of a business carried on by him. There is no statutory definition of plant and machinery although certain rules have evolved through decided cases.

Prescribed accounting periods   A VAT term for periods covered by VAT returns. Normally periods are of three months' duration ending on the dates notified in the certificate of VAT registration.

Potentially exempt transfers (PETs)   An outright gift made by one individual to another or to an interest in possession or accumulation and maintenance trust is a PET. This means that the gift is exempt from IHT provided the donor survives seven years. If the donor does survive for that period the PET becomes an actually exempt transfer. If he dies during the period the transfer proves not to have been exempt.

Pre-emption   The right to purchase property before or in preference to other property eg shares or premises.

Pre-sale dividends   Where a group of people are about to sell their shares in a private company, it may be more tax efficient for them to extract part of the value from the company by taking a dividend immediately before the sale takes place.

Pre-trading expenditure   Certain expenditure incurred in connection with a trade which is about to be carried on may qualify for tax relief once the trade is commenced.

Premium   A lump sum payment to a landlord to obtain a lease is regarded as a premium for tax purposes. Where the lease is for a period of less than 50 years, part of the premium is normally treated as income for the landlord.

Private company   Under company law, this is a company which is not a public company. The Financial Services Act 1986 prohibits a private company from issuing any advertisement under which the public may invest in its securities.

Privity of contract   This is a rule under English contract law that only a party to a contract may sue under the contract. It is, however, subject to the provisions of the Contracts (Rights of Third Parties) Act 1999.

Public company   A company which uses the suffix plc and which has a minimum share capital of £50,000, at least a quarter of which is paid up, and which observes certain requirements under the Companies Acts.

Purchase of own shares   A company may purchase its own shares. A public company is normally permitted to do so only in so far as it has distributable profits or the purchase of own shares is being funded by the proceeds from an issue of new shares. A private company may purchase its own shares out of capital.

In all situations, there is a set procedure which must be followed for the purchase to be in accordance with company law. A special tax treatment may apply where a private trading company purchases its own shares.

Qualifying corporate bonds   A loan stock issued by a company may be an exempt asset for CGT purposes (ie it qualifies for exemption). On the other hand, any loss realised on a disposal of a QCB is not normally allowable for CGT purposes.

Qualifying loans   An individual who is a partner is entitled to relief for interest paid on qualifying loans, ie loans used to acquire an interest in the firm or loans which have been taken to enable the individual to make a loan to his firm for use in the ordinary course of the firm's business. Shareholders in a close company may also be able to raise qualifying loans to acquire shares or make loan capital available to the company.

Quiet enjoyment   The right of a tenant of premises to occupy the premises without any lawful interruption or disturbance by the landlord or his agent.

Rebasing   This is a technical term for CGT purposes whereby an individual who held an asset at 31 March 1982 may have his capital gain computed as if his cost were the market value of the asset at that date.

Receiver   An official appointed by the court or by a debenture holder to take charge of the company's affairs and realise its assets. Following the Insolvency Act 1986, the proper term is an administrative receiver.

Relevant earnings   Schedule D profits and earnings from a non-pensionable employment. An individual may make contributions into a personal pension scheme based on a percentage of his relevant earnings for a tax year.

Relief for reinvestment in unquoted shares   CGT relief may be obtained where an individual or trust invests in a qualifying unquoted trading company within three years of the date of a disposal which gave rise to a capital gain.

Rescission   The revocation of a contract eg where the seller rescinds a contract relating to land where the purchaser raises an objection in the title.

Reservation of benefit   This is an IHT term. Where a person makes a gift but reserves a benefit, the transaction is not regarded as a PET. The asset remains part of the individual's estate for as long as he continues to reserve a benefit. If he has not relinquished his reserved benefit by the time of his death, the asset's market value is brought into account for IHT purposes just as if he still owned the asset.

Resolution   A decision of a company's members at a general meeting or of directors at a Board of Directors meeting.

Retirement annuity   These are similar to personal pension schemes. In effect, they are approved contracts under which a person who was self-employed or in non-pensionable employment could provide for their retirement prior to the introduction of personal pension schemes in July 1988. Many retirement annuity policies make provision for premiums to be paid in subsequent years and, whilst no new retirement annuity policies are now issued, contributions under existing policies thus continue to attract relief for some years to come.

Retirement relief   This is a special relief for CGT purposes which applies where an individual aged 55 or over disposes of his business or an interest in a business (eg an interest in a firm).

Revenue expenditure   Expenditure which is deductible in arriving at a company's profits. Contrast capital expenditure.

Reverse charge   A VAT charging mechanism which obliges the customer to account to Customs for VAT on the price charge for goods or services. The VAT charged is recoverable as input VAT, subject to the normal rules.

Roll-over relief   This is a CGT relief which applies where an individual disposes of a business or an asset used in a business and spends the proceeds on acquiring replacement assets during a qualifying period (normally up to one year before and up to three years after the date of disposal of the original asset).

Romalpa clause   A term under a sale contract under which the vendor reserves legal title over the assets which have been sold until he receives payment.

Salaried partner   An individual subject to the supervision and direction of equity partners and who is therefore no more than a very senior employee. Salaried partners are assessable under Schedule E rather than under Schedule D.

Scientific research allowances   Certain expenditure incurred by traders on scientific research may attract allowances. Revenue expenditure is allowed in full. Capital expenditure may attract 100% capital allowances.

Self-administered pension scheme   A pension scheme with no more than 12 members where one or more of the members is a trustee or the company which established the scheme is a trustee.

Schedule D   A self-employed person's profits are assessed under Schedule D.

Schedule E   Directors and employees are assessed under Schedule E. The normal basis of assessment for Schedule E income is the receipts basis, ie an individual is assessed according to remuneration received by him during the year.

Share capital   See Capital.

Shares valuation division   A specialist section of the Capital Taxes Office which negotiates valuations of unquoted shares where such a valuation is required for tax purposes.

Small companies rate   Corporation tax is charged only at 20% unless the company concerned has profits in excess of the lower limit (at present £300,000 provided that there are no associated companies). There is marginal relief up to £1.5m. If there are associated companies, the lower limit is divided by the number of associated companies.

Sole traders   An individual is a sole trader if he carries on business on his own account rather than in partnership or through a company.

Specific performance   An order for a party who has defaulted to carry out the obligations that he has entered into under a contract.

Stamp duty   A duty payable at 0.5% on transfers of shares and at 1% to 4% on transfers of property.

Table A   Table A of the Companies (Tables A to F) Regulations 1985 (SI No 805), a standard form of articles of association which are adopted in many companies' articles.

Target company   Where it is intended that a company should be purchased, the company concerned is often referred to as the 'target company'. This helps to distinguish it from other companies such as where the person making the acquisition is itself a company.

Tax invoice   An invoice issued by a supplier which must show specific information. It is the docuement on which VAT accounting and control procedures are based.

Tax point   The time at which a transaction is regarded as taking place for VAT purposes, and when VAT becomes payable or recoverable.

Title   The right of ownership in property.

Time apportionment basis   Where an asset was owned at 6 April 1965, and no universal rebasing election has been made, it is sometimes possible for a capital gain to be computed on the time apportionment basis. This means that only a proportion of the gain achieved over the total period of ownership is brought into charge.

Tort   A civil wrong committed against another party, eg negligence or trespass. This is different from a liability under a contract since a person may be liable under the law of tort where there is no contractual relationship.

Ultra vires   A doctrine in company law that a company must keep within its registered objects.

Unfair dismissal   A dismissal of an employee contrary to the Employment Rights Act 1996.

Unfair prejudice   In company law, a minority shareholder may have a claim against the company's directors if they exercise their powers unfairly to the prejudice of minority shareholders.

Unincorporated businesses   A company is an incorporated business. Businesses carried on by a sole trader or by a partnership are unincorporated businesses.

Universal rebasing election   An irrevocable election which may be made under which the 31 March 1982 value of assets held by that person is treated as if it were the original cost.

Venture capital loss relief   Where an individual has subscribed for shares in an unquoted trading company, any losses may be set against the individual's income for the year in which the loss is realised. This is known as venture capital loss relief.

Venture capital trust   A new type of investment trust established under the Finance Act 1995 provisions. VCTs must invest in unquoted trading companies with net assets of no more than £10m.

Vicarious liability   Where a party is liable for the acts of others even though that party did not commit the act or omission.

Warranty   In contract law, a term of a contract which is breached entitles the injured party to sue for damages but not to repudiate the contract.

Wasting assets   A wasting asset is an asset with an expected useful life of less than 50 years.

Wrongful dismissal   A term in employment law describing a situation where an employee is dismissed in breach of contractual rights under common law.

Zero-rating   A VAT term for a sale on which no VAT is charged. A person making zero-rated supplies may nevertheless still be able to recover input VAT.

INDEX